THE RUSSIAN INTELLIGENTSIA
MYTH, MISSION, AND METAMORPHOSIS

Myths and Taboos in Slavic Cultures

Series Editor
Alyssa Dinega Gillespie

Editorial Board

David Bethea (University of Wisconsin, Madison)
Eliot Borenstein (New York University, New York)
Julia Bekman Chadaga (Macalester College, St. Paul, Minnesota)
Nancy Condee (University of Pittsburg, Pittsburg)
Caryl Emerson (Princeton University, Princeton)
Bernice Glatzer Rosenthal (Fordham University, New York)
Marcus Levitt (USC, Los Angeles)
Alex Martin (University of Notre Dame, South Bend, Indiana)
Irene Masing-Delic (Ohio State University, Columbus)
Joe Peschio (University of Wisconsin-Milwaukee, Milwaukee)
Irina Reyfman (Columbia University, New York)
Stephanie Sandler (Harvard University, Cambridge)

Other Titles in this Series

Queer(ing) Russian Art: Realism, Revolution, Performance
Edited by Brian James Baer & Yevgeniy Fiks

Belomor: Criminality and Creativity in Stalin's Gulag
Julie S. Draskoczy

Shapes of Apocalypse: Arts and Philosophy in Slavic Thought
Edited by Andrea Oppo

THE RUSSIAN INTELLIGENTSIA
MYTH, MISSION, AND METAMORPHOSIS

Edited by Sibelan Forrester
and Olga Partan

ACADEMIC STUDIES PRESS
BOSTON
2025

Names: Forrester, Sibelan E. S. (Sibelan Elizabeth S.), editor. | Simonova-Partan, Ol'ga, editor.
Title: The Russian intelligentsia : myth, mission, and metamorphosis / edited by Sibelan Forrester and Olga Partan.
Description: Brookline, MA : Academic Studies Press, 2025. | Series: Myths and taboos in Slavic cultures | Includes bibliographical references and index.
Identifiers: LCCN 2024033495 (print) | LCCN 2024033496 (ebook) | ISBN 9798887196695 (hardback) | ISBN 9798887196701 (adobe pdf) | ISBN 9798887196718 (epub)
Subjects: LCSH: Intellectuals--Russia (Federation)--History. | Intellectuals--Russia (Federation)--Attitudes. | Authors, Russian--Attitudes. | Russia (Federation)--Civilization. | Russia (Federation)--Intellectual life.
Classification: LCC DK510.32 .R869 2024 (print) | LCC DK510.32 (ebook) | DDC 947--dc23/eng/20240814
LC record available at https://lccn.loc.gov/2024033495
LC ebook record available at https://lccn.loc.gov/2024033496

Copyright © Academic Studies Press, 2025
ISBN 9798887196695 hardback
ISBN 9798887196701 ebook PDF
ISBN 9798887196718 epub

Book design by Lapiz Digital Services
Cover design by Ivan Grave

Published by Academic Studies Press
1007 Chestnut Street
Newton, MA 02464, USA
press@academicstudiespress.com
www.academicstudiespress.com

Contents

Acknowledgements   vii

1. Introduction: The Intelligentsia in Russia: Shifting Terms, History, and Scholarly Approaches   ix
   Olga Partan and Sibelan Forrester

Part One: Pre-Nineteenth Century   1

2. An Essay on the Origins of the Intelligentsia: Catherine the Great and Her Relations with Novikov and Radishchev   3
   Marcus Levitt

Part Two: The Nineteenth Century   27

3. The Intelligentsia in the Russian Press of the 1860s and 1870s   29
   Konstantine Klioutchkine

4. Dostoevsky and the Intelligentsia   44
   Alexander Burry

5. Accommodating the Intelligentsia: Tolstoyan Nonresistance as a Response to the Russian Intelligentsia   62
   Michael Denner

6. The Russian Intelligentsia and Western Intellectuals: Through the Prism of Chekhov   80
   Svetlana Evdokimova

Part Three: The Twentieth Century   103

7. Merchants vs. the Intelligentsia: The Case of the Moscow Art Theatre   105
   Maria Ignatieva

8. A Bridgeable Schism? The Russian Silver Age Intelligentsia Holds Its Ground, Spruces up, and Proselytizes   123
   Irene Masing-Delic

9. *Landmarks* (Vekhi)—the Russian Intelligentsia at a Crossroads Olga Sobolev	149
10. The End of the Classical Intelligentsia? Gary Hamburg	165
11. The Russian Knights Templar: A Secret Mystical Order and Its Legacy Olga Partan	188
12. Remaking the Literary Intelligentsia (1930s-1940s) Carol Any	211
13. The Soviet Intelligentsia and Thaw-Era Science Fiction Sibelan Forrester	229
14. The Intelligentsia and the "Thick Journal" Marina Adamovich	245
15. A Romantic Ironist or a New Intellectual? Tatyana Tolstaya and Her Critique of the Russian Intelligentsia Alexandra Smith	264

Part Four: The Twenty-First Century — **287**

16. Ulitskaya and Pelevin on the *Shestidesiatniki* Sofya Khagi	288
17. The Intelligentsia and the Intellectuals: A History of Two Terms in Russian Philosophical Discourse Alyssa DeBlasio	312
18. Legacy and Denial: Russian Intelligentsia on Screen and Online in the First Two Decades of the Twenty-First Century Tatiana Smorodinska	334

Contributors — **350**

Index — **352**

Acknowledgements

We wish to acknowledge support from various institutions and to recall the helpful experiences of conference panels and roundtables as we gathered and prepared the chapters in this book.

The volume was generously supported by the Office of the Provost at Swarthmore College and by the McFarland Center for Religion, Ethics and Culture at the College of the Holy Cross. We express our particular gratitude to Thomas Landy, McFarland Center Director, for his enthusiastic support of this project and his help in organizing the two-day online conference in 2021, which brought together all the participants and got us all acquainted with one another's topics. Sibelan Forrester is grateful to the Summer Language Workshop at Indiana University for the chance to present some of early research for her chapter in the summer of 2018. The College of the Holy Cross Research and Publication Award allowed Olga Partan to conduct research and several interviews in Moscow in June 2018 at the initial stage of this project.

Our collaboration included the following panels and roundtables at the annual conventions of the Association for Slavic, East European and Eurasian Studies (ASEEES):

- 49th Annual Convention, Chicago, IL, November 9–12, 2017; "The Intelligentsia in Russia: Have Rumors of its Death Been Exaggerated?" (roundtable)

• 50th Annual Convention, Boston, December 6–9, 2018; "The Intelligentsia in Russia I: End of the 19th and Early 20th Century" (panel), "The Intelligentsia in Russia II: The Intelligentsia in the Soviet Union" (panel), and "The Intelligentsia in Russia III: The Intelligentsia and Intellectuals in Russia after 1991" (panel)

• 51st Annual Convention, San Francisco, November 23–26, 2019; "Rethinking the Role of the Intelligentsia on the Post-Soviet Cultural Stage" (panel)

The two-day online conference, "The Intelligentsia in Russia: Spiritual and Moral Values," was held on March 12 and 13, 2021. We thank all our collaborators for their participation and for keeping things interesting!

The COVID pandemic significantly delayed our work on the project, and among other things it meant that our work was completed quite a while after Russia's invasion of Ukraine in early 2022. Although this event also delayed our work and required significant revision of some of the contributions, it has also clarified some important questions about the current nature of the Russian intelligentsia.

We wish to commemorate Italian scholar Claudia Pieralli of the University of Florence, whose illness and untimely death meant that she did not contribute a chapter on the Russian intelligentsia and Masonry, which would have been a valuable part of the collection. We regret that one of our contributors felt compelled to withdraw from participation—perhaps in fear of repercussions at home in Russia in this time of war.

Finally, we owe many thanks to our editors at Academic Studies Press. The extended period of our work on this volume meant that we had the pleasure of working with Daniel Frese, Alana Felton, Alessandra Anzani, Sasha Shapiro, Daria Nemtsova, Kate Yanduganova, and our Series Editor Alyssa Gillespie. Two anonymous readers for ASP gave us thoughtful and helpful comments and suggestions and helped to improve the collection. We are very grateful to Igor Nemirovsky for his support over the years.

Introduction

The Intelligentsia in Russia: Shifting Terms, History, and Scholarly Approaches

Olga Partan and Sibelan Forrester

The intelligentsia in Russia has been both scorned and admired, alternately blamed for Russia's tragic fate and cherished for its cultural uniqueness. While the Russian intelligentsia is traditionally defined as a well-educated social class engaged in complex intellectual labor, the concept of the class has evolved over time along with its role in Russian society.[1] It developed and evolved chronologically from the eighteenth century to today, originating in education and philosophy and playing a distinct spiritual and moral role in Russian society. The contributors to this collection discuss the essential elements of the *myth* of the Russian intelligentsia as both a distinctive social group and a spiritual formation that claims high moral standards and expectations for the self and for society. They explore how representatives of the intelligentsia have seen their *mission* on various historical stages. Moreover, the chapters address the intelligentsia's *metamorphosis* over time

---

1 The Merriam-Webster dictionary defines the word *intelligentsia* as "intellectuals who form an artistic, social, or political vanguard or elite," webster.com/dictionary/intelligentsia. The Cambridge dictionary provides a similar definition: "very educated people in a society, especially those interested in the arts and in politics," dictionary.cambridge.org/us/dictionary/english/intelligentsia, accessed November 10, 2023. In Ozhegov's explanatory dictionary, it is "People of intellectual labor and educations, who have special knowledge in various fields of science, technology and culture; a social stratum of people engaged in such work," *Tolkovyi slovar' russkogo iazyka*, 249.

and through different historical eras: how socio-political factors have shaped its persistence alongside its perpetual transformation. The collection will address the intelligentsia's complex and ambiguous role, articulating the term's fluidity in different socio-political surroundings.

This volume takes a multidisciplinary approach, combining literary, philosophical, cultural, historical, mythological, and anthropological studies. Because of the intelligentsia's logocentric nature, many of the articles focus on its depiction or activities in literature, which served as a venue for discussion of social and political issues under Russian and Soviet censorship.

The intelligentsia in Russia and the Soviet Union has played a significant role in creating and interpreting the cultural riches we study—the works that ensure Russia's reputation for outstanding artists, dancers, scientists and writers. These individuals never worked in a vacuum or in isolation, but rather in the matrix of values and expectations largely shaped by the intelligentsia. After the end of the Soviet Union, it seemed that the intelligentsia and its traditional role, part oppositional and part aspirational, had been consigned to the past, but more recent political and social events have reopened questions about the place, significance and impact of the intelligentsia in Russia—and for readers and observers elsewhere.

The Intelligentsia: Origins and Transformations

The term originates from the Latin noun *intelligentia* and the verb *intelligere* "to understand;"[2] it belongs to the vocabulary that has been assimilated into Russian from Western European languages. Despite its Latin etymology, the intelligentsia is frequently seen as a particularly Russian phenomenon, especially by scholars of Russian history and culture. Like the term, with its Western origin, the intelligentsia in Russia has strong cultural, spiritual, and intellectual ties to the West, inspired by Western ideals of individual freedom, enlightenment, and equality. Eighteenth-century poet, playwright, and theoretician Vasily Tredyakovsky (1703–1769) associated the Latin word *intelligentia* with reason and translated it as *razumnost'*.[3] Philosopher Isaiah Berlin noted:

---

2 "Intelligentsia," in *Oxford Learner's Dictionaries*, accessed on January 11, 2024, https://www.oxfordlearnersdictionaries.com/us/definition/english/intelligentsia?q=intelligentsia.

3 G. M. Hamburg, "Russian Intelligentsia," in *A History of Russian Thought*, ed. William Leatherbarrow and Derek Offord (Cambridge: Cambridge UP, 2012), 44.

"Intelligentsia" is a Russian word invented in the nineteenth century that has since acquired worldwide significance. The phenomenon itself, within historical and literally revolutionary consequences, is, I suppose, the largest single Russian contribution to societal change in the world.[4]

Martin Malia said of the intelligentsia, "No class in Russian history has had a more momentous impact on the destinies of that nation or indeed of the modern world."[5] The intelligentsia as a social group sprang from Peter the Great's early eighteenth-century Westernizing and educational reforms. The first Russian universities were founded in the eighteenth century with largely foreign professors, and by the end of the eighteenth century they had produced a new, though still quite small, generation of educated and enlightened Russians.

The perpetual transformation and fluidity of the term "intelligentsia" in Russian culture are remarkable; how the term acquired its modern sense is still debated. Some scholars believe that it was popularized in the 1860s by the writer Piotr Boborykin, who borrowed it from German to describe an educated, thinking, progressive group. However, an 1836 entry from poet Vasily Zhukovsky's diary (first published only in 1994) reveals the term in use earlier. Describing a fire at St. Petersburg's famous Leman *balagan*, where many spectators perished in the flames, Zhukovsky criticized the Russian aristocratic Europeanized elite for its lack of empathy for the common people's hardship:

> Через три часа после общественного бедствия, почти рядом с тем местом, на коем еще дымились сожжённые тела 300 русских, около которого выли не допускаемые к мертвым полицией родственники, осветился великолепный Энгельгардтов дом, и к нему потянулись кареты, все наполненные лучшим петербургским дворянством, тем, которое у нас представляет всю русскую европейскую интеллигенцию; никому не пришло в голову (есть исключения), что случившиеся несчастие есть общее, танцевали и смеялись и бесились до 3-ех часов и разъехались, как будто ничего не было…

---

4 Isaiah Berlin, "A Remarkable Decade: 'The Birth of the Russian Intelligentsia,'" in *Russian Thinkers*, ed. Isaiah Berlin (New York: Penguin Classics, 1998), 133.
5 Martin Malia, "What is the Intelligentsia?," in *The Russian Intelligentsia*, ed. Richard Pipes (New York: Columbia UP, 1961), 4.

В Англии это не могло бы случиться; а если бы случилось, то народ бы выбил все окна освещенной залы. Это ругательство над народным несчастьем.⁶

Three hours after the societal disaster, almost next door to the place where the burned bodies of 300 Russians were still smoldering, and police were not letting the wailing relatives approach the dead bodies, the magnificent Engelhardt mansion was lit up, and carriages filled with the best representatives of the St. Petersburg nobility, who for us represent the whole Russian European intelligentsia, were lined up headed for the mansion. It did not occur to anyone (with some exceptions) that the misfortune that had occurred was a shared one; everyone danced, laughed and raved until 3 o clock and left as if nothing had gone on . . .

This could not have happened in England; and if it had happened, the people would have knocked out all the windows of the illuminated hall. It is a desecration of the people's misfortune.⁷

Zhukovsky condemns the aristocratic intelligentsia for their indifference to the common folk's tragedy. He portrays a Russian elite preoccupied with its own entertainment and pleasure, incapable of showing compassion and empathy towards its own people. Furthermore, there are sinister prophetic overtones in those lines: the "intelligentsia" is oblivious as its surroundings burn down (in the case Zhukovsky describes, literally; in the case of Russian history, metaphorically). Zhukovsky's words also juxtapose the Russian "European" elite to the common people of Russia, and he uses this tragic event to reflect on the gap between Russian and (superior) Western societal norms: here, Russian versus British. It is significant that the first known use of the term is linked to two main themes: the intelligentsia's responsibility to the common people, and juxtaposition of the Russian mentality to the Western one.

The intelligentsia's reputation developed during the reign of Catherine the Great through individuals such as Russian author and social critic Aleksandr Radishchev (1749–1802) and the writer, journalist, and philanthropist Nikolai Novikov (1744–1818).⁸ The Decembrists and their revolt under Nicholas

---

6   V. A. Zhukovskii, *Dnevniki. Zapisnye knizhki (1834–1847)* (Moscow: Direct-Media, 2012), 40.
7   Translation by the editors—SF, OP. All translations here are ours unless otherwise noted.
8   See Marcus Levitt's chapter in this volume.

I in 1825 became, in retrospect, models of the intelligentsia's self-sacrificing commitment to political progress. The intelligentsia was further shaped in the 1830s and 1840s by fascination with German idealist philosophy, and then by enthusiasm for the Great Reforms that started in 1855, leading up to the abolition of serfdom in 1861. Ivan Turgenev's 1862 novel *Fathers and Children* (also translated as *Fathers and Sons*) famously reflects the antagonistic world outlook of two generations—summarizable as the clash of idealism with materialism. By the 1860s, the term "intelligentsia" began to gravitate toward the *raznochintsy*, people who no longer fit within traditional divisions of Russian society into aristocracy, clergy, merchantry and peasantry. As this collection will show, by the end of the nineteenth century the term had acquired a variety of competing definitions.

After the 1917 Bolshevik revolution, perceptions of the intelligentsia changed dramatically. Vladimir Lenin, in a 1919 letter to Maxim Gorky, characterized the intelligentsia harshly:

> Интеллектуальные силы рабочих и крестьян растут и крепнут в борьбе за свержение буржуазии и её пособников, интеллегентиков, лакеев капитала, мнящих себя мозгом нации. На деле это не мозг, а говно.[9]

> The intellectual forces of the workers and peasants are growing and strengthening in the struggle to overthrow the bourgeoisie and its accomplices, the little *intelligenty*, the lackeys of capital, who imagine themselves the brain of the nation. In fact, they're not the brain, but the shit.

Nevertheless, the Soviet government later proclaimed the intelligentsia "one of the three pillars of the socialist order, together with the proletariat and the toiling peasantry."[10] Revolutionary connections to the materialist intelligentsia of the 1860s must have redeemed the term from opinions like Lenin's. In the Soviet era, the "intelligentsia" officially signified all those who worked not so much with their hands as with their minds—including the rural, urban, scientific, and creative intelligentsia. As under Catherine II and then Alexanders I and II, emphasis on European-style education and cultural production encouraged

---

9   V. I. Lenin's letter to A. M. Gorky, written September 15, 1919, Biblioteka gazety "Revolutsiia," accessed February 11, 2022, http://revolucia.ru/lenin51_47.html.
10 Malia, "What is the Intelligentsia?," 3.

the formation and emergence of a group that was both knowledgeable and critical of social phenomena, and especially of the government, its stances and actions. At the same time, as Mark Lipovetsky, Pavel Khazanov, and others have shown, a sizable part of the Soviet intelligentsia (especially, per Lipovetsky, the ITR engineering and technical workers) adopted a detached attitude toward the Soviet Government and the Communist Party, keeping their "heads down" in exchange for the benefits of work in their chosen fields.[11] The traditions of the classic critical intelligentsia were actually continued more by Soviet dissidents. Nevertheless, the gradual historical transformation included the "Thaw" generation of the 1960s (the *shestidesiatniki*), and then the liberal intelligentsia of the 1980s, allies of Mikhail Gorbachev in his attempts to reform the Soviet system.[12]

The Intelligentsia in the Era of Putin

The new metamorphoses of the intelligentsia in the era of Putinism deserve special attention, as we are completing our introduction in the midst of a full-scale war in Ukraine unleashed by Russian President Vladimir Putin. Over the last decade of Putin's reign, and particularly since that invasion, Russia has turned into an authoritarian state with punitive organizations, where parliamentary institutions, law enforcement agencies and systems of justice are mere tools in the hands of the ruling elite. Post-Soviet public discourse had already consistently signaled that as a class or social group the intelligentsia in Russia had left the historical arena for good. While there are still individual *intelligenty* (*intelligentnye liudi*), the intelligentsia as a sacred moral order has frequently been declared dead.[13] At a 2016 literary evening at Brandeis University, the well-known Russian writer Lyudmila Ulitskaya insisted that there is NO more intelligentsia in Russia at the current historical stage. In turn, Russian state media have offered heated discussions asserting, mourning, or celebrating the intelligentsia's demise. Recent articles include "The new intelligentsia—it's no longer a purely Russian phenomenon" (Novaia intelligentsiia—eto uzhe

---

11 Mark Lipovetsky, "The Poetics of ITR Discourse: In the 1960s and Today," *Ab Imperio* 1 (2013): 109–131; Pavel Khazanov, *The Russia That We Have Lost: Pre-Soviet Past as Anti-Soviet Discourse* (Madison: U of Wisconsin Press, 2023).
12 See Vladislav Zubok, *Zhivago's Children: The Last Russian Intelligentsia* (Cambridge, MA: Harvard UP, 2011) for detailed discussion of the intelligentsia's degeneration and disappearance as the Soviet system collapsed.
13 Note for example Masha Gessen's book, *Dead Again: The Russian Intelligentsia after Communism* (London: Verso Books, 1997)—the title underlines the repeated demise of the intelligentsia.

ne chisto russkoe iavlenie), "Do we need the intelligentsia?" (Nuzhna li nam intelligentsiia?), and "The *intelligent* is dead, but why is the disdain for him so lively?" (Intelligent mertv, no pochemu prezrenie k nemu tak zhivo?).[14]

Russian-Swiss author Mikhail Shishkin (born in 1961) identifies the intelligentsia as "the most progressive group of the Russian population that historically would oppose the ruling class."[15] By that definition, it is still alive even if the name has changed. Today, in fact, the intelligentsia in Russia has split into two antagonistic camps largely defined by conflicting views about the annexation of Crimea in 2014 and differing attitudes toward the war in Ukraine. The saying: "Skazhi mne chei Krym i ia skazhu kto ty/Tell me who Crimea belongs to, and I'll say who you are" (based on the Russian proverb: "Skazhi mne kto tvoi drug i ia skazhu kto ty/Tell me who your friend is, and I'll say who you are") reflects the dramatic juxtaposition of those who enthusiastically support the Kremlin's political agenda and those who are appalled by it—each group seeing itself as the progressive representatives of Russian society. Does the contemporary intelligentsia see opposition to the ruling class as a prerequisite for belonging in the group? Or has political participation become so ineffective that citizens turn away from it and back to art and literature in order to debate significant social issues? Can we even use the term intelligentsia to refer to a present-day cultural elite that actively supports Putinism?

Over the last several years, the intelligentsia has undergone yet another metamorphosis. Eminent journalists, writers, and human right activists in the Russian Federation and elsewhere are increasingly being declared "foreign agents" (in Russian, *inoagenty*). The 2012 law on Foreign Agents is also an attack on Russian civil society, giving the authorities new opportunities to prosecute political dissent. Prominent opposition journalist Viktor Shenderovich was declared a foreign agent on December 30, 2021. With characteristic wit, Shenderovich noted the equal sign established between the concepts of foreign agent and representative of the intelligentsia:

---

14 For media debates on the intelligentsia see Elena Barysheva's interview with Vladimir Pozner: "Novaia intelligentsiia—eto uzhe ne chisto russkoe iavleniie," *Moscow News*, November 7, 2012, http://www.mn.ru/society/84702; Mikhail Deliagin, "Nuzhna li nam intelligentsiia," *Moskovskii komsomolets*, February 18, 2012, https://www.mk.ru/social/2018/02/18/nuzhna-li-nam-intelligenciya.html; Andrei Arkhangel'skii, "Intellegentsiia—eto cool," Colta.ru, http://www.colta.ru/articles/society/13865, accessed January 5, 2022.
15 Mikhail Shishkin, interview with Olga Partan, April 2018.

сегодняшнее наполнение понятия «иноагент» почти совпадает с понятием «интеллигентный человек», «приличный человек».[16]

[T]oday's meaning of the concept "foreign agent" almost coincides with the concept of "an *intelligent*," "a decent person."

Receiving the Theater Star award in December, 2021, actor Liya Akhedzhakova gave an emotional speech on the paradox of labeling representatives of the intelligentsia as "foreign agents":

Вот—потерян смысл. Что такое, «иноагент»? Ну это же шпион, который вообще на эти деньги тут ходит, нюхает, на нас доносит и разрушает нашу жизнь. Вот это «иноагент». Почему звание иноагента присваивается лучшим людям профессии? Лучшим! Лучшие журналисты, лучшие правозащитники.[17]

There, the meaning is lost. What is a "foreign agent'? Well, in general it's a spy who walks around using this money, sniffs things out, denounces us, and destroys our life. That's a "foreign agent." Why is the title of foreign agent attached to the best people in the profession? The best! The best journalists, the best human rights defenders.

Akhedzhakova expresses her admiration for and pride in the so-called foreign agents, emphasizing that they represent truth and high moral values as well as high professional competence.

Since the Russian invasion of Ukraine in February of 2022, the split between the Putin regime's supporters and those who condemn his military aggression has become even more drastic. Anti-war statements by Russian journalists, writers, scientists, human rights activists, and representatives of Russian pop culture vividly demonstrate that many members of the Putin-era intelligentsia feel

---

16 Sofiia Rogacheva, "Rezhim Putina nesovmestim so svobodoi. Viktor Shenderovich stal inoagentom," *Sibir' Realii*, December 31, 2021, https://www.sibreal.org/a/viktor-shenderovich-stal-inoagentom/31634081.html.
17 Deutsche Welle na russkom, "Akhedzhakova emotsional'no raskritikovala prisvoenie statusa 'inoagentov' zhurnalistam i pravozashchitnikam," *DW na russkom*, accessed on January 9, 2024, https://www.youtube.com/watch?v=57iz9Iele7E.

responsible for the future of their homeland and publicly protest against official state propaganda. The falsehood of the so-called "Special Military Operation" for the "de-Nazification of Ukraine" is juxtaposed to narratives exposing the horror of the war and the Russian nation's historic responsibility for its outcomes. After the invasion, Ulitskaya wrote:

> Безумие одного человека и преданных ему подсобников руководит судьбой страны. Можно только делать догадки о том, что будет написано об этом в учебниках истории через 50 лет. Боль, страх и стыд—вот чувства сегодняшнего дня.[18]

> The madness of one man and his devoted accomplices directs the fate of the country. One can only speculate about what history textbooks will write about this in 50 years. Pain, fear, and shame are the feelings of today.

While public opinion polls conducted in Russia during the first weeks of the war in Ukraine suggest that 83% of the Russian population support Putin's leadership, Mikhail Shishkin reflects, "Do a dictatorship and a dictator give a birth to a slave population, or does a slave population give birth to a dictatorship and a dictator? The chicken and the egg. How can this vicious circle be broken? How can a new Russia begin?"[19] Shishkin believes that "Russia's fate depends on de-Putinisation."[20]

Today Russia is experiencing a multi-generational exodus as hundreds of thousands of highly educated and free-thinking Russians abandon their homeland, moving beyond the reach of Putin's dictatorship.[21] Press reports indicate that about fifteen thousand people were arrested for anti-war protests in Russia in March 2022 alone, as new laws make anti-war statements and even use of the

---

18 L. Ulitskaia, "Bezumie odnogo cheloveka i predannykh emu podsobnikov rukovodit sud'boi strany," *Gazetaby.com*, March 14, 2022, https://gazetaby.com/post/uliczkaya-bezumie-odnogo-cheloveka-i-predannyx-emu/184027.
19 Ivan Nechepurenko, "Faced with Foreign Pressure, Russians Rally around Putin, Poll Shows," *New York Times*, March 31, 2022, https://www.nytimes.com/2022/03/31/world/europe/putin-approval-rating-russia.html; Mikhail Shishkin, "Neither NATO nor Ukraine can de-Putinise Russia," *The Guardian*, published March 28, 2022, https://www.theguardian.com/commentisfree/2022/mar/28/nato-ukraine-vladimir-putin-russia-democratic-national-guilt.
20 Shishkin, "Neither NATO nor Ukraine."
21 Sophie Pinkham, "'They're Willing to Risk Ruining Their Lives.' Putin's War Is Driving Russians Out," *New York Times*, March 17, 2022, https://www.nytimes.com/2022/03/17/opinion/russian-migrants-putin-war-ukraine.html.

word "war" a form of criminal offense that can result in fifteen years in prison. The country is facing a new reality of dictatorship with brutal state control of traditional and social media, along with forceful propaganda based on Soviet-era ideology, nationalism, and anti-western rhetoric. How can the intelligentsia, already undermined by post-Soviet changes, respond to this?

Reflecting on the official pro-military position of the Russian Orthodox Church, Mikhail Epstein points to the phenomena of "sacromania"—obsession with one's own holiness or the sanctity of one's principles and beliefs—in the Russian Orthodox Church's support for Putin through sermons and public statements. Yet, despite the bent of both church and official media, many in the young generation of Russian citizens do not want to kill or to be killed, according to Dmitri Muratov, editor in chief of *Novaia gazeta* and co-recipient of the 2021 Nobel Peace Prize.[22]

What is happening to the intelligentsia of Russia amid this new historical tragedy? What choices face the intelligentsia in the third decade of the twenty-first century? What is the position of young, educated people whose future has been stolen by the Kremlin regime? There are not many options to choose from: protest, joining the dissidents within the country, and thus face arrest and imprisonment; silently disagree with the regime but remain in the country for the sake of family or personal stability; emigrate, perhaps permanently, leaving Russia for an unknown period of time; or publicly support the "Special Military Operation" and call those who left the homeland or made public anti-war statements traitors or foreign agents. Alas, more than ever the intelligentsia in Russia is split into antagonistic camps.

Today, dissidents who speak out against the war, fight corruption, or defend civil liberties and human rights in the Russian Federation face absurd fabricated accusations, criminal prosecution and imprisonment. In fact, the majority of those who can think independently unavoidably become dissidents in Putin's Russia. Here is Andrei Sinyavsky's definition of dissidence:

> диссидентство—это прежде всего, на мой взгляд, движение интеллектуальное, это процесс самостоятельного и

---

22 Dmitrii Muratov, "Okno v Evropu zakryto, i na nem ustanovleny reshetki," YouTube, accessed December 15, 2023, https://youtu.be/KMKpK_gD784. Another outcome of Putin's war in Ukraine is a sharpened distinction between the Russian intelligentsia and analogous groups in Ukraine and in other former Soviet republics, which Russo-centric Imperial and Soviet practice had tended to fold into the Russian phenomenon when that was convenient, even when members of non-Russian intelligentsia groups tended to prefer not to assimilate and Russify. But this is a topic for another project.

бесстрашного думания. И вместе с тем эти интеллектуальные или духовные запросы связаны с чувством моральной ответственности, которая лежит на человеке и заставляет его независимо мыслить, говорить и писать, без оглядки на стандарты и подсказки государства.

[D]issidence is first of all, in my opinion, an intellectual movement; it is a process of independent and fearless thinking. And at the same time, these intellectual or spiritual demands are associated with a sense of moral responsibility that is incumbent on a person and makes him think, speak and write independently, without regard to the standards and prompting of the state.[23]

The international non-profit human right group "Memorial," founded in 1987 by Andrei Sakharov and Lev Ponomariov and long involved in studying political repression in the USSR and contemporary Russia society, was also declared a foreign agent and dissolved in April 2022. Memorial supported rehabilitation of persons who had undergone political repression, gathering artifacts and information, and resurrecting names and personal stories from oblivion. Memorial's activities were historical and educational, as the organization paid respect to repressed individuals and their relatives, working to make authorities accountable for violations of human rights. Current statistics on the numbers of political prisoners in Russia are chilling; according to a document prepared jointly by the Independent Human Rights Project "Political Prisoners Support Memorial" and "Memorial Human Rights Defense Center," the numbers of arrests and imprisonments for political reasons dramatically increased over the last five years, particularly after the Russian invasion of Ukraine.[24]

---

23 Andrei Siniavskii, "Dissidenstvo kak lichnyi opyt," *Bookshaker.net*, accessed December 10, 2023, https://bookshaker.net/r/dissidentstvo-kak-lichnyy-opyt-abram-terc?page=2.

24 Even though "Memorial" was officially shut down on April 5, 2022, by a decision of the Moscow City Court, the organization continues to monitor political repressions and was a co-recipient of the Nobel Peace Prize the same year. According to "Memorial" documents, on September 1, 2018, "the list of political prisoners contained 46 individuals, while the list of those persecuted for exercising freedom of religion and belief included 137 individuals, for a total of 183 people." Shortly after February 24, 2022, the list of political prisoners tripled: "As of 5 April 2023, the 'general' list of political prisoners has grown to 141 individuals, and the list of those persecuted for exercising their freedom of religion and belief has increased to 410 individuals, making a total of 558 people." See the pdf from Memorial: Tsentr zashchity prav cheloveka, "Polozheniie politicheskikh zakliuchennykh v Rossii," April 12, 2023, https://memorialcenter.org/analytics/polozhenie-politicheskih-zaklyuchennyh-v-rf, accessed December 11, 2023.

The majority of these political prisoners are representatives of the intelligentsia and are well-educated free thinkers. In today's Russia, anti-war public statements are categorized as discrediting the Russian military and seen as high treason, as in the case of Vladimir Kara-Murza, the Russian-British journalist, political activist and author, who in April 2023 was sentenced to twenty-five years in prison, then released in a prisoner exchange in August 2024. As absurd as it sounds in the context of the largest war on the European continent since World War II, one can be sentenced to seven years in prison for simply using the word "war."[25] In May 2023 two young women—theater director and poet Evgeniya Berkovich and playwright Svetlana Petriichuk—were arrested and imprisoned, accused of justifying terrorism for their critically acclaimed 2020 production of the play "Finist the Brave Falcon," written by Petriichuk and awarded a prestigious Golden Mask award in Russia. The production was based on documentary material, telling the stories of Russian women who married Islamic extremists, but the legal persecution was undoubtedly connected with Berkovich's anti-war position, expressed in poems and interviews.

To the international community that wonders why the Russian populace is so obedient, does not rebel, but rather appears as a silent, amorphous mass, Muratov clarifies:

> The most difficult question, I am often asked: "Why are the Russians silent? Why don't they rebel? And what, are all Russian slaves?" I will not avoid this question and will ask in response: "Where to speak? Where to protest? Rallies are banned, 600 political prisoners are in prison, 20 thousand cases against peace supporters, 300 non-state media have been closed, there is not a single parliament member who advocates peace, those people who are in prison should command our respect, compassion and desire to help them."[26]

Aleksei Navalny's tragic destiny is a terrifying demonstration of how the Kremlin deals with political dissidence in Russia. Navalny's sudden death on February 16, 2024, in a corrective colony north of the Arctic Circle was perceived by the Russian opposition and the Western press as a possible political assassination. For more than a week after his death, Navalny's mother Lyudmila Navalnaya was not allowed to claim her son's body for a Christian burial. A group of liberal

---

25 There were even cases when street protesters were arrested for holding blank pieces of paper.
26 Muratov, "Okno v Evropu zakryto."

representatives of the Russian intelligentsia, mourning Navalny's death, released videos with the demand that the son's body be returned to his mother.[27] These video addresses included speeches by public intellectuals and artists, including by two recent Nobel Prize recipients, Belarusian journalist and essayist Svetlana Alexievich and Russian journalist Dmitri Muratov, film director Andrei Zviagintsev, and dancer and choreographer Mikhail Baryshnikov. Navalny's funeral in Moscow was attended by thousands of Russians, becoming one of the most powerful open manifestations of public support, respect and admiration for his life journey. Ignoring the risk of detention and political repercussions, a multigenerational procession mourned this opposition leader who had dared to challenge the status quo and had become President Putin's most outspoken and well-known political opponent.

The current wave of emigration from Russia has been compared to the "White" emigration following the October Revolution of 1917 and the Civil War. According to data from the Red Cross, about two million people left Russia or were expelled during that period. Emigration data of the present so-called fifth wave is not fully known, but even official Russian sources confirm that hundreds of thousands of people have left Russia since the start of the war in Ukraine. The authors of an OutRush study believe that those who have left are mostly young, educated and better-off—members of the Russian middle class.[28] This group is defined as "politicized, active and sad."[29] According to *Forbes* magazine, 700,000 to 1,000,000 people left Russia after the announcement of partial mobilization on September 21, 2023.[30]

The new wave of emigrants spans generations and different socio-economic strata, with destinations as diverse as Western and Eastern Europe, Israel, the Caucasus and Middle East, Central Asia, and North America. Recent emigrants belong to the Russian intellectual and artistic elite, with leading writers, journalists, theater and film directors, actors, classical musicians as well as rock and pop stars. The list includes such writers as Lyudmila Ulitskaya and Vladimir Sorokin; theater and film directors such as Andrei Zvyagintsev, Dmitri Krymov,

---

27 "'Otdaite telo!' Izvestnye politiki, zhurnalisty i artisty trebuiut vydat' telo Naval'nogo ego materi," *BBC News Russkaia Sluzhba*, accessed May 10, 2024, https://www.youtube.com/watch?v=3ofdNSkzGVc.

28 Mariia Kiseleva and Viktoriia Safronova, "Novye rossiiskie emigranty. Kto oni, skol'ko ikh i kuda uekhali?," *BBC News Russkaia Sluzhba*, May 5, 2023, https://www.bbc.com/russian/features-65686712.

29 Ibid.

30 Andrei Zlobin, "Kreml' nazval 'utkoi' dannye Forbes o 700,000 uekhavshikh iz Rossii posle 21 sentiabria," *Forbes*, October 6, 2022, https://www.forbes.ru/society/479089-kreml-nazval-utkoj-dannye-forbes-o-700-000-uehavsih-iz-rossii-posle-21-sentabra.

and Kirill Serebrianikov; actors Chulpan Khamatova and Anatoli Bely; the tsarina of Russian pop culture Alla Pugacheva and her husband Maxim Galkin, a standup comedian; leaders of the legendary rock bands *Akvarium* and *Mashina vremeni*—Boris Grebenshchikov and Andrei Makarevich respectively; film star, director and writer Renata Litvinova, rock singer Zemfira; and popular journalists Yury Dud and Ksenia Larina, to name just a few. They have joined prominent writers such as Dmitri Kuzmin and Mikhail Shishkin, who have lived outside Russia for many years while continuing to write in Russian.[31]

Regrettably, the list of representatives of the cultural elite who publicly support the invasion of Russian troops in Ukraine, those who incite hatred and in one way or another support the war, is also substantial. However, as editors of this volume we cannot include these individuals in the intelligentsia as it is defined here. The usual traits of the intelligentsia have always included not just disaffection from the misdeeds of political powers and actors but also dissent and resistance, an oppositional stance, and willingness to pay the price for resistance. Active vocal supporters of a war initiated by a criminal regime cannot be seen as any kind of moral compass or consciousness of the nation and should instead be seen as anti-intelligentsia.[32]

In an atmosphere of mass emigration and censorship of all independent media, the Russian diaspora scattered around the world finds many ways to exchange information, creating new internet platforms and publishing houses for discussion and reflection on the historical tragedy that Russia has initiated. The Internet's unlimited possibilities provide opportunities for the Russian-speaking diaspora abroad to receive information that contradicts Kremlin propaganda; people living in Russia can receive it too—as long as they know how to set up a virtual private network.

While the format of this introduction does not provide room to discuss the wide variety of Internet programs, independent media, and publications, it is worth mentioning a few. The radio station Echo of Moscow, beloved by the freethinking intelligentsia, ceased to exist on March 1, 2022, when it went off the air by order of the Prosecutor General's Office of Russia. Despite this, Echo's

---

31 The new diaspora joins the many émigré cultural figures of the fourth wave, which we could say left mostly for economic reasons, and the many cultural figures who have moved between Russia and other countries since 1991, with their cultural production and communication increasingly taking place online.

32 A list of more than 150 people who support President Putin's decision to start his "Special Military Operation" may be found in "Svyshe 150 deiatelei kul'tury podderzhali prezidenta i spetsoperatsiiu na Ukraine," *Regnum*, March 4, 2022, https://regnum.ru/news/3524646, accessed December 22, 2023.

editor in chief Aleksei Venediktov and his colleagues created a new program, *The Living Nail* (Zhivoi gvozd'), that continues to broadcast on a YouTube channel. Another renowned Echo of Moscow journalist, Ksenia Larina, left Russia and now lives in Portugal, with her own YouTube programs. Popular journalist and blogger of a younger generation, Yury Dud, who created a popular YouTube show *vDud'*, continues work outside Russia, making documentaries and conducting interviews, with over two billion views and 10.3 million subscribers.[33] The independent television channel *TV Rain* (Dozhd'), which began broadcasting in Russia in 2010, had to suspend work in Russia and move first to Latvia and then, after controversy over a broadcast, to the Netherlands. These and many other independent media actively oppose state propaganda and support the intelligentsia mission of enlightening audiences with meaningful programming.

The start of the war and severe tightening of censorship negatively impacted publishing in Russia as well. This has encouraged the revival of so-called tamizdat (publication of uncensored Russian-language literature outside Russia), under conditions of greater freedom of expression.[34] The widely known publisher, producer, and journalist Georgy Urushadze recently founded a new publishing house, Freedom Letters, for non-censored literary works that can be purchased worldwide online. Recently published and forthcoming works include books in Russian, Ukrainian, Belarusian, and English.[35]

New literary magazines published abroad bring together members of the intelligentsia who find themselves in internal or external exile. For example, the *Fifth Wave/Piataia volna* literary journal, recently founded by the émigré writer and cardiologist Maxim Osipov, addresses its artistic and civic mission by writing:

> The contributions will be solicited from authors living in Russia and abroad, all of whom are united by their rejection of war and totalitarianism, their love for Russian culture as part of European culture, their sense of personal involvement in and responsibility for what is happening, and their desire to see Russia as a free, peace-loving country, no matter how far-fetched this wish may seem.[36]

---

33 Wikipedia, https://ru.wikipedia.org, s.v. "Iurii Aleksandrovich Dud'," accessed December 2, 2023. Both Dud' and his show are labeled as "media foreign agents" by the Russian government.
34 On the model of "samizdat" from *sam-* ("self-") and *izdat* (short from *izdatel'stvo*, "publishing house"), using the word *tam* ("there").
35 For more information see the publishing house's website at www.freedomletters.org.
36 Maxim Osipov, "About," *Fifth Wave Independent Russian Writing*, accessed on June 22, 2024, https://www.5wave-ru.com/en/about.

The current stage of Russian history and the massive fifth wave of emigration from Russia is a great displacement, but we also see a new metamorphosis within the growing Russian intelligentsia living outside Russia—what we would hope to call the unification of people with strong moral and civil positions who refuse to co-exist or cooperate with the Kremlin's political agenda and are ready to risk their lives, comfort, and careers for freedom. The annual forum of free Russian culture in Europe, "SlovoNovo" in Budva, Montenegro, is a striking example of the consolidation of leading representatives of the liberal anti-Putin intelligentsia that have scattered around the world.[37] In September 2023, the eighth yearly forum was devoted to discussions of Russian culture and politics during the challenging time when the invasion of Ukraine brought irreparable changes to the whole world. Participants include many of the cultural figures listed above. The forum's founder—impresario, gallerist, and art collector Marat Gelman—has succeeded in creating a significant annual event in the life of the growing diaspora of the Russian intelligentsia.

Earlier Scholarship

A substantial body of Russian and Western publications has been dedicated to the intelligentsia, with striking diversity of definitions and terms. Studies by Western scholars flourished during the Cold War, when expertise on Soviet Russia was supported in the United States and other Western countries by government funding, and cultural historians were fascinated by the intelligentsia. Both the "classic" Russian intelligentsia of the nineteenth century and the Soviet intelligentsia have been studied by Russian and Western scholars. A wave of significant works was published during the Cold War (Isaiah Berlin, Richard Pipes, Marc Raeff, Marshall Shatz, Andrei Sinyavsky).[38] Feminist historiography has addressed the place of women in the intelligentsia (Barbara Engel).[39] The apparent demise of the Russian intelligentsia after perestroika inspired more recent

---

37 For more information about SlovoNovo forum see the event's website at www.slovonovo. me. In 2022, funds raised at the forum were used to provide food packages for residents of Ukrainian cities bombed by Russian troops.

38 See Isaiah Berlin, ed., *Russian Thinkers* (New York: Penguin Classics, 1978); Richard Pipes, ed., *The Russian Intelligentsia* (New York: Columbia UP, 1961); Mark Raeff, *Origins of the Russian Intelligentsia* (New York: Harcourt Brace & Company, 1966); Marshall Shatz, *Soviet Dissent in Historical Perspective* (Cambridge: Cambridge UP, 1980); Andrei Sinyavskii, *The Russian Intelligentsia*, trans. Lynn Visson (New York: Columbia UP, 1997).

39 See Barbara Alpern Engel, *Mothers and Daughters: Women of the Intelligentsia in Nineteenth-Century Russia* (Cambridge: Cambridge UP, 1983).

studies (Masha Gessen, Vladislav Zubok, Inna Kochetkova), while others have ranged from additional histories (Laurie Manchester) to surveys over the long term (Vladimir Nahirny) and analyses of the current situation (Dmitri Shalin, Mark Lipovetsky).[40] Denis Sdvizhkov investigates the Russian intelligentsia's interaction with its European counterparts in his recently published, provocative *Know-It-Alls and Their Friends* (Znaiki i ikh druz'ia), using a mocking term taken from a popular Soviet children's book series.[41]

Richard Pipes, editor and contributor to an influential 1961 collection on the Russian intelligentsia, argues that the term itself is "inherently vague and evolving" and thus "cannot be directly studied."[42] In turn, Gary Hamburg suggests using the term in its plural form—intelligentsias—to avoid confusion between various groups of *intelligenty* at different stages of Russian social, cultural, and political development and to denote the constant transformation and evolution of this societal group.[43]

Debates on the intelligentsia are inseparable from the rich body of scholarship on Russian intellectual history and Westernization. Contributors to the volume *A History of Russian Thought* address the role of the intelligentsia in the history of ideas that shaped Russia's social and political landscape.[44] Without discussing the intelligentsia per se, the collection *The Europeanized Elite in Russia 1762–1825: Public Role and Subjective Self*[45] investigates what it meant to be the enlightened Westernized nobility of a nation "outside European civilization,"

---

40 See Masha Gessen, *Dead Again: The Russian Intelligentsia after Communism* (New York: Verso, 1997); Vladislav Zubok, *Zhivago's Children: The Last Russian Intelligentsia* (Cambridge, MA: The Belknap Press, 2009); Inna Kochetkova, *The Myth of the Russian Intelligentsia: Old Intellectual in the New Russia* (London: Routledge, 2010); Laurie Manchester, *Holy Fathers, Secular Sons: Clergy, Intelligentsia, and the Modern Self in Revolutionary Russia* (DeKalb: Northern Illinois UP, 2011); Vladimir Nahirny, *The Russian Intelligentsia: From Torment to Silence* (New York: Routledge, 2018); Dmitri Shalin, ed., *Russian Intelligentsia in the Age of Counterperestroika: Political Agendas, Rhetorical Strategies, Personal Choices* (New York: Routledge, 2019); Mark Lipovetsky, "Intelligentsia Narratives," in Andrew Kahn et al., *A History of Russian Literature* (Oxford: Oxford UP, 2018), 739–769.

41 See Denis Sdvizhkov, *Znaiki i ikh druz'ia: Sravnitel'naia istoriia russkoi intelligentsii* (Moscow: Novoe literaturnoe obozrenie, 2021). Znaika is a protagonist of Soviet children's books by Nikolai Nosov, based on the adventures and misadventures of Neznaika ("Dunno") and his friends.

42 Richard Pipes, "Historical Evolution," in *The Russian Intelligentsia*, ed. R. Pipes, 49.

43 Hamburg, "Russian Intelligentsias," 44–69. Hamburg points out such multifaceted social groups as the "early intelligentsia" in the eighteenth century, the "classical intelligentsia" that originated between 1815 and 1860, "revolutionary intelligentsia," "zemstvo intelligentsia," "serf intelligentsia," "village intelligentsia," "intelligentsia from the people," and so forth.

44 Leatherbarrow and Offord, *A History of Russian Thought*.

45 Andreas Schönle, Andrei Zorin, and Alexei Evstratov, eds., *The Europeanized Elite in Russia 1762–1825: Public Role and Subjective Self* (DeKalb: Northern Illinois UP, 2016).

illuminating the public and private domains of the post-Petrine educated elite that paved the way for the intelligentsia.[46]

Contributions to this Collection

The scholars contributing to this volume are mainly specialists in Russian literature and cultural history, which is appropriate given the logocentric nature of the Russian intelligentsia. Berlin defines the early members of intelligentsia as

> a small group of *littérateurs*, both professional and amateurs, conscious of being alone in a bleak world, with a hostile and arbitrary government on the one hand, and a completely uncomprehending mass of oppressed and inarticulate peasant[s] on the other, conceiving of themselves as a kind of self-conscious army, carrying a banner for all to see—of reason and science, of liberty, of a better life.[47]

Gary Saul Morson echoes Berlin's words, pointing out the almost priestly role of literary figures as bearers of the nation's highest moral standards:

> In Russia this [idealized biographical] approach to writers' lives continued long after Romanticism and, indeed, has never ceased. As poets and novelists became the national consciences, or what Solzhenitsyn called a "second government," tradition required them not only to create great works but also to live appropriately high-minded lives. When the novelist Mikhail Sholokhov joined in the condemnation of dissident writers Andrei Sinyavsky and Yuli Daniel, and regretted that they had only been imprisoned rather than summarily executed, the editor and author Alexander Tvardovsky wrote in his diary that "Sholokhov is now a former writer."[48]

Books are a necessary sign of culture—the "book wallpaper" of stuffed shelves in a small apartment immediately identifies the resident—but they are also a

---

46 Ibid., 4.
47 Berlin, "A Remarkable Decade 'The Birth of the Russian Intelligentsia,'" 144.
48 Gary Saul Morson, "Dostoevsky and His Demons," *New York Review of Books*, July 1, 2021, https://www.nybooks.com/articles/2021/07/01/dostoevsky-and-his-demons/.

proven way to preserve and pass knowledge and history to the next generation, to evade censorship. Today the internet offers ways to manipulate and quickly disseminate thoughts expressed in language or images, but books remain important: a chapter or a series of poems that first appears on the Russian Live Journal or on Facebook will still appear as a book (if the author has enough cachet, and if the work pleases a publisher). This makes sense if one thinks of the censorship of information online, which with the right tools and collaborators can take place quickly, easily, and without notice or trace. The private library is once again a defense against Newspeak or information blockades, especially when it preserves information from the past.

The logocentric and even literature-centric quality of intelligentsia discourse was strongly present in the nineteenth and twentieth centuries; even the philosopher Aleksandr Herzen wrote a novel to engage in debates over how life should be lived, with the provocative title *Who Is to Blame*? Many courses in Russian history have novels on the syllabus: they illustrate the social conditions of the time and show students how those conditions were depicted and debated. Even when artists and writers were not themselves *intelligenty*, their work spoke to the intelligentsia and was treasured by these consumers and preservers of culture. Authors who would never have described themselves as members of the intelligentsia, such as Marina Tsvetaeva, were retroactively claimed by later *intelligenty*. The importance of literature is recognized on all sides: anyone who watched television coverage of the opening ceremony of the 2014 Winter Olympics may recall how it dwelt on the writers who established Russia's reputation as a source of world culture as well as world-class athletes. The ceremony was widely viewed as a strong nationalist statement.

This volume not only offers focused descriptions of the intelligentsia's place in the work of some crucial writers or groups, and a chance to understand public discourse in and outside Russia today with greater subtlety. It also casts light on the relationship between literature and politics—the fluidity of the phenomenon of the intelligentsia—and the power of discourses from the past to shape debate today and to reappear in transformed or appropriated ways.

Part 1: Pre-Nineteenth Century

Marcus Levitt's chapter "An Essay on the Origins of the Intelligentsia: Catherine the Great and Her Relations with Novikov and Radishchev" accentuates the intelligentsia's eighteenth-century roots, focusing on the relationships of Catherine the Great (who ruled Russia 1762–1796) and two men who are often named progenitors of the Russian intelligentsia—Nikolai Novikov (1744–1818) and Aleksandr Radishchev (1749–1802). Levitt argues that these figures, who both famously suffered from Catherine's repression, may serve as prototypes for two later types of *intelligent*. Novikov faced the difficult challenge of helping to create a socially conscious, enlightened reading public; Radishchev openly challenged state power (especially over serfdom) in the name of suffering humanity and social good. Both found support for their positions in Catherine's early pro-Enlightenment position but were caught by the sharp change in political climate following the French Revolution.

Part 2: The Nineteenth Century

In his chapter "The Intelligentsia in the Russian Press of the 1860s and 1870s," Konstantine Klioutchkine explores the broad use of the word "intelligentsia" in literary and journalistic debates of the second half of the nineteenth century. He argues that while the language of the Russian public sphere would undergo continuous changes in the following decades and beyond, the notion of the intelligentsia would continue to generate debates about progressive intellectuals in a technologically mediated world whose apparently self-evident goal should be the improvement of life for all.

Nineteenth century literature is represented by case studies dedicated to Lev Tolstoy, Fyodor Dostoevsky, and Anton Chekhov in their attitudes toward the intelligentsia. In "Dostoevsky and the Intelligentsia," Alexander Burry traces the gradual evolution of Dostoevsky's attitude toward various members of the intelligentsia throughout his creative career. Dostoevsky was involved in a revolutionary circle in the late 1840s, but he had a lifelong preference for peaceful, non-violent reform rather than revolution. At the same time, both early and late in his career, Dostoevsky displayed a principled refusal to inform on more revolutionary actors, even if he disagreed with their ideas.

In his "Accommodating the Intelligentsia: Tolstoyan Nonresistance as a Response to the Russian Intelligentsia," Michael Denner explores Count Lev Tolstoy's conflicted relationship with the intelligentsia. Denner suggests that Tolstoy's rejection of the intelligentsia had its roots in Tolstoy's rejection of human agency *per se*. In place of the intelligentsia's foundational faith in its own right to govern (*gosudarstvo*), Tolstoy argued that absolute, abject submission to the most arbitrary, absolute law was in fact desirable. Tolstoy embraced this rejection of human agency quite early, as we see in his pedagogical writings from the 1850s, his later striving for "self-abolition" or emptiness, decades-long fascination with Buddhism and Taoism, and public writings on non-resistance to evil.

In "The Russian Intelligentsia and Western Intellectuals: Through the Prism of Chekhov," Svetlana Evdokimova considers Anton Chekhov's complex and ambivalent relationship with the Russian intelligentsia in the context of the concept's continuous evolution throughout the nineteenth century, as well as Western European notions of the "intellectual." While Chekhov was considered a "typical representative" of the intelligentsia, he simultaneously embodied qualities that seemed contrary to the intelligentsia's behavior and style of thought.

Part 3: The Twentieth Century

Maria Ignatieva's chapter on "Merchants vs. the Intelligentsia: The Case of the Moscow Art Theater" reevaluates the role that merchants played in the creation and the financial, organizational, spiritual, and artistic aspects of that exemplary institution, the Moscow Art Theater. If today's popular subject of "identity" is applied to the Moscow Art Theater, we may say that the *identity* of the Moscow Art Theater, from its opening in 1898 until 1917, was shaped not only by the intelligentsia, but also by merchants who contributed greatly to all facets of its well-being, in particular the merchants Konstantin Alekseev (better known as Stanislavsky), Savva Morozov, and Nikolai Tarasov.

Irene Masing-Delic's contribution, "A Bridgeable Schism? The Russian Silver Age Intelligentsia Holds Its Ground, Spruces up, and Proselytizes," presents the ideological and philosophical schism between two camps of the intelligentsia that formed at the beginning of the 20th century. Masing-Delic demonstrates that this schism in Russian intelligentsia circles was a struggle between *two* religions: a "religion without god" and a religion *with* God. It was a confrontation between materialist philosophy that attacked faith in "spirits" and any form of spirituality and a *determinedly* dualistic philosophy that posited the existence of both material and spiritual realities (this and "other" worlds).

In her chapter "*Landmarks* (Vekhi)—the Russian Intelligentsia at a Crossroads," Olga Sobolev focuses on *Landmarks*, the volume of seven essays released in 1909 by eminent thinkers of the time, widely regarded as the first major attempt to reflect on the phenomenon of the Russian intelligentsia in its socio-philosophical, cultural and political standing. Sobolev analyzes the volume's account of the intelligentsia and surrounding questions from a modern critical perspective (including issues of self-definition, critical appraisal, and social impact) and explores its relevance for Russian realities of the present day.

Gary M. Hamburg's chapter "The End of the Classical Intelligentsia?" focuses on the "thick journal" *Voice of the Past* (Golos minuvshago) from 1913 to 1923, asking whether Soviet power brought the classical intelligentsia, and with it this journal and others, to an untimely end. Publishing "thick journals" on literature and politics was a central element of classical intelligentsia activity in the nineteenth and early twentieth centuries. Hamburg's reconstruction of the journal and its social and cultural significance emerges in parallel with the destiny of its editorial board, which included the literary critic Pavel Sakulin and historians such as Aleksei Dzhivelegov, Vasily Semevsky, and Sergei Melgunov.

Olga Partan's chapter "The Russian Knights Templar: A Secret Mystical Order and Its Legacy" traces the surprising story of the secret Order of the Knights Templar, which formed after 1917 and united a large group of the artistic and scientific intelligentsia. Partan underlines the post-revolutionary intelligentsia's continued high moral, ethical and spiritual mission, as well as its political escapism and helplessness when confronted by the Soviet state and its punitive organizations. Membership in the Order reflected moral, spiritual and creative dimensions of its members' lives: it represented a form of resistance to the totalitarian state, filling life with meaning and purpose hidden from the uninitiated, though much of the surviving evidence of its existence was preserved in secret police archives.

Moving later in the twentieth century, Carol Any in her "Remaking the Literary Intelligentsia (1930s–1940s)," analyzes the social engineering of the literary intelligentsia that the Communist party needed in order to foster a reliable cohort of writers. Any identifies four strategies: recruitment, education, unionization, and the purges. The new literary intelligentsia had to redefine its mission, shaping writing careers to fit the expectations of censorship and other forms of literary oversight. In the 1930s, Stalin gave particular weight to writers whose books he hoped would spread Soviet values among the reading public and promote Soviet achievements abroad.

Sibelan Forrester's chapter "The Soviet Intelligentsia and Thaw-Era Science Fiction" notes the origin of most science fiction authors of the time outside the Writers' Institutes that had shaped so many Soviet writers in earlier decades. Most Thaw-era science fiction (SF) writers had scientific and technical educations, and their writing could offer both more interesting adventure plots (along with typical intelligentsia discussion of Big Questions in literary works, less censored because SF was considered a genre for children and adolescents) and ways for rising members of the technical intelligentsia to acquire intelligentsia culture. Sometimes the authors graduated into critical approaches to Soviet reality, though at the same time they had to accommodate to the changes of the era of Stagnation if they hoped to continue successful literary careers.

Marina Adamovich's "The Intelligentsia and the Thick Literary Journals" describes the history of the Russian periodicals known as "thick journals," which have traditionally published literary works alongside various genres of journalism. The Russian thick journal represents a unique cultural phenomenon with the mission to express the main humanitarian values and cultural tendencies of the epoch. Historically speaking, the "thick journal" has been a tribune for intelligentsia self-expression and intellectual debates. This chapter approaches the thick journal as a reflection of the intellectual spiritual elite's self-consciousness and a mirror of national discourse.

In her contribution to the volume, "A Romantic Ironist or a New Intellectual? Tatyana Tolstaya's Critique of the Russian Intelligentsia," Alexandra Smith focuses on Tolstaya's essay "The Perils of Utopia: The Russian Intelligentsia under Communism and Perestroika," arguing that Tolstaya's analysis of the Russian intelligentsia as a cultural myth appears ambivalent. While Tolstaya criticizes the Russian democratic intelligentsia of the 1990s as too idealistic and incapable of solving important social problems, she asserts her belief in the moral superiority of Russian writers and artists over the rest of the population. Tolstaya attempts to read her personal narratives in relation to collective ones as part of the post-Soviet nostalgic yearning for a special relationship between texts and life that can ensure the survival of spiritual and moral values.

Part 4: The Twenty-First Century

The three final essays discuss twenty-first-century debates on the role of the intelligentsia in Russian society. In "Ulitskaya and Pelevin on the *Shestidesiatniki*," Sofya Khagi explores portrayals of the liberal intelligentsia of the 1960s—the influential generation known as the *shestidesiatniki*—by two major post-Soviet writers: Lyudmila Ulitskaya in *The Big Green Tent* (Zelenyi shater, 2010), and Victor Pelevin in *Generation "П"* (1999). Khagi shows that these novels present a spectrum of post-Soviet responses to the myth of the s*hestidesiatniki*: Ulitskaya provides an earnest if tempered tribute that contrasts with Pelevin's satirical interrogation of their political and ethical principles.

Alyssa DeBlasio's chapter on "The Intelligentsia and the Intellectuals: A History of Two Terms in Russian Philosophical Discourse" centers on discourse around the words "intelligentsia" and "intellectual" in Russian philosophical thought from the first decade of the twenty-first century. DeBlasio sees the discussion of "intelligentsia" vs "intellectuals" as a mirror for broader debates over the future of the Russian academy—addressing questions of politics in the academy, the role of scholars and philosophers in twenty-first-century Russia, and how scholars and institutions should meet the demands of the digital age.

Tatiana Smorodinska's "Legacy and Denial: Russian Intelligentsia on Screen and Online in the First Two Decades of the Twenty-First Century" focuses on how the perspective of a young generation of Russians, born in the decade before or after the collapse of the Soviet Union, is presented in various digital media projects and contemporary cinema. Smorodinska observes that in post-Soviet Russia the term "intelligentsia" is either used ironically, referring to the Soviet intelligentsia's compromised integrity, or applied to saintly heroes of the past whose high moral ground is out of reach for cynical and self-absorbed contemporaries. Paradoxically, the new generation of Russian intellectuals who deny and discredit the old Russian intelligentsia myth and refuse to self-identify as "intelligentsia" are in fact building on the old intelligentsia in their activities and so continuing its legacy.

We hope that this volume will serve readers who want to read it in its entirety or in individual chapters. Therefore, we have deliberately left some recurrent definitions and concepts associated with the intelligentsia, trying to preserve the autonomy of each chapter as well as the coherence of the whole sequence.

Bibliography

Berlin, Isaiah, ed. *Russian Thinkers*. New York: Penguin Classics, 1998.

———. "A Remarkable Decade 'The Birth of the Russian Intelligentsia', in *Russian Thinkers*, edited by I. Berlin, 130–154. New York: Penguin Classics, 1998.

Engel, Barbara Alpern. *Mothers and Daughters: Women of the Intelligentsia in Nineteenth Century Russia*. Cambridge: Cambridge UP, 1983.

Gessen, Masha. *Dead Again: The Russian Intelligentsia after Communism*. London: Verso Books, 1997.

Khazanov, Pavel. *The Russia That We Have Lost: Pre-Soviet Past as Anti-Soviet Discourse* Madison: U of Wisconsin Press, 2023.

Kochetkova, Inna. *The Myth of the Russian Intelligentsia: Old Intellectual in the New Russia*. London and New York: Routledge, 2010.

Lipovetsky, Mark. "The Poetics of ITR Discourse: In the 1960s and Today." *Ab Imperio* no. 1 (2013): 109–131.

———. "Intelligentsia Narratives." In Andrew Kahn et al., *A History of Russian Literature*, 739–769. Oxford: Oxford UP, 2018.

Hamburg, G. M. "Russian Intelligentsia." In *A History of Russian Thought*, edited by William Leatherbarrow and Derek Offord, 44–69. Cambridge: Cambridge UP, 2012.

Malia, Martin. "What is Intelligentsia?" In *The Russian Intelligentsia*, edited by Richard Pipes, 1–18. New York: Columbia UP, 1961.

Manchester, Laurie. *Holy Fathers, Secular Sons: Clergy, Intelligentsia, and the Modern Self in Revolutionary Russia*. DeKalb: Northern Illinois UP, 2011.

Morson, Gary Saul. "Dostoevsky and His Demons." *New York Review of Books*. July 1, 2021. https://www.nybooks.com/articles/2021/07/01/dostoevsky-and-his-demons/.

Nahirny, Vladimir. *The Russian Intelligentsia: From Torment to Silence*. New York: Routledge, 2018.

Pipes, Richard, ed. *The Russian Intelligentsia*. New York: Columbia UP, 1961.

Raeff, Mark. *Origins of the Russian Intelligentsia*. New York: Harcourt Brace & Company, 1966.

Shalin, Dmitri, ed. *Russian Intelligentsia in the Age of Counterperestroika: Political Agendas, Rhetorical Strategies, Personal Choices*. New York: Routledge, 2019.

Shatz, Marshall. *Soviet Dissent in Historical Perspective*. Cambridge: Cambridge UP, 1980.

Sinyavskii, Andrei. *The Russian Intelligentsia*. Translated by Lynn Visson. New York: Columbia UP, 1997.

Zhukovskii, V. A. *Dnevniki. Zapisnye knizhki (1834–1847)*. Moscow: Direct-Media, 2012.

Zubok, Vladislav. *Zhivago's Children: The Last Russian Intelligentsia*. Cambridge, MA: Harvard UP, 2011.

Part 1

PRE-NINETEENTH CENTURY

An Essay on the Origins of the Intelligentsia: Catherine the Great and Her Relations with Novikov and Radishchev

Marcus C. Levitt

A major paradox of Catherine the Great's rule (1762–1796) consists in the fact that in the first part of her reign she encouraged the development of a "public sphere" in Russia and laid the institutional and intellectual basis for it, while in her later years, shocked by revolutionary events in France, she asserted autocratic prerogative to try curtailing its would-be autonomy. She thus set in motion a kind of "scissors crisis" in which the state's ongoing need for educated servitors and citizens came into conflict with the absolutist imperative for total social and political control. The working thesis of this chapter is that the "intelligentsia" was the product of this dilemma, as a group of citizens committed to serve what they considered society's good yet frustrated by official constraint from above as well as a lack of support from below. Both the nature of the social good and the degree of constraint changed over time; in general, the harsher the restrictions became, the more revolutionary-minded was the response.

The story of Catherine the Great's relationship to the two men often named as progenitors of the Russian intelligentsia—Nikolai Novikov (1744–1818) and Aleksandr Radishchev (1749–1802)—brings this problem into sharp relief and accentuates the intelligentsia's roots in the eighteenth century. These two major intellectual figures who famously suffered Catherine's repression may serve as prototypes for two types of later *intelligent*. Novikov faced the difficult challenge of creating a socially conscious, enlightened reading public and was a kind of *Kulturträger avant la lettre*; Radishchev openly challenged state power (especially serfdom) in the name of suffering humanity and the social good. Both found support for their positions in Catherine's early pro-Enlightenment position but were caught up in the sharp change in political climate sparked by the French Revolution. It is a mark of the embryonic state of the Russian public sphere and Catherine's central role in its formation that their story plays out somewhat like a Neoclassical tragedy in which a ruler, starting out with the best of intentions and great confidence, feels compelled to adopt the role of a despot under the inexorable pressure of unforeseeable external forces.

The main issues overshadowing scholarship on both Novikov and Radishchev concern the degree or nature of their opposition to autocracy. The basic interpretive issue may be seen in terms of the difference between what Habermas characterizes as a pre-political "literary public sphere," pioneered by Novikov, and a public sphere proper: that is, one that asserts a right to political influence, as in Radishchev's case.[1] The issue could also be framed in terms of the difference between early or moderate and late Enlightenment thinking, where the first—represented by Novikov—focuses on individual moral improvement and social amelioration, within a pious religious framework, while the second—represented by Radishchev—has a more rationalist and radical bent and considers evil on a global, systemic and institutional level, decrying both church and state.[2] A further question involves Catherine the Great: while traditionally many historians have seen Catherine's gestures toward liberal Enlightenment policies, including her initial trial balloons exploring an end to serfdom, as pure hypocrisy (e.g., Pushkin's lapidary formulation of her character as "a Tartuffe in skirts"), more recent scholarship has recognized "Catherine's sustained and deep engagement with the ideas of the Enlightenment."[3]

Colum Leckey has summed up the recent wave of scholarly interest "in Russian public culture under Catherine" by such scholars as Elise Wirtschafter,

---

1 Jürgen Habermas, *The Structural Transformation of the Public Sphere: An Inquiry into a Category of Bourgeois Society*, trans. Thomas Burger (1962; Cambridge, MA: MIT Press, 1989). For a recent discussion, including criticism of Habermas's formulation, see the special issue of *Culture Unbound: Journal of Current Cultural Research* 2, no. 4 (2010), ed. Torbjörn Forslid and Anders Ohlsson, dedicated to literary public spheres; and Kevin Pask, "The Bourgeois Public Sphere and the Concept of Literature," *Criticism* 46, no. 2 (2004): 241–256.

2 The canonical work on what I am calling the "high" Enlightenment, associated with the French *philosophes*, is Peter Gay's *The Enlightenment: An Interpretation*, 2 vols. (New York: W. W. Norton, 1966–1969).

3 Douglas Smith, "Attached to the Party of Humanity: On Robert Zaretsky's 'Catherine & Diderot,'" *Los Angeles Review of Books*, March 1, 2019, https://lareviewofbooks.org/article/attached-party-humanity-robert-zaretskys-catherine-diderot/. In particular, Smith cites the works of historian Isabella de Madariaga.

Cynthia Whittaker, and Douglas Smith as fascination with "a rare moment when educated society and government were in fundamental agreement on policies and principles."[4] Arguably, Catherine the Great's relationship to Novikov, while subject to some disagreement among historians,[5] best represents this "rare moment." During the period following her coup, Catherine strove to justify her assumption of power by reference to Enlightenment principles and actively encouraged the emergence of public opinion.

Catherine and Novikov

Novikov, whose career almost completely coincided with—and was determined by—Catherine's time in power, took up the challenge, leading an effort to nurture and expand the fledgling Russian reading public. Novikov began his adult life as an officer in the Izmailovsky Regiment of the imperial guard, in which he had been enrolled as a child (a common practice for Russian noble boys). Within half a year of his entry, in late June 1762, the *Izmailovtsy* helped engineer the military coup that put Catherine on the throne, and Novikov was among those who swore allegiance to the new empress. A few years later, when Catherine summoned the regiment to Moscow for the meeting of the Commission to Create a New Law Code (1767–1769), Novikov was selected to serve as one of its recording secretaries, responsible for transcribing the daily debates which were to be reported in the newspaper, on the model of English parliamentary practice.[6] Catherine's Commission thus served "as a training-ground for young Russian writers,"[7] including Novikov. Although the Commission was cut short

---

4 Colum Leckey, "Patronage and Public Culture in the Russian Free Economic Society, 1765–1796," *Slavic Review* 64, no. 2 (2005): 355–79; here, 357. See also his *Patrons of Enlightenment: The Free Economic Society in Eighteenth-Century Russia* (Newark, NJ: U of Delaware Press, 2011). Dmitry Kalugin registers the new equilibrium in terms of a differentiation within the public sphere so that it "is no longer a homogeneous, artificially created milieu ... [and] embodies that difference which is necessary for the exchange of information, dialogue, and, finally, argument" (Dmitrii Kalugin, "'A Society That Speaks Concordantly,' or Mechanisms of Communication of Government and Society in Old and New Russia," in *Public Debate in Russia: Matters of (Dis)Order*, ed. Nikolai Vakhtin and Boris Firsov [Edinburgh: Edinburgh UP, 2016], 52–84; here, 65).
5 See, for example, Barbara Maggs, review of *Un publiciste frondeur sous Catherine II: Nicolas Novikov* by André Monnier, *Comparative Literature Studies* 22, no. 2 (Summer 1985): 272–274.
6 W. Gareth Jones, "Novikov's Naturalized Spectator," in *The Eighteenth Century in Russia*, ed. John G. Garrard (Oxford: Clarendon Press, 1973), 149–165; here, 149. See also his *Nikolay Novikov, Enlightener of Russia* (Cambridge: Cambridge UP, 1984).
7 Jones, "Novikov's Naturalized Spectator," 149. Delegates included Prince M. M. Shcherbatov, I. P. Elagin, A. V. Naryshkin, A. A. Rzhevsky, A. A. Nartov, V. I. Bibikov, S. G. Domashnev, G.

by war with Turkey and did not produce a new law code, it was "a significant landmark in that it provided a public sounding board and thereby educated a large segment of Russian society to the notions of free debate and circulation of secular ideas."[8] Furthermore, Catherine's widely publicized *Nakaz* (Instruction) to the delegates, based on the works of Montesquieu and Beccaria, provided an inspirational justification for her Enlightened rule and validated Russian civil society.[9] The *Nakaz* served as a formative document for many in Novikov's generation, including Radishchev.

Catherine made use of the impetus that the Commission had given to the awakening of Russian public opinion by initiating the publication of the so-called satirical journals, aka moral miscellanies, modelled on Addison and Steele's the *Tattler* and the *Spectator* of 1709–1714. Catherine's choice of satirical journalism was not fortuitous, as it had helped expand the English reading public and continued to inspire similar periodicals across Europe. Habermas noted the key role of these journals in creating a public sphere in England.[10] W. Gareth Jones has argued that Russia's satirical journals served as a "demonstration of the concept of freedom of expression promulgated in the *Nakaz*."[11] He also noted that Catherine thus helped shape the self-consciousness of Novikov's cohort as "a distinct literary coterie" which could be conceived of as analogous to the English socially conscious combined "parliamentary reporter and magazine essayist."[12]

A vital feature of satirical journalism was its projection of a literate community exchanging ideas, a virtual reading public in microcosm. Like the *Spectator*,

---

I. Poletika, N. N. Motonis, Ia. P. Kozelsky, L. V. Tatishchev, and G. V. Kozitsky; F. A. Kozelsky, M. I. Popov, and A. O. Ablesimov served as secretaries.

8 Marc Raeff, book review of *Freedom of Expression* by K. A. Papmehl, *Jahrbücher für Geschichte Osteuropas*, Neue Folge 20, no. 3 (1972): 446. Catherine's attempt to create a "society" by shaping the delegates' political vocabulary and behavior is analyzed by Kalugin in "'A Society That Speaks Concordantly,'" 62–64.

9 K. A. Papmehl, "The Problem of Civil Liberties in the Records of the 'Great Commission,'" *Slavonic and East European Review* 42, no. 99 (June 1964): 274–291; and his *Freedom of Expression in Eighteenth-Century Russia* (The Hague: Nijhoff, 1971), 47–70. See also: Kenneth Craven, "Publish and Languish: The Fate of Nikolai Ivanovich Novikov (1743–1818), Propagator of the Enlightenment under Catherine II," *Archives et Bibliotheques de Belgique Archief en Bibliotheekwezen in Belgie* (1983): 173–189, esp. 178; and Douglas Smith, "Alexander Radishchev's *Journey from St. Petersburg to Moscow* and the Limits of Freedom of Speech in the Reign of Catherine the Great," in *Freedom of Speech: The History of an Idea*, ed. Elizabeth Powers (Lanham, MD: Rowman & Littlefield, 2011), 61–74.

10 Habermas, *Structural Transformation*, 42.

11 W. Gareth Jones, "Russian Literature in the Eighteenth Century," in *Reference Guide to Russian Literature*, ed. Neil Cornwell (London: Routledge, 2013), 17.

12 Idem, "Novikov's Naturalized Spectator," 150.

the Russian satirical journals featured a cluster of contributors orchestrated by an editor and included anecdotes, short essays, poems and satirical pieces. They also featured letters to the editor, often from idiosyncratic and allegedly out of town readers, both men and women, which contributed to the sense (or illusion) of "a common body of shared opinion."[13] It was never fully clear to what extent the varied contributors, published anonymously or given transparently fictional "speaking names" (e.g., G. Pravdolyubov, or "Mr. Truth Lover"), represent real people or were creations of the writer-editor. The play of names constituted part of the journals' charm and humor.

The tone of the satirical journals was conversational, half-jocular, half-serious, and touched on a large variety of issues, including fashion, social behavior, moral philosophy, and social ills. The latter included the mistreatment of serfs, bribe taking, thievery, corrupt judges, flattery, and maladministration. A further set of issues addressed problems of writing, authorship, readers, and patronage, as well as the internecine "war" among writers and the journals themselves. The anonymity of the satirical journals allowed, even encouraged, frank criticism, the more so since Catherine had given permission for them to be published (at least initially) anonymously and without censorship.[14] Catherine's own journal, *Vsiakaia vsiachina* (translated variously as "All sorts of things," "All sorts," and "Odds and ends"), which had initiated the flowering of the periodicals by inviting them to publish, also came out anonymously, though her identity was more or less an open secret.[15] The Russian satirical journals, like the *Spectator*, belong to what we have referred to as moderate Enlightenment thought that focused on individual moral improvement and social amelioration. The issue for scholars

---

13 Michael G. Ketcham, *Transparent Designs: Reading, Performance, and Form in the "Spectator" Papers* (Athens: U of Georgia Press, 1985), 127. Cf. Goodman, *Republic of Letters*, 172: "Journals served as a meeting ground for a public seeking a forum and their model was the *Spectator*." Gary Marker notes that "The blossoming of Russian journals [in the second half of the eighteenth century] was thus, in a certain sense, indistinguishable from the overall coming of age of Russia's educated society ... [T]he pursuit of a public voice through the press ... was part of an ideological mission" ("The Creation of Journals and the Profession of Letters in the Eighteenth Century," in *Literary Journals in Imperial Russia*, ed. Deborah A. Martinsen [New York: New York UP, 1997], 14–15).

14 See V. P. Semennikov, *Russkie satiricheskie zhurnaly 1769–1774 godov: Razyskaniia ob izdateliakh i sotrudnikakh* (St. Petersburg, 1914), 4–5; according to this scholar, censorship was reinstated after an article appeared in *Smes'* (Miscellany) that was offensive to the clergy (7).

15 Ever since P. Pekarsky discovered evidence of her participation in the empress's own hand (P. Pekarskii, "Materialy dlia istorii zhurnal'noi i literaturnoi deiatel'nosti Ekateriny II," *Zapiski Akademii nauk* 3 [1863], *Prilozhenie* 6, 1–87), scholarly consensus has been that Catherine, together with her secretary G. V. Kozitsky, wrote and edited *Vsiakaia vsiachina*. For a skeptical view, see Michael Von Herzen, "Catherine II—Editor of *Vsiakaia Vsiachina*? A Reappraisal," *The Russian Review* 38, no. 3 (1979): 283–297.

has been whether Novikov crossed the line and challenged Catherine's autocratic power or whether the controversy he provoked (as W. Gareth Jones has argued) was "willed by the official journal and ... waged under her [Catherine's] tutelage ..., an act of collaboration rather than defiance."[16] "This is the moment," comments a recent scholar, "when the right to transmit the bearings of power is delegated to society, or rather to private individuals."[17]

The series of satirical journals that Novikov created—the *Drone* (Truten', 1769–1770), the *Tattler* (Pustomelia, 1770), the *Painter* (Zhivopisets, 1772), and the *Hairnet* (Koshelek, 1774)—represent his most significant work as a writer. In the opening of the *Painter*, the most successful of them,[18] he dedicated the journal to the anonymous author of the comedy, *Oh, the Times!* that had recently been staged. That this was another covert composition by the empress gave him the opportunity not only to sing her praises in a playful way, but also to justify his own satirical undertaking, to claim her support, and to align his authorial activity, and those of his fellow writers, with hers:

> You are admirable as the first to show that the liberty granted to Russian minds can be used for the good of the fatherland. But, my dear sir, why do you hide your name, a name worthy of our thanks? I can find no reason. In reviling vice so harshly and giving the vice-ridden reason to attack you, are you really fearful of their abuse? No, such a weakness can never have a place in your heart. And can such a noble boldness fear oppression at a time when, to Russia's happiness and the *well-being* of the human race, the *most wise* Catherine rules over us? The satisfaction she demonstrated at the performance of your comedy attests to her patronage of those like you, of writers. . . .
>
> You opened up for me a path I always feared; you awoke in me the desire to emulate you in the admirable feat of correcting the

---

16 Jones, "Novikov's Naturalized Spectator," 353. See also his "The Polemics of the 1769 Journals: A Reappraisal," *Canadian-American Slavic Studies* 16, nos. 3–4 (Winter 1982): 432–43. The main controversy was over the nature of satire; where Catherine advocated "'good manners,' 'meekness' and 'mercy' . . . as the prime elements governing social interaction," Novikov promoted "critical invective ['personal satire'] characteristic of groups fighting for the right to an official designation in the public sphere" (Kalugin, "'A Society That Speaks Concordantly,'" 62).
17 Kalugin, "'A Society That Speaks Concordantly,'" 62.
18 It underwent five editions in twenty years (M. N. Longinov, *Novikov i moskovskie martinisty* [Moscow: Tip. Gracheva, 1867], 22–23, n.1).

morals of our countrymen; you roused me to try my own hand at it; and, God willing, readers will find in my sheets even a little resemblance to the wit and salt that enliven your composition. If I will have some success in my undertaking and if these sheets bring benefit and pleasure to readers, for this the credit should go to you, not to me, because without your example I would not have had the courage to attack vice.[19]

Novikov thus openly acknowledged his profound debt to Catherine, and his collaboration with her was to continue for more than another decade.[20] In the early 1770's he embarked on several projects aimed at both expanding readership and bolstering a sense of national and social self-awareness. Together with a bookseller he founded the Society Striving for Printing Books which partnered with the Academy of Sciences and the Society for the Translation of Foreign Books, which Catherine had created in 1768 and personally subsidized as "probably the leading Russian voice for the French Enlightenment."[21] He launched the *Ancient Russian Library* (Drevniaia rossiiskaia vivliofika, 10 vols., 1773–1775; 2nd rev. ed. 1788–1791), a compendium of historical materials which Catherine supported by giving Novikov access to imperial archives and by providing a financial subsidy. In 1772, Novikov published his *Attempt at a Historical Dictionary of Russian Writers*, which featured 317 writers; most were contemporaries, but the number included translators, preachers, and scholars, as well as many neophytes that (in his repeated phrase) "hold out very great hopes." It was thus both a declaration of Russia's current happy state and of its great potential.[22]

---

19 P. N. Berkov, *Satiricheskie zhurnaly N. I. Novikova* (Moscow: Izdatel'stvo Akademii nauk, 1951), 283–4; italics in the original. See Jones, *Nikolai Novikov*, 62–63, who notes that the "anonymous author" was asked for a contribution and may have provided one. Passing along issues of *Koshelek* to Catherine, Novikov wrote to her secretary G. V. Kozitsky to see if she approved of them, "for this one thing is my goal: to always do what is pleasing to her" (delat' ei ugodnoe)." N. I. Novikov, *Pis'ma N. I. Novikova* (St. Petersburg: Izdatel'stvo imeni N. I. Novikova, 1994), 11.
20 On the collaboration, see esp.: Craven, "Publish and Languish," 173–189.
21 Gary Marker, *Publishing, Printing, and the Origins of Intellectual Life in Russia* (Princeton, NJ: Princeton UP, 1985), 92. Several scholars have recently described the emergence of learned and "friendly" societies in Russia from the perspective of Russia's developing public sphere and Catherine's role in it; see: Joseph Bradley, *Voluntary Associations in Tsarist Russia* (Cambridge, MA: Harvard UP. 2009); Colum Leckey, "Patronage and Public Culture" and *Patrons of Enlightenment*; Vera Kaplan, *Historians and Historical Societies in the Public Life of Imperial Russia* (Bloomington: Indiana UP, 2017).
22 Kalugin notes that for Novikov a "writer" here meant anyone who published a book, including sermons ("'A Society That Speaks Concordantly,'" 76 n. 23). See also: S. I. Nikolaev,

Most of Novikov's undertakings in the 1770s proved financially precarious and short-lived. Despite an active marketing campaign, the publishing society, for example, only lasted about two years. In a moment of dejection in 1775 he wrote to Catherine's secretary, G. V. Kozitsky, that "without [your] help, I will be under extreme pressure to abandon all of my undertakings unfinished; what can I do when my keenness to render service to my fatherland is so poorly received by my fellow citizens!"[23] Novikov was fighting an uphill battle; Russia was overwhelmingly illiterate; the reading public such as it was seemed more interested in cheap translated novels and chapbooks (the one area of profitable commercial publishing in Russia) than in serious literature; and his efforts at enlightenment often met with apathy from below while encountering conservative pushback from above.[24]

In 1775, Novikov became a Freemason, which supplied spiritual succor and a network for his publishing and philanthropic efforts. Most notable in the latter case was his publication of what is considered the first Russian Masonic journal, *Morning Light* (Utrennii svet, 1777–1780), the subscriptions to which publicly supported two "charity schools"—an "attempt to draw a whole society into social action."[25] At the same time, Novikov and his colleagues founded the Society for Establishing Schools (Obshchestvo staraiushchikhsia o spomoshchestvovanii zavedeniiu uchilishch).[26] The charity schools, like many of Novikov's projects, sought support via subscription—a practice that originated in England and spread in eighteenth-century Europe as a form of collective, public patronage.[27] Even here Novikov largely depended on court circles and

---

"'Prevelikie nadezhdy' russkoi poezii v slovare pisatelei N. I. Novikova," *Russkaia literatura* 2 (2020): 35–39; and Colum Leckey, "What Is 'Prosveshchenie?' Nikolai Novikov's 'Historical Dictionary of Russian Writers' Revisited," *Russian History* 37, no. 4 (2010): 360–377.

23 Novikov, *Pis'ma Novikova*, 12.

24 The negative response from nobles, albeit fictionalized, may be gleaned from the satirical journals themselves. See Jones, *Novikov*, 70. Marker comments on the "limited and unrewarding market" that put a brake on professionalization ("The Creation of Journals," 27 and 29); "intellectual life and institutions evolved ... far more rapidly than readership did," engendering a frustrating "sense of isolation and superfluousness" (29).

25 Jones, *Nikolai Novikov*, 145–148. See also his article, "The 'Morning Light' Charity Schools, 1777–80," *The Slavonic and East European Review* 56, no. 1 (1978): 47–67.

26 Vera Kaplan, *Historians and Historical Societies*, 23–79; here, 46–49. Kaplan asserts that "The Society for Establishing Schools ... can be seen as an additional site in the landscape of the early Russian public sphere, signifying another deliberate attempt to expand the community of the educated" (48). The charity schools were absorbed into Catherine's new state system of public schools in 1784, and Jones speculates (*Nikolai Novikov*, 148) that Catherine may have been motivated by Novikov's work.

27 On the importance of subscriptions for the public sphere, see Dena Goodman, *The Republic of Letters: A Cultural History of the French Enlightenment* (Ithaca, NY: Cornell UP, 1994), 175–82.

on Catherine's personal backing, although his Masonic contacts and active marketing efforts helped increase subscriptions across the country, including from among clergymen and provincial administrators.[28]

Freemasonry, like the many new societies and private associations that appeared in Catherine's Russia, offered islands of relative autonomy that featured a new kind of Enlightenment sociability; they were both self-governing (often with constitutions, elections, and careful attention to due process) as well as egalitarian, offering a haven from rank-conscious officialdom (although membership was nevertheless overwhelmingly aristocratic).[29] With the help of his Masonic colleagues, in 1779 Novikov assumed a ten-year lease of Moscow University Press, the largest publishing house in the Russian Empire, at which time he moved his operations from Petersburg to the old capital. The historian V. O. Klyuchevsky dubbed this period of 1779–1789—the height of Novikov's activity as a publisher—the "Novikov decade,"[30] as he went on to establish "a new publishing career of national scope."[31] The lease of the Moscow University Press included the responsibility for publishing textbooks as well as the newspaper *Moscow News* (Moskovskie vedomosti), whose circulation under Novikov, according to N. M. Karamzin, "increased spectacularly."[32] He capitalized on the university's community of faculty and students, many of whom were Freemasons, to procure writing and translations for the large number of new journals and serial publications he sponsored.[33] In addition, he helped establish

---

28 Jones, *Nikolai Novikov*, 147. On Novikov's subscribers, see Gary Marker, "Novikov's Readers," *The Modern Language Review* 77, no. 4 (October 1982): 894–905.

29 On learned and "friendly" societies, see n. 21. Raffaella Faggionnato (*A Rosicrucian Utopia in Eighteenth-Century Russia: The Masonic Circle of N. I. Novikov* [Dordrecht: Springer, 2005], 11) notes that Russian Masonic lodges "allowed members to be part of a microsociety whose organisation was evidently modeled on the new political principle of representation at a time when constitutionalism had become the symbol of modernity and progress in the European political debate"; the starting point to which they strove "was a radical reform of the reigning mental universe" (121). See also Douglas Smith, *Working the Rough Stone: Freemasonry and Society in Eighteenth-Century Russia* (DeKalb, IL: Northern Illinois UP, 1999).

30 V. O. Kliuchevskii, "Vospominaniia o N. I. Novikove i ego vremeni," in idem, *Sochineniia*, vol. 8 (Moscow: Izdatel'stvo sotsial'no-ekonomicheskoi literatury, 1959), 249.

31 Craven, "Publish or Languish," 182.

32 Nikolai Karamzin asserted in his well-known essay "O knizhnoi torgovle i liubvi ko chteniiu v Rossii" (1802), in idem, *Sochineniia*, (Leningrad: Khudozhestvennaia literatura, 1984), vol. 2, 117, that under Novikov the newspaper's subscriptions went from no more than 600 to 4000. Gary Marker notes that if Karamzin's figures were correct, Novikov's "was far and away the most widely disseminated periodical of its day" ("The Creation of Journals," 17).

33 These included: the *Economic Magazine* (*Ekonomicheskii magazin*, 1780–1789); *Moscow Monthly Publication* (*Moskovskoe ezhemesiachnoe izdanie*, 1781) and *Evening Twilight* (*Vecherniaia zaria*, 1782), which continued *Morning Light*; *Town and Country Library* (*Gorodskaia i derevenskaia biblioteka*, 1782-6); the *Supplement to Moscow News* (*Prilozheniie k*

a series of seminars at Moscow University and societies such as the Friendly Learned Society, which had both educational and philanthropic aims. In 1784, Novikov, together with his fellow Masons, many also in the Friendly Learned Society, founded the Typographical Company, a private joint stockholding concern made possible by the Free Press Law of 1783 that allowed individuals to operate their own printing presses.[34] The Typographical Company was a commercial venture but also had a secret press for "in house," uncensored (and illegal) Masonic literature. Novikov's association with the Masons, whose extensive roster of adherents embraced many of Russia's leading literary, intellectual, and political figures, including at court, in the university and in the church, greatly facilitated the expansion of Novikov's new "publishing empire." His many ambitious projects in editing, publishing, philanthropy, and education often intersected with his personal search for religious and philosophical truth. The degree to which Novikov's commitment to Rosicrucianism, an esoteric, hermetic subset of Freemasonry which he joined in 1784, came into conflict with his Enlightenment, rationalist position, remains unclear.[35] Printing forbidden texts "for private use"; efforts to involve tsarevich Pavel Petrovich in the movement; connections with European colleagues that had political overtones;[36] as well as secret, mystery cult-like rituals, laid Rosicrucianism open to

---

"Moskovskim vedomostiam," 1783–1784); *Diligent Repose* (*Pokoiashchiisia trudoliubets*, 1784–1785); the first children's journal, *Children's Reading for Heart and Mind* (*Detskoe chtenie dlia serdtsa i razuma*, 1785–1789, for which N. M. Karamzin worked); and *Magazine of Natural History, Physics and Chemistry* (*Magazin natural'noi istorii, fiziki i khimii*, 1788–1790). Faggionato surveys the journals (*A Rosicrucian Utopia*, 18–27) and notes that "the project to which all of the voices contributed was the construction of an individual ethical code upon which the reform of social and political life was to be founded" (121). Their collective program, together with that of the Typographical Company, "was directed toward spreading the language and concepts inspired by constitutionalism, democracy and the guiding ideal of tolerance" (123).

34 As Marker has written, the new private presses "were required to submit their publications to the local prefects of police, but the police had neither the means nor the interest to become actively engaged in censorship. For all practical purposes, therefore, Russia had acquired a relatively free press—a further indication of the continued amity between empress and literati" ("Nikolai Ivanovich Novikov," in *Early Modern Russian Writers, Late Seventeenth and Eighteenth Centuries*, vol. 150, *The Dictionary of Literary Biography* [Detroit, MI: Gale, 1995], 255). See also Faggionato, *A Rosicrucian Utopia*, 127.

35 Faggionato, *A Rosicrucian Utopia*, is the most thorough examination of Novikov's "Masonic Circle."

36 Novikov's circle was under the broad jurisdiction of the Berlin Rosicrucians and its representatives in Russia technically had the right to intervene in his publishing activities, although Novikov would not relinquish control over the presses. See Jones, *Nikolai Novikov*, 178–179. For a reading that casts negative light on the German involvement, see In-ho L. Ryu, "Moscow Freemasons and the Rosicrucian Order: A Study in Organization and Control," in *The Eighteenth Century in Russia*, ed. John G. Garrard (Oxford: Clarendon Press, 1973), 198–232.

accusations of conspiracy and connection to the banned Bavarian Illuminati, who had sought to undermine organized religion and transform Freemasonry into a political system.[37] Novikov's large-scale famine relief effort in his home province in 1787 that "gave the masonic brotherhood an opportunity of demonstrating their pietistic philanthropy"[38] also provoked some suspicion. It is quite clear, however, that Novikov's Masonic interests (at least in his eyes) had no basic doctrinal quarrel with Russian Orthodoxy, and there is no tangible evidence of any conscious ideological opposition to Catherine's regime.[39]

Catherine had long been an outspoken critic of Freemasonry,[40] but the precise reasons for and timing of her turn against Novikov just about at the time of his greatest success remain obscure. A series of repressive measures including repeated raids and book confiscations, interrogations, a ban on secular presses' publication of religious subject matter, followed by the refusal to renew Novikov's lease of the university press, finally led to his financial ruin and arrest.[41] It also remains a question why Novikov was singled out for such harsh punishment (fifteen years in the Shlisselburg Fortress) while his colleagues were

---

Faggionato, *A Rosicrucian Utopia*, rejects this argument, as well as Ryu's view of Rosicrucianism as "the most esoteric and reactionary branch of the extremely multifarious spiritual and social phenomenon which went by the name of Freemasonry" (Ryu, "Moscow Freemasons," 198; see Faggionato, *A Rosicrucian Utopia*, 115 and passim). Ryu thus considers Catherine's actions against Novikov "completely justified" and argues that Rosicrucianism "promoted... anything but critical social consciousness or independent civic initiative" (232).

37 See Reinhart Koselleck, *Critique and Crisis: Enlightenment and the Pathogenesis of Modern Society* (Cambridge, MA: MIT Press, 1988) for a stimulating analysis of the intellectual and political implications of Masonic secrecy in the context of Absolutism.

38 Jones, *Nikolay Novikov*, 203.

39 This is the basic argument of both Jones and Faggionatto. For a differing opinion, see the work of Ryu cited above in n. 36. G. P. Makagonenko, a major exponent of the view of Novikov as oppositionist, noted "a strikingly paradoxical phenomenon: while the collection of facts cited to prove one or another argument always remains the same, the conclusions scholars draw about the nature of Novikov's activity differ" radically (*Nikolai Novikov i russkoe prosveshchenie XVIII veka* [Moscow: Nauka, 1952], 16).

40 She wrote three comedies with anti-Masonic content in the mid-1780s, which give us clues as to her changing (but consistently negative) attitude toward the phenomenon. See Lurana Donnels O'Malley, *The Dramatic Works of Catherine the Great: Theatre and Politics in Eighteenth-Century Russia* (Burlington, VT: Ashgate, 2006), 73–96.

41 For analysis of Novikov's arrest, interrogation, and imprisonment, see: Faggionato, *A Rosicrucian Utopia*, 205–216; Jones, *Nikolai Novikov*, 206–215; Isabel de Madariaga, *Russia in the Age of Catherine the Great* (London: Phoenix Press, 2002), 521–531, and her review of Faggionato in *The Slavonic and East European Review* 85, no. 2 (2007): 349–352; Gilbert H. Mc Arthur, "Catherine II and the Masonic Circle of N. I. Novikov," *Canadian-American Slavic Studies* 4, no. 3 (1970): 529–546; Craven, "Publish and Languish"; and K. A. Papmehl, "The Empress and 'Un Fanatique': A Review of the Circumstances Leading to the Government Action against Novikov in 1792," *The Slavonic and East European Review* 68, no. 4 (1990): 665–691.

treated quite leniently; a year before Radishchev had only been sentenced to ten years of exile (after a commuted death sentence) and was able to live a more or less normal life in Siberia.[42] The wretched end to Novikov's career followed from a variety of reasons, the most important of which were the changing political climate that came with the revolutionary events in France and the "scissors crisis" mentioned earlier—the latent clash between Absolutism and the autonomous social activity that Freemasonry represented, which in Catherine's opinion had now come to a head.

Catherine and Radishchev

Radishchev's career, no less than Novikov's, was launched by Catherine the Great, although before the publication of his *Journey from St. Petersburg to Moscow* in 1790 Radishchev had played only a very minor role in Russian literary life. At age thirteen, he had begun service as a page at Catherine's court, and four years later, in 1766, on the empress' personal command he was sent along with nine other young noblemen to study in Germany, at Leipzig University. There he became absorbed by the works of French Enlightenment thinkers, especially Helvétius, Mably, and Rousseau.[43] This was a formative experience for Radishchev, who wrote a memoir about it many years later in the form of a biography of a fellow student, entitled *The Life of Fyodor Vasilyevich Ushakov* (Zhitie Fedora Vasil'evicha Ushakova, 1789), published anonymously.[44] The main drama of *The Life* revolves around the Russian students' revolt against the despotic acts of their official director, as a result of which the students were thrown

---

42 Notably, Radishchev was tried and sentenced, while Catherine simply condemned Novikov, who had not been charged with breaking any specific laws. I. Z. Serman noted that the issue "continues to surprise" scholars ("Imperatritsa i poruchik Novikov," *XVIII vek* 25 [2008]: 347).

43 Notably, Catherine also approved of most of these authors, with the exception of Rousseau. On the closeness of their "philosophical assumptions," see Allen McConnell, "The Empress and Her Protégé: Catherine II and Radishchev," *The Journal of Modern History* 36, no. 1 (1964): 14–27, esp. 21. McConnell has a series of articles on Radishchev's thought: "Radishchev's Political Thought," *American Slavic and East European Review* 17, no. 4 (1958): 439–453; "Helvetius' Russian Pupils," *Journal of the History of Ideas* 24, no. 3 (1963): 373–386; "Rousseau and Radishchev," *The Slavic and East European Journal* 8, no. 3 (1964): 253–272; "Abbé Raynal and a Russian Philosophe," *Jahrbücher Für Geschichte Osteuropas* 12, no. 4 (1965): 499–512. See also his *A Russian Philosophe: Alexander Radishchev, 1749–1802* (The Hague: M. Nijhoff, 1964).

44 Barbara Walker has described this work as first in a line of "intelligentsia memoirs" that provide insight into the question of intelligentsia identity. See "On Reading Soviet Memoirs: A History of the 'Contemporaries' Genre as an Institution of Russian Intelligentsia Culture from the 1790s to the 1970s," *The Russian Review* 59, no. 3 (2000): 327–352.

in jail and just barely avoided recall to Russia. The episode led Radishchev to thoughts about the pernicious nature of autocracy, and he compared the conflict to the French parlements' conflict with Louis XVI.[45] He wrote that

> The example of the absolute power (or autocracy [*samovlastie*]) of the sovereign, having no law to follow, not even in the application of his other rules, apart from his will or whims, encourages every person in charge to think that in using his share of power without limits he is the same ruler in the particular case as is [the sovereign] in the general. And this is so true that it is often accepted as a rule, that contradicting the power of the person in charge is an insult to the supreme power. [This is] an unhappy thought that imprisons thousands of people who love the fatherland in jail, and condemns them to death, suffocating the spirit and mind, and in the place of greatness, inculcates timidity, slavery and confusion under the guise of order and peace! Yes, this could not be otherwise according to the striving for power (*samovlastie*), characteristic of all people, that confirms Helvetius' opinion at every step.[46]

Characteristically, Radishchev sees the workings of autocratic power as a far-reaching structure that has specific pernicious effects on its subordinates,

---

45 A. N. Radishchev, "Zhitie Fedora Vasil'evicha Ushakova," in idem, *Polnoe sobranie sochinenii* (Moscow and Leningrad: Izdatel'stvo Akademii nauk SSSR, 1938–1952), vol. 2, 153–212; here, 168. This reference is obviously anachronistic for the 1760s, but it does indicate Radishchev's early attraction to the radical Enlightenment. He wrote that he and his fellow students had "learned to think" from Helvetius's *De l'esprit* (1758). Allan McConnell asserts that "Catherine had not only permitted Helvetius' books into Russia, but had them translated into Russian" ("Helvetius' Russian Pupils," 373–386; here, 373–374). However, I have not been able to identify any published translations apart from an excerpt that appeared in *Sobranie novostei* (March 1776): 3–12 ("Ob ume, pervonachal'nyia poniatiia"); and an abridgement-paraphrase (*Dukh Gel'vetsiia* [Tambov: Vol'naia tip. [Nilova], 1788], cf. *Svodnyi katalog russkoi knigi grazhdanskoi pechati XVIII veka* [Moscow: Izdanie Gosudarstvennoi biblioteki SSSR imeni V. I. Lenina, 1962], vol. 1, no. 2064, 319). On the French parlements' conflict with Louis XVI, see William Doyle, "The Parlements of France and the Breakdown of the Old Regime 1771–1788," *French Historical Studies* 6, no. 4 (1970): 415–458.
46 A. N. Radishchev, *Polnoe sobranie sochinenii* (Moscow and Leningrad: Izdatel'stvo Akademii nauk SSSR, 1938–1952), vol. 1, 162. Notably, Radishchev also translated "despotism" as *samoderzhavie*. A. M. Kutuzov, to whom the *Zhitie* was dedicated, noted that Radishchev's political outspokenness shocked many people, but that, since Catherine said nothing (*svyshe molchali*), its critics fell silent (Radishchev, *Polnoe sobranie sochinenii*, vol. 1, 463–464 [commentary by Ia. L. Barskov]).

both on those to whom power is delegated and on those who are subjected to it. He is particularly attuned to the functioning and abuse of the law, which can condemn a person to jail or death for merely "contradicting the power of the person in charge." At the same time, the human striving for power (*samovlastie,* the same word used here for autocracy) is acknowledged as a universal truth with which political thinkers must reckon.

Before his arrest, Radishchev had dabbled in literature while working as a civil servant—a common situation for writers of the era.[47] Among other things, he contributed to Novikov's satirical journals (according to his son); he belonged to the Society for Printing Books and the Society for the Translation of Foreign Books; he completed several translations, including Mably's *Obervations sur les Grecs*;[48] and he subscribed to the *Ancient Russian Library.* Whereas Novikov's career spanned many activities over decades that promoted the public sphere, the publication of Radishchev's book *A Journey from Saint Petersburg to Moscow,* an outspoken condemnation of serfdom and autocracy, represents his almost exclusive claim to fame, which earned its author exile to Siberia and the reputation of a revolutionary martyr in the later tradition. Whereas, as noted, there is no solid evidence of Novikov's ideological opposition to Catherine's regime, the question for Radishchev concerns whether his was a loyal opposition, a warning about the revolutionary danger posed by the evils of serfdom and autocracy, or a more or less explicit justification, even encouragement, of revolt.

Many writers have seen Radishchev as the prototype *intelligent,* speaking in the name of society and poised ambiguously between loyal and hostile opposition. This ambiguity—the degree to which the Russian intelligentsia was revolutionary—reverberates throughout its subsequent history. Whereas the pathos of Novikov's career was to work within the ground rules as laid out by Catherine, Radishchev's thinking, following French "late" Enlightenment ideas, tended toward fundamental, systemic political critique. Where Novikov

---

[47] From 1771 to 1775 he served as a secretary in the Senate, from 1777 to 1780 as an official in the Board of Commerce, and from 1780 he worked at the St. Petersburg Customs House, where he became official manager not long before his arrest. On the conflicting demands of writing and service, see Irina Reyfman, "To Serve or to Write? Noble Writers in the Eighteenth Century," in eadem, *How Russia Learned to Write: Literature and the Imperial Table of Ranks* (Madison: U of Wisconsin Press, 2016), 20–43.

[48] The book, which had received imperial funding and passed censorship, included sharp criticism of autocracy. In particular, a footnote described autocracy as "the state of affairs most repugnant to human nature . . . The injustice of the sovereign gives the people, who are his judges, the same or an even greater right over him than the law gives him to judge criminals." Radishchev, *Polnoe sobranie sochinenii,* vol. 2, 282; quoted in Allen McConnell, "The Empress and Her Protégé," 21.

sought the moral amelioration of society, the expansion of a Habermasian-type public sphere and personal illumination via Rosicrucianism, Radishchev's intellectual trajectory reflects Reinhart Koselleck's analysis of high Enlightenment "criticism" that prepared the way for "crisis"—revolution, dictatorship, and even totalitarianism.[49] According to Koselleck, absolutist ideology, as a response to the seventeenth-century religious wars, claimed the sole right to rule for the throne and divorced political power from questions of morality. Hence the rationalist, Enlightenment critic, excluded from the practical exercise of power, claimed the possession of (allegedly "apolitical") moral truth. According to Koselleck, he thus became victim of "moral dualism": "Convinced of his own moral innocence, the rationalist critic condemned an amoral, calculating, power-hungry state and made the abuse of power identical with its very exercise."[50]

In her marginal notes on the *Journey*, Catherine recognized this zero-sum moral righteousness that (as in the case of *The Life of Fyodor Vasilyevich Ushakov*) held the monarch entirely responsible for social and legal abuses, which, arguably, followed logically from the nature of autocracy. "The author's purpose," she correctly divined, ". . . is to point out the defects of the present form of government and its vices." But the author has "eaten up [i.e., claimed] all the wisdom, and the Sovereign is only left with a grain of [common] sense" (that is, the Sovereign is wrong by definition). She argued that the morality of revolutionary violence is warped: "if someone does evil, does that give someone else the right to do an even greater evil? Answer: of course not." Furthermore, "Everything in the world . . . is established and ordered by experience, which demands that everything be based on precedent, and not on arbitrary will. If it were otherwise, it would be worse, for the better is the enemy of what is good today."[51] In other words, Radishchev's overly utopian position failed to take the

---

49 Koselleck, *Critique and Crisis*. For an analysis and survey of critical reaction to this work, see Niklas Olsen, *History in the Plural: An Introduction to the Work of Reinhart Koselleck* (New York: Berghahn Books, 2014), 41–100. See also Anthony J. La Vopa, "Conceiving a Public: Ideas and Society in Eighteenth-Century Europe," *The Journal of Modern History* 64, no. 1 (1992): 79–116.

50 La Vopa, "Conceiving a Public," 84. Cf. Koselleck, *Critique and Crisis*, 118. This for Koselleck constitutes the fatal flaw of Enlightenment (and by extension, modern totalitarian) political thought that claims to be the mouthpiece for public opinion and self-righteous truth yet is hypocritically blind to its own will to power. "Criticism goes far beyond that which had occasioned it and is transformed into the motor of its own self-righteousness. It produces its own self-delusion" (119). Radishchev's political views, like those of most of his contemporaries, were based on morality and mostly ignored the practical obstacles to governing. Koselleck's argument seems quite applicable to the nineteenth-century Russian "revolutionary intelligentsia."

51 D. S. Babkin, *Protsess Radishcheva* (Moscow: Izdatel'stvo Akademii nauk SSSR, 1952), 158–159; the translation is from Alexander Radishchev, *A Journey from St. Petersburg to Moscow*, trans. Leo Weiner, ed. Roderick Page Thaler (Cambridge, MA: Harvard UP, 1969),

realities of the Russian situation into account. To some degree, Catherine's angry response probably reflected her own frustration at the outcome of her earlier, overly ambitious, pro-Enlightenment positions. She had had to come to terms with the practical limitations of her position. This was best formulated in her famous alleged response to Denis Diderot, who had given her untenably radical political advice on his trip to Petersburg in 1773–1774: "You write on paper, which can tolerate anything," she said she told the *philosophe*, "while I, poor empress—work on human skin, which is much more sensitive and prickly."[52]

Catherine herself took Radishchev's criticism very personally, and in her marginal notes on the *Journey* she responded defensively.[53] She wondered "whether I in some way have offended" the author, and guessed that he was taking revenge for thwarted ambition to serve at court. She attacked his motives and defended her own: "The author is maliciously inclined . . . I do not know how great the lust for power is in other rulers; in me it is not great. . . . *Malice* is in the malicious; I have none of it." She claimed that Russia's problems were due to "the poor execution of our commands," so that her critics were "accusing themselves. . . . They are criticizing society, and not the Sovereign's good heart or intentions."[54] One of the major ironies here was that Radishchev's critique of Catherine's rule was based in large part on the liberal Enlightenment principles expressed in her own *Nakaz*, to which he referred in the *Journey* more than once. Allen McConnell goes as far as to call Radishchev "Catherine's protégé" and notes "the many parts of the *Nakaz* that formed points of departure for Radishchev's *Journey*; the latter was partly an attack on the *Nakaz* (its defense of autocracy) but mainly [it was] a criticism of Catherine's failure to carry out the *Nakaz*'s promises."[55]

240–242. Catherine's notes were first published by O. M. Bodianskii in *Chteniia* 54, kn. 3 (1865): otd. 5, 67–77.

52 As she described her response to Diderot in a letter to Count L. P. de Ségur in 1785 (*Mémoirs ou Souvenirs et Anecdotes*, 3 vols. [Paris, 1827], vol. 3:37, quoted in de Madariaga, *Russia in the Age*, 33). On Catherine and Diderot, see, most recently: Robert Zaretsky, *Catherine and Diderot: The Empress, the Philosopher, and the Fate of the Enlightenment* (Cambridge, MA: Harvard UP, 2019).

53 She had also framed the mission of the Commission to Compose a New Law Code in very personal terms. She declared that "God forbid! that after finishing this legislation, there should be a people more just, and of course flourishing on earth. Otherwise the intention of our laws would not be fulfilled, a misfortune which I would not live to see" (*Catherine the Great's Instruction [Nakaz] to the Legislative Commission, 1767*, ed. Paul Dukes [Newtonville, MA: Oriental Research Partners, 1977], 108; capitalization normalized).

54 Babkin, *Protsess Radishcheva*, 157–58; translation from Radishchev, *A Journey*, 240. Catherine refers to "the author" because Radishchev's authorship had not yet been established; the book had been published anonymously.

55 McConnell, "The Empress and Her Protégé," 16.

As a work of literature, the *Journey* has been both denigrated as bad literature and acclaimed as a masterpiece, mostly for political reasons.[56] Among various debated issues—apart from that of its political stance—are the nature of its "sentimentalism" (especially as contrasted to the work's alleged "utilitarianism" and materialism)[57] and its complex narrative structure. Many readers have responded negatively to the book's often heavily archaic style.[58] Its use of multiple narrators may be seen as a strategy for self-protection that arguably has its roots in satirical journalism. The *Journey* is loosely structured and consists in chapters ostensibly corresponding to stops on a journey that feature essays and short narratives on various subjects as well as inserted narratives, including a powerful history of censorship, a plan for the gradual elimination of serfdom, and a long ode ("Freedom" [Vol'nost'], which Catherine considered "most clearly, manifestly revolutionary" because "tsars are threatened with the block"[59]). As N. I. Gromov argues, the book presents a multi-voiced dialogue, presenting differing opinions about serfdom, including the desire for the violent destruction of the existing order, in which group he puts the book as a whole.[60] The language of the *Journey* and its contrasting styles underscore the moral hypocrisy of official high discourse that is used to justify morally low activities.[61]

The *Journey from Saint Petersburg to Moscow* somewhat unexpectedly ends with another inserted text, the "Slovo o Lomonosove." Radishchev had worked on the "Slovo" since 1780, before the rest of the *Journey* was begun, and its placement at the end of the work (even if it was a late addition) suggests its importance as culmination of the work.[62] The "Slovo" takes place at Lomonosov's grave in St. Petersburg and contrasts his stone monument to his "life and works." "Slovo"

---

56 Political interpretations of the work are reviewed in K. Iu. Lappo-Danilevskii, "Plan postepennogo osvobozhdeniia krest'ian v 'Puteshestvii iz Peterburga v Moskvu' A. N. Radishcheva," *XVIII vek* 25 (2008): 206–232.
57 See the works of Tanya Page, especially "Radishchev's Polemic Against Sentimentalism in the Cause of Eighteenth-Century Utilitarianism," in *Russian Literature in the Age of Catherine the Great*, ed. Anthony Cross (Oxford: Meeuws, 1976), 141–172.
58 I have given my own take on these issues in *The Visual Dominant in Eighteenth-Century Russia* (DeKalb, IL: Northern Illinois UP, 2011), 222–252.
59 Babkin, *Protsess Radishcheva*, 163; Radishchev, *A Journey*, 248.
60 N. I. Gromov, "O kompozitsii 'Puteshestviia iz Peterburga v Moskvu,'" in *A. N. Radishchev: Stat'i i materialy* (Leningrad: Leningradskii universitet, 1950), 129–147; here, 142.
61 In this, Radishchev's stylistic practice may be compared to that of Derzhavin as described by Anna Lisa Crone in *The Daring of Derzhavin: The Moral and Aesthetic Independence of the Poet in Russia* (Bloomington, IN: Slavica, 2001), 38–45 and passim.
62 For scholarship on the "Slovo," see Steven A. Usitalo, *The Invention of Mikhail Lomonosov: A Russian National Myth* (Boston, MA: Academic Studies Press, 2013), 118 n. 96. Usitalo focuses on Radishchev's criticism of Lomonosov as a scientist; see my comments on this in my book review in *The Slavic and East European Journal* 58, no. 2 (Summer 2014): 333–335.

in the title may signify a eulogy, a panegyric (*pokhval'noe slovo*), a speech, sermon, discourse, or simply "a word." In this the "Slovo o Lomonosove" is generically ambiguous, like the *Journey* as a whole. However, this unusual take on the Horatian "exegi monumentum" theme makes the case for Lomonosov's transcendent significance as a poet (to which we shall return) but also refuses to refrain from some very pointed criticism.[63] The narrator asserts that he is "a foe to servility not only in what may arouse our awe, but even in our love," and declares (in words that uncannily look forward to Tolstoy and Dostoevsky): "Truth is our highest divinity, and if the Almighty Himself should wish to change its aspect by no longer revealing Himself in it, we would turn our face away even from Him."[64] The criticism of Lomonosov includes negative assessments of his work as a scientist (he was unoriginal), as an historian, as an orator and scholar of rhetoric, and as a writer of drama and epic. Despite the "countless beauties" and "uninterrupted harmony" of his odes, they "sometimes employed more words than ideas."[65] But, most cuttingly, Radishchev criticizes the odes—for which Lomonosov the poet earned his greatest glory—for their sycophancy, because, "following the common custom of flattering kings, who are frequently unworthy" of any praise, Lomonsov had extolled Empress Elizabeth.[66]

On the other hand, Radishchev champions Lomonosov as a truly "great man" (*velikii muzh*). This had to do first of all with his "unconquerable passion for learning." "Endowed by nature with creative power" and "the priceless right to influence his contemporaries..., [he] acted in various ways upon his fellow citizens, by opening up the people's minds [to] the various paths to learning."[67] Lomonosov, the son of peasants, helped create "fellow citizens" of them, something which complemented the *Journey*'s advocacy of equal rights for the "simple" Russian people (also a central concern of the later intelligentsia). Second and most important, Lomonosov was the creator of Russian literature:

> Your word, living now and evermore in your creations, the word of the Russian nation (*plemia*), which you have regenerated in

---

63 Pushkin commented (in an article that could not be published until after his death due to censorship) that "Radishchev had the secret intention of striking a blow against the unassailable glory of *the Russian Pindar*. It is worth noting that Radishchev carefully concealed this intention with feigned respect and treated Lomonosov's fame much more carefully than he did the supreme authority which he attacked with such insane impudence" (A. S. Pushkin, *Polnoe sobranie sochinenii*, 10 vols. [Leningrad: Nauka, 1978], vol. 7, 190).
64 Radishchev, *A Journey*, 235; I have made some minor changes in this translation.
65 Ibid., 237.
66 Ibid., 233.
67 Ibid., 232.

our tongue, will fly on the lips of the people beyond the illimitable horizon of the centuries. Let the elements in their compound fury burst open the earthly abysses and swallow this magnificent city whence your loud song rang out to the far corners of vast Russia; let some ferocious conqueror destroy even the name of our dear fatherland: but as long as the Russian word will strike an ear, you will live and will not die.[68]

Radishchev's verbal monument to Lomonosov, "an optimistic ending to a tragic book,"[69] combines these two elements: it champions both his "fellow citizens" (constituting society) and Russian letters, from now on dedicated to "the service of society"[70] rather than serving the court and imperial culture, as had mostly been the case hitherto. Radishchev presents a kind of Declaration of Independence of modern Russian literature, and as such may be seen as a counterpart to Novikov's efforts to expand the literary public sphere and its moral influence. Both men may be seen as making a first attempt, however problematical, to establish the rights of an actual, political public sphere; the appearance of the intelligentsia may be seen as a consequence of their failure.

Bibliography

Babkin, D. S. *Protsess Radishcheva*. Moscow: Izdatel'stvo Akademii nauk SSSR, 1952.

Berkov, P. N. *Satiricheskie zhurnaly N. I. Novikova*. Moscow: Izdatel'stvo Akademii nauk, 1951.

Bradley, Joseph. *Voluntary Associations in Tsarist Russia*. Cambridge, MA: Harvard UP, 2009.

Craven, Kenneth. "Publish and Languish: The Fate of Nikolai Ivanovich Novikov (1743–1818), Propagator of the Enlightenment under Catherine II." *Archives et Bibliotheques de Belgique / Archief en Bibliotheekwezen in België* 1–4 (1983): 173–190.

---

68 Ibid., 223. The "Russian word"—still another, quasi-mystical meaning of "slovo," here and in the later tradition often associated with the divine Logos. In particular, the passage brings to mind places in Gogol''s *Dead Souls* and *Selected Passages from Correspondence with Friends*.
69 L. I. Kulakova, "A. N. Radishchev o M. V. Lomonosove," in *Literaturnoe tvorchestvo M. V. Lomonosova: Issledovaniia i materialy*, ed. P. N. Berkov and I. Z. Serman (Moscow and Leningrad: Izdatel'stvo Akademii nauk, 1962), 219–236; here, 236.
70 Radishchev, *A Journey*, 224.

Crone, Anna Lisa. *The Daring of Derzhavin: The Moral and Aesthetic Independence of the Poet in Russia*. Bloomington, IN: Slavica, 2001.

de Madariaga, Isabel. *Russia in the Age of Catherine the Great*. London: Phoenix Press, 2002.

Doyle, William. "The Parlements of France and the Breakdown of the Old Regime 1771–1788." *French Historical Studies* 6, no. 4 (1970): 415–58.

Dukes, Paul, ed. *Catherine the Great's Instruction (Nakaz) to the Legislative Commission, 1767*. Newtonville, MA: Oriental Research Partners, 1977.

Faggionato, Raffaella. *A Rosicrucian Utopia in Eighteenth-Century Russia: The Masonic Circle of N. I. Novikov*. Dordrecht: Springer, 2005.

Gay, Peter. *The Enlightenment: An Interpretation*, 2 vols. New York: W. W. Norton, 1966–69.

Goodman, Dena. *The Republic of Letters: A Cultural History of the French Enlightenment*. Ithaca, NY: Cornell UP, 1994.

Gromov, N. I. "O kompozitsii 'Puteshestviia iz Peterburga v Moskvu.'" In *A. N. Radishchev: Stat'i i materialy*, edited by N. P. Alekseev, 129–147. Leningrad: Leningradskii universitet, 1950.

Habermas, Jürgen. *The Structural Transformation of the Public Sphere: An Inquiry into a Category of Bourgeois Society*. Translated by Thomas Burger. Cambridge, MA: MIT Press, 1989.

Jones, W. Gareth. "Novikov's Naturalized Spectator." In *The Eighteenth Century in Russia*, edited by J. G. Garrard, 149–65. Oxford: Clarendon Press, 1973.

———. "The 'Morning Light' Charity Schools, 1777–80." *The Slavonic and East European Review* 56, no. 1 (1978), 47–67.

———. "The Polemics of the 1769 Journals: A Reappraisal." *Canadian-American Slavic Studies* 16, nos. 3–4 (1982), 432–43.

———. *Nikolay Novikov, Enlightener of Russia*. Cambridge: Cambridge UP, 1984.

———. "Russian Literature in the Eighteenth Century." *Reference Guide to Russian Literature*, edited by Neil Cornwell, 13–18. London: Routledge, 2013.

Kalugin, Dmitrii. "'A Society That Speaks Concordantly,' or Mechanisms of Communication of Government and Society in Old and New Russia." In *Public Debate in Russia: Matters of (Dis)Order*, edited by Nikolai Vakhtin and Boris Firsov, 52–84. Edinburgh: Edinburgh UP, 2016.

Kaplan, Vera. *Historians and Historical Societies in the Public Life of Imperial Russia*. Bloomington: Indiana UP, 2017.

Ketcham, Michael G. *Transparent Designs: Reading, Performance, and Form in the "Spectator" Papers*. Athens: U of Georgia Press, 1985.

Kliuchevskii, V. O. "Vospominaniia o N. I. Novikove i ego vremeni." In idem, *Sochineniia*, vol. 8, 223–253. Moscow: Izdatel'stvo sotsial'no-ekonomicheskoi literatury, 1959.

Koselleck, Reinhart. *Critique and Crisis: Enlightenment and the Pathogenesis of Modern Society*. Cambridge, MA: MIT Press, 1988.

Kulakova, L. I. "A. N. Radishchev o M. V. Lomonosove." In *Literaturnoe tvorchestvo M. V. Lomonosova: Issledovaniia i materialy*, edited by P. N. Berkov and I. Z. Serman, 219–236. Moscow and Leningrad: Izdatel'stvo Akademii nauk, 1962.

La Vopa, Anthony J. "Conceiving a Public: Ideas and Society in Eighteenth-Century Europe." *The Journal of Modern History* 64, no. 1 (1992): 79–116.

Lappo-Danilevskii, K. Iu. "Plan postepennogo osvobozhdeniia krest'ian v 'Puteshestvii iz Peterburga v Moskvu' A. N. Radishcheva." *XVIII vek* 25 (2008): 206–232.

Leckey, Colum. "Patronage and Public Culture in the Russian Free Economic Society, 1765–1796." *Slavic Review* 64, no. 2 (2005): 355–79.

———. "What Is 'Prosveshchenie?" Nikolai Novikov's 'Historical Dictionary of Russian Writers' Revisited." *Russian History* 37, no. 4 (2010): 360–77.

———. *Patrons of Enlightenment: The Free Economic Society in Eighteenth-Century Russia*. Newark, NJ: U of Delaware Press, 2011.

Levitt, Marcus C. *The Visual Dominant in Eighteenth-Century Russia*. DeKalb, IL: Northern Illinois UP, 2011.

———. Review of *The Invention of Mikhail Lomonosov*, by Steven A. Usitalo. *The Slavic and East European Journal* 58, no. 2 (2014): 333–335.

Longinov, M. N. *Novikov i moskovskie martinisty*. Moscow: Tip. Gracheva, 1867.

Maggs, Barbara. Review of *Un publiciste frondeur sous Catherine II: Nicolas Novikov* by André Monnier. *Comparative Literature Studies* 22, no. 2 (1985): 272–274.

Makagonenko, G. P. *Nikolai Novikov i russkoe prosveshchenie XVIII veka*. Moscow: Nauka, 1952.

Marker, Gary. "Novikov's Readers," *The Modern Language Review* 77, no. 4 (1982), 894–905.

———. *Publishing, Printing, and the Origins of Intellectual Life in Russia*. Princeton, NJ: Princeton UP, 1985.

———. "Nikolai Ivanovich Novikov." In *Early Modern Russian Writers, Late Seventeenth and Eighteenth Centuries*. Vol. 150, *The Dictionary of Literary Biography*, 249–59. Bruccoli Clark Layman, Gale Research, 1995.

———. "The Creation of Journals and the Profession of Letters in the Eighteenth Century." In *Literary Journals in Imperial Russia*, edited by Deborah A. Martinsen, 14–33. New York: New York UP, 1997.

McArthur, Gilbert H. "Catherine II and the Masonic Circle of N. I. Novikov." *Canadian-American Slavic Studies* 4, no. 3 (1970): 529–46.

McConnell, Allen. "Radishchev's Political Thought." *American Slavic and East European Review* 17, no. 4 (1958): 439–53.

———. "Helvetius' Russian Pupils." *Journal of the History of Ideas* 24, no. 3 (1963): 373–86.

———. *A Russian Philosophe: Alexander Radishchev, 1749–1802*. The Hague: M. Nijhoff, 1964.

———. "Rousseau and Radishchev." *The Slavic and East European Journal* 8, no. 3 (1964): 253–72.

———. "The Empress and Her Protégé: Catherine II and Radishchev." *The Journal of Modern History* 36, no. 1 (1964): 14–27.

———. "Abbé Raynal and a Russian Philosophe." *Jahrbücher Für Geschichte Osteuropas* 12, no. 4 (1965): 499–512.

Nikolaev, S. I. "'Prevelikie nadezhdy' russkoi poezii v slovare pisatelei N. I. Novikova." *Russkaia literatura* 2 (2020): 35–39.

Novikov, N. I. *Pis'ma N. I. Novikova*. St. Petersburg: Izdatel'stvo imeni N. I. Novikova, 1994.

Olsen, Niklas. "Explaining, Criticizing, and Revising Modern Political Thought." In *History in the Plural: An Introduction to the Work of Reinhart Koselleck*, 41–100. New York: Berghahn Books, 2014.

O'Malley, Lurana Donnels. *The Dramatic Works of Catherine the Great: Theatre and Politics in Eighteenth-Century Russia*. Burlington, VT: Ashgate, 2006.

Page, Tanya. "Radishchev's Polemic Against Sentimentalism in the Cause of Eighteenth-Century Utilitarianism." In *Russian Literature in the Age of Catherine the Great*, edited by Anthony Cross, 141–172. Oxford: Meeuws, 1976.

Papmehl, K. A. *Freedom of Expression in Eighteenth-Century Russia*. The Hague: Nijhoff, 1971.

———. "'The Empress and 'Un Fanatique': A Review of the Circumstances Leading to the Government Action against Novikov in 1792." *The Slavonic and East European Review* 68, no. 4 (1990): 665–91.

———. "The Problem of Civil Liberties in the Records of the 'Great Commission.'" *Slavonic and East European Review* 42, no. 99 (1964): 274–91.

Pask, Kevin. "The Bourgeois Public Sphere and the Concept of Literature." *Criticism* 46, no. 2 (2004): 241–56.

Pushkin, A. S. *Polnoe sobranii sochinenii*, 10 vols. Leningrad: Nauka, 1978.

Radishchev, Aleksandr [Radishchev, Alexander]. *A Journey from St. Petersburg to Moscow*. Translated by Leo Weiner, edited by Roderick Page Thaler. Cambridge, MA: Harvard UP, 1969.

——— [Radishchev, A. N.]. *Polnoe sobranie sochinenii*. 3 vols. Moscow and Leningrad: Izdatel'stvo Akademii nauk SSSR, 1938–1952.

Reyfman, Irina. *How Russia Learned to Write: Literature and the Imperial Table of Ranks*. Madison: U of Wisconsin Press, 2016.

Ryu, In-ho L. "Moscow Freemasons and the Rosicrucian Order: A Study in Organization and Control." In *The Eighteenth Century in Russia*, edited by John G. Garrard, 198–232. Oxford: Clarendon Press, 1973.

Serman, I. Z. "Imperatritsa i poruchik Novikov." *XVIII vek* 25 (2008): 346–353.

Smith, Douglas. *Working the Rough Stone: Freemasonry and Society in Eighteenth-Century Russia*. DeKalb, IL: Northern Illinois UP, 1999.

———. "Alexander Radishchev's *Journey from St. Petersburg to Moscow* and the Limits of Freedom of Speech in the Reign of Catherine the Great." In *Freedom of Speech: The History of an Idea*, edited by Elizabeth Powers, 61–74. Lanham, MD: Rowman & Littlefield, 2011.

———. "Attached to the Party of Humanity: On Robert Zaretsky's 'Catherine & Diderot,'" *Los Angeles Review of Books*, March 1, 2019. https://lareviewofbooks.org/article/attached-party-humanity-robert-zaretskys-catherine-diderot/.

Usitalo, Steven A. *The Invention of Mikhail Lomonosov: A Russian National Myth*. Boston, MA: Academic Studies Press, 2013.

Von Herzen, Michael. "Catherine II—Editor of *Vsiakaia Vsiachina*? A Reappraisal." *The Russian Review* 38, no. 3 (1979): 283–297.

Walker, Barbara. "On Reading Soviet Memoirs: A History of the 'Contemporaries' Genre as an Institution of Russian Intelligentsia Culture from the 1790s to the 1970s." *The Russian Review* 59, no. 3 (2000): 327–352.

Zaretsky, Robert. *Catherine and Diderot: The Empress, the Philosopher, and the Fate of the Enlightenment*. Cambridge, MA: Harvard UP, 2019.

Part 2

THE NINETEENTH CENTURY

The Intelligentsia in the Russian Press of the 1860s and 1870s

Konstantine Klioutchkine

This essay describes the development of the notion of the intelligentsia in the period between the 1860s and 1870s, identifying the moment in 1868 when the word itself entered wide circulation in progressive publications. The history of the intelligentsia during that period was bound up with the rapid growth of the press, which gained lasting economic viability based on the commercial success of its leading cultural form, the encyclopedic "thick journal." I argue that the critics of the progressive journals *Notes of the Fatherland* and *The Cause* introduced the term intelligentsia as part of reconsolidating their audiences. Imagining and organizing audiences had been essential to the functioning of thick journals since the creation of *The Library for Reading* in 1834 and, in particular, since the appearance of the model progressive journal *The Contemporary* in 1847. This essay traces the history of the terms by which progressive journals had described their readership on the way to employing the word intelligentsia in 1868.

An important part of my argument is that the meanings of the word intelligentsia, in order to be effective, had to be sufficiently ambivalent in order to address diverse experiences, ideologies, and political views of potential readers. Even as the progressive critics agreed, in 1868, as to the social and economic status of what they called the intelligentsia, they disagreed with each other as to what personalities, what experiences, and what political programs their particular intelligentsia readers had to develop. In the course of the 1870s, as the press continued to grow, the notion of the intelligentsia became increasingly ambivalent, especially as writers from the full ideological spectrum of the Russian press joined the public discussion with their alternative descriptions of the intelligentsia. Having emerged from progressive thick journals, the term, originally working to consolidate particular audiences, came to function as a notion that described an increasingly vague diversity of educated persons in the Russian public sphere. This notion gained lasting cultural currency precisely by generating ongoing attempts to define what its meaning might be. These attempts would be as unsuccessful at achieving a consensus as they would be productive for continuing the often lucrative public discussion of this issue.

The Intelligentsia of 1868 in the Cultural and Economic Context of the 1860s and 1870s

One of the few points of agreement in the intelligentsia debates has been the assumption that this notion emerged as part of Russia's transition to modernity.[1] The country's entry into modern life was marked by a particularly prominent role of the press, represented especially by the leading thick journals. The press gained outsize cultural influence in the context of a relatively slow pace that modernization took in the very large territory beyond St. Petersburg and Moscow in such aspects of life as education, technology, business, politics, and the liberal professions. As young educated people sought self-realization in modern life, they first were able to gain it primarily by way of reading and writing in the field of high journalism. Only gradually did they gain fulfillment beyond the medium of print by pursuing sustainable intellectual careers in the general economy of developing capitalism. The prominence of the press in addressing the precarious social condition of Russian intellectuals encouraged journalists continuously to cultivate new and resonant terms that negotiated the experience of their readers as representative subjects of modernity.

Insofar as the transition from traditional to modern life involved uncertainty and confusion, it is instructive that the authorship and the origin of the word intelligentsia remain unclear. However, consistent use of the word can be dated

---

1 E.g., *The Russian Intelligentsia*, ed. Richard Pipes (NY: Columbia UP, 1961), v-viii; V. R. Leikina-Svirskaia, *Intelligentsia v Rossii vo vtoroi polovine XIX veka* (Moscow: Mysl', 1971), 3–4; Marc Raeff, *Origins of the Russian Intelligentsia: The Eighteenth-Century Nobility* (NY: Harcourt, Brace and World, 1966), 1–13.

to 1868 when it was taken up by the publicists of the progressive journals *The Cause* and *Notes of Fatherland*. These journals, advocating the values of equality, democracy, and rapid social improvement, dominated the country's high journalism: they were more economically successful and culturally influential than their liberal, conservative, and nationalist ideological opponents. Their influence was especially pronounced among several generations of young readers entering Russia's modern life by way of the growing number of educational institutions across the country.

1868 was the year of a new consolidation of Russian progressive discourse in the two aforementioned journals. Progressive journalism had come to dominate the country's press in the late 1850s when Emperor Alexander II, succeeding the conservative Nicholas I, introduced sweeping liberal reforms. By 1860, the broad cultural impulse toward progressive speech coalesced in two journals, *The Contemporary* and *The Russian Word*. In 1866, the assassination attempt by Nikolai Karakozov against Alexander II led to government reaction forcing the closure of progressive publications. By the turn of 1868, however, the two progressive journals reinvented themselves under the new titles. It was at that moment that their journalists came to reassess the status of writers and readers by using the word intelligentsia.

In that year, the first Russian Marxist critic Pyotr Tkachyov (1844–1886) defined the intelligentsia as an increasingly prominent group of people whose distinction was that they could rely only on their intellectual skills to survive in the modernizing world. Tkachyov described the new generation of intellectuals coming of age after 1860 as distinctive in lacking the economic resources that their predecessors had derived from their respective positions in the traditional social world as members of the gentry, clergy, merchantry, or state bureaucracy. Tkachyov wrote about a difficult challenge: there was still little demand for intellectual skills in the as-yet underdeveloped economy. Accordingly, he explained that the self-realization "of our intelligentsia" was bound up with its own effort to effect social change. The first step in that had to involve learning from independent sources of knowledge, such as Tkachyov's own writing, about the principles of social science, such as the Marxist vision of historical development.[2] Tkachyov's fellow critic Nikolai Shelgunov (1824–1891), a seasoned progressive publicist, deplored the rifts between Russian intellectuals and blamed the failure of schools and universities to provide their graduates with appropriately unifying education. He called on "representatives of the

---

2   P. N. Tkachev, "Podrastaiushchie sily" [Rising forces], *Delo* [The Cause] 9 (1868): 1–28, esp. 3–8.

intelligentsia" to join forces in developing and disseminating the scientific knowledge that would lead to readers' uniform engagement in the country's social progress.[3] Nikolai Mikhailovsky (1842–1904), the future leading Populist critic, wrote in his "Notes on the Russian Intelligentsia" that as a member of the intelligentsia himself he published his work for other members of the intelligentsia: the identity as readers and writers in "his" press was a key criterion in the true intelligentsia's identification.[4]

In the texts of these progressive critics, the intelligentsia gained a consistent meaning describing educated persons alienated from the state, society, and the means of production. With these forms of alienation in mind, the critics emphasized that the intelligentsia found its primary existential home, its intellectual experience, and its means of self-realization in the progressive press, as its readers and writers. As traditional educational institutions lagged behind the "current" standards of knowledge, as state bureaucracy offered existentially unsatisfying careers, and as the economy failed to provide rewarding jobs—the press promised the knowledge, the community, and the visions of a better future that readers could not find elsewhere.

Conceptual Genealogy of the Term

The 1868 definition of the "intelligentsia" absorbed a range of ideological, cultural, and behavioral values developed in the progressive press of the preceding years. Envisioning their readers as socially alienated, progressive journals had long repudiated the "old-world" spiritual, intellectual, and cultural assumptions—including faith in God, Christian ethics, philosophical idealism, Romantic aesthetics, political liberalism, and the conventions of polite society. Instead, they invited readers to cultivate a new set of values. In the new framework, human experience was viewed as subject to the determinations of natural and social sciences—physiology, anthropology, sociology, history, and economics most prominent among them. These sciences informed the progressive ethics prescribing that a person rely on the utilitarian calculus of pleasure and pain to understand his or her experience and to work out the rules of conduct. In particular, scientific calculations appeared to have proven that true happiness

---

3 N. V. Shelgunov, "Russkii individualizm" [Russian individualism], *Delo* 7 (1868): 1–23, esp. 2–3.
4 N. K. Mikhailovskii, "Ocherki obshchestvennoi zhizni: Pis'ma ob russkoi intelligentsii" [Sketches of social life: Notes on the Russian intelligentsia], *Sovremennoe obozrenie* [Contemporary review] 6 (1868): 336–355.

was predicated on a person's understanding that his or her individual realization centrally derived from altruistic work to improve life for all. Accordingly, one was expected to gain pleasure in self-abnegating effort on behalf of social progress with a view toward rewards in the future. In everyday behavior, the new ethic translated into performative rejection of social conventions, as well as of upper-class fashions: the new person cultivated coarse and direct behavior, alternative styles of dress, and sartorial symbols of diverse emancipatory and revolutionary movements, such as the Italian Risorgimento and Polish Liberation.

The central notions in the conceptual genealogy of the "intelligentsia" were the "nihilists" following Ivan Turgenev's novel *Fathers and Sons* (1862), the "new people" in Nikolai Chernyshevsky's novel *What Is to Be Done* (1863), and the "intellectual proletariat" in Dmitry Pisarev's criticism in the mid-1860s. Turgenev's figure of the nihilist became a topic of intense critical debate, and his cultural influence led a generation of young readers to describe themselves with this word. These debates focused on Turgenev's hero Bazarov, a medical student who believed that the natural sciences would resolve the questions of human existence once scientific knowledge became sufficiently advanced. Working toward that knowledge, Bazarov occupied himself on a summer vacation by dissecting frogs whose physiology, he thought, would offer insights into the functioning of any living being. Away from his experiments, Bazarov ridiculed his gentry hosts for their attachment to art and literature, social conventions, and polite conversation. Furthermore, he shocked them by denying the values of human affection and love. His crude manners, chapped hands, unkempt hair, and slovenly dress emphasized his nihilist disdain for prevailing cultural standards.

Whereas Bazarov's nihilism stopped short of providing the answers for those who sought meaningful social action beyond the cultivation of scientific knowledge, Chernyshevsky's *What is To Be Done?* spelled out those answers for the "new people" it described, offering them an overall program of personal life conducive to wholesale social change. Like Bazarov, Chernyshevsky's two leading male characters were medical students committed to the development, dissemination, and application of scientific knowledge. They relied on the ethics of "rational egoism" that taught them that attaining true happiness involved calculating how to constrain one's immediate desires in a way that generated longer-term individual and social rewards. The novel's main new person, however, was its heroine Vera Pavlovna, who proved best able to translate the new worldview into practical life. She did so by organizing economically profitable women's communes, which combined productive labor with mutual education and support. The novel also featured a hero of the future, presumably a revolutionary, whose ethics, the novel hinted, led him to radical activities among the underprivileged masses. Ultimately, the novel provided a vision of communist utopia that would result from the new people's combined effort, a vision that came to its heroine in one of her prophetic dreams.

A leading critic who championed the nihilists and the new people was Dmitri Pisarev: his articles, including those on Turgenev's and Chernyshevsky's characters, became so influential that the new people chose the self-designation of *pisarevtsy* nearly as often as "nihilists." Pisarev's influence derived from his ability to take the rhetoric of the new people to the extreme. As early as 1861, his language on the rejection of existing values called for destroying "anything that could be destroyed" in order to test what remained with a view to its value as a foundation for progress.[5] Writing about the new people's devotion to science, Pisarev called on his readers to treat the anatomized frog as the symbolic source of salvation and renewal of the Russian people.[6] Developing the economic aspect of Chernyshevsky's vision, Pisarev described the new people as the "intellectual proletariat." In 1864, he argued that the intellectual capital embodied in such persons was the leading force of social transformation.[7] Pisarev had not read Karl Marx, but his language provided a bridge to Marxist discussions of the intelligentsia by Pyotr Tkachyov and later critics.

The language of the new people in the progressive journals of the 1860s tracked back for its originary inspiration to the work of Vissarion Belinsky in the 1840s. Especially productive was Belinsky's conception of a new kind of public expression that would rely on the involvement of a new type of writers and readers. His conception served as the basis for the reorganization in 1847 of *The Contemporary*, which became the paradigmatic progressive journal in the late 1850s. Belinsky rejected the aesthetic and social hierarchies of his day in order to foreground the "ordinary readers and writers" whom he expected to join forces in a shared ideological effort. That effort would emphasize the role of criticism, both aesthetic and social. Adopted by later progressive journalists, Belinsky's language became especially resonant in Nikolai Dobrolyubov's discussions of "realist criticism" at the turn of the 1860s, and in Pyotr Lavrov's descriptions of "critically thinking persons" in 1868.[8]

---

5   Daniel Brower, *Training the Nihilists: Education and Radicalism in Tsarist Russia* (Ithaca, NY: Cornell UP, 1975), 15.
6   Irina Paperno, *Chernyshevsky and the Age of Realism: A Study in the Semiotics of Behavior* (Stanford, CA: Stanford UP, 1988), 17.
7   D. I. Pisarev, "Tsvety nevinnogo iumora" [The flowers of harmless humor], *Russkoe slovo* [The Russian Word] 2 (1864): otd. 2, 41–42.
8   On Belinsky's new conceptualization of writers and readers, see, e.g., Mikhail Makeev, *Nikolai Nekrasov, poet i predprinimatel': Ocherki o vzaimodeistvii ekonomiki i literatury* (Moscow: MAKS Press, 2009), 77–80. On Dobrolyubov's "realist criticism" see, e.g., Aleksei Vdovin,

Ambivalence of Meaning

Though the progressive critics shared broad epistemic assumptions, they came to compete with one another by envisioning different ideological particulars as organizing their respective prescriptions for readers. The competition became especially prominent in 1862 when the critics of *The Contemporary* battled those of *The Russian Word* over correct interpretation of Turgenev's Bazarov. *The Contemporary* rejected Turgenev's description of the nihilists, considering it a caricature of the new generation. By contrast, *The Russian Word* embraced Turgenev's character as a largely true representation of the new progressive person. It was in that journal that Pisarev gained his lasting cultural influence by championing Turgenev's hero but rewriting him in his own more radical terms. The conflict in the progressive camp was viewed as "the split among the nihilists," according to Fyodor Dostoevsky's idiom. Dostoevsky suggested that disagreements within the camp of his ideological opponents would undermine their cultural influence.[9] This suggestion proved wrong. The ability of progressive critics to envision different kinds of new people within a shared epistemic framework continuously attracted new readers to their publications. Ultimately, the ongoing debates about the new people within the progressive press functioned to increase the influence of its discourse as a dominant force in the country's cultural economy.

Debates about progressive educated people continued in discussions of the intelligentsia in 1868 and following years, while adjusting some of the ideological premises. The earlier models foregrounded individual or small-group scientific enlightenment, combined with communal economic enterprise, as the everyday activity that would engender social change largely of itself. By 1868, these principles appeared to have fallen short. The intelligentsia was now expected to evolve a greater moral responsibility beyond the frameworks of the natural sciences and economics. The new moral position had to derive from the intelligentsia's recognition of its own social status as the product of historical development. In particular, the *intelligent* had to acknowledge his or her debt to the laboring classes, whose manual work made it possible for the educated to gain their intellectual skills. Accordingly, the intelligentsia had to commit to a broader social engagement, and one that was now predicated on the new

---

Dobroliubov: Raznochinets mezhdu dukhom i plot'iu (Moscow: Molodaia gvardiia, 2017), 133–160.
9 F. M. Dostoevskii, "G-n Shchedrin ili raskol v nigilistakh" [Mr. Shchedrin, Or the split among the nihilists], *Epokha* [The epoch] 5 (1864): 274–294.

spiritual, rather than narrowly scientific, values emanating from the acknowledgement of the intellectuals' calling in human history.

Despite the recognition of the intelligentsia's high purpose, it remained a matter of acute debate as to what kind of social action the proper progressive person was required to adopt—especially as the *intelligent* was also expected to cultivate individual freedom and self-development. In that latter vein, Shelgunov's prescriptions for the intelligentsia focused on personal development along the earlier scientific lines of the 1860s. By contrast, Lavrov emphasized that "critically thinking persons" had to recognize their debt to the people and return it by extensive but peaceful philanthropic work. Such "gradualism" did not satisfy Tkachyov, who advocated for radical action beyond philanthropy, enlightenment, and propaganda: especially once he emigrated to Europe in 1873, he called for inciting riots and perpetrating acts of terror in order to unhinge the existing social framework. Mikhailovsky, whose journalism was the most abundant and influential among these critics, wavered as to the proper modes of his readers' engagement in the social world. Uncertain on that count, Mikhailovsky developed a new prescriptive iteration of the truly progressive figure as a "harmoniously" or "integrally developed personality." That figure had to resist the growing specialization of labor in the world of capitalism by cultivating his or her diverse human faculties and by engaging in a variety of activities.[10] This vision of a harmonious experience was at obvious variance with its author's own life, which was one-sidedly committed to constant writing for the press. The discrepancy between Mikhailovsky's theoretical model and his actual experience highlighted the tension that haunted the progressive tradition: its critics' models of personality could be as compelling to their audiences as they were impossible to translate into viable practical lives beyond reading and writing.

Despite the diversity of models for intelligentsia personalities, the core ideological framework remained consistent in the discourse of progressive journals during the 1860s and 1870s. In particular, the emphases on criticism, as well as on the shared effort of "ordinary" intellectuals, continued to condition the formative role of critics and publicists in dictating who the new people were supposed to be. Progressives' didacticism worked to exclude the leading fiction writers, future Russian literary classics among them, from membership in the intelligentsia. At best, these writers were viewed as capable of contributing cultural material for critical interpretation, and Turgenev's *Fathers and Sons* was the main instantiation of such treatment. More commonly, progressive critics approached the future

---

10 N. K. Mikhailovsky, "Bor'ba za individual'nost'" [The struggle for individuality], *Otechestvennye zapiski* [Notes of the Fatherland] 10 (1875): 613–656.

classics with extreme animosity, especially when commenting on the trend of "anti-nihilist" novels, questioning the progressive cultural assumptions about human personality. Such texts included Nikolai Leskov's *No Way Out* (1864), Dostoevsky's *Notes from Underground* (1864) and *Crime and Punishment* (1866), and Ivan Goncharov's *The Precipice* (1869). The leading progressive journals, didactically opposed to aestheticism in art, let alone anti-nihilist prose, published no canonical Russian fiction between 1860 and 1880.[11]

However, the format of the thick journal demanded a significant proportion of creative literature, and progressive journals did publish an abundant amount of fiction that even at the time was broadly understood to be aesthetically second-rate. Amid that fiction, an especially prominent genre was the novel about progressive young people. The number of such novels peaked at the turn of the 1870s, shortly after the critics theorized the new iteration of new people as the intelligentsia. These novels continuously re-envisioned particulars of the ordinary lives of those who adopted progressive ideological schemata. The master-narrative of this genre introduced young men and women informed by the canon of progressive texts and followed them as they acted on that education by resisting prevalent social conventions and by pursuing the prescribed range and kind of social engagement. They worked as teachers, doctors, and nurses among the lower classes both in the capitals and in the provinces, helped to liberate women from oppressive social conditions, organized cooperatives, and participated in publishing enterprises that disseminated the new knowledge.

For all its aspirations, however, this master-narrative led its characters to a dead end: the progressive novel was unable to imagine ideologically appropriate development for its characters. Government censorship prevented descriptions of radical social change or revolutionary activity beyond rather vague hints. More importantly, the expectations of literary realism demanded that the novel place its characters in the existing social and economic circumstances if it were to envision those characters' sustainable existence. Where Chernyshevsky's utopia offered fantasies of rapid economic success, and where Pisarev hoped for swift progress actuated by intellectual capital, the progressive novel struggled: it had to describe its "intellectual proletarians" supporting themselves by ordinary intellectual careers in a slowly developing modern economy. Even as these characters continued to espouse their ideological commitments, they had

---

11 The most notable exception was Dostoevsky's *The Raw Youth*, published by *Notes of the Fatherland* in 1873. M. E. Saltykov-Shchedrin, a classic of Russian satirical prose who has been less popular in the West, was an editor at *Notes of the Fatherland* and published most of his work in that journal.

to resort to mundane survival in their present lives. The discrepancy between ideological dreams and ordinary existence proved disheartening. Some progressive characters were driven to suicide and other forms of self-destruction, especially alcoholism. Most had to make peace with what amounted to ordinary bourgeois life. The viable characters increasingly pursued careers without a clear philanthropic aspect, taking jobs as bank executives, lawyers, and factory managers.[12] The novel's difficulty in imagining inspiring character development caused progressive critics to recognize that fiction about the new people described how "the mountain" of ideological aspirations produced "the mouse" of banal existence.[13] Ultimately, this novel suggested that, while the broad ideological assumptions of the progressive critics became commonplace among their readers, the growing intelligentsia was constituted by ordinary educated people coming of age after the turn of the 1860s. Moreover, the novel expressed a mounting concern that progressive language became so culturally ubiquitous that it ceased to work as a distinguishing feature of any truly progressive faction within the educated public.[14]

Alternative Meanings

Beyond treatment of the intelligentsia in the progressive journals, two competing uses of the word with far vaguer meanings became common during the

---

12 The master narrative of the progressive novel gained expression in the titles of the more prominent texts of the era. The life of the characters begins in the *Putrid Marshes* (*Gnilye bolota*, A. K. Sheller-Mikhailov, 1864) of traditional Russian life before the liberal reforms. Once social change is underway, the heroes engage in the struggle between *The Old and the New Russia* (*Staraia i novaia Rossiia*, D. K. Girs, 1868) and go through *Hard Times* (*Trudnoe vremia*, V. A. Sleptsov, 1865). Yet they move forward *Step by Step* (*Shag za shagom*, I. V. Omulevsky, 1870–1871), improving themselves and trying to effect social change while also organizing cooperative enterprises, as in *A Story of a Cooperative* (*Istoriia odnogo tovarishchestva*, N. F. Bazhin, 1869). These projects, however, lead to *No Exodus* (*Bez iskhoda*, K. M. Stanyukovich, 1873) as characters ultimately fail in their quest for transformation. In 1877, Ivan Turgenev's novel *Virgin Soil* (*Nov'*, 1877) absorbed the narrative tradition of the progressive industrial novel in order to show that the only viable character in that tradition would become an ordinary intellectual professional in the world of general capitalism: Turgenev presented this figure as a progressively minded but pragmatic factory manager, Solomin.
13 This was the view of the critic A. M. Skabichevsky regarding the novels of one of the more prolific fiction writers, A. K. Sheller-Mikhailov. Quoted in *Istoriia russkoi literatury XIX v.*, vol. 4, ed. D. N. Ovsianiko-Kulikovskii (Moscow: Mir, 1908–1910), 137.
14 Concerns about the bourgeois outcome of commonplace progressive ideas were registered as early as the influential novella *Bourgeois Happiness* (Meshchanskoe schast'e) by N. G. Pomyalovsky (published in the *Contemporary* in 1860) and found a representative manifestation, for instance, in K. M. Stanyukovich's novel *No Exodus* (Bez iskhoda, 1873).

period, and especially in the 1870s. Gentry fiction-writers, including Turgenev, Lev Tolstoy, and Leskov, used the term ironically to ridicule unfounded intellectual pretensions among members of any social group. Tolstoy, publishing his *War and Peace* in the conservative journal *The Russian Messenger*, employed the word, anachronistically, to satirize the vacuity of Petersburg's high society in the early 1800s.[15] Turgenev, in a short story for the liberal *Messenger of Europe*, made fun of the gentry in a provincial Russian town.[16] Leskov referred to provincial intelligentsia as consisting of bureaucrats and clergy alien to the core of traditional Russian life. He wrote that most of this intelligentsia was distinguished by its idleness, although the idleness of some was compounded by their rhetorical "protestation" against traditional social values.[17]

Another broad use of the word intelligentsia was featured in texts on history and sociology describing the educated strata of any social, ethnic, or national group. This application could refer to the Russian clergy as the stratum essential to the bureaucratic functioning of the pre-modern Russian state. Similarly, it could describe literate peasants as capable of expressing the otherwise inarticulate interests of Russian peasantry as a social estate. In this broader sense, the word was common in reference to the educated strata of Slavic peoples in Europe, including the Czechs, Serbs, and especially Poles.[18] Evocations of the Polish intelligentsia could be particularly prominent because the word intelligentsia had existed in Polish before it appeared in Russian, prompting the later scholarly opinion that the word had come to Russia from Poland, an opinion that remains as plausible as it is impossible to verify.[19]

---

15 Lev Tolstoi, *Polnoe sobranie sochinenii*, vol. 9 (Moscow: Gosudarstvennoe izdatel'stvo khudozhestvennoi literatury, 1935-ë964), 12 (first book form edition in 1868).

16 I. S. Turgenev, *Polnoe sobranie sochinenii i pisem v dvadtsati vos'mi tomakh* (Moscow: Akademiia nauk, 1960–68), vol. 8. Originally "Strannaia istoriia" [A strange story], *Vestnik Evropy* [The Messenger of Europe] 1 (1870).

17 Nikolai Leskov, *Chaiushchie dvizheniia vody* [Those hoping for water to flow], *Otechestvennye zapiski* [Notes of the Fatherland] 4, kn. 1 (April 1867): 491–492.

18 E.g., N. Ia. Danilevskii, *Rossiia i Evropa* [Russia and Europe], *Zaria* [Dawn] 1–6 and 8–10 (1869).

19 For a more recent version of this claim, see Nathaniel Knight, "Was the Intelligentsia Part of the Nation? Visions of Society in Post-Emancipation Russia," *Kritika: Explorations in Russian and Eurasian History* 7, no. 4 (Fall 2006): 733–758; and Boris Kolonitskii, "Identifikatsiia rossiiskoi intelligentsii i intellegentofobiia: Kon. XIX—nachalo XX v.," in *Intelligentsiia v istorii: Obrazovannyi chelovek v predstavleniiakh i sotsial'noi deistvitel'nosti*, ed. D. A. Sdvizhkov (Moscow: IVI RAN, 2001), 151–171. For an alternative view that the word came to Russian from German, see, e.g., Richard Pipes, "'Intelligentsia' from the German 'Intelligenz'? A Note," *Slavic Review* 30, no. 3 (1971): 615–618. For a general survey of the uses of the word intelligentsia in Russia in a broad Western context, see Otto Wilhelm Müller, *Intelligencija: Untersuchungen zur Geschichte eines politischen Schlagwortes* (Frankfurt: Athenäum Verlag, 1971).

All the meanings of the term intelligentsia would coexist in the public discourse of the 1870s, as represented, for one prominent instance, in Dostoevsky's *Diary of a Writer* (1873, 1876–1877, 1880–1881), a running journalistic commentary on the country's life and times. Like Mikhailovsky, Dostoevsky was capable of addressing his readers as "we, the members of the intelligentsia," though in his treatment this identification was less a matter of appealing to his audience than of warning it about the dangers of such an identification. His argument was that whatever the intelligentsia might be, both its definition and its failure consisted in its separation from ordinary people. Within the framework of that argument, Dostoevsky cast blame on all the intelligentsia social "strata" or "classes" for their alienation from the nation's spiritual force. Among the educated, he easily distinguished the younger intelligentsia as defined by the country's progressive journalists, but he then described their susceptible readers as especially likely to have been corrupted by spiritual alienation. When Dostoevsky turned to the topic of the Slavic peoples, such as the Poles and Czechs, he raised the same concern as he did with regard to Russians, questioning the distance between educated segments of Slavic societies and their respective peoples.[20]

The End of the "Classical Intelligentsia" Period

The turn of the 1880s marked a range of interrelated changes in the Russian press, the country's general economy, and its cultural landscape. The press had proven its commercial viability and continued its rapid expansion. Thick journals lost their cultural prominence, yielding to newspapers, weekly magazines, and mass-circulation journals. The press's audiences expanded from the tens of thousands of relatively highly educated people to hundreds of thousands of readers with varying degrees of education. In the meantime, the young educated readers of the 1860s and 1870s increasingly found professional careers in the general economy and looked beyond the journals for self-identification and self-realization. Consolidating larger and variously educated audiences in the growing sphere of print ceased being a matter of describing the relatively clear ideological assumptions of alienated intellectuals. The set of cultural values that could be envisioned as consistent and distinctive of the earlier intelligentsia became increasingly vague, fragmentary, and commonplace in the public discourse of the Russian press as a whole.

---

20 F. M. Dostoevskii, *Dnevnik pisatelia*, in idem, *Polnoe sobranie sochinenii v tridtsati tomakh* (Leningrad: Nauka, 1972–1990), vols. 21–27.

In the last two decades of the nineteenth century, references to the intelligentsia became so routine that most educated people came to view themselves through this term. The challenges inherent in such routinization appeared especially pronounced in the writings of Anton Chekhov (1860–1904), entering the field of the press around 1880 (see Svetlana Evdokimova's chapter in this collection). Chekhov himself came to be celebrated as a representative intelligentsia figure on account of his humanitarian projects, the humanity of his art, and his status as a leading Russian writer. However, he treated the term with intense aversion, insisting—especially in his correspondence—that the aura of the intelligentsia's distinction concealed its moral failure, lack of true education or intelligence, and inability to engage in meaningful social action. His stories and plays repeatedly describe that pattern as haunting the lives of the intellectual professionals he represents.[21] One of the central features of Chekhov's art is the sense of the prison-house of intelligentsia assumptions: his characters struggle in vain to find an alternative language by which to make sense of their experience. Chekhov's relation to the notion of the intelligentsia can be taken as indicative of the term's future in Russian and Soviet society: its intellectual professionals, regardless of their attitude toward this word, would find it hard to avoid the cultural expectation that they define themselves and be viewed by others through the demanding standards of this inherently ambivalent term.

The end of what I have been calling the "classical period of the intelligentsia" featured the publication of Pavel Annenkov's (1813–1887) memoir *A Remarkable Decade: 1838–1848* in 1880. Annenkov's text established a model for treatment of the intelligentsia as a historical, cultural, or social category. Remembering the intellectual "circles" of his youth, Annenkov, aware that the term "intelligentsia" was anachronistic, easily used it to describe progressively minded intellectual elites as a long-ranging feature of Russian culture and society. Annenkov's interest was historicist and analytical: he looked to describe distinct generations of intellectuals as members of different cultural formations at different periods in Russian history. His conceptual approach emphasized the recognition that there was not one Russian intelligentsia but rather different intelligentsias in different periods: each with its own social status and functions, with its own relation to the state; its own engagement with the means of production; and its own set of cultural values. Thus, the very title of his memoir

---

21 For instance, his play *Uncle Vanya* (*Diadia Vania*, 1897) features a range of intelligentsia types: a self-important and vacuous professor of philology; Uncle Vanya's mendacious mother, continuously reading what she views as progressive journalism; a provincial doctor disillusioned by his work and succumbing to alcoholism; and Uncle Vanya and his niece, who selflessly toil to maintain their familial estate but fail to find meaning in this barely sustainable enterprise.

highlighted the intelligentsia of the 1840s as distinct from that of the 1860s and 1870s. Even as Annenkov's analytical and historicist view would influence future scholarship, his practical use of the term invited less discriminating treatment of the intelligentsia as a word that purported to describe a continuous, coherent, and somehow uniform phenomenon, distinctive of Russian life and its educated persons.

Bibliography

Brower, Daniel. *Training the Nihilists: Education and Radicalism in Tsarist Russia*. Ithaca, NY: Cornell UP, 1975.

Danilevsky, N. Ia. *Rossiia i Evropa* [Russia and Europe]. *Zaria* [Dawn] 1–6, 8–10 (1869).

Dostoevskii, F. M. "G-n Shchedrin ili raskol v nigilistakh" [Mr. Shchedrin, Or the split among the nihilists]. *Epokha* [The epoch] 5 (1864): 274–294.

———. *Polnoe sobranie sochinenii v tridtsati tomakh*. Leningrad: Nauka, 1972–1990.

Knight, Nathaniel. "Was the Intelligentsia Part of the Nation? Visions of Society in Post-Emancipation Russia." *Kritika: Explorations in Russian and Eurasian History* 7, no. 4 (2006): 733–758.

Kolonitskii, Boris. "Identifikatsiia rossiiskoi intelligentsii i intellegentofobiia: Kon. XIX—nachalo XX v." In *Intelligentsiia v istorii: Obrazovannyi chelovek v predstavleniiakh i sotsial'noi deistvitel'nosti*, ed. D. A. Sdvizhkov, 151–171. Moscow: IVI RAN, 2001.

Leikina-Svirskaia, V. R. *Intelligentsia v Rossii vo vtoroi polovine XIX veka*. Moscow: Mysl', 1971.

Leskov, Nikolai. *Chaiushchie dvizheniia vody* [Those hoping for the flow of water]. *Otechestvennye zapiski* [Notes of the fatherland] 4, kn. 1 (1867): 491–492.

Makeev, Mikhail. *Nikolai Nekrasov, poet i predprinimatel': Ocherki o vzaimodeistvii ekonomiki i literatury*. Moscow: MAKS Press, 2009.

Mikhailovskii, N. K. "Ocherki obshchestvennoi zhizni: Pis'ma ob russkoi intelligentsii" [Sketches of social life: Notes on the Russian intelligentsia]. *Sovremennoe obozrenie* [Contemporary review] 6 (1868): 336–355.

———. "Bor'ba za individual'nost'" [The struggle for individuality]. *Otechestvennye zapiski* [Notes of the Fatherland] 10 (1875): 613–656.

Müller, Otto Wilhelm. *Intelligencija: Untersuchungen zur Geschichte eines politischen Schlagwortes*. Frankfurt: Athenäum Verlag, 1971.

Ovsianiko-Kulikovskii, D. N., ed. *Istoriia russkoi literatury XIX v.* Moscow: Mir, 1908–1910.

Paperno, Irina. *Chernyshevsky and the Age of Realism: A Study in the Semiotics of Behavior.* Stanford, CA: Stanford UP, 1988.

Pipes, Richard, ed. *The Russian Intelligentsia.* New York: Columbia UP, 1961.

Pipes, Richard. "'Intelligentsia' from the German 'Intelligenz'? A Note." *Slavic Review* 30, no. 3 (1971): 615–618.

Pisarev, D. I. "Tsvety nevinnogo iumora" [The flowers of harmless humor]. *Russkoe slovo* [The Russian Word] 2 (1864): otd. 2, 41–42.

Raeff, Marc. *Origins of the Russian Intelligentsia: The Eighteenth-Century Nobility.* New York: Harcourt, Brace and World, 1966.

Shelgunov, N. V. "Russkii individualizm" [Russian individualism]. *Delo* [The Cause] 7 (1868): 1–23.

Tkachev, P. N. "Podrastaiushchie sily" [Rising forces]. *Delo* [The Cause] 9 (1868): 1–28.

Tolstoi, Lev. *Polnoe sobranie sochinenii.* Moscow: Gosudarstvennoe izdatel'stvo khudozhestvennoi literatury, 1935–1964.

Turgenev, I. S. *Polnoe sobranie sochinenii i pisem v dvadtsati vos'mi tomakh.* Moscow: Akademiia nauk, 1960–1968.

Vdovin, Aleksei. *Dobroliubov: Raznochinets mezhdu dukhom i plot'iu.* Moscow: Molodaia gvardiia, 2017.

Dostoevsky and the Intelligentsia

Alexander Burry

Fyodor Dostoevsky's relationship with the intelligentsia is more difficult to categorize than, for instance, that of his contemporary Lev Tolstoy, who worked in isolation at Yasnaya Polyana, at a great distance from other Russian writers and thinkers. A journalist as well as a novelist, Dostoevsky interacted closely with various members of the intelligentsia. Derek Offord justifiably defines Dostoevsky as an *intelligent* himself, "both inasmuch as he made a livelihood by intellectual activity and ... in that it was his vocation, or perhaps mission is a more apt word, to help to construct a broad, humane culture characterized by passionate engagement with ideas, moral commitment, a quest for the integration of reason and faith, and great, even millenarian, expectations."[1] Although Dostoevsky articulated sharp and substantive disagreements with members of the radical intelligentsia of the 1860s such as Nikolai Chernyshevsky, Nikolai Dobrolyubov, and Dmitry Pisarev, he can be considered part of the conservative intelligentsia that polemicized with these radicals and sometimes also with Slavophiles and other conservatives in the 1860s–1870s. Moreover, attention to Dostoevsky's changing ideas as well as his lifelong values reveals a certain closeness of thought and some shared interests even with the radical intelligentsia, along with his clear opposition to their political program.

---

1 Derek Offord, "Dostoevskii and the Intelligentsia," in *The Cambridge Companion to Dostoevskii*, edited by W. J. Leatherbarrow (Cambridge, UK: Cambridge University Press), 115.

Dostoevsky underwent considerable ideological changes in his career, including an oft-discussed conversion experience in prison in the early 1850s. Nevertheless, if we trace his thinking from his youth to the end of his life, certain values stand out as stable and consistent. First and foremost, perhaps, is his devotion to Christ as an exemplar for humanity. Despite his wavering religious belief—Dostoevsky famously claimed that his faith had passed through a furnace of doubt—he never abandoned his spiritual attachment to Christ. Dostoevsky also was a firm defender of the peasantry throughout his life. In his *Writer's Diary*, he twice cites as a formative event his experience, decades earlier, on his way to St. Petersburg to enter the Imperial Engineering Academy, of seeing a government courier beating a peasant driver, who then in turn beat his horses. Despite Dostoevsky's involvement in a revolutionary circle in the late 1840s, he also exhibited a lifelong preference for peaceful, non-violent reform rather than revolution. At the same time, both at the beginning and end of his career, as I discuss below, Dostoevsky displayed a principled refusal to inform on more revolutionary actors, even if he disagreed with their ideas.

Early Career, Imprisonment, and Exile

Dostoevsky's literary debut, his 1845 epistolary novel *Poor Folk*, won him the praise of premier literary critic Vissarion Belinsky and thereby turned him into a celebrity.[2] It also gained for him the mentorship of the radical critic, who attempted to guide his young protégé, with mixed results. Dostoevsky started to diverge considerably from Belinsky's point of view early on, and a break took place between them in 1847. By the late 1840s, Belinsky had abandoned the utopian socialism he had embraced early in the decade in favor of the left-Hegelian philosopher Ludwig Feuerbach, who in *The Essence of Christianity* argued that God is a human invention onto which human beings project their positive qualities. Despite his agreement with Belinsky and other members of the radical intelligentsia on many points, Dostoevsky could never accept the absence of a transcendent force.[3] Joseph Frank sums up their differences: "As a moral religious progressive influenced by French utopian socialism, Dostoevsky considered his social idealism to be an up-to-date version of Christ's messages of brotherly love,

---

2 Dostoevsky's subsequent works of the 1840s, including *The Double*, met with less success, and were harshly reviewed by Belinsky and other critics.
3 Dostoevsky misleadingly claimed, in the 1870s, that Belinsky had converted him from Christianity to radical socialism. In reality, he remained a believer while awaiting what he thought was his certain execution on Semyonovskaya Square in 1849.

and he stubbornly refused to be converted to the atheism advocated by Belinsky in the late 1840s after becoming acquainted with Left Hegelian thought."[4] Thus, a combination of literary, philosophical, and personal circumstances distanced Dostoevsky from his erstwhile mentor, and led him to other circles of the intelligentsia in the late 1840s. After joining a more moderate group headed by fellow Engineering Academy cadet Aleksei Beketov, in Spring 1847 he found his way to the fateful Petrashevsky Circle, led by Mikhail Butashevich-Petrashevsky, who was influenced by the utopian socialist ideas of Charles Fourier but did not share Dostoevsky's Christianity. Dostoevsky's account of the Petrashevsky Circle meetings is somewhat withering: he accuses various members of "playing with liberalism." His common ground with the Petrashevtsy consisted of his outrage at serfdom and ill treatment of the peasantry; however, while agreeing that the French utopian socialists had a noble aim, he was skeptical of the possibility of any of their plans being put into effect.

Perhaps the figure who had the most impact on Dostoevsky while he was in the Petrashevsky Circle was the aristocratic political activist Nikolai Speshnev. Unlike Petrashevsky, who believed in gradual, long-term revolution and did not support violent overthrow of the government, Speshnev openly called himself a Communist, and believed in violent revolution. He formed a secret society, which included Dostoevsky, as early as January 1849. According to Dostoevsky's first biographer, Orest Miller, the novelist told him the secret society intended to spread discontent with the existing order. Within this society, Dostoevsky expressed some of his most revolutionary sentiments. When asked what should be done if the serfs could not be freed except by an uprising, Dostoevsky reportedly responded, "so let there be an uprising."[5] Thus, Speshnev converted Dostoevsky from peaceful utopian socialism to a more revolutionary approach, which accepted violence as a last resort.

Early in 1849, the Petrashevsky Circle split into the Kashkin Circle, which consisted of Fourierists, and the Palm-Durov Circle, which Dostoevsky joined along with all members of Speshnev's secret society. While their meetings included literary readings and musical performances, Dostoevsky participated in conspiratorial activity as well, discussing the liberation of the serfs and the tyranny of censorship, reciting Aleksandr Pushkin's 1819 poem "The Village," with its invocation of the abolition of serfdom, agreeing to write articles on socialism,

---

[4] Joseph Frank, *Dostoevsky: The Years of Ordeal, 1850–1859* (Princeton, NJ: Princeton UP, 1983), 43.
[5] Quoted in Joseph Frank, *Dostoevsky: The Seeds of Revolt, 1821–1849* (Princeton, NJ: Princeton UP, 1976), 270.

which he never produced, and reading aloud and circulating Belinsky's July 15, 1847 letter to Nikolai Gogol, which denounces the writer for the conservative views he reveals in *Passages from Correspondence with Friends*. The charges against Dostoevsky, when he was brought in for questioning by the authorities, also included illegally distributing writings and developing his own printing press. During the interrogations, he attempted to minimize his role by characterizing the Petrashevsky Circle as lacking seriousness and being more of a social and aesthetic group than a political one. Unlike other defendants, who blamed themselves for their actions under questioning, Dostoevsky never showed any remorse, and never implicated Speshnev's secret group or anyone else.

As a convict from 1850 to 1854, and an exile until his return to St. Petersburg in late 1859, Dostoevsky was largely cut off from the changes taking place in European Russia: the disastrous Crimean War, the death of Nicholas I, the succession to the throne of the reform-minded Alexander II, and the rise of the *raznochintsy*, or people of mixed classes, as an intellectual force. However, changes took place within him that would drastically affect his engagement with the intelligentsia once he returned to Petersburg. His involuntary close encounters with members of the *narod*, or common people, in prison reshaped both his view of the lower classes and his Christianity. In particular, he came to see the *narod* as a repository of true Christian faith, and viewed them as displaying potential for goodness despite all their faults. His newfound understanding of the peasantry, expressed most directly in his quasi-fictional prison memoir *Notes from the House of the Dead* (1860–1862) resulted in some key disagreements with Chernyshevsky and other radicals on two points in particular. Chernyshevsky argued in favor of a rational, mathematical reorganization of society that would reconcile its members' selfish urges in order to achieve economic equality, rather than relying on Christian charity to help the poor, and viewed crime solely as a product of the environment. Dostoevsky, by contrast, praised Christian charity in *Notes*, and while acknowledging the role played by the environment in crime, noted that the peasants understood themselves to be criminals, even if they never repented their transgressions, and thus demonstrated the important role of personal responsibility. In keeping with the knowledge he gained of the peasants' character, Dostoevsky's approach to Christianity changed in prison as well. Frank describes his conversion as "from a semi-secularized Christian socialism to a reverence for the people and their 'childish faith.'"[6] While his effort to paint his own experience as a dramatic conversion has led scholars to exaggerate the

---

6 Joseph Frank, *Dostoevsky: The Miraculous Years, 1865–1871* (Princeton, NJ: Princeton UP, 1995), 310.

impact of Siberia on his religious development, he came to see the importance of the peasantry in the transmission of Orthodox faith over the centuries, and thus moved closer to the Slavophile position than he had been in the 1840s. Finally, Dostoevsky's period of imprisonment and exile also witnessed a shift in his thinking on the question of nationhood, from universal socialism to an emphasis on Russian national culture.

Return to the Fray: the 1860s

Although the various radical, liberal, and conservative journals of the 1860s would eventually polemicize fiercely against one another, the late 1850s and early 1860s saw a brief period of relative comity, with the various members of the intelligentsia sharing the hope that Alexander II's reforms would succeed in solving the problems that plagued Russia under the reactionary reign of Nicholas I. Indeed, Dostoevsky believed at this time that the period of ideological disagreement among the various factions of Russian intellectual life would soon come to an end, and his two journals of the 1860s, *Time* and *Epoch*, were produced with this goal of reconciliation in mind. His more conservative colleagues at the journals, the critics Apollon Grigoryev and Nikolai Strakhov, on the other hand, were skeptical that there could be any reconciliation with the nihilists, given their wholesale rejection of all authorities and traditions.

Dostoevsky's ideology in the early 1860s was known as *pochvennichestvo*, which loosely translates to "return to native soil." This movement, which he developed along with his older brother Mikhail, Grigoryev, and Strakhov, attempted to steer a middle ground between the radicalism of Chernyshevsky, editor of *The Russian Word* (Russkoe slovo), and the conservatism of Slavophiles like Ivan Aksakov, editor of *Day* (Den'). Unlike the radicals, who viewed improvement of the peasantry's position as the most important task, Dostoevsky and his fellow *pochvenniki* aimed for a kind of cultural synthesis, the fusion of the upper classes with the *narod*. They insisted that both classes had something to offer each other: the *narod* had preserved Orthodoxy and Russian customs such as the *obshchina*, or peasant village community, while the upper classes, in turn, could offer the benefit of their Western education.[7]

---

7 Nor did his *pochvennik* convictions ever entirely disappear. In *A Writer's Diary*, he continues to urge a kind of give-and-take between the upper classes and the *narod*, in encouraging his contemporaries to bow down before the People: "But, on the other hand, we should bow down on only one condition, and that is a sine qua non: the People must accept much of what

Dostoevsky's *pochvennik* phase was notable—in light of his later polemics with radicals in *Notes from Underground*, *Crime and Punishment*, and *Demons*—for his disinclination to attack his opponents on the left. *Time* was initially considered a progressive journal. With Dostoevsky's approval, its authors advocated for the abolition of corporal punishment, hospital and prison reforms, and for Jews to be given full rights as citizens. It sided with the left-wing journals *The Contemporary* and *The Russian Word* on the question of women's emancipation, and defended student demonstrations at St. Petersburg University in 1861 and the nihilists against charges of arson in 1862. Strakhov and Grigoryev, in fact, were upset by Dostoevsky's refusal to attack Chernyshevsky and Dobrolyubov more directly. Dostoevsky did, however, criticize aspects of the radical agenda even in this period. Although he spoke favorably of Chernyshevsky, Dobrolyubov, and Mikhail Saltykov-Shchedrin, a writer favored by radicals at *The Contemporary*, he critiqued the left for their extreme positions, such as Chernyshevsky's fervent defense of the rights of women to be unfaithful to their husbands after centuries of social acceptance of male infidelity.[8] But in many ways he sympathized with the radicals' antipathy to superfluous men, attacks on those who opposed the spread of peasant literacy, and other issues. The radicals, in turn, welcomed *Time*, as Ivan Panaev and Nikolai Nekrasov wrote complimentarily about it, although Chernyshevsky, who disliked *pochvennichestvo*, was more reserved. And Dostoevsky was revered by the young radicals, particularly for *Notes from the House of the Dead*, which began to appear in Fall 1861, and which gave him the reputation of a martyr for his suffering in prison.

Along with his points of agreement with left-wing thought, Dostoevsky also expressed strong disagreement with conservative members of the intelligentsia. He critiqued the Slavophiles for what he saw as an unhealthy attachment to the past. Unlike the Slavophiles, who felt that the upper classes had been separated from their Russian nationality with the reforms of Peter I, and that only the lower classes retained true Russian characteristics, the *pochvenniki* argued that the upper classes had not been cut off from their nationality by the reforms, despite their trend toward Westernization. For Dostoevsky and the other *pochvenniki*, Peter's reforms were absolutely necessary to Russia's development, as they allowed the nation to absorb the ideals of Western Europe. Nor did Dostoevsky agree with the Slavophiles that most nineteenth-century literary output was alien to Russian traditions. Here, following Grigoryev's influential

---

we bring with us." See Fyodor Dostoevsky, *A Writer's Diary*, trans. Kenneth Lantz (Evanston: Northwestern UP, 1993), 350.
8   Dostoevsky did, however, favor women's emancipation, likening it to Christian love of humanity.

essay on Pushkin, he cited his predecessor as an example of the Russian capacity to adopt foreign genres, styles, and customs, yet remain thoroughly Russian in character (anticipating his later remarks on Pushkin in his legendary 1880 speech). Dostoevsky disagreed with Aleksei Khomyakov's statement that "With us, because of the divisions between life and knowledge, art is impossible,"[9] continually praising the works of Pushkin, Gogol, Turgenev, and other nineteenth-century writers. In addition, Dostoevsky did not emphasize Orthodoxy as much as the Slavophiles, viewing it as only one of many manifestations of Russia's uniqueness (he would change his position on Orthodoxy as he gradually embraced Slavophilism in the mid-1860s).

Dostoevsky's polemic with the radicals, though, eventually became more bitter, and his tolerance for their views gradually decreased, especially in light of the revolutionary disturbances taking place in 1861–1862: the peasant revolts around the countryside, the fires spreading in St. Petersburg, and the various leaflets circulating in Moscow and St. Petersburg, most notoriously "Young Russia" by Pyotr Zaichnevsky, which called for bloody revolution.[10] As Wayne Dowler notes, Dostoevsky did not disagree with the nihilists' goals so much as the revolutionary means they were willing to undertake to achieve them.[11] He diverged sharply from the radicals on their solution to the peasant question, and especially on the scope of their plans. This took the form of differing attitudes to Alexander II's 1861 emancipation of the serfs. The radicals opposed the economic terms of the emancipation, viewing them as disadvantageous to the peasantry, and did not think that suitable reforms could come from above; hence, their desire for revolution. Dostoevsky, on the other hand, saw the emancipation as a "sublime event," felt that continued reforms by the monarchy were the best vehicle for change, and reproached the radicals for their impatience, and their desire to bring about changes that were not yet possible.

Dostoevsky especially disagreed with the nihilists on aesthetic issues. Chernyshevsky and Dobrolyubov, in their essays on art and literature, took a utilitarian approach to aesthetics. In "The Aesthetic Relations of Art to Reality," Chernyshevsky describes a seascape as desirable only as a substitute for seeing

---

9 Quoted in Wayne Dowler, *Dostoevsky, Grigor'ev, and Native Soil Conservatism* (Toronto: U of Toronto Press, 1982), 119.
10 Upon seeing "Young Russia," Dostoevsky ran to Chernyshevsky's apartment in a panic to ask if he had played any part in it; Chernyshevsky responded that he had not. Dostoevsky also discussed it with Aleksandr Herzen while visiting him in London during his trip to Europe in summer 1862. Herzen, who shared Dostoevsky's faith in the *obshchina*, agreed that the pamphlet showed the need for the educated class to come closer to the *narod*.
11 Dowler, *Dostoevsky, Grigor'ev, and Native Soil Conservatism*, 132.

the ocean itself. Dobrolyubov, in his articles on works such as Ivan Goncharov's *Oblomov*, Ivan Turgenev's *On the Eve*, and Aleksandr Ostrovsky's *The Storm*, describes them in terms of their usefulness for Russian society, ignoring their aesthetic value. Dostoevsky responds to this evaluation of art in the second issue of *Time* with a characteristically paradoxical approach in his article "Mr. D-bov and the Question of Art," bringing the nihilist critics' emphasis on utility to its logical conclusion. He takes an even-handed position, critiquing not only the utilitarian approach to art, but also that of "art for art's sake" critics of the time such as Aleksandr Druzhinin, Pavel Annenkov, and Vasily Botkin. In doing so, as Frank points out, he "establishes his credentials as a nonpartisan commentator who, even if picking a quarrel with Dobrolyubov, can hardly be considered to belong to the party of the enemy."[12] Despite praising Dobrolyubov on some counts in the course of the article, he attacks the nihilist on the level of his own claims. For art to be truly useful, Dostoevsky argues, it must have aesthetic value; otherwise, it cannot achieve its goal of moving readers. As an example, he cites Homer's epics, whose relevance for current times could not have been predicted when they were written, but which because of their aesthetic beauty have accrued new significance (and thereby usefulness) over time.

Dostoevsky's essay *Winter Notes on Summer Impressions*, published in *Time* in 1863 and based on his trip to Europe in summer 1862, crystallizes his opposition to the radicals. In this work, he criticizes the tendency of educated Russians in general, and nihilists such as Chernyshevsky in particular, to idealize Western Europe. He rejects Chernyshevsky's reverence for the achievements of Western technology, especially the Crystal Palace (designed by Joseph Paxton for the Great Exhibition of 1851 in London), which he goes on to critique in *Notes from Underground* as well, and his belief in the advantages of scientific progress in general. Mocking the attempts of French utopian socialists to put their schemes into practice, he argues that they are trying to create brotherhood where none exists. He proposes instead that Russia, whose peasants have kept alive traditional forms of socialism such as the *obshchina*, and have preserved the Orthodox faith, provides more fertile ground for brotherhood. Dostoevsky met the émigré Aleksandr Herzen during his stay in London, and *Winter Notes* shows the influence of the older writer's works. Like Herzen, an erstwhile Westernizer who later expressed an aversion to Western society, and a sense that Europe was at the end of its historical development while Russia was just starting its own, Dostoevsky critiques European bourgeois society, castigating what

---

12 Joseph Frank, *Dostoevsky: The Stir of Liberation, 1860–1865* (Princeton, NJ: Princeton UP, 1986), 78.

he views as the falseness of French society while attacking English capitalism. At the same time, Dostoevsky also gradually drew closer to Slavophilism in the early 1860s. In his article "Two Camps of Theoreticians" in *Time* in 1862, he focuses on the role of the *narod* in Russia's future, siding with the Slavophiles over the Westernizers. In the aforementioned *Winter Notes*, his warnings to Russia against Western influences parallel the writings of Khomyakov, and his counterposing of synthesis as a positive ideal toward which people should strive recalls Ivan Kireevsky's ideal of *tsel'nost'* (wholeness).[13]

Dostoevsky's growing opposition to the radical intelligentsia, and his gradual embrace of Slavophilism, with its identification of Russian culture with Orthodoxy, are abundantly reflected in *Notes from Underground* and *Crime and Punishment*. *Notes from Underground*, published in *Epoch* in 1864, represents the best known of the many literary critiques of nihilism as expressed in Chernyshevsky's 1863 novel *What is To Be Done?* This novel promulgated the ideology of "rational egoism," a type of utilitarianism that suggests mathematically organizing the various selfish urges among human beings in a society so that they are mutually beneficial. Dostoevsky's anti-hero embodies a critique of nihilism from within, as the Underground Man accepts Chernyshevsky's premises but draws on their logical conclusions to show that they are untenable in human society. As a critique of Chernyshevsky's assumption that people always act according to their individual advantages, the Underground Man proposes the "most advantageous advantage," which involves expression of irrational urges and desires. One example he gives is his impulse to stick out his tongue at the Crystal Palace, praised by Chernyshevsky in *What is To Be Done?* as a symbol of a future utopia. Indeed, the anti-hero's actions, beginning with his announcement in the opening of the novella that he is refusing to see a doctor even though there is something wrong with his liver, amount to a kind of trap for himself: by continually going against his self-interest, he ends up embracing almost equally predictable self-sabotage. Dostoevsky originally included a Christian solution to the Underground Man's sense of entrapment, but the censor removed it since it appeared blasphemous in the mouth of such an unappealing character. Thus, only with his next major work, *Crime and Punishment*, was Dostoevsky able to go beyond attacking the views of the left-wing intelligentsia, and to provide concrete alternatives to their utopian vision.

To an extent, *Crime and Punishment* represents a continuation of Dostoevsky's critique of Chernyshevskian nihilism, as Raskolnikov justifies his murder of the

---

13 See Sarah Hudspith, *Dostoevsky and the Idea of Russianness: A New Perspective on Unity and Brotherhood* (London: Routledge Curzon, 2004), 49–55.

pawnbroker in part based on utilitarian calculations. He overhears a student at a tavern telling an officer that murdering the pawnbroker Alyona Ivanovna would improve the lives of thousands, which strikes Raskolnikov as uncanny, since he has just been thinking the same thing. Dostoevsky thus implies that Chernyshevsky's ideology, taken to its logical conclusion, is potentially murderous. In addition, through the character Lebezyatnikov, he satirizes Chernyshevsky's philosophy by putting it in the mouth of a vulgar, not-too-intelligent radical who does not quite grasp the import of the ideas he is regurgitating.

However, *Crime and Punishment* goes beyond this critique to attack the ideas of Dmitry Pisarev, who brought nihilism to a new stage: one that privileged the strong individual who has the will to take matters into his own hands, even if it comes to murder. Where Chernyshevsky interpreted Ivan Turgenev's nihilist hero Bazarov, from *Fathers and Children*, as a lampoon of contemporary nihilists (specifically Dobrolyubov), Pisarev viewed him more positively, praising him as an individual who acts according to his own values, and recognizes no moral law above him. The core of Raskolnikov's theory, as discussed with the detective Porfiry Petrovich in Part 3 of the novel, relies heavily on this conception, as Raskolnikov claims that extraordinary men are justified in committing murder, and perhaps even must do so, to ensure that they are able to say a "new word" of their own.

Revolutionary Dmitry Karakozov's April 4, 1866 attempt on the life of Alexander II distanced Dostoevsky further from the radicals, as he feared being associated with them. However, he continued to view the youth who turned to nihilism as innocent and well-meaning people who were being misled, and he believed that government repression of their ideas was not the best way to oppose their convictions. His portrait of the young nihilist Ippolit Terentiev in *The Idiot* demonstrates this view. Ippolit and his associates, Burdovsky, Doktorenko, and Keller, are depicted as hapless scoundrels rather than a potential threat to the Russian order, and as an eighteen-year-old consumptive with only months left to live, Ippolit embodies the existential angst typical of Dostoevsky's searching heroes, as he wonders what purpose living in the face of certain death can have. Indeed, *The Idiot* was not received entirely negatively by radicals. In the early 1870s, Saltykov-Shchedrin, who had dueled with Dostoevsky in the pages of the *Contemporary*, praised his artistic achievements in this novel even as he rejected its world view: "To judge by the profundity of Dostoevsky's artistic scheme, by the range of the spiritual world which he makes the field of his examination, Dostoevsky stands by himself in the whole of our literature."[14]

---

14 Quoted in Temira Pachmuss, "Dostoevsky in the Criticism of the Russian Radical Intelligentsia," *The Russian Review* 21, no. 1 (1962): 62.

Aleksandr Skabichevsky also praised Dostoevsky as an artist and psychologist, while criticizing him as a social critic. However, Temira Pachmuss's observation on the radical intelligentsia's reception of Dostoevsky's works holds true: "with the possible exception of Shchedrin and Skabichevsky, Dostoevsky's work was rarely approached from an aesthetic viewpoint. The social-minded critics displayed their implacable and uncompromising hostility toward Dostoevsky's philosophy and, almost with one voice, they emphasized the writer's inability to understand the social and economic nature of a bourgeois society."[15]

The Last Decade: the 1870s

Dostoevsky's involuntary period abroad in the late 1860s and early 1870s, even more than his trip to Europe early in the 1860s, inspired not only a critique of the West but also idealization of Russia. His relations with Turgenev, which had soured due to a longstanding debt Dostoevsky owed him, grew worse. In a well-known interaction between them abroad, Dostoevsky claimed that Turgenev considered himself a German rather than a Russian. At the same time, Dostoevsky was embracing the movement of Pan-Slavism, with Nikolai Danilevsky as its intellectual leader. Danilevsky's book *Russia and Europe*, which appeared in 1869, posited Russia's imminent rise to power, with European civilization on the decline, and proposed a Slavic federation of states. Dostoevsky agreed that Russia was preparing a renovation of the Western world, but saw its role as more ambitious. He disagreed with Danilevsky's proposal that the Slavic federation be jointly governed, insisting that Russia must be at the head of such a federation, and also thought Russia must control Constantinople rather than, as Danilevsky proposed, making it a common city for all Eastern nationalities.

The Nechaev Affair of 1869 further reinforced Dostoevsky's growing antipathy toward the radical intelligentsia. Sergei Nechaev, a young radical, murdered a student named Ivanov for protesting Nechaev's methods in the student revolutionary movement in St. Petersburg. Dostoevsky responded with *Demons*, a political satire of nihilism with the terrorist Pyotr Verkhovensky as a partial representation of Nechaev. The novel includes other portraits of members of the intelligentsia, as Pyotr's father, Stepan Trofimovich, resembles the liberal historian Timofei Granovsky, and the pretentious writer Semyon Karmazinov is a caricature of Turgenev. The murder of disillusioned radical Ivan Shatov by members of Pyotr Verkhovensky's circle parallels Nechaev's murder of Ivanov.

---

15 Ibid., 73–74.

Radical critics such as Nikolai Mikhailovsky and Pyotr Tkachyov accused Dostoevsky of slandering nihilists, but as Frank shows, the portraits of the revolutionaries actually closely reflect reality. Nechaev was not just a revolutionary but a manipulator of others, who would not hesitate, for example, to dig up dirt on an accomplice to ensure his or her loyalty. Verkhovensky, who tries to gain control of Stavrogin through knowledge of his secret marriage to Marya Lebyadkina, performs the same actions that Nechaev did, or would have done.[16] *Demons* marked Dostoevsky for radicals as a renegade, as did his editorship of the *Citizen* under the direction of the conservative Prince Vladimir Meshchersky.

Dostoevsky's return to Russia in 1871, his resumption of journalism, and his interaction with young people in the 1870s substantially changed his views on the radical youth over the course of the decade. If in the 1860s he had reacted against the utilitarianism and rejection of Christianity by Chernyshevsky, Dobrolyubov, Pisarev, and others, he found that the Populists had a different program that was closer to his in many respects. Although the Populists, too, supported revolution, they understood socialism not as an atheist movement but rather similarly to the way Dostoevsky himself had in the 1840s, as the realization of Christian ideals on earth. Like Dostoevsky, the Populists desired to protect peasant life, with its traditional socialist institutions, from the encroachment of capitalist forces from the West, and believed that the Russian peasant represented a higher type than the European industrial worker. These were certainly principles with which Dostoevsky, an ardent anti-capitalist, could agree. In his *Historical Letters*, Pyotr Lavrov encouraged a movement to go to the people (*khozhdenie v narod*) in order to repay the masses for their hard labor, which enabled the intelligentsia to cultivate itself. In *What Is Progress?*, Mikhailovsky expressed his disillusionment with the West, arguing that it could no longer serve as a template for the Russian search for social and economic justice. Like Dostoevsky, these thinkers rejected a worship of science and progress that left no room for the development of the individual personality. Further, as the trial of the Nechaevists in 1871 showed, many Populists and even terrorists, such as Vera Figner and Pyotr Kropotkin, disapproved of Nechaevism. This confirmed Dostoevsky's belief in the purity and capacity for self-sacrifice of the Russian youth and increased his desire to enter into dialogue with the Populists.

As a consequence, his harsh critique of radicals in *Demons* was considerably reduced in his next novel, *The Adolescent*. Dostoevsky even arranged to publish this work not in the *Russian Messenger*, where his novels usually appeared, but in *Notes of the Fatherland*, the progressive journal headed by Nekrasov. It is telling

---

16 Frank, *Dostoevsky: The Miraculous Years*, 438–452.

that, whereas *Demons* was inspired by the Nechaev affair, with its ruthless, brutal approach, one of the episodes that interested Dostoevsky while writing *The Adolescent* was the Dolgushin trial of 1874. Aleksandr Dolgushin and his Group of Twenty-Two, who planned to foment peasant rebellion, drew on writings of Lavrov, Mikhailovsky, and other Populist thinkers, and made proclamations based on moral appeal and Christian principles, which contrasted heavily with Nechaev's incitement to destroy all enemies. As with the Nechaev Affair in *Demons*, Dostoevsky incorporates this affair of the young radical intelligentsia into his novel as the "Dergachyov Group." Frank calls *The Adolescent* "a kind of Trojan horse introduced into the very journalistic citadel of the former enemy to undermine its last defenses."[17] The hero, Arkady Dolgoruky, claims to be preaching absolute communism, which aligns him with the Populists. At the same time, he undermines the radicals' agenda, albeit much more gently than in *Demons*, critiquing the acceptance of Christian moral ideas without concomitant belief in God. In the novel, Kraft, a member of the Dergachyov Group, commits suicide as a result of his lack of faith in Russia. Arkady's natural father Versilov, a typical member of the generation of the '40s, gives an impassioned speech about the Golden Age in which he acknowledges his own need for faith. And as in his other mature novels, Dostoevsky includes a Christ figure in the wandering peasant Makar, Arkady's legal father, as a positive counterpart to the young radicals. Nevertheless, Dostoevsky's fellow conservative *intelligenty* reacted strongly to the publication of *The Adolescent* in *Notes from the Fatherland*, as Strakhov and Apollon Maikov viewed it as the novelist's betrayal of his former convictions.

A Writer's Diary, Dostoevsky's major journalistic project of the 1870s, served as a forum in which he could express his disagreement with, among other people, members of the radical intelligentsia. In the article "Environment," for instance, he continues his polemic against Chernyshevskian ideas on crime and human responsibility, criticizing lawyers who plead for the exoneration of criminals using the "environmental defense." Dostoevsky objects that this defense argues against the very existence of crime, and also ignores the views of lower-class criminals, who often acknowledge their guilt. Elsewhere in *A Writer's Diary*, Dostoevsky clearly refers to the Populists' "go to the People" movement in critical terms:

> Our revolutionaries are saying the wrong things and are wasting their time, and have been doing so for a whole century now....

---

17 Joseph Frank, *Dostoevsky: The Mantle of the Prophet, 1871–1881* (Princeton, NJ: Princeton UP, 2002), 173.

> Nowadays we have a type of Russian revolutionary who is so distinct from the People that each is utterly and completely incapable of understanding the other: the People understand absolutely nothing of what the revolutionaries want, while the revolutionaries have become so out of touch with the People that they are not even aware of their alienation from them.[18]

In *A Writer's Diary* and elsewhere, Dostoevsky opposes both the radical propensity for violent revolution and the liberal solution of a constitutional monarchy, proposing instead that the law of Christian love needs to penetrate every level of public life, including the monarchy, which should behave in a Christian manner even toward its terrorist enemies. Dostoevsky was convinced that this utopian ideal was approaching, and that it would take place through a meeting of the young members of the intelligentsia (the Populists) and the *narod*: "Our People and the young generation of our intelligentsia will suddenly come together and understand one another in many things, and much more closely and readily than was the case in our day and in our generation."[19]

Dostoevsky's last novel, *The Brothers Karamazov*, reveals the extent of the novelist's softening toward the radical intelligentsia of the 1870s. To be sure, there is a blistering portrait of seminarian and aspiring journalist Rakitin as a petty opportunist. However, Dostoevsky also gives Ivan Karamazov, ostensibly a nihilist and atheist, many of his cherished convictions. For instance, in justifying to his novice brother Alyosha his desire to "return his ticket" to paradise, Ivan contends that paradise cannot be built on the tears of one suffering child, having just recited several anecdotes of children being tormented, an argument that Dostoevsky borrows from Belinsky's 1841 rejection of Hegel's teleological view of history. Early in the novel, summarizing his article on ecclesiastical courts in Father Zosima's cell, Ivan essentially voices Dostoevsky's own theoretical argument, claiming that the church should absorb the state in itself, and that the law of Christian love should be infused throughout secular society. On the other hand, Ivan's maxim, "If there is no immortality, then everything is permitted" serves as the impetus for the illegitimate Smerdyakov to murder Fyodor Pavlovich. Dostoevsky here embodies his conviction that the radicals' perhaps well-meaning desire to reconstruct Russia on humanitarian principles of equality will inevitably fail if these principles are not accompanied by belief in God.

---

18 Dostoevsky, *A Writer's Diary*, 837.
19 Dostoevsky, *A Writer's Diary*, 978.

Perhaps the most intriguing aspect of *The Brothers Karamazov* in light of Dostoevsky's ongoing dialogue with the radical intelligentsia is its proposed continuation, the second book referred to in the "Author's Foreword" of the novel. Although there are no written notes for the sequel, Igor Volgin has demonstrated that, based on Dostoevsky's reported conversations with journalist and publisher Aleksei Suvorin and others in the last year of his life, the novelist was considering various plans, including one in which Alyosha would attempt to assassinate the tsar and be executed.[20] Such a plan would seem out of character for the Christ-like Alyosha, but Dostoevsky's point, according to Volgin, is precisely that for such a pure-hearted Christian youth, this type of martyrdom was the only possible response to the present state of affairs in Russia. This plan, combined with Dostoevsky's description of himself in these later years as a "Russian Socialist," reflects the novelist's gradual progress back to the Christian socialism of his youth, and a degree of identification with his ostensible radical opponents.[21]

These changes can be linked with Dostoevsky's dispirited view of the autocracy during this period, which similarly indicates some sympathy toward the radical intelligentsia's views. His jubilee address to Tsar Alexander II on the occasion of the twenty-fifth anniversary of his accession to the throne, presented on behalf of the Slavic Benevolent Society, boldly conveys his desire for the tsar to take an active role in repairing the rift between the *narod* and the intelligentsia, immediately following the bombing of the Winter Palace by members of the People's Will. After praising the tsar for the emancipation of the serfs and other reforms, he mentions the perpetrators of this bombing without denouncing them strongly, and even refers to them as "young Russian energies" with sincere motives who have gone astray. He also admonishes Alexander to consult his subjects and allow them to express their wishes to him freely and without formality, which aligned him with the radicals who were calling for a Constituent Assembly.

The day after the tsar's anniversary celebration, Dostoevsky had a well-known conversation with Suvorin that reveals his disappointment with the tsarist regime, and his sympathy with the young radicals who were trying to destroy

---

20 Igor' Volgin, *Poslednii god Dostoevskogo* (Moscow: Sovetskii pisatel', 1991), 23–37.
21 The novelist S. I. Smirnova-Sazonova reported hearing Dostoevsky whisper to Suvorin in 1880 that he was a "Russian socialist," which for him involved the sharing of the state with the Church. The term recalls Herzen's earlier use of it to mean the application of Christian love to social injustices. Elsewhere, Dostoevsky defines it as follows: The Russian people "believe that salvation is ultimately to be found only in *worldwide union in the name of Christ*. That is our Russian socialism!" See Dostoevsky, *A Writer's Diary*, 1351.

it. Dostoevsky asked Suvorin whether, were he to overhear a plot to blow up the Winter Palace, he would report it to the police. Suvorin said he would not, and Dostoevsky said that he would not, either. This conversation magnified the moral discredit into which the tsarist regime had fallen, among conservative as well as liberal and radical members of the intelligentsia. Dostoevsky's disagreement with the monarchy—and sympathy for the radicals—was also inspired by the increasing number of executions carried out by the tsar. On the day of his conversation with Suvorin, the young radical Ippolit Mlodetsky attempted to assassinate Minister of the Interior Mikhail Loris-Melikov and was condemned to death. Dostoevsky attended the execution on Feburary 22, 1880, and was reported to be in low spirits as a result later that evening; he went so far as to depict the execution in detail at a gathering the following day that included members of the royal family.

Dostoevsky's "Pushkin Speech" in June, 1880 represents the culmination of his public career, and his polemic with other members of the intelligentsia. The festival itself was seen as a hopeful sign of better relations between the tsar and the intelligentsia, as censorship of the speeches had been relaxed, and official approval of the event given. Dostoevsky's speech represented a continuation, among other things, of his "duel" with Turgenev and the liberal Westernizers. Whereas in his speech, Turgenev refused Pushkin the title of "national poet," Dostoevsky firmly and unambiguously praised Pushkin as the embodiment of Russian brotherhood and pan-humanism. The speech had an inspirational effect on its audience, uniting the crowd in enthusiastic cheering and even sobbing, and according to Dostoevsky, even reconciling longstanding enemies. Ivan Aksakov declared to the audience that it was not a speech, but a historical event, and Dostoevsky himself was viewed as symbolically inheriting Pushkin's mantle as prophet of Russia. Following its ecstatic reception, however, the "Pushkin Speech" was critiqued from all political sides. M. A. Antonovich argued that Dostoevsky's advice to the intelligentsia to "humble yourself" went against the spirit of progress and science; Gleb Uspensky similarly critiqued Dostoevsky's preaching of submissiveness and humility. The liberal Russian jurist Aleksandr Gradovsky's critique of the speech made such a strong impression on Dostoevsky that he responded to it in his *Writer's Diary*. Gradovsky argues, among other points, that Dostoevsky's prescription of "humbling oneself," that is, working on one's own virtues, is not enough to improve social conditions. Dostoevsky retorts in his article that it indeed is: that social and civic ideals do not exist separately, apart from moral ideals. As always in the *Writer's Diary* and elsewhere, Dostoevsky insists here—contrary to much of the intelligentsia—that social activism without religious belief is insufficient to effect change for the better. The

"Pushkin Speech" was attacked from the right as well, as Konstantin Leontiev found it incompatible with Christianity, and critiqued Dostoevsky's desire to create an earthly paradise through human wisdom. A speech that united so many warring factions of the intelligentsia during the presentation itself turned out to be equally controversial and divisive in its aftermath.

Had he lived to March 1, 1881, Dostoevsky would undoubtedly have been horrified, but not surprised at the assassination of Alexander II by the so-called *pervomartovtsy* ("First-of-Marchers"). Throughout his career, he argued that he understood the radical intelligentsia all the better for having been a part of it himself in his youth. For this reason, he was able to polemicize with them while also sharing some common hopes for Russia. As Volgin notes, Dostoevsky's death and funeral succeeded in uniting not only thousands of his countrymen, but various members of the intelligentsia and royal family: conservatives such as Konstantin Pobedonostsev and Strakhov attended; so did radicals like Mikhailovsky and Saltykov-Shchedrin.[22] These visitors to Dostoevsky's funeral—like the motley crowd of exultant listeners to his "Pushkin Speech"—exemplify the diversity of the Russian intelligentsia, with their varied opinions on the political, social, economic, and cultural questions of their time. Despite this diversity, though, they came together in a shared concern for the good of Russia and its people, and perhaps no one depicted this mixture of ideas more vividly than the deceased novelist. Dostoevsky spent his entire career acting as a kind of middleman between Slavophiles and Westernizers, extreme monarchists and left-wing revolutionaries. And he united these warring factions, at least temporarily, in his death.

Bibliography

Dostoevskii, Fedor [Dostoevsky, Fyodor]. *A Writer's Diary*. Translated by Kenneth Lantz. Evanston: Northwestern UP, 1993.

Dowler, Wayne. *Dostoevsky, Grigor'ev, and Native Soil Conservatism*. Toronto: U of Toronto Press, 1982.

Frank, Joseph. *Dostoevsky: The Seeds of Revolt, 1821–1849*. Princeton, NJ: Princeton UP, 1976.

———. *Dostoevsky: The Years of Ordeal, 1850–1859*. Princeton, NJ: Princeton UP, 1983.

---

22 Volgin, *Poslednii god Dostoevskogo*, 454.

———. *Dostoevsky: The Stir of Liberation, 1860–1865*. Princeton, NJ: Princeton UP, 1986.

———. *Dostoevsky: The Miraculous Years, 1865–1871*. Princeton, NJ: Princeton UP, 1995.

———. *Dostoevsky: The Mantle of the Prophet, 1871–1881*. Princeton, NJ: Princeton UP, 2002.

Hudspith, Sarah. *Dostoevsky and the Idea of Russianness: A New Perspective on Unity and Brotherhood*. London: Routledge Curzon, 2004.

Offord, Derek. "Dostoevskii and the Intelligentsia." In *The Cambridge Companion to Dostoevskii*, edited by W. J. Leatherbarrow, 111–130. Cambridge: Cambridge UP, 2002.

Pachmuss, Temira. "Dostoevsky in the Criticism of the Russian Radical Intelligentsia." *The Russian Review* 21:1 (1962): 59–74.

Volgin, Igor'. *Poslednii god Dostoevskogo*. Moscow: Sovetskii pisatel', 1991.

Accommodating the Intelligentsia: Tolstoyan Nonresistance as a Response to Russian Intelligentsia

Michael A. Denner

Tolstoy and Landmarks

The writers who contributed to the 1909 volume of articles *Landmarks* (Vekhi) sought to explain the failure of the 1905 Russian Revolution. Their collective assessment was that the Revolution's failures could be attributed to a group of self-nominated persons, "intelligentsia," who sought to improve society in the name of the people (*narod*). The book could be subtitled: *What's the Matter with the Intelligentsia?*

This intelligentsia had lost its way morally, having cast aside any system that did not serve the people's interest. S. L. Frank, in his contribution to the collection ("The Ethics of Nihilism"), would seem to speak for all the contributors when he asserts that the intelligentsia embraced a mentality (*umonastroenie*) of "nihilistic moralism" (*nigilisticheskii moralizm*):

> Nihilistic moralism is the basic and deepest feature of the spiritual physiognomy of the Russian *intelligent*: the denial of objective values leads to the deification of the subjective interests of one's neighbor ("the people" [*narod*]), and hence follows the recognition that the highest and only human task is serving the people, and this, in turn, leads to an ascetic hatred of everything

> that hinders or even fails to contribute to the accomplishment of this task.... A person must therefore devote all their strength to the improvement of the fate of the majority, and everything that distracts one from this aim is evil, and must be ruthlessly exterminated.... Nihilistic moralism is the peculiar, rationally incomprehensible, and at the same time compelling and lively fusion of [otherwise] antagonistic motivations into a [coherent] powerful psychological force.[1]

Frank here makes what I think is an uncontroversial claim, that being an *intelligent* in the nineteenth and twentieth centuries in the Russian Empire—and subsequently in the Soviet Union—entailed embracing a morality that is "against the system" and "for the people." Being an *intelligent* means opposition to the current situation and dedication to overthrowing the current State.

This attitude of "nihilistic moralism" differentiates intelligentsia from the "merely" educated. This distinction between "the educated class" and the intelligentsia isn't mine but belongs to the historian and KD politician Pavel Nikolaevich Milyukov, from the beginning of his popular rebuttal to *Landmarks*, "The Intelligentsia and the Historical Tradition" (Intelligentsiia i istoricheskaia traditsiia, 1910).

One charge that Milyukov leveled at the authors in *Landmarks*—who were themselves reappraising the intelligentsia after the 1905 revolution—is the idea, bandied about in *Landmarks*, that the intelligentsia is "a-" or "anti-governmental." Milyukov disagrees with this claim and counters with a fine but important distinction that relies on Russian terms, both translated as State: The intelligentsia is anti-State, in the sense of *pravitel'stvo*, the institutions governing Russia; but the intelligentsia is pro-government, in the sense of *gosudarstvo*, of a truly legal, rightful (*pravovoe*) government. In other words, the intelligentsia rejects the present government, but *their* government, government by the intelligentsia, is fine.[2] This attitude is, essentially, Bolshevism.[3]

In any case, I think it is accepted that the intelligentsia was (is?) a class of people that embraces, among other things, an active opposition to the existing state apparatus, its laws and operations, because they are unjust; but concomitantly

---

1 Semen Frank, "Etika nigilizma," in *Vekhi: Intelligentsiia v Rossii: sborniki statei, 1909–1910*, ed. Valentin Shelokhaev and Nataliia Kazakova (Moscow: Molodaia gvardiia, 1991), 162.
2 Pavel Miliukov, "Intelligentsiia i istoricheskaia traditsiia," in *Vekhi: Intelligentsiia v Rossii: sborniki statei, 1909–1910*, ed. Valentin Shelokhaev and Nataliia Kazakova (Moscow: Molodaia gvardiia, 1991), 337.
3 Ibid.

it supports a "truly legal" government. In this embrace of a *potentially* legitimate government, the intelligentsia is not anarchical. (This distinction, essentially the dispute whether "legitimate government" is a *contradictio in terminis*, was far more important in 1910 than it seems to be today.)

The intelligentsia is, philosophically, quite amenable to rules, hierarchy, and power. To be an *intelligent* is to resist, to be part of a politicized vanguard of a revolution that aims to bring down the existing authority and replace it with... itself. At that point, they will become the State. (In a nutshell, this is what "syndicalism" or even "Machism" means.)

What Lev Tolstoy most stridently repudiated in the intelligentsia, at least in 1909, was exactly *this* belief in their own agency, in the intelligentsia's faith that it *could* affect some desirable change at will. Contra Frank, who accused the intelligentsia of nihilism because they devoted themselves to the improvement of the people (understood on every level—their moral improvement, their empowerment, etc.) without regard for the morality of their own acts, Tolstoy believed that the intelligentsia was insufficiently nihilistic: they believed that someone *could* improve the people.

We might think of this conflict between Tolstoy and the intelligentsia as a meta-quarrel about metaphysics: Tolstoy's rejection of the intelligentsia wasn't exactly about "who should rule," but instead had its roots in Tolstoy's rejection of human agency *per se*. In place of the intelligentsia's foundational faith in their own right to rule, Tolstoy offered the belief that absolute, abject submission to the most arbitrary, absolute law was, in fact, desirable. (What is this claim if not an enigmatic refiguring of the paradoxical assertion from *War and Peace* that "kings are the slaves of history"?) Tolstoy evidently embraced this rejection of human agency quite early: it is evident in his pedagogical writings from the 1850s. It is refigured, later in his career, as a Schopenhauerian "self-abolition" or emptiness, is reflected in Tolstoy's decades-long fascination with Buddhism and Taoism, and finds its place in Tolstoy's public writings as non-resistance to evil.

Tolstoy wrote an unpublished response to *Landmarks* in May of 1909. The editors of the *Jubilee* edition, where the piece was first published, dwell extensively on Tolstoy's rejection of the collection's cliquish language: Tolstoy indeed called the authors "illiterate" and devoted much of his review of the book to what, to his mind, was the use of an artificial and mostly imported lexicon. (The word "existential" bothered him in particular.) But, especially in the context of his late essays (e.g., "Edinoe na potrebu," 1905; "Konets veka," 1905; and especially "Pis'mo k kitaitsu," 1906; all collected in vol. 36 of his *Polnoe sobrane sochinenii*), Tolstoy's central criticism of *Landmarks* was that the authors on the one hand rejected the intelligentsia's outsized estimation of its ability to effect external change, but on the other failed to offer an alternative *internal* approach:

There was extreme self-confidence, both on the part of the authors of the book and on the part of the caste intellectual [the intellectuals who were criticized by the intellectuals in *Landmarks*]. Thus on page 59 one finds: "Whether for bad or good, the fate of Russia is in the hands of the intelligentsia . . . how grand and terrifying is this historical responsibility, intellectually how enormous and terrifying is its historical responsibility to the future of our country, both near and far.

So in the collection there were a lot of things that were superfluous, but it lacked the one thing that I and every person who recognizes the justice of hundreds of times before the birth of Christ, the thought expressed by all the wise men of the world that the improvement of human life is not accomplished by external, but by internal change.[4]

Tolstoy decided against publishing his review of *Landmarks*, citing the same French saying that Kutuzov favored in *War and Peace*: "*Dans le doute abstiens toi*" [sic].[5] The self-abolition implied by this saying (when in doubt, do nothing, don't even exist) is both a rationale for not publishing the review—he confided to his secretary Gusev that he didn't want to antagonize the "young intelligentsia"—but also a rejection of the fundamental rationale of the intelligentsia, that *something* can be done, that resistance is not futile, that it can produce an intentional and positive change.

People and Power

This attitude that underlies the very existence of the intelligentsia implies a binary distinction between resistance and nonresistance, between opposition and complicity, between "people and power" (*narod i vlast'*) that I think was the locus of Tolstoy's anti-statist and anarchical writing during the waning decades of the nineteenth and first decade of the twentieth centuries—writings best

---

4 Lev Tolstoi, *Polnoe sobranie sochinenii: Akademicheskoe iubileinoe izdanie*, 90 vols., ed. V. G. Chertkov (Moscow and Leningrad: Khudozhestvennaia literatura, 1928–1958), vol. 38, 26–27. All translations from Russian are mine, unless otherwise noted. Where unclear, I also indicate the nature of the citation (e.g., letter, diary, etc.)
5 Ibid., vol. 28, 572.

typified by his book *The Kingdom of God Is within You* (Tsarstvo bozh'e vnutri vas, 1894) and *What, Then, Shall We Do?* (Tak chto zhe nam delat'?, 1881–1886).

Opposition to the State, argued Tolstoy, always eventuated in the justification or rationalization of State because the State is ultimately nothing more nor less than violence directed at those who would undermine the existing order. In other words, the State is a recursive structure, an organization whose sole purpose is the maintenance of that organization, and always through coercion. (Tolstoy consistently uses the word *nasilie*; "coercion" expresses the word's complex meaning, which includes but is not limited to physical violence.)

Even if the opposition were to be successful, even if "the old State" were to be overturned and a new one, founded on claims to improved justice, were founded, Tolstoy remarks, the same system of violence/coercion would reinstate itself with the new system, only the violence against the subalterns would be "more despotic and vicious" because, as a result of the struggle, "the mutual hatred people hold towards one another would be intensified, and likewise would be intensified and new forms of oppression would be devised (*vyrabotaiutsia novye sredstva poraboshcheniia*)."[6] (Tolstoy was right: The Russian Empire was brutal and coarse in its institutionalized violence; the Soviet Union was even more brutal and more coarse. And the Russian Federation today is far more brutal and coarse than the USSR.)

Tolstoy calls this the "circle of coercion" (*krug nasiliia*) and remarks that "there is no way to break out of this circle by using force" (*vyrvat'sia iz nego siloi net nikakoi vozmozhnosti*) because opposition always justifies violence, and the State is both ruthlessly effective and the sole (legal) agent of violence.[7] Perversely, the State is an organization that collapses the distinction between opposition to the State and collaboration with the State. Opponents of the State are its best supporters. (Again, this is how Vladimir Lenin and Aleksandr Bogdanov understood revolution, as an assumption of authority and violence, not its disruption.[8])

If the state (power, authority—all structures based on coercion/violence) forms a dense, overwhelming web of apparatuses and institutions exclusively founded on the preservation of the status quo, and which are therefore activated by all attempts to alter the status quo, how then does one effectively resist the state? Given these theses, is true opposition even possible? This question brings

---

6 Ibid., vol. 28, 198.
7 Ibid., vol. 28, 155.
8 Robert C Williams, "Collective Immortality: The Syndicalist Origins of Proletarian Culture, 1905–1910," *Slavic Review* 39, no. 3 (1980): 389–402.

to mind Colin Gordon's rejection of this binary in his afterword in Michel Foucault's *Power/Knowledge*:

> The binary division between resistance and non-resistance is an unreal one. The existence of those who seem not to rebel is a warren of minute, individual, autonomous tactics and strategies which counter and inflect the visible facts of overall domination, and whose purposes and calculations, desires and choices resist any simple division into the political and the apolitical. The schema of a strategy of resistance as a vanguard of politicization needs to be subjected to re-examination, and account must be taken of resistances whose strategy is one of evasion of defense... the Schwejks [sic] as well as the Solzhenitsyns. There are no good subjects of resistance.[9]

I want to point at this idea, this desimplifying of the distinction between resistance and non-resistance. If you think of resistance as *La Résistance*, as a group of active opposers to an authoritarian regime—precisely as the intelligentsia saw itself (at least according to Milyukov and Tolstoy)—then the tendency is to think of the nonresistors as latent, as inactive, unconcerned with change. There's a vanguard, and no one else matters; they are just material or matériel. Again, this is very much the mindset of the Russian intelligentsia from, say, 1860 onwards, for instance as they are depicted in *Landmarks*.

Gordon claims though that there is no binary distinction between resistance and nonresistance and its role in change, that in fact non-rebellion is, as he says, "a warren of minute and individual tactics and strategies" that "counter overall domination," and that these strategies defy any simple division between political and apolitical. This focus is the essence of Foucault-based governability studies, as well as the heart of James Scott's anarchism: tactics and strategies for opposing overall domination.

I don't know whether Gordon was alluding here to Tolstoy, or even knows anything about Tolstoy's view on non-resistance to evil, but this quotation about resisting or non-resisting evil and corrupt regimes, about the strategy of resistance as basically synonymous with politicization... Tolstoy himself could have written it, and mutatis mutandis, he did write it, over and over again, in *War and Peace*:

---

9   Colin Gordon, "Afterword," in Michael Foucault, *Power/Knowledge—Selected Interviews and Other Writings*, ed. C. Gordon (New York: Vintage, 1980), 257.

> The French, retreating in 1812—though according to tactics they should have separated into detachments to defend themselves—congregated into a mass because the spirit of the army had so fallen that only the mass held the army together. The Russians, on the contrary, ought according to tactics to have attacked in mass, but in fact they split up into small units, because their spirit had so risen that separate individuals, without orders, dealt blows at the French without needing any compulsion to induce them to expose themselves to hardships and dangers. . . . A lump of snow cannot be melted instantaneously. There is a certain limit of time in less than which no amount of heat can melt the snow. On the contrary the greater the heat the more solidified the remaining snow becomes.[10]

How, then, do you truly resist an unjust system through nonresistance; how can you accommodate the heat without turning to ice?

I'm tempted to say something like this: Tolstoy goes one further than Foucault, who, inverting Clausewitz, claimed that politics, state policy, is war by other means.[11] Tolstoy would have said that our social existence, our economic life, our modern identity itself is war carried out by other means. We are constantly subjected to the coercive power of the system, although we remain mostly unconscious of that coercion. (As I'll argue later, it's this "official coercion" that ultimately allows us to sense our own existence and that perhaps, paradoxically, holds the key to true freedom.) Given this world, this social system, how do we resist it? How do we rebel against the system, if we *are* the system?

There are two separate but connected questions at play here: on the one hand, how has state coercion become so damn effective? And on the other, how is it that we, the subjects of authority and objects of violence, are largely insensible to that coercion? We cannot fight it if we are unaware of it.

The Place of Violence

Tolstoy spent five hundred pages providing an etiology of state violence and its terrible effectiveness in *What, Then, Shall We Do?* and another five hundred

---

10 Leo Tolstoy, *War and Peace*, trans. Louise Maude and Aylmer Maude, Project Gutenberg, 2001, 12 and 115, https://www.gutenberg.org/cache/epub/2600/pg2600-images.html.
11 Michel Foucault. *"Society Must Be Defended,"* trans. David Macey (Toronto, ON: Picador, 1997), 16.

pages in *The Kingdom of God Is within You*. Tolstoy developed his theory of the awful power of the modern State while a subject of the Russian Empire, a particularly stupid and savage example of state authority, outstripped perhaps only by the current Russian Federation.

Tolstoy advances the notion that all state authority depends on coercion and violence and that this violence, though mostly untapped by the system, is systemic, no matter how insignificant. (Tolstoy always uses the word *nasilie*, not necessarily physical violence but the imposition of one's will on another.)

The history of modernity and the West is, for Tolstoy, the steady and uninterrupted discovery of new modes of control without need for recourse to bodily violence. The State has discovered essentially that coercion works best specifically when *physical* violence remains, as it were, the ghost of a threat.[12]

We know this is true, insists Tolstoy, because the threatened violence is always sourced in the armed organs of society, in the police and military. Like some law of physics, as the coercion necessary for the functioning of a system increases, so must the potential for physical violence. The reverse holds true, too, a sort of substitution principle: As the potential for effective violence increases, according to Tolstoy, the system must become effective and coercive. In his assertion that the potential for violence has increased, he is irrefutably correct: those organizations sanctioned by the State to deal in violence—the police, the military—are now much more deadly and effective than they were when Tolstoy was alive.

Yet we are largely unaware of the role of violence and coercion in maintaining the system. Tolstoy's uses the metaphor of the wicker basket for the ways social organization hides the means and culpability for violence and coercion, for the ways that authority ultimately gets exercised:

> Just as in a wicker basket all the ends are so hidden away that it is hard to find them in the state organization the responsibility for the crimes committed is so hidden away that men will commit the most atrocious acts without seeing their responsibility for them: . . . One set of people have suggested, a second set have proposed, a third have reported, fourth have decided, a fifth have confirmed, sixth have given the order, and a seventh set of men have carried it out. They hang, they flog to death women, old men, and innocent people.[13]

---

12 Tolstoi, *Polnoe sobranie sochinenii*, vol. 25, 276.
13 Ibid., vol. 28, 250.

Systemic power, modern authority, operates most effectively when it does not outright or violently repress dissentient forces but instead organizes and channels them through systems of exchange that offer the illusion of freedom and improvement.

Tolstoy was one of the great anarchists of the nineteenth century, and one way to think of anarchism is not as simple rebellion against the routines and rituals of social structures but instead as a technique for undermining dominant value systems by revealing the moments of coercion, moments that make the system robust. What emerges is a liberation of sorts for the coerced and dominated but not necessarily the kind of liberation the intelligentsia imagines.

And this brings me to the next accommodation and how it operates, according to Tolstoy. One way to phrase the question is: Why are we insensate to the coercion enacted upon us? Why are we so accommodating to being re-accommodated?

Tolstoy Does Women's Work

Let me overanalyze a justly famous diary entry Tolstoy made in the spring of 1897, the period when he was working on aesthetic theories that would inform *What Is Art?* It centers on Tolstoy's sofa, his *kushetka*, upon which he was born, and where all his children were born. In that sense, at least, the couch is very much a woman's place:

> I was walking around dusting things off in my room, I came to the sofa and I couldn't recall whether I had already dusted it off or not. Since such movements are habitual and unconscious, I felt that it was already impossible to remember. If I had in fact dusted the sofa and forgotten that I had done so, i.e., if I had acted unconsciously, then this is tantamount to not having done it at all. If someone conscious had seen me doing this, then it might have been possible to restore this in my mind. If, on the other hand, no one had been observing me or observing me only unconsciously, if the complex life of so many people takes place entirely on the level of unconsciousness [habit, routine], then it's as if this life had never been. Therefore life is only life when it's illuminated by consciousness. What is consciousness? What is an act that is illuminated by consciousness? Acts illuminated by consciousness are acts that we perform freely, that is, we perform

them knowing that we could have acted differently. Therefore, consciousness is freedom. (If we undergo coercion, and we have no choice over how we bear this violence/coercion, then we will not feel [it]).[14]

Tolstoy sets up two opposed phenomenological "clusters," two ways of experiencing time that involve concomitant ethical awareness-of-the-world and awareness-of-ourselves-in-action/movement. The first mode or cluster is ordinary life governed by "established procedures" . . . habit and unconsciousness, the "default" manner of acting, seeing, being, and knowing . . . *Zugzwang*. We are forced to act, even when our act is contrary to our eventual best interest. In this mode, we participate in Tolstoy's wicker basket of coercion and violence but remain largely unaware of it. This phenomenological state is also notably lonely, sealed off from contact with other consciousnesses.

The second mode occurs on those rare occasions when we return our attention, or more exactly our attention is turned by an observer, to our actions, to movements that are habitual, and we realize that we are not acting freely but rather according to habit, ritual, unconsciously; we are made aware of our complicity, our participation in socially conditioned activity, we become aware of ourselves as acting in a context of rules and regulations and, simultaneously, we are made aware of our experience of coercion/violence at the hands of the State.

What separates these two modes is awareness of choice, the possibility of agency, of other-doing. That awareness is maybe always subsequent, secondary, and deeply paradoxical. Perhaps we truly know ourselves only by the bite and weight of the chains we wear.

If someone conscious had seen me doing this, then it might have been possible to restore it in my mind.

A maximalist reading of this passage would lead one to say that true consciousness requires multiple awarenesses of the world . . . community and co-operation. We need another consciousness to turn our attention back there, back to our action.

Two notable concepts: The knowledge that we could have acted differently is the knowledge that we do not have to do what unconscious habit dictates, that we do not have to participate. Tolstoy uses the word *nepodchinenie*, noncompliance. It is Gordon's nonresistance. The second concept is the binary of loneliness and communion in the diary.

---

14 Ibid., vol. 53, 141–142.

The scene begins in solitude, as both the writing of the entry and the dusting take place maximally alone, isolated, in the count's chamber, on his seigneurial estate, upon *that couch*. But it's convoluted: Tolstoy, the alpha-male count, dusts his own room, doing the work of a servant, woman's work: not production but maintenance of the things our life requires. Tolstoy then imagines himself overseen, observed, and the moment is redeemed. "Solitude calls out for solidarity."[15] "The Stranger" oversees himself in isolation, in the first person "I," and then "The Resident" imagines another, a companion (this is Gustafson's formulation). The conscious observer, the "true" master, emancipates the unconscious servant/lord, the duster, revealing to the servant the servant's freedom, his ability to act differently. Master and slave become one, both share freedom, only to lose it again. (Very, very Hegelian for someone who claimed not to understand Hegel.)

Isolation leads to failure, to being trapped and enslaved; for freedom, the unconscious consciousness needs the surveillance of another, superior consciousness, a conscious consciousness. Consciousness is the observer, observed. Our freedom always (only?) means a sudden awareness of our true state, of our subjectedness to violence and coercion. We are who we are, we can perceive the world, because of the violence done to us, done to our bodies.

Our freedom is, as it were, returned to our awareness by some second conscious consciousness, but with our freedom comes also the *awareness* of our own unfreedom, the violence being done to us.

Look, if you've read *War and Peace* . . . bells should be ringing. War and violence, the "complex life of so many people," "the inevitable course of events" versus "individual freedom" and "consciousness," human bodies. "What force (*sila*) makes people move?"[16] Which of our actions are pre-determined, and when do we exert agency?

Birds are Free

Let me bring together the varied strands of this essay: The intelligentsia, Foucault's and Gordon's notion of nonresistance and resistance to authority, the pervasive, systemic violence in Tolstoy's basket, and Tolstoy's theory of conscious action and freedom, played out on his couch. How do we *effectively* rebel against an unjust system without ourselves becoming the system? Maksim Gorky, the Russian/Soviet writer and Marxist thinker, spent time with Tolstoy

---

15 Richard Gustafson, *Leo Tolstoy: Resident and Stranger* (Princeton, NJ: Princeton UP, 1986), 20.
16 Tolstoi, *Polnoe sobranie sochinenii*, vol. 12, 322.

late in Tolstoy's life, in 1901 and 1902, when both of them were living in Gaspra, in the Crimea. Like everyone else around Tolstoy, including Tolstoy, Gorky kept notes on everything Tolstoy said, publishing them not long after Tolstoy's death.

One passage in particular came to mind when thinking about freedom, isolation, rebellion, and accommodations. It's a conversation Gorky had with Tolstoy and Leopold Sulerzhitsky. Sulerzhitsky (they called him Suler) subsequently became a theatrical director until his sudden death in 1916. He's largely responsible for the introduction of yoga to Europe and America through his work with Stanislavsky:

> I remember that Suler once got ahold of a little brochure by Kropotkin [the famous Russian anarchist and naturalist] that fired him up and he spent all day telling everyone about the wisdom of anarchy.... "Stop it, Leopold, would you? I'm sick and tired of it," said Tolstoy. "You keep repeating like a parrot one word, freedom freedom ... and where, what's the sense? If you get this freedom, in your sense of it, what comes of it? In a philosophical sense, it's just a bottomless pit. And in life, in a practical sense, you'd just become an idler, a bum (*lentiai, pobirokha*). How would you connect with people, with life, if you were free in your sense? Look, birds are free, and still they build nests. You wouldn't even bother with nests, you'd just fuck around, like some hound dog. Think about it seriously and you'll see, you'll feel, that freedom is just another word for emptiness, endlessness.[17]

Suler's idea of freedom, just acting according to your own free will, roughly Berlin's definition of negative liberty, is undesirable because such freedom leaves you alone: "How would you connect with people, with life, if you were free in your sense?" Building nests—Tolstoy uses the Russian expression *vit' gnezdo*, to weave or braid or twist a nest—has to be understood fully here. Birds weave accommodations ... they build a place for more birds, they weave relationships and thereby overcome isolation. Birds are born free, yet they build nests. (Sulerzhitsky loved to draw birds and was himself often compared to a bird.) Humans unchained, though, are like male dogs, *kobeli*, which means in this context something like "stud muffin," the opposite of communal, reproductive birds with their nests. Freedom can only exist when we act communally, a Tolstoyan riff on J. J. Rousseau's "everywhere in chains."

---

17 *L. N. Tolstoi v vospominaniiakh sovremennikov*, vol. 2 (Sankt Peterburg: Pal'mira, 2017), 481–483; the translation is mine (MAD).

Tolstoy went on, still responding to Suler's apotheosis of freedom:

> [Tolstoy] frowned angrily, sat quietly for a moment, and quietly added: "Christ was free, Buddha was too, and they both took upon themselves the sins of the world, voluntarily they became captives of this worldly life.... What about you? And us? What's there to say. We all seek freedom from responsibility to our neighbors, all the while it's these very feelings of responsibility that make us people, and were it not for such feelings, we'd all live like animals.[18]

Maximal freedom for Tolstoy always leads the truly emancipated—perfect individuals like Jesus and Buddha—back into the world, into social obligations. In Tolstoy's world, again, back on the couch, we constantly and sharply vacillate between two poles. Freedom isolates us until it reaches its extremes, and like the black bag where Ivan Ilych is trapped (in *Death of Ivan Ilych*), suddenly we fall through into a new existence, into communion with others: it is only our freedom that reveals the always-already extant chains that bind us, the ones called back to our consciousness when the conscious consciousness, our own (but not ours), reminds us of ourselves. We are always and everywhere determined by the system, by its violence and its established procedures, but also by the chains of responsibility to our neighbors.

We can recognize the truth and become free in our unfreeness, *aware* of servitude. Or we can remain unaware of the violence done to us and continue to be subject to the coercion of the State. Tolstoy offers this choice in a metaphor:

> A horse harnessed with others to a cart is not free to refrain from moving the cart. If he does not move forward the cart will knock him down and go on dragging him with it, whether he will or not. But the horse is free to drag the cart himself or to be dragged with it. And so it is with man.
>
> Whether this is a great or small degree of freedom in comparison with the fantastic liberty we should like to have, it is the only freedom that really exists...[19]

---

18 Ibid., 481–483. The translation is mine.
19 Tolstoi, *Polnoe sobranie sochinenii*, vol. 28, 282.

Resistance is futile, and frankly so is nonresistance. You can drag the cart or get dragged by it. The cart is going to go forward either way. There's your freedom.

Negative Narration

In the conclusion of *The Kingdom of God Is within You,* Tolstoy tells two stories about how the State exerts its authority and the possibility of resistance.

The 1890s in Russia were a time of droughts, famines, crop failures, peasant insurrections and social rebellion. Alexander III and Nicholas II regularly sent out armed troops to clamp down on unrest. Tolstoy begins with the story of what had recently happened in Oryol, to the south of Moscow. Briefly, peasants had risen up against their landlord when he diverted water from their irrigation system. Unidentified peasant women had overturned the landlord's carts, so police were instructed to arrest one woman per household, randomly chosen. Predictably, the peasants resisted the arrest of their sisters, mothers, wives, and daughters, and they beat the State's representatives. The governor of the province got involved. Tolstoy describes the horrible flogging in Oryol, punishment meted out because the peasants refused to allow their women to be arrested, and then remarks coolly that this is how state authority *always* works:

> And if there is no need to imprison, beat, and kill men every time the landlord collects his rents, every time those who are in want of bread have to pay a swindling merchant three times its value . . . it is because so many men have been beaten and killed for trying to resist these demands, that the lesson has now been learnt very thoroughly.[20]

Tolstoy turns from the story of how the peasant rebellion was punished in Oryol to another peasant uprising in Tula, a town about 100 miles south of Moscow, very near Yasnaya Polyana, Tolstoy's ancestral estate. We could think of this story in narratological terms, as a variety of what Saul Morson calls negative narration that Tolstoy perfected in *War and Peace*: He tells a counter-story, the story that had most or all the same elements as Oryol but with a different ending.[21] He tells us what *did not* happen.

---

20 Ibid., vol. 28, 228.
21 Gary Saul Morson, *Hidden in Plain View* (Stanford, CA: Stanford UP, 1987), 130.

Tolstoy is traveling on September 9, 1894, and on the train platform encounters soldiers sent to punish peasants in Tula; just as in Oryol, the peasants in Tula had rebelled over property rights, and again the State had dispatched soldiers to flog them. Tolstoy wonders how this could happen: the soldiers, who seem so *normal* and happy, like boys everywhere—how could they possibly "assist at the murder of their fathers and grandfathers"? A general sits at a table chatting about the weather "as though the business he was on was of so simple a character that it could not disturb his serenity." Officers stand around eating cake. How can they act so normally when "they all know that they are going to torture, perhaps to kill, their famished fellow-creatures within an hour?" How could the other passengers on the platform not exclaim "No! Flog and kill starving men!... We won't allow it!"[22]

But no one does this. Everyone, like in *War and Peace* or in the Sevastopol port during the Crimean War, is "calmly going about their daily routine,"[23] pursuing their own private affairs but doing the true work of history, unconsciously. (Dusting their couches.)

But there emerges in Tolstoy's narrative of ordinary life—for Tolstoy ordinary life is a welter of violence, isolation, authority—on the platform, that there are tiny, critical moments, turning points. None of them, he is at pains to emphasize, are *per se* important. A "lady of liberal views" (our *intelligentka*) on the platform began to complain about the existing order of things, confronting the soldiers. A merchant begins praising the soldiers, and a few soldiers turn away, embarrassed by the lies and deception repeated by the merchant. Tolstoy remarks that lately there had been a shift in public opinion and that more often the authorities had been subjected to "public opinion." The governor knew that there was an international press "that may report the affair and cover him in ignominy forever." One company commander criticizes the governor's demand, saying that they shouldn't be "butchers." Among the ranks there are soldiers who are "free-thinking," and some young officers hold "liberal ideas." The general is aware of a change in public opinion, and worries perhaps that his soldiers will not "at the last minute obey him." Everyone questions the legitimacy of state authority, though they proceed anyway, albeit in doubt.[24]

The train of soldiers and officials all act "bold and composed," but Tolstoy proposes that the bolder they seemed, the more they inwardly suffered, and that as the train approached Tula, "this feeling [of suffering] increased." Tolstoy repeatedly remarks, as he tells the story of the train's approach to "the scene

---

22 Tolstoi, *Polnoe sobranie sochinenii*, vol. 28, 229–230.
23 Ibid., vol. 4, 6.
24 Ibid., vol. 28, 231–233.

of the action," that since the men are in a state of inward agitation, prompted by their doubts, "no one knows what each soldier will do at the last minute." They are "hypnotized," he repeats, and wonders, will they wake up? The State's authority depends on the wicker basket scheme, and the exercise of violence and coercion depends on human connections, with each set of actors ignoring the actual significance of their decision. In other words, between the initial decision to use violence and the actual exercise of violence, there are many possibilities of failure. As authority gets further and further from the source and closer and closer to the "scene of the action," the possibility for failure increases, which is what happened, or more exactly did not happen, in Tula:

> It was enough for a few men, some personally concerned in the affair and others simply outsiders, to express their disapproval... their contempt and loathing for those who had taken part in inflicting them ... thanks to these and a few other seemingly insignificant influences brought to bear on these hypnotized men, the affair took a completely different turn, and the troops, when they reached the place, did not inflict any punishment.[25]

We can be Tolstoy's higher consciousness. We can recall to the minds of others that they can act differently, that they do not have to follow established procedure. That's what fascinates Tolstoy here: the story of what did not happen.

Tolstoy is unproblematically associated with the origin of non-resistance to evil, a concept he transmitted directly to Gandhi and through Gandhi into the post-colonial world. But, importantly, Tolstoy's non-resistance is *not* what is commonly thought of as non-resistance, if you think of it as principled pacifism, as a conscious movement of protest against an unjust regime. Tolstoyan non-resistance looks like ordinary life, unorganized, undirected, like the activity of Muscovites before Napoleon's attack in *War and Peace*, like Gordon's notion of the non-resistance as a strategy "of evasion of defense." Like Schwejk not Solzhenitsyn.

Of course, individual actions precipitate the non-event in Tula: the event is highly charged, it reverberates with potential. But no one *knows* what's going to happen. What seems like boldness and composure is actually agitation and doubt. Tolstoy remarks that "seemingly insignificant influences" turn out to have profound, radical results.[26] The system changes *suddenly*.

---

25 Ibid., vol. 28, 263–264.
26 Ibid., vol. 28, 264.

Sandpiles

There's a concept in statistics and physics called self-organized criticality: A system independently reaches a critical state, where there is no correlation between the system's response to a perturbation and the actual effect of that perturbation. The textbook example of this is the sandpile in which the addition of one more grain of sand may cause nothing to happen, or it may cause the entire pile to collapse, a cascading effect. On the one hand, statistically at least, the length and time of the system are infinite . . . if we did enough simulations, in one of them, you could keep adding grains of sand forever and the pile would never collapse. Extreme stability.

You can understand critical state or criticality as the latent potentiality of sudden changes that are caused by seemingly insignificant perturbations. Here, the important Tolstoyan concept is the relationship between individual agency and group behavior, the play between freedom and history writ large in *War and Peace*.

I'll leave you with the closing words of *The Kingdom of God Is within You*, words that seem to uncannily reflect the notion of "criticality" and the interaction between individuals and groups:

> Just as a single shock may be sufficient, when a liquid is saturated with some salt, to precipitate it at once in crystals, a slight effort may be perhaps all that is needed now that the truth already revealed to men may gain a mastery over hundreds, thousands, millions of men, that a public opinion consistent with conscience may be established, and through this change of public opinion the whole order of life may be transformed. And making that effort depends upon us.[27]

Bibliography

Foucault, Michael. *Power/Knowledge—Selected Interviews and Other Writings*. Edited by C. Gordon. New York: Vintage, 1980.

———. *"Society Must Be Defended."* Translated by David Macey. Toronto, ON: Picador, 1997.

Frank, Semen. "Etika nigilizma." In *Vekhi: Intelligentsiia v Rossii: sborniki statei, 1909–1910*. Edited by Valentin Valentinovich Shelokhaev and Nataliia Aleksandrovna Kazakova, 153–185. Moscow: Molodaia gvardiia, 1991.

---

27 Ibid., vol. 28, 284.

Gordon, Colin. Afterword to *Power/Knowledge—Selected Interviews and Other Writings*, by Michael Foucault, edited by C. Gordon. New York: Vintage, 1980.

Gustafson, Richard F. *Leo Tolstoy: Resident and Stranger*. Princeton, NJ: Princeton UP, 1986.

Miliukov, Pavel. "Intelligentsiia i istoricheskaia traditsiia." In *Vekhi: Intelligentsiia v Rossii: sborniki statei, 1909–1910*, edited by Valentin Valentinovich Shelokhaev and Nataliia Aleksandrovna Kazakova, 294–382. Moscow: Molodaia gvardiia, 1991.

Morson, Saul. *Hidden in Plain View*. Stanford, CA: Stanford UP, 1987.

Tolstoi, Lev. *Polnoe sobranie sochinenii. Akademicheskoe iubileinoe izdanie.* 90 vols. Edited by V. G. Chertkov. Moscow and Leningrad: Khudozhestvennaia literatura, 1928–1958.

Zueva, Ekaterina, ed. *L. N. Tolstoi v vospominaniiakh sovremennikov*. Sankt Peterburg: Pal′mira, 2017.

The Russian Intelligentsia and Western Intellectuals: Through the Prism of Chekhov[1]

Svetlana Evdokimova

In the 1860s two new terms—"intelligentsia" and "culture"—entered the Russian language. Both became widely used in the course of the nineteenth-century, culminating, by the end of the nineteenth century, in passionate polemics about the role of the intelligentsia in Russia, on the one hand, and about what constitutes culture, on the other. Chekhov's birth and development as a writer run parallel to the evolution of these concepts, and his literary career illuminates major debates around the concept of the intelligentsia, its goals, and its responsibilities.

Chekhov's association with the Russian intelligentsia is both indisputable and controversial. A typical representative of the intelligentsia by birth and by profession, Chekhov made the intelligentsia the main protagonist of his art. By depicting a host of typical representatives of the intelligentsia in his works (doctors, lawyers, teachers, professors, students, engineers, writers, artists, etc.), Chekhov himself undoubtedly contributed to the general perception that he was a model *intelligent*.[2] His collaboration with the Moscow Art Theater further

---

1 A large part of this essay was written during my residency stay at the Bogliasco Study Center on the Ligurian coast of Italy in 2018. My profound thanks go to the Bogliasco Foundation for hosting me during my six weeks stay at the Center and providing an ideal environment in which this work could develop.
2 In his 1999 essay "The Intelligentsia and Freedom: Toward an Analysis of the Intelligentsia's Discourse," Mikhail Lotman formulates the conviction that Chekhov is the writer of and

contributed to his appropriation by the intelligentsia.[3] However, the everlasting debates about what constitutes a true *intelligent*, and the fact that the intelligentsia also included those who openly criticized it, made it difficult to fit Chekhov into the narrow frame of any one definition of the intelligentsia.[4] Indeed, while the intelligentsia turned Chekhov into its ideal and appropriated his image as a model of *intelligentnost'* (literally, intelligentsia-ness, or the highest degree of being an *intelligent*), Chekhov's portrayals of the intelligentsia and his frequent references to it are highly ambiguous: on the one hand, he uses the concept of *intelligentnost'* almost invariably in a positive sense; on the other, his portrayals of members of the intelligentsia in his prose and plays are, for the most part, unflattering. In his letters, he also frequently expresses critical and caustic sentiments about the Russian intelligentsia. Thus, a counter-opinion that viewed Chekhov as a passionate critic of the intelligentsia—in many ways like the one later articulated in *Vekhi* (Landmarks, 1909)—emerged almost simultaneously with the intelligentsia's eulogization of Chekhov. The nature of Chekhov's association with the intelligentsia was questioned not only by later generations of readers, but by his contemporaries, who noted that he depicted it as whining and spineless. In his 1905 essay "Chekhov and Gorky," Dmitry Merezhkovsky delineates the major paradox of Chekhov's appropriation by the intelligentsia: the intelligentsia loves and appreciates Chekhov for those same ideals that he, in

---

for the intelligentsia: "Even more paradoxical is the treatment of Chekhov, the most typical *intelligent* (*samogo intelligentskogo*) of all Russian writers, a singer of *intelligentnost'* and the intelligentsia's favorite: regardless of differences in taste and ideology, for members of the Russian intelligentsia Chekhov was and remains one of the very few 'indisputable' authors" (Mikhail Lotman, "Intelligentsiia i svoboda (k analizu intelligentskogo diskursa)," in *Russkaia intelligentsiia i zapadnyi intellektualizm: Istoriia i tipologiia*, ed. B. A. Uspenskii [Moscow: O.G.I., 1999], 1250). Similarly, Vladimir Kataev eloquently expresses the common view of Chekhov as a model of *intelligentnost'*: "It was none other than Chekhov who not only with his oeuvre, but also with his very life became a model of true *intelligentnost'*" (Vladimir Kataev, "Boborykin i Chekhov [K istorii poniatiia 'intelligentsiia' v russkoi literature]," in *Chekhov plius . . . Predshestvenniki, sovremenniki, preemniki* [Moscow: Iazyki slavianskoi kul'tury, 2004], 145).

3 The prominent Silver Age poet Maksimilian Voloshin's observations about peculiarities of the Russian theater shed light on Chekhov's role in creating a "theater for the intelligentsia": "The Russian theater used to be an everyday theater for one or another class of society—for the merchant class, for the nobility, for the clerks: it used to be either a theater of Ostrovsky or of Griboedov and Turgenev, or of Gogol. The Russian intelligentsia, due to its universal, all-inclusive nature, managed to unify these types of theater and, for one moment, created its own theater—the theater of Chekhov" (M. Voloshin, "Mysli o teatre," *Apollon* 5 [1910]: 38).

4 Kataev formulates the dilemma as follows: "Chekhov is the quintessence of Russian *intelligentnost'*. Yet he is also an antipode of the Russian *intelligent*. One must admit that such contradictory conclusions could be drawn on the grounds both of the writer's fictional texts and of his open pronouncements" (Kataev, "Boborykin i Chekhov," 146).

fact, seems to reject—"without even being aware of this, these writers [Chekhov and Gorky] do nothing but undermine and destroy all the beliefs, all the ideals and idols of the Russian intelligentsia."[5] The authors of *Landmarks*, who viewed Chekhov as an ally in their indictment of the intelligentsia, expressed similar sentiments. This view culminated in some later scholars' asserting that Chekhov "might properly be called anti-intelligentsial."[6]

How could Chekhov be simultaneously the intelligentsia's very embodiment, its spokesman, and the "destroyer" of its beliefs? How could he both castigate the intelligentsia for its multiple flaws and use the terms *intelligentnost'/intelligentnyi* approvingly as a marker of refinement and culture? Obviously, the reason for this seeming contradiction is not so much Chekhov's inconsistency, but the confusion around the term "intelligentsia" and especially what it meant for Chekhov. The term clearly does not mean the same thing for those who view Chekhov as "the most typical *intelligent* of all Russian writers" (M. Lotman)[7] and those who perceive him as "anti-intelligentsial" (Morson). While Gary Saul

---

5   Merezhkovsky acknowledges that Chekhov and Gorky were central literary figures of the Russian intelligentsia and "spokesmen of the intellectual (*intelligentnaia*) middle of the Russian middle class." He emphasizes, however, that he is speaking only about the "average" Russian *intelligent*'s appreciation of these writers, which points to the central question that plagues historians and literary scholars delving into the subject of the intelligentsia: what does this term mean? Can one define what constitutes an "average" member of the intelligentsia? The intelligentsia's love of Chekhov and Gorky, according to Merezhkovsky, is based on these writers' presumed "humanitarian ideas" (understood as faith in progress, science, and reason), which represent the sacred values of the intelligentsia, whereas in fact both Chekhov's and Gorky's literary works demonstrate the very opposite—the impossibility of faith in these "humanitarian ideas." See D. S. Merezhkovskii, "Chekhov i Gor'kii," in *A. P. Chekhov: Pro et Contra*, ed. D. K. Bogatyrev (St. Peterburg: Izdatel'stvo Russkogo Khristianskogo gumanitarnogo instituta, 2002), 692.
6   Morson included Chekhov among what he calls "counter-traditional thinkers" and observed that some *Landmarks* authors expressed criticism of the intelligentsia similar to Chekhov's. See Gary Saul Morson, "The Intelligentsia and Its Critics," in *A Companion to Russian History*, ed. Abbott Gleason (Chichester, UK: Wiley-Blackwell, 2009), 267–268. Indeed, many of Chekhov's contemporaries observed his critical attitude toward the intelligentsia. S. Severny insisted, along with the authors of *Landmarks*, that Chekhov displayed a "harsh and profoundly critical attitude toward the Russian intelligentsia"; see "'Vekhi' i Chekhov," in *Vekhi: Pro et Contra, Antologiia*, ed. V. V. Sapov (St. Peterburg: Izdatel'stvo Russkogo khristianskogo gumanitarnogo instituta, 1998), 315. Morson further points out that Chekhov's criticism of the intelligentsia, including his brother Nikolai, "can be read as a counter-statement to intelligentsial morals" (Morson, "The Intelligentsia and Its Critics," 267). Morson, however, almost exclusively identifies the intelligentsia's ideas with nihilism and does not address Chekhov's frequent use of the term intelligentsia in a positive sense. On Chekhov's concept of the intelligent, see also S. Evdokimova, "Russian Binaries and the Question of Culture: Chekhov's True Intelligent," in *Chekhov's Letters: Biography, Context, Poetics*, ed. Carol Apollonio and Radislav Lapushin (Lanham: Lexington Books, 2018), 173–192.
7   Lotman, "Intelligentsiia i svoboda," 125.

Morson essentially identifies the intelligentsia with nihilism and radicalism, other scholars interpret it as a broader category referring to a cultured educated stratum of society. Pyotr Boborykin (1836–1921), for example, passionately objected to the narrowing of the term in the aftermath of *Landmarks*: "One thing is clear—that the authors of the collection have given a concept of 'intelligentsia' a meaning that is either too narrow or too flexible.... The intelligentsia for them is both 'nihilists' and 'social democrats' and 'socialist revolutionaries' and circles of all kinds, literary and underground."[8]

Which intelligentsia shall we then consider when discussing Chekhov's relations with the intelligentsia and his self-awareness as an *intelligent*? In order to disentangle Chekhov's attitude to the intelligentsia, it is necessary to determine how the concept of the intelligentsia was understood by Chekhov and his contemporaries. The division along ideological lines—insisting that only a particular group adopting "Western" and "progressive" values constituted the intelligentsia—contributed to the confusion about who could be viewed as a member of the intelligentsia, because it automatically excluded writers and thinkers holding more conservative and right-wing views. An attempt to present the Russian intelligentsia as a peculiarly Russian phenomenon characterized by a very specific ideology, protest, opposition, uprootedness, and by adherence to broadly understood "ethics" and values, reveals the conceptual weakness of the definition and of the proclaimed distinction between the intelligentsia and intellectuals. Although the myth of the uniqueness of the Russian intelligentsia was set already by Pyotr Boborykin, the opposition between the intelligentsia and intellectuals in the European sense of the word became routine only in studies dedicated to the intelligentsia in the aftermath of *Landmarks*; it then was quickly adopted by Western scholars. This opposition did not exist for Chekhov. The present essay attempts to disentangle Chekhov's complex association with the intelligentsia, delineating its inherent contradictions and tracing its evolution in a larger European context.

The Intelligentsia's Toads and Crocodiles

Based on Chekhov's fictional and non-fictional work we can distinguish at least three distinct groups to which Chekhov refers as the intelligentsia. First,

---

8 Petr Boborykin, "Podgnivshie 'Vekhi' (Konspekt publichnoi lektsii)," in *Vekhi: Pro et Contra, Antologiia*, ed. V. V. Sapov (St. Peterburg: Izdatel'stvo Russkogo khristianskogo gumanitarnogo instituta, 1998), 202.

there is the intellectual elite and carriers of culture and tradition who (perhaps erroneously) regard themselves as autonomous and independent of the dominant social group. This group includes prominent cultural figures who create the intellectual and moral foundations of society through their creative and intellectual activity, through their dissemination of ideas and worldviews. According to its self-proclaimed godfather, Pyotr Boborykin, the intelligentsia was represented by people "of high intellectual and moral culture."

The second meaning of the word "intelligentsia," for Chekhov, refers to a group of professional people, variably educated, such as doctors, teachers, veterinarians, and priests, who may or may not be characterized by the highest degree of culture. The notion of the intelligentsia as a social group that incorporated people of the so-called "various ranks" (*raznochintsy*)—that is, individuals drawn from the non-gentry strata—bears additional relevance for Chekhov, who was extremely class conscious and frequently commented on the significance of his own lower-middle-class origins for his development as a writer and human being.

Thirdly, Chekhov also describes an ideologically driven faction of the intelligentsia that established itself in opposition to the state and that might include members from the first two groups. This is the intelligentsia in the narrow sense (as classically defined by Richard Pipes among many others),[9] which in the aftermath of *Landmarks* was frequently identified—erroneously—with the Russian intelligentsia as such. It is this latter group that received the most criticism from Chekhov.

Chekhov's letters and fictional writings record hundreds of instances of biting criticism of the Russian intelligentsia, which attracted the attention of his readers. A self-made man, Chekhov was probably Russia's most consistent individualist, and he resented the Russian radical intelligentsia as a fundamentally anti-individualist movement. The core of his criticism of this faction within the intelligentsia rested on the intelligentsia's party and group mentality, its militant rhetoric, and its hypocrisy that stemmed from the disparity between the intelligentsia's lofty rhetoric and its actual passivity. Chekhov was sensitive to all forms of tendentiousness and hypocrisy, whether conservative or liberal.[10] As he puts it in his frequently quoted letter to Ivan

---

9 Richard Pipes, "The Historical Evolution of the Russian Intelligentsia," in *The Russian Intelligentsia*, ed. Richard Pipes (New York: Columbia UP, 1961), 48.
10 Cf., for example, Chekhov's comments about Russian liberal writer Dmitry Grigorovich: "He himself is a tendentious writer and only pretends to be the enemy of tendentiousness" (A. P. Chekhov, *Polnoe sobranie sochinenii i pisem*, 30 vols., ed. N. F. Bel'chikov [Moscow: Nauka, 1974–1983]; here, vol. P3, 130). Or Chekhov's famous confession to Pleshcheev:

Orlov of February 1899: "All of the intelligentsia is to blame, all of it.... I despise our hysterical and hypocritical intelligentsia. I don't believe in it even when it suffers and complains. I believe only in separate individuals, and it does not matter whether they are peasants or intelligentsia."[11] Anticipating some of the criticism of *Landmarks*, Chekhov blamed this intelligentsia for betraying its mission of disinterested enlightenment for the sake of expedient political truths and for its sectarian nature.[12] He valued the intelligentsia as individuals, but not *en masse*, as a group. Extremely sensitive to the rapid social changes taking place in pre-revolutionary Russia and to new activist trends within the intelligentsia—what we could call the elements of the organic intelligentsia (in Gramscian terms) struggling for hegemony and their special interests—Chekhov objected as early as 1888 to the intelligentsia's search for global solutions and totalitarian methods. Referring to the intelligentsia of the liberal Russian journal *Russkaia mysl'* as "toads and crocodiles" who "under the banner of science, art, and suppressed freedom will rule here, in Russia, in ways not known even at the time of the Inquisition in Spain," Chekhov lamented the manipulation of the press and mass media for political goals.[13] Apprehensive of the intelligentsia's conformity, on the one hand, and of its quest for power, on the other, Chekhov was especially critical of those involved in the production and dissemination of ideology, that is, men of letters, professors, publicists, journalists, and literary critics. Recoiling from the intelligentsia's party mentality, Chekhov regarded inner freedom as inseparably connected to culture and valued individual liberty above all. Emphasis on inner freedom and a personal code of behavior rather than a desire to form "community of interests" and "solidarity" constitutes the core of Chekhov's criticism of the contemporary literary intelligentsia in his letter to Ivan Leontyev (Shcheglov) of May 3, 1888:

> Are not you suffocated by such words as solidarity, the unity of young writers, community of interest, and so on? ... there is

---

"I have no particular liking either for the gendarmes, or the butchers or the scientists, or the writers, or for the young. I consider labels and tags a prejudice" (ibid., vol. P3, 11). Cf. also: "I do not think about either conservatism or liberalism, but about their [the characters he depicts—SE] stupidity and pretentiousness" (ibid., vol. P3, 19).

11 Ibid., vol. P8, 101.

12 Cf. Berdyaev's criticism of the intelligentsia giving up on truth: "Love for egalitarian justice, for the general good and national wellbeing has paralyzed love of truth, has almost destroyed any interest in truth." N. A. Berdiaev, "Filosofskaia istina i intelligentskaia pravda," in *Vekhi: Sbornik statei o russkoi intelligentsii* (Moscow: M. V. Sablin, 1909), 8.

13 Chekhov, *Polnoe sobranie*, vol. P2, 316–317.

> nothing to which this solidarity might attach itself securely . . . And do we need it? No . . . Let's be ordinary people, let's treat all equally and then you won't need an artificially wrought solidarity."[14]

Significantly, Chekhov stresses that inner un-freedom is characteristic not only of "merchants' houses and police stations"—that is, of not any particular "class," but rather of those who lack culture, even if they may belong to the educated classes: "Pharisaism, dull-wittedness and tyranny reign not only in merchants' houses and police stations. . . . I see them in science and literature among the younger generation. I look upon tags and labels as prejudices."[15] Only through sustained personal effort to rid oneself of qualities incompatible with inner freedom may one become a man of culture and a true *intelligent*.

By no means, however, did Chekhov identify the intelligentsia solely with nihilists and radicals, whom the authors of *Landmarks* painted as intolerant, fanatical, belligerent, and slovenly. Most of those to whom Chekhov refers as "the intelligentsia"—doctors, engineers, writers, professors, actors—were hardly nihilists with dirty fingernails, and Chekhov unhesitatingly considered himself an integral part of this group. Although critical of the Russian intelligentsia as an ideology-oriented group, Chekhov never completely severed his bond with the intelligentsia in a broader sense, and was supportive of the intelligentsia's project of general enlightenment and social improvement. He always differentiated between the professional intelligentsia and the intelligentsia that was motivated by specific ideologies. In a letter to Dmitry Grigorovich of January 12, 1888, he writes:

> We'll be drinking a lot of toasts tonight to the people who taught me to cut up corpses and write prescriptions. . . . We drink to Turgenev, Tolstoy and you. Men of literature (*literatory*) drink to Chernyshevsky, Saltykov and Gleb Uspensky, but the public (students, doctors, mathematicians and so on) to which I belong as an Aesculapius, still holds fast to the good old days and refuses to betray the much beloved names.[16]

---

14 Ibid., vol. P2, 262.
15 Ibid., vol. P3, 11.
16 Ibid., vol. P2, 175.

Chekhov's juxtaposition of "men of letters," or literati (*literatory*)—he means here a particular group of liberal and radical men of letters—to a more general public of educated people and professionals (students, doctors, mathematicians, etc.) reveals his awareness not only of the existence of distinct groups within the educated classes, but also of their diverging aesthetic and moral tastes and values. The socially and ideologically oriented literary intelligentsia tended to worship the radicals: Chernyshevsky, Saltykov, and Uspensky. Indeed, they were emblems of the Russian intelligentsia in its narrower sense. They formed a group of "men of ideas and convictions" ideologizing every sphere of human relations.[17] Chernyshevsky's demand that an artist should have a distinct "world outlook" was further emphasized by Nikolai Dobrolyubov and Dmitry Pisarev, and it lingered in the literary criticism of Chekhov's time. The insistence on a distinct "world outlook" by this kind of literary intelligentsia was precisely what plagued Chekhov throughout his literary career. Chekhov struggled with the demand that literature must express a particular ideology, exhibit social criticism, and show the path to social wellbeing.[18] It is significant that Chekhov does not include himself among those who drink to the more radical part of the Russian intelligentsia, but associates himself with a more diverse group of educated people (the so-called free professions), who were less politically oriented. The idols of these professionals were the Russian classics—Turgenev and Tolstoy, that is, gentlemen-littérateurs and individualists—rather than the propagators of populism and progressivism. This "public" that Chekhov identifies with, and which includes students and doctors, was also part of the broader intelligentsia, although a less vocal one. It is obvious that Chekhov is fully conscious of these distinct factions within the intelligentsia.

---

17 Chekhov frequently mocks these "people of conviction." See, for example, his highly ironic portrayal of Maria Vasilyevna, who blames Voinitsky for no longer being "a man of ideas and convictions" in *Uncle Vanya*.
18 Chekhov subtly mocks ideological demands on literature in his fictional and non-fictional works. Cf., for example this conversation in his novella *Three Years* (*Tri goda*, 1985): "'A work of literature cannot be significant or useful unless its basic idea contains some meaningful social task,' Konstantin was saying looking at Yartsev angrily." As Simon Karlinsky observes, "Konstantin's views on the uses of literature are a minute summary of the one of the basic theses of Peter Lavrov's *Historical Letters* (1870, final version 1891), which is perhaps the most representative, influential and widely read single document of Russian nineteenth-century anti-government dissent... Yulia's reasons for rejecting literature that deals with love... are a simple-minded paraphrase of the reasons advanced by the Populist critics of Chekhov's time when they dismissed Tolstoy's *Anna Karenina* as socially irrelevant" (Simon Karlinsky, *Anton Chekhov's Life and Thought: Selected Letters and Commentary* [Evanston, IL: Northwestern UP, 1997], 8–9).

It is no coincidence that Chekhov, who undoubtedly was aware that the earlier split in the *Contemporary* (Sovremennik) was caused by the increasing influence of Chernyshevsky and Dobrolyubov in the journal, mentions specifically those gentry writers who had left *Sovremennik*—Grigorovich, Turgenev, and Tolstoy. The division between radical "men of literature" (*literatory*) and "the public (students, doctors, mathematicians and so on)" ran along the frontline separating the supporters of *Sovremennik* (Saltykov was part of the journal's editorial board from 1863 to 1884; both Saltykov and Uspensky published in the post-split *Sovremennik*) from its critics in the late 1850s and early 1860s. Probably not incidentally, Chekhov omits here the name of Dostoevsky who was neither a liberal aristocrat nor a representative of a radical camp, but who was no less a "man of ideas" than his radical opponents. Dostoevsky's *pochvennichestvo* (native-soil conservatism) had little appeal for Chekhov, who was far from idealizing either "native soil" or the Russian peasant, for as he confessed he could never forget about "peasant blood" in his own veins.

Describing the divide within the intelligentsia, Chekhov clearly juxtaposed the gentlemen-littérateurs to the ideologically committed representatives of the literary intelligentsia (headed by N. Nekrasov, who belonged to the landed gentry but supported the "revolutionary democrats"). Chekhov clearly distinguishes three groups within the intelligentsia: the bearers of tradition (that is, Russian classical writers); the educated class of various ranks ("students, doctors, mathematicians" who venerated the Russian cultural elite); and the radical intelligentsia, represented by "men of ideas," whose models are Chernyshevsky, Saltykov, and Uspensky. The intelligentsia understood in its broader sense as "free professionals" appears to be less ideologically engaged than its purely literary faction; it holds classical Russian culture in the highest esteem, while the "men of literature" constitute the part of the intelligentsia that favors ideas and specific ideology over art and personal interests. In a sense, one could see the division of *Sovremennik* as beginning the split among Russian intellectual circles that created distinct groups of the intelligentsia: on the one hand, an ideologically engaged, radical minority core, including men from all classes but increasingly more representatives of the *raznochintsy*, and which was struggling for "hegemony"; on the other, a group of submerged gentry intellectuals who represented the nation's intellectual elite in the more universal, western sense of the word. Regardless of its aristocratic origins (*Sovremennik* was after all founded by Pushkin), the journal was gradually overpowered by its "revolutionary democratic" faction and exhibited the fissure between the traditional intelligentsia, Western-style intellectuals, and a newer group of more militant and socially oriented literati of "various ranks," a group that gradually usurped the title "intelligentsia."[19]

Closer to the *raznochintsy* in his social background, Chekhov clearly gravitated to the others in his artistic sensibility and overall outlook. Conceding that the era of the sixties was "sacred," Chekhov at the same time criticized what it came to represent among epigones and zealots. What Chekhov clearly objected to were not particular ideas but ideas turned into ideology; not ideals, but the fanaticism with which these ideals were imposed on others—that is, tendencies that became prominent among the radical intelligentsia in the aftermath of the sixties.

The Intelligentsia and the Question of Culture

With great disapproval Chekhov observed that the radical Russian intelligentsia frequently opposed not only Western intellectuals but also traditional culture in general. Unlike the radical and liberal intelligentsia of his time, Chekhov believed that the genuine intelligentsia and culture must be inseparable. Moreover, the main task of the intelligentsia as Chekhov sees it should be precisely the defense of culture and integration of culture into everyday life. Thus the quality of being a member of the intelligentsia—*intelligentnost'*—is identified in Chekhov's usage with culture, good manners, and attention to ethics. In fact, originally, those who could be considered members of the intelligentsia, even when the term had not yet entered into wide circulation, were preoccupied primarily with problems of education, enlightenment, and culture (note that the latter term also became widely deployed only later in the 1860s).[20] The educated elite of the first third of the 19th century considered

---

19 The very way the journal formulated their differences with Turgenev and his group and explained the split between them delineates the ideological tendency of the group that constituted the intelligentsia as later understood by Fedotov and others: "Regretting the loss of their cooperation, the editors, however, did not want . . . to sacrifice the main ideas of the publication, which seem to it fair and honest, and the service to which attracts and will attract new, fresh figures to it." We see how they put the notion of "service" to "ideas" at the center of their concerns. See "Zhurnal Sovremennik (1847–1866)," Russkaia literatura XIX veka, http://russkay-literatura.ru/zhurnalistika-xix-veka/66-zhurnal-sovremennik-1847-1866.html.

20 Moreover, the very word "culture" came into use in Russia rather late. As noted by scholars, it first appears only in the mid-1830s. The dictionary of I. Renofants in 1837 (*Pocket Book for Lovers of Reading Russian Books, Newspapers, and Magazines*) distinguishes two meanings: "arable farming, agriculture" and "education." See P. Chernykh, *Istoriko-etimologicheskii slovar' sovremennogo iazyka* (Moscow: Russkii iazyk, 1999), 453. Even Vladimir Dal's dictionary of

enlightenment its main task and engaged with liberal ideas, but did not necessarily oppose political powers and undoubtedly was not characterized by "rootlessness." The intellectual elite was radicalized only in the 1860s, when the term "intelligentsia" became widely propagated. Paradoxically, interest in the concept of culture and wide circulation of the term arose at about the same time, simultaneously with social change within the Russian educated classes and the emergence of the intelligentsia as a distinct social group. We may recall that Boborykin merged these two terms in his definition of the intelligentsia as people "of superior intellectual and ethical culture." However, gradually a small but vocal part of the intelligentsia started to oppose itself to merely educated people and even occasionally expressed animosity to culture. Thus, an older contemporary of Chekhov, Piotr Kropotkin, ruminating on new trends within the intelligentsia, observed that "Nihilism first of all declared a war on the so-called conventional lies of cultured life."[21] By contrast, Chekhov repeatedly identifies *intelligentnost'* with culture.[22] The intelligentsia's main task, according to Chekhov, is the defense of culture, which according to him merges moral and aesthetic values. Frequently criticizing his brothers, as well as many other members of the intelligentsia, for their lack of culture, and lamenting Russian disrespect for formal and aesthetic aspects of life, which he considered integral parts of culture and *intelligentnost'*, he expressed admiration for Western culture, good manners, and the overall refinement characteristic of European life.[23] Chekhov's feuilleton "In Moscow" (1891),

---

1866 marked the term "culture" as "French," and its first meaning is related to agriculture, while only the second meaning is "education, intellectual and moral." This suggests that up to the sixties the word's second meaning was not widespread. Although Russians knew this word in its Latin, German, or French variants, the category of culture was not in the spotlight, and therefore was not reflected accordingly in the lexicon. As L. A. Sugai notes, the word is not found in Dobrolyubov, Pisarev, or Chernyshevsky; see L. A. Sugai, "Terminy 'kul'tura', 'tsivilizatsiia' i 'prosveshcheniie' v Rossii nachala veka (Vellanskii, Pushkin, Gogol', simvolisty)," Smekni, http://mirznanii.com/a/131047/terminy-kultura-tsivilizatsiya-i-prosveshchenie-v-rossii-xix-nachala-xx-veka-vellanskiy-pushkin-gogol-simvolisty. However, it is precisely from the end of the 1860s and 1870s, and especially in the 1880s—the years of Chekhov's formation—that the concept of "culture" finally becomes widespread.

21 Petr Kropotkin, *Zapiski revoliutsionera* (Moscow: Moskovskii rabochii, 1988), 283–285.
22 Cf. "The passengers in the train speak about commerce, new singers, about Franco-Russian sympathies; one feels everywhere a lovely, cultured, enlightened (*intelligentnaia*) buoyant life" ("The Duel"). Writing from Nice, he praises French culture and refined manners (Chekhov, *Polnoe sobranie*, vol. P7, 98, 64). Both in his letters and in his fiction, the word "culture" features prominently and plays an important role in Chekhov's criticism of the intelligentsia's lack of culture. (See "Ariadne," "House with a Mezzanine," "The Duel," "Three Years," "My Life," among many other texts).
23 For more detail on the problem of culture, see S. Evdokimova, "Chekhov i problema kul'tury," in *Izuchenie chekhovskogo naslediia na rubezhe vekov: vzgliad iz XXI stoletiia (Materialy XXXVIII*

which as he explained was intended "to depict the Moscow *intelligent* in a few strokes," parodies the Russian *intelligent*'s complete lack of culture, education, and respect for the aesthetic aspects of life: "Because I know nothing, I am completely uncultured . . . nothing offends my sense of aesthetics."[24] This feuilleton could be quoted almost in its entirety as a biting parody of the type of *intelligent* who is utterly uncultured, that is, who lacks *intelligentnost'*. Connecting the notion of culture to the concept of cultivation, education, and formation in general, Chekhov frequently uses this term in its initial etymological sense, referring to agriculture, as well as in its secondary meaning related to education and cultivation of the senses. Culture for Chekhov implies a perpetual struggle with wild untamed nature and with all forms of barbarism. The narrator of "In Moscow" implicitly suggests the tasks of the intelligentsia as combining education, good manners, skills, hygiene, and other achievements of European civilization. Admitting his moral and aesthetic flaws, this Moscow *intelligent* acknowledges the superiority of European culture and longs to bring the Russian *intelligent* closer to European models: "And yet I could study and get to know everything; if I liberated myself from my 'Asian' quality, I could learn and love European culture, trade, crafts, agriculture, literature, music, painting, architecture, hygiene."[25] Sensitive to the split within the intelligentsia and its alienation from culture, Chekhov advocated for cultivation of the soul, respect for the aesthetic aspect of life and a code of behavior that he considered an integral part of true *intelligentnost'*.[26] Firmly believing that as a carrier of culture and enlightenment the true intelligentsia was supposed to be universal, Chekhov strove to "cultivate" the Russian *intelligent* and bring him closer to the Western educated classes.

---

mezhdunarodnoi konferentsii "Chekhovskie chteniia v Ialte," 2017), ed. O. O. Pernatskaia (Simferopol: Arial, 2019), 13–31.
24 Chekhov, *Polnoe sobranie*, vol. S7, 501–502.
25 Ibid., vol. S7, 506–507. Multiple examples in Chekhov's prose and letters reveal his concern for the lack of culture among the new intelligentsia. Cf., for example, how in "My Life" Dr. Blagovo complains about the lack of culture among the intelligentsia: "There is no end to what the new literature has invented! It has invented intelligentsia workers in the country. . . . Cultured life has not yet begun among us. There's the same savagery, the same uniform boorishness, the same triviality, as five hundred years ago. . . . Civilized life has not yet begun among us. Old people console themselves by making out that if there is nothing now, there was something in the forties or the sixties. . . . The beginning of Russia was in 862, but the beginning of cultured Russia has not come yet" (ibid., vol. S9, 230, 258).
26 On the code of behavior that Chekhov advocates, see Evdokimova, "Russian Binaries."

"All the European Intelligentsia": The Responsibility of Intellectuals[27]

Chekhov's understanding of the intelligentsia's role in society was not limited to the propagation of culture. Although he emphatically rejected those "toads and crocodiles" among the intelligentsia who strove for hegemony and the advancement of a particular ideology, he did not advocate indifferentism and withdrawal from a civic stance. Rather his models were those members of educated classes—both Russian and Western—who did not hesitate to interfere and publicly denounce injustice: Voltaire, Dr. Friedrich Haass (known as the "holy doctor of Moscow"), Herzen, Korolenko, and Zola.

Indeed, for Chekhov the notion of the genuine, true intelligentsia—as opposed to the intelligentsia in the narrow sense of the word—was not a purely Russian phenomenon, but a universal one. Moreover, Chekhov's concept of the responsibility of the intelligentsia was, in fact, very close to what emerged in the 1890s in Europe in connection with the notorious Dreyfus affair. Chekhov praises Zola's nobility and French writers for their support of Dreyfus ("France is a wonderful country, and its writers are wonderful").[28] In a frequently quoted letter to Suvorin of February 6 (18), 1898, from Nice, Chekhov not only outlines his uncompromised position in respect to the Dreyfus affair and his admiration for Zola's courageous open letter of protest, but also comments on the moral and civic responsibilities of the educated classes in general. According to Chekhov, "the best people, leading the nation" must respond to injustices and persecutions, as did Zola and before him Voltaire, who interfered in the Jean Calas case, achieving his posthumous exoneration through a public campaign, and—in the Russian context—as did the philanthropist and humanist of German origin, Dr. Haass, advocating on behalf of prisoners of the Russian empire, and as did Vladimir Korolenko, defending the Udmurt minority peasants of the Stary Multan village, who were falsely accused of committing ritual murders (in the so-called Multan Affair):

> Yes, Zola is not Voltaire, and we are all not Voltaires, but there are such circumstances in life when the reproach that we are not Voltaires is least appropriate. Remember Korolenko, who

---

27 "The Responsibility of the Intellectual" is Noam Chomsky's famous essay, written during the Vietnam War, which pertains to the tradition of protest by public intellectuals described in this section of my essay.
28 Chekhov, *Polnoe sobranie*, P7, 143.

defended the Multan pagans and saved them from hard labor. Dr. Haass is also not Voltaire, and yet his wonderful life passed and ended quite happily.[29]

Chekhov emphasizes the responsibility of the intelligentsia to fight against injustices, but insists on the need to abstain from political hatreds and engagements: "The business of writers is not to blame, not to prosecute, but to intercede ... They will say: what about politics? the interests of the state? But great writers and artists should only be involved in politics to the extent that they have to defend themselves against it."[30] His position vis-à-vis the intelligentsia is very close to the way intellectuals as a group were interpreted in France in the late 19th century. Significantly, writing to Fyodor Batyushkov from Nice in 1898, Chekhov not only expresses his support of Dreyfus and Zola, but also does not differentiate between the French and Russian intelligentsia so long as in both cases the educated classes defend truth and justice. In fact, he refers to French intellectuals as intelligentsia:

> Here [in France] Zola and Dreyfus are at the center of discussions. The majority of the intelligentsia is on Zola's side and believes in Dreyfus's innocence.... Every Frenchman feels that, thank God, there is still justice in the world, and if someone innocent is accused then there are those who would intervene on his behalf.[31]

A month later he reiterates his opinion about Zola's public role: "You ask my opinion about Zola and his trial. My primary consideration is evidence: all the European intelligentsia is on his side, while all that is repulsive and dubious is against him."[32] Clearly, for Chekhov, the intelligentsia in its best aspirations and its service to the ideas of enlightenment, culture, and justice, is not a uniquely Russian phenomenon, but a universal one.

Who then are those to whom Chekhov refers as "all the European intelligentsia" and of whom he considers himself a part? Russian and Western authors of the myth of the uniqueness of the Russian intelligentsia insist that the concept of the intelligentsia was borrowed by Western countries from Russia and that

---

29 Ibid., vol. P7, 167–168.
30 Ibid., vol. P7, 168.
31 Ibid., vol. P7, 157.
32 Ibid., vol. P7, 173.

it was distinct from intellectuals.[33] Claiming that the Russian intelligentsia was "the *largest* single *Russian contribution* to social change in the *world*," Isaiah Berlin explains this "contribution" in this way:

> The concept of intelligentsia must not be confused with the notion of intellectuals. Its members thought of themselves as united by something more than mere interest in ideas; they conceived themselves as being a dedicated order, almost a secular priesthood, devoted to the spreading of a specific attitude to life, something like a gospel."[34]

However, this widely accepted view is not completely accurate as it takes into account only a small faction within the intelligentsia and identifies that part with the whole. The intelligentsia thinking of itself as united by "something more than mere interest in ideas" was not a uniquely Russian phenomenon among European intellectual elites. Many French intellectuals at the end of the nineteenth century, both liberal and conservative, pointed out that the French educated classes were inspired by the ideas of the Great French Revolution, and became deeply politicized especially after 1848. The Russian intelligentsia's oppositionism, considered its unique feature, also at least in part, grew out of the spirit of Romanticism and infatuation with the ideals of the French Revolution, which influenced nineteenth-century French writers no less than their Russian counterparts.[35]

---

33 Thus, Isaiah Berlin asserts that "the word 'intelligentsia,' like the concept, is of Russian origin and was invented sometime in the 1860s or 1870s. It did not mean simply educated persons. It certainly did not mean merely intellectuals as such. . . . Russian society in the nineteenth century was, to use a contemporary term, underdeveloped. It was a backward society, consisting to a vast extent of a mass of illiterate, semi-starved peasants, a certain number of bureaucrats holding them down with various degrees of efficiency, and a small class of persons who had received sufficient education either to be officials, administers or clerks, or to form that minimum number of lawyers, doctors, land surveyors and teachers without which even so backward a mass as the Russians could scarcely be expected to get on" (Isaiah Berlin, *The Power of Ideas* [Princeton, NJ: Princeton UP, 2000], 103).
34 Isaiah Berlin, ed., *Russian Thinkers* (New York: Viking Press, 1978), 115–116.
35 French conservative and nationalist thinkers described the "intellectuals" as an elite group of educated classes who opposed themselves to the state and commented on it as a phenomenon that developed in the aftermath of the French revolution. For example, Charles Maurras, an influential reactionary and monarchist French writer, already refers to the term "intelligentsia" (*l'intelligence*) as "used in St. Petersburg" in his book *L'avenir de l'intelligence* (1904/1905), as a phenomenon characteristic of the last two centuries in the history of French writers: "Tout d'abord, précisons. Nous parlons de l'Intelligence, comme on en parle à Saint-Pétersbourg, du métier, de la profession, du parti de l'Intelligence. Il ne s'agit donc pas de l'influence que peut,

It is also important to keep in mind that, although the Russian intelligentsia as a distinct group may have emerged in the 1860s (or even before, as some scholars argue), the theoretical conceptualization of the role of the intelligentsia/intellectuals in both Russia and France occurs at approximately the same time, that is, in the period from 1890s to 1920s. In France—even prior to the Russian debates about the intelligentsia that culminated in the publication of *Landmarks*—passionate polemics emerged during the Dreyfus Affair, which stimulated the educated classes' self-awareness as a group and led to fiery discussions, both left and right, of intellectuals' role in public life. The French concept of "intellectuals" as a group characterized by a particular set of ideas and dedication to higher ideals fully crystallized toward the end of 1890s. French historians Pascal Ory and Jean-François Sirinelli define the intellectuals in terms that could as well be applied to the intelligentsia: "a man of culture, creator or mediator, placed in the situation of a man of politics, producer or consumer of ideology."[36] They note that although the word "intellectual" was not extensively employed as a noun in French until the 1890s, it became widely accepted after Zola's famous open letter "J'accuse . . . !" published in *L'Aurore* (the Paris daily newspaper) in connection with the Dreyfus Affair. Scholars agree that the intellectual, in a modern sense, was born in the course of the Dreyfus Affair and the public uproar around it.[37] It has also been said that Zola was responsible for the figure of the intellectual, capable somehow of bringing an artist and writer closer to those with direct access to political decision-making. An intellectual becomes someone who shapes public opinion. Christophe Charles, one of the authors outlining this process, describes the period between 1880 and 1900 as a turning point in the course of the history of the intellectual,

---

en tout temps, acquérir par sa puissance l'intelligence d'un lettré, poète, orateur, philosophe. . . . Nous traiterons du *genre* écrivain. . . . Nous traitons de la destinée commune aux hommes de lettres, du sort de leur corporation et du lustre que lui valut le travail des deux derniers siècles" (Charles Maurras, *L'avenir de l'intelligence* [Paris: Nouvelle librairie nationale, 1925], 17–19. Maurras's discussion of the intelligentsia makes an interesting counterpart to *Landmarks*. Though Maurras suggests he is using the term "intelligentsia" as it is used in Russia, he insists that the concept itself (not to be confused with the term) has existed in France for at least two centuries and that it implies a particular group of writers, even a sort of "corporation." A closer look at Maurras's arguments suggests that the differences in perception of Russian and French "intelligentsias" might not have been as prominent as most scholars, including Berlin, tend to claim. The critique of the intelligentsia by French conservatives, such as Maurras, shares many points with criticism of the intelligentsia by the authors of *Landmarks*.

36 Pascal Ory and Jean-François Sirinelli, *Les intellectuels en France, de l'affaire Dreyfus à nos jours* (Paris: Armand Colin, 1986), 10.

37 There is a vast literature on the subject of French intellectuals and their origin as a distinct group. See in particular, among many others, a classical study by Christophe Charles, *Naissance des 'intellectuels', 1880–1900* (Paris: Les Éditions Minuit, 1990), 19–65.

culminating in the moment of particular mobilization among writers, journalists, students, academics and politicians, lending support to the Dreyfusard cause. The day after Zola's "J'accuse . . . !" was published, George Clemenceau printed in *L'Aurore* a collective petition in support of Dreyfus signed by a large group of eminent writers, artists, scholars, and academics, under the headline "Manifestes des intellectuels," and shortly after he referred to them as "all these intellectuals coming from all corners of the horizon who united around an idea." Clemenceau invested the term with a particular ideological connotation, which was quickly picked up by arch-conservative anti-Dreyfusard Maurice Barrès (1862–1923); Barrès vehemently attacked those *intellectuels* and his rebuke, "La protestation des intellectuels," led to wide deployment of the term from both left and right.[38] Barrès specifically attacked the concept of intellectuals as a group "united around an idea," in Clemenceau's approving definition, and wrote: "the intellectual defines himself as a cultured individual, but without a mandate, who claims to apply his intelligence to effectively resolve the various cases pertaining to the Dreyfus Affair."[39] Like Boborykin, who insisted that he endowed the German term *die Intelligenz* with a particular ethical and ideological connotation, Barrès detects ideological undertones in the term "intellectuals," who, according to him, usurp the right of fair judgment by pretending to be a group of high-minded individuals. Thus, with on the one hand the joint efforts of such antagonistic figures as Zola and Clemenceau, who introduced the term, and on the other Barrès, who publicized the term, the term "intellectual" acquired distinct ideological connotations, referring not so much to intellectual properties as to a collective of people unified by dedication to a particular ideal.[40] Barrès

---

38 Barrès picked up on Clemenceau's use of the term but used it against the signatories and accused them of uprootedness. He also mocked Clemenceau's use of the term as a noun rather than an adjective, arguing that it was against the rules of the French language. Although the adjective *intellectuel* had obviously been used before, the noun (in both French and English) was not. However, in fact, according to J. Julliard and M. Winock, the term had occurred before in Guy de Maupassant and was used for the first time by Saint-Simon in *Du système industriel* (1821): "D'une part, j'invite les intellectuels positifs à s'unir et à combiner leurs forces pour faire une attaque générale et définitive aux préjugés, en commençant par l'organisation du système industriel" (Henri Saint-Simon, *Œuvres*, vol. 3 [Paris: Anthropos, 1966], 189–191, quoted in Jacques Julliard and Michel Winock, eds., *Dictionnaire des intellectuels français* [Paris: Le Seuil, 1996], 14). In this sense the term signifies individuals distinguished by their intellectual properties and capable of serving the responsibilities of social utopia. Yet only in the course of the Dreyfus affair, and to a large extent due to Barrès's attention to the term, did it become fashionable, albeit first employed in a derogatory way.
39 Mauris Barrès, *Scènes et doctrines du nationalisme* (Paris: Elibron), 44.
40 Just as Boborykin might be considered the godfather of the term "intelligentsia," the godfathers of the term "intellectual" were Clemenceau and Boborykin's younger French contemporary, Barrès. One a moderate liberal and westernizer, the other a staunch conservative and

might have inadvertently popularized the term (which for him had emphatically negative connotations), but it was Zola who stimulated ideological and political unity among the educated French elite, leading to the concept of intellectuals as a group. It is undoubtedly this group that Chekhov refers to as "all the European intelligentsia." This context is crucial to understanding Chekhov's unique view of the intelligentsia's role and responsibility.

By the end of the nineteenth century, important parallels emerge in Russia and Europe in the formation of the terms "intelligentsia" and "intellectuals" and the polemics surrounding the concepts these terms defined. Similar to Russian claims that conservative writers could not be considered members of the intelligentsia, some French leftist intellectuals such as Jean Jaurès (1859–1914) would also insist that a right-wing intellectual is almost a contradiction in terms. Regardless of the term used to refer to them ("intellectuals," "the intelligentsia", *les clercs*) from the end of nineteenth century, in both Russia and France intellectuals were perceived as a group endowed with a certain collective responsibility, and this responsibility was not simply a matter of personal opinion. Intellectuals start thinking about their particular function and their role in society. Both the Russian intelligentsia and French intellectuals found their ardent defenders, as well as vehement detractors and critics, who blamed them for "rootlessness," cosmopolitanism, opposition to the state, and party mentality. In both cases there was debate about whether an *intelligent* or an intellectual was supposed to be motivated by a particular ideology or by universal values.

I will conclude my discussion of Chekhov's interpretation of the intelligentsia with a brief reference to one of Chekhov's French contemporaries, the devoted Dreyfusard Julien Benda (1867–1956), whose position was in many ways similar to Chekhov's. In his influential book *La trahison des clercs* (published only in 1927), Benda commented on the particular role of the intelligentsia (to whom he refers as "clerks") as people with the duty and responsibility to

---

nationalist, Boborykin and Barrès had little in common in their literary, social, and political orientations. Yet, ironically, both were responsible for popularizing the terms "intelligentsia" and "intellectuals," respectively. Neither of them "invented" these terms, but both facilitated their wide circulation, albeit from drastically different ideological positions: Boborykin, from the liberal camp, introduced the term "intelligentsia" approvingly, referring to its particular lofty role in society, while Barrès, from the far right, used the term "intellectuals" disparagingly and mocked their "elitism" and disconnectedness from the national soil.

It is interesting that Russian and French criticism of the intelligentsia/intellectuals also shares many common features, especially the notion of presumed "rootlessness" and separation from national interests. Much the way some conservative critics of the intellectuals in France, such as Barrès and Charles Maurras, criticized the intellectuals for their opposition to the state, many authors of *Landmarks* blamed the Russian intelligentsia for "rootlessness" and defined it through its opposition to power and the official state.

serve the ideals of reason and higher spiritual values. He insists that the Dreyfus Affair marked not the "birth" of the intellectual, but rather the culmination of a process that he associated with Enlightenment ideals. Not unlike his Russian counterparts discussing the high calling of the intelligentsia, Benda spoke about the strict moral demands that their vocation as intellectuals imposed. However, like Chekhov, he believed the intellectuals betrayed their service to the values of universal humanity inherited from the Enlightenment in favor of political hatreds, which he saw as a distortion of the spirit of the Dreyfusard intellectuals. It is no coincidence that Benda prefers to use the term "clerks" in "the medieval sense," that is, referring to intellectuals as a group united by their dedication to universal values rather than to the newly emerging politicized groups that let political commitment determine their understanding of the intellectual vocation as such, thus discarding the ideal of disinterestedness and the universality of truth.[41] Ethnic and political hatreds, according to Benda, contaminated the intellectual's high vocation. Like Chekhov, he makes clear that he does not view true intellectuals as indifferentists who avoid a public role and distinct political stance. However, he insists that their social awareness stems not from nationalist group passions but from dedication to the universal values of reason and of the Enlightenment:

> [W]hen Voltaire fought for the Calas family; when Zola and Duclaux came forward to take part in a celebrated lawsuit (the Dreyfus affair); all these "clerks" were carrying out their functions as "clerks" in the fullest and noblest manner. They were the officiants of abstract justice and were sullied with no passion for a worldly object.[42]

We see that Benda's model intellectuals (who include Voltaire and Zola) and Chekhov's models of the true intelligentsia (Voltaire, Dr. Haass, Korolenko,

---

41 Serving the high goal of universal values, intellectuals of past centuries were able to mitigate evil ("It may be said that thanks to the 'clerks,' humanity did evil for two thousand years but honored good"), but the adoption of "political passions" led to corrosion of this lofty cause. Benda specifically attacks right wing nationalists and conservatives for their "political passions" betraying universal values: "Today, if we mention Mommsen, Treitschke, Ostwald, Brunetière, Barrès, Lemaître, Péguy, Maurras, D'Annunzio, Kipling, we have to admit that the 'clerks' now exercise political passions with all the characteristics of passion—the tendency to action, the thirst for immediate results, the exclusive preoccupation with the desired end, the scorn for argument, the excess, the hatred, the fixed ideas." Julien Benda, *The Treason of the Intellectuals* (*La trahison des clercs*) (New York: W. W. Norton & Company, 1969), 44, 46.
42 Ibid., 50–51.

Zola) are selected on a common principle: serving truth and justice. However, both resented militant groups within the intelligentsia who subordinated objective truth and universal values to narrow political goals. In one letter to Suvorin, Chekhov speaks about the need to rise above the particular and subjective for the sake of the universal in all spheres of life, be it religion, science, medicine, or literature: "The term 'tendentiousness' has at its foundation the inability of people to rise above the particulars."[43] Similarly, Benda denounces intellectuals taking parts in political passions at the expense of their primary goal of being guardians of universal justice, but he insists that the intellectual must intercede on behalf of abused truth. Such ideal intellectuals for him are Zola and the Dreyfusards.

A true intellectual, according to both Chekhov and Benda, is one who defends the truth, who stands firm in his fight against any kind of injustice, but who does so in a disinterested way. Absorbed by national passions, by blind patriotism, interests of the state or a struggle for hegemony, the modern intellectual becomes completely politicized. Trying to defend the vocation of the clerks as an expression of "disinterested intelligence," Benda—much like Chekhov—laments the contamination of art and even of philosophy, history, and criticism by ideology and political "passions." Chekhov criticized the "toads and crocodiles" of the radical but conformist Russian intelligentsia of *Russian Thought*, as well as conservatives like the contributors to Suvorin's *New Times*. Benda denounced the betrayal of the intellectuals by conservative elements that surfaced during the Dreyfus Affair. Both of them deplored the politicization of the educated elite that would lead to horrific events in Russia and Europe in the not-so-distant future. Although each country and each country's intelligentsia had its own history, Chekhov's case suggests that the boundary separating the Russian intelligentsia and European intellectuals is rather artificial and fluid—Chekhov was both an intellectual and a member of the intelligentsia in the broad European sense of the word.

---

43 Chekhov, *Polnoe sobranie*, vol. P3, 37. Referring to Jesus's famous dictum "Love thy neighbor as thyself," Chekhov makes an insightful comment about the significance of paying attention to general and universal aspects rather than picking out "particulars." The neighbor, he argues, refers to the universal, while an "enemy" is merely a particular. "Christ, standing above enemies and not noticing them, was a courageous nature, even and broad-minded, and he hardly attached importance to the difference, which is in the particulars of the concept of 'neighbor'... In medicine this is similar. He who does not know how to think medically, but judges by particulars, denies medicine" (ibid., vol. P3, 36–37).

Bibliography

Barrès, Maurice. *Scènes et doctrines du nationalisme*. Paris: Elibron, 2007.

Benda, Julien. *The Treason of the Intellectuals* (*La trahison des clercs*). New York: W. W. Norton & Company, 1969.

Berdiaev, Nikolai N. "Filosofskaia istina i intelligentskaia pravda." In *Vekhi: Sbornik statei o russkoi intelligentsii*, 1–22. Moscow: M. V. Sablin, 1909.

Berlin, Isaiah, ed. *Russian Thinkers*. New York: Viking Press, 1978.

Berlin, Isaiah. *The Power of Ideas*. Princeton, NJ: Princeton UP, 2000.

Boborykin, P. "Podgnivshie 'Vekhi' (Konspekt publichnoi lektsii)." In *Vekhi: Pro et Contra, Antologiia*, edited by V. V. Sapov, 201–207. St. Petersburg: Izdatel'stvo russkogo khristianskogo gumanitarnogo instituta, 1998.

Charle, Christophe. *Naissance des "intellectuels," 1880–1900*. Paris: Les Editions de Minuit, 1990.

Chekhov, A. P. *Polnoe sobranie sochinenii i pisem*. Edited by N. F. Bel'chikov. 30 vols. Moscow: Nauka, 1974–1983.

Chernykh, P. *Istoriko-etimologicheskii slovar' sovremennogo iazyka*. Moscow: Russkii iazyk, 1999.

Evdokimova, S. "Chekhov i problema kul'tury." In *Izuchenie chekhovskogo naslediia na rubezhe vekov: Vzgliad Iz XXI stoletiia (Materialy XXXVIII mezhdunarodnoi konferentsii "Chekhovskie chteniia v Ialte," 2017)*, edited by O. O. Pernatskaia, 13–31. Simferopol: Arial, 2019.

———. "Russian Binaries and the Question of Culture: Chekhov's True Intelligent." In *Chekhov's Letters: Biography, Context, Poetics*, edited by Carol Apollonio and Radislav Lapushin, 173–192. Lanham: Lexington Books, 2018.

Julliard, Jacques, and Michel Winock, eds. *Dictionnaire des intellectuels français*. Paris: Le Seuil, 1996.

Karlinsky, Simon. *Anton Chekhov's Life and Thought: Selected Letters and Commentary*. Evanston: Northwestern UP, 1997.

Kataev, Vladimir. "Boborykin i Chekhov (K istorii poniatiia 'intelligentsiia' v russkoi literature)." In *Chekhov Plius . . . Predshestvenniki, sovremenniki, preemniki*. Moscow: Iazyki slavianskoi kul'tury, 2004.

Kropotkin, Petr. *Zapiski revoliutsionera*. Moscow: Moskovskii rabochii, 1988.

Lotman, Mikhail. "Intelligentsiia i svoboda (k analizu intelligentskogo diskursa)" [The intelligentsia and freedom: Toward an analysis of the intelligentsia's discourse]. In *Russkaia intelligentsiia i zapadnyi intellektualizm: Istoriia i tipologiia. Materialy mezhdunarodnoi konferentsii*, edited by B. A. Uspenskii, 122–150. Moscow: O.G.I., 1999.

Maurras, Charles. *L'avenir de l'intelligence*. Paris: Nouvelle librairie nationale, 1925.

Merezhkovskii, D. S. "Chekhov i Gor'kii." In *A. P. Chekhov. Pro et Contra*, edited by D. K. Bogatyrev, 692–672. St. Petersburg: Izdatel'stvo russkogo khristianskogo gumanitarnogo instituta, 2002.

Morson, Gary Saul. "The Intelligentsia and Its Critics." In *A Companion to Russian History*, edited by Abbott Gleason, 261–278. Chichester, UK: Wiley-Blackwell, 2009.

Ory, Pascal, and Jean-François Sirinelli. *Les intellectuels en France, de l'affaire Dreyfus à nos jours*. Paris: Armand Colin, 1986.

Pipes, Richard. "The Historical Evolution of the Russian Intelligentsia." In *The Russian Intelligentsia*, edited by Richard Pipes. New York: Columbia UP, 1961.

Saint-Simon, Henri. *Œuvres*. Vol. 3. Paris: Anthropos, 1966.

Sapov, V. V., ed. *Vekhi: Pro et Contra, Antologiia*. St. Petersburg: Izdatel'stvo russkogo khristianskogo gumanitarnogo instituta, 1998.

Sugai, L. A. "Terminy 'kul'tura', 'tsivilizatsiia' i 'prosveshcheniie' v Rossii nachala veka (Vellanskii, Pushkin, Gogol', simvolisty)." Smekni. Accessed May 10, 2024. https://smekni.com/a/131047/terminy-kultura-tsivilizatsiya-i-prosveshchenie-v-rossii-xix-nachala-xx-veka-vellanskiy-pushkin-gogol-simvolisty/.

Voloshin, Maksimilian. "Mysli o teatre." *Apollon* 5 (1910): 32–40.

"Zhurnal Sovremennik (1847–1866)." Russkaia literatura XIX veka. Accessed May 10, 2024. http://russkay-literatura.ru/zhurnalistika-xix-veka/66-zhurnal-sovremennik-1847-1866.html.

Part 3

THE TWENTIETH CENTURY

Merchants vs. the Intelligentsia: The Case of the Moscow Art Theatre[*]

Maria Ignatieva

"Just give them [the merchants, MI] a chance, and they will buy the intelligentsia one by one . . . " Anton Chekhov[1]

This chapter will reevaluate the role that two merchants, Konstantin Alekseev (Stanislavsky) and Savva Morozov, played in the creation and functioning of the Moscow Art Theatre between the years 1898 and 1905. The pre-1917 October Socialist Revolution Moscow Art Theatre has always been identified as the theatre of the Russian intelligentsia. It is the theater of Chekhov, Pushkin, Griboedov, Aleksei Tolstoy and Lev Tolstoy, Dostoevsky, Gorky, and Leonid Andreev. The fact that the Moscow Art Theatre as an institution was created by merchants' financial support is well known; however, the extent to which the cultural influence of the merchants affected and shaped the theater has not been investigated sufficiently. During the Soviet era of theatrical historiography, the role that Konstantin Alekseev-Stanislavsky (not in his role as an actor and director of the Art Theatre, indeed) and Savva Morozov[2] played *as merchants* in

---

[*] The spelling "theatre" is used throughout the article when referring to the Moscow Art Theatre, as this is part of its official name.
[1] A. Serebrov, *Vremia i liudi: Vospominaniia* [Time and people: Memoirs] (Moscow: Moskovskii Rabochii, 1960), 212.
[2] Tatyana Klevantseva, "Prominent Russians: Savva Morozov," Russiapedia, accessed June 24, 2024, https://russiapedia.rt.com/prominent-russians/art/savva-morozov/.

the creation and functioning of the Moscow Art Theatre (MAT) was narrowed down to their financial and organizational contributions.

In the years since the collapse of the Soviet Union, Russian researchers from different spheres have focused on the restoration and rehabilitation of the Russian merchants as a class and their contributions to various spheres of Russian life. Hundreds of books have been written, including serious monographs, about the role of merchants in literature, music, and art, and about their lifestyle. In theatre history, the most significant, eye-opening books include those by Galina Brodskaya, *Alekseev-Stanislavsky, Chekhov, and Others, from the Middle of the Nineteenth Century to 1898* and *Alekseev-Stanislavsky, Chekhov, and Others, from 1902 to the 1950s* (Agraf, 2000), and Olga Radishcheva's trilogy about Stanislavsky and Nemirovich-Danchenko's artistic relationships. Radishcheva has carefully examined Savva Morozov's role in the history of MAT up to Morozov's death in 1905. To illustrate Radishcheva's point of view, it would be important to outline two episodes that throw new light on the theatre history. The first episode took place during the early years of the Moscow Art Theatre and shows how essential the involvement of Savva Morozov, a merchant turned wealthy industrialist, was to the theatre and to Stanislavsky. When in 1900 Savva Morozov became one of the co-directors of the Art Theatre, Vladimir Nemirovich-Danchenko rebelled against both Morozov's new authority and Stanislavsky's unconditional support of him. Nemirovich-Danchenko gave Stanislavsky an ultimatum, demanding that he choose between the two, Nemirovich-Danchenko and Morozov. Stanislavsky's response to Nemirovich-Danchenko must have sounded startling: "Without you, I don't want to stay in this venture ... Without Morozov ... —I definitely cannot [stay]."[3] The second episode took place during the celebration of the theatre's twentieth anniversary, in 1928. Recalling the financial uncertainty of the Moscow Art Theatre's first years, Stanislavsky asked the audience to stand and observe a minute of silence in memory of Savva Morozov and his contribution to the theatre. In 1928, with all the top Soviet government officials present at the celebration, it was a challenge to the authorities, albeit perhaps not intended as such. Asking Bolsheviks to stand up in memory of a capitalist was not just daring but dangerous. This noble gesture placed Stanislavsky's life and those of his extended family members in jeopardy; some of them, as former merchants and thus enemies of the Soviet people, were already exiled, imprisoned, or killed. (His brother, Georgy, and Georgy's three sons had been executed in 1920.) Radishcheva connects "the

---

3 Irina Vinogradskaia, *Letopis' zhizni i tvorchestva Stanislavskogo* [Stanislavsky's life and times], 2nd ed., 4 vols. (Moscow: Khudozhestvennyi teatr, 2003), vol. 1, 280.

Morozov moment" with Stanislavsky's massive heart attack, which happened less than an hour after his speech and terminated his acting career.[4] Describing these two episodes, Radishcheva emphasizes Stanislavsky's noble striving to publicly recognize the role Morozov had played in the Moscow Art Theatre, even if it meant challenging the Soviet regime.

Soviet historiography (including theater historiography) always wrote favorably about individual merchants who had generously given their collections to the Soviet State, such as Pavel Tretyakov, Aleksei Bakhrushin, and Savva Mamontov, or who had helped the revolutionaries, as Savva Morozov did with financial support of the Bolsheviks. But those were the exceptions. Merchants and wealthy farmers (*kulaks*), just like the aristocracy and bourgeoisie, were not to be portrayed in a sympathetic light: they were ideological enemies, hostile to the proletariat and peasantry and not players for the team of socialist utopians. Konstantin Alekseev-Stanislavsky, a scion of the merchant dynasty of the Alekseevs,[5] developed into a theatrical and cultural icon in the Soviet Union despite his merchant origins, and his status as the icon of the great Russian realistic theatre was even sanctioned by Stalin. Nevertheless, Stanislavsky commemorated his childhood as a wealthy merchant's son in his memoirs *My Life in Art*. In the book, he described the Alekseevs' rich household, where children were given great opportunities to succeed in everything they did, be it dancing, fencing, acting, writing, music, or languages. It is important to remember that the book was written and published in the United States in 1924, when Stanislavsky was welcomed as an international theatrical authority who represented the great Russian culture. Stanislavsky's status as a legend, which was bolstered by the enthusiastic reception in America, allowed him to write freely about his background. Most likely, it would have been hard for him to write this book in Russia with many events still fresh in his memory: the complete expropriation of his family business, his own recent arrest and release, the accusations that he was an enemy of the Soviet state, newspapers' mockery of the Moscow Art Theatre, and uncertainty about its future. The book was published in Russian in 1926, and, after adding just a few facts in 1928, Stanislavsky never revised it.

Merchant in Russia traditionally meant more than a person who buys and sells: merchants were in trade, owners of factories and manufactures, financial negotiators, entrepreneurs, industrialists, and so on, and the word itself was

---

4   Olga Radishcheva, *Stanislavskii i Nemirovich-Danchenko: Istoriia teatral'nykh otnoshenii* [Stanislavsky and Nemirovich-Danchenko. A history of theater relationships], 3 vols. (Moscow: Artist. Rezhisser. Teatr, 1997), vol. 1, 3.
5   Evgeniia Gershkovich, "Moskovskaia dinastiia: Alekseevy-Chetverikovy," *Moskvich*, February 16, 2023, https://moskvichmag.ru/lyudi/moskovskaya-dinastiya-alekseevy-chetverikovy/.

associated with a wide economic activity. In the second half of the 19th century, the merchants' estate (*kupechestvo*) combined a patriarchal approach to life and love for tradition with a vibrant, dynamic striving for economic and social changes, and educated merchants established themselves as influential social newcomers. Moscow, the old capital of Imperial Russia, became an industrial, cultural, and ideological center of the merchantry, and the Moscow merchants formed a very special establishment. Unlike other merchants of Imperial Russia,

> They did not depend upon foreign capital and state orders to build their economic power.... The combination of their Great Russian ethnic stock and the almost exclusively indigenous character of their economic life supplied them with a rationalization of and a justification for their separateness and their mission.[6]

Among these wealthy merchants-industrialists, who became generous patrons of hospitals and orphanages, the arts and educational institutions, were members of the so-called *patrician circle* of the Moscow merchants, whose names are known to anyone even slightly familiar with Russian culture. These names (some already mentioned above) included the Morozovs, Bakhrushins, Tretyakovs, Mamontovs, Botkins, Khludovs, and, indeed, Alekseevs. Amongst the most-celebrated cultural institutions that were sponsored by their money are the Bakhrushin Theatre Museum, the Tretyakov Gallery, the Mamontov Opera, and, of course, the Moscow Art Theatre. Members of the Moscow patrician merchants' circle were interconnected in business, intermarried, and interrelated; their economic ties were strengthened through families. Merchants and their families, the new types of people in Russian society, were depicted in numerous plays by Aleksandr Ostrovsky, most familiar in translation being *The Storm* (sometimes *The Thunderstorm*, 1859), *Enough Stupidity in Every Wise Man* (1868), *The Forest* (1871), and *Without a Dowry* (1878). Ostrovsky's plays, successfully performed in both Imperial theatres, the Aleksandrinsky and the Maly, gave Russian theatre long-awaited national, realistic plays and new types of characters: the city and provincial merchants, lower- and upper-middle-class schemers and upstarts, and wealthy guardians of the Russian tradition of *Domostroi*. Dobrolyubov wrote well-known essays about Ostrovsky's plays ("The Dark Kingdom," 1859 and "A Ray of Light in the Dark Kingdom," 1860). Interestingly, many people soon forgot that the playwright's theatrical

---

6 Alfred J. Rieber, *Merchants and Entrepreneurs in Imperial Russia* (Chapel Hill: U of North Carolina Press, 1982), 135.

characters were not the same as the real people. Dobrolyubov, who described merchants living in "the dark kingdom," unintentionally coined the term that became popular lore to describe merchants in general. The *samodur*, describing the merchants' willful, stubbornly unreasonable behavior (it translates as "a petty tyrant," "a stubborn tyrant") was often added to the *dark kingdom*. There are several explanations for this. Merchant society was closed to outsiders, and Ostrovsky's realistic, multidimensional characters were perceived by theatre audiences as real people, and the plays—as study guides to merchants' lifestyle. However, the aforementioned essays were written not about the generation of Konstantin Alekseev and Savva Morozov, but about their fathers and grandfathers: when Dobrolyubov published his essays, the boys were not even born yet (Savva was born in 1862, Konstantin in 1863). In fact, Konstantin Stanislavsky's and Savva Morozov's upbringing followed the examples of the Russian aristocracy, with only one, but an essential exception: merchants' children were trained in the family businesses beginning when they were teenagers. Hence, the sons of the not-so-well educated Sergei Alekseev and Timofei Morozov, Konstantin Alekseev and Savva Morozov, knew foreign languages, were familiar with Western economy and culture, frequently travelled abroad, and experienced first-hand the fruits of contemporary European civilization. They were also eager to adopt, adapt, and use their knowledge of European technical and cultural advancements at home, in Russia, be it in industry or in arts and culture. But merchants' industrial and financial successes, especially as compared to the impoverished aristocracy and struggling intelligentsia, made Dobrolyubov's "definitions" very popular once again. The word *samodur* followed both Morozov and Stanislavsky their entire lives. The meaning of the word could be altered: for example, there could be a good *samodur* (when one gave millions to hospitals, schools, orphanages, art institutions, and other ventures) or a bad *samodur* (when Morozov bought the most expensive pieces of art to decorate his house). However, regardless, they would be *samodurs*. One explanation of this stigma lies in the fact that, although a foreign education and experience abroad widened their horizons, many remained faithful to the ideals, principles, and customs of their clans. Many of them were the Old Believers (the pre-Petrine wing of the Russian Orthodox church, often called *raskol'niki*), such as the Morozovs, the Tretyakovs, and the Shchukin family. Some others—like the Alekseevs—were not Old Believers but were still deeply religious, with religion at the foundation of their family life and ethics. Although these different wings of Russian Orthodox Christianity kept merchant clans from religious uniformity, it did not diminish their religious zeal and belief in the importance of religion in society. With the same singlemindedness, they believed in the high mission of the arts and the importance of their patronage, be it of an individual artist or of new ventures. The tension between the Russian intelligentsia, aristocracy, and educated merchants was gradually softening by the last quarter of the nineteenth century, but the merchants' big money and extravagant behavior could immediately trigger traditional name-calling, such as *samodury*, in response. Stanislavsky was correct in *My Life in Art*, saying that the borders between classes were blurring—in the 1870s, wealthy merchants' children were often placed in the same educational institutions as children of the Russian aristocracy: both Konstantin Alekseev and Savva Morozov studied (not in the same year) at the well-known private Pokrovskaya Gymnasium No. 4, alongside children of the aristocracy.[7] Although Konstantin Alekseev struggled in the gymnasium and transferred to the Lazarevsky Institute (which he left after the seventh year), Savva Morozov successfully finished the gymnasium, continued his education at Moscow University, and then was accepted at Cambridge University, in the United Kingdom, where he studied chemistry.

It would be important to mention that both Konstantin Alekseev and Savva Morozov had, since the age of twelve, worked in their fathers' factories as apprentices, learning the family's traditional craft firsthand. Morozov, while studying in Cambridge, investigated the specifics of manufacture at Manchester and Liverpool textile factories to incorporate it later into the family business. Both Morozov and Alekseev loved theatre and believed in its educational mission through entertainment. In 1896, already a successful entrepreneur, Savva Morozov (and his cousin) invested 200,000 rubles to build a theatre for the Morozov workers in Orekhovo-Zuevo. In 1897, when this wooden summer theatre was completed, Feodor Chaliapin sang at its opening.[8] In the same year, Konstantin Alekseev-Stanislavsky invited Savva Morozov to invest in the future Moscow Art Theatre. When Morozov informed his family about it, his mother, the head of the Morozov clan, approved of his new venture, saying that she had known Kostya Alekseev since his boyhood and could trust him unreservedly. Such was Savva Morozov's path towards the Moscow Art Theatre. As Alfred J. Rieber wrote about Russian merchants of the last quarter of the 19th century, "They claimed to place industry at the service of culture and, where possible, culture at the service of industry."[9] Savva Morozov was certainly one of them.

Konstantin Alekseev-Stanislavsky's path to the Moscow Art Theatre was different, because it came from his unrelenting passion for theatre since childhood

---

7 Anna Fedorets, *Savva Morozov* (Moscow: Molodaia gvardiia, 2013), 35.
8 Fedorets, *Savva Morozov*, 152.
9 Rieber, *Merchants and Entrepreneurs*, 170.

and was wholeheartedly supported by his parents: the children had their own theatre, specially built to satisfy their thirst to perform. The eighteen-year-old Alekseev became a full-time worker at his uncle's factory but continued performing and directing under the stage name of Stanislavsky, so as not to compromise the reputation of his clan. It took him seven years to create (with A. Fedotov) the Society of Art and Literature, and sixteen years to become a highly respected amateur actor and director, to the extent that he was invited to perform with professional actors at the Imperial Maly Theatre. A comparative overview of Konstantin Alekseev and Savva Morozov's careers suggests that their collaboration in the creation of the Moscow Art Theatre was almost inevitable. One trait in their personalities, though, was radically different: unlike the merchant Savva Morozov, Alekseev-Stanislavsky was an artist, and this shaped the outcome of their collaboration. In 1897, Stanislavsky and Vladimir Nemirovich-Danchenko (a theater critic, playwright, and theater pedagogue) petitioned the Moscow City Council to grant them a piece of land to build a new Public Theatre, with a yearly subsidy. Stanislavsky wrote that if the projected new theater were announced as a private venture, "Moscow would claim that my participation in a private enterprise . . . was nothing short of a merchant's craze, while if it is a Public theatre that means it would serve the higher purposes of the public enlightenment."[10] Not quite believing in government support (and rightly so, as the petition was not granted), Stanislavsky approached several members of his patrician merchant circle at the same time. Morozov was one of the industrialists he targeted. Not all representatives of the merchants' clans were enthusiastic. Aleksei Bakhrushin, for example, a well-known collector known for his passion for theatre, refused to invest, and we can only speculate as to why: most likely, Bakhrushin, while respecting Alekseev as a merchant and a talented theatre amateur, doubted his ability to become a professional actor and director. Perhaps Stanislavsky's dream of his own professional theatre could be compared to Pavel Tretyakov exhibiting a painting of his own at the Tretyakov gallery? Stanislavsky was so shocked by Bakhrushin's rejection that he almost cried from disappointment.[11] Unlike Bakhrushin, Savva and his brother Sergei Morozov were eager to invest and gave 5,000 rubles each. The group of merchant-founders established the new theater's unique organizational structure, which followed the industrial business model of a syndicate, not that of typical Russian private theater companies.

---

10 Vinogradskaia, *Letopis' zhizni i tvorchestva Stanislavskogo*, 203.
11 Vladimir Nemirovich-Danchenko, *Pis'ma*, 4 vols. (Moscow: Khudozhestvennyi teatr, 2003), 1:754.

> Thirteen sharers concluded an agreement on 10 April 1898....
> The enterprise was to belong to the sharers, not to the acting company, whose interests were represented by both co-founders (i.e., Stanislavsky and Nemirovich-Danchenko, M. I.).... The long-term aim, however, was to transfer control of the Theatre to the acting troupe itself.[12]

Nemirovich-Danchenko had no money to spare and, thus, was a shareholder who "in lieu of a financial contribution, was to provide professional literary, consulting, and administrative services."[13]

First called the Moscow Art Public All-Accessible Theatre, MAT opened on October 14, 1898. The new theater's first production, Aleksei Tolstoy's play *Tsar Fyodor Ioannovich*, received glorious reviews. *Shylock*, based on Shakespeare's *The Merchant of Venice*, premiered on October 21, 1898, and was harshly criticized. The critics immediately assumed that the person to blame was Alekseev-Stanislavsky because of his merchant origins. That would become a popular trend: while the MAT was establishing itself, negative aspects of its activity, either creative or administrational, would be blamed on the merchants involved; that is, Morozov and Alekseev-Stanislavsky. Stanislavsky's fault, in this case, was that he, as the director of the show, insisted that M. Darsky as Shylock speak with a heavy Jewish accent. Vlas Doroshevich, a critic and a writer, who, in just a few years, would change his attitude towards Stanislavsky and become a fervent defender, wrote a satirical pamphlet in the newspaper *Russkoe Slovo*. "I confess I like much better our 'gentlemen's' fathers, those Tit Titych Prutkovs, who only smashed mirrors but did not mess with Shakespeare."[14] Doroshevich's reasoning summarized the typical prejudices against merchants. But, in fact, Shylock's speaking with a Jewish accent was not something unheard-of on the Russian stage: Germans were played with a German accent, French characters with a French accent, and so on.

Not only the critics, but the MAT actors too mocked Stanislavsky's merchant's habits. His diaries and letters clearly indicate that he was used to it. Only once he was deeply hurt to find out that a person he worshipped, Anton Chekhov, also explained his artistic flaws by his merchant origins. Chekhov was a close friend of Nemirovich-Danchenko and allowed himself to write without

---

12 Nick Worrall, *The Moscow Art Theatre* (London: Routledge, 1996), 40.
13 Iurii Orlov, *Moskovskii khudozhestvennyi teatr, 1898–1917. Tvorchestvo. Organizatsiia. Ekonomika* (Moscow: RATI-GINIS, 2011), 54.
14 Olga Radishcheva, Iurii Vinogradov, and Ekaterina Shingareva, *Moskovskii khudozhestvennyi teatr v russkoi teatral'noi kritike 1898–1905* (Moscow: Artist. Rezhisser. Teatr, 2005), 46–47.

concealing his feelings in their correspondence. After reading reviews of *The Death of Ivan the Terrible* by A. Tolstoy, he wrote that "Alekseev should not have played Ivan the Terrible. It is not in his line. When he directs, he is an artist; when he acts, he looks like a young, rich merchant who decided to indulge himself in the art [of theater, MI]."[15] It was a merciless verdict. Chekhov's father, as we remember, was a déclassé Taganrog merchant; having overcome his own social origins, Chekhov became a symbol of the Russian intelligentsia. Still, in 1899 Chekhov refused to believe that Stanislavsky, too, could reach beyond the limitations of his milieu. Later Chekhov admired Stanislavsky's Astrov in *Uncle Vanya* and Vershinin in *The Three Sisters*. Nevertheless, his skepticism re-emerged during rehearsals of *The Cherry Orchard* in 1904. Stanislavsky did not and could not know that the co-founder of the Art Theatre, Nemirovich-Danchenko, in his letters to Chekhov and Olga Knipper, also complained about Stanislavsky's willfulness and stubbornness, typical, as he thought, of wealthy merchants. Nemirovich-Danchenko, who prided himself on being a member of the Russian intelligentsia, at the same time never completely shed his own prejudices against Stanislavsky's background. Even in 1936, while writing his memoirs *From the Past*, Nemirovich-Danchenko tried to figure out which was "the most essential part of Stanislavsky ... out of his four personalities: #1—an artist, #2—a merchant, #3—a child, #4—a wise man."[16] Obviously, to Nemirovich-Danchenko the merchant component remained one of the most essential parts of Stanislavsky's personality.

Yet Stanislavsky's views and habits, those of a merchant, contributed to the greatness of the Art Theatre. The Alekseevs, like many Russian merchants, knew how to work together as a family and with the family, in literal and metaphorical meanings of the word, and with the head of the family at the helm of a venture. Many family members were involved in the creation and functioning of the Moscow Art Theatre. Stanislavsky's wife, Maria Lilina, his brothers Vladimir, Georgy, and Boris, and his sisters Anna, Lyubov, and Zinaida, were all involved in the Moscow Art Theatre at different times and in various capacities. Lilina, besides acting, helped with costumes; Anna acted, Zinaida also acted, directed, and later became one of the best teachers of the Stanislavsky System; Vladimir assisted Stanislavsky and became a director of the musical theatre, Boris went to collect materials for *The Snow Maiden*, and so on.

Another striking similarity to the merchants' traditional establishments could be found in the fact that, from the start, the MAT was closed to outsiders, and

---

15 Radishcheva, *Stanislavskii i Nemirovich-Danchenko*, vol. 1, 94.
16 Ibid., vol. 1, 224.

especially to the press. As a result, in the style of many wealthy merchants, the MAT actors behaved like members of a sacred society, religious cult, and privileged sect, openly opposing themselves to other theater companies. The reasons for this "sect-like" isolation were different from those of the merchants: from the very beginning, Stanislavsky emphasized the idea of the theater's Promethean mission, where they were all serving the highest goals of enlightening and bringing the truth. Stanislavsky, like many merchants, was deeply religious, and since the theater was his second (or first?) home, he started the initial meeting of the troupe in Pushkino with a liturgical service. This was an extraordinary innovation: In traditional Christianity, theatre and religion were not on friendly terms. However, for Stanislavsky this ceremony signified the establishment of the highest goals of the theatre, serving humanity with religious fervor and devotion. But these innovations introduced by Stanislavsky, important as they were for the reformation of theatre as an institution, just emphasized Stanislavsky's difference from the rest of the group, and first and foremost from his co-founder, Nemirovich-Danchenko. Nemirovich-Danchenko belonged to the Russian intelligentsia, while Stanislavsky did not. The only other person in the theatre who grasped Stanislavsky's ways of life was another merchant, Savva Morozov. As wealthy industrialists, they understood each other well, they did not need to sign financial documents: A merchant's word was a word of honor. (In A. Ostrovsky's play *Without a Dowry*, one of the merchants says at the end, "I gave my merchant's word!" Nothing could tempt a real merchant to break his promise.) For Stanislavsky, for Morozov, there was no such a thing as "dirty work": both men started as clerks at the lowest level in their family businesses, gradually moving up to the top. "I would like to recall our beloved S. T. Morozov, who was not only the co-director but also the electrician, who additionally worked in the dressing rooms . . . painted, installed light bulbs, worked in the shop on props . . ."[17] True: the first building that MAT rented was the Hermitage Theater, and Savva Morozov not only paid for its renovation and enlargement of its seating capacity in 1900 but also dressed in his overalls, like a hired worker, to help with the construction. That was part of the merchants' work ethic that both Stanislavsky and Morozov firmly believed in. On the other hand, Nemirovich-Danchenko, as a member of the intelligentsia, envisioned his duties as administrative and literary, as "delegating" and guiding rather than hammering nails and creating new sound machines.

---

17 Konstantin Stanislavskii, *Stat'i. Rechi. Besedy. Pis'ma* [Essays. Speeches. Conversations. Letters] (Moscow: Iskusstvo, 1953), 286.

"Further financial backing was sought during the summer of 1899 when, eventually, Savva Morozov advanced an additional 21,000 rubles and persuaded the remaining shareholders . . . to reengage themselves for sums equivalent to the initial outlay of each. The third season was to cost Morozov alone some 120,000 rubles," Nick Worrall writes.[18] Having invested a lot of money in the theatre, Morozov became its active and energetic co-director, both in word and in deed. He developed a taste for running MAT's daily life, despite not being a theatre practitioner and not understanding its artistic demands. The MAT daily conflicts at that time, which could be, perhaps, considered petty and non-essential, concealed the class struggle behind them: the views of the intelligentsia clashed with the merchants' ideas about theatre repertoire, artistic directions, and its resonance in Russian society. Once incident almost forced the co-directors to quit. In 1900, Morozov, without asking the two other co-directors, cancelled a few appointments previously scheduled by Nemirovich-Danchenko. Nemirovich-Danchenko was deeply offended. As he wrote in a letter to Stanislavsky, he did not want to be treated by Morozov as his literary secretary and demanded to be given equal rights with the other two co-directors *in writing*. He complained that, unlike Stanislavsky, he needed to have a signed document specifying his rights and responsibilities. Nemirovich-Danchenko emphasized, "The instructions are absolutely necessary. Without them, I refuse to grant Savva Timofeevich the right [to make a single-handed decision, MI]. I don't know him as well as I know you, and thus, I am not willing to put my blind trust in him."[19] It was the first clash of ambitions. Who was in charge? Two merchants or a playwright, a member of the Russian intelligentsia?

The nobleman Nemirovich-Danchenko, from Morozov's point of view, did not devote as much time and effort to the venture as he and Stanislavsky had. But neither Morozov nor Stanislavsky could compete with Nemirovich-Danchenko's literary education and experience. Anton Chekhov was on Nemirovich-Danchenko's side: "Morozov is a good man, but he should not be allowed to get too close to the essence of the venture. He judges acting, actors, and plays like a member of the audience but not like a theatre director."[20] Nemirovich-Danchenko, supported by Chekhov, tried to limit the power that "the merchant's money" gave Morozov: be it a small cancellation of auditions or the choice of plays, Nemirovich-Danchenko would not let Morozov make decisions without his approval. As a member of the intelligentsia,

---

18 Worrall, *The Moscow Art Theatre*, 41.
19 Nemirovich-Danchenko, *Pis'ma*, vol. 1, 328.
20 Radishcheva, *Stanislavskii i Nemirovich-Danchenko*, vol. 1, 208.

Nemirovich-Danchenko became the censor of his merchant-colleagues. Gorky admired Morozov's activities, too, when he saw "Morozov in the backstage areas, all covered in dust and on edge about the success of the play." But, unlike Gorky, Nemirovich-Danchenko was not ready "to forgive him all his factories . . . and to love him because he loves the art [of theatre, MI] selflessly, with all his greedy, mercantile, and *muzhik*'s soul" [meaning *peasant*'s, MI].[21]

Morozov's upbringing made him feel odd in the actors' milieu, and, as Nemirovich-Danchenko wrote, "while talking to theatre personnel, Morozov's . . . tone is a bit funny and awkward."[22] But Morozov steadily tried to promote his repertory line in the theatre, which, he thought, would bring the MAT great recognition. Neither of the plays he supported brought the theater either special public appreciation or profit. Among the plays that MAT produced, two were particularly important to Morozov. The first production was A. Ostrovsky's *The Snow Maiden*. Unlike Ostrovsky's other plays, *The Snow Maiden* does not give realistic portrayals of the *dark kingdom*, for which he was so well known to the public: he defined the genre of the play as "a spring fantasy." Ostrovsky created the pagan kingdom of the Berendeys, based on the folk legend of the snow maiden. Passionately observing pagan rituals, the Berendeys live in tune with and in fear of nature, expressing natural cycles through their rituals, songs, and dances. The Snow Maiden, the daughter of Spring and Father Frost, comes from the forests to live with the Berendeys, inadvertently causing conflicts in the Berendeys' well-established life. Dazzling the Berendey men by her beauty, the Snow Maiden remains cold and is unable to fall in love herself. She likes the shepherd and musician Lel best but still is unable to feel anything special. However, the same night when she finally falls in love and is consumed by desire, the morning sun, the Berendeys' god Yarilo, touches her, and the Snow Maiden evaporates.

In 1885, Savva Mamontov, another well-known merchant industrialist and great benefactor of artists, produced *The Snow Maiden* with scenery by V. Vasnetsov, K. Korovin, and I. Levitan. Morozov and Stanislavsky were both infatuated with the play and the idea of opening the 1900–1901 season with it. For Morozov, as for Savva Mamontov, *The Snow Maiden* embodied the quintessence of the Russian national spirit. The importance of this play in the MAT repertoire was understood differently by the two groups: Stanislavsky and Morozov—the merchants—were in one, with Nemirovich-Danchenko and Chekhov—the intelligentsia—in the other. For Morozov and Stanislavsky, the future of MAT

---

21 Fedorets, *Savva Morozov*, 248.
22 Nemirovich-Danchenko, *Pis'ma*, vol. 1, 349.

was tied to the "the Russian theme": in two of Aleksei Tolstoy's plays, *Tsar Fyodor Ioanovich* and *The Death of Ivan the Terrible*, and in Ostrovsky's *The Snow Maiden*. The other group, including Nemirovich-Danchenko and Anton Chekhov, believed that *The Snow Maiden* was an outdated piece and recommended a contemporary one, like those of Hauptmann, Ibsen, and Strindberg.[23] Morozov, firmly believing that it was the Russian theme that had defined and would define MAT's national identity, invested money in renovating the stage and enlarging the seating capacity of the auditorium. He paid for new electricity and lighting equipment and single-handedly installed them to facilitate the exquisite lighting effects the show required. The audience was mesmerized by Stanislavsky's directorial fantasy ("*The Snow Maiden* is the creation of a director with a colossal, boisterous, and exuberant fantasy")[24] but the production was not a success, and audience interest declined soon after the opening night. Therefore, Nemirovich-Danchenko and Chekhov, the intelligentsia, proved the merchants wrong: the latter did not sense "*l'air du temps*" as well as the former.

Another production, generously sponsored by Morozov, deepened the contradictions further. In 1901, Savva Morozov invested thousands of rubles in another production, Nemirovich-Danchenko's play *In Dreams*. Meyerhold thought that the play was "talentless, petty, and falsely pious."[25] At the same time, the scenery and costumes were elaborate, chic, and very expensive. Nadezhda Lamanova, the most fashionable Moscow couturier, who also made dresses for their Imperial highnesses, created the costumes for the female actors, among whom were Maria Andreeva, Olga Knipper, and Maria Lilina. Knipper wrote to Chekhov about the rehearsals of *In Dreams*: from one of her letters, we learn that the administration (in this case, Morozov) had paid 1,200 rubles for her character's three costumes.[26] It is important to keep in mind that at the time the yearly salaries of the second-best MAT actors were 1,200 to 1,500 rubles.[27] One review by Pack (Ashkenazi) was titled, "Merchants' Money Down the Drain!" The critic wrote: "Four acts … of the most excellent furniture."[28]

There was another reason for Morozov's support of the play: he was passionately in love with the MAT actress, Maria Andreeva. Against the policy of the

---

23 Radishcheva, *Stanislavskii i Nemirovich-Danchenko*, vol. 1, 111.
24 Radishcheva, Vinogradov, and Shingareva, *Moskovskii khudozhestvennyi teatr*, 133.
25 Radishcheva, *Stanislavskii i Nemirovich-Danchenko*, vol. 1, 128.
26 Nadezhda Lamanova, "Spektakl' 'V mechtakh' na stsene MKhT" [The play 'In dreams' on the scene of MAT], Virtual'nyi muzei Nadezhdy Lamanovoi, accessed June 24, 2024, https://lamanova.com/17_in-dreams.html.
27 Orlov, *Moskovskii khudozhestvennyi teatr*, 40.
28 Radishcheva, Vinogradov, and Shingareva, *Moskovskii khudozhestvennyi teatr*, 256–259.

Moscow Art Theatre, Morozov's actions were based on his favoritism, which was obvious to the entire troupe and the co-directors. "Morozov fell under her influence, like a schoolboy, like a simpleton," wrote Nemirovich-Danchenko.[29] Maria Andreeva, a well-known amateur actress before the Moscow Art Theatre opened, started her career as one of its female leads, but her popularity was gradually declining. There were various reasons behind this, but Morozov, who fanatically believed in her genius, strove to give Andreeva a chance to show herself as the MAT's prime actress and the most beautiful woman in Moscow. Ironically, Morozov's behavior in this case resembled that of merchants in Ostrovsky's plays, who would shower their kept actresses with gifts and beautiful clothes. Stanislavsky, on the other hand, found nothing wrong in Morozov's behavior: he saw Morozov's attitude towards Andreeva in a different light. He wrote, "Savva Timofeevich's feelings for you are exceptional. His devotion [to you, MI] is the kind for which people ruin their lives and make sacrifices."[30] While the show was unfavorably reviewed by the press, it gathered full houses, and Andreeva created a sensation as Princess Starocherkasskaya. "Ms. Andreeva played incredibly, [showing] the character's genuine depth, wittiness, and finesse. However, despite all that, her heroine is psychologically vague. And we have only the author to blame for that."[31] For the first time in the young theater's history, the production was booed. Despite bad reviews, *In Dreams* became a very fashionable show in Moscow, although not for the reasons the Moscow Art Theatre wanted to be remembered. In Spring 1902, during their annual tour to St. Petersburg, MAT presented *In Dreams* for Nicholas II and the Imperial family at the Mikhailovsky Theater.[32] Morozov, who had insisted that no aristocrats should be among the shareholders, must have felt the bitter irony of performing for the Tsar's family.

In 1902, Morozov initiated a reorganization of the MAT syndicate. "However, the changed conditions still required working capital.... Once again, Morozov took it upon himself to finance the company, lending various sums on credit for a three-year period."[33] Neither Vsevolod Meyerhold nor Aleksandr Sanin was included in the group of shareholders; obviously, Stanislavsky and Morozov had agreed upon this. When the new MAT arrangement became known to the press, Vlas Doroshevich wrote an angry pamphlet:

---

29 Nemirovich-Danchenko, *Pis'ma*, vol. 1, 491.
30 Konstantin Stanislavskii, *Sobranie sochinenii*, 9 vols. (Moscow: Iskusstvo, 1989–1999), vol. 7, 438.
31 Radishcheva, Vinogradov, and Shingareva, *Moskovskii khudozhestvennyi teatr*, 255.
32 Stanislavskii, *Sobranie sochinenii*, vol. 7, 440.
33 Worrall, *The Moscow Art Theatre*, 71.

> Hey, they have a merchant who is fixing electricity under the ceiling! He is the master of the bells! He is the boss of the electric wiring and the light bulbs! . . . But don't believe the merchant, even if he is sitting quietly under the ceiling of the theatre. Be afraid of a merchant even when he gives you those beautiful stage effects . . . ! Because, out of the blue, this very merchant decided: from now on, I want this theater to be a shareholding institution! . . . And then our merchant-benefactor, like a magpie in a children's tale, says: this one would have a share, and that one—would not. . . . Enough of this humiliation. Theatres, please stay away from the merchant-benefactors. Especially from the chintz barons.[34]

Morozov was, indeed, as Stanislavsky repeated in his letters and speeches many times, a *God-sent gift*. Not everyone felt the same, as we know, and disagreements between the three directors were happening more often, reaching a peak by 1904. In 1903, MAT finally received Chekhov's last play *The Cherry Orchard*. Chekhov recommended that Stanislavsky play Lopakhin, a merchant. Chekhov explained that Lopakhin was not a merchant in *the vulgar meaning* of the word. In his letter to Stanislavsky, he wrote that "yes, he is a merchant *but* a decent man in all senses who behaves *almost impeccably, intelligentsia-like*, not trivial, without any eccentricity, and it seems to me that this role is the central part in the play, and you could play it brilliantly" (my italics, MI).[35] Stanislavsky rehearsed Lopakhin for a little while but ended up playing Gaev, a member of the Russian nobility, and the role became one of the best in his career. Thus, there is another ironic twist in the situation: a merchant by birth and social status, Stanislavsky created the role of a nobleman who was being pushed out of his family estate by the merchant Lopakhin.

After Chekhov's death, during the directors' discussions of the coming 1904–1905 season, Morozov firmly disagreed with Nemirovich-Danchenko's suggestion that they include *Ivanov* in the MAT repertoire. In particular, he voiced his concern against Olga Knipper being cast as Sarah. He dared to criticize Chekhov's widow and the top actress, saying that "Knipper is too old for Sarah," but also that "she would fail it the way she failed Ranevskaya in *The Cherry Orchard*."[36] Morozov's shocking judgment was disregarded: *Ivanov* was included

---

34 Radishcheva, Vinogradov, and Shingareva, *Moskovskii khudozhestvennyi teatr*, 268.
35 Stanislavskii, *Sobranie sochinenii*, vol. 7, 676.
36 Nemirovich-Danchenko, *Pis'ma*, vol. 1, 533.

in the 1904–1905 season, and Knipper was cast as Sarah. As for Morozov, not only did he think that Chekhov's time had passed; he was also a great admirer of Maxim Gorky's plays. The success of *The Lower Depths* convinced him that Gorky could become the leading playwright at MAT. Without support of the whole MAT troupe, Morozov, Andreeva, and Gorky openly opposed the other two co-directors' artistic policy. Nemirovich-Danchenko begged Stanislavsky in a letter in October 1903, "Let's not allow our theatre to be devoured by those mad dogs!"[37] But the group failed to influence Stanislavsky's and Nemirovich-Danchenko's long-term decisions about the general artistic direction of the Moscow Art Theatre. At the end of 1903, Andreeva informed the administration that she would be leaving the theatre. In April 1904, Gorky read his new play, *The Summer Folks*. The whole troupe disliked his merciless portrayal of the Russian bourgeois intelligentsia. After Nemirovich-Danchenko wrote a review of the play with significant editorial suggestions, Gorky took a stand and replied that he would never return to the Moscow Art Theatre as long as Nemirovich-Danchenko remained one of the co-directors. Just as Stanislavsky had firmly supported Morozov in the conflict between Morozov and Nemirovcih-Danchenko during the first seasons, this time Stanislavsky defended Nemirovich-Danchenko against Gorky and Morozov. The first time, in order to save the theatre, he took the merchants' side; the second time, to save the spirit of the already famous theatre, he was with the intelligentsia, although clearly understanding that his position might ruin MAT financially. It almost did, but another merchant would rescue the theatre, further tying this ironic knot that was already so tightly tangled between merchant and intelligentsia influences upon the Moscow Art Theatre.

Shortly afterwards, Morozov resigned his position in the theatre and was no longer willing to pay for the rent and maintenance of the building. For the Moscow Art Theatre, his decision was a serious financial blow. Upon Stanislavsky and Nemirovich-Danchenko's request, Morozov generously left his share of 14,800 rubles for three more years, waiving his rights to be involved in any artistic decisions. In his parting address to the Moscow Art Theatre, Morozov wrote: "Please, take good care of Stanislavsky."[38]

In 1905 Savva Morozov committed suicide (according to the official version); his relatives, however, were always sure that he had been murdered by the Bolsheviks. It was a convenient coincidence, following Morozov's death, that his beneficiary Maria Andreeva, a Bolshevik agent whom Lenin called *a*

---

37 Ibid., 494.
38 Radishcheva, *Stanislavskii i Nemirovich-Danchenko*, vol. 1, 224.

phenomenon, gave most of the sum Morozov had left her (approximately sixty thousand rubles) to the Bolsheviks. Stanislavsky, more than anyone else, mourned Morozov's resignation and his death. The second time around the Moscow Art Theatre was also rescued by a merchant: this happened in Germany in 1906. Nikolai Tarasov, who had just inherited an enormous fortune from his relatives, Armenian gas and oil magnates, contributed 30,000 rubles and saved the theater from bankruptcy. Unlike Savva Morozov, who was a workaholic, Tarasov led the life of a refined dandy. He was later the co-founder of, and a contributing member (design, literary sketches, and parodies) to, the cabaret *The Bat*. At the age of twenty-eight, in 1910, Tarasov, too, committed suicide.

In conclusion: studies of the early history of the Moscow Art Theatre, the theatre of the Russian intelligentsia, show the great influence of Russian merchants upon its formation and functioning. The merchants' impact was not limited to the theatre's financial well-being but was connected to its overall artistic policies, successes, and failures. In 1904, Stanislavsky wrote that "we have to observe the rule that is most beneficial . . . for our theatre: artistic and humanistic matters always come first, while the financial (materialistic) . . . [comes] second."[39] However, the merchants, such as Stanislavsky himself, Savva Morozov, and later Nikolai Tarasov, made this highly unrealistic principle possible; in Soviet times, the Moscow Art Theatre became a State institution and was subsidized by the government. But behind the practical and artistic matters in the ideological struggle between members of the intelligentsia and merchants for the leading role in MAT, we should not miss the cultural processes described by Yury Lotman:

> Culture is a complicated entity, consisting of many strata, where each layer [of this entity, MI] functions at its own pace, and, therefore, any vertical dissection [of culture, MI] uncovers the simultaneous co-existence of each stratum's development.[40]

Studies of the subject *Merchants vs. The Intelligentsia* brought forward those existing cultural strata at different stages of their development, all of which would be abruptly stopped by the 1917 Socialist revolution.

---

39 Radishcheva, *Stanislavskii i Nemirovich-Danchenko*, vol. 1, 232.
40 Iurii Lotman, "Kul'tura i vzryv," in idem, *Semiosfera* (St. Petersburg: Iskusstvo, 2000), 21.

Bibliography

Fedorets, Anna. *Savva Morozov*. Moscow: Molodaia gvardiia, 2013.

Gershkovich, Evgenia. "Moskovskaia dinastiia: Alekseevy-Chetverikovy." *Moskvich*, February 16, 2023. https://moskvichmag.ru/lyudi/moskovskaya-dinastiya-alekseevy-chetverikovy/.

Klevantseva, Tatyana. "Prominent Russians: Savva Morozov." Russiapedia. Accessed June 24, 2024. https://russiapedia.rt.com/prominent-russians/art/savva-morozov/.

Lamanova, Nadezhda. "Spektakl' 'V mechtakh' na stsene MKhT" [The play 'In dreams' on the scene of MAT]. Virtual'nyi muzei Nadezhdy Lamanovoi. Accessed June 24, 2024. https://lamanova.com/17_in-dreams.html.

Lotman, Iurii. "Kul'tura i vzryv." In idem, *Semiosfera*, 11–148. St. Petersburg: Iskusstvo, 2000.

Nemirovich-Danchenko, Vladimir. *Pis'ma*. 4 vols. Moscow: Khudozhestvennyi teatr, 2003.

Orlov, Iurii. *Moskovskii khudozhestvennyi teatr, 1898–1917. Tvorchestvo. Organizatsiia. Ekonomika*. Moscow: RATI-GITIS, 2011.

Radishcheva, Olga. *Stanislavskii i Nemirovich-Danchenko: Istoriia teatral'nykh otnoshenii*. 3 vols. Moscow: Artist. Rezhisser. Teatr, 1997–1999.

Radishcheva, Olga, Iurii Vinogradov, and Ekaterina Shingareva. *Moskovskii khudozhestvennyi teatr v russkoi teatral'noi kritike 1898–1905*. Moscow: Artist. Rezhisser. Teatr, 2005.

Rieber, Alfred J. *Merchants and Entrepreneurs in Imperial Russia*. Chapel Hill: U of North Carolina Press, 1982.

Serebrov, Aleksandr. *Vremia i liudi: Vospominaniia*. Moscow: Moskovskii rabochii, 1960.

Stanislavskii, Konstantin. *Stat'i. Rechi. Besedy. Pis'ma*. Moscow: Iskusstvo, 1953.

———. *Sobranie sochinenii*. 9 vols. Moscow: Iskusstvo, 1989–1999.

Vinogradskaia, Irina. *Letopis' zhizni i tvorchestva Stanislavskogo*. 2nd ed. 4 vols. Moscow: Khudozhestvennyi teatr, 2003.

Worrall, Nick. *The Moscow Art Theatre*. London: Routledge, 1996.

A Bridgeable Schism? The Russian Silver Age Intelligentsia Holds Its Ground, Spruces up, and Proselytizes

Irene Masing-Delic

"There is in every child the essentially human urge to reshape the earth, to act upon a friable environment (unless he is a born Marxist or a corpse and meekly waits for the environment to fashion *him*)."
Vladimir Nabokov, *Speak, Memory*.[1]

"Let us discard the old coat of grey materialism."
Anatoly Lunacharsky, *Religiia i sotsializm*[2]

"Only as a holy beast could Russia righteously sin."
A. S. Askoldov, "The Religious Meaning of the Russian Revolution."[3]

1　Vladimir Nabokov, *Speak, Memory. An Autobiography Revisited. Novels and Memoirs 1941–1951* (New York: The Library of America, 1996), 621.
2　Anatolii Lunacharskii, *Religiia i sotsializm*, part 1 (St. Petersburg: Shipovnik, 1908), 160. All translations from Russian are mine, unless otherwise indicated.
3　Sergei Alekseevich Askol'dov [Alekseev], "The Religious Meaning of the Russian Revolution," in *Out of the Depths (De Profundis): A Collection of Articles on the Russian Revolution*, trans. and ed. William F. Woehrlin (Irvine, CA: Charles Schlack Jr., Publisher, 1986), 21.

Introduction

This chapter aims to characterize some ideological conflicts within the Russian intelligentsia of the first quarter of the twentieth century. During this period the new faction of neo-Kantian idealists within the Russian intelligentsia stirred controversies that confirmed the materialists in their assumptions and inspired the so-called "god-builders" (*bogostroiteli*) to "spruce up" socialist doctrines, using pseudo-religious and pseudo-philosophical metaphor-laden language. They took note of idealist "taunts" that socialist writing was inept and dreary and were eager to prove the opposite.[4] The idealists in turn criticized the aggressive atheism and materialism of hardline Marxists and populists. The idealist faction in the intelligentsia had emerged at the turn of the century and included numerous "apostates" of Marxism. It was viewed with deep distrust by Marxists proper and other socialist groupings, which rejected dualist idealism and uncompromisingly defended their monist-materialist postulates.

This chapter argues that, despite their critique, the idealists kept channels open for potential reconciliation with the Marxists, making numerous attempts to "win over" the old guard; even as late as 1909, in the controversial collection of articles *Landmarks* (Vekhi), they blamed their opponents for contributing decisively to the outbreak of the 1905 revolution but assumed that most of them were horrified by actual events. The idealists therefore asked them to consider rapprochement with "true" religion, as their own ideology was so clearly false. These proselytizing efforts arose from the notion that they shared important values and characteristics with the materialist intelligentsia, such as a "religious" attitude to their mission. The atheist and materialist old intelligentsia, formed in the 1860s and still thriving in the 1900s, was in essence religious, the idealists argued. They saw additional commonality with the materialists in their shared abhorrence of the bourgeois mentality, its spiritual obtuseness, emotional shallowness and all the other features of *poshlost'*. They deemed these bourgeois characteristics prevalent in Western Europe, with its egotistic individualism and ambitions to thrive in *this* world, but largely absent in Russia, where the People was indifferent to material prosperity. The idealist camp was similarly convinced that the "universal" Russian nation (Dostoevsky famously saw it so)[5] had a

---

4 Christopher Read, *Religion, Revolution and the Russian Intelligentsia 1900–1912: The Vekhi Debate and Its Intellectual Background* (Basingstoke: The MacMillan Press, 1979), 77.
5 In his so-called "Pushkin Speech" of June 1880, during celebrations of the poet's birth, Dostoevsky declared that no nation had produced a genius with such "capacity for universal sympathy as our Pushkin." This meant that, "beyond all doubt, the destiny of a Russian is pan-European and universal. To become a true Russian, to become a Russian fully . . . , means

God-given mission to unify all humankind in a spirit of free unity (some form of *sobornost'*) while spurning "lukewarm" bourgeois attitudes. They took note that unification of humankind was an important goal of socialism too, however differently envisioned. Given these potential commonalities, leading members of the idealist faction believed that they merely needed to redirect their opponents' misguided faith in scientific utopianism toward Russian Orthodoxy and Russian patriotism (seen as embracing universality) and divert their commitment to justice for the People toward new—religious—expressions. On this platform, the idealist camp saw opportunity for reeducating the "self-hypnotized"[6] and a path to reunify the intelligentsia. In short, the "Russian Idea" of universalism/internationalism, and rejection of Western individualism,[7] could resolve the ideational *schism* within the intelligentsia.[8] The Marxist and populist socialist factions, however, were not ready to be redirected and reeducated. When the Marxist-Leninists emerged victorious in the Civil War and took charge of the country, they sent the intelligentsia's idealist and religious wing into exile, most famously in 1922 on the "philosophers' ships."[9] Even the innocuous "god-builders," who never departed from socialist doctrines in attempting to create a sexier socialism with romantic and religious imagery to "spice up" classical Marxist Socialism, were unacceptable to the Marxist establishment. Georgy Plekhanov and Vladimir Lenin had already rejected them before World War I.

The idealist faction did not lose hope for a long time, however; it was guided by Dostoevsky's idea that maximalist convictions could swing to diametrically opposite positions in a dialectic mode that spurned synthesis. As we know, the idealists were eventually forced by circumstances to renounce attempts at making a "real" religion out of the "fake" socialist one and realized that their

---

only to become the brother of all men, to become, if you will, a universal man." Quoted from "Celebration of Pushkin's Birth. June 8, 1880. Feyodor Dostoevsky," Speech Vault, accessed July 8, 2024, http://www.speeches-usa.com/Transcripts/feyodor_dostoevsky-pushkin.html. This became a cornerstone concept of the idealist-religious philosophers' views of Russian Orthodoxy's mission in the world.

6   S. N. Bulgakov, "Basic Problems of the Theory of Progress," in *Problems of Idealism: Essays in Russian Social Philosophy*, trans. and ed. Randall A. Poole (New Haven, CT: Yale UP, 2003, 1st ed., 1977), 37.

7   The idealist camp's critique of the bourgeois West was sometimes modified by acknowledging Europe's culturally valid past—which, as Dostoevsky's Ivan Karamazov put it, was a beloved "cemetery."

8   One could argue that the term "schism" is inappropriate in this context: an established creed is here challenged not by heretics, but by a "religious war" between "progressive" Orthodoxy and "conservative" Marxist materialism. Still, "schism" is a good term for the rift within the intelligentsia, because of the unshakable "faith" both intelligentsia camps embraced.

9   In 1922 the Soviet government exiled hundreds of prominent intellectuals using ships for their transport to Europe.

positions were irreconcilable. The materials used here to show the struggle between factions are essays from the first publications in *Problems of Idealism* (Problemy idealizma, 1902), essays from *Landmarks* and the collection *Out of the Depth* (Iz glubiny, 1918), as well as overviews of basic Marxist and populist postulates from a variety of sources. I discuss only a few important participants in the debates in detail: Sergei Askoldov, Sergei Bulgakov, Nikolai Berdyaev, Georgy Plekhanov, and Anatoly Lunacharsky, leaving out numerous others. Left out too is the creative intelligentsia. Most of them were passionately involved in exploring more communal and fraternal forms of government, plumbing the soul of the folk or the "new class" of the proletariat, but even Maxim Gorky's novels of his god-building period, however didactic, are too fictional to offer suitable material.

Basic Materialist Concepts and the Idealist Critique

By the early 1900s the Russian intelligentsia from the 1860s had established its profile as adamantly materialist and atheist. Though it opposed all forms of reactionary "animism" (Plekhanov's term), the idealist intelligentsia camp yet saw the Marx-Engels-based socialist faction of the intelligentsia as propagating a religion rather than an objective and scientific ideology, as claimed—a dogmatic pseudo-religion that eliminated the "deity" but otherwise raided traditional faith for "contraband" (Bulgakov's term) ideational goods. They did not mince words in confronting their opponents' "dishonest" strategies but kept hoping to set them straight.

The Existence of God

One disputed issue, obviously, was the existence or not of a creator deity. Marxism upholds the notion that matter was never created but was itself the substance that constitutes reality, i.e., of everything that exists. It is not God but Matter that is eternal and omnipresent, having no beginning and no end.[10] Eternal Matter in its unstoppable dialectical motion and constant flux is the one and only matrix of all that exists, including all human thought, scientific and philosophical, and all artistic creativity, even the most sophisticated. All historical and cultural phenomena are engendered by the brain, a biological (i.e.,

---

10 Frederick Engels, *Anti-Dühring* (Moscow: Foreign Languages Publishing House, 1959), 465.

material) organ. "Being" is the cause of "knowing"—contrary to idealistic perceptions, for which "knowing" explains "being." Plekhanov, "Father of Russian Marxism," said "there are no inborn ideas"[11]—hence, no soul or spirit where they could dwell; there is only the human brain, which learned to think long after life emerged.[12] This organ of thought eventually transcended nature and its laws by "a long historical process of *autocreation*," largely through "collective labor," translating current labor practices into institutions of self-organization, science and art (author's italics).[13] It was "in the essence of matter to evolve into thinking beings," capable of "developing history."[14]

This total servitude of the human mind to external material conditions might be seen as a dreary master-slave relationship (as Nabokov indicates in my first epigraph). Engels's *Anti-Dühring* (1878) counter-argued, however, that human brains were learning to "desire change before it forces itself upon them."[15] Expanding on Engels's statement, Plekhanov states: "we are empowered in proportion to what we know," with science as a means to control the material world.[16] Lenin agreed. In *Materialism and Empiriocriticism* (1909), in the chapter "Freedom and Necessity," he approvingly quotes Engels's dictum that necessity rules us "*only insofar as it is not understood*" (his italics). Knowing the laws of matter and nature brings the possibility "of systematically making them work towards definite ends" that humanity is learning to desire. Lenin adds: "The development of consciousness in each human individual and the development of the collective knowledge of humanity at large presents us at every step with examples of the transformation of the unknown 'thing-in-itself' (Kant's *Ding an sich*) into the known 'thing-for-us.'"[17] Trustfully desiring changes that necessity imposes, gaining ever more empirical knowledge of material laws, enables the leap from necessity to freedom. Changes in evolving matter itself help too, as when quantity turns into a new and better quality. Summing up, subordination to matter and its laws develops into observation, anticipation,

---

11 Georgii Plekhanov, *Izbrannye filosofskie proizvedeniia*, 5 vols., vol. 1: *K voprosu o razvitii monisticheskogo vzgliada na istoriiu* (Moscow: Gosudarstvennoe izdatel'stvo politicheskoi literatury, 1936), 510.
12 Engels, *Anti-Dühring*, 115.
13 Andrzej Walicki, *Marxism and the Leap to the Kingdom of Freedom: The Rise and Fall of the Communist Utopia* (Stanford, CA: Stanford UP, 1995), 45–46.
14 David McLellan, *Friedrich Engels* (New York: Viking Press, 1978), 87. If this is a correct rendering of Marxist thought, it endows matter with a certain entelechy, as a "deity in the making."
15 Engels, *Anti-Dühring*, 475.
16 G. V. Plekhanov, *Ob ateizme i religii v istorii obshchestva i kul'tury* (Moscow: Mysl', 1977), 274.
17 Vladimir Lenin, *Materialism and Empirio-Criticism* (New York: International Publishers, 1927), 191.

and understanding, thus to increasing control over the material world. Humans can learn to manipulate inescapable causality, steadily growing the sector of freedom. Similarly, knowing economic laws and historical modes of production and trade makes their development predictable, thus controllable, especially since history is more dynamic than nature, set in motion by humankind that has learnt to observe and draw inferences—in other words, to think. Thus, a perfect (yet forever perfectible) socialist society can be *planned* and realized according to predictions by those who fully *understand* economic development and thus are able to steer it toward socialism. The inevitable result is a society that completely realizes humanity's quest for fair distribution of goods, health and happiness: humanity transforms collective labor into a "miracle-working" force (as god-building Gorky perceived it). Naturally the arts are useful too: they inspire labor and exalt scientific accomplishments. The idealist, religious position emerges from a critique of these assumptions.

Idealist-Religious Critique

Sergei Bulgakov

For the religious idealists God's existence is an axiom and a *sine qua non*. In his "Basic Problems of the Theory of Progress," first published in the collection *Problems of Idealism*,[18] Bulgakov states that God is Creator of the world and cosmos in their ideal form before their present "fallen" state, disputing the Marxist vision of eternal and uncreated matter. He is baffled by the notion that unconscious matter, ruled by implacable causality as well as chance, would suddenly "decide" to create human reason that would gradually but determinedly introduce "rational purposiveness."[19] How would a "dead mechanism gradually giv[e] way to . . . its complete antithesis," the thinking human being, without supra-material prodding? How could causation "cause" human consciousness and "create . . . human reason"? In his later "Heroism and Asceticism," Bulgakov pokes fun at the notion that "the individual" (*lichnost'*) is merely a product of

---

18 It was republished in Bulgakov's *From Marxism to Idealism* (1903), a title that "immortalized the whole development" of the "autonomization of ideals and values" taking place at the time (Randall Poole, *Neo-Idealist Philosophy in the Russian Liberation Movement: The Moscow Psychological Society and Its Symposium, Problems of Idealism* [Washington, D.C.: Kennan Institute for Advanced Russian Studies, 1996], 34). Bulgakov's article is here quoted from the 2003 English translation of the collection.
19 Bulgakov, "Basic Problems of the Theory of Progress," 91.

its material environment yet tasked with improving it; that is, changing the very "cause" that caused him/her. It strikes him as following R. E. Raspe's mendacious Baron von Münchhausen who pulled himself and his horse out of a swamp by his own hair.[20]

Bulgakov also wonders why the Marxists still view the cosmos as ruled by pure causality, where life emerged by chance and coincidence, in teleological terms. How can they be sure that a "bright future" of peace and well-being awaits future generations if Marxism decries any "teleology," suspecting that the concept inevitably implies a supra-material design for the world?[21] The Marxists answer, as we know, that the developed human brain can manipulate the laws of nature, outfoxing and reversing the master-slave relation, making nature the slave. Bulgakov counter-argues that the theory of endless progress achieved by Reason was a "theodicy," called upon to replace "metaphysics and religion, or more precisely, . . . [take] . . . the form of both."[22] For him, Marxist theodicy is based on "pure religious faith," which has crept in "clandestinely, as contraband."[23] The progressivists smuggled the religious notion of a *beyond* into their scientific theories, a *beyond* where their ideals would be realized. True, their *beyond* was not in "other worlds," but just the Future, where it would take the form of an ideal universal state (and also no longer a state). Bulgakov, however, warned the Marxists that their conviction that the struggle with necessity would result in happiness and (virtual) Freedom was on shaky grounds. If progress was "pure contingency," why would the same contingency not redirect itself and, having "extoll[ed] reason today, ruin it tomorrow"?[24] Why not stop pretending that there was no science in Marxist "prophecies" and admit that claiming science as guarantor of their truths was meant to inspire confidence in this future's inevitability, to assure believers that Marxist predictions would become reality as surely as a lunar eclipse calculated by astronomers.[25] The Marxist answer would be that they knew the laws of motion in time—the latter a function of motion, a mode of matter (Spirkin)—and how to manipulate them.

---

20 See Sergei Bulgakov, "Heroism and Asceticism: Reflections on the Religious Nature of the Russian Intelligentsia," in *Landmarks. A Collection of Essays on the Russian Intelligentsia*, ed. Boris Shragin and Albert Todd, trans. Marian Schwartz (New York: Karz Howard Publishers, 1977), 47, 91.
21 Alexander Spirkin, *Dialectical Materialism* (Moscow: Progress Publishers, 1983), 95.
22 Bulgakov, "Basic Problems of the Theory of Progress," 91.
23 Ibid., 96.
24 Ibid., 95.
25 Ibid., 92.

Besides positing a deity that encourages free theurgical creativity,[26] as opposed to manipulation of necessity, Bulgakov critiques the role of ethics in Marxism. This philosophy openly required sacrificing previous generations for the benefit of future ones, relying on their readiness for martyrdom. Why, however, should earlier generations "be manure for future harmony," as Ivan Karamazov asked in *The Brothers Karamazov*, Bulgakov wonders.[27] In his view, this was sheer "vampirism."[28] Accumulating wealth to create and satisfy ever new needs of an inevitably materialist nature would also ironically mean that the victorious proletariat, allegedly untainted by bourgeois *poshlost'*, would become a full-fledged bourgeoisie. If the class struggle became "a form of sharing in life's goods," then "it is obvious that a new bourgeoisie [could] be raised on naked class interest."[29] Socialist struggles for "justice" would result in *embourgeoisement*; that is, the very social phenomenon that both Marxists and idealists allegedly abhorred. Bulgakov concludes that "the attempt to construct a 'scientific religion' failed from all perspectives, not least ethical ones. This emphasis on ethics implied that radical materialists were misguided but decent human beings who failed to think their premises out to their logical end.

Landmarks (Vekhi)

The contentious dialogue between these intelligentsia factions across the ever-widening schism of idealism versus materialism reached a well-known peak in the publication of *Landmarks* (Vekhi, 1909), in which the idealists criticized the virtually sacrosanct atheist intelligentsia and their claimed monopoly on political martyrdom. They did not deny that the materialist intelligentsia had suffered for the exploited Russian folk but objected to their "appropriating" martyrdom for self-romanticizing purposes. As the contributors expected, *Landmarks* met with a storm of indignation in the materialist camp and beyond. Bulgakov contributed his essay "Heroism and Asceticism. Reflections on the Religious Nature of the Russian Intelligentsia." As the title indicates, his critique of the materialist atheists was counterbalanced by acknowledging their misguided, yet unmistakably, "religious nature." Including laudatory remarks on the materialists' moral stamina during tsarist persecution and praising their

---

26 *Theurgical* activity is humankind's voluntary and free co-creativity with God in transforming earthly reality.
27 Bulgakov, "Basic Problems of the Theory of Progress," 103.
28 Ibid.
29 Ibid.,102.

contempt for philistinism, Bulgakov yet makes plain that he will not mince words about their flaws, which, in his view, stem from their notion of man-Godhood, making humankind the deity of the future, with themselves, the radical intelligentsia, as its prophetic precursors.

Repeating that seeking the "happiness of the last generations who will triumph on the bones and blood of their forebearers" was ethically unacceptable, Bulgakov pleads with the materialists to return to "faith in the universal resurrection" by correcting misconceptions that had arisen via western enlightenment theories, often simplistically interpreted, and Russian positivist thinkers like Pyotr Lavrov and Nikolai Mikhailovsky.[30] Sweetening the pill, he however praises the old intelligentsia for not having become philistines like their socialist European counterparts; the Russian materialists' deep "'anti-bourgeois'" feelings clearly resemble "religious revulsion toward spiritual philistinism, toward the 'kingdom of this world.'"[31] This essentially religious "revulsion" promised that the materialists could be redeemed, once they understood where they went wrong and ceased indoctrinating the young with misconceptions. Bulgakov did not hide that they would have to spend "years of salutary repentance" to become true (Russian Orthodox) *intelligenty*, but he held out the hope of redemption. However, he added one more reason why they were led astray: their largely homegrown cult of false heroism.[32]

This cult was linked to embracing man-Godhood, "belief in man's natural perfection" achieved "through man's own powers;" humanity's self-created divine status would begin to manifest itself once the materialists had toppled tsarist rule and seized power. This cult of intelligentsia potential made them see themselves as saviors of the Russian folk and proletariat, nay of all humankind.[33] Unfortunately, they had also led the new generation into the temptation of "spiritual arrogance" and to adopting the "theatrical trappings of heroism."[34] Flattered by the conviction that salvation depended on them alone, the young accepted that the price for "self-worship" could be death—a heroic one, naturally, after a life free from "the bonds of ordinary morality."[35] Enchanted by the spectacle of revolutionary romanticism, their elders fully encouraged the "spiritual pedocracy" that happily replaced "the Christian saint" with "the

---

30 Bulgakov, "Heroism and Asceticism," 37.
31 Ibid., 27–28.
32 Ibid., 26.
33 Ibid., 33–34.
34 Ibid., 35–36.
35 Ibid., 35, 42.

revolutionary student" in their iconostasis.[36] Bulgakov pleads with his opponents to abandon this vision of themselves as melodramatic participants in historical drama. If they returned to Christian virtues of perseverance and patience in the quest for social change, they would realize that non-spectacular humility (asceticism) was not "reconciliation to evil, inertia and even servility," as they usually claimed.[37] Bulgakov clearly meant to reach the younger generation of populist/Marxist socialists who saw spectacular death as the proper exit from life, tending subconsciously toward suicide. Ending his essay, he asserted once more that "the nature of the Russian [materialist, IMD] intelligentsia [was] religious" and, therefore, their "intense search for the City of God on earth, this desire to execute the will of God on earth as in heaven" were profoundly distinct from bourgeois culture's "attraction to solid worldly prosperity."[38] Though their maximalism could be called "abnormal" and "a result of religious perversion," there was no reason not to expect a "recovery of religious health."[39] He pleaded for ending the intelligentsia's "split," which had resulted from its ideological divisions, exploited by "fishermen in troubled waters."[40]

Nikolai Berdyaev

Berdyaev agreed that Marxism and socialist populism were contraband religions.[41] In the chapter "Socialism as Religion," from his book *The New Religious Consciousness and Society* (1907/1999), he unambiguously declared that, "Social Democracy cares very much about religion, since it itself wants to be one."[42] It virulently opposes Christianity because the latter acknowledges the "absolute value" of each individual, whereas Marxism takes no interest in personality and actively dislikes outstanding creative artists and independently thinking scientists.[43] It claims to cherish the proletarian collective, which will save the world from iniquity, but actually Marxism wishes to extend their destruction of "evil" to all classes, eventually even to the "deified proletariat." Once classless society has come into existence, the proletariat will join those who "fertilize[d]

---

36 Ibid., 40–41.
37 Ibid., 49.
38 Ibid., 62.
39 Ibid.
40 Ibid., 61.
41 ??
42 Nikolai Berdiaev, "Socialism as Religion," in *A Revolution of the Spirit: Crisis of Value in Russia 1890–1924*, ed. Bernice Glatzer Rosenthal and Martha Bohachevsky-Chomiak, trans. Marian Schwartz (New York: Fordham UP, 1990), 110.
43 Ibid., 111.

the soil for future generations," preparing the advent of a super-humanity that will become "God."[44] In this "beyond-the-future," humanity will be the "earthly god" of "self-satisfied humanity," directing infinite and tedious progress.[45]

Certainly, Marxism has no interest whatsoever in righting past wrongs, Berdyaev insists, and the "tiny tear of the once tormented child" is not a problem since, unlike Ivan Karamazov, Marxist ideologues are not interested in "tiny tears" (*slezinki*).[46] Marxist thinkers do not ask themselves how children's sufferings will be justified to the mothers of tortured children in the realm of eternity: their eternity is a strictly linear, endless future. They are more concerned about future super-generations, not yet born, than about struggling against current evil and rectifying past—or current—wrongs. In reality the "specter of an endless, but temporal future" that they yearn for is the "evil infinity" of endless temporality, opposed to the Christian eternity as timelessness where God will redeem even incomprehensible suffering. Choosing the allegedly bound-to-be-perfect future, theoreticians of endless progress fail to see that it would be excruciatingly dull. Life in a world of ongoing technological progress, with more and more art glorifying meaningless events, inevitably bores even the most dedicated engineer.[47] The famous "leap into the realm of freedom" means no more than increased mobility in space. Berdyaev predicts that the alleged titans will lead a life of "bourgeois satiety," the superman of future socialist society turning into merely the "consistent, definitive 'bourgeois.'"[48]

Like Bulgakov, Berdyaev points to the role of *prophecy* in socialist religion. It clings to "collapse-theories"—the present world order *will* self-destruct—that are pure "eschatology."[49] Beyond visions of social catastrophes and destruction of the past, socialist prophets discern the end of history in the "'millennial kingdom' of socialism."[50] Linear socialist "bad" endlessness, promising merely ever-growing

---

44 Ibid., 112–113.
45 Ibid., 113.
46 Ibid., 115.
47 Marxists sometimes also considered this question of eternal boredom in their paradise. In A. Bogdanov's short story "Immortality Day" (1914), the excruciating boredom of forever the same leads the inventor of the immortality serum to suicide (at the age of one thousand years and after scores of marriages). See Airin Masing-Delich, *Uprazdnenie smerti. Mif o spasenii v russkoi literature XX veka* (Boston, MA: Academic Studies Press, 2020), 420–422.
48 Berdyaev, "Socialism as Religion," 120, 122. Berdyaev had not changed his mind on this by the early 1930s, when he wrote that the Soviet communist was a bourgeois of the "parvenu type" (Nicholas Berdyaev, *The Bourgeois Mind and Other Essays* [London: Sheed & Ward, 1934/1966], 21), communism the "sinister" successor of capitalism, and communist man a hypocrite who "makes hell on earth," claiming "to be preparing a future earthly paradise" (24).
49 Berdyaev, "Socialism as Religion," 116.
50 Ibid., 117.

control over blind Mother Matter and material comfort for mortals rehearsing the same "new facts," contrasts with eternal spiritual verticality. The vertical axis presents a tension-filled existence, full of conflicts between real and ideal, material and spiritual, one's better and one's darker self, "here" and "there." Verticality, as just defined, lets the individual form him/her/self into a unique personality, capable of eternally meaningful existence in other dimensions. Marxist mortals will merge with matter (sprouting Bazarov's famous burdock, IMD), but the idealists claim existence in the "good eternity" of what Symbolists called *realiora*. In his discussion of the "Legend of the Grand Inquisitor" (in *The New Religious Consciousness*), Berdyaev uses Dostoevsky's famous chapter from *The Brothers Karamazov* to reinforce his view of socialism as bent on "forcing humankind to be happy by taking its freedom."[51] The series of inquisitors had not ended. Karl Marx was followed by Konstantin Pobedonostsev, Ober-Procurator of the Most Holy Synod, also bent on sparing humanity the sufferings that independent moral choices inevitably bring. Coercion of the spirit was a greater crime than outright rebellion against God, in Berdyaev's view. Nietzsche, Byron, Ivan Karamazov, and other spiritual rebels against God, historical and fictitious, pose no threat to religion—rather, a revitalizing challenge. The "violation of conscience" endorsed by Plekhanov and other Marxists presents a clear danger, however.[52]

Given this caustic critique that views socialists as destined for bourgeois *poshlost'*, led astray less by European thinkers than by themselves, and working to enslave humanity—did Berdyaev then, unlike Bulgakov, see the intelligentsia schism as unbridgeable? His *Landmarks* article, "Philosophic Truth and the Moral Truth of the Intelligentsia" (Filosofskaia istina i intelligentskaia pravda), begins as highly critical of the materialist intelligentsia. Pointing out the difference between situational truth (*pravda*) and actual verity (*istina*), he charges the left intelligentsia with supporting only the former, enforcing its utility for their own aspirations in the process.[53] The *intelligentshchina*—he uses the derogatory term that idealists would apply to hardcore socialist *intelligenty*—ignored this distinction. In fact, they were "prepared to accept any philosophy on faith, provided it sanction[ed] [their] social ideals," and were equally prepared to repudiate any that did not.[54]

---

51 Nikolai Berdiaev, *Novoe religioznoe soznanie i obshchestvennost'* (St. Petersburg: Izdanie N. V. Pirozhkova, 1907/1999), 63.
52 Ibid., 104.
53 Nikolai Berdyaev, "Philosophic Truth and the Moral Truth of the Intelligentsia," in in *Landmarks. A Collection of Essays on the Russian Intelligentsia*, ed. Boris Shragin and Albert Todd, trans. Marian Schwartz (New York: Karz Howard Publishers, 1977), 8.
54 Ibid.

Berdyaev does not only criticize, however. Like Bulgakov, he sees virtues in the traditional intelligentsia's ideological stance, such as distrust of "abstract academicism," the demand "for an integral worldview in which theory merges with life," and "thirst for faith."[55] It is socialist dogma in their case, but faith nevertheless. Berdyaev could acknowledge "unconscious religiosity" in these features.[56] Continuing to emphasize his opponents' need for self-criticism and repentance, he still intersperses reconciliatory remarks amid criticism. The "thirst for justice on earth ... in the soul of the Russian intelligentsia" is "essentially holy," even if not immune to perversion."[57] Seeing his own philosophical faction as reconciling "knowledge and faith" and granting the materialists' striving for a *pravda* that could do without lying, he believes in collaborating for a "national philosophical tradition that we need so much."[58] In other words, Berdyaev invites the old intelligentsia to join ranks with the idealists in the *common* creation of a Russian integral philosophy to complement rationalistic European philosophical systems. This is clearly an invitation to close the intelligentsia's ranks and establish a common task, at least if the materialists "can move on to a new consciousness" founded on the synthesis of knowledge and faith, and the acquisition of inner freedom too long sacrificed.[59] The rewards would be enormous, he promises, at the end of his essay: "Then shall be born the new soul of the intelligentsia."[60]

God-Building

God-building, mainly the creation of Anatoly Lunacharsky and Maxim Gorky, had its heyday in the middle of the first decade of the twentieth century and declined around 1911–1912, when Lenin ridiculed it and insisted that its adherents forswear it.[61] I discuss god-building here because it, uniquely among the time's ideological factions, heeded the opinions of other ideological camps and reacted to accusations of dullness by creating a sexier socialism, spicing up not the essence but the *style* of the socialist message. Not deviating from essential Marxist doctrines, certainly not from atheism, the god-builders' deity was not

---

55 Ibid., 9.
56 Ibid.
57 Ibid., 11.
58 Ibid., 19.
59 Ibid., 21.
60 Ibid., 22.
61 Some Gorky scholars argue that the writer never renounced this splinter group, especially when he fused his liking for Fyodorovism with Nietzschean visions of the new Soviet man as the new "overman."

"socialist-Christian," but solely the traditional cult object: the *narod*. Its sacredness even intensified as it was seen as the guarantor of generational continuity (*rod na rod: narod*, as Gorky put it in *Confession*) and thus a form of eternity. Since the god-builders saw themselves as Marxists, adding but a random dash of contemporary philosophy chosen for a fashionable touch—what was their goal in creating a separate "branch" of the original doctrine? Marxist philosopher Roland Boer answers concisely, defining god-builders as "atheists who sought to increase the emotional power of Marxism by drawing upon positive elements from religion, especially Christianity."[62] Lunacharsky, their "most articulate spokesman," was critical of Plekhanov's emphasis on "pure rationalism" taken from later Engels, which had robbed Marxism of the "'warm stream' of Marx's own thought and practice."[63] The god-builders' goal was to inspire rediscovery of "the heart of his system."[64]

This rediscovery could be made by absorbing "the utopian dimension of religious belief" and presenting Marxism as the surest path to "making fairytales come true."[65] This entailed instilling the vision of a Nietzschean godlike mankind: "Our ideal is the image of man, of man like a god, in relation to whom we are all are but raw material, mere ingots waiting to be given shape, living ingots that bear their own ideal within themselves," Lunacharsky promised.[66] The phrase "bearing their own ideal within themselves," as Boer points out, harkens back to the Christian notion of the human being "created in the image of God."[67] The god-building branch of Marxism accepted, as did their fellow-socialists, that their own and perhaps many subsequent generations would but *imagine* the future ideal world, inhabited by overmen, since they would not live to see it, but Lunacharsky sweetened the pill. Assuming that the essence of Marxism was "emotional collectivism," he defined it as "the feeling of being linked to one's species and its history," the ecstasy of anticipating a future "when we will no longer exist."[68] He knows it may seem "irrational from the perspective of egoism" to be indifferent to personal rewards in a celestial paradise and to accept mortality without any resurrections with equanimity, but selfless collectivists

---

[62] Roland Boer, "Utopia, Religion and the God-Builders: From Anatoly Lunacharsky to Ernst Bloch," in *From Francis Bacon to William Golding: Utopias and Dystopias of Today and of Yore*, ed. Ligia Tomoiaga et al. (Newcastle upon Tyne: Cambridge Scholars Publishing, 2012), 2.
[63] Ibid., 4.
[64] Ibid., 9.
[65] Ibid. For socialist visions of collectively realizing the myths and "fairytales" of Christianity through science, see my *Uprazdnenie smerti* (2020), or *Abolishing Death* (1992).
[66] Boer, "Utopia, Religion and the God-Builders: From Anatoly Lunacharsky to Ernst Bloch," 9.
[67] Ibid., 10.
[68] Lunacharskii, *Religiia i sotsializm*, part 1, 354, 357.

who embrace the "religion of Species, Progress and Labor" find service to the future more joyous than Christian bliss in heaven.[69] God-building was free of the "vices" of traditional religion, such as the personal relationship with God, its "narrow-mindedness" (*uzkodushie*) and "cowardly fear of death." The bliss of salvation that believers expect after death—but never will experience, since it does not exist—the god-builders find in this life. They find it in the "absolutely unique experience of the boundaries of the individual being dissolved and of having his/her vital energies overflow the rims of the corporeal vessel," in ecstatic transports of self-sacrifice.[70] Lunacharsky invites the human collective to outdo Christ's self-sacrifice by living and dying for the "human gods" of post-eschatological times, not for recompense, but out of love for their species.

Arguably, Lunacharsky resolved the problem the idealists raised—that past generations would be reduced to "fertilizing the future"—by claiming that self-sacrifice in this life was more rewarding than (non-existing) celestial bliss. The generations who created gods and titans were not victims of Marxist vampires, since they could benefit, while on earth, from "the gold of pure science, the incense of inspired art and the myrrh of sacred enthusiasm."[71] Science would learn to control the weather, to summon and subdue rain, snow, and hail, control all nature's whims. Science would offer the fruits of its discoveries throughout the process. God-building would offer the joys of inspired creativity "carried by the wings of creative dreams" to all generations.[72] *Building* divine humankind was joyful in the present; it made "hearts beat in joyful unison" at every new accomplishment.[73] Freedom from egotism and fear as well as love for the human-divine species meant not renunciation, but the Schillerian joy of loving interconnectedness, celebrated in the poet's *Ode to Joy* and Beethoven's Ninth Symphony.

Genuine Marxists did not desire the personal immortality and eternal celestial bliss that the idealists claimed to offer. Or was there a non-verbalized hope that future human gods might achieve the immortality that behooves gods, but on earth? Lunacharsky's prediction that humankind would learn to control the climate sounds very Fyodorovian; climate control was one of the immortality

---

69 Ibid., 357. In other words, believers in traditional Christian religions lacked true religiosity: yearning for personal rewards, they hoped to keep their individual ego forever; guaranteed immortality was capitalist property.
70 Ibid., 363.
71 Ibid.,105.
72 Ibid., 90.
73 Ibid.

philosopher's main goals.[74] He also believed that united humankind could accomplish the "task" (*delo*) of achieving physical immortality, and although he was a devout Orthodox Christian, his ideas stirred utopian dreams among many socialist god-builders, notably Maxim Gorky. To discuss Fyodorovism and god-building would exceed the limits of this essay. Suffice it to say that some builders of divine humankind were certain that omnipotent science would prove able to create immortal humans, unlike the deity that "did not exist"—the Christian God. The funeral rites and history of Lenin's posthumous existence as a corpse in a glass sarcophagus exude the aura of Soviet Fyodorovism: surely Lenin would become the first man in history to rise from the dead! Spiced-up socialism thus offered both ecstasies and inspiration to compensate for the knowledge that many generations would not know ultimate perfection before realization of the Perfect World.

Was God-Building Convincing as "Sexy Socialism"?

In his *Landmarks* article, "Philosophic Truth and the Moral Truth of the Intelligentsia," Berdyaev mentions that the fashionable European philosophers Avenarius and Mach were "proclaimed the philosophical saviors of the proletariat" and that "Messrs. Bogdanov and Lunacharskii [who discovered them for Marxism, IMD] made them the philosophers of the Social-Democratic intelligentsia."[75] Apparently this foursome did not impress Berdyaev, who noted that they hardly impacted Marxist philosophy in any constructive way, as it remained unchanged and "true to its old faith."[76] This reaction was to be expected, but what did the classical Marxists, for instance, the "father of Russian Marxism," Plekhanov, think of god-building ambitions? Plekhanov did not approve of Lunacharsky's attempt to add another "religion" to the rich assortment available at the time. In his view, Lunacharsky was trying to sugar the pill of human mortality and lift "the drooping spirits of the Russian intelligentsia" after the failed 1905 revolution, wrapping a heart-warming vest (*dushegreika*) of religious imagery around Marxist truths.[77] Lunacharsky wanted to finish off (*dokonat'*) the Christian God by divinizing Humankind, but what he did was to reintroduce

---

74 See Nikolai Fyodorov's thoughts on achieving immortality and control of nature, in *The Philosophy of the Common Task* (vol. 1, 1906/1907; vol.2, 1911).
75 Berdyaev, "Philosophic Truth," 8.
76 Ibid.
77 Plekhanov, *Ob ateizme i religii*, 250–251.

"animism."[78] It was certainly laudable to continue Feuerbach's legacy, to kill deistic religion, but restoring humankind's self-respect should not take the form of self-divinization: the dignity of mankind could well do without divine accoutrements. As for "discarding the coat of grey Marxism," as Lunacharsky's article "Atheism" recommended,[79] Plekhanov was determined to keep wearing that "old coat."[80] He was baffled by god-building's attempts to make the human being into a god while stating that god is a fiction. If God does not exist, why did god-builders declare humankind divine? Humankind was not a fiction, so why call it god, knowing *he* is a fiction while *it* is not? Lenin utterly repudiated god-building, as already stated. In short, it was at best a qualified success.

The End of the Trilogy: Out of the Depths

To return to the materialist-idealist controversy—specifically, to the situation after the October Revolution, which marked the political defeat of the idealist cause—it continued for some time, until the expulsion of those idealists who had not yet left by 1922. In *Out of the Depths, Articles on the Russian Intelligentsia* (Iz glubiny, 1918), the mainly former *Landmarks* contributors continued to believe that their camp would eventually triumph.[81] True, there was consensus that the Revolution was "a profound spiritual catastrophe," but also shared faith in "Russia's future rebirth," which would be "linked to its return to the religious foundations of life."[82]

Naturally, new political circumstances were reflected in *Out of the Depths*, the collection that completed the "trilogy" begun by *Problems of Idealism* and continued by *Landmarks*. There was a stronger focus on the *narod*'s role in the catastrophic events of 1917: their apparent approval of triumphant socialism had surprised religious idealists, who had accepted Dostoevsky's notion of the Russian folk as God-bearing. In his essay, "The Religious Meaning of the Russian Revolution," Sergey Askoldov tried to explain why the Russian people, against expectations, had turned atheist and socialist.[83]

---

78 Ibid., 233, 245.
79 Lunacharskii, *Religiia i sotsializm*, part 1, 251.
80 Ibid., 253.
81 The collection was typeset in 1918 but confiscated. In 1921, the typesetters printed it on their own initiative, but distribution was prevented and sales forbidden; only a few copies survived. It was eventually published in Paris in 1967.
82 See Nikita Struve's introductory "Proroscheskaia kniga," in *Iz glubiny. Sbornik statei o russkoi revoliutsii* (Paris: YMCA-Press, 1967).
83 Sergei Askol'dov, "The Religious Meaning of the Russian Revolution."

According to him, all souls have a tripartite structure: there is "the *holy* principle, the *human* one, and the *bestial* one" (author's italics).[84] In different national cultures the proportions of these components vary. In the Russian soul the *human* aspect is weakly developed, whereas in European nations it usually dominates, leading to spiritual triviality even in altruistic people. The prevalence of the *human* creates a mentality whose banality evokes "revulsion" (*protivnost'*) in Russians, since it causes inability to register life's spiritual beauty" and its "heights and depths."[85] Always "living on the plane of *cultural* benefits, such as science, technology, and the improvement of society, precludes understanding *mystery*, such as the Russian simple folk's unfathomable bond with Christ," and the Russian peasant—in all his beastliness—being "mystically united with the cross borne by Him."[86] The folk co-experienced His suffering in their own life and thus partook of His holiness. This unique bond of the beastly *and* the divine enabled the folk to retain their inner purity even when steeped in misdeeds. This notion was beyond the grasp of civilized Europeans, but it was this truth which justified Russia referring to herself as "Holy Rus." Identification with Christ's suffering enabled the people and the nation to feel for all who suffer, and their "co-suffering" with all people in pain and need made the Russian soul a "universal" one, from peasants to non-atheistic elites.

Askol'dov does not deny that humanistic culture has some positive aspects: inspired by European ideas, Alexander II abolished serfdom, and rightly so—but European humanism usually relies on purely rationalistic, not religious, principles, which explains its detrimental impact on the Russian psyche. Thus, "no sooner did humanistic consciousness [represented by the atheist intelligentsia, IMD] declare its [the people's, IMD] rights" without heeding its religious bonding with Christ's passion than populist beastliness was released. The Russian soul's naïve innocence became perverted when humanistic concepts such as "legal rights," replaced "sacred justice." In other words, it was the westernized intelligentsia, which deprived the Russian soul of both its holiness and beastliness and thereby destroyed its sense of empathy with humankind's sufferings and sins, eliminating the best part of its spiritual make-up, thus opening the floodgates for revolutionary violence.

Beastliness and holiness can coexist, however, Askoldov argues, but humanism does not overlap with either. Saintly people are usually holy, but they can also break moral codes while still remaining saintly. The beastly part

---

84 Ibid., 12.
85 Askol'dov, "The Religious Meaning of the Russian Revolution," 15.
86 Ibid., 20.

of the soul, in turn, is not devoid of "softness, timidity, meekness, and good nature," but, indisputably, there is also "fury and ferocity" in that aspect of the soul.[87] Humanism is neither holy nor ferocious—it wants to improve society by introducing rational and gradual reforms that, lacking in identification and empathy, prove unproductive. As long as holiness, protected by religion, counteracted the "beastly" aspect of the soul of the people and vibrant Orthodoxy challenged humanistic pretensions to be the ultimate arbiter of ethics, there had been no problems. When the intelligentsia's materialist wing triumphed and the religious intelligentsia was decried by public opinion, revolutionary forces corrupted and eventually destroyed the spiritual life of the masses. Instigators of revolutions are always "humanitarians"—in Russia too it was nihilistic oratory that joined the people's thirst for vengeance, and the "beast" was let loose in its worst manifestations. Askoldov was convinced, however, that this was but a temporary state. Following Dostoevskian thought, he trusted the "law of antagonism of forces," to bring out a reaction against the "city of the Prince of the World" and replace it with "the invisible City of God, which [was] being built" in Russia despite resistance from the Bolshevik State.[88] Askoldov trusted that even the 1917 revolutions had not destroyed the Russian spiritual uniqueness that guaranteed the ultimate triumph of good.

Berdyaev's "Specters of the Russian Revolution" (Dukhi russkoi revoliutsii) credits Gogol and, especially, Dostoevsky with unmasking the future makers of Russian revolutions in works such as *Dead Souls* (Mertvye dushi, 1842) and *The Demons* (Besy, 1872). While Gogol revealed flaws of the Russian mentality without offering hope for their eradication, Dostoevsky showed both the root cause of the evil that befell Russia and how it could be overcome. Unlike European revolutions, the Russian variety was never solely, or even at all, concerned about social reforms, never settling for less than "universal happiness."[89] Thus it impinged on the sphere of religion without offering a creative-redemptive vision of the immortality of the soul, but only a nihilistic "universal levelling."[90] This levelling creed viewed itself as exactly that, however—as a creed. Berdyaev argues that "in Russia, a special cult of revolutionary holiness arose" with its own saints, legends and dogmas.[91] This cult led to a curious phenomenon: a

---

87 Ibid., 12.
88 Ibid., 22.
89 Nikolai Aleksandrovich Berdiaev, "Specters of the Russian Revolution," in *Out of the Depths (De Profundis): A Collection of Articles on the Russian Revolution*, trans. and ed. William F. Woehrlin (Irvine, CA: Charles Schlacks Jr., Publisher, 1986), 46.
90 Ibid., 50.
91 Ibid., 63.

kind of "false Russian sensitivity and sentimentalism" that could not tolerate the slightest criticism, implying that its [socialist] saints and teachings were without flaws, their every statement sacrosanct.[92] The failures and excesses of the 1905 revolution changed little in either their self-estimation or the perceptions of broad sectors of educated elites who continued to regard socialist pronouncements as revelations. Society at large respected "socialist martyrs," even when not sharing their convictions. The "deceptive appearance of revolutionary holiness was sent to the Russian people as a temptation, and as a trial of its spiritual strength," Berdyaev concludes, adding that Russians did "not pass this trial."[93] Despite their failure, Berdyaev could not believe that they would be prey to misconceptions forever. Faithful to Dostoevsky's notion of Russia's God-given destiny to lead the world spiritually, Berdyaev argues that Russia is too great a nation to succumb to a false religion forever. "The idea of a people, the divine concept of it remains, even after a people has fallen, has betrayed its goals, and has subjected its national and state dignity to the greatest humiliation."[94] Berdyaev trusts that once the "demonic specters" that haunt the land have been identified, a new Russia will realize its divinely ordained destiny.[95]

Bulgakov's dramatized "symposium essay" "At the Feast of the Gods" (Na piru bogov, 1918) presents six characters in its cast: Diplomat, Writer, Public Figure, General, Lay Theologian (the translator has "Worldly Divine"), and Refugee, who debate the situation in Russia in 1918.[96] As William Woehrlin has pointed out, Bulgakov takes a detached position, letting each man, including the reactionary General, have his say; at times it is even "difficult for the reader to identify Bulgakov's own position."[97] Still, there are signs that the Writer, the Refugee and the Lay Theologian carry the most privileged ideas.[98] The Refugee (*Bezhenets*), apparently, at some stage, fled from the Bolsheviks, but he is more than a fugitive. The Russian word has the root *beg/bezh* (i.e., *run*) in it and he may be seen as a modern version of a *begun*, who refuses to ever settle down in a fixed place or spiritual position in his search for the Ideal Church and Redeemed Russia. The Refugee makes the piece's final statement: Russia is

---

92 Ibid., 45.
93 Ibid., 64.
94 Ibid.
95 Ibid.
96 This "essay" is in the tradition of Vladimir Solovyov's dramatized *Three Conversations* (*Tri razgovora*), discussing the future of Russia and the world from the perspective of Eternity.
97 William F. Woehrlin, "Introduction: Voices from Out of the Depths," in *Out of the Depths (De Profundis): A Collection of Articles on the Russian Revolution*, trans. and ed. William F. Woehrlin (Irvine, CA: Charles Schlacks Jr., Publisher, 1986), xxix.
98 Bulgakov himself was a lay theologian until he was ordained for the priesthood in 1918.

saved "by the power of the Mother of God," which everyone, except the worldly and Europeanized Diplomat, confirms by stating, "Christ is truly risen."[99] This concluding demonstration of near unity is not the only affirmation of religious faith. As Woehrlin remarks, "the pages of *Out of the Depths* contain more than a few examples of the kind of religious thinking that moves with breathtaking speed from despair at Russia's sins and suffering to the possibility and advantage of God's salvation, with its implication that Russia has a special mission in world history."[100] The last point is important, since conviction of Russia's special historical role in God's divine plan permeates Bulgakov's dramatic dialog, justifying its optimistic message that current tribulations yet pledge the appearance of a great new era. "Proof" is the fact that Europe "was a spiritually moribund land," that the Constitutional Democrats (the Kadets) had been thwarted in their plans to build a "repulsive" democratic Russia (as the reactionary, but not entirely misguided, General puts it), and that the demonic forces aiming to annihilate God's plan for Russia are hatching a "mystical plot," that will be uncovered and exposed.[101] The Writer confirms that it is not "petty middle-class decency, moderation and tidiness" that will resolve Russia's current crisis, but the Russian people that, contrary to all evidence, still believes in Christ: "the people's ideal is Christ, it has no other."[102] Bulgakov seems to share his privileged characters' sentiment that 1918 is not the year to analyze social problems, historical mistakes and other "petty" issues. Transcendental events—and the October Revolution is a negative one—can only be dealt with in a religious spirit. "Humanism," as Askoldov termed it, does not measure up to the giant apocalyptic events looming ahead. The only concrete measure considered is to help the radical intelligentsia atone for introducing "the idols of humanism" into Russian culture.[103] The Writer clothes the vision of renewal for all in literary language, evoking Fyodor Tyutchev's famous poem "Cicero" (1831), specifically the lines about being witnesses at the "divine feast" of momentous historical events.[104] The Public Figure is uneasy for a moment, but the Writer and Refugee reassure him that Russia lives and that Christ still walks his beloved land of Russia. He is won over, and only the Diplomat remains a liberal sceptic.

---

99 Sergei Bulgakov, "At the Feast of the Gods," in *Out of the Depths (De Profundis): A Collection of Articles on the Russian Revolution*, trans. and ed. William F. Woehrlin (Irvine, CA: Charles Schlacks Jr., Publisher, 1986), 118.
100 Woehrlin, "Introduction," xxviii.
101 Askol'dov, "The Religious Meaning of the Russian Revolution," 71, 75.
102 Ibid., 90.
103 Ibid., 99.
104 "Schastliv kto posetil sei mir / V ego minuty rokovye. / Ego prizvali vseblagie / Kak sobesednika na pir."

Concluding Remarks

In the schism outlined above, idealists and Orthodox thinkers, undoubtedly, represent the more complex and stimulating sector of the Russian Silver Age intelligentsia. Their "early and perceptive critique of twentieth-century political religions," elegantly and wittily presented, plus their vision of two realities, the "merely real" and the "supra-real," created thought systems that eschewed utopian visions of eternal material progress and defended the absolute value of the individual and his/her right to follow independent decisions, with however the caveat that an individual could only be truly free if s/he fervently embraced Orthodoxy.[105]

This theocratic insistence on Orthodoxy as the *sine qua non* of Russian culture undermines the spiritual freedom the idealists claim as one of their virtues and points to nationalism/chauvinism as embedded in their creed. The character of the Refugee in Bulgakov's "At the Feast of the Gods," voicing Dostoevsky's views, speaks of the Russian nation as "the only people in the world of universal consciousness, free from nationalism," but the very statement exudes what it denies: nationalism.[106] The Writer believes "that the salvation of the world will come through the Russian people, and that to it belongs not only a great future, but a decisive word in the fates of the world."[107] Even the old-fashioned General prefers Russian Bolsheviks to Europeanized Kadets, the former displaying *style russe*, while the liberals of the constitutional party evoke distrust, attempting to introduce "European parliamentarism."[108] In fact, the symposium participants seem most of all to deplore the loss of the mighty empire that Russia once was—they fear the Bolsheviks would be unable to restore it. Some even regret that losing World War I thwarted imperial Russia's attempt to take Constantinople —Istanbul after 1930—and make it the Center of Orthodoxy once more.

Of the two intelligentsia faiths presented above, socialism was stauncher in the sense that it never included the idealists in its strategies and plans, whereas the religious flank, as we have seen, kept inviting the old intelligentsia to join them. Even in the final statement of *Pir bogov*, Bulgakov lets the Refugee perceive universality "flicker[ing] through the deformities of present-day

---

105 Randall Poole, "Russian Political Theology in an Age of Revolution," in *Landmarks Revisited. The Vekhi Symposium One Hundred Years On*, ed. Robin Aizlewood and Ruth Coates (Boston, MA: Academic Studies Press, 2013), 154.
106 Bulgakov, "At the Feast of the Gods," 88.
107 Bulgakov, "At the Feast of the Gods," 90.
108 Ibid., 81.

internationalism."[109] Later, already in emigration, Berdyaev, impacted by Fascism's rise in Europe, came for a time to view the events of 1917 as a mere dialectical link in development of his "Russian idea" (of the nation's uniqueness and divine mission); the October Revolution, in his later émigré years, lost the demonic aspects so vividly demonstrated in "Specters of the Russian Revolution." According to Poltoratsky, Berdyaev came to view "the communists as continuators of Russian Messianism," maintaining the idea of "Moscow, the Third Rome" in its new incarnation of Moscow, the Third International.[110] Idealist proselytizing met little receptivity in the materialist camp, however. Many decades later, Church and State have made their peace in today's Russia, and the Russian Idea, in spite of the lapse of time, hovers over both in forms that, most likely, would be unacceptable to most of the religious idealists of *Out of the Depths*.[111]

Bibliography

Askol'dov [Alekseev], Sergei Alekseevich. "The Religious Meaning of the Russian Revolution." In *Out of the Depths (De Profundis): A Collection of Articles on the Russian Revolution*, translated and edited by William F. Woehrlin, 1–32. Irvine, CA: Charles Schlack Jr., Publisher, 1986.

Berdiaev, Nikolai. *Novoe religioznoe soznanie i obshchestvennost'*. St. Petersburg: Izdanie N. V. Pirozhkova, 1907/1999.

Berdiaev, Nikolai. "Socialism as Religion." (1906) In *A Revolution of the Spirit. Crisis of Value in Russia 1890–1924*, edited by Bernice Glatzer Rosenthal and Martha Bohachevsky-Chomiak, translated by Marian Schwartz, 107–133. New York: Fordham UP, 1990.

——— [Berdyaev, Nikolai]. "Philosophic Truth and the Moral Truth of the Intelligentsia" (1909). In *Landmarks: A Collection of Essays on the Russian Intelligentsia*, edited by Boris Shragin and Albert Todd, translated by Marian Schwartz, 3–22. New York: Karz Howard Publishers, 1977.

——— [Berdyaev, Nikolai]. *The Bourgeois Mind and Other Essays*. London: Sheed & Ward, 1934/1966.

---

109 Ibid., 88.
110 N. P. Poltoratskii, *Berdiaev i Rossiia: Filosofiia istorii Rossii u N. A. Berdiaeva* (New York: Obshchestvo druzei russkoi kul'tury, 1967), 88.
111 Berdyaev showed signs of disillusionment when voicing disapproval of Politburo member Andrei Zhdanov's "dressing-down" of Anna Akhmatova and Mikhail Zoshchenko in 1946.

——— [Berdiaev, Nikolai Aleksandrovich]. "Specters of the Russian Revolution." In *Out of the Depths (De Profundis): A Collection of Articles on the Russian Revolution*, translated and edited by William F. Woehrlin, 33–64. Irvine, CA: Charles Schlack Jr., Publisher, 1986.

Boer, Roland. "Utopia, Religion and the God-Builders: From Anatoly Lunacharsky to Ernst Bloch." In *From Francis Bacon to William Golding: Utopias and Dystopias of Today and of Yore*, edited by Ligia Tomoiaga, Minodora Barbul, and Ramona Demarcsek, 2–20. Newcastle upon Tyne: Cambridge Scholars Publishing, 2012.

Bulgakov, Sergei [Bulgakov, S. N.]. "Basic Problems of the Theory of Progress." (1902) In *Problems of Idealism: Essays in Russian Social Philosophy*, translated and edited by Randall A. Poole, 85–123. New Haven, CT: Yale UP, 2003.

———. "Heroism and Asceticism. Reflections on the Religious Nature of the Russian Intelligentsia." In *Landmarks: A Collection of Essays on the Russian Intelligentsia*, edited by Boris Shragin and Albert Todd, translated by Marian Schwartz, 23–63. New York: Karz Howard Publishers, 1977.

———. "At the Feast of the Gods." In *Out of the Depths (De Profundis): A Collection of Articles on the Russian Revolution*, translated and edited by William F. Woehrlin, 65–118. Irvine, CA: Charles Schlack Jr., Publisher, 1986.

Dostoevskii, Fedor. "Celebration of Pushkin's Birth. June 8, 1880. Feyodor Dostoevsky." Speech Vault. Accessed July 8, 2024. http://www.speeches-usa.com/Transcripts/feyodor_dostoevsky-pushkin.html

Engels, Frederick. *Anti-Dühring*. Moscow: Foreign Languages Publishing House, 1959.

Izgoev, Aleksandr. "On Educated Youth: Notes on Its Life and Sentiments." In *Landmarks: A Collection of Essays on the Russian Intelligentsia*, edited by Boris Shragin and Albert Todd, translated by Marian Schwartz, 88–111. New York: Karz Howard Publishers, 1977.

Lenin, V. I. *Materialism and Empirio-Criticism*. New York: International Publishers, 1927.

Lunacharskii, A. *Religiia i sotsializm*. Part 1. St. Petersburg: Shipovnik, 1908.

Masing-Delic, Irene [Masing-Delich, Airin]. *Uprazdnenie smerti. Mif o spasenii v russkoi literature XX veka*. Boston, MA: Academic Studies Press, 2020.

———. *Abolishing Death. A Salvation Myth of the Twentieth Century*. Stanford, CA: Stanford UP, 1992.

McLellan, David. *Friedrich Engels*. New York: Viking Press, 1978.

Nabokov, Vladimir. *Speak, Memory. An Autobiography Revisited. Novels and Memoirs 1941–1951*. New York: The Library of America, 1996.

Plekhanov, G. V. *Izbrannye filosofskie proizvedeniia*. 5 vols. Vol. 1: *K voprosu o razvitii monisticheskogo vzgliada na istoriiu*. Moscow: Gosudarstvennoe izdatel'stvo politicheskoi literatury, 1936.

———. *Ob ateizme i religii v istorii obshchestva i kul'tury*. Moscow: Mysl', 1977.

Poltoratskii, N. P. *Berdiaev i Rossiia. Filosofiia istorii Rossii u N. A. Berdiaeva*. New York: Obshchestvo druzei russkoi kul'tury, 1967.

———. "Sbornik 'Iz glubiny' i ego znachenie." In *Iz glubiny. Sbornik statei o russkoi revoliutsii*. Paris: YMCA-Press, 1967.

Poole, Randall. *Neo-Idealist Philosophy in the Russian Liberation Movement: The Moscow Psychological Society and Its Symposium, Problems of Idealism*. Washington, D.C.: Kennan Institute for Advanced Russian Studies, 1996.

———. "Philosophy and Politics in the Russian Liberation Movement." In *Problems of Idealism: Essays in Russian Social Philosophy*, translated and edited by Randall A. Poole, 1–78. New Haven, CT: Yale UP, 2003.

———. "Russian Political Theology in an Age of Revolution." In *Landmarks Revisited: The Vekhi Symposium One Hundred Years On*, edited by Robin Aizlewood and Ruth Coates, 146–169. Boston, MA: Academic Studies Press, 2013.

Read, Christopher. *Religion, Revolution and the Russian Intelligentsia 1900–1912. The* Vekhi *Debate and its Intellectual Background*. London: The MacMillan Press, 1979.

Rosenthal, Bernice Glatzer, and Martha Bohachevsky-Chomiak, eds. *A Revolution of the Spirit: Crisis of Value in Russia 1890–1924*. Translated by Marian Schwartz. New York: Fordham UP, 1990.

Shragin, Boris, and Albert Todd, eds. *Landmarks. A Collection of Essays on the Russian Intelligentsia*. Translated by Marian Schwartz. New York: Karz Howard Publishers, 1977.

Spirkin, Alexander. *Dialectical Materialism*. Moscow: Progress Publishers, 1983.

Struve, Nikita. "Prorocheskaia kniga," In *Iz glubiny. Sbornik statei o russkoi revoliutsii*. Paris: YMCA-Press, 1967.

Tiutiukin, S. V. *G. V. Plekhanov: Sud'ba russkogo marksista*. Moscow: Rosspen, 1987.

Walicki, Andrzej. *Marxism and the Leap to the Kingdom of Freedom. The Rise and Fall of the Communist Utopia*. Stanford, CA: Stanford UP, 1995.

Woehrlin, William F. "Introduction: Voices from Out of the Depths." In *Out of the Depths (De Profundis): A Collection of Articles on the Russian Revolution*, translated and edited by William F. Woehrlin, xvii-xxxiii. Irvine, CA: Charles Schlacks Jr., Publisher, 1986.

Landmarks (Vekhi)— the Russian Intelligentsia at a Crossroads

Olga Sobolev

The notion of the Russian intelligentsia, with a variety of aspects related to its ideology, its function, and its social ontology, constitutes one of the main narratives of the social and cultural history of the present day. All quintessential nineteenth- and twentieth-century political concepts—such as the notions of "power," "people," "society," "revolution"—made sense only in connection with the so-called "intelligentsia narrative," perpetuated by generations of Russian thinkers for more than a century and a half. This narrative's history is interwoven into literary images, political appeals, philosophical manifestos, and journalistic polemics, praising, accusing, analyzing, or cursing the "intelligentsia" in the process of this largely self-imposed and auto-reflective discourse. The collection *Landmarks* was a major milestone in the course of these polemics, for it is commonly regarded as the first major critical attempt to reflect on the social standing of the Russian intelligentsia: on its objectives, its function, and essentially its self-identification as a social group.

The collection was published in March 1909 on the initiative of Mikhail Gershenzon. It consisted of seven essays contributed by leading thinkers of the day, including Semyon Frank, Nikolai Berdyaev, and Sergei Bulgakov, who offered their account of the intelligentsia question in the aftermath of the tragic defeat of the Revolution of 1905. Its contents are as follows:

- Mikhail Gershenzon, "Preface to the First Edition";
- Nikolai Berdyaev, "Philosophical Verity and Intelligentsia Truth";
- Sergei Bulgakov, "Heroism and Asceticism: Reflections on the Religious Nature of the Russian Intelligentsia";
- Mikhail Gershenzon, "Creative Self-consciousness";
- Aleksandr Izgoev (Aron Lande), "On Educated Youth: Notes on Its Life and Sentiments";
- Bogdan Kistyakovsky, "In Defence of Law: The Intelligentsia and Legal Consciousness";
- Pyotr Struve, "The Intelligentsia and Revolution";
- Semyon Frank, "The Ethics of Nihilism: A Characterization of the Russian Intelligentsia's Moral Outlook."[1]

The appraisal in *Landmarks* came as a shock to mainstream Russian liberal forces. Rather than expressing solidarity with the pro-revolutionary tendencies and discussing new tactics for revolt, the volume urged liberals to move away from an active pro-revolutionary position. It emphasized reflective consolidation, the need for the intelligentsia's moral and political re-education, and its emancipation from the outworn legacy of the pre-1905 world.[2] Each of the contributors examined a different angle of the problem, and each of these contributions brought an impressively fresh note to the ongoing debate concerning the intelligentsia's identity and self-image.

To use a term coined by Svetlana Boym, the project of *Landmarks* can be seen as one of the first detours into the "off-Modern"[3]—the unexplored potentials of a mainstream narrative, probing lateral and unforeseen paths of critical thought. According to Boym, the term can be understood as a detour from any "deterministic narrative" of its own time,[4] and as the starting point of a broader, theoretically based analysis or discourse. Both characteristics are

---

1 *Vekhi* (Moscow: Izdatel'stvo Sablina, 1909). Here and hereafter textual references (retaining the translators' syntax and punctuation) are to *Vekhi*. *Landmarks: A Collection of Articles about the Russian Intelligentsia*, ed. and trans. Marshall S. Shatz and Judith E. Zimmerman (London: M. E. Sharpe, 1994).
2 In their reflection, the attempt made in *Landmarks* can hardly be regarded as systematic: the contributors were deliberately kept unaware of the overall content of the volume, as the editor wanted to avoid any kind of internal argument and pre-publication polemics. The collection, nonetheless, offered a remarkably focused and incisive critical analysis, as well as a very broad platform for further discussion. For modern scholarly reception of *Vekhi* see Robin Aizlewood and Ruth Coates, eds., *Landmarks Revisited: The Vekhi Symposium 100 Years On* (Boston, MA: Academic Studies Press, 2013).
3 Svetlana Boym, *The Future of Nostalgia* (New York: Basic Books, 2002), xvii.
4 Ibid.

germane to the analysis offered in *Landmarks*, manifesting in the long-term ramifications of the volume's ideas, which have been gaining currency over the course of the history of Russian liberal thought. Examples of this are manifold and include the 1918 collection *Out of the Depth* (Iz glubiny), which appraised the intelligentsia's impact on and involvement in the Bolshevik revolution.[5] It was followed by *Change of Landmarks* (Smena vekh) released in 1921 at the high tide of Bolshevik hostility towards the country's intellectuals, leading to their mass deportation (the "philosophers' ships") some fourteen months later in the autumn of 1922.[6] In 1974, amid the suffocating decades of Brezhnev-era stagnation, a new collection appeared, *From under the Rubble* (Iz-pod glyb). Authored by a group of Soviet intellectuals, the volume criticized the intelligentsia's passive position and appealed for their leadership in the revival of Orthodoxy, formation of a nation-state, and cultural rebirth. The early 1990s saw three new reprints of the *Landmarks* collection,[7] which was not entirely surprising: the country was making a fresh start after the collapse of the Soviet system, and the intelligentsia had to redefine their identity and their social goals.

Landmarks offered the notion of a political culture based on liberal practices, humanism, a solid moral framework, and spiritual worth, which has no less appeal today than it had in 1909, not least due to striking similarities with the post-1905 political context. Modern-day Russian authoritarianism lends itself to comparison with the reactionary years of the 1900s, when a comment or a literary text was equated with an act of political insurgence, and severe repressions were likely to be inflicted after an enlightened observation or a liberal word. In

---

5 *Out of the Depth: A Collection of Articles about the Russian Revolution* (Moscow-Petrograd: Russkaia mysl', 1918) was edited by Pyotr Struve; it was the culmination of his trilogy of edited volumes, following *Problems of Idealism* in 1902 and *Vekhi* in 1909. The collection included eleven essays, five authored by contributors to *Landmarks* (Nikolai Berdyaev, Sergei Bulgakov, Aleksandr Izgoev, Pyotr Struve, and Semyon Frank). The edition was widely disseminated during the anti-Bolshevik Kronshtadt uprising of 1921. It was later reprinted in Paris in 1967. For a more detailed analysis of the philosophical platform of these volumes see Caryl Emerson, "Foreword," in *Problems of Idealism: Essays in Russian Social Philosophy*, ed. and trans. Randall A. Poole (New Haven, CT: Yale UP, 2003), x-xvii; Leonard Shapiro, "The Vekhi Group and the Mystique of Revolution," *The Slavonic and East European Review* 34, no. 22 (1955): 69-71.
6 Published in July 1921 (Prague: Logos), *Change of Landmarks* offered a highly controversial stance on the possibility of collaboration with the Bolsheviks, in order to avoid a damaging division of Russian intellectual and liberal forces. For further analysis see Shapiro, "The Vekhi Group," 71-73.
7 These editions (with a considerable print run of 50,000 copies) were followed by an impressive anthology on the polemics around *Vekhi*: *Vekhi: pro et contra*, ed. Vadim Sapov (St Petersburg: Izdatel'stvo Russkogo khristianskogo gumanitarnogo instituta, 1998) and *Anti-Vekhi*, ed. Vadim Sapov (Moscow: Astrel', 2007).

light of these parallels, the volume's ideas sound remarkably relevant for Russia's realities of the present day; reading *Landmarks* through the lens of a more recent perspective may offer new points of reference for the ongoing debate on the intelligentsia's social impact. In pursuing this task, we shall proceed with a twofold examination: first contextualizing the controversy that surrounded the volume's release, and then moving to a comparative analysis of contemporary and modern readings of *Landmarks*.

The Unacknowledged Legislators of People's Minds

The release of *Landmarks* was a major literary sensation in its time. The first edition (3000 copies) sold out in two days; the second (another 3000 copies) disappeared from shelves in a couple of weeks. It was followed by three more consecutive editions, amounting to a total print run of 16,000 copies that sold out over approximately six months. To give an idea of the resonance evoked by this publication, one can refer to the critical bibliography appended to the fourth and fifth reprints of the volume. The bibliography comprised no fewer than 217 review articles published in 80 periodicals between March 23, 1909 and February 15, 1910,[8] which even the most eminent scholars in the context of today's electronic communications would envy.

As for the content of these reviews, the contemporary response to *Landmarks* was crushingly negative.[9] Attacks came from all existing political parties (the Constitutional Democrats, the Octobrists, the Socialist Revolutionaries, etc.), as well as from a whole number of affronted individuals, including such major figures as Lenin and Dmitry Merezhkovsky (albeit, obviously, from completely different standpoints). Pavel Milyukov, leader of the Constitutional Democrats, even took the trouble of going on tour throughout the country to disclaim the

---

[8] Publication of *Vekhi* was announced on March 15, 1909 in the newspaper *Russian News* (*Russkie vedomosti*). The reception statistics (for an average of 20 entries per month) are as follows: March—8 articles; April—35 articles (April 23—6 articles); May—49 articles; June—23 articles; July–December—20 articles per month on average; January–mid-February—22 articles (Vadim Sapov, "Vokrug Vekh," in *Vekhi: pro et contra*, ed. Vadim Sapov (St Petersburg: Izdatel'stvo Russkogo khristianskogo gumanitarnogo instituta, 1998), 3.

[9] Those few who raised their voices in support of *Landmarks'* position included Prince Evgeny Trubetskoi, founder of the minor political Party of Peaceful Renewal, the Metropolitan Antony Khrapovitsky, as a mouthpiece of the Church, and the eminent Russian author Vasily Rozanov, who called *Landmarks* "a pedagogical and philosophical book" (Vasilii Rozanov, "Mezhdu Azefom i 'Vekhami,'" *Novoe vremia*, August 20, 1909, 4).

position of *Landmarks*; and, according to Semyon Frank's memoirs, he never encountered a lack of listeners.[10]

On the one hand, the reception of *Landmarks* was evidently a *succès de scandale*. However, it is worth looking deeper into the underlying reasons for this scandal, because the unparalleled controversy and heated debates surrounding this publication testified to the great urgency of the volume's ideas, as well as their relevance for the liberal intelligentsia's fundamental questions and concerns. These concerns, now exposed with remarkable clarity for the first time, drew attention to the fundamental paradox in the paradigm of the intelligentsia's social metaphysics, namely to an intrinsic contradiction between their collective intentionality (or self-perception) and their *modus operandi* as a social group.

Examining this contradiction, it is worth noting that the status of the intelligentsia, be it social, legal, or political, was not firmly and formally established at the time (which nowadays, arguably, can be regarded as a *de facto* position). The first decade of the twentieth century was characterized by rapid growth of the educated classes. In 1897 the number of students in Russia was recorded at 31,427; by 1908, there were about three times more, reaching a figure of 92,697.[11] The most popular Higher Educational Establishments of the capital included the Mining Institute, the Electrotechnical Institute, and the State Institute of Railway Communication. Their graduates were known to have excellent prospects of employment, as well as relatively high salaries at the start of their jobs.

These growing numbers of educated intellectuals, however, found themselves completely removed from government activity and its structures. There were only four establishments that historically supplied the generations of Russian statesmen (the Imperial Aleksandrovsky Lyceum; the Imperial School of Jurisprudence; the Page Corps; and the Nikolaevsky Cavalry School). All of these catered exclusively to descendants of the old Russian aristocracy; for those outside their circle, pursuing a political career was strictly speaking out

---

10 S. L. Frank, *Biografiia P. B. Struve* (New York: Izdatel'stvo imeni Chekhova, 1956), 84. Milyukov was outraged by the disengagement of *Landmarks* from the revolutionary movement, claiming that their emphasis on people rather than institutions did not correspond to the current political context (Pavel Miliukov, "Intelligentsia i istoricheskaia traditsiia," in *Intelligentsia v Rossii*, ed. K. Arsen'ev et al. [St. Petersburg: Zemlia, 1910], 105). According to Milyukov, one needed to capitalize on the "cracks" produced in the tsarist monarchy by the October Manifesto (October 17, 1905), which promised basic civil rights, universal men's suffrage, and an elected parliament—the first Duma. The Constitutional Democrats (led by Milyukov) had a majority, or near majority, in the first three Russian Dumas (1906–1912).
11 A. E. Ivanov, *Vysshaia shkola Rossii v kontse XIX-nachale XX veka* (Moscow: Institut istorii AN SSSR, 1991), 254.

of reach.[12] The rift between the government and the intelligentsia was therefore carefully maintained. Such a position was aggravated by the vaguely formalized legal status of the latter. The social value of the intelligentsia's education was acknowledged by their exemption from certain taxes, but, unlike the nobility and the burghers, the intelligentsia was deprived of representation in local government (*zemstvo*). Any attempts to introduce educational qualification (along with property status) as a basis for election to these bodies (as was the case in Germany after the 1848 revolution) were to no avail, and intellectuals (with some rare exceptions) were effectively denied political participation up until the revolution of 1905–1907.

As regards the intelligentsia's self-perception, several aspects traditionally featured in this type of discourse. The first concerned *the gulf between the intelligentsia and those in power, which was characterized by antagonism and hostility to the existing political order. The second juxtaposed the intelligentsia against the people: emphasis shifted to their missionary* role (though not without political undertones)—the intelligentsia as a "defender of the people" (*zastupnik narodnyi*)[13] against the anti-democratic and tyrannical state. In addition, one should also mention the intelligentsia's ethical function, associated with shaping the domain of social morals. This role would commonly be ascribed to religion, but in the Russian Empire the Orthodox Church was under strict state control and, thus, heavily politicized. (In this respect the parallel with modern-day Russia is difficult to miss.)[14]

---

12 There were some rare exceptions involving those who managed to build a state career after graduating from other Institutions. Examples include Pyotr Stolypin, who graduated from St. Petersburg University, and Sergei Vitte—a graduate of Novorossiysky University of Odessa. Both of them, however, had very strong personal connections among the governing elite: Pyotr Stolypin's family dated back to the old aristocrats of the sixteenth century and were as eminent as the Counts Tolstoy. In the same vein, Vitte's mother belonged to one of the oldest noble families, the princely Dolgorukys.

13 The term was widely used among members of the 1860s-1870s Populist Movement (*narodniki*). In the words of Mikhail Protopopov, an ardent populist, influential journalist, and literary critic, "'defending the people' (*narodozastupnichestvo*) is not so much a matter of political calculation as of personal moral satisfaction" of the intelligentsia (Mikhail Protopovov, "Posledovatel'nyi narodnik," *Russkaia mysl'* 5 [1891]: 117).

14 It is also worth mentioning the opposition of the Russian intelligentsia to Western intellectuals, which substantiates the claimed uniqueness of this Russian phenomenon and its manifestations. Perpetrators of this idea commonly refer to the fact that English borrowed the term "intelligentsia" from Russian, although in Russian and in English this word arose primarily to refer to Polish and generally Central and Eastern European intellectuals ("Etimologicheskie online-slovari russkogo iazyka," Lexicography Online, accessed July 24, 2023, https://lexicography.online/etymology/).

In their attempt to unite their diverse functions, members of the intelligentsia saw themselves, to paraphrase Shelley's expression, as the unacknowledged legislators of people's minds.[15] At the turn of the century, however, these "legislators" found themselves in a fairly weak position. They had no access to real power and no experience of political activity in its practical sense. As regards their populist mission, and more specifically the intelligentsia's major project of "going to the people" (*khozhdenie v narod*),[16] by the 1890s this venture had turned into a fiasco due to poor organization, ideological diversity, and the illiterate peasant masses' lack of receptiveness to socialist ideals. That failure only intensified public rhetoric about the rift between the intelligentsia and the people, *drawing attention to the marginality of the former's social position*. In the words of Semyon Frank: "To 'them' were opposed 'we,' the 'people,' and above all the 'caste' of the intelligentsia, concerned with the welfare of the people and devoted to its service, but due to their lack of rights capable only of criticizing the authorities, arousing oppositional sentiments, and secretly getting ready for a revolt."[17]

By the turn of the twentieth century, therefore, the intelligentsia constituted a rapidly growing, but in the main hermetic social layer; and the metaphor of being "split off" (*otshchepenstvo*)[18] was increasingly cited as their common characteristic. The intellectuals could no longer be regarded as located between the state and the people, but effectively found themselves outside the former and the latter. At the same time, within the framework of their identity discourse, the intelligentsia's self-perception was still largely validated through their outward social functions: that is, derived from their relation to their main counterparts—the state and the people. Considering that these functions were not underpinned by any meaningful social interactions, such an approach rendered worthless the intelligentsia's appraisal of all other aspects of their social metaphysics.

---

15 "*Poets* are the unacknowledged *legislators of the world*" (Percy B. Shelley, "A Defence of Poetry," in idem, *Essays, Letters from Abroad, Translations and Fragments* [London: William Smith, 1845], vol. 1, 15).

16 Widespread in the 1860s-1870s, *khozhdenie v narod* was a mass movement of educated young people who believed that socialist propaganda among the peasant masses would lead to their awakening and through this to liberalization of the tsarist regime. "Enlightenment" here meant not only elimination of the illiteracy of the population or the creation of public schools, but also the improvement of the peasants' economic life: the organization of cheese dairies, savings and loan banks, labor cooperatives, and other initiatives borrowed from Western books on farming.

17 Frank, *Biografiia Struve*, 75.

18 The contemporary connotations of this term were discussed in works by Pavel Milyukov ("Intelligentsiia i istoricheskaia traditsiia," 128–129) and Nikolai Berdyaev (*Dukhovnyi krizis intelligentsii* [St. Petersburg: Obshchestvennaia pol'za, 1910], 61–72).

It was this kind of paradox that was highlighted by the authors of *Landmarks*, who saw the intelligentsia's revolutionary zeal as a mere substitute for an authentic cultural mission, as well as a major obstacle to becoming a leading political player. This zeal, though not without its appeal, was seen in *Landmarks* as rooted in the intelligentsia's political non-involvement—their estrangement from government activity, with which they had no concern except hoping to overthrow it by a revolt. "*Landmarks* embodied criticism of the basic sacred dogma of the radical intelligentsia," Frank wrote,

> ...the 'mystique' of revolution. This was regarded as an audacious and quite intolerable betrayal of the age-old sacred testament of the Russian intelligentsia, the betrayal of the tradition handed down by the prophets and saints of Russian social thought—Belinsky, Granovsky, Chernyshevsky, Pisarev—and a betrayal of the age-old striving for liberty, enlightenment, and progress, and a going over to the side of black reaction.[19]

The Russian intelligentsia believed passionately in perfecting human society, in the rationalism of enlightenment, and in social progress. The nobility, the state, and its supporting bureaucracy were all abhorrent, and not joining forces against them was to betray everything that was honorable in man. An attempt to separate the intelligentsia's collective intentionality from these, so to speak, progressive forces was the major reason for public rejection of *Landmarks*, especially if one adhered to the positivist version of enlightenment typically professed by the intelligentsia during the decades around the turn of the twentieth century. In order to ascertain whether there were any real grounds for such a rejection, it is worth looking into the question of whether *Landmarks*' critique of established discourse was directed towards the intelligentsia's immanent or transcendent characteristics. Given that the Enlightenment has, it must be stressed, always been associated with both the intelligentsia's identity and its populist mission, this question essentially amounts to interpreting their intention to separate the two, seeing it either as an urgent call for a more profound self-reflection or as a regressive counter-Enlightenment stance. In this connection, it would also be useful to consider whether the critique offered by *Landmarks* is still relevant for the Russia of the present day, and, if so, to reflect on the grounds for its current importance.

---

19 Vasilii Zen'kovskii, ed., *Sbornik pamiati Semena Liudvigovicha Franka* (Munich: Izdatel'stvo sem'i Franka, 1954), 11.

"If We Could Change Ourselves, the World Would Also Change"[20]

As Gershenzon claimed in his foreword to the volume, the common platform for all seven essays was "the theoretical and practical primacy of spiritual life over external forms of community." The authors believed "that the individual's inner life is the sole creative force in human existence, and that this inner life, and not the self-sufficient principles of the political realm, constitutes the only solid basis on which a society can be built."[21] According to *Landmarks*, the intelligentsia's main weakness lay in its low degree of self-understanding—in the absence of this solid inner core that could shape and support their outward social functions and allow them to react meaningfully to the changing political context. This weakness manifested itself most clearly in the intelligentsia's caricatural, not to say catastrophic, performance in the first (1906) and second (1907) State Dumas when driven by the inertia of their revolutionary persuasions, the intelligentsia proved completely incapable of taking the lead in the aftermath of the 1905 Revolution (a time when the government agreed to respond to the new constitutional demands put forward by liberal forces).

The idea in *Landmarks*, therefore, was to re-direct the general vector of the intelligentsia's social involvement from outward to inward and to place emphasis on their moral re-education. The pervasive sense of intellectual orthodoxy—a single-minded dedication to the idea of revolt—endowed *Landmarks'* appeal to broaden the ontological platform of the intelligentsia's self-reflection, while maintaining distance from a definitive political stance. To use the wording coined by Frank, this was an attempt to re-examine the question of the intelligentsia from a vantage standpoint outside of "the right and the left."[22] The aim was to return to spiritual and moral values embodied in liberally thinking individuals, who were open to aesthetic and philosophical innovations (symbolism, existentialism, neo-Kantianism, etc.) and empowered to devise constructive alternatives for social transformation. According to *Landmarks*, this would facilitate a welcome shift from the intelligentsia's "degrading slave-mentality" of outsiders towards that of active participators and legislators[23] (some sort of

---

20 Mahatma Gandhi, "General Knowledge about Health XXXII," in *The Collected Works of Mahatma Gandhi* (Delhi: Government Publications Division, 1958–1964), vol. 12 (1964), 158.
21 *Vekhi. Landmarks*, xxxvii.
22 S. L. Frank, "Po tu storonu 'pravogo i levogo,'" *Novyi mir* 4 (1990): 226.
23 *Vekhi. Landmarks*, 131–2. As Frank put it in his comments on Struve's statements: "*He always discussed politics not from 'below,' but from 'above,' not as a member of an enslaved society,*

working agreement with the monarchy, so that reform could take place on a solid foundation of law, was not entirely dismissed).

Concerning the general framework of this moral re-education, what was offered was essentially a neo-enlightenment project based on the intelligentsia's own acculturation, which was seen as an alternative to existing populist and nihilist outreach programs. More specifically, Berdyaev outlined the importance of expanding the intelligentsia's attitude towards various philosophical systems, as the value of the latter was typically narrowed down to the social and utilitarian aims that those systems could serve (a different outlook was labelled reactionary and instantly dismissed). He considered this step toward pluralism as first and foremost necessary for reviving the intelligentsia's freedom of thinking. "We called true that philosophy which furthered the struggle with autocracy in the name of socialism," he claimed, "and we made the obligatory profession of such 'true' philosophy an essential part of the struggle itself."[24] The intelligentsia had to cure themselves of such a state of inner slavery, for only by doing this could they emancipate themselves from the external oppression they were used to blaming for all their own failures and misfortunes. "Love for egalitarian justice, for social good, for the people's welfare paralyzed love for the truth, has almost destroyed any interest in truth,"[25] he wrote.

While advocating pluralism as the general principle of their campaign, *Landmarks* saw religious humanism rather than positivism and utilitarian ethics as the basis of their social metaphysics. This seemingly regressive turn inevitably came under attack from their rationalist opponents. But in relation to this point, it is worth bearing in mind that *Landmarks* emphasized spiritual rather than dogmatic aspects of religious concerns. Paramount was freedom of choice in accepting and internalizing Christian ideals; their understanding of religion was akin to that projected in the writings of Dostoevsky (*The Brothers Karamazov*)—a subconscious inner connection with the divine, independent of the rigid system of ecclesiastical structures and institutions. As Bulgakov put it in his essay:

> A church intelligentsia combining true Christianity with a clear and enlightened understanding of cultural and historical tasks (which contemporary churchmen so often lack), were one to

---

but conscious of the fact that he was a potential participant in positive state construction" (Frank, *Biografiia Struve*, 76).
24 *Vekhi. Landmarks*, 12.
25 Ibid., 6.

arise, would meet an urgent historical and national need. And even if it had to suffer in its turn the persecution and oppression which the intelligentsia endures for the sake of atheistic ideals, this would have enormous historical and religio-moral significance and would find a very special response in the people's souls.[26]

Atheism, commonly associated with the positivist version of enlightenment, provided, in his view, a false premise for configuring both the intelligentsia's self-conception and their attitude towards people. He drew attention to the fact that, within the framework of this approach, the humanistic notion of "living a fulfilling life" had been gradually replaced by purely functional activity, which Bulgakov defined as "living for."[27] Being born from the intelligentsia's unrestrained passion for perfecting mankind, and like any mission focusing on outcomes, it was essentially hubristic, aiming at victory rather than reconciliation and thus never hesitating to sacrifice the means to the desired end. Such "heroism," Bulgakov argued, was drawn from self-gratification ("from a false image of oneself as the unacknowledged saviour of the world"), in contrast to the true humility of "Christian askesis."[28]

Moreover, according to Berdyaev, the intelligentsia's predilection for social utilitarianism, supplanting Christian morality, altered their overall humanistic life stance, and in particular their perception of "genuine love for people."[29] Within the framework of this new ethics, he claimed, the Christian idea of wholesome compassion found its positivist substitute in pity for the deprived—hence the urge to put oneself at the disposal and service of the latter. Berdyaev perceived certain condescending, top-down undertones in such an intention, which, unsurprisingly, met no resonance in the masses and paved the way for the intelligentsia's social isolation. "Genuine love for people . . . is not in pity that denies one's dignity, but in recognition of God's own image in every human being," he wrote.[30]

---

26 Ibid., 47–48.
27 Ibid., 67.
28 Ibid., 27, 35, 37.
29 Ibid., 8.
30 Ibid., 8. This lack of Christian "sense of community" (*sobornost'*) was regarded in *Landmarks* as a major factor in widening the rift between the intelligentsia and the people. This rift, in Gershenzon's infamous assertion (for which he never ceased to provide endless apologies and clarifications), had already reached the stage of such irrevocable hatred that a barrier was required to keep both sides securely apart. "Such as we are," he wrote, "we not only cannot dream of merging with the people, but we must fear them more than all the government's

Frank and Struve in their essays severely criticized the attempt to seek moral grounding in atheism and the consequentialism of utilitarian ethics. Considering that any utilitarian standpoint had intrinsic difficulties accounting for such values as individual rights and justice, Frank defined it as "nihilistic moralism"[31] in order to highlight the platform's fundamental hollowness. He drew attention to the precariousness of rooting the intelligentsia's identity in such morally flawed ethics, based, as he put it, on "the notion that society's progress need not be the fruit of human improvement, but could be instead a jackpot to be won at the gambling table of history by appealing to popular unrest."[32]

In a passage of extraordinary foresight and insightfulness, especially if one recollects the date when his essay was written, Frank outlined the long-term implications of one's adherence to, so to speak, null and void systems:

> The socialist is not an altruist. True, he too is striving for human happiness, but he does not love living people, only his idea, the idea of universal human happiness. Since he is sacrificing himself for the idea, he does not hesitate to sacrifice others as well. He can see his contemporaries only as victims of the world's evil that he dreams of eradicating, or as perpetrators of that evil . . . It is this feeling of hatred for the enemies of people [sic.] that forms the concrete, active psychological foundation for his life. Thus, great love for future humanity engenders great hatred for people [sic.].[33]

These implications, when reviewed from today's vantage point, manifested themselves, first, in the outrage of the Bolshevik terror, and then in the *hostis publicus* rhetoric of Stalin's purges. Subsequently, this led to the overtly grotesque *simulacrum*-state of the late-Soviet era, and one can only admire the lucidity with which *Landmarks* got to the roots of this pitiful evolution back in 1909. "We accepted," Bulgakov wrote, a hollow shell of "atheistic socialism" without "the roots which feed the tree" of European civilization, without its important

---

executions, and we must bless this government which alone, with its bayonets and prisons, still protects us from the people's wrath" (Ibid., 64).

31 Ibid., 141. Semyon Frank saw the contemporary intelligentsia as an order of militant monks "of the nihilistic religion of earthly well-being" (ibid., 150).
32 Ibid., 125.
33 Ibid., 143.

Christian substratum, "powerful spiritual tendencies," social morality, and the rule of law. "No culture has yet been built upon such a foundation."[34]

A hundred and fifteen years after the volume's first release, this statement by Bulgakov sounds both surprisingly visionary and remarkably modern, not least because nowadays Russian intellectuals are once again bound to reflect on the project of their "fathers," who at the beginning of the 1990s tried to implant Western economic values in the dry soil of the outworn Soviet system. The social outcomes of this project—the formation of a civil society rooted in humanism, solid education, and the rule of law—were deemed questionable already in the early 2010s. Moreover, it is highly ironic (not to say dispiriting) with regard to the implementation of this project that *Landmarks*' appraisal of the post-1905 situation has retained its actuality all the way through the last thirty years and up to the present-day *status quo*. To give but a few examples, one can refer, for instance, to a brief account of public legal awareness offered by Kistyakovsky: "The Russian, whatever his class, breaks the law wherever he can do so with impunity; the government acts in the same way."[35] Likewise, Aleksandr Izgoev's comment on the level of competence in Russian political

---

34 Ibid., 23.
35 Ibid., 94. Here, Kistyakovsky uses a quote from Aleksandr Herzen's work *On the Development of the Revolutionary Ideas in Russia*, first published in German in 1851. "Historically," Kistyakovsky continues, "our public consciousness never advanced the ideal of the legal person. Both aspects of this ideal, the person disciplined by law and by a stable legal order, and the person endowed with all rights and freely enjoying them, are alien to our intelligentsia's mentality" (ibid., 94). In a playful mode, he refers to a verse parody by Boris Almazov (Adamontov) satirizing the intelligentsia's denial of the need for legal guarantees, regarded by Slavophiles (Konstantin Aksakov and others) as a manifestation of Russia's spiritual authenticity:

> По причинам органическим,
> Мы совсем не снабжены
> Здравым смыслом юридическим
> Сим исчадьем Сатаны.
>
> Широки натуры русские—
> Нашей правды идеал
> Не влезает в формы узкие
> Юридических начал. (*Vekhi*, 103)
>
> For reasons quite historical
> We have a lack intense
> Of that quality diabolical,
> Juridical common sense.
>
> Too lofty is our sense of right
> In this broad-natured nation
> To fit within the confines tight
> Of legal codification. (*Vekhi. Landmarks*, 95)

circles requires no further elucidation; and one would not be surprised to see it in today's headlines, subject to some minor changes in the names of political players: "We must have the courage to admit that, aside from some thirty or forty Kadets and Octobrists, the overwhelming majority of the deputies in our State Dumas have not exhibited the knowledge necessary to undertake the administration and reconstruction of Russia."[36]

One of the most striking predictions, however, was put forward by Pyotr Struve, who drew attention to the process of "reformatting" the intelligentsia under the proliferation of capitalist relations or the advance of the market economy, to put it in the modern-day sense of the term. "As economic development proceeds," he wrote, "the intelligentsia will be 'bourgeoisified'; that is, through a process of social adjustment it will become reconciled with the state, and it will organically and spontaneously be drawn into the existing social structure and distributed among the different classes of society."[37] In 1905, this type of scenario did not come into being,[38] but post-Soviet developments bore witness to the predictive power of Struve's thought. Quite a few modern-day intellectuals, especially those from high quarters, could hardly use the word 'intelligentsia' as a means of self-identification. This applies to such members of the cultural elite as Stanislav Govorukhin or Nikita Mikhalkov, as well as those from the neo-Stolypinist consensus who until recently held together Putin and his 'liberal tower' à la Aleksei Kudrin, Anatoly Chubais, and Egor Gaidar.

Further to the point, not unlike the aftermath of the 1905 revolution, the socio-political climate of modern Russia can be characterized as a time of reactionary depression, not to mention striking similarities in severe censorship and a complete absence of pluralism and freedom of speech. Even the vast and rapid revival of religious consciousness in the post-Soviet decades can hardly be seen as a solid platform for fostering free and independent moral thinking, largely because a firm political alliance has been formed between the Russian state and the Russian Orthodox Church. Present-day Russian intellectuals are once again at a crossroads, tormented by the same perennial questions of whether to radicalize or to avoid rocking the boat. The old Soviet era's legacy has been effaced; the new values are unclear and far from being shaped in any meaningful sense. Considering this, it is not difficult to see why debates on the intelligentsia's current strategies and the ways of emerging unscarred from the murky years of reaction still retain their thought-provoking quality today, as they did before.

---

36 Ibid., 89.
37 Ibid., 128.
38 Russia went along a different path, prophetically outlined in Struve's reflections: "The crisis of socialism must . . . have a greater ideological impact in Russia than elsewhere" (ibid., 129).

Bibliography

Aizlewood, Robin, and Ruth Coates, eds. *Landmarks Revisited: The Vekhi Symposium 100 Years On*. Boston, MA: Academic Studies Press, 2013.

Berdiaev, Nikolai. *Dukhovnyi krizis intelligentsii*. St Petersburg: Obshchestvennaia pol'za, 1910.

Boym, Svetlana. *The Future of Nostalgia*. New York: Basic Books, 2002.

Emerson, Caryl. "Foreword." In *Problems of Idealism: Essays in Russian Social Philosophy*, edited and translated by Randall A. Poole, vii-xviii. New Haven, CT: Yale UP, 2003.

"Etimologicheskie online-slovari russkogo iazyka." Lexicography Online. Accessed July 24, 2023. https://lexicography.online/etymology/.

Frank, S. L. *Biografiia P. B. Struve*. New York: Izdatel'stvo imeni Chekhova, 1956.

———. "Po tu storonu 'pravogo i levogo.'" *Novyi mir* 4 (1990): 226–233.

Gandhi, Mahatma. "General Knowledge about Health XXXII." In *The Collected Works of Mahatma Gandhi*, edited by Indian Ministry of Information and Broadcasting, vol. 12, 156–160. Delhi: Government Publications Division, 1964.

Ivanov, A. E. *Vysshaia shkola Rossii v kontse XIX-nachale XX veka*. Moscow: Institut istorii AN SSSR, 1991.

Miliukov, Pavel. "Intelligentsia i istoricheskaia traditsiia." In *Intelligentsiia v Rossii*, edited by K. Arsen'ev et al, 89–191. St Petersburg: Zemlia, 1910.

Protopovov, Mikhail. "Posledovatel'nyi narodnik." *Russkaia mysl'* 5 (1891): 113–130.

Rozanov, Vasilii. "Mezhdu Azefom i 'Vekhami.'" *Novoe vremia* 20 (1909): 3–4.

Sapov, Vadim, ed. *Vekhi: pro et contra*. St Petersburg: Izdatel'stvo Russkogo khristianskogo gumanitarnogo instituta, 1998.

———. *Anti-Vekhi*. Moscow: Astrel', 2007.

Sapov, Vadim. "Vokrug Vekh." In *Vekhi: pro et contra*, edited by Vadim Sapov, 2–17. St Petersburg: Izdatel'stvo Russkogo khristianskogo gumanitarnogo instituta, 1998.

Shapiro, Leonard. "The *Vekhi* Group and the Mystique of Revolution." *The Slavonic and East European Review* 34, no 22 (1955): 56–76.

Shelley, Percy B. "A Defence of Poetry." In idem, *Essays, Letters from Abroad, Translations and Fragments*, vol. 1, 1–15. London: William Smith, 1845.

Shatz, Marshall S., and Judith E. Zimmerman, eds. and trans. *Vekhi. Landmarks: A Collection of Articles about the Russian Intelligentsia*. London: M. E. Sharpe, 1994.

Vekhi. Moscow: Izdatel'stvo Sablina, 1909.

Zen'kovskii, Vasilii, ed. *Sbornik pamiati Semena Liudvigovicha Franka*. Munich: Izdatel'stvo sem'i Franka, 1954.

The End of the Classical Intelligentsia?

G. M. Hamburg

The publication of "fat journals" on literature and politics was a central element of the classical intelligentsia's activity in the nineteenth and early twentieth century.[1] The present article, which focuses on *Voice of the past* (Golos minuvshago) from 1913 to 1923, asks whether Soviet power brought the classical intelligentsia, and with it this journal and others, to an untimely end.

I

Golos minuvshago's first editorial board included the literary critic Pavel Nikitich Sakulin and the historians Aleksei Karpovich Dzhivelegov, Vasily Ivanovich Semevsky, and Sergei Petrovich Melgunov. Sakulin was a distinguished historian of nineteenth-century Russian literature whose massive 1913 study of Prince Vladimir Odoevsky merited the simultaneous granting of a master's and doctoral degree at Moscow University.[2] In the two decades preceding the

---

1 Gary M. Hamburg, "A Russian Triptych: Intellectuals before and after 1917," *Journal of Modern Russian History and Historiography* 16 (2023): 50–64.
2 Pavel N. Sakulin, *Iz istorii russkogo idealizma: Kniaz' V. F. Odoevskii. Myslitel'-pisatel'*, vol. 1, part 2 (Moscow: Izdatel'stvo Sabashnikovykh, 1913).

publication of this book, Sakulin had involved himself in political protests, starting with the student protests of 1890 for which he was arrested, and ending most dramatically with his resignation, with over 100 other instructors, from the Moscow University faculty in 1911 over the attempt of the ministry of education to limit assemblies and to delegate the prerogative of closing the university to local police (the so-called "Kasso affair"). In 1917, he published a fascinating book on the introduction of a reformed Russian *Schrift* that examined justifications for the reform and the psychological objections to it.[3] After 1917, Sakulin taught literature and linguistics at Moscow University and continued his research into nineteenth-century literary history.

Dzhivelegov, at Moscow University a protégé of the great historian Pavel Gavrilovich Vinogradov, was a historian of late medieval and Renaissance cities in Western Europe. His early works analyzed urban social history.[4] Like Sakulin, Dzhivelegov was politically active, in this case through membership on the Central Committee of the Constitutional Democratic party and via a book on the introduction of universal suffrage in Germany.[5] Just before the founding of *Golos minuvshago*, he co-edited with Melgunov and Vladimir Ivanovich Pecheta a multi-volume work on the Great Reform of 1861, and a seven-volume work on the Napoleonic war and Russian society.[6] These publications, landmarks in Russian social and political history, were probably the most important collective works on modern Russia to appear before the end of the old regime. Both Sakulin and Dzhivelegov left the editorial board of *Golos minuvshago* in 1914, so their leadership lasted barely a calendar year. After the revolution, Dzhivelegov continued to write on the late Middle Ages and Renaissance. He shifted from liberalism to Marxism.

The senior member of the editorial board was Semevsky, probably the most accomplished social historian of Russia under the old regime. Semevsky was born into a petty gentry family in Vitebsk province. At the Petersburg classical *gimnaziia* from 1863 to 1866, he studied under Vasily Ivanovich Vodovozov, a

---

3 Pavel N. Sakulin, *Reforma russkogo pravopisaniia* (Petrograd: Parus, 1917).
4 Aleksei Karpovich Dzhivelegov, *Gorodskaia obshchina v srednie veka: nekotoryia novyia teorii o proiskhozhdenii srednevekovykh gorodov* (Moscow: Izdatel'stvo magazina "Knizhnoe delo," 1901); idem, *Srednevekovyia goroda v Zapadnoi Evrope* (St. Petersburg: Brokgauz-Efron, 1902); idem, *Nachalo ital'ianskago Vozrozhdeniia* (Moscow: Pol'za, 1908).
5 Idem, *Bismark i Lassal': K istorii vseobshchego izbiratel'nogo prava* (Moscow: Trud i volia, 1906).
6 Aleksei Karpovich Dzhivelegov, Sergei Petrovich Mel'gunov, and Vladimir Ivanovich Pecheta, eds., *Velikaia reforma: 1861–1911, Russkoe obshchestvo i krest'ianskii vopros v proshlom i nastoiashchem*, 6 vols. (Moscow: Izdatel'stvo Sytina, 1911); idem, eds., *Otechestvennaia voina i russkoe obshchestvo, 1812–1912*, 7 vols. (Moscow: Izdatel'stvo Sytina, 1911–1912).

well-known translator of European literature and one of the capital's best theorists of education.[7] Vodovozov's Tuesday circle introduced Semevsky to leading Russian populists, such as Pyotr Lavrovich Lavrov, and Nikolai Konstantinovich Mikhailovsky.[8] It is likely that, under Vodovozov but also through the auspices of his older brother Mikhail Ivanovich, Semevsky encountered the thinking of Nikolai Gavrilovich Chernyshevsky, whose ideas of social justice would influence him the rest of his life.[9] On completing *gimnaziia*, Semevsky enrolled in the Petersburg Medical-Surgical Academy, where he studied natural sciences and medicine for two years. He then transferred to Petersburg University's department of history and philology and graduated in 1872.

As a graduate student, Semevsky focused on the history of the eighteenth-century Russian peasantry. In a general way, he may have followed in the scholarly footsteps of his older brother, who published a series of articles, and later books, on the late seventeenth and early eighteenth century.[10] However, Vasily's concentration probably owed more to two other factors. The first was educated society's obsessive interest in the peasant question, an interest manifested in the debates over peasant emancipation and implementation of the peasant reforms of the 1860s, but also fanned by the burgeoning populist movement. As the historian Aleksandr Aleksandrovich Kizevetter noted, the early and mid-1870s were the years when the "going to the people" occurred. Semevsky did not join the hundreds of students who journeyed to peasant villages to raise the peasants' consciousness, but he "went to the people" through his research in libraries and archives.[11] The second factor was Semevsky's realization that Russian historians had done little work on the enserfed peasantry under Catherine II, that is, during the apogee of serf system. Ivan Dmitrievich Belyaev's pioneering *Peasants in Old Russia* (Krest'iane na Rusi, (1860) had devoted only one chapter to the late eighteenth century.[12] Aleksandr Vasilyevich Romanovich-Slavatinsky's book on the eighteenth- and nineteenth-century nobility primarily treated the peasantry

---

7   Vasilii I. Vodovozov, *Izbrannye pedagogicheskie sochineniniia*, ed. Vasilii Zakharovich Smirnov (Moscow: Izdatel'stvo Akademii pedagogicheskikh nauk RSFSR, 1958).

8   Sergei Vladimirovich Gavrilov, "V. I. Vodovozov i V. I. Semevskii: ot istoricheskoi biografii pedagoga k vnutrennei biografii istorika," *Vestnik Severnogo federal'nogo universiteta. Seriia gumanitarnoi i sotsial'noi nauki* 4 (2017): 5–15.

9   Ol'ga Borisovna Kokh, "Geroi svoego vremeni (shtrikhi k portretu M. I. Semevskogo)," *Pskov* 14 (2001): 44–60.

10 Mikhail Semevskii, *Slovo i delo! 1700–1725. Tainaia kantseliariia pri Petre Velikom*, 2nd ed. (St. Petersburg: Tipografiia V. S. Balasheva, 1884).

11 Aleksandr A. Kizevetter, "V. I. Semevskii v ego uchenykh trudakh," *Golos minuvshago* 1 (1917): 201.

12 Ivan D. Beliaev, *Krest'iane na Rusi. Izsledovanie o postepennom izmenenii znacheniia krest'ian v russkom obshchestve* (Moscow: v Universitetskoi tipografii, 1860), 312–316.

from the legal perspective: it dealt with nearly two centuries of evidence on the material position of the peasantry in just forty pages.[13]

In 1881, Semevsky published his candidate's dissertation, *Peasants under Catherine II* (Krest'iane v tsarstvovanie Imperatritsy Ekateriny II), a massive volume that constituted a landmark in Russian historical scholarship.[14] In 1901, he saw into print an even more massive sequel, dealing with other categories of peasants under Catherine—those under royal control, state peasants, those under Church jurisdiction, and so on.[15] He drafted a third volume summarizing the peasant economy under Catherine but never managed to publish it.

Analyzing Semevsky's capital work, Kizevetter pointed to its four major conclusions:

1. the serfs' deprivation of liberty reached its height late in the eighteenth century;
2. the serf regime alienated Russian landowners from efficient estate management, turning them "not into rural entrepreneurs, but rather into petty rulers over their serfs";
3. the serfs "lived at the mercy of their lords," so that the material wellbeing of most privately owned peasants was "hanging by a thread";
4. non-serf peasants lived under "the same norms of unfreedom" experienced by serfs.[16]

To these conclusions should be added another: Semevsky's positive assessment of the peasant commune and of communal assemblies, which he saw as limiting the lords' authority over distribution of land resources.[17] Between the lines Semevsky maintained that the imperial government and the nobility had reduced the peasantry to penury, but that peasants, left to their own devices, might have fashioned an equitable, dignified way of life.

Semevsky's master's thesis proved so controversial that his conservative advisor, Konstantin Nikolaevich Bestuzhev-Ryumin, "in horrified panic," decided

---

13 Aleksandr V. Romanovich-Slavatinskii, *Dvorianstvo v Rossii ot nachala XVIII veka do otmeny krepostnago prava* (St. Petersburg: Tipografiia Ministerstva vnutrennikh del, 1870), 306–369.
14 Vasilii I. Semevskii, *Krest'iane v tsarstvovanie Imperatritsy Ekateriny II* (St. Petersburg: v Tipografii F. S. Sushchinskago, 1881).
15 Idem, *Krest'iane v tsarstvovanie Ekateriny II*, vol. 2 (St. Petersburg: Tipografiia M. M. Stasiulevicha, 1901).
16 Kizevetter, "V. I. Semevskii v ego uchenykh trudakh," 208–210.
17 Boris P. Baluev, "Iskrennii i pravdivyi drug naroda: Vasilii Ivanovich Semevskii," in *Istoriki Rossii: XVIII–nachalo XX veka*, ed. A. N. Sakharov (Moscow: Skriptorii, 1996), 458; Semevskii, *Krest'iane v tsarstvovanie Imperatritsy Ekateriny II*, 101–138.

not to approve it. After defending the thesis at Moscow University, an unusual step permitted by Russian university regulations, Semevsky was allowed to teach at Petersburg University, but the authorities soon dismissed him, again for political disloyalty.

After losing his university job, Semevsky devoted the bulk of his time to research concerning governmental and social attitudes toward the peasant question. He divided the history of the debates over the peasantry into three periods: the eighteenth century, during which certain officials and intellectuals strove to limit the scope of the serf system; the first half of the nineteenth century, during which political and social actors strove to liberate the peasants, but without land; and the brief period starting in 1858, when the objective of many actors shifted to peasant emancipation with land.[18] He published his two-volume monograph, *The Peasant Question in Russia in the Eighteenth Century and the First Half of the Nineteenth Century* in 1888, and the next year at Moscow University defended it as a doctoral dissertation.[19]

Semevsky devoted roughly the first half of volume 1 to eighteenth-century views on the peasant question, starting with the age of Peter I and ending with Catherine II's death. In the remainder, he discussed governmental projects under Pavel I and Alexander I, as well as projects for emancipation developed in the Free Economic Society, in the work of scholars and poets, and by the Decembrists. He concentrated in the second volume on Nicholas I's reign. He analyzed its nine secret committees on the peasant question, the tsar's and nobility's reluctance to support serfdom's abolition, the intelligentsia's advocacy of a landed emancipation, and the serfs' growing resistance to serfdom. The picture that emerged in the two volumes was of initially isolated but later orchestrated challenges to a devastating system of forced labor, a picture of a government afraid of fundamental social change and therefore ineffectual in its implementation.

From the 1870s Semevsky had tried to hasten Russia's transformation. He helped send books from Petersburg to the countryside, and he took part in discussions on the country's possible political reform. From 1891 to 1897 he served on the fund to aid needy Russian writers, and from 1897 in the Mutual Aid Union for Russian writers. In 1895, he signed a petition demanding freedom of the press, and in November 1904 protested the beating of students on Kazanskaya

---

18 Baluev, "Iskrennii i pravdivyi drug naroda: Vasilii Ivanovich Semevskii," 461.
19 Semevskii, *Krest'ianskii vopros v Rossii v XVIII i pervoi polovine XIX veka* (St. Petersburg: Obshchestvennaia pol'za, 1888).

Square.[20] On January 8, 1905, Semevsky and other prominent intellectuals from the journal *Son of the Fatherland* (Syn otechestva) went to the chair of the Committee of Ministers, Sergei Yulyevich Vitte, to ask that the tsar receive the workers' petition and not station soldiers in front of the Winter Palace. He was arrested after this meeting and briefly jailed.[21] Later in 1905, Semevsky became chair of the Committee to Aid in the Release of Prisoners from Shlisselburg Prison, and in 1907 he co-edited a book on that prison's history.[22] He also became a member of the Committee for the Assistance of Political Exiles.

After the century's turn, Semevsky no longer sharply contrasted social change and political liberty, instead seeing them as inextricably related.[23] Throughout his life, he had rejected revolutionary populism on the grounds that revolutions do not foster major improvements in the lives of common people.[24] Now, therefore, he belonged in the liberal-populist camp.[25]

In June 1906, the populist Venedikt Aleksandrovich Myakotin invited Semevsky to stand for election to the organizing committee of a new political party, the Party of Popular Socialists. Later that year he joined the board of *Popular-Socialist Review* (Narodno-sotsialisticheskoe obozrenie).[26] The Popular Socialists stood for equality under the law; civil rights; separation of Church and state; ending private property in Russia; bolstering the peasant commune; distribution of land to peasants by the state; introduction of an eight-hour day for factory workers; amnesty for political prisoners; abolition of capital punishment in the empire; and the extension of mandatory, free education to all citizens.[27] Although this program was in various respects radical, the Popular Socialists wanted to implement it by non-violent means.

---

20 Sergei Ivanovich Volkov, "V. I. Semevskii (k nauchnoi biografii)," *Istoriia SSSR* 5 (1959): 120–121.

21 Anna Sergeevna Mel'nikova, "Nauchnaia i obshchestvenno-politicheskaia deiatel'nost' istorika V. I. Semevskogo," in *Kopytinskie chteniia. III: sbornik statei Mezhdunarodnoi nauchno-prakticheskoi konferentsii, Mogilev, 28 fevralia–1 marta 2019* (Mogilev: MGU imeni A. A. Kuleshova, 2020), 85–87.

22 Nikolai Fedorovich Annenskii et al., *Galereia shlissel'burgskikh uznikov*, part 1 (St. Petersburg: Tipografiia M. M. Stasiulevicha, 1907).

23 Gennadii Abramovich Nevelev, "Istoriia dekabristov v trudakh V. I. Semevskogo," *Istoriia i istoriki. Istoriograficheskii ezhegodnik* (1973): 246–247.

24 Oleg Vladimirovich Sidorenko, *Istoriografiia IX–nachala XX vv. Otechestvennoi istorii (uchebnoe posobie)* (Vladivostok: Izdatel'stvo Dal'nevostochnogo universiteta, 2004), 202.

25 Boris Petrovich Baluev, *Liberal'noe narodnichestvo na rubezhe XIX–XX vekov* (Moscow: Nauka, 1995).

26 Mel'nikova, "Nauchnaia i obshchestvenno-politicheskaia deiatel'nost' istorika V. I. Semevskogo," 86.

27 Anna Sergeevna Mel'nikova, "Narodno-sotsialisty i trudoviki v poiskakh putei preobrazovaniia Rossii nachala XX veka: programmnye osnovy," *Vesnik Magilewskaga dziarzhawnaga universiteta imia A. A. Kuliashova. Seriia A, Gumanitarnyia navuki* 2 (2016): 12–15.

Along with Semevsky, Mel'gunov was the driving force on *Golos minuvshago*. Mel'gunov was born in Moscow in December 1879, into a prominent noble family. His father Pyotr Petrovich had trained as a historian at Moscow University alongside Vasily Osipovich Klyuchevsky. Sergei Petrovich studied history at the same institution from 1901 to 1904. An early interest was the history of the seventeenth-century Church schism and of the Old Believer sects that emerged from it; however, Mel'gunov found more exciting the practical task of organizing the university's "secret archive"—its disciplinary records and its position papers on student organizations.[28]

Like many young people after the century's turn, Mel'gunov was politically active. In 1906, he joined the Constitutional Democrats, largely out of his commitment to freedom of conscience, but also because he wanted to push liberal constitutionalists to the left—that is, toward support of radical social reforms. By 1907, without abandoning his liberal principles, he gravitated toward the Popular Socialists. His activism attracted attention from the police, who authorized surveillance of his movements and perlustration of his correspondence.[29] His positions on political questions were close to those of Semevsky, and so was his supra-party orientation.

Between 1911 and 1915, Mel'gunov and other scholars collectively financed three major projects.[30] Semevsky contributed essays to two of them. *Great Reform* (Velikaia reforma) (1911), on the peasant emancipation of 1861, carried in volume one his essay on the peasant question in eighteenth-century literature;[31] in volume two, his essay on the Decembrists and the peasant question;[32] and in volume three, his essay on the Petrashevsky Circle and the peasant question.[33] Mel'gunov edited these volumes and provided articles in two of them.[34]

---

28 Iurii Nikolaevich Emel'ianov, *S. P. Mel'gunov: V Rossii i emigratsii*, 2nd edition (Moscow: URSS, 2011), 20–21.
29 Ibid., 28–36.
30 Sergei P. Mel'gunov and Nikolai Pavlovich Sidorov, eds., *Masonstvo v ego proshlom i nastoiashchem, v dvukh tomakh* (Moscow: Izdatel'stvo "Zadrugi" i K. F. Nekrasova, 1914–1915), 5.
31 Vasilii Ivanovich Semevskii, "Dekabristy i krest'ianskii vopros," in *Velikaia reforma. Russkoe obshchestvo i krest'ianskii vopros v proshlom i nastoiashchem. Iubileinoe izdanie*, 6 vols., vol. 2 (Moscow: Izdatel'stvo Sytina, 1911), 176–193.
32 Idem, "Krest'ianskii vopros v literature Ekaterininskogo vremeni," in *Velikaia reforma. Russkoe obshchestvo i krest'ianskii vopros v proshlom i nastoiashchem. Iubileinoe izdanie*, 6 vols., vol. 1 (Moscow: Izdatel'stvo Sytina, 1911), 218–240.
33 Idem, "Petrashevtsy i krest'ianskii vopros," in *Velikaia reforma. Russkoe obshchestvo i krest'ianskii vopros v proshlom i nastoiashchem. Iubileinoe izdanie*, 6 vols., vol. 3 (Moscow: Izdatel'stvo Sytina, 1911), 205–220.
34 Sergei Petrovich Mel'gunov, "Dvorianin i rab na rubezhe XIX veka," in *Velikaia reforma. Russkoe obshchestvo i krest'ianskii vopros v proshlom i nastoiashchem. Iubileinoe izdanie*, 6 vols., vol. 1 (Moscow: Izdatel'stvo Sytina, 1911), 241–260; idem, "Epokha 'ofitsial'noi narodnosti'

Patriotic war and Russian society (Otechestvennaia voina i russkoe obshchestvo, 1911–1912) printed Semevsky's long essay on peasant disturbances during the 1812 invasion.[35] Melgunov co-edited the volume along with Dzhivelegov and Vladimir Ivanovich Pecheta. The planning and production of these projects gave Semevsky and Melgunov a chance to collaborate before the formation of their journal, *Golos minuvshago*.

The members of the journal's editorial board were important scholars. Semevsky, with his publications on the peasantry, the peasant question, and Russian social thought was unquestionably the most remarkable of them, but Sakulin's contributions to the history of modern Russian literature and Dzhivelegov's to Renaissance studies made marks in those disciplines. Melgunov was, at this early stage in his life, a scholar-activist, but after 1917 he would become one of the great historians of the Russian revolution. All the editors had engaged in Russian political life: Semevsky as critic of the government's peasant policies and as part of the Popular Socialist party; Sakulin and Melgunov were student activists, and Melgunov had, like Semevsky, gravitated toward the Popular Socialists. Dzhivelegov was a Kadet, one of the party's chief theoreticians of popular suffrage and perhaps its leading expert on city life. All the editors belonged to liberal or moderate socialist elements on the political spectrum, and all were temperamentally disposed to reach across partisan political lines in order to facilitate the end of autocracy.

II

In the first number of *Golos minuvshago*, the editors promised a historical journal that would make scholarly insights on modern history accessible to the Russian public, while maintaining the scholarly character of each article. The editors also pledged to treat the history of art seriously, to provide "illustrations, portraits, reproductions of paintings and drawings that are unknown or little known to the public." According to the editors, "the journal will be impartial/non-partisan (*bezpartiinyi*), because scholarship itself stands above party affiliations (*bezpartiina sama nauka*)." At the same time, the journal would serve "not the select few, but the toiling majority."[36]

---

    i krepostnoe pravo," in *Velikaia reforma. Russkoe obshchestvo i krest'ianskii vopros v proshlom i nastoiashchem. Iubileinoe izdanie*, 6 vols., vol. 3 (Moscow: Izdatel'stvo Sytina, 1911), 1–21.

35 Vasilii I. Semevskii, "Volneniia krest'ian v 1812 g. i sviazannye s Otechestvennoi voinoiu," in *Otechestvennaia voina i russkoe obshchestvo*, ed. Aleksei Karpovich Dzhivelegov, Sergei Petrovich Mel'gunov, and Vladimir Ivanovich Pecheta, vol. 5 (Moscow: Tipografiia Sytina, 1911), 74–113.

36 "Ot redaktsii," *Golos minuvshago* 1 (January 1913): 5–6.

Translated into more concrete language, the editors' statement pledged to treat modern history of interest to the Russian reading public, broadly understood, through articles written by progressively minded writers, regardless of their political affiliations. This ambition echoed the objectives of two earlier journals, the *Past* (Byloe, published in Russia by Vasily Yakovlevich Bogucharsky and Pavel Eliseevich Shchyogolev, 1906–1907; published abroad by Vladimir Lvovich Burtsev, 1900–1904, 1908–1912) and the *Past Years* (Minuvshie gody, published in Russia, again by Bogucharsky and Shchyogolev, in 1908). In spite of the partisan debates in the Third State Duma, it was still possible in early 1913 for the moderate left to aspire to create a non-party journal.

In 1973 Yury Mikhailovich Kritsky analyzed *Golos minuvshago*'s treatment of Russian social thought and the history of the revolutionary movement.[37] He noted the journal's interest in Aleksandr Nikolaevich Radishchev and late eighteenth-century ideas, but suggested that its authors "paid insufficient attention" to this period. Kritsky was happier with the treatment of the Decembrists, although he faulted it for supporting Semevsky's supposed approach to Decembrism as a movement of the classless intelligentsia.[38] Kritsky praised Semevsky's articles on the Petrashevsky Circle for their "rich factual material" and for his attempt to distinguish different tendencies among circle members.[39] Kritsky found great value in the journal's publications on Russian populism, particularly its articles on Mikhail Aleksandrovich Bakunin, Lavrov, and Mikhailovsky, even though he was unsympathetic to the journal's support for Mikhailovsky's critique of Marxism.[40] Toward the end of his article, Kritsky tried to divide the publication into two periods: the initial period of 1913–1916, in which the editors pursued their liberal-populist, anti-Marxist lines, and a second period of 1917–1923 in which they "took an openly hostile line toward Soviet power."[41] On Kritsky's evidence, this latter characterization is not terribly convincing. Rather, Semevsky and others tried to remain true to the journal's original mission, at a moment when the awkwardness of a non-partisan historiography had become acute.

Kritsky briefly noted disagreements between Semevsky and Melgunov over the journal's contributors. For example, Semevsky promoted articles by Marxist historians, such as Mikhail Nikolaevich Pokrovsky, by younger scholars

---

37 Iurii Mikhailovich Kritskii, "Voprosy istorii russkoi obshchestvennoi mysli i revoliutsionnogo dvizheniia v Rossii XVIII–nachala XX v. v zhurnale 'Golos minuvshago' v 1913–1923 gg.," in *Istoriia i istoriki. Istoriograficheskii ezhegodnik* (1972): 78–106.
38 Ibid., 81–82.
39 Ibid., 85–86.
40 Ibid., 93–97.
41 Ibid., 100.

such as Sigismund Natanovich Valk, and articles of a polemical nature, while Melgunov preferred to publish liberals such as Aleksandr Aleksandrovich Kornilov and Aleksandr Aleksandrovich Kizevetter.[42] More recently, Sergei Vladimirovich Gavrilov and Irina Aleksandrovna Gavrilova have suggested that Semevsky and Melgunov disagreed over *Golos minuvshago*'s chronological range: Semevsky insisted on publications primarily illuminating the nineteenth century, while Melgunov wanted to include more material from the twentieth century.[43] Semevsky demanded contributors adhere to proper scholarly norms, while Melgunov was willing to publish articles without full footnotes. In the end, Semevsky saw *Golos minuvshago* as an instrument for raising the public's democratic consciousness, while Melgunov had less cosmic political ambitions and embraced the reality that the journal would fail if it lacked readers.[44] The Gavrilovs therefore attributed Melgunov's interest in liberal contributors partly to the desire to broaden the journal's subscription base among well-educated moderates, while Semevsky was convinced that the journal should find readers among the growing opposition to autocracy.[45]

Golos minuvshago therefore offered a history of the Russian intelligentsia written by *intelligenty* from the liberal-populist perspective, a history with immense value in terms of its factual content that aimed mainly at the pro-revolutionary public and only secondarily at the educated liberals who came to power briefly in February/March 1917.

III

After the February/March revolution, Melgunov negotiated the right to investigate materials in two secret archives: the archives of Moscow Spiritual Consistory and Missionary Council and the archives of the Moscow Okhrana.[46] He planned to use materials from the Spiritual Consistory to write about the necessity of separating Church and state. On the basis of materials in the police archive, he planned a series of publications on autocratic censorship, on the Holy Retinue (Sviashchennaia druzhina), on Loris-Melikov's "dictatorship of the

---

42 Ibid., 102.
43 Sergei Gavrilovich Gavrilov and Irina Aleksandrovna Gavrilova, "V. I. Semevskii versus S. P. Mel'gunov: kontseptsii razvitiia 'vnepartiinogo' zhurnala 'Golos minuvshago' v 1913–1916 godakh," *Vestnik TGPU* 5 (2016): 198.
44 Ibid., 200.
45 Ibid., 199.
46 Emel'ianov, *S. P. Mel'gunov*, 44–5.

heart" in 1881–1882, on the Khodynka Field catastrophe, on 1905, on police provocations, on the May 1915 pogrom, and on the history of political parties seen from the Okhrana's perspective. As Emelyanov has noted, only one of these volumes appeared in print, a documentary history of the Bolshevik party.[47] In April 1918, the Soviet authorities asserted the new government's control over historical archives, and in May the historian Pokrovsky informed Melgunov of the government's displeasure over the volume on the Bolsheviks. Pokrovsky characterized the book as the result of "journalists openly hostile to Soviet power, who see the archive as an instrument of struggle with that power."[48]

During 1917, Melgunov wrote articles for the newspaper *Power of the People* (Vlast' naroda), joined the Council of Deputies of the Laboring Intelligentsia, and stood for election to the Central Committee of Workers Popular-Socialist Party. He spoke in favor of freedom of conscience, advocated free elections to the Constituent Assembly, and in November protested Bolshevik infringements on those elections. In 1918, he joined the Union for the Resurrection of Russia—a body with representatives from the Popular Socialists, Socialist Revolutionaries, and Kadets who opposed the Bolsheviks' "anti-democratic" policies.[49] Thus, his consistency in supporting liberal populism put him on a collision course with the Soviet regime.

Between August 31, 1918, and August 31, 1921, the Soviet authorities arrested Melgunov five times. The first two arrests occurred in the wake of Fania Kaplan's attempt to assassinate Lenin, an event with which Melgunov had no connection. The third arrest, in spring 1919, was likely meant to intimidate him into dropping his opposition to the new regime. The fourth arrest, in 1920, was bound up with suppression of the Zadruga publishing cooperative (sixty of its members were rounded up, starting in August 1919) and with his alleged support for the so-called "Tactical Center," a group that recognized Admiral Kolchak as the sovereign authority in Russia.[50]

In August 1920, the Supreme Revolutionary Tribunal tried Melgunov and other defendants belonging to the "Tactical Center." As a supposed leader of this organization, he was sentenced to death by shooting, but was released from prison on February 13, 1921, on the petition of the anarchist Pyotr Alekseevich Kropotkin, the populist Vera Nikolaevna Figner, and the populist writer

---

47 Ibid., 45; S. P. Mel'gunov, M. A. Tsiavlovskii, eds., *Materialy po istorii osvoboditel'nogo dvizheniia v Rossii*, vol. 1: *Bol'sheviki. Dokumenty po istorii bol'shevizma s 1903 po 1917 god byvshego Moskovskogo okhrannogo otdeleniia* (Moscow: Zadruga, 1916).
48 Emel'ianov, *S. P. Mel'gunov*, 46.
49 Ibid., 47–51.
50 Ibid., 54–55.

Vladimir Galaktionovich Korolenko.[51] Melgunov rejected the prosecutors' account of his political activity.

During his 1920 detention and interrogation, Melgunov kept a diary in which he recorded his impressions of Lubyanka prison and of his interrogator Yakov Saulovich Agranov. Melgunov wondered how it had transpired that he was being questioned by someone "from our circle, a person of identical educational background, a person from the same civic traditions and the same status, and, finally, in the last analysis, of the same ideology." Melgunov sensed that he and his wife had been naive about the solidarity that they had presumed bound together all *intelligenty*. He wrote: "Trust in customary intelligentsia honesty, to a certain way of thinking and its entire psychology—here was the root of all naivety."[52] In other words, Melgunov had acted consistently with the code of the classical intelligentsia but felt his interrogator had betrayed that code.

In a 1923 article, written in emigration, Melgunov claimed that the Cheka fabricated evidence, that it accused defendants of crimes they had not committed. He described the indictment as "an illiterate, false, and in places a fantastical piece of work, thrown together hastily from testimony in the preliminary investigation done in the bowels of the Special Bureau of the Cheka." He asserted that the entire trial would not have passed scrutiny in any "bourgeois court."[53] The chief prosecutor, Nikolai Vasilyevich Krylenko, presented the case as a trial of the intelligentsia: "The materials of this case clearly show how the Russian intelligentsia, entering the whirlwind of revolution of with slogan of the people's power, exited it as an ally of obscurantist generals, as a hired and obedient agent of European imperialism. The intelligentsia defiled its banner and hurled it onto the mud.... This group has outlived its era, so it seems to me, we have no need to add to its representatives in the future."[54] In making this accusation against the intelligentsia, Krylenko only repeated what the Cheka investigator, Agranov, had told Melgunov at his first interrogation: "I must say here is the flower of the Moscow intelligentsia and the Moscow professorate."[55]

During the interrogation, Melgunov described his own politics as support of the "democratic" coalition, and therefore as opposition to "every kind of

---

51 Ibid., 58–60.
52 I. Iu. Berezhanskaia and V. S. Khristoforov, eds., *Tiuremnye zapiski S. P. Mel'gunova. 1920 god. Sbornik dokumentov* (Moscow: Izdatel'skii tsentr Instituta rossiiskoi istorii RAN, 2015), 64.
53 Sergei P. Mel'gunov, "Sud istorii nad intelligentsiei (k delu 'Takticheskogo Tsentra')," in *Politicheskie partii Rossii. Konets XIX–pervaia tret' XX veka. Takticheskii tsentr. Dokumenty i materialy* (Moscow: ROSSPEN, 2012), 631; original in *Na chuzhoi storone. Istoriko-literaturnye sborniki* (Berlin: Izdanie "Vataga" i "Plamia," 1923), 137–163.
54 Mel'gunov, "Sud istorii nad intelligentsiei," 632.
55 Ibid., 643.

demagogy." He admitted that his attitude toward the Bolshevik coup (*perevorot*) was "extremely negative." He denied taking overt action to subvert the Soviet government but testified: "I considered it my duty to take part in every sort of conversation. In the absence of the press, this was the only channel to exert influence public opinion, if not of the country at large, then at least of a group of the intelligentsia, and thereby to counteract views I considered harmful."[56] He predicted the Soviet government would inevitably fall. He characterized the government not as a class dictatorship, but rather as a kind of "pretorianism":

> The Soviet government will nurture in Russia not communists, but a new bourgeoisie. This class of new property owners, raised on the bread of communists, will, in defense of its own interests, in precise accord with the Marxist theory of class struggle, put an end to Soviet power. Here there will be an inevitable 9th of Thermidor.[57]

In August 1921, the Soviet authorities arrested Melgunov for a fifth time. He was exiled to Cherdyn in the northern Perm province. After the intervention of the Political Red Cross, he was released from exile and then was forcibly expelled from Soviet Russia, on October 10, 1922.[58] According to historian Stuart Finkel, Melgunov was part of a group of close to one hundred intellectuals expelled from Soviet Russia in fall 1922 and winter 1923.[59]

IV

From 1916 onward, Mstislav Aleksandrovich Tsyavlovsky contributed to *Golos minuvshago* several articles on the history of Russian literature and three specialized articles on Pushkin.[60] He was also the chief researcher in the Moscow Okhrana archives on the 1918 volume concerning the Bolshevik party that led to Melgunov's censure by Pokrovsky. In the years when Melgunov faced arrests

---

56 Ibid., 645.
57 Ibid., 646.
58 Emel'ianov, *S. P. Mel'gunov*, 60–61.
59 Stuart Finkel, *On the Ideological Front: The Russian Intelligentsia and the Making of the Soviet Public Sphere* (New Haven, CT: Yale UP, 2007), 229–234.
60 Mstislav Aleksandrovich Tsiavlovskii, "Toska po chuzhbine u Pushkina," *Golos minuvshago* 1 (1916): 35–60; idem, "'Dnevnik Vul'fa.' 'Duel' Pushkina.' (Iz novykh knig o Pushkine)," *Golos minuvshago* 2 (1917): 279–294; idem, "Pushkin i gr. Fikel'mon," *Golos minuvshago* 2 (1922): 108–123.

and police harassment, Tsyavlovsky played an important role in seeing *Golos minuvshago* into print. When the authorities expelled Melgunov from Soviet Russia, Tsyavlovsky assumed the journal's editorship.

Tsyavlovsky was born in 1883 into an old noble family, was educated in Warsaw at *Gimnaziia* No. 6, then at Moscow University's Historical-Philological Faculty, from which he graduated in 1910.[61] At Moscow University, Tsyavlovsky studied with Aleksandr Ivanovich Kirpichnikov, a distinguished professor with publications on Pushkin and Gogol.[62] From 1903 to 1906, Tsyavlovsky was active in the Moscow political underground, as a member of the Russian Social Democratic Workers Party. In December 1906 he was arrested in Tver on suspicion of involvement in the assassination of Count Aleksei Pavlovich Ignatyev. Although he had nothing to do with the killing (performed by his cousin Sergei Ilyinsky, a member of the Socialist-Revolutionary "Battle Organization"), Tsyavlovsky was incarcerated in Moscow for six months, then exiled for six months to Vologda.[63]

Tsyavlovsky's career as a Pushkinist began with publication of a chronological catalogue of Pushkin's works, in 1914, and his first scholarly article in the same year.[64] He brought to bear in his scholarship unusual factual rigor and objectivity. His colleague Sergei Mikhailovich Bondi later wrote of him: "In his articles he laid out scrupulously selected and carefully verified facts and provided the strictest possible argumentation in support of his proposed conclusions.... Reading Tsyavlovsky's articles, one found it easy to understand the reason for their rigorous facticity and external dryness and to assess their genuine significance."[65] At the same time, political engagement fueled Tsyavlovsky's interest in police archives as a historical source on current politics but also on the politics of the Pushkin era.[66]

---

61 *Otchet o sostoianii i deistviakh Imperatorskago Moskovskago Universiteta za 1910 god* (Moscow: Tipografiia Imperatorskago Moskovskago Universiteta, 1911), 74.
62 Mstislav Aleksandrovich Tsiavlovskii and Tat'iana Grigorievna Tsiavlovskaia, *Vokrug Pushkina* (Moscow: Novoe literaturnoe obozrenie, 2000), 207.
63 Kseniia Petrovna Bogaevskaia, "Kommentarii," in *Vokrug Pushkina*, ed. Mstislav Tsiavlovskii and Tat'iana Tsiavlovskaia (Moscow: Novoe literaturnoe obozrenie, 2000), 208.
64 Nikolai Aleksandrovich Siniavskii and Mstislav Aleksandrovich Tsiavlovskii, *Pushkin v pechati. 1814–1837. Khronologicheskii ukazatel' proizvedenii Pushkina, napechatannykh pri ego zhizni* (Moscow: L. E. Bukhgeim, 1914); Mstislav Aleksandrovich Tsiavlovskii, "Zametki o Pushkine," in *Pushkin i ego sovremenniki* 17–18, ed. Boris L'vovich Modzalevskii (1914): 45–73.
65 Sergei Mikhailovich Bondi, "M. A. Tsiavlovskii i ego stat'i o Pushkine," in *Stat'i o Pushkine*, ed. Mstislav Tsiavlovskii (Moscow: Izdatel'stvo AN SSSR, 1962), 4–5.
66 Ibid., 8.

Tsyavlovsky's factological approach to literary scholarship, his rigorous scholarly objectivity, and his leftist political identity apparently endeared him to Semevsky. So did Tsyavlovsky's family background. Semevsky's wife, Elizaveta Nikolaevna, a distinguished memoirist and educator, also the widow of his old teacher Vodovozov, had been born Tsyavlovskaya.[67] Thus, by scholarly genealogy, disposition, and personal ties, Tsyavlovsky belonged organically to Semevsky's circle.[68]

Two questions should be asked about the transition between Melgunov's and Tsyavlovsky's editorship of *Golos minuvshago*. The first is whether after 1917, and especially in the years 1922 and 1923, contributors who belonged to the Bolshevik Party and those who had arranged positions in the Soviet institutions "exited" the journal. Kritsky's 1973 article on the journal claims that nine contributors ceased to send articles to the journal, and instead favored new journals, such as *Proletarian Revolution* (Proletarskaia revolutsiia), *Hard Labor and Exile* (Katorga i ssylka), and *Red Chronicle* (Krasnaia letopis') that were published "on a higher scholarly level" and "recognized the victory of Marxism on the historical front."[69] However, Emelyanov has argued that Kritsky's contention was unjustified, for two reasons: the journal was consistent in its programmatic mission across the ten years of its existence, and no "exit" of authors out of political calculation can be observed. According to Emelyanov, the journal's transformation, if it occurred, was the result of pressure from the Soviet authorities, not of the authors' political indisposition to Marxism.[70] Emelyanov should have added that Tsyavlovsky, a Bolshevik, maintained his association with journal throughout the civil war period. His editorship should therefore be read as a sign that, after Semevsky, the journal was not at all "anti-Marxist" in its coloration.

The second question is whether Tsyavlovsky's editorship brought a change in *Golos minuvshago*'s program. The short answer is that there was no evidence of a new mission on the journal's pages. In the January 1923 issue, Tsyavlovsky inserted an editorial comment on the journal's first decade: "Looking back now on the past ten years, we can assert with calm confidence that *Golos minuvshago* did not alter its goals, and that it fulfilled its potential to the best of its ability." Tsyavlovsky added that the journal remained open to "various political and social perspectives," and that it published "not for the edification of a selected

---

67 Elizaveta Nikolaevna Vodovozova, *Na zare zhizni i drugie vospominaniia*, 2 vols. (Moscow: Khudozhestvennaia literatura, 1964).
68 Tsiavlovskii and Tsiavlovskaia, *Vokrug Pushkina*, 40.
69 Kritskii, "Voprosy istorii russkoi obshchestvennoi mysli," 103.
70 Emel'ianov, *S. P. Mel'gunov*, 311–4.

audience, but for the laboring majority. . . . These general tasks and principles guided the editorial staff ten years ago. To them it remains dedicated today."[71]

Under Tsyavlovsky, the journal carried fewer articles and fewer portraits, because of the paper shortage affecting the country. Tsyavlovsky acknowledged that censorship regulations had changed in 1917, but he tried to interpret the new censorship positively—that is, as a green light to publish materials on the history of Russia's "liberation movement."[72] Of the articles in the January 1923 number, several were installments of memoirs, three focused on Russian writers (Pushkin, Nekrasov, and Lev Tolstoy), and one on Kizevetter's history of courts of conscience under Catherine II.[73] The March-April issue included memoirs and documentary publications, and the conclusion of Kizevetter's history.[74] The journal's final issue, dated May-October 1923, again carried several excerpts from memoirs, but also very important literary and political documents, such as fragments of Dushan Petrovich Makovitsky's diaries from Lev Tolstoy's household in Yasnaya Polyana for October 1905—one of the crucial junctures of the 1905 revolution.[75] It was possible that, in mid-1923, Tsyavlovsky was attempting to move the journal deeper into literary history, without altering its general historical orientation or its political coloration. If so, this path remained consistent with the Semevsky-Melgunov program of 1913. However, Soviet literary authorities decided to close the journal.

V

Did the "classical intelligentsia" (the broad subject of this essay) come to an end at some point before the end of Russia's civil wars? What part, if any, did *Golos minuvshago* play in this process?

From 1913 to 1923, *Golos minuvshago* pursued a consistent editorial policy promoting understanding of modern Russian history, including the history of the literary intelligentsia. The journal advertised itself as non-partisan, or rather supra-partisan. Because it invited contributions from the left and therefore

---

71 Mikhail Aleksandrovich Tsiavlovskii, "1913–1923," *Golos minuvshago* 1 (1923): ii.
72 Ibid., iii.
73 Aleksandr A. Kizevetter, "Sovestnye sudy pri Ekaterine II," *Golos minuvshago* 1 (1923): 134–160.
74 Aleksandr A. Kizevetter, "Sovestnye sudy pri Ekaterine II (okonchanie)," *Golos minuvshago* 2 (1923): 3–34.
75 Nikolai Nikolaevich Gusev, "1905–1906 god v Iasnoi Poliane (iz zapisok Makovitskogo)," *Golos minuvshago* 3 (1923): 3–29.

from Bolsheviks as well as populists and liberals, its existence was helpful to the Bolshevik cause from 1913 to 1917. Because its editorial board after 1917 included Tsyavlovsky, and because, after Melgunov's banishment, Tsyavlovsky became sole editor, *Golos minuvshago* remained useful to the Soviet government. The journal's repression—witness the repeated arrests of Melgunov and the journal's closure in 1923—suggests the authorities' hostility toward independent or semi-independent *intelligenty*.

The closure of the journal, however, cannot be regarded as a definitive end to its operation. For one thing, Tsyavlovsky stood near the top of the Soviet literary profession, participating in publication of the Academy of Sciences' jubilee edition of Lev Tolstoy's works as well as in publication of the Academy edition of Pushkin's works. From 1925 to his death, he kept a diary of discoveries about Pushkin, a diary to which his second wife, Tatyana Grigoryevna, contributed and which she continued until 1971.[76] The diary makes clear he was aware that "Pushkin's manuscripts were governmental property (*gosudarstvennoe dostoianie*), which must not be in private hands."[77] Indeed, he knew that the government was in the process of "nationalization of Pushkin's manuscripts in private hands,"[78] and that he was acting on behalf of the state in procuring manuscripts for scholarly institutions. In the diary, Tsyavlovsky recorded documentary finds by other Pushkinists, such as the discovery of the "lost" manuscript of the poem, "The monk" (Monakh) in 1928;[79] rumors about manuscripts, such as the existence of a diary by Pushkin in the possession of his granddaughter Elena Aleksandrovna;[80] unpublished Pushkin manuscripts abroad;[81] the discovery of Pushkin's letters to the Slavophile Ivan Vasilyevich Kireevsky;[82] the finding in 1931 of Pushkin manuscripts in Simbirsk;[83] the discovery in 1931 of four love letters from Pushkin to a young Armenian woman;[84] of letters by Pushkin in French held abroad;[85] and so on. From a much later dissident perspective, Andrei Donatovich Sinyavsky argued that many members of the intelligentsia who remained in the Soviet

---

76 Tsiavlovskii and Tsiavlovskaia, *Vokrug Pushkina*, 67–147.
77 Ibid., 74.
78 Ibid., 77.
79 Ibid., 71–78; Pavel Eliseevich Shchegolev, "Poema A. S. Pushkina 'Monakh,'" *Krasnyi arkhiv* 6 (1928): 60–201; Sergei Aleksandrovich Fomichev, "Pervaia poema Pushkina," in *Pushkinskaia perspektiva* (Moscow: Znak, 2007), 52–61.
80 Tsiavlovskii and Tsiavlovskaia, *Vokrug Pushkina*, 79–81, 99–100, 103.
81 Ibid., 105–106.
82 Ibid., 87.
83 Ibid., 89–95.
84 Ibid., 98.
85 Ibid., 115.

Union betrayed the intelligentsia's classical mission by becoming "courtiers" in the new order.[86] Whether Tsyavlovsky's post-1923 life constituted a "betrayal" is a complicated matter, but there is no doubt he behaved as a courtier.

For another thing, after his expulsion from the Soviet Union, Melgunov settled in Berlin. There he set up a new publishing house, The Gang (Vataga), and began publication of a new journal, *On a Foreign Shore* (Na chuzhoi storone). From 1923 to 1925, he edited thirteen issues of the journal—the first from Berlin and the others from Berlin and Prague, where his collaborator Evgeny Aleksandrovich Latsky ran a sister concern, The Flame (Plamia). In 1926, Melgunov relocated his operation to Paris, where he published still another journal, this one combining the titles of its predecessors, *Voice of the Past on a Foreign Shore* (Golos minuvshago na chuzhoi storone). This last journal, published from 1926 to 1928, consisted of six "books," numbered fourteen to nineteen. In a sense, Melgunov's European journals were continuations of *Golos minuvshago*: they combined the history of the nineteenth-century intelligentsia and the history of literature; they published analytical articles, *belles lettres*, and historical memoirs. Melgunov sought through these journals to appeal to people of various political parties and to serve the Russian people.

Thus the history of *Golos minuvshago* demonstrated both the continuation of the intelligentsia inside the Soviet Union, albeit under constrained circumstances, and the continuation of the intelligentsia in the Russian diaspora. Did the Russian revolutions of 1917 precipitate the "end of the classical intelligentsia?" Yes and no.

Bibliography

Annenskii, Nikolai Fedorovich, and Vasilii Iakovlevich Bogucharskii, *Galereia shlissel'burgskikh uznikov*. Part 1. St. Petersburg: Tipografiia M. M. Stasiulevicha, 1907.

Baluev, Boris Petrovich. *Liberal'noe narodnichestvo na rubezhe XIX–XX vekov*. Moscow: Nauka, 1995.

———. "Iskrennii i pravdivyi drug naroda: Vasilii Ivanovich Semevskii." In *Istoriki Rossii: XVIII–nachalo XX veka*, edited by A. N. Sakharov, 446–485. Moscow: Skriptorii, 1996.

---

86 Andrei Siniavsky, *The Russian Intelligentsia* (New York: Columbia UP, 1997).

Beliaev, Ivan Dmitrievich. *Krest'iane na Rusi. Izsledovanie o postepennom izmenenii znacheniia krest'ian v russkom obshchestve*. Moscow: v Universitetskoi tipografii, 1860.
Berdiaev, Nikolai Aleksandrovich. *Vekhi. Sbornik statei o russkoi intelligentsii*. 2nd ed. Moscow: s.p., 1909.
Bogaevskaia, Kseniia Petrovna. "Kommentarii." In *Vokrug Pushkina*, edited by Mstislav Tsiavlovskii and Tat'iana Tsiavlovskaia, 203–306. Moscow: Novoe literaturnoe obozrenie, 2000.
Bondi, Sergei Mikhailovich. "M. A. Tsiavlovskii i ego stat'i o Pushkine." In *Stat'i o Pushkine*, edited by Mstislav Tsiavlovskii, 3–10. Moscow: Izdatel'stvo AN SSSR, 1962.
Burbank, Jane. *Intelligentsia and Revolution: Russian Views of Bolshevism, 1917–1922*. Oxford: Oxford UP, 1986.
Chamberlain, Lesley. *Lenin's Private War: The Voyage of the Philosophy Steamer and the Exile of the Intelligentsia*. New York: St. Martin's Press, 2007.
Dzhivelegov, Aleksei Karpovich. *Gorodskaia obshchina v srednie veka: nekotoryia novyia teorii o proiskhodenii srednevekovykh gorodov*. Moscow: Izdatel'stvo magazina "Knizhnoe delo," 1901.
Dzhivelegov, Aleksei Karpovich, and Sergei Petrovich Mel'gunov. *Srednevekovyia goroda v Zapadnoi Evrope*. St. Petersburg: Brokgauz-Efron, 1902.
———. *Bismark i Lassal'. K istorii vseobshchego izbiratel'nogo prava*. Moscow: Trud i volia, 1906.
———. *Nachalo ital'ianskago Vozrozhdeniia*. Moscow: Pol'za, 1908.
Dzhivelegov, Aleksei Karpovich, Sergei Petrovich Mel'gunov, and Vladimir Ivanovich Pecheta, eds. *Velikaia reforma. 1861–1911. Russkoe obshchestvo i krest'ianskii vopros v proshlom i nastoiashchem*. 6 vols. Moscow: Izdatel'stvo Sytina, 1911.
———. *Otechestvennaia voina i russkoe obshchestvo, 1812–1912*. 7 vols. Moscow: Izdatel'stvo Sytina, 1911–1912.
Emel'ianov, Iurii Nikolaevich. *S. P. Mel'gunov: v Rossii i emigratsii*. 2nd ed. Moscow: URSS, 2011.
Emmons, Terence, ed. *Time of Troubles, The Diary of Iurii Vladimirovich Got'e: Moscow, July 8, 1917 to July 23, 1922*. Princeton, NJ: Princeton UP, 1988.
Finkel, Stuart. *On the Ideological Front: The Russian Intelligentsia and the Making of the Soviet Public Sphere*. New Haven, CT: Yale UP, 2007.
Fomichev, Sergei Aleksandrovich. "Pervaia poema Pushkina." In *Pushkinskaia perspektiva*, edited by S. A. Fomichev, 52–61. Moscow: Znak, 2007.

Gavrilov, Sergei Gavrilovich, and Irina Aleksandrovna Gavrilova. "V. I. Semevskii versus S. P. Mel'gunov: kontseptsii razvitiia 'vnepartiinogo' zhurnala 'Golos minuvshago' v 1913–1916 godakh." *Vestnik TGPU* 5 (2016):196–203.

Gavrilov, Sergei Vladimirovich. "V. I. Vodovozov i V. I. Semevskii: ot istoricheskoi biografii pedagoga k vnutrennei biografii istorika." *Vestnik Severnogo federal'nogo universiteta. Seriia gumanitarnoi i sotsial'noi nauki* 4 (2017): 5–15.

Gusev, Nikolai Nikolaevich. "1905–1906 god v Iasnoi Poliane (iz zapisok Makovitskogo)." *Golos minuvshago* 3 (1923): 3–29.

Hamburg, Gary M. "A Russian Triptych: Intellectuals before and after 1917." *Journal of Modern Russian History and Historiography* 16 (2023): 50–64.

Ivanov-Razumnik, Razumnik Vasil'evich. *Istoriia russkoi obshchestvennoi mysli.* Parts 5–8. Petrograd: Revoliutsionnaia mysl', 1918.

Kizevetter, Aleksandr Aleksandrovich. "V. I. Semevskii v ego uchenykh trudakh." *Golos minuvshago* 1 (1917): 199–222.

———. "Sovestnye sudy pri Ekaterine II." *Golos minuvshago* 1 (1923): 134–160.

———. "Sovestnye sudy pri Ekaterine II (okonchanie)." *Golos minuvshago* 2 (1923): 3–34.

Kokh, Ol'ga Borisovna. "Geroi svoego vremeni (shtrikhi k portretu M. I. Semevskogo)." *Pskov* 14 (2001): 44–60.

Kritskii, Iurii Mikhailovich. "Voprosy istorii russkoi obshchestvennoi mysli i revoliutsionnogo dvizheniia v Rossii XVIII–nachala XX v. v zhurnale 'Golos minuvshago' v 1913–1923 gg." *Istoriia i istoriki. Istoriograficheskii ezhegodnik* (1972): 78–106.

Lenin, Vladimir Il'ich. Letter to A. M. Gor'kii, September 15, 1919. Biblioteka gazety "Revolutsiia." Accessed February 11, 2022. http://revolucia.ru/lenin51_47.html.

Makarov, Vladimir Gennad'evich, and Vasilii Stepanovich Khristoforov, eds. *Vysylka vmesto rasstrela: deportatsiia intelligentsii v dokumentakh VChK-GPU, 1921–1923.* Moscow: Russkii put', 2005.

Materialy po istorii osvoboditel'nogo dvizheniia v Rossii. Vol. 1: Bol'sheviki. Dokumenty po istorii bol'shevizma s 1903 po 1917 god byvshego Moskovskogo okhrannogo otdeleniia. Moscow: Zadruga, 1916.

Mel'gunov, Sergei Petrovich. "Dvorianin i rab na rubezhe XIX veka." In *Velikaia reforma. 1861–1911. Russkoe obshchestvo i krest'ianskii vopros v proshlom i nastoiashchem,* vol. 1, ed. Aleksei Dzhivelegov and Vladimir Pecheta, 241–260. Moscow: Izdatel'stvo Sytina, 1911.

———. "Epokha 'ofitsial'noi narodnosti' i krepostnoe pravo." In *Velikaia reforma. 1861–1911. Russkoe obshchestvo i krest'ianskii vopros v proshlom i nastoiashchem*, vol. 3, ed. Aleksei Dzhivelegov and Vladimir Pecheta, 1–21. Moscow: Izdatel'stvo Sytina, 1911.

———. "Sud istorii nad intelligentsiei (k delu 'Takticheskogo Tsentra')." In *Politicheskie partii Rossii. Konets XIX–pervaia tret' XX veka. Takticheskii tsentr. Dokumenty i materialy*, 629–658. Moscow: ROSSPEN, 2012.

———. *Tiuremnye zapiski S. P. Mel'gunova. 1920 god. Sbornik dokumentov*. Edited by I. Iu. Berezhanskaia and V. S. Khristoforov. Moscow: Izdatel'skii tsentr Instituta rossiiskoi istorii RAN, 2015.

Mel'gunov, Sergei Petrovich, and Nikolai Pavlovich Sidorov, eds. *Masonstvo v ego proshlom i nastoiashchem*. 2 vols. Moscow: Izdatel'stvo "Zadrugi" i K. F. Nekrasova, 1914–1915.

Mel'nikova, Anna Sergeevna. "Narodno-sotsialisty i trudoviki v poiskakh putei preobrazovaniia Rossii nachala XX veka: programmnyi osnovy." *Vesnik Magilewskaga dziarzhawnaga universiteta imia A. A. Kuliashova. Seriia A, Gumanitarnyia navuki* 2 (2016): 12–15.

———. "Nauchnaia i obshchestvenno-politicheskaia deiatel'nost' istorika V. I. Semevskogo." In *Kopytinskie chteniia. III: sbornik statei Mezhdunarodnoi nauchno-prakticheskoi konferentsii, Mogilev, 28 fevralia–1 marta 2019*, 85–87. Mogilev: MGU imeni A. A. Kuleshova, 2020.

Miliukov, Pavel Nikolaevich. *Iz istorii russkoi intelligentsii. Sbornik statei i etiudov*. St. Petersburg: Tipografiia A. E. Kolpinskago, 1902.

Nevelev, Gennadii Abramovich. "Istoriia dekabristov v trudakh V. I. Semevskogo." *Istoriia i istoriki. Istoriograficheskii ezhegodnik* (1973): 232–257.

Nikolaev, Petr Alekseevich. "Pavel Nikitich Sakulin." *Voprosy literatury* 4 (1969): 112–122.

Novgorodtsev, Pavel Ivanovich, ed. *Problemy idealizma. Sbornik statei*. Moscow: Izdatel'stvo Moskovskago psikhologicheskago obshchestva, 1903.

"Ot redaktsii." *Golos minuvshago* 1 (1913): 5–6.

Otchet o sostoianii i deistviakh Imperatorskago Moskovskago Universiteta za 1910 god. Moscow: Tipografiia Imperatorskago Moskovskago Universiteta, 1911.

Read, Christopher. *Religion, Revolution, and the Russian Intelligentsia, 1900–1912: The Vekhi Debate and Its Intellectual Background*. Totowa, NJ: Barnes and Noble, 1979.

Romanovich-Slavatinskii, Aleksandr Vasil'evich. *Dvorianstvo v Rossii ot nachala XVIII veka do otmeny krepostnago prava*. St. Petersburg: Tipografiia Ministerstva vnutrennikh del, 1870.

Sakulin, Pavel Nikitich. *Iz istorii russkogo idealizma. Kniaz' V. F. Odoevskii. Myslitel'-pisatel'.* Vol. 1, parts 1–2. Moscow: Izdatel'stvo Sabashnikovykh, 1913.

———. *Reforma russkogo pravopisaniia*. Petrograd: Parus, 1917.

Semevskii, Mikhail Ivanovich. *Slovo i delo! 1700–1725. Tainaia kantseliariia pri Petre Velikom*. 2nd ed. St. Petersburg: Tipografiia V. S. Balasheva, 1884.

Semevskii, Vasilii Ivanovich. *Krest'iane v tsarstvovanie Imperatritsy Ekateriny II*. St. Petersburg: v Tipografii F. S. Sushchinskago, 1881.

———. *Istoriia krest'ianskogo voprosa v sviazi s istoriei vnutrennego byta Rossii v XVIII i pervoi polovine XIX v. Lektsii, chitannye vo vtoroi polovine 1882–1883 gg. privat-dotsentom S.-Pb. Universiteta Semevskim*. St. Petersburg: n.p., 1883.

———. *Krest'ianskii vopros v Rossii v XVIII i pervoi poloviny XIX veka*. St. Petersburg: Obshchestvennaia pol'za, 1888.

———. *Krest'iane v tsarstvovanie Ekateriny II*. Vol. 2. St. Petersburg: Tipografiia M. M. Stasiulevicha, 1901.

———. *Politicheskie i obshchestvennye idei dekabristov*. St. Petersburg: Tipografiia Pervoi Spb. Trudovoi Arteli, 1909.

———. "Dekabristy i krest'ianskii vopros." In *Velikaia reforma. 1861–1911. Russkoe obshchestvo i krest'ianskii vopros v proshlom i nastoiashchem*, vol. 2, ed. Aleksei Dzhivelegov and Vladimir Pecheta, 176–193. Moscow: Izdatel'stvo Sytina, 1911.

———. "Krest'ianskii vopros v literature Ekaterinskogo vremeni." In *Velikaia reforma. 1861–1911. Russkoe obshchestvo i krest'ianskii vopros v proshlom i nastoiashchem*, vol. 1, ed. Aleksei Dzhivelegov and Vladimir Pecheta, 218–240. Moscow: Izdatel'stvo Sytina, 1911

———. "Petrashevtsy i krest''ianskii vopros." In In *Velikaia reforma. 1861–1911. Russkoe obshchestvo i krest'ianskii vopros v proshlom i nastoiashchem*, vol. 3, ed. Aleksei Dzhivelegov and Vladimir Pecheta, 205–220. Moscow: Izdatel'stvo Sytina, 1911.

———. "Volneniia krest''ian v 1812 g. i sviazannye s Otechestvennoi voinoiu." In *Otechestvennaia voina i russkoe obshchestvo*, edited by Aleksei Karpovich Dzhivelegov, Sergei Petrovich Mel'gunov, and Vladimir Ivanovich Pecheta, vol. 5, 74–113. Moscow: Tipografiia Sytina, 1911.

Shchegolev, Pavel Eliseevich. "Poema A. S. Pushkina 'Monakh.'" *Krasnyi arkhiv* 6 (1928): 60–201.

Sidorenko, Oleg Vladimirovich. *Istoriografiia IX–nachala XX vv. Otechestvennoi istorii (uchebnoe posobie)*. Vladivostok: Izdatel'stvo Dal'nevostochnogo universiteta, 2004.

Siniavskii, Nikolai Aleksandrovich, and Mikhail Aleksandrovich Tsiavlovskii. *Pushkin v pechati. 1814–1837. Khronologicheskii ukazatel' proizvedenii Pushkina, napechatannykh pri ego zhizni*. Moscow: L. E. Bukhgeim, 1914.

Siniavsky, Andrei. *The Russian Intelligentsia*. New York: Columbia UP, 1997.

Soifer, Valerii. "Lenin: 'Opirat'sia na intelligentsiiu my ne budem nikogda." Troitskii variant. October 2018. Accessed July 10, 2024. https://www.trv-science.ru/2018/10/lenin/.

Tsiavlovskii, Mstislav Aleksandrovich. "Zametki o Pushkine." *Pushkin i ego sovremenniki* 17–18, edited by Boris L'vovich Modzalevskii (1914): 45–73.

———. "Toska po chuzhbine u Pushkina." *Golos minuvshago* 1 (1916): 35–60.

———. "'Dnevnik Vul'fa.' 'Duel' Pushkina.' (Iz novykh knig o Pushkine)." *Golos minuvshago* 2 (1917): 279–294.

———. "Pushkin i gr. Fikel'mon." *Golos minuvshago* 2 (1922):108–123.

———. "1913–1923." *Golos minuvshago* 1 (1923): i–ii.

Tsiavlovskii, Mstislav Aleksandrovich, and Tat'iana Grigorievna Tsiavlovskaia. *Vokrug Pushkina*. Moscow: Novoe literaturnoe obozrenie, 2000.

Vinogradov, Vladimir Konstantinovich. *Arkhiv VChK: Sbornik dokumentov*. Edited by Alter L'vovich Litvin and Vasilii Stepanovich Khristoforov. Moscow: Kuchkovo pole, 2007.

Vitte, Sergei Iul'evich. *Vospominaniia tsarstvovaniia Nikolaia II*. Vol. 1. Moscow and Petrograd: Gosudarstvennoe izdatel'stvo, 1923.

Vodovozov, Vasilii Ivanovich. *Izbrannye pedagogicheskie sochineniniia*. Edited by Vasilii Zakharovich Smirnov. Moscow: Izdatel'stvo Akademii pedagogicheskikh nauk RSFSR, 1958.

Vodovozova, Elizaveta Nikolaevna. *Na zare zhizni i drugie vospominaniia*. 2 vols. Moscow: Khudozhestvennaia literatura, 1964.

Volkov, Sergei Ivanovich. "V. I. Semevskii (k nauchnoi biografii)." *Istoriia SSSR* 5 (1959): 113–123.

The Russian Knights Templar: A Secret Mystical Order and its Legacy

Olga Partan

> Воздух дома не буржуазный, не интеллигентский—рыцарский. Жизнь на высокий лад.
>
> The air of the household was neither that of the bourgeoisie nor that of the intelligentsia—it was knightly. An elevated way of life.
> Marina Tsvetaeva[1]

The story of the secret Order of the Knights Templar in Soviet Russia contains some of the most enigmatic pages in the history of the Russian intelligentsia. The order's activities shed light on the post-revolutionary intelligentsia's high moral, ethical, and spiritual mission as well as its political escapism and helplessness when confronted by the many-faced hydra of the Soviet state and its punitive organizations. Membership in the order represented a form of resistance to the totalitarian state, filling life with hidden meaning and purpose unknown to the uninitiated.

---

1 Marina Tsvetaeva, "Otvet na anketu" [Answer to the questionnaire], in eadem, *Sobranie sochinenii v semi tomakh*, ed. Anna Saakiantz and Lev Mnukhin (Moscow: Ellis Lak, 1994), vol. 4, 622. All translations from Russian into English are my own unless otherwise noted.

The Russian Knights Templar chivalrously carried their high ideals through brutal interrogations, imprisonments, exile, and even executions of comrades by Soviet inquisitors in the midst of the Stalinist Great Terror. Hamlet's moral dilemma, "To be or not to be," would become once again crucially important for the arrested and imprisoned Templars. While some of them were ready to die for their beliefs and ideals, others chose the path of collaboration and cooperation, becoming informers of the OGPU/NKVD/NKGB and various later incarnations. Such cooperation could make it possible to save one's life and family, to be released from the labor camps, and even to pursue a successful career.

The secret files and archival documents about the Knights Templar, which existed in Soviet Russia from about 1918 until about 1930, became available only in the late 1990s and early 2000s thanks to the remarkable research and numerous publications of the Russian scholar Andrei Nikitin (1935–2005), who opened the veil of secrecy, revealing the Templars' spiritual and moral resistance to the New Soviet World. Andrei Nikitin's father—the theater designer Leonid Nikitin (1896–1942)—was a Templar of a high degree who was arrested and sent into exile twice, first in 1930 and then in 1941; he died in a GULag infirmary in 1942.[2] Nikitin's work, unique in its scope and analysis, resurrected for posterity the history of the Russian Templars, illuminating the phenomena of the Soviet spiritual underground and continuing the spiritual relay race of the Russian intelligentsia, with the continuity of its idealistic mission passed from one generation to another. At the end of his life, Nikitin was certain that thanks to his work the phenomenon of the Order of Knights Templar had already entered the history of Russia of the twentieth century, becoming the subject of further scholarship.[3] Nevertheless, two decades later the rich history of the order and the spiritual quest of its members has not had a significant impact on Western scholarship, and its legacy has never been fully evaluated. The topic of mystical secret societies, orders, groups, and circles in Soviet Russia remains understudied to this day.[4]

---

2 Thanks to Nikitin Jr.'s scholarly reputation and the fact that his father was posthumously rehabilitated, he was able to access the archives of the OGPU/NKVD/NKGB. On numerous occasions, Nikitin admits, he was not allowed full access to the Templars case materials. As a rule, materials confiscated during arrests were not available to researchers.
3 Andrei Nikitin, "Tsvety iz pepla" [Flowers from the ash], in *Rosa Mystica*, ed. Andrei Nikitin (Moscow: Agraf, 2002), 3. Despite Nikitin's numerous publications in recent decades, his work still seems to be outside the mainstream of Western Russian Studies.
4 Birgit Menzel observes that "it is quite remarkable how little scholarly attention has been given to spiritual and occult practices and thought in Soviet and post-Soviet society." Menzel explains this deficiency as due to the many problems that scholars encounter in their work on this topic, such as scattered materials, largely inaccessible sources, and mystifications and

Structured in two parts, this essay first concentrates on the order's history and its transmission to Russian soil by Apollon Karelin (1863–1926), who had a special mission: to open an Eastern branch of the order in Soviet Russia. I pay special attention to the ideals, rituals, and organizational structure of the order. The second part of the essay traces the legacy of the Knights Templar in the artistic milieu of the Moscow Art Theater Studios, paying tribute to celebrated cultural figures who were very close to the Knights Templar: the poet Marina Tsvetaeva (1892–1941) and the modernist director Evgeny Vakhtangov (1883–1922). I aim to demonstrate how, at a time when the revolutionary whirlwind was sweeping away centuries-old foundations and beliefs, the ancient knights' order supported the values of the post-revolutionary intelligentsia, helping them rise above everyday reality, and connecting them to the universal history of world culture. Georgy Fedotov defines the intelligentsia's consciousness/self-identification as almost a kind of order, suggesting that "although it does not have external forms, but has its own unwritten code of honor, morality, its vocation, its vows."[5] Yet, to say "the Order of Knights Templar in Soviet Russia" sounds bizarre, if not oxymoronic. After all, how could medieval knights, whose order was defeated in the fourteenth century, reappear in post-revolutionary Russia? What was so attractive to the Russian intelligentsia in the spiritual and moral dimensions of the order's credo?

Part 1: A Brief History of the Knights Templar and Their Transposition on Russian Soil

To better understand the medieval roots of the order in Soviet Russia, it is important to briefly discuss the history of the Knights Templar, which has fascinated scholars and the public for centuries. The monastic Order of the Knights Templar—the Templars—was founded in Jerusalem in 1118, receiving a charter from medieval theologian Saint Bernard de Clairvaux the same year. The Templars represented a new type of knighthood, since they were simultaneously monks and warriors who, in addition to taking vows of poverty, chastity and obedience, were entrusted with the protection of pilgrims on their way to the Holy Land. The order acquired incredible power and wealth during the Middle Ages: "At their peak in the

---

mythologizing. Birgit Menzel, "Introduction," in *The New Age of Russia: Occult and Esoteric Dimensions*, ed. Birgit Menzel, Michael Hagemeister, and Bernice Glatzer Rosenthal (Munich and Berlin: Otto Sagner, 2012), 18.

5 G. P. Fedotov, "Tragediia intelligentsii," LiveJournal.com, accessed August 1, 2021, https://intelligentsia1.livejournal.com/11813.html.

12th century, the Templars became the largest, richest organization the Western world had ever seen, something akin to a wealthy modern day multinational corporation."[6] Characterized by ritualistic secrecy, the Templars introduced to the Western world such modern practices as a banking system, diplomacy, property development, agriculture, and commerce. While creating their international Templar Empire, the brothers also helped the poor and sick. By the fourteenth century, there was an army of fifteen thousand knights in France alone.[7]

The Templars were defeated by the French King Philippe IV (1268–1314), often called the Fair. Since the King's treasury was experiencing serious problems, he decided to take possession of the Templars' wealth and enlisted the support of his obedient Pope, Clement V. Mass arrests took place on Friday, October 13, 1307 (the notoriously unhappy Friday the 13th). Templars were arrested, accused of heresy, idolatry, secrecy of proceedings, sodomy, and corruption; many were tortured and burned alive. Pope Clement V officially abolished the order in 1312, and Jacques de Molay, the twenty-second grand master of the order, was burned at the stake in March of 1314 in front of Notre Dame de Paris after spending six and a half years in prison and enduring torturous interrogations. Right before his death in front of a Parisian crowd, de Molay declared his innocence, denying all accusations of heresy. In Karen Ralls's words: "The medieval definition of what exactly constitutes 'heresy' was rarely very specific; it was molded and shaped according to how the prosecutors wanted to create their case and who was in power at the time."[8] In this way, the medieval inquisition was akin to the Stalinist show trials, where executioners skillfully constructed both the guilt and the verdict.

There has been much speculation over the years suggesting that the order did not disappear, since surviving Templars were accepted into various other existing orders and religious societies or organized new ones under different names, continuing their activities. The order was formally restored in 1743 in Paris, with the new organization closely associated with Freemasonry rather than with the medieval Templars.[9]

---

6 Karen Ralls, *Knights Templar Encyclopedia* (Newburyport: New Page Book, 2007), 132.
7 This brief historical overview of the Medieval Knights Templars is based on Fedor Fortinskii, "Novye otkrytiia v oblasti istorii ordena tamplierov," in *Mistiki, rozenkreitsery i tampliery v sovetskoi Rossii*, ed. Andrei Nikitin (Moscow: Agraf, 2000), 279–302; Dan Jones, *The Templars: The Rise and Spectacular Fall of God's Holy Warriors* (New York: Viking, 2017); Ralls, *Knights Templar Encyclopedia*; Malcolm Barber, *The New Knighthood: A History of the Order of the Temple* (Cambridge: Cambridge UP, 1994).
8 Ralls, *Knights Templar Encyclopedia*, 50–51.
9 Tim Wallace-Murphy explains that "while Freemasonry is not the child of the medieval Templar Order, it is a branch from the same genealogical tree; both the Templars and Freemasonry were created by the family group of Rex Deus and, while separated by several

Apollon Karelin and Bringing the Order to Russia

The founder and commander in chief of the Eastern Order of the Knights Templar in Soviet Russia was Apollon Karelin, a westernized Russian *intelligent*, mystical anarchist, and nobleman who on his mother's side was related to the poet Mikhail Lermontov (1814–1841). An active revolutionary, Karelin was arrested numerous times by tsarist police and had the reputation of being the second most influential figure in Russian anarchism after Pyotr Kropotkin (1842–1921). After the revolution of 1905, Karelin was forced to flee to Europe, settling in France. Discussing Karelin's spiritual ideals, Nikitin writes: "unlike Kropotkin, Karelin was, as one might think, a deeply religious person, although his faith had nothing to do with Orthodoxy or Catholicism and was of an anti-Church nature."[10]

While in Paris, Karelin enjoyed great respect among the Russian émigré community and was able to unite rival groups of Russian anarchists into a single "Brotherhood of free community members" (Bratstvo vol'nykh obshchinnikov) that had a clear linguistic connection to the Brotherhood of Free Masons (Bratstvo vol'nykh kamenshchikov).[11] Karelin's spiritual search eventually brought him to the secret French societies. He was initiated into the Knights Templar and returned to Russia in 1917 not only as an anarchist, but as Knight Santei—a messenger of the Western Order of the Knights Templar that was considered a continuation of the original medieval Templars' tradition and had ties with French Masonic lodges.[12]

Seemingly, mystical anarchism was for a while a solid cover for the order's work to train future Templars among the creative and scientific intelligentsia and university students in Russia. In Karelin's close circle, anarchist ideas about universal equality and brotherhood and the rejection of all forms of state power as an apparatus of violence and suppression of individual freedom were discussed along with mystical teachings of the East, the ancient legends of the Templars, and the history of art, philosophy, and literature. It is no surprise that mystical and anarchic ideas attracted young representatives of the

---

centuries, both nonetheless embody the same spiritual principle." Tim Wallace-Murphy, *The Enigma of the Freemasons: Their Historical and Mystical Connections* (New York: The Ivy Press Limited, 2006), 124.
10 Nikitin, *Mistiki, rozenkreitsery i tampliery v sovetskoi Rossii*, 56.
11 Nikitin, "Tsvety iz pepla," 15–16.
12 Nikitin, *Mistiki, rozenkreitsery i tampliery v sovetskoi Rossii*, 58.

post-revolutionary intelligentsia, since individual freedom had always been a core value for a real *intelligent*.[13]

It is not clear when Karelin took the first steps to found the Order of Templars in Russia, but most likely the first knights in Russia were initiated no later than 1919.[14] Having experienced the collapse of his revolutionary ideals and horrified by the red terror and violence, Karelin felt that "the revolution had been crushed by the Bolsheviks."[15] As he was preaching anarchist ideals, he started work on the spiritual enlightenment and education of young representatives of the Russian intelligentsia. The question of Karelin's political intentions cannot be unequivocally answered: did the group discuss counter-revolutionary and clearly anti-Soviet issues? Despite the fact that most of the confiscated materials were destroyed, surviving evidence clearly signals that materialist philosophy and the Marxist worldview were alien to the Russian Templars.[16]

The Russian Knightly Order and Its Members

Historically speaking, the notion of a new form of Russian knighthood uniting a group of free-thinking, enlightened Russian intellectuals fascinated by esoteric knowledge was not novel for Westernized post-Petrine Russia: It shares some historical parallels with the aristocratic intelligentsia involved in the Decembrist movement. Like the secret society of the Russian Templars, many Decembrists were members of Masonic lodges and saw their organization as a brotherhood of knights of freedom. Yury Lotman points out that "The interpretation of the Decembrist movement as the knighthood of freedom was typical for Dmitriev-Mamonov, one of the founders of the Decembrist organization 'Order of Russian Knights.'"[17] According to Lotman, the Order of Russian Knights remained surrounded by an aura of mystery but its plan of action was influenced by the

---

13 In his 1907 essay "What is the Intelligentsia?," Razumnik Ivanov-Razumnik states that one of the main characteristic of the intelligentsia is its striving toward the personal liberation of the individual. See Razumnik Ivanov-Razumnik, "Chto takoe intellegentsiia?," in *Intelligentsiia, vlast', narod* (Moscow: Nauka, 1993), 80.
14 Nikitin, *Mistiki, rozenkreitsery i tampliery v sovetskoi Rossii*, 98.
15 Evgenii Moravskii, "Apollon Andreevich Karelin. Nekrolog," in *Orden rossiiskikh tamplierov*, ed. Andrei Nikitin (Moscow: Minuvshee, 2003), vol. 1, 48.
16 See Aleksei Solonovich, "Kritika materializma" [Critique of materialism], in *Orden rossiiskikh tamplierov*, ed. Andrei Nikitin (Moscow: Minuvshee, 2003), vol. 3, 443–514.
17 Iurii Lotman, "Dekabrist v povsednevnoi zhizni," in idem, *Besedy o russkoi kul'ture* (St. Petersburg: Iskusstvo, 1994), 376. The Order of Russian Knights was one of the pre-Decembrist organizations. It was founded in 1815 by Count Matvei Dmitriev-Mamonov (1790–1863) and Mikhail Orlov (1788–1842).

French revolution and included overthrowing the existing political system and autocracy and creating a new societal structure based on a constitution. Lotman clarifies that the concept of "the new knighthood" was widespread among the educated elite as "the idea of a worldwide brotherhood of enlightened wise men."[18] Unlike the Decembrists, the Russian Templars did not leave evidence to suggest that they were actively planning to overthrow the existing political system; rather, they were searching for ways to coexist with the oppressive regime, juxtaposing their moral values to communist ideology. The Russian Templars' moral code was based on Christian values, and their intellectual pursuits (reading and retelling ancient texts and legends) established their connection with world history and culture. In distinction from the Masonic lodges of the Decembrist era, the organization of the Knights Templar was gender inclusive and relied heavily on the membership of female knights.

When Karelin returned to Russia from exile in 1917, his activity and publications abroad clearly contributed to the foundation of the Eastern Order of Knights Templar. In 1919 or 1920, the order already consisted of several groups of knights, and it reached the peak of its activity in the 1920s. The main organization of the Knights Templar, "The Order of Light," was based in Moscow and included leading representatives of the artistic intelligentsia, many of whom were associated with the Moscow Art Theater and its studios. The list of initiated Knights Templar included the actor and director Mikhail Chekhov (1891–1955), several of Vakhtangov's students who were also Tsvetaeva's close friends—the poet Pavel Antokolsky (1896–1978), actor and director Yury (Georgy) Zavadsky (1894–1977), and his sister Vera Zavadskaya (1895–1930), and such members of the MAT Third Studio as Ruben Simonov (1899–1968), Anna Orochko (1898–1965), and Vera Lvova (1898–1985).[19] Among the Knights Templar of high degree were the Moscow Art Theater actor and director Valentin Smyshlyaev (1891–1936), poet, translator, and orientalist Pavel Arensky (1887–1941), and composer Sergei Kondratyev (1896–1970), as well

---

18 Ibid.
19 Among the first knights who received their initiations from Karelin were young representatives of the artistic intelligentsia: actors, directors, musicians, poets, and painters who in 1918 founded the concert association Centipede (Sorokonozhka) in Moscow. Centipede's activities laid a foundation for the future charitable and educational activities of the Russian Templars. The concerts were held in worker's districts, poor housing, workers' clubs, and military units. The Centipede existed for one year and rallied participants, whose activities and camaraderie fell just as creation of the Eastern Order of Templars was beginning. Members of this associations included Chekhov, Antokolsky, Zavadsky, Nikitin, Smyshlyaev, and other Knights Templar.

as respected scholars such as the art historian Aleksei Sidorov (1891–1978) and the philologist Dmitry Blagoi (1893–1984), just to name a few.

The order was alienated from its historical surrounding, and this alienation seems to have been a form of spiritual refuge from the chaos and devastation of the revolution and Civil War. Similarly, Martin Malia emphasizes the alienation of the Russian intelligentsia as one of its distinguishing features, suggesting that it was a result of "a tension between the ideal and the real, or between what the individual wishes to become and what society permits him to be. In Russia this phenomenon was pushed to its ultimate development."[20] One of the arrested Knights Templar, Evgeny Smirnov, stated that:

> The purpose of the "Order of Light" is purely ethical: moral self-improvement of the individual through the perception of Christian foundations and the cultivation of knightly Christian virtues in oneself. The knight is an ethical concept, as a person who commits moral deeds. Cleansing the Christian foundations from the dogmas that have accumulated over the centuries, obscuring the face of Christ the knight, and sometimes the deception of the church—these are the aspirations of members of the order.[21]

This testimony clarifies that in their worldview the Russian Templars made a clear distinction between Christ as a knight, Christianity as his true teaching, and the Church.

The organization was a hybrid of mystical anarchism with ideas and symbols signaling the influence of the historic Knights Templar and Freemasonry.[22] The order's main moral and spiritual mission included two main tasks that mirrored core values of the Russian intelligentsia: work on self-perfection in order to serve society and humankind and combining mystical and scientific knowledge of the world to participate in the struggle between the light of knowledge and the darkness of ignorance.[23]

---

20 Martin Malia, "What is Intelligentsia?," in *The Russian Intelligentsia*, ed. Richard Pipes (New York: Columbia UP, 1961), 4.
21 See Andrei Nikitin, ed., *Orden rossiiskikh tamplierov* (Moscow: Minuvshee, 2003), vol. 2, 131. This statement by one of the arrested Knights Templar, Evgeny Smirnov, was made during his interrogation on November 23, 1930.
22 Nikitin, *Mistiki, rozenkreitsery i tampliery v Sovetskoi Rossii*, 79, 127.
23 Ibid., 35.

The same notion is illustrated in Zavadskaya's June 29, 1929, poem dedicated to Karelin. Mourning Karelin's death, the poetic persona nostalgically describes the earlier knightly gatherings, emphasizing the fight against evil as the Templars' main mission:

> Ты нас учил со злом бороться,
> Быть гордым, смелым и прямым.
> В часы, когда смеркалось солнце,
>
> Внимали мы речам твоим.
> Твоя душа—звезда над мглою.
> И жертвой освящен твой меч.
> Твой дух над нашею землею
> Взошел как огнезарный смерч![24]
>
> You taught us to fight against evil,
> To be proud, bold, and straightforward.
> In the hours when the sun went down
> We would listen to your speeches.
>
> Your soul is a star above the gloom
> And your sword is sanctified by sacrifice.
> Your spirit over our land
> Arose like a fiery whirlwind!

An interconnected mystical worldview, sense of high ethical responsibility of each member, and anarchic rejection of any political power as an apparatus meant to repress individual freedom lay at the very heart of the Order's doctrine. Yulia Nazarova observes:

> Just like Russian Freemasonry, the Order of the Knights Templar paid a lot of attention to the moral improvement of the individual, which is in general uncharacteristic for the Russia mentality with its ideal of "community," common moral responsibility, and was even more uncharacteristic for the Soviet mentality.[25]

---

24 Vera Zavadskaiia, "A. A. Karelinu," in *Rosa Mystica*, ed. Andrei Nikitin (Moscow: Agraf, 2002), 142.

25 Iuliia Nazarova, "Etiko-misticheskoe soderzhanie kontseptsii rossiiskogo ordena tamplierov," *Gumanitarnye vedomosti TGPU im. L. N. Tolstogo* 1 (2018): 7.

The whole concept of knighthood was very appealing to the Russian intelligentsia, given its noble agenda with romantic overtones, and the knightly code of honor in many ways mirrored the unwritten spiritual and moral code of the intelligentsia. Nikitin writes:

> The knight appeared to be a person who voluntarily took upon himself the mission of serving good and light in the world, a symbol of honor, fortitude, courage, and strict fulfillment of duty: he turned out to be the most vivid and all-embracing ideal image, understandable to every young, intellectually developed and well-read person.[26]

The fact that Darkness had triumphed over Light in Soviet Russia was seen as a part of the historic worldwide struggle between Good and Evil, Light and Darkness. The knightly initiation was perceived as a spiritual awakening that would define the physical and spiritual existence of the knight until the end of his/her days on earth and in the hereafter. Earthly suffering and torturous interrogations were as an unavoidable component of the fate of Knights Templar:

> Initiation is what distinguished the life of a Knight from that of a regular person. In terms of its significance, it stands alongside two others—birth and death. A symbolic touch on the shoulder awakens the spirit of a person, returning it to the realm of true life.[27]

While some Templars denied their association with the order during their brutal interrogations, in their poetic legacy they clearly identified themselves as Knights Templar. A poem by Boris Vlasenko associates the Soviet regime with Lucifer, while the Russian knight identifies himself as a direct descendant of medieval knighthood:

> Пусть мир лежит во зле покорно
> И торжествует Люцифер,
> Как прежде я борюсь упорно,
> Я—рыцарь Храма, тамплиер.[28]

---

26 Nikitin, *Orden rossiiskikh tamplierov*, vol. 2, 24.
27 Aleksandr Uittenkhoven, "Rytsari p'iut kiprskoe," in *Rosa Mystica*, ed. Andrei Nikitin (Moscow: Agraf, 2002), 283.
28 Boris Vlasenko, "Tamplier," in *Rosa Mystica*, ed. Andrei Nikitin (Moscow: Agraf, 2002),199.

> Let the world lie in evil submissively
> And Lucifer celebrate his triumph,
> As before, I struggle tenaciously,
> I'm a knight of the Temple, a Templar.

Comparing the Russian Knights Templar with other esoteric groups and circles of Soviet Russia, Konstantin Burmistrov emphasizes their good organizational structure, clearly defined mission and orientation toward Gnosticism, while many other secret societies showed serious interest in the occult and magic.[29] One of the main requirements for newly initiated Knights was a sincere belief in immortality and the eternal life of the human soul—and *not* being a member of the Communist Party. Initiatory formulas, preserved in the memory of some Templars, are of particular interest for their spiritual and religious poetics, striving upward toward eternity and at the same time preparing for earthly martyrdom. At the initiation, Russian Templars took an oath of absolute secrecy; even the closest family members were not allowed to know about their knighthood, and all materials and legends were passed from mouth to mouth, or hand to hand via samizdat (underground publishing typed on thin paper). After repressions began, private letters and other incriminating documents were destroyed, and pages from diaries with names and references to meetings were torn out and burned. Moreover, the Templars themselves did not always know who exactly was a member of their order, though knights knew others in their own groups.

Burmistrov defines the Templars as "the cream of the contemporary intelligentsia," summarizing that they were especially active in such organizations as the State Institute of the Word, the Oriental Institute, Institute of Living Oriental Languages, Bauman Technical High School in Moscow, Moscow Conservatory, State Academy of Artistic Science, Moscow Art Theater, Third Studio, and Second Moscow Art Theater, Kropotkin Museum, and the Tolstoy society.[30] It is impossible to know with precision how many members of the intelligentsia were initiated into the order, but, by the late 1920s when the mass arrests and repressions began, the organization had a well-established structure with centers in Moscow, Sergiev Posad, Leningrad, Nizhny Novgorod, Sochi, Novorossiysk, the North Caucasus, Sverdlovsk, Central Asia, and the Belorussian Soviet Socialist Republic. Not all the groups had similar missions and methods. Nikitin notes a striking contrast between the Moscow and Nizhny Novgorod organizations:

---

29 Konstantin Burmistrov, "The History of Esoterism in Soviet Russia in the 1920s-1930s," in *The New Age of Russia: Occult and Esoteric Dimensions*, ed. Birgit Menzel, Michael Hagemeister, and Bernice Glatzer Rosenthal (Munich and Berlin: Otto Sagner, 2012), 73–74.

30 Burmistrov, "The History of Esoterism in Soviet Russia in the 1920s-1930s," 77–78.

> In contrast to the Moscow mystics, who were more engaged in theory and work on self-perfection and in terms of social activity directed their efforts to educational and charitable work, the Nizhny Novgorod anarcho-mystics undertook attempts to "go out to the people," influencing the masses by distributing not only illegal literature, but also outright flyers.[31]

The flyers called readers to fight for freedom of religion and to unite around the Church to fight the devilish Soviet regime.[32]

The miraculously surviving segments of Knights Templar poetic heritage published by Nikitin in *Rosa Mystica* give us a glimpse of the secret spiritual life of the Russian Knights. In these poetic texts, the knight is depicted as a defender of the temple of faith, fighting any kind of oppression and injustice in his/her surrounding, and this image is militant rather than peaceful. Swords, spears, and shields are persistently mentioned, allegorically representing the necessary knightly ammunition in a war against evil. Such imagery raises doubts about the veracity of the testimony of the arrested Templars, who claimed there was no agenda for an ideological struggle against Soviet power.

The symbols of the order included a light blue eight-pointed star, or sometimes a light blue aster, symbolizing the infinite universe of eight dimensions. Initiations were made with a white rose, a symbol of purity of thought and striving for infinity. Judging from several testimonies, Karelin always appeared at meetings and lectures with a white rose. During their testimony, some Templars used military terminology, referring to their groups as divisions (*otriady*) and the order's senior knights as commanders (*komandory*). Divisions consisted of no more than eight to ten knights, and frequently representatives of the groups did not know one another or the commanders of other groups.

Activities of the order included educational lectures on the history and philosophy of art, secret gatherings with meditation, and charity concerts to help those disadvantaged by the Revolution and Civil War—this last very much in the spirit of the pre-Revolutionary intelligentsia. Financial help for the poor and disadvantaged was provided by monthly contributions from each member, consisting of 1–1.5% of their income. All these factors demonstrate that the Order of Knights Templar in Soviet Russia was a well-organized secret society that united a large group of the post-revolutionary intelligentsia, searching for the meaning of existence and self-identification in the new Soviet surroundings,

---

31 Nikitin, *Orden rossiiskikh tamplierov*, vol. 1, 121.
32 Ibid., 121–122.

facing at the same time unavoidable dangers of arrest and persecution. Mass arrests, imprisonment, and exile of the Templars occurred at the end of the 1920s and in the fall of 1930, but the repressions were frequently perceived as a knightly initiation.

Part 2: The Cultural Legacy of the Russian Knights Templar

The above information on the existence and activities of the order gives a researcher of Russian culture a rather unexpected arsenal of knowledge, hinting at completely new meanings and interpretations in the work of the artistic intelligentsia who were, in one way or another, related to the order. Did the punitive organs of the Soviet Inquisition manage to defeat the order during mass arrests and repressions and stop its activities completely, or did the knights, like some of the medieval Templars, manage to disperse and continue their activities throughout their lives? What legacy did the order leave in Soviet culture?

Marina Tsvetaeva's Poetic Drama Snowstorm: A Message to Two Knights Templar?

During Tsvetaeva's life in post-revolutionary Moscow between 1917 and 1922, three Knights Templar of high degree were in her inner circle—Vera and Yury Zavadsky and Pavel Antokolsky. Tsvetaeva dedicated her dramatic cycle *Romantika* and several poetic cycles to Zavadsky and Antokolsky, and her relationships with some of them did not end when she emigrated from Russia in 1922. Tsvetaeva met the actors of the Third Moscow Art Theater Studio in October 1918 when Karelin was apparently already actively working on his organizing mission. Tsvetaeva's daughter, Ariadna Efron, recalled:

> In 1919, we had a lot of people, actors, friends, lovely Sonechka had been visiting. She was charming. The handsome Zavadsky also visited, his sister Vera was friends with mother, and we were also friendly with her later on, in France.[33]

---

[33] Veronika Losskaia, *Marina Tsvetaeva v zhizni. Vospominaniia sovremennikov* (Moscow: PROZAiK, 2011), 65. The "lovely Sonechka" is Sofia Gollidei (1894–1934), an actress and Vakhtangov's pupil in the MAT's Third Studio.

Zavadskaya was Tsvetaeva's school friend, and their friendship continued in the 1920s in Paris. Another knight, Antokolsky, met Tsvetaeva again in Paris in 1929; recollecting this meeting, Tsvetaeva writes: "I am walking with my two-year-old son in Bellevue Park—Observatoire. Next to me, at my other hand, in step with my two-year-old son is Pavlik A., who came [to Paris] with Vakhtangov's Studio."[34]

In her *Tale of Sonechka* Tsvetaeva recalls:

> It was winter 1918–1919, still winter 1918, December. In some theater, on some stage, I read my play *Snowstorm* to the Third Studio students. In an empty theater, on a full stage. My *Snowstorm* had a dedication: To Yury and Vera Z., my love—to their friendship.[35]

An analysis of *Snowstorm* through the prism of the Knights Templar mysteries, legends, and rituals can provide a new interpretation for some mysterious images, passages, and phrases in the play. The nature of *Snowstorm* is transcendental; it echoes Vakhtangov's artistic search for new theatrical forms that would reflect the eclectic spirituality of the modernist era. The play's heroine, the Lady in the Cloak, a young, beautiful aristocrat, decides to escape the comfortable boredom of married life and finds herself in a small tavern, lost in the forests of Bohemia. Under mystical circumstances, the Lady in the Cloak meets the Gentleman in the Cloak who arrives at the tavern, introducing himself as "Prince of the Moon, Rotunda Cavalier, and Knight of the Rose."[36] This introduction echoes initiation into the Knights Templar that was made, as mentioned before, with a white rose. Experiencing an inexplicable sense of spiritual kinship, the Lady in the Cloak feels that she once knew this man: "Prince, resolve for me one problem:/ Where and when have I already met you?"[37] The metaphysical nature of love is reflected in the meeting of lovers who exist in two different dimensions and are destined to meet in the earthly realm only for a short period of time. The play depicts the notion of Templars' legends in which the soul could descend to earth in the form of a knight.

---

34 Marina Tsvetaeva, "Povest' o Sonechke" [The tale of Sonechka], in eadem, *Sobranie sochinenii v semi tomakh*, ed. Anna Saakiantz and Lev Mnukhin (Moscow: Ellis Lak, 1994), vol. 4, 410.
35 Ibid., 293.
36 Marina Tsvetaeva, *Metel'*, in eadem, *Sobranie sochinenii v semi tomakh*, ed. Anna Saakiantz and Lev Mnukhin (Moscow: Ellis Lak, 1994), vol. 3, 366.
37 Ibid., 370.

One gets the impression that in the end of the play the Gentleman, a Templar of high degree, is performing the sacrament of initiation to a female novice. As mentioned before, unlike Masonic lodges at that time, which usually limited their membership to men, the Russian Templars attracted many women. In her remarks, Tsvetaeva points out that, while pronouncing the following phrase, the Gentleman is addressing someone invisible in the highest spheres:

> Освободи! Укрепи!
> Дай ей Свободу и Силу!
> Юная женщина, спи!
>
> Free her! Strengthen her!
> Give her Freedom and Power!
> Young woman, sleep![38]

Spiritual freedom and strength were core aspects of the Russian Templars' morality, resonating in phrases such as "Above the heart! Forward to the spirit!" Moreover, immediately after that, the Gentleman commands the Lady to forget their meeting, which corresponds to the Templars' oath to keep their membership in the order secret.[39] The Lady in the cloak is destined to remember the meeting only as a magical dream.

> ГОСПОДИН
> И не помни!
>
> ДАМА
> (Чуть слышно)
> Забыла!
>
> GENTLEMAN:
> And do not remember!
>
> LADY:
> (barely audible)
> I've forgotten![40]

---

38 Ibid.
39 Nikitin, *Orden rossiiskikh tamplierov*, vol. 2, 188–189.
40 Tsvetaeva, *Metel'*, vol. 3, 371.

Such intertextual connections between *Snowstorm* and the Templars' rituals and symbols suggests that Tsvetaeva was aware of the spiritual quest of her friends, the Knights Templar. It could also suggest that her friends trusted the poet with quite a few details that were otherwise supposed to be kept secret.

The Knights Templar around Vakhtangov

Driven by spiritual hunger and searching for answers to existential questions amidst historic turmoil, the artistic intelligentsia was susceptible to esoteric teachings and sought membership in various secret societies. As mentioned earlier, many young actors associated with the Moscow Art Theater and its studios joined the Order of Light. As Maria Ignatieva notes in her article for this volume, the Moscow Art Theater (MAT) has the status of a theater of the intelligentsia. While working on his famous system, Konstantin Stanislavsky creatively revised MAT's societal mission and carried on his pedagogical role as an educator of young actors. In 1911, Stanislavsky gathered the young people in MAT and talked about the importance of conveying on stage the nuances of their characters' spiritual lives in addition to physical expressiveness. Stanislavsky urged his actors to move away from "external realism" to the "realism of the inner truth of the human spirit." It is in this direction that young Vakhtangov, who transcribed his teacher's whole lecture, directed his creative quest. The experimentation and artistic quest of the First MAT Studio was of a spiritual and philosophical nature. Together with a group of young actors and directors who were experimenting with various stage techniques, both Vakhtangov and Michael Chekhov were searching for ways to express the life of the human spirit on stage and were drawn toward transcendental theatricality. Vakhtangov admits, "I love theater in all forms, but most of all I am attracted not by everyday moments (I love them too if there is humor or humorous tragedy in them), but moments when the human spirit is especially alive."[41] For Chekhov, "the true artist functioned as a medium, envisioning the spiritual world and expressing its messages in the world of reality."[42]

The fact that several of Vakhtangov's most intimate friends and disciples were Knights Templar of a high degree opens up new perspectives on the director's

---

[41] Vakhtangov's letter to A. Cheban, written August 3, 1917, in *Evgenii Vakhtangov: Dokumenty i svidetel'stva*, ed. Vladislav Ivanov (Moscow: Indrik, 2011), vol. 1, 444.
[42] Marie-Christine Autant-Mathieu and Yana Meerson, eds., *The Routledge Companion to Michael Chekhov* (London: Routledge, 2015), 2.

creative career.[43] The stage practitioners involved with the Order of Light viewed the theater stage as an arena for transmitting "the mystery of theatrical art in general and the catharsis of the actor, acting as a mediator between the spectator and the transcendent world."[44] The Templars advocated apolitical purity of stage art designed to serve humanity, and such mission was in harmony with Vakhtangov's artistic credo, seeking to touch the souls of spectators exhausted by the hardships of the revolution and Civil War. The knightly code of honor with its high morality, as well as the very concept of knighthood with its rituals and symbols, were undoubtedly attractive to the young theater practitioners not only from a moral and spiritual perspective but also from a theatrical point of view, since the Templars' practice contains an element of role-playing and performativity.

Mikhail Chekhov, Vakhtangov's very close friend and colleague in MAT, was initiated by Karelin himself and had the highest twelfth degree in the Order of Light hierarchy. Zavadsky and Simonov, Vakhtangov's two close disciples who assisted during rehearsals of his legendary 1922 production of Carlo Gozzi's *Princess Turandot* were both Knights Templar as well. Mirroring the Templars' view of the Russian Revolution of 1917, Vakhtangov and his intimate surrounding viewed the revolution as not a political, but rather a mystical event. This notion was vividly illustrated after the fact by Zavadsky who, during his 1930 arrest and interrogations, provided testimony to the Soviet secret police (OGPU) about his personal views and artistic evolution.[45] It is notable that while answering investigators' questions about the Order of Light, Zavadsky spoke about Vakhtangov as his spiritual teacher:

> I can talk about my inner ideological evolution: I entered the revolution as an idealist—I was a student of Vakhtangov, Stanislavsky's student, and this period included the elements of pure idealism with a bias towards mysticism. This is how I entered the revolution—as an idealist with a mystical bias.[46]

---

43 There is a more detailed discussion of the possible connections between Vakhtangov's artistic credo of *fantastic realism* and the artistic mission of the Order of Light in my article "Evgenii Vakhtangov's Fantastic Realism: Evolving Interpretations of a Term," in a special edition of *Arti dello Spettacolo/Performing Arts* 7 (2021): WORD><STAGE: Stage Words: Inter-semiotic and Inter-linguistic Translation of Dramaturgic, Literary and Theater Theory Text, 45–55.
44 Nikitin, *Mistiki, rozenkreitsery i tampliery v Sovetskoi Rossii*, 108.
45 The OGPU was the Soviet Union's secret police from 1924–1934. It was previously known as the Cheka and was later renamed the NKVD.
46 Nikitin, *Orden rossiiskikh tamplierov*, vol. 2, 56. Zavadsky's interrogation was on September 14, 1930.

Unlike many other Knights Templar who were sent into exile, Zavadsky was released from prison, possibly due to the help of Konstantin Stanislavsky (1863–1938) and Avel Yenukidze (1877–1937), the latter of whom was a prominent Georgian Bolshevik and member of the Soviet Central Committee in Moscow.[47]

An examination of personal correspondence, diaries, and biographical facts suggests that Vakhtangov could have had some ties to the order and was aware of its mission and ideals. On a biographical level, Vakhtangov's preoccupation with immortality during the last years of his life would make the order's main rule for membership—belief in immortality and the eternal life of the human soul—very comforting. One of the most significant documents is Vakhtangov's letter to Zavadskaya, the object of his platonic fascination, written in June 4, 1919. Striking in its poetic beauty, this letter seems to contain some secret knowledge that the two correspondents are aware of, as well as an almost tangible faith in their future meeting in the hereafter. Vakhtangov, who was married and had a son, addresses Vera, a knight of a high degree of the Order of Light as "the only one and beautiful" who was "sent to earth to bring Light..."[48] Vakhtangov continues:

> In my life You—are the only one.
> You—were sent.
> My mother, those who I loved, the mother of my son, my son—
> did not open the meaning of life for me at all, since I have not experienced such pure and delightful excitement.

These lines are ambiguous, since they not only signal a declaration of platonic love and devotion, but also suggest that Vera is some sort of carrier of the highest level of spiritual enlightenment that brought new light to Vakhtangov's life. Vakhtangov concludes his poetic and enigmatic letter with the lines:

> And You—Light like the Sun.
> And You—Great like God.
> And You—The only one like Life.
> And You—Unavoidable like Death
> Do not be sad. [...]
> Let us live out our days as long as we are destined to.[49]

---

47 Nikitin, *Mistiki, rozenkreitsery i tampliery v Sovetskoi Rossii*, 161.
48 *Evgenii Vakhtangov: Dokumenty i svidetel'stva*, vol. 2, 294–296.
49 Ibid., 296.

Undoubtedly, Vakhtangov was a Knight of Theater, but was he himself a Knight Templar? Or, if not, was he aware of the activities of the Order of Light, its spiritual and moral doctrine, and the fact that his leading pupils were Knights Templar who passionately believed in their mission to fight the evil of darkness and ignorance and to bring Light to the world through artistic creation? While his studios and then his theater were frequently mentioned in the interrogations of arrested Russian Templars, Vakhtangov's name *per se* was cited only by Zavadsky. Curiously, in his 1933 interrogation the Knight Templar Mikhail Sizov admits that, despite the fact that the order had twelve degrees, the identity of the knights of the highest degree remained unknown, and Karelin took this secret to his grave.[50]

While Chekhov emigrated to the West and later taught acting to leading Hollywood stars, the majority of Vakhtangov's pupils became Soviet theater practitioners and acting teachers who educated and enlightened several generations of Russian stage and film actors and directors. Vakhtangov's students sacredly kept their secret, and neither family members nor colleagues knew about their knighthood. Was such secrecy self-protection, loyalty to the oath, or belief in an afterlife where they would be asked about their earthly journey? The Soviet Secret police was clearly aware of their past association with the order and was watching them. Questions about Vakhtangov's pupils, Zavadsky and Simonov, resurfaced in 1962 during the KGB interrogation of Aleksandr Paul (1897–1965). Paul was a Knight Templar who was arrested and sent to the GULag, but then became an informer who was allowed to teach Western literature in a leading Moscow theater institution and hold a permanent position in the Shchukin Theater School, associated with the Vakhtangov Theater. It is important to emphasize that at this time both Zavadsky and Simonov were People's Artists of the USSR and artistic directors of Moscow's leading cultural institutions—the Mossovet Theater and the Vakhtangov Theater, respectively. In response to an interrogator's question: "Which Knights Templar, members of the Order of Light do you know, who would be members of the Order of Light and currently reside in Moscow?" Paul replied:

> I already showed that the organization of the knightly Order of Light was secret and therefore not all members knew each other . . . I can name Zavadsky, head of the Moscow Mossovet Theater . . . and Simonov, Ruben Nikolaevich, People's Artist of the USSR, Head of the E. Vakhtangov Theater.[51]

---

50 Andrei Nikitin, ed., *Rozenkreitsery v Sovetskoi Rossii* (Moscow: Minuvshee, 2004), 233.
51 Nikitin, *Orden rossiiskikh tamplierov*, vol. 2, 189.

The timeframe of this interrogation suggests that Zavadsky and Simonov's artistic biographies must be reevaluated through the prism of their dedication both to the credo of their teachers (Karelin and Vakhtangov) and to their knightly ideals, removing the layers of ideological makeup. The rich and understudied topic of the Knights Templar in Vakhtangov's close surroundings can shed new light on how his pupils remained active as knights of stagecraft until the ends of their lives, teaching, directing, acting, and nurturing generations of students and spectators. As for Paul himself, his role in the history of the order is rather enigmatic, since on one hand he was collaborating with the Soviet secret police, while on the other hand his apartment had been, in Nikitin's words, "a little island of the Knights Templar" throughout 1940s and 1950s."[52] Along with Paul, one of the oldest Knights Templar, Maria Dorogova (1889–1981 or 1982), who had met Karelin abroad before World War I, also gave lectures on secret societies, esoteric knowledge and occultism.[53]

I would like to pay tribute to Nikitin's publications and findings not only as a scholar but also as a descendent of a Knight Templar: my paternal grandfather, the actor and director Ruben Simonov, was one of Vakhtangov's favorite students and took to his grave his secret affiliation with the Knights Templar. Nobody in my family knew anything about the Order of Light or my grandfather's knighthood until June 2020, when in the course of my research I came across several volumes of Nikitin's publications. The same was true of another Knight Templar, Vera Lvova (1898–1985), who was Vakhtangov's pupil in the Third MAT Studio and for many years was a leading acting professor in the Shchukin Theater Institute.[54] When during an online meeting in early 2021 I informed Lvova's granddaughter Anna Brusser that her grandmother and other Vakhtangovites had been Knights Templar, Anna was flabbergasted: she had lived with her grandmother her whole youth and never knew anything about her knighthood. During our conversation, we discussed the knighthood of our grandparents as a moral shield of the real Russian *intelligenty* that protected them against their surroundings, providing a moral compass to navigate Soviet cultural waters, as they strove for higher artistic and spiritual mission.

In their spiritual quest, the Russian Knights Templar followed the *code d'honneur* of the Russian intelligentsia—resisting the darkness and ignorance of an oppressive Soviet regime, juxtaposing it to intellectual and spiritual

---

52 Ibid., 324.
53 Ibid.
54 Anna Brusser is currently a professor of stage voice and speech and the head of the Speech Department at the Boris Shchukin Theater Institute.

enlightenment. The cosmopolitanism and spiritual eclecticism of members of the order made them true citizens of the world who strove for personal freedom, rejecting any form of political or religious dogmatism and repression. While some important issues will forever remain secret and enigmatic, a great deal of scholarly work lies ahead to identify the full extent of the Templars' influence on their cultural surrounding, tracing their cultural legacy in such domains as literature, culture, performing arts, and education of new generations of the intelligentsia.

Bibliography

Autant-Mathieu, Marie-Christine, and Yana Meerson, eds. *The Routledge Companion to Michael Chekhov*. London: Routledge, 2015.

Barber, Malcolm. *The New Knighthood: A History of the Order of the Temple*. Cambridge: Cambridge UP, 1994.

Burmistrov, Konstantin. "The History of Esoterism in Soviet Russia in the 1920s-1930s." In *The New Age of Russia: Occult and Esoteric Dimensions*, edited by Birgit Menzel, Michael Hagemeister, and Bernice Glatzer Rosenthal, 52–80. Munich and Berlin: Otto Sagner, 2012.

Evgenii Vakhtangov: Dokumenty i svidetel'stva. Edited by Vladislav Ivanov. Vol. 1. Moscow: Indrik, 2011.

Evgenii Vakhtangov: Dokumenty i svidetel'stva. Edited by Vladislav Ivanov. Vol. 2. Moscow: Indrik, 2011.

Fedotov, G. P. "Tragediia intelligentsii." LiveJournal.com. Accessed August 1, 2021. https://intelligentsia1.livejournal.com/11813.html.

Fortinskii, Fedor. "Novye otkrytiia v oblasti istorii ordena tamplierov." In *Mistiki, rozenkreitsery i tampliery v sovetskoi Rossii*, edited by Andrei Nikitin, 279–302. Moscow: Agraf, 2000.

Ivanov-Razumnik, Razumnik. "Chto takoe intellegentsiia?" In *Intelligentsiia, vlast', narod*, edited by L. I. Novikova and I. N. Sizemskaia, 73–80. Moscow: Nauka, 1993.

Jones, Dan. *The Templars: The Rise and Spectacular Fall of God's Holy Warriors*. New York: Viking, 2017.

Losskaia, Veronika. *Marina Tsvetaeva v znizni. Vospominaniia sovremennikov*. Moscow: PROZAiK, 2011.

Lotman, Iurii. "Dekabrist v povsednevnoi zhizni." In idem, *Besedy o russkoi kul'ture*, 331–384. St. Petersburg: Iskusstvo, 1994.

Malia, Martin. "What is Intelligentsia?" In *The Russian Intelligentsia*, edited by Richard Pipes, 1–18. New York: Columbia UP, 1961.

Menzel, Birgit. "Introduction." In *The New Age of Russia: Occult and Esoteric Dimensions*, edited by Birgit Menzel, Michael Hagemeister, and Bernice Glatzer Rosenthal, 11–28. Munich and Berlin: Otto Sagner, 2012.

Moravskii, Evgenii. "Apollon Andreevich Karelin. Nekrolog." In *Orden rossiiskikh tamplierov*, edited by Andrei Nikitin, vol. 1, 47–49. Moscow: Minuvshee, 2003.

Nazarova, Yulia. "Etiko-misticheskoe soderzhanie kontseptsii rossijskogo Ordena tamplierov." *Gumanitrnye vedomosti TGPU im. L. N. Tolstogo* 1 (2018): 5–10.

Nikitin, Andrei. *Mistiki, rozenkreitsery i tampliery v sovetskoi Rossii*. Moscow: Agraf, 2000.

Nikitin, Andrei. "Tsvety iz pepla." In *Rosa Mystica*, edited by Andrei Nikitin, 3–10. Moscow: Agraf, 2002.

Nikitin, Andrei, ed. *Orden rossiiskikh tamplierov*. Vol. 1: *Dokumenty 1922–1930*. Moscow: Minuvshee, 2003.

Nikitin, Andrei, ed. *Orden rossiiskikh tamplierov*. Vol. 2: *Dokumenty 1930–1944*. Moscow: Minuvshee, 2003.

Nikitin, Andrei, ed. *Orden rossiiskikh tamplierov*. Vol. 3: *Dokumenty 1922–1930*. Moscow: Minuvshee, 2003.

Nikitin, Andrei, ed. *Rozenkreitsery v Sovetskoi Rossii*. Moscow: Minuvshee, 2004.

Partan, Olga. "Evgenii Vakhtangov's Fantastic Realism: Evolving Interpretations of a Term." *Arti dello Spettacolo/Performing Arts* 7 (2021): 45–55.

Ralls, Karen. *Knights Templar Encyclopedia*. Newburyport, MA: New Page Book, 2007.

Solonovich, Aleksei. "Kritika materializma." In *Orden Rossijskikh Tamplierov*, edited by Andrei Nikitin, vol. 3, 443–514. Moscow: Minuvshee, 2003.

Tsvetaeva, Marina. "Otvet na anketu." In eadem, *Sobranie sochinenii v semi tomakh*, edited by Anna Saakiantz and Lev Mnukhin, vol. 4, 621–624. Moscow: Ellis Lak, 1994.

Tsvetaeva, Marina. "Povest' o Sonechke." In eadem, *Sobranie sochinenii v semi tomakh*, edited by Anna Saakiantz and Lev Mnukhin, vol. 4, 293–416. Moscow: Ellis Lak, 1994.

Tsvetaeva, Marina. "Metel'." In eadem, *Sobranie sochinenii v semi tomakh*, edited by Anna Saakiantz and Lev Mnukhin, vol. 3, 358–372. Moscow: Ellis Lak, 1994.

Wallace-Murphy, Tim. *The Enigma of the Freemasons: Their Historical and Mystical Connections*. New York: The Ivy Press Limited, 2006.

Remaking the Literary Intelligentsia (1930s–1940s)

Carol Any

In the autumn of 1922, the fledgling Bolshevik state loaded 160 intellectuals onto a pair of steamboats and deported them. The "philosophers' ships" were an early step in ensuring an intelligentsia compatible with Bolshevism. The passengers included philosophers, theologians, scientists, professors, and journalists, along with a few writers.[1] By the 1930s, Stalin, who had been charged with overseeing the philosophers' ships, was giving especially great weight to writers, whose books he hoped would spread Soviet values among the reading public and promote Soviet achievements abroad. To engineer a new literary intelligentsia, eliminating suspect writers would not be enough. The party would also need to foster a reliable cohort to replace them. How did it go about achieving this goal? What were the challenges and results? This essay will identify four strategies that were implemented to insure the social engineering of the literary intelligentsia. These were recruitment, education, unionization, and the purges. The essay will also briefly consider how the new literary intelligentsia saw its mission and what new features accrued to the intelligentsia myth.

---

1 V. G. Makarov and V. S. Khristoforov, "Passazhiry 'filosofskogo parokhoda' (sud'by intelligentsii, repressirovannoi letom–osen'iu 1922 g.)," Institut istorii estestvoznaniia i tekhniki imeni S. I. Vavilova RAN, accessed May 12, 2024, https://ihst.ru/projects/sohist/papers/mak03vf.htm.

Recruitment

In the 1920s and well into the thirties, the party mounted an energetic effort to recruit proletarians into literature by establishing literary circles at factories and encouraging workers to try their hand at writing short pieces for their factory newspaper. This effort was implemented through RAPP (the Russian Association of Proletarian Writers), whose leadership circle under Leopold Averbakh served as an unofficial literary office for the Communist Party.[2] Literary consultants were brought in to help the most promising of these worker-writers improve their grammar and writing skills, and two journals for "mass literature," the *Chisel* (Rezets) and *Growth* (Rost), were founded in the mid-1920s as a publishing platform for these so-called "literary shockworkers."

Neither the aspiring writers nor most of the consultants were up to their task,[3] but most party leaders favored recruiting factory workers, reasoning that they could learn to write well. The minority of party leaders who valued literary quality, such as Trotsky, Bukharin, Lunacharsky, and Voronsky, were out of power by the late twenties and early thirties. But there was still one more obstacle to a wholesale importation of workers from the factory circles. This was Maxim Gorky. Stalin was determined to lure Gorky back to the Soviet Union and position him as the public face of Soviet literature and guarantor of its distinction. To persuade Gorky to return, he was prepared to make concessions.

Gorky shared the party's goal of bringing workers into literature. But he was appalled that *Rezets* and *Rost* were providing a forum for substandard "literature," and he called for the elimination of the factory circles. He expected aspiring proletarian writers to dedicate themselves to study, and he had his own more realistic vision of a path forward for them. Their first steps into literature would be as contributors to collaborative volumes that gave them a role they were suited for. Gorky designed at least four of these: *History of the Civil War* (Istoriia grazhdanskoi voiny), *Our Achievements* (Nashi dostizheniia), *People of the First and Second Five-year Plans* (Liudi pervoi i vtoroi piatiletki), and *History of Factories and Plants* (Istoriia fabrik i zavodov). The material for each was

---

2 T. M. Goriaeva, ed., *Mezhdu molotom i nakoval'nei: Soiuz sovetskikh pisatelei SSSR; Dokumenty i kommentarii*, vol. 1: *1925–June 1941* (Moscow: Rosspen, 2011), 48, 58, 167; S. I. Sheshukov, *Neistovye revniteli: Iz istorii literaturnoi bor'by dvadtsatykh godov* (Moscow: Moskovskii rabochii, 1970), 297.

3 Evgeny Dobrenko, *The Making of the State Writer: Social and Aesthetic Origins of Soviet Literary Culture*, trans. Jesse M. Savage (Stanford, CA: Stanford UP, 2001), 332.

provided by workers; then it was shaped by historians; finally, it was polished by established writers.[4]

Gorky and his opponents were locked in a struggle for the heart and soul of the Soviet literary intelligentsia-to-be. The party prioritized the literary intelligentsia's social composition, which would determine the kind of writing it produced. Gorky prioritized literature itself. He hoped that a significant portion of its authors would be from the working class, but this would depend on their dedication to study.

The dispute over who to recruit was entangled with the question of how future writers should be educated. RAPP won permission to open the Workers' Evening Literary University (Vechernii rabochii literaturnyi universitet), whose mission was to provide a basic literary education to factory recruits.[5] Its opening in Leningrad in spring 1931 was a defeat for Gorky, who wanted to ensure that all aspiring writers would be educated at a specialized institute of higher education. The power struggle was reflected in the pages of the *Literary Gazette* (Literaturnaia gazeta), which argued against the creation of a new institute.[6]

Eighteen months later, the landscape of literary politics had changed, enabling Gorky to win a victory of his own. Dissatisfied with the insubordination of the RAPP leadership, the party dissolved RAPP and all other literary groups in favor of a single Writers' Union. Stalin's desire to teach the RAPP leaders a lesson in party obedience coincided with his efforts to win over Gorky. On September 16, 1932, the Central Committee passed a resolution to create a Literary Institute named for Gorky.[7] The wording, however, invited dispute. It stated that applicants from the working class and peasantry would have priority in admissions, but it also said that the Institute would aim at those who had already demonstrated their creative ability (*pisateliam, tvorcheski sebia proiavivshim*). Most importantly, the resolution did not explicitly state that the Institute would be an institution of higher education (*VUZ*).

---

4 Dobrenko, *Making of the State Writer*, 369.
5 A. S. Kurilov, "Gor'kii i Vechernii rabochii literaturnyi universitet (VRLU)," *Literaturovedcheskii zhurnal* 29 (2011): 266.
6 L. Subotskii, ed., *Sovetskaia literatura na novom etape: Stenogramma pervogo plenuma orgkomiteta Soiuza sovetskikh pisatelei (29 oktiabria–3 noiabria 1932)* (Moscow: Sovetskaia literatura, 1933), 52–53, 190; Dobrenko, *Making of the State Writer*, 339. Kurilov ("Gor'kii i Vechernii rabochii literaturnyi universitet," 270) argues that the VRLU was not necessarily at odds with Gorky's vision: factory writers who completed the basic education provided by the VRLU could potentially continue their education at the Litinstitut.
7 Andrei Artizov and Oleg Naumov, comps., *Vlast' i khudozhestvennaia intelligentsiia: Dokumenty TsK RKP(b), VChK–OGPU–NKVD o kul'turnoi politike 1917–1953 gg.* (Moscow: Mezhdunarodnyi fond "Demokratiia," 2002), 182–183.

The Literary Institute

Exploiting the resolution's ambiguous wording, supporters of the factory circles went to work to implement their own vision. They had backing in the Communist Party secretariat and the Commissariat of Enlightenment.[8] When the Institute opened its doors on December 3, 1933, it was called the Workers' Evening Literary University, a name which suggested that it was a sister school to the one in Leningrad, and many or most of its students were from the factory circles. It even appears that this was done behind Gorky's back.[9]

The inaugural class seems to have been composed mostly or entirely from the factory circles.[10] Vladimir Stavsky, a former RAPP leader who now had a seat on the *orgkomitet* of the incipient Writers' Union, placed a newspaper announcement while Gorky was away from Moscow, just weeks before the first class was to be held. Out of three hundred applicants, 130 were admitted.[11] There was no entrance examination or interview; had there been one, none of this cohort could have gained admission.[12] The application consisted of a questionnaire plus at least one work, which could be a single newspaper feuilleton.[13]

The incoming class attended an orientation meeting with Stavsky and the literary critic Gavriil Sergeevich Fedoseev. One of the students, Zinovy Fazin, later recalled the reaction of the assembled applicants to Fedoseev's remarks:

---

8 Viacheslav Ogryzko, "Bez lishnikh slovesnykh igr. Kto rukovodil Litinstitutom v pervye desiatiletiia ego sushchestvovaniia," *Literaturnaia Rossiia* 2 (2017), https://litrossia.ru/item/9644-bude-zhiv-orekh-bude-vsjo-pomre-orekh-ne-bude-nichego-zhizn-russkoj-provintsii/.

9 Kurilov, "Gor'kii i Vechernii rabochii literaturnyi universitet (VRLU)," 273–274, offers evidence that the Moscow VRLU was completely separate from the Literary Institute. If so, this was never acknowledged by the Litinstitut administration. V. F. Pimenov, the Literary Institute's rector from 1964 to 1985, cites the December 1933 date as its first matriculation, and Margarita Aliger recalled, "My nazyvalis' VRLU—Vechernii Rabochii Literaturnyi Universitet imeni M. Gor'kogo." See Margarita Aliger, "Chernyi khleb s gorchitsei," in *Vospominaniia o Litinstitute, 1933–1983,* ed. V. F. Pimenov (Moscow: Sovetskii pisatel', 1983), 40.

10 Wikipedia, https://ru.wikipedia.org, s.v. "Literaturnyi institut imeni A. M. Gor'kogo," accessed August 19, 2022.

11 V. F. Pimenov, "Shkola Gor'kogo," in *Vospominaniia o Litinstitute, 1933–1983,* ed. V. F. Pimenov (Moscow: Sovetskii pisatel', 1983), 7; Ogryzko, "Bez lishnikh slovesnykh igr.," n.p.

12 Z. Fazin, "To, chego ne zabyt'," in *Vospominaniia o Litinstitute, 1933–1983,* ed. V. F. Pimenov (Moscow: Sovetskii pisatel', 1983), 52.

13 Aliger, "Chernyi khleb s gorchitsei," 40. When Aliger matriculated in 1934, the Institute offered a degree in two and a half years for on-site students or three and a half years for correspondence students (Pimenov, "Shkola Gor'kogo," 7). By the 1940s it had grown into a full-time, five-year higher education degree program; see "Literaturnyi institut," *Bol'shaia sovetskaia entsiklopediia,* Academic, http://dic.academic.ru/dic.nsf/bse/104020/Literaturnyi.

He spoke about the great significance and worldwide impact of classic and contemporary Russian literature. Citing Gorky, he said that the artistic image was a particular form of organizing thought, and that according to Tolstoy, the linking of thoughts and images is more or less the fundamental creative method in the mind of a writer. While saying this, Gavriil Sergeevich used words that were incomprehensible to many of us (there's no doubt about that!), like "association" (*assotsiatsiia*), "apperception" (*appertseptsiia*), and the like; and I saw the future students of the Workers' Literary University exchanging perplexed glances.[14]

Here was Fedoseev, a forty-year-old intellectual, making contact with young proletarians hoping to become writers. He was speaking to them across multiple divides of class, education, and generation. According to Fazin, Fedoseev made a positive impression on them with his "noble, professorial appearance."[15]

The students included lathe operators (turners), smiths, miners, mine surveyors (colliery surveyors), engineers, and sailors.[16] They also included many from the non-Russian nationalities,[17] as well as *besprizorniki* like Viktor Avdeev, who made his way to Moscow as a stowaway on freight trains and slept on benches along Tverskoi Boulevard.[18] That *besprizorniki* could avail themselves of a Litinstitut education was a point of pride. The rest of the world could not boast such egalitarianism; Gorky himself as a young man in tsarist Russia had been denied entry to the University of Kazan. Gorky now arranged publication of works by the *besprizorniki* in a collective volume titled *Yesterday and Today* (Vchera i segodnia).[19]

These students arrived with varying degrees of literary consciousness. Semen Babaevsky, who would go on to win a Stalin Prize for his 1949 novel *Knight of the Golden Star* (Kavaler zolotoi zvezdy), recalled taking a story of his that had been rejected by a journal to his teacher, the literary critic Leonid Ivanovich

---

14 Fazin, "To, chego ne zabyt'," 51.
15 Ibid., 52. See Ogryzko, "Bez lishnikh slovesnykh igr," on the unfulfilled expectation that Fedoseev would become the director of the Litinstitut.
16 Lev Oshanin, "Chetvertyi nabor," in *Vospominaniia o Litinstitute, 1933–1983*, ed. V. F. Pimenov (Moscow: Sovetskii pisatel', 1983), 71.
17 Aleksandr Vlasenko, "Ot komsomol'skoi iunosti—k zreloi pore," in *Vospominaniia o Litinstitute, 1933–1983*, ed. V. F. Pimenov (Moscow: Sovetskii pisatel', 1983), 77.
18 Viktor Avdeev, "Studencheskii bilet," in *Vospominaniia o Litinstitute, 1933–1983*, ed. V. F. Pimenov (Moscow: Sovetskii pisatel', 1983), 29.
19 Ibid., 29.

Timofeev. Timofeev's observation came as a revelation: in a story something has to *happen*.[20] A similar dynamic may have been what prompted Konstantin Paustovsky in 1938 to tell his seminar students, "without imagination there is no authentic prose and there is no poetry."[21]

Starting with the second class of students, who matriculated in Autumn 1934, the social composition of the student body was vastly different, with many students coming from the *sluzhashchie*, although the application remained the same. This class included Margarita Aliger and Evgeny Dolmatovsky, whose fathers were lawyers, and Konstantin Simonov, whose parents came from the *dvorianstvo*. Students from old intelligentsia white-collar families, like Aliger, Simonov, and Antonina Koptiaeva, mingled with students from the working class and from the new technical intelligentsia. Some of the Institute's graduates did not become writers, but filled posts elsewhere in literature, for example as editors in the press and in radio.[22]

Many students from the proletariat took their literary inspiration from the works of writers whose lives they could identify with, starting with Gorky and including others like Aleksei Ivanovich Svirsky. Nonetheless, the Litinstitut's project was about students from the ranks of workers receiving instruction and mentoring from members of the old intelligentsia. Babaevsky, recalling his acquaintance with Vladimir Lidin, reflected,

> to this day I cannot understand how it was that I, to some extent still a farm lad, a peasant's peasant, could have made a good impression on this elegant, urban intellectual (*intelligent*) ... Vladimir Germanovich showed me my literary errors as carefully and clearly as if he were going through his own stories, and he talked to me as an equal.[23]

The required core curriculum included literature of antiquity, political economy, history of philosophy, history of the Middle Ages, stylistics, folklore, old Russian literature, nineteenth-century Russian literature, Western literature, and history of the Russian novel. Students also studied historical materialism, dialectical

---

20 Semen Babaevskii, "Prokhozhu po Tverskomu...," in *Vospominaniia o Litinstitute, 1933–1983*, ed. V. F. Pimenov (Moscow: Sovetskii pisatel', 1983), 61.
21 Anatolii Mednikov, "Na urokakh Paustovskogo," in *Vospominaniia o Litinstitute, 1933–1983*, ed. V. F. Pimenov (Moscow: Sovetskii pisatel', 1983), 86.
22 Pimenov, "Shkola Gor'kogo," 8.
23 Babaevskii, "Prokhozhu po Tverskomu...," 59.

materialism, and the history of the Communist Party.[24] Many students from the ranks of the factory circles expected the Institute to be a kind of beefed-up version of those.[25] These students protested against the curriculum. They had their supporters in the literary power apparatus, but the faculty stood up for Gorky's vision.[26]

During the 1934–1935 academic year, the Institute sought to assess the literacy level of its students by having them take dictation as they listened to two literary excerpts read out loud, one from Gogol and one from Gorky. The results were so embarrassing that they were concealed.[27]

The core courses were taught by highly qualified specialists, but it was in the specialty seminars, under the tutelage of an established writer, that the students learned their craft and formed personal relationships with the instructor. Students could specialize in prose, poetry, drama, or literary criticism and, from 1939, children's literature.[28] Seminar instructors eventually included Konstantin Fedin, Veniamin Kaverin, Konstantin Paustovsky, Ilya Selvinsky, and Mikhail Zoshchenko; the chair of the examination committee was Vsevolod Ivanov.[29] This company of non-party writers must also be explained by Gorky's influence. Indeed, a non-party writer might be teaching at the Institute while getting panned in the press, as happened with Paustovsky.[30] From these non-party, old intelligentsia writers, students learned literary values that sometimes were in stark contrast to Soviet literary policy. Paustovsky taught that it was impossible

---

24 Pimenov, "Shkola Gor'kogo," 7; Oshanin, "Chetvertyi nabor," 71; Abdurakhman Absaliamov, "My—iz Litinstituta," in *Vospominaniia o Litinstitute, 1933–1983*, ed. V. F. Pimenov (Moscow: Sovetskii pisatel', 1983), 82.
25 Fazin, "To, chego ne zabyt'," 52.
26 Ibid., 52–53.
27 Ibid., 52.
28 A specialization in translation was added in 1955, but it seems to have existed unofficially from the thirties. Abdurakhman Absaliamov, who attended the Litinstitut from 1936 to 1940, wanted to specialize in creative writing, but was channeled into translation. He took a course in translating from Tatar to Russian, and a separate course with a different instructor in translating from Russian to Tatar. Clearly, he was needed for the mammoth undertaking of translating the national literatures into Russian (and vice versa), an important part of creating a Soviet literature. See "V Polpredstve Tatarstana v RF proshla vstrecha s rektorom Literaturnogo instituta," Tartar-inform.ru, December 3, 2014, https://www.tatar-inform.ru/news/v-polpredstve-tatarstana-v-rf-proshla-vstrecha-s-rektorom-literaturnogo-insti-tuta-433129, https://www.tatar-inform.ru/news/science/03-12-2014/v-polpredstve-tatar-stana-v-rf-proshla-vstrecha-s-rektorom-literaturnogo-instituta-5276124; and Absaliamov, "My—iz Litinstituta," 82–83.
29 Babaevskii, "Prokhozhu po Tverskomu . . . ," 58.
30 Mednikov, "Na urokakh Paustovskogo," 88. Reacting to the prevailing practice in book reviews, Paustovsky told his students, "In a literary work one must look first of all for what is in it, and not what isn't in it."

to write a story based on second-hand knowledge (an implicit criticism of the party practice of sending writers to visit collective farms and factories so that they could write a novel about them).[31] Selvinsky tried to inculcate in his students the value of "disinterested poetry" (*beskorystnaia poeziia*).[32] When one student, following authoritative statements, declared that "thought [should] dissolve form," Selvinsky refuted the idea, pointing to *Eugene Onegin* (Evgenii Onegin), *The Bronze Horseman* (Mednyi vsadnik), *The Novice* (Mtsyri), and Goethe's *Faust*. Fedin advised his students to read the stories of Ivan Bunin, the émigré Nobel laureate, to learn how to construct a phrase.[33]

Instructors seem to have encouraged debate among different viewpoints while upbraiding students for unduly harsh, disrespectful, or unfounded criticisms. When Sarra Matveevna Shtut made mincemeat out of a fellow student's essay, the instructor, S. M. Breitburg, made her feel she had behaved badly. When Kaverin expressed contempt for a fellow-student's poem, Zoshchenko took him aside afterwards with an admonition: "Don't walk into literature by elbowing people out of your way."[34] Zoshchenko and Breitburg were teaching their students not to follow the practice of the Soviet press. In some cases, the extent of mentoring was extraordinary. Narovchatov, a poet who in the 1970s became chief editor of *New World* (Novyi mir), recalled that his cohort of budding poets met with Selvinsky at least once a week for three years.[35]

These intelligentsia writers provided a wider aesthetic berth for the rising generation, even managing to extend it beyond the walls of the Institute. Selvinsky, who headed the prose department at Gosizdat (the state publishing house) made safe space available for young writers to hold literary meetings, and so did editors at *October* (Oktiabr'), *Flame* (Ogonek), *Youth Communist Pravda* (Komsomol'skaia pravda), and other press offices. One participant recalled ten literary circles in Moscow in these years, describing them as noisy and contentious.[36] Some students attended several of these circles. Unlike the literary groupings of the 1920s and early thirties, they were not distinguished from one another by separate literary credos; but it is nonetheless surprising

---

31 Ibid., 89.
32 Sergei Narovchatov, "Gody ucheniia," in *Vospominaniia o Litinstitute, 1933–1983*, ed. V. F. Pimenov (Moscow: Sovetskii pisatel', 1983), 106.
33 Iurii Trifonov, "Seminar Fedina," in *Literaturnyi institut imeni A. M. Gor'kogo Soiuza pisatelei SSSR, 1933–1973*, ed. V. F. Pimenov et al. (Moscow: s.n., 1974), 60.
34 S. Shtut, "O proshlom dlia nastoiashchego," in *Vospominaniia o Litinstitute, 1933–1983*, ed. V. F. Pimenov (Moscow: Sovetskii pisatel', 1983), 69.
35 Narovchatov, "Gody ucheniia," 102.
36 Ibid., 101–102.

to discover the existence of literary clubs that at any moment could have been flagged as illegal private groups and worse.[37]

Unionization

While a next-generation literary intelligentsia was in the making, the existing intelligentsia, inherited from pre-Soviet times, had to be managed. The Union of Soviet Writers was created in 1932 for this purpose. A party-funded, universal writers' organization, it emerged from the confluence of three factors: Stalin's dissatisfaction with Averbakh's power grabs, his pursuit of Gorky, and his decision to replace the mantra of class struggle with a policy of national Bolshevism. Under national Bolshevism, writers, regardless of their class background, had only to declare themselves loyal Soviet citizens to secure a place at the literary table. This was an anodyne after the abuses of RAPP, and yet it also raised fraught questions about the tradition of intellectual independence and moral leadership that had been handed down from pre-revolutionary Russian literature. The establishment of the Writers' Union rendered all other literary associations illegal. Literature was to join education and the press as part of an infrastructure meant to deliver communist values. The turn to national Bolshevism brought writers of suspect class origin into the fold while turning on its head the idea of an intelligentsia as a moral counterweight to political authority. That mission, embraced by Pushkin, Dostoevsky and Tolstoy, was no longer needed—so went the argument.

Gorky and others tried to make their peace with this notion, especially in the two years following the 1932 annunciation of the Writers' Union. There was considerable appeal in the idea of writing books that would seed the young Soviet culture with the fictional characters who would become its cultural signposts.[38] And where RAPP's abusive literary pygmies had been calling the shots, suddenly there was Gorky, whose credibility with writers legitimized the new union and made them feel their interests would be safeguarded. In this way, Stalin got a

---

37 Although literary groups other than the Writers' Union were illegal after April 1932, private social gatherings were common among writers living in the same apartment building or even at salons such as that of Tatiana Shchepkina-Kupernik. Such gatherings were not groups of like-minded writers. But this could potentially have opened up a gray area in which the distinction between a private gathering and a literary group could have been unclear.
38 The idea that an educated elite would shape and improve the masses was well established in Russia before the revolution; see Jeffrey Brooks, *When Russia Learned to Read: Literacy and Popular Literature, 1861–1917* (Princeton, NJ: Princeton UP, 1985), 295–96.

critical mass of writers to give the Writers' Union a chance. Meanwhile, its social engineering was undertaken through class-conscious admissions, a network of benefits calculated to make literature an attractive career choice, and the purges.

The initial admissions process in 1934 accepted about 2,200 members. We do not have nationwide figures for the social origins of this first cohort, but in the Moscow branch only one-fifth of members were of worker or peasant origin, while more than half were from the *sluzhashchie*.[39] These statistics reflected the demographic reality in 1934, when there had not yet been enough time to educate and recruit a generation of young communists. Only twenty to twenty-five per cent of the initial cohort were Communist Party members.

At the Seventeenth Party Congress in 1934, Stalin declared that most intellectuals were now "working within Marxist parameters."[40] Writers' Union statistics, however, suggest that this putative reality had not yet been achieved in the literary sector. To bring it about, Stalin used both the extraordinary violence of the Great Purge and institutionalized procedures to guide the functioning of the literary industry. An intricately tentacled pre-publication review that sent manuscripts to an editorial board and then on to *Agitprop* and the censorship office tamped down writers' literary aspirations, gradually creating a more docile, self-censoring literary intelligentsia. (Plays, besides going through these channels, also had to be approved by the Arts Committee.) The Writers' Union, the Central Committee secretaries, and *obkom* and *gorkom* secretaries could also get involved. Each reprinting of a novel entailed a completely new censorship review.[41]

It did not take long for writers to feel aggrieved at such treatment. Hard controls like censorship, however, were not the only complaint. By 1936, the transactional nature and corrupting effect of the Writers' Union had become obvious. This situation prompted the prolific and popular novelist Marietta Shaginian to announce her departure from the Writers' Union. Shaginian, a non-party writer considered "close" to communism, had applied for party membership a couple of years earlier (her application languished unanswered along with many others which had been submitted during a period when review of applications was held up pending purges of the membership rolls). She was on the list of writers slated to receive one of the first Peredelkino dachas, and

---

39 *Pervyi vsesoiuznyi s"ezd sovetskikh pisatelei, 1934: Stenograficheskii otchet* (Moscow: Khudozhestvennaia literatura, 1934), 663, 697.
40 Katerina Clark, *Moscow, the Fourth Rome: Stalinism, Cosmopolitanism, and the Evolution of Soviet Culture, 1931–1941* (Cambridge, MA: Harvard UP, 2011), 129.
41 Herman Ermolaev, *Censorship in Soviet Literature, 1917–1991* (Lanham, MD: Rowman and Littlefield, 1997), 58–59.

so she had a lot to lose by leaving the Writers' Union. What tipped the balance was that she felt the dachas were intended to buy writers off. Under pressure from Aleksandr Shcherbakov, the Writers' Union's first secretary who outranked Gorky, she eventually retracted her declaration of withdrawal from the Union (Shcherbakov threatened to have her conduct declared anti-Soviet).[42]

Although Gorky prevailed in barring the factory writers' privileged entry into the Writers' Union, recruitment of working-class writers remained a goal, and the Writers' Union undertook its own work with beginning writers, who sometimes had only a primary school education, some of them union members and others who aspired to join.[43] In contrast to the literary consultants used by RAPP, the Writers' Union referred novices' manuscripts to qualified writers who offered critiques and guidance. In one case, a reviewer expressed amazement at a beginning writer who had been in literature for ten years and had publications to his name (probably in small local newspapers), but was still a "beginning writer."[44] The reviewer noted that it would be cruel, after ten years, to tell him to find another profession. In the best cases, a reviewer would recommend publication of a manuscript conditional upon having the author work with an established writer. In other cases, the reviewer found the work either too ungrammatical, lacking in "literary taste," or without any human interest. When the Writers' Union decided that a worker's manuscript merited publication, there would follow a negotiation with *Sovetskii pisatel'*, the publishing house that was attached to the Writers' Union. At one point, *Sovetskii pisatel'* agreed to publish a manuscript, but when the Writers' Union recommended a second manuscript by the same author the publisher balked.[45]

In 1936 Aleksei Surkov lamented that the working class had yet to produce a single writer of note;[46] and more than a decade later, the head of the Writers' Union admissions committee, Leonid Sobolev, noted that the committee had had to stand firm in rejecting the application of a recruit "fresh from the lathe,"

---

42 A. S. Shcherbakov, letter to M. Gorky, written February 28, 1936, Arkhiv Gor'kogo, Institut mirovoi literatury imeni A. M. Gor'kogo, f. 1330/6, no. KG-17 90–4–18, l. 1.
43 The Writers' Union *orgkom* in its first six months oversaw an increase in factory literary circles and literary consultations (see Subotskii, *Sovetskaia literatura na novom etape*, 52–53), or possibly it was merely claiming credit for creating circles that in fact already existed; see ibid., 196.
44 "Komissiia po literaturnoi konsul'tatsii i ekspertize pri Prezidiume SSP," Rossiiskii gosudarstvennyi arkhiv literatury i iskusstva (hereafter RGALI), f. 631, op. 10, ed. khr. 2 (1940), l. 58.
45 Ibid., l. 39.
46 A. A. Surkov, letter to A. S. Shcherbakov [written no earlier than 1936], RGALI, f. 1712, op. 1, ed. khr. 64, l. 2 verso.

who had applied seven times.[47] A sign of how much the party struggled to create an intelligentsia to its liking was the increasingly common use of the phrase "real writers." The phrase was itself an acknowledgment of the opposite—of just how many Writers' Union members did not rise to the level of being writers. Even an Agitprop official, in a seeming slip of the pen, sent off a memo in which he referred to "real writers."[48]

The Great Purge

Some twenty-five percent of Writers' Union members were arrested from 1936 through 1938, and these were disproportionately critical and independently minded. The rolls were replenished by new admissions, younger and more fully acculturated to Soviet mores, who therefore could be expected to be more compliant. Writers' privileged status and access to housing, goods, and services reshaped the literary profession by attracting people who chose literature as a lucrative career rather than as a calling.

It is striking that the Writers' Union managed to grow handily from the original number of 2,200 members, in spite of severe depletion resulting from the purges and the war. In 1936, Gorky used a ballpark membership figure of 3,000. This was likely an overstatement, but certainly new members were continually being admitted. About six hundred writers were arrested, however, in the years 1936 through 1938. Using Gorky's figure, this would have amounted to one-fifth of the membership. However, in January 1938, the recent head of the Writers' Union party committee I. Marchenko estimated the number of Writers' Union arrests counting from summer 1936 at one-third of the membership. A conservative estimate of Great Purge arrests would seem to be twenty-five to thirty percent of the membership.[49] Even without accounting for natural deaths,

---

47 Protokoly nos. 37–38 i stenogrammy, September 19–December 6, 1947, RGALI, f. 631, op. 15, ed. khr. 816, l. 49.
48 D. L. Babichenko, comp., *"Shchast'e literatury": Gosudarstvo i pisateli, 1925–1938; Dokumenty* (Moscow: Rosspen, 1997), 269.
49 "Almost one-third of the membership" was the estimate given by R. A. Medvedev, *K sudu istorii: genezis i posledstviia stalinizma* (New York: Knopf, 1974), 445, cited in John Garrard and Carol Garrard, *Inside the Soviet Writers' Union* (New York: Free Press, 1990), 260. Among those arrested were some fifty students of the Literary Institute; see Goriaeva, *Mezhdu molotom i nakoval'nei*, 733–734. Marchenko dated the student arrests to the period 1935–1937. Audrey L. Altstadt, *The Politics of Culture in Soviet Azerbaijan* (London: Routledge, 2016), 200–202, provides figures for Azerbaijan's branch in line with the upper end of this estimate. She counts the number of expelled members at thirty-seven percent, the great majority of them also arrested. Seven new members were admitted in 1937, as against twenty-four expulsions.

this would have shrunk the Writers' Union to between 1,850 and 2,250 members, ground which had to be made up through acceptance of new members.[50] If we use the low estimate, an average of sixty-one new acceptances per year from 1935 to the outbreak of war in June 1941 would have brought the membership back to the original number of 2,200. In fact, however, wartime admissions statistics allow us to deduce that membership at the outbreak of war had surged to 2,850, a remarkable number even if we use the high estimate (2,250) as a baseline.[51] By 1946, although nearly four hundred writers had perished in the war, the 1934 initial membership of 2,200 had risen by twenty-five percent, to 2,760.[52] Population growth of sixteen percent between 1926 and 1939 helped enable the increase in the Writers' Union ranks.[53]

Vitaly Shentalinsky estimates that, overall, 1,500 members perished in the GULag. (This does not count the five hundred who survived.) When the Writers' Union finally held its second congress in December 1954, however, it had grown to 3,700 members (of whom ten percent had been in the 1934 cohort).[54] What all these numbers mean is that in those two decades the Writers' Union added not 1,500 members (which is the difference between the 1954 and the 1934 figures) but 3,000 members. To this number we must add perhaps as many as another five hundred to replace the five hundred writers who survived the GULag,[55] many of whom would not have been reinstated in the union by December 1954.

The twenty-five to thirty percent of the membership arrested from 1936 through 1938 was disproportionately independent-minded and critical of the regime, including many from the old intelligentsia. Stalin alluded to the younger, more Sovietized members who replaced them and their counterparts

---

50 The 2,250 figure presupposes an arrest rate of twenty-five percent among a membership of 3,000. The 1,850 figure presupposes a thirty-three percent arrest rate among a membership of 2,800 (to adjust for possible overstatement in Gorky's round number figure).
51 From 1942 through 1946, the union added 317 new members (RGALI, f. 631, op. 15, ed. khr. 816, l. 47). With the statistics available to us from D. L. Babichenko, *Pisateli i tsenzory* (Moscow: Rossiia molodaia, 1994), 111 and 117, that four hundred writers were killed in the war and that in 1946 the Writers' Union reached 2,760 members, we arrive at 2,843 as the number of members at the outbreak of war in 1941.
52 Babichenko, *Pisateli i tsenzory*, 111, 117. More than a third of members belonged to the Moscow branch, which had eight hundred members in 1941; see RGALI, f. 631, op. 15, ed. khr. 576, l. 4. This was a reflection both of demographics and of the desirability of Moscow; many writers who had the opportunity to relocate to the capital did so.
53 Iu. A. Poliakov et al., eds., *Vsesoiuznaia perepis' naseleniia 1939 goda: Osnovnye itogi* (Moscow: Nauka, 1992), 21. The statistic for the RSFSR was nearly identical at 17%.
54 Garrard and Garrard, *Inside the Soviet Writers' Union*, 241.
55 Vitaly Shentalinsky, *Arrested Voices: Resurrecting the Disappeared Writers of the Soviet Regime* (New York: Free Press), 1996, 6.

across all Soviet institutions, at the Eighteenth Party Congress in March 1939, when he stated that the intelligentsia had received fresh blood as a result of "hundreds of thousands of young people who had joined its ranks," altering its social composition and intellectual character and remaking it into a "new, people's, socialist intelligentsia."[56] Demographics and the purges contributed to this shift. In 1939, 63% of the population of the USSR was under thirty, 18.1% was between twenty and twenty-nine years old, 15% was between thirty and thirty-nine, 9% between forty and forty-nine, 6.4% between fifty-and fifty-nine, and 6.6% were sixty or older.[57]

Certainly, many applicants were fast-tracked in order to regain lost ground. These fast-tracked beneficiaries of the purges became known by a neologism, *vydvizhentsy*. Leonid Batkin pointed out that this word reflected something more than a mere fast-tracking. The "[old] intelligentsia" and the thin layer of "party intelligentsia" were wiped out and replaced by the *vydvizhentsy*, who constituted an intelligentsia in name only.[58]

Packing the Writers' Union with young writers presumed to be loyalist was perhaps less straightforward a process than we might think. The *vydvizhentsy* did include young liberals. Katerina Clark cautions that many of the young writers who were fast-tracked to Writers' Union membership were advocates of sincerity in literature.[59] Konstantin Simonov, who after the war became a key figure in the Writers' Union leadership, published his first poems and was admitted to the Writers' Union in 1936, when he was just twenty-one years old and still a student at the Literary Institute. Three years later he published an article in *Literaturnaia gazeta* arguing for "the right to the lyric," which Clark sees as an argument against the official view of socialist realism.[60]

The Literary Institute came to be seen as a breeding ground for unsound thought. Party officials grew concerned in 1941–1942, when six of its 115 students were arrested,[61] and positively alarmed in 1943, when it came to light

---

56 I. Stalin, *Voprosy leninizma* (Moscow: Partiinoe izdatel'stvo, 1932), 646–649, cited in *Osmyslit' kul't Stalina*, comp. Juan Cobo (Moscow: Progress, 1989), 33.
57 Poliakov, *Vsesoiuznaia perepis' naseleniia 1939 goda*, 28.
58 L. Batkin, "Son razuma," in *Osmyslit' kul't Stalina*, comp. Juan Cobo (Moscow: Progress, 1989), 46.
59 Clark, *Moscow the Fourth Rome*, 338. This was tied to the "campaign for the lyric."
60 Konstantin Simonov, "Zametki o poezii," *Literaturnaia gazeta*, December 31, 1939, cited in Clark, *Moscow the Fourth Rome*, 331.
61 Gennadii Kostyrchenko, *Tainaia politika Stalina: Vlast' i antisemitizm; Novaia versiia* (Moscow: Mezhdunarodnye otnosheniia, 2015), vol. 1, 476; idem, *Stalin protiv kosmopolitov* (Moscow: Rosspen, 2009), 106–7. I extrapolate the number 115 from figures given for 1944 in Kostyrchenko, *Tainaia politika Stalina*, vol. 1, 479.

that one of its students, Arkady Belinkov, had written a novel that he termed a "neobaroque" alternative to socialist realism. He submitted the manuscript as his diploma work; it then caught fire and was read by some 250 people. Fanning the flames for party officials was the involvement of prominent non-party writers. Belinkov's supervisor was Viktor Shklovsky; the head of the creative writing department was Selvinsky; and the novel's title, *A Rough Draft of Feelings* (Chernovik chuvstv), had been suggested by Mikhail Zoshchenko.[62]

Belinkov was arrested in January 1944. Another student, Genrikh Elshtein, who had written a novel called *Eleven Doubts* (Odinnadtsat' somnenii)—another red flag of a title—was arrested in April. The Central Committee secretariat responded by passing a resolution on July 26, 1944 to shutter the Institute, but Simonov convinced Stalin to annul the resolution.[63]

Leading roles in the Writers' Union were assigned as a means of coopting members of the literary intelligentsia. A Politburo resolution (of January 25, 1939), which named Fadeev as Writers' Union head, also named a new Writers' Union presidium of fifteen members.[64] In July 1939, Andreev informed Stalin about thirty-one writers on whom the NKVD had compromising material. Of the fifteen members named to the presidium, eight were on the "compromised" list.[65] Three of them (Fedin, Valentin Kataev, and Pyotr Pavlenko) were Fadeev's closest advisers. Two others (Nikolai Tikhonov and Surkov) would in the future be chosen to lead the Writers' Union. Fear of *kompromat* made for an obedient and therefore valuable official.

How, then, should we assess the party's attempt to build and coopt a pliant literary intelligentsia? By the measure of pure numbers, Stalin's implementation strategy for building a cadre of writers was a success. Many young writers had their careers boosted by the vacancies created by the purges, and the Writers' Union's closed distribution system of privileges assured a ready supply of new members, many of whom received both literary and ideological training at the Literary Institute. By 1967, the percentage of Writers' Union members who were Communist Party members had risen to fifty-five percent. Even those who were not party members were probably more inclined to see literature as a pragmatic career choice rather than a deeply felt calling. Nearly one third of Writers' Union members had the privilege of living in Moscow, and most of the rest lived

---

62 Kostyrchenko, *Tainaia politika Stalina*, vol. 1, 476–477.
63 Ibid., 479.
64 *Vlast' i khudozhestvennaia intelligentsiia*, 424.
65 These figures may be arrived at by comparing *Vlast' i khudozhestvennaia intelligentsiia*, 424, and Babichenko, *Pisateli i tsenzory*, 15.

in other major cities.[66] The membership would more than double through the next decades, reaching 9,500 in 1986.[67] The unspoken trade-off between upward mobility and individual authority, exposed by the indignant Shaginian in 1936, was on a firm footing.

This success in creating a state-friendly intelligentsia, even aided by the purges, was not unqualified. As these young writers embarked on their careers, censorship and other forms of literary oversight eroded their belief in their mission. And they were decisively shaped by the concession that Stalin made to Gorky when he needed him most. Gorky, through his dogged insistence on a higher literary education as the gateway to Writers' Union membership, and through his persistence in battling the advocates of a lesser educational standard, ensured that the next generation of writers would be exposed to diverse influences, especially from old intelligentsia writers, whose books they read and who were their teachers and mentors.

Bibliography

Aliger, Margarita. "Chernyi khleb s gorchitsei." In *Vospominaniia o Litinstitute, 1933–1983*, edited by V. F. Pimenov, 39–50. Moscow: Sovetskii pisatel', 1983.

Altstadt, Audrey. *The Politics of Culture in Soviet Azerbaijan, 1920–40*. London: Routledge, 2016.

Artisov, Andrei, and Oleg Naumov, eds. *Vlast' i khudozhestvennaia intelligentsiia: Dokumenty TsK RKP(b), VChK–OGPU–NKVD o kul'turnoi politike; 1917–1953 gg*. Moscow: Mezhdunarodnyi fond "Demokratiia," 2002.

Avdeev, Viktor. "Studencheskii bilet." In *Vospominaniia o Litinstitute, 1933–1983*, edited by V. F. Pimenov, 29–38. Moscow: Sovetskii pisatel', 1983.

Babaevskii, Semen. "Prokhozhu po Tverskomu…" In *Vospominaniia o Litinstitute, 1933–1983*, edited by V. F. Pimenov, 57–64. Moscow: Sovetskii pisatel', 1983.

Babichenko, D. L. *Pisateli i tsenzory*. Moscow: Rossiia molodaia, 1994.

Babichenko, D. L., ed. *"Shchast'e literatury": Gosudarstvo i pisateli, 1925–1938; Dokumenty*. Moscow: Rosspen, 1997.

Batkin, L. "Son razuma." In *Osmyslit' kul't Stalina*, edited by Juan Cobo, 9–53. Moscow: Progress, 1989.

---

66 Mikhail Sholokhov, "Rech' na XX s"ezde KPSS," ENI Sholokhova, http://feb-web.ru/feb/sholokh/texts/sh0/sh8/sh8-317-.htm.
67 Garrard and Garrard, *Inside the Soviet Writers' Union*, 241.

Brooks, Jeffrey. *When Russia Learned to Read: Literacy and Popular Literature, 1861–1917*. Princeton, NJ: Princeton UP, 1985.

Clark, Katerina. *Moscow, the Fourth Rome: Stalinism, Cosmopolitanism, and the Evolution of Soviet Culture, 1931–1941*. Cambridge, MA: Harvard UP, 2011.

Dobrenko, Evgeny. *The Making of the State Writer: Social and Aesthetic Origins of Soviet Literary Culture*, trans. Jesse M. Savage. Stanford, CA: Stanford UP, 2001.

Ermolaev, Herman. *Censorship in Soviet Literature, 1917–1991*. Lanham, MD: Rowman and Littlefield, 1997.

Fazin, Z. "To, chego ne zabyt'." In *Vospominaniia o Litinstitute, 1933–1983*, edited by V. F. Pimenov, 51–56. Moscow: Sovetskii pisatel', 1983.

Garrard, John, and Carol Garrard. *Inside the Soviet Writers' Union*. New York: Free Press, 1990.

Goriaeva, T. M., ed. *Mezhdu molotom i nakoval'nei: Soiuz sovetskikh pisatelei SSSR; Dokumenty i kommentarii*. Vol. 1: *1925–June 1941*. Moscow: Rosspen, 2011.

Kostyrchenko, Gennadii. *Stalin protiv kosmopolitov*. Moscow: Rosspen, 2009.

———. *Tainaia politika Stalina: Vlast' i antisemitizm; Novaia versiia*. Moscow: Mezhdunarodnye otnosheniia, 2015.

Kurilov, A. S. "Gor'kii i Vechernii rabochii literaturnyi universitet (VRLU)." *Literaturovedcheskii zhurnal* 29 (2011): 259–281.

"Literaturnyi institut." *Bol'shaia sovetskaia entsiklopediia*. Academic. Accessed April 29, 2024. http://dic.academic.ru/dic.nsf/bse/104020/Literaturnyi.

Makarov, V. G., and V. S. Khristoforov. "Passazhiry 'filosofskogo parokhoda' (sud'by intelligentsii, repressirovannoi letom–osen'iu 1922 g.)." Institut istorii estestvoznaniia i tekhniki imeni S. I. Vavilova RAN. Accessed May 12, 2024. https://ihst.ru/projects/sohist/papers/mak03vf.htm.

Mednikov, Anatolii. "Na urokakh Paustovskogo." In *Vospominaniia o Litinstitute 1933–1983*, edited by V. F. Pimenov, 85–91. Moscow: Sovetskii pisatel', 1983.

Medvedev, R. A. *K sudu istorii: genezis i posledstviia stalinizma*. New York: Knopf, 1974.

Narovchatov, Sergei. "Gody ucheniia." In *Vospominaniia o Litinstitute, 1933–1983*, edited by V. F. Pimenov, 96–110. Moscow: Sovetskii pisatel', 1983.

Ogryzko, Viacheslav. "Bez lishnikh slovesnykh igr. Kto rukovodil Litinstitutom v pervye desiatiletiia ego sushchestvovaniia." *Literaturnaia Rossiia* 2 (2017): n.p. Accessed April 29, 2024. https://litrossia.ru/item/9644-bude-zhiv-orekh-bude-vsjo-pomre-orekh-ne-bude-nichego-zhizn-russkoj-provintsii/.

Oshanin, Lev. "Chetvertyi nabor." In *Vospominaniia o Litinstitute 1933–1983*, edited by V. F. Pimenov, 71–72. Moscow: Sovetskii pisatel', 1983.

Pervyi vsesoiuznyi s"ezd sovetskikh pisatelei, 1934: Stenograficheskii otchet. Moscow: Khudozhestvennaia literatura, 1934.

Pimenov, V. F. "Shkola Gor'kogo." In *Vospominaniia o Litinstitute, 1933–1983*, edited by V. F. Pimenov, 5–14. Moscow: Sovetskii pisatel', 1983.

Poliakov, Iu. A., ed. *Vsesoiuznaia perepis' naseleniia 1939 goda: Osnovnye itogi.* Moscow: Nauka, 1992.

Shcherbakov, A. S., letter to M. Gor'kii. February 28, 1936. Arkhiv Gor'kogo, Institut Mirovoi Literatury imeni A. M. Gor'kogo, f. 1330/6, no. KG-17 90–4–18.

Shentalinsky, Vitaly. *Arrested Voices: Resurrecting the Disappeared Writers of the Soviet Regime.* New York: Free Press, 1996.

Sheshukov, S. I. *Neistovye revniteli: Iz istorii literaturnoi bor'by dvadtsatykh godov.* Moscow: Moskovskii rabochii, 1970.

Sholokhov, Mikhail. "Rech' na XX s"ezde KPSS." ENI Sholokhova. Accessed April 29, 2024. http://feb-web.ru/feb/sholokh/texts/sh0/sh8/sh8-317-.htm.

Shtut, S. "O proshlom dlia nastoiashchego." In *Vospominaniia o Litinstitute, 1933–1983*, edited by V. F. Pimenov, 65–70. Moscow: Sovetskii pisatel', 1983.

Simonov, Konstantin. "Zametki o poezii." *Literaturnaia gazeta*, December 31, 1939.

Stalin, Iosif. *Voprosy leninizma* (Moscow, 1932). In *Osmyslit' kul't Stalina*, edited by Juan Cobo. Moscow: Progress, 1989.

Subotskii, L., ed. *Sovetskaia literatura na novom etape: Stenogramma pervogo plenuma orgkomiteta Soiuza sovetskikh pisatelei (29 oktiabria–3 noiabria 1932).* Moscow: Sovetskaia literatura, 1933.

Trifonov, Iurii. "Seminar Fedina." In *Literaturnyi Institut imeni A. M. Gor'kogo Soiuza Pisatelei SSSR, 1933–1973*, edited by V. F. Pimenov and A. N. Vlasenko, 59–61. Moscow: s.n., 1974.

"V Polpredstve Tatarstana v RF proshla vstrecha s rektorom Literaturnogo instituta." Tartar-inform.ru. December 3, 2014. https://www.tatar-inform.ru/news/v-polpredstve-tatarstana-v-rf-proshla-vstrecha-s-rektorom-literaturnogo-instituta-433129

Vlasenko, Aleksandr. "Ot komsomol'skoi iunosti—k zreloi pore." In *Vospominaniia o Litinstitute 1933–1983*, edited by V. F. Pimenov, 77–80. Moscow: Sovetskii pisatel', 1983.

The Soviet Intelligentsia and Thaw-Era Science Fiction

Sibelan Forrester

The intelligentsia in Russia, as well as its broader Soviet incarnation, has been known both for political ambitions and for valuing, creating and consuming cultural products. As other chapters in this collection underline, the intelligentsia has been active at multiple historical moments, usually following state support and expansion of education. The Thaw years (roughly 1957–1966) saw marked growth in the number of educated citizens who by definition formed the Soviet intelligentsia,[1] including the technical intelligentsia who had been trained to support Soviet industrialization and, of course, the famous early successes of the Soviet space program. Education under and after Stalin also positioned a new generation as authors and readers of science fiction; this restored the genre, encouraged its writing and publication, and drew its writers into relationship with the Soviet literary bureaucracy. Indeed: if authors were to be understood as "engineers of human souls," than who could depict the future better than actual engineers?

---

1 "Stalin and the Central Committee in 1935 put forward the view that the new technical intelligentsia would be a model for the development of a Communist (classless) society in the USSR, in which the working class would eventually be raised to the level of the technical intelligentsia." See Kendall Bailes, *Technology and Society under Lenin and Stalin: Origins of the Soviet Technical Intelligentsia, 1917–1941* (Princeton, NJ: Princeton UP, 1978), 410.

Science fiction (SF) was present in Russia and then the USSR well before the Khrushchev years. Some Russophone proto-SF appeared in the nineteenth century; most important of these for the Soviet period was Nikolai Chernyshevsky's 1863 novel *What Is to Be Done?* (Chto delat'?).[2] The novel is subtitled "From Stories about New People" (Iz rasskazov o novykh liudiakh), while the chapter "Vera Pavlovna's Fourth Dream" foretells the wonderful arrangement of life in the (utopian socialist) future, matching the progressive tendency of later non-dystopian SF. Jules Verne remained very popular with Soviet readers, and H. G. Wells even more so: his Fabian politics fit well with Soviet doctrine, and he had even met Vladimir Lenin. Anindita Banerjee has shown the importance of SF and popular science discourse in the late Imperial period;[3] Bolshevik Aleksandr Bogdanov chose the genre of SF to reach out to workers and persuade them of socialism's promise in his 1908 novel *Red Star* (Krasnaia zvezda).[4]

SF was a distinct element in the burgeoning Soviet literary scene of the 1920s (including, among other things, 1918 and 1922 reprints of Bogdanov's *Red Star*). Many early Soviet SF writers (Bogdanov, Mikhail Bulgakov, Andrei Platonov, Aleksei N. Tolstoy, Evgeny Zamyatin) were educated as scientists or technical specialists (doctor, doctor, engineer, [sometime] engineer, and naval engineer, respectively), foreshadowing the Thaw-era SF readers and writers who emerged from the technical intelligentsia. The genre would logically appeal to readers as well as authors who had scientific backgrounds, offering writers a strong connection with imagined or actual readers, especially when so many Bolshevik plans for the new USSR relied on science and technology (electrification, prospecting for resources, industrialization, etc.). As a lively part of the early Soviet literary polysystem, SF functioned as a genre that a writer might choose for a particular purpose—much as it did in the *oeuvre* of Czech author Karel Čapek, popular in the USSR in translation—more than one that fully characterized a writer.

Obligatory socialist realism, officially introduced at the first Congress of the Soviet Writers' Union (1934), excluded SF from the properly literary sphere. The models chosen for socialist realism differed markedly from previous SF

---

2 In English, see: Nikolai Chernyshevsky, *What Is to Be Done?*, trans. Michael Katz (Ithaca, NY: Cornell UP, 1989).
3 The title of Anindita Banerjee's *We Modern People* (Middletown, CT: Wesleyan UP, 2012) points up the impact of popular science as well as nascent SF on public opinion in the late Imperial period.
4 In English see: Alexander Bogdanov, *Red Star: The First Bolshevik Utopia*, trans. Charles Rougle, ed. Loren Graham and Richard Stites (Bloomington: Indiana UP, 1984). The translation was made from the original edition of *Krasnaia zvezda*, and it includes elements that were censored out of the Soviet editions.

works; reprints of *Red Star* paused after 1922.⁵ Indeed, Zamyatin's dystopian *We* (written in Modernist prose atypical for SF) first appeared in English translation (1924), becoming a formative pre-text for Anglophone dystopian fictions such as *Brave New World* and *1984* rather than for later Soviet SF. The best-known SF author of the Stalin era, Aleksandr Belyaev (1884–1942), was loved by readers but then largely forgotten until the Thaw period. At the same time, ideas of rocketry and space exploration were far from taboo,⁶ and stories (mostly forgettable) with SF elements did appear in journals aimed at young geeks, such as *Technology to Youth* (Tekhnika—molodezhi) and *Knowledge is Power* (Znanie—sila). The journals played an increasingly important role as SF later revived.

For something over two decades, from the early 1930s to the mid-1950s, *nauchnaia fantastika* ("scientific/scholarly fantasy") in the USSR was restricted to the so-called "proximate goal" (*blizhnii pritsel*): narratives of the present or very near future.⁷ Readers' testimonies suggest that this writing was not considered science fiction, or rather: not considered *fantastika*. Anatoly Britikov's 1970 study of SF beautifully critiques the near-goal authors,⁸ who in essence wrote the usual socialist realist stuff, just set on the moon or in hostile terrestrial environments (e.g., under the sea; in the Arctic). It is no surprise that these men and their allies in the literary bureaucracy resisted when SF reemerged from technical magazines and young adult literature a few years after Stalin's death. A watershed moment was the publication of Ivan Efremov's tremendously popular SF novel *The Andromeda Nebula* (Tumannost' Andromedy) in 1957. And with that my story here begins.

Years of emphasis on producing highly educated Soviet citizens had raised the numbers of university-educated professionals from 233,000 or so

---

5   Some commonly cited exemplars of socialist realism were Maxim Gorky's *Mother* (1905), Fyodor Gladkov's *Cement* (1925), and Valentin Kataev's *Time, Forward!* (1932).

6   See Asif Siddiqi, *The Red Rockets' Glare: Spaceflight and the Russian Imagination, 1857–1957* (Cambridge: Cambridge UP, 2010).

7   "Proximate goal" authors included Vladimir Nemtsov (1907–1994), Aleksandr Studitsky (1908–1991), Nikolai Toman (1911–1974), and most especially Aleksandr Kazantsev (1908–2002). They came of age in the late 1920s and early 1930s; like many other authors in this chapter, all of them had technical or scientific educations.

8   A. F. [Anatolii Fedorovich] Britikov, *Russkii sovetskii nauchno-fantasticheskii roman* (Leningrad: Nauka, 1970), 186 ff. Britikov worked at the Institute of Russian Literature in Leningrad, familiarly known as the Pushkin House; his study was one of several Soviet publications on SF in the 1960s and 1970s, which showed the genre taken seriously as a topic of academic, or at least critical, study. Where Anglo-American SF had a large component of pulp, the less palatable part of Soviet *fantastika* that the (non-)market offered was essentially socialist realist, often barely reimagined after authors who pursued the "proximate goal."

in 1928 to around 3,500,000 in 1960.[9] Under Khrushchev a confluence of greater though inconsistent freedom of discourse and admiration of scientists, researchers and cosmonauts as culture heroes contributed to a sudden flowering of Soviet SF, largely written by people (men mostly, but women too) with scientific and technical backgrounds.[10] SF in this period, alongside children's literature, historical fiction, and literary translation, offered an kind of literary discourse that was both politically safer and artistically less confining for writers with aesthetic ambitions or the desire for a rollicking plot. Indeed, as suggested above, the genre could be said to have re-emerged out of children's literature: early Thaw SF stories were printed in journals for young readers with scientific interests, and the main Soviet publishers of SF books continued to be Children's State Publisher (DetGIz), later Children's Literature (Detskaia literatura), and The Young Guard (Molodaia gvardiia), the latter aimed at readers of Komsomol age, fourteen to twenty-eight years old.[11] Translation played an important role in the development of Soviet SF too, as more recent works from around the world became available to readers, and fans and authors with the necessary language proficiency read foreign works—in English, German, or Japanese. Sometimes readers with good foreign language knowledge, like Arkady Strugatsky, also translated the foreign SF works they admired. Just as historical fiction allowed a thrilling plot to be set in an era where historical materialism would not compel socialist realism, SF could set stories in distant places or (future) times and free them to some extent from stultifying requirements. This was an important part of the appeal to many new readers in the quickly growing Soviet intelligentsia: SF had to be fun to read, even if the introductions tended to stress the authors' scientific *bona fides*. Many SF works had roots in adventure literature, as well as the pre-Stalinist Russophone SF that might now be accessed again.

---

9 Vladislav Zubok, *Zhivago's Children: The Last Russian Intelligentsia* (Cambridge, MA: Harvard UP, 2011), 124). The increase is even more impressive than it first looks, since some of those earlier thousands would have died or been purged from the statistics.
10 A scientific background did not necessarily lead to writing SF, of course; mathematician Elena Ventsel wrote largely "women's prose" in the Thaw era, under the punning pseudonym I. Grekova (*igrek* in Russian means the variable y).
11 The Soviet Union had a limited number of state publishing establishments, each with its own profile, but all facing the same rules of censorship and central approval. It was easier to get an ambiguous, non-socialist-realist short story into print than to publish a novel of the same constitution. The compromises required (whether imposed by censors or editors or observed by authors who internalized the system's demands) were compensated for by the enormous print runs that acceptable authors could enjoy.

For this study, I selected a group of representative Thaw SF authors cited in Anatoly Britikov's 1970 study, *Russkii sovetskii nauchno-fantasticheskii roman*;[12] if writers had made an impression on Britikov (a literary scholar who sincerely admired the genre) by 1970, they could be considered major SF authors of the day. Moreover, Britikov focuses on *novels*, which had higher status than the short stories a beginner or amateur might write, and which demanded bigger investment from publishers and, no doubt, attracted more attention from censors. The authors he discusses were fairly established and aesthetically if not professionally successful by the time he wrote his book, a few years after the Thaw ended. Like Eastern Europe in general, the USSR took SF more seriously than did the United States and some other literary/linguistic markets, where SF was considered "genre fiction" if not "pulp" (named after the poor-quality paper of the magazines where stories were printed). Britikov surely intended to support SF and its authors with his serious and detailed study at a moment when the Thaw's end put their work at risk, and his book appeared nine years before Darko Suvin's groundbreaking 1979 study, *Metamorphoses of Science Fiction*, which laid the foundation for serious academic study of SF in the Anglophone world and, among many other things, made several important Soviet and East European SF authors part of that conversation from the beginning.

I began to research the SF authors expecting that the Thaw must have propelled people born in the 1930s and even 1940s (those who became the *shestidesiatniki*, "people of the sixties," a vital new stage of the Soviet intelligentsia) into writing expansive, "far-aim" SF—what we would all recognize as proper science fiction, not production novels set on the moon—as young adults, much as authors born in the late 1890s and early 1900s had leapt into writing amid the cultural ferment of the Soviet 1920s. In fact, however, Britikov's authors are much more widely distributed in age. Of forty-seven authors whose dates I could confidently locate,[13] one was born before 1900, eleven were born between 1900

---

12 The Thaw era authors I found in Britikov are: Altov, Amatuni, Amosov, Bakhnov, Bovin, Chernenko, Davydov, Dneprov, Efremov, Emtsev, Gansovsky, Gor, Gorbovsky, Granin, Gromova, Gurevich, Lagin, Larionova, Liapunov, Lukodyanov, Lukovsky, Martynov, Meerov, Melentyev, Mikhailov, Nevinsky, Obukhova, Parnov, Pavlovsky, Poleshchuk, Rich, Rosokhvatsky, Savchenko, Shalimov, Shefner, Snegov, Sokolova, Strugatsky (twice), Varshavsky, Voiskunsky, Volkov, Volkov, Zakharchenko, Zhemaitis, Zhuravleva, and Zuev-Ordynets. (Some names are *noms de plume*, and in some cases two of the writers regularly wrote together.) In a few cases my numbers will vary, because for some authors certain kinds of information were lacking. A few writers glancingly mentioned in Britikov lacked enough of a footprint elsewhere for me to include in this data.

13 Besides the forty-seven authors cited in Britikov, *Russkii sovetskii nauchno-fantasticheskii roman*, I have added Kir Bulychyov—pen name of Igor Mozheiko (1934–2003)—whose success as a screenwriter and SF author was established a bit later.

and 1910, fifteen between 1911 and 1920, twelve between 1921 and 1930, and only eight between 1931 and 1940, the decade I had expected to be most richly represented. The group born before 1910—in the same era as the "near-goal" writers who dominated the pseudo-genre in the Stalin years[14]—includes one of the most groundbreaking, Ivan Efremov, author of *The Andromeda Nebula*. Younger writers were important too (including another of the best known, Boris Strugatsky, born in 1933), but apparently a number of SF writers had been waiting for a more encouraging situation, had been writing (and even publishing) works of other kinds,[15] or were simply inspired by new literary works they saw being published and wanted to join in.[16] Surely a few had been writing what we would consider SF "for the desk drawer." More than a few of the writers Britikov mentions (at least six) had spent time in prison or GULag camps, obviously not favorable places for literary work.

Significantly, less than half of these SF authors received higher education at the Literary Institutes that prepared new generations of Soviet writers for the command literary economy.[17] Most of these authors had instead scientific educations of some kind. Those who joined the Writers' Union (most of the successful ones did; membership is confirmed for twenty-seven of forty-three

---

14 See note 7 above for details.
15 Note the publication dates of books by Georgy Gurevich:
    a. *The Rocket Man* (Chelovek-raketa, 1947)
    b. *The Fast-growing Poplar* (Topol' stremitel'nyi, 1951)
    c. *Frost on Palm Trees*
    d. *An Underground Storm* (Podzemnaia nepogoda, 1956)
    e. *The Birth of the Sixth Ocean* (Rozhdenie shestogo okeana, 1960)
    f. *The Transit of Nemesis* (Prokhozhdenie Nemezidy, 1961)
    g. *Captives of the Asteroid* (Plenniki asteroida, 1962)
    h. *On a See-through Planet* (Na prozrachnoi planete, 1963)
    i. *We Are from the Solar System* (My—iz Solnechnoi sistemy, 1965)
    j. *Non-linear Fiction* (Nelineinaia fantastika, 1978)
    k. *Tempocity* (Tempograd, 1980)
    l. *Only to Overtake* (Tol'ko obgon, 1985)
    m. *Schoolbooks for a Magician* (Uchebniki dlia volshebnika, 1985)
    n. *Youth Warrant* (Order na molodost', 1990)
    Some writers of "near-goal" works switched to more interesting work once it was safer to do so. One might still note that Gurevich's books came thicker and faster in the Thaw years.
16 The story is that Ilya Varshavsky (1908–1974) saw his son, an engineer and cyberneticist, reading a science fiction book and asked with irritation how he could waste his time on such nonsense. The son replied that he should try to write some himself rather than criticizing, and the rest is history. Thus, Varshavsky's writerly origin story points to serendipity rather than a longstanding interest in or desire to write SF.
17 Biographical information for this section was taken mostly from the rich website FantLab.ru, though sometimes also from Wikipedia, *Kratkaia literaturnaia entsiklopediia*, or introductions to published work.

writers I investigated, and Britikov himself was a member)[18] did so only after they had published quite a bit, enjoyed some recognition as authors, and could see a prospect of making a living as writers. Acceptance into the Union was a prerequisite for earning a living from literary work, as opposed to occasional honoraria.[19] The varied original professions include astronomy, biology, ceramics, chemistry, engineering (electrical or mechanical), medicine, paleontology, pharmacy, physics, pilot, radio, river transport, rocketry, surgery, and general "technical sciences." In short, the majority of Thaw-era SF authors came from the *technical* intelligentsia and became writers without having passed through the pipeline that supplied the Soviet literary economy. This could have various consequences: perhaps these writers were less trained in the habits of socialist realism; their previous SF reading had probably emphasized Verne, Wells, and Soviet authors of the 1920s. Even if they began writing with an aim to entertain or provide (popular science) infotainment, in the USSR literature was still a prestigious venue for asking big questions, and the best Thaw-era SF dug into that.

Related to (and in many ways springing from) adventure literature, SF works prioritize engaging plots, often with striking and exotic imagined settings: outer space or other planets. Scholars of SF have noted that its style in general (not only in Russophone SF) tends to be realistic,[20] so the new body of works emerging during the Thaw suited editors' stylistic preferences: realism was familiar and generally approved. This simpler style also made SF more accessible to readers who had not grown up in logocentric intelligentsia families with "book

---

18 Twenty-five writers had "technical" backgrounds, versus eighteen who did not (numbers here are reduced because of lack of information for some writers). Kir Bulychyov was an exception: since he belonged to the Screenwriters' Union, he could make money from writing without being accused of being a "drone." Moreover, as fans eventually discovered, he was really Dr. Igor Mozheiko, a respected scholar and specialist on Southeast Asia.
19 It is more difficult now than before to determine when and even whether a writer joined the Writers' Union, though in the Soviet era this was a ritual part of any author's biography. Many writers listed in Britikov, *Russkii sovetskii nauchno-fantasticheskii roman*, were not famous enough to merit entries in reference works. My plan for archival research was thwarted by the pandemic (2020–2021). Scientific or technical education would naturally not include practice of creative writing; students with an itch to write postponed it or wrote in their free time. Soviet educational institutions required earlier specialization, though students of natural sciences who loved non-scientific activities could pursue them in amateur groups sometimes based at their institutes. During and after the Thaw, SF "circles" formed in some cities, where aspiring writers gathered with more established ones to get advice and criticism and to make connections in the field.
20 "Literary sf follows in the stylistic tradition of the realistic novel, despite its many quasi-marvelous elements." See Istvan Csicsery-Ronay, Jr., *The Seven Beauties of Science Fiction* (Middletown, CT: Wesleyan UP, 2008), 83.

wallpaper" in their homes and experience of Silver Age authors. Setting situations on distant planets, even perhaps in different millennia, let authors depict issues that would have been too close to home for higher-status and more closely censored genres, even given the increased literary freedom of the first Thaw years. A few examples of relatively frank depiction of recognizably Soviet problems include the underhanded competition among several secondary, otherwise not villainous characters to obtain "deficit" *ulmotron* hardware in the Strugatskys' 1963 novel *Far Rainbow* (Dalekaia raduga), or the mockery of character Eibi See's attempts to speed a backward planet's development from primitive matriarchy to slave-holding, the obligatory next step according to Marxist historical materialism, in Vladlen Bakhnov's 1970 story "Fifth on the Left" (Piataia sleva).[21] Bakhnov's story describes "progressor" capitalists eager to sell products to the new planets, but capitalists would surely be happy to sell to planets at any stage of development, including the most primitive. They would not respect the Marxist historical stages—or depict them in paintings on the walls of their meeting hall.

If scientific or technical education and experience made writers familiar with astronomical, physical, or biological issues likely to arise in SF and thus qualified them to write it, the (relative) freedom to engage with moral questions or social issues that could not be discussed in other Soviet venues turned out to make it worth writing—and reading. For the intelligentsia the point, of course, is not merely to see one's name in print or even to make a living in literature, but to make a difference in society, with identifying and discussing the issues before them as the first step. As in the nineteenth century, lack of opportunities for uncensored public debate kept Soviet literature vibrant as a place for ideological as well as psychological and aesthetic work, even if readers first had to learn to read between the lines. In fact, the need to write "Aesopian" prose to address current issues despite Soviet censorship encouraged writing (and not only in SF) that rewards multiple approaches and even multiple re-readings—in other words, complex and engaging literary works.

For some years SF became popular even among writers who did not make the cut in Britikov's study. It is always hard to know how much Soviet publishing decisions corresponded to readers' interests, as opposed to guidance from above, but print runs for Soviet SF were often enormous, into hundreds of thousands of copies, even though the books might be printed on terrible quality paper

---

21 Bakhnov did attend the Gorky Literary Institute, but his involvement in the script for the charming part-SF, part-historical fantasy film *Ivan Vasilyevich meniaet professiiu* (Ivan Vasilyevich changes profession, translated as *Ivan Vasilyevich: Back to the Future*, 1973) suggests a genuine interest in, and knack for, SF topics.

(pulp indeed). Either good quality, acid-free paper was not available, or perhaps no one expected the books to be sought by library patrons and customers in antiquarian book shops decades after they were published.

Paleontologist Ivan Efremov's *The Andromeda Nebula* (1957) was not the only example of early Thaw SF that moved beyond the "near-goal" works of quasi-SF that preceded it,[22] but it strikingly leapt into a distant future, millennia from the present; the novel could hardly have presented a greater challenge to late Stalinist quasi-SF. Tellingly, it was first serialized in a journal,[23] only later clearing the higher hurdle of approval for a bound volume (the first book publication was in 1958). Although "near-goal" writers objected, readers reacted with great enthusiasm, many explicitly linking their pleasure as readers with their identity as working or budding scientists. The well-known aircraft designer Oleg Antonov commented,

> Нравится все: особенно отношение людей будущего к творческому труду, к обществу и друг к другу.... Ради такого будущего стоит жить и работать.
>
> Everything is pleasing: especially the way the people of the future relate to creative labor, to society, and to one another.... It's worth living and working for the sake of such a future.

Student V. Alkhimov wrote: "We have the impression that *The Andromeda Nebula* is addressed to us, the young romantics of technology."[24] Britikov quotes these examples from a book of reactions to Efremov's novel—which were perhaps gathered and published to advance the exciting new kind of SF Efremov presented and to quash objections. Literature featuring space travel was unusually suitable for the late 1950s and early 1960s, as the Soviet space program led

---

22 Ilya Kukulin also mentions Georgy Martynov's novella *Callisto*, published in 1957. Il'ia Kukulin, "Periodika dlia ITR: Sovetskie nauchno-populiarnye zhurnaly i modelirovanie interesov pozdnesovetskoi nauchno-tekhnicheskoi intelligentsii," *Novoe literaturnoe obozrenie* 3 (2017), accessed May 6, 2024. https://www.nlobooks.ru/magazines/novoe_literaturnoe_obozrenie/145_nlo_3_2017/article/12478.

23 Excerpts of Efremov's novel, written in 1955–1956, were published in the newspapers *Pioneer Pravda* (children would join the Young Pioneers before becoming Komsomol—Communist Youth—members at fourteen) and *Komsomol Pravda*; the whole novel first appeared serially in the journal *Tekhnika—molodezhi* [Technology for youth] in 1957.

24 Britikov, *Russkii sovetskii nauchno-fantasticheskii roman*, 221–222, quotes from E. Brandis and V. Dmitrevskii, *Cherez gory vremeni: Ocherk tvorchestva I. Efremova* (Moscow and Leningrad: Sovetskii pisatel', 1963), 209 and others. Here and elsewhere all translations are mine unless otherwise noted.

the world. SF contributed to enthusiasm for the space program and for scientific and technical education (again, even as SF was considered a "youth" genre) and therefore won support from journal editors and the literary bureaucracy, even if the latter were unlikely to read it themselves.

Readers' comments foreground the link between appreciating SF and intelligentsia ideals—"creative labor," the "youthful romantic[ism] of technology," the idea of making the USSR and indeed the whole world better through one's inspiration and effort, and maintaining high standards of morality and behavior alongside one's own morale. Benjamin Tromly's study of the educational formation of the Soviet intelligentsia under Stalin and Khrushchev notes that "the very contours of Soviet history" ensured that "fast-changing ideas about what intelligentsia should mean ensured that the term would carry myriad associations in any given period, let alone across a longer time span."[25] At the same time, Slava Gerovitch shows a telling slippage among various ways the term "intelligentsia" is used and offers three distinct definitions: first, the intelligentsia as well-educated, effective specialists in science and technology; second, the self-directed, frequently oppositional Soviet group in the 1960s and especially the 1970s that more resembled the "classic" intelligentsia of the nineteenth century, with top scientists like Andrei Sakharov asserting the right and ability to judge Soviet practices and find them wanting; and third, the intelligentsia as possessors of cultural polish and "people skills" that set them apart from many purely technical specialists, especially those from lower-class backgrounds who had undergone practical training and lacked the comfort and suavity that an intelligentsia family could provide.[26] Obviously, an individual might fit into only one of these categories, though some individuals would fit all three. Perhaps the ability to move from science and technology into literary authorship, with its emphasis on mastery of style and language, shows that Soviet SF authors could encompass all three varieties of intelligentsia belonging.

Introductions to anthologies and novels stress the importance of the Soviet way of life (Efremov is especially given to this in his own forewords and

---

25 Benjamin Tromly, *Making the Soviet Intelligentsia: Universities and Intellectual Life under Stalin and Khrushchev* (Cambridge: Cambridge UP, 2014), 3–4.
26 "Boris Chertok stressed that rocket engineers often lacked the cultural sophistication usually associated with the intelligentsia: 'To act, not to chat; to take risks; to make a decisive impact on the course of events—such was our work style. Those who did not care left very quickly. Many in our group lacked such intelligentsia traits as cultured conversation, tactfulness, or politeness. But we appreciated the sense of humor and were attentive to each other's work, trying to help if necessary.' See Slava Gerovitch, "Stalin's Rocket Designers' Leap into Space: The Technical Intelligentsia Faces the Thaw," *OSIRIS* 23 (2008): 207; citing Boris E. Chertok, *Rakety i liudi*, vol. 4: *Lunnaia gonka* (Moscow: Mashinostroenie, 2002), 356.

explanations *ot avtora*: his introduction to *Hour of the Bull* (Chas byka, 1970) describes America as full of fascist gangsters) but also the importance of the authors' currency with the latest science,[27] often mentioning even their membership in the technical and scientific professional unions. The introductions offered a chance to put some propaganda in the books' apparatus, advancing both political and scientific values and ensuring a warmer welcome from literary censors, even though many readers surely skipped the introductions.

Nevertheless, the 1960s Soviet intelligentsia in general shared a commitment to truth, progress, and equality, like the nineteenth-century intelligentsia whose striving gave the world a Russian name for the phenomenon. Like earlier incarnations in Russia and the USSR, the technical intelligentsia under Khrushchev was encouraged to study and work hard, to imbibe and exude the romanticism of technology, and to enjoy the privileges afforded by their position in society, earned by hard work, intellectual gifts, and cultivation of their minds. Some of them moved away from the state's ideological guidance once the Brezhnev era of Stagnation began, assuming an oppositional stance in the name of higher values.[28] Some authors of SF did this too, though not all; for example, the cheerful and optimistic early works of the Strugatskys quickly gave way to a much darker mood,[29] and they began to encounter difficulties with Soviet censorship that

---

27 From "Ob avtorakh," in Mikhail Emtsev and Eremei Parnov's collection of stories *Padenie sverkhnovoi* (Moscow: Znanie, 1964): "The young authors, who themselves work on the forefront of science, have mastered the material well and know the fundamental directions of contemporary science." The print run was 180,000 copies. See also V. Frolov on Daniil Granin in *Posle svad'by* (After the wedding, 1958): "D. Granin came to literature in 1949. He wanted, as an engineer, a scientific worker, to tell about those people he worked with, whom he know well—about young scholars, their brave daring and quests" (Daniil Granin, *Posle svad'by*, book 1, accessed July 11, 2024, https://readli.net/chitat-online/?b=874168&pg=1).

28 Patrick Major notes, "From 1969 there was a renewed clamp-down on Soviet SF works. In the 1970s *Molodaia gvardiia* suspended its SF series, and the 'Leningrad Collection' fell into abeyance, as did SF stories in the magazines *World of Adventure* and *Seeker*. 'Stalinist' authors such as Nemtsov and Kazantsev regained a certain editorial influence, while 'oppositional' SF authors such as Emtsev, Mirer, Yuryev, Larionova, Altov, Savchenko, Snegov, and Berdnyk abandoned writing altogether after failing to find an outlet for publication. Others, such as Parnov, allegedly sold out, becoming the acceptable face of Soviet SF at international conventions. The Strugatskys remained *personae non gratae* until the breakthrough of their classic *Roadside Picnic* (1972), which gained them an international reputation, especially once filmed by Tarkovsky as *Stalker* (1979). But only in the late 1980s could even these stars publish other 'top drawer' works, such as *Crooked Destiny* (1989), a metafictional account of their tribulations with the censor." See Patrick Major, "Future Perfect? Communist Science Fiction in the Cold War," *Cold War History* 4, no. 1 (2003): 89. This was not necessarily a move away from state ideology, but it could be a decision not to participate—or inability to write according to the new and more oppressive standards of the era of Stagnation.

29 Vladislav Zubok cites an attempted 1963 crackdown where precisely "near-goal" author and literary gatekeeper Kazantsev plays the heavy: "Arkady Strugatsky recalled another inquisitorial

Boris Strugatsky later described in eloquent detail. Nevertheless, readers whose educations had made them new members of the intelligentsia could begin with the Strugatskys' more optimistic and utopian works, then follow over time, learning to "read between the lines" but also to recognize and describe problems they saw around them, many of them philosophical or political rather than technical or scientific. Elana Gomel suggests that the Strugatskys' use of allegory to convey elements that could not be openly stated under Soviet censorship eventually froze them in that Aesopian posture even as the era of glasnost' and perestroika made it possible to write more critically and openly.[30] By then, however, they had exerted a tremendous influence on their readers, which helps explain their continuing post-Soviet popularity.

How did the best Soviet SF combine greater discursive/intellectual/philosophical freedom with engaging plots, attracting readers with its attention to big issues, as well as scientific and technical details that move beyond socialist realist clichés? Efremov's groundbreaking novel presents a future where most remaining obstacles encountered by humanity are caused by nature, especially the rigors and dangers of space travel, described without romanticizing. (Mostly.) Many of his ideas recall Bogdanov's *Red Star*, whether because he read the novel in his youth (he was seventeen when the third edition was published in 1922) or because ideas such as switching jobs for intellectual and psychological refreshment fit standard socialist ideology. SF conventions let authors leap over *how* an international crew or group of scientists would come to be working together in a relatively near future: economic and political transformations on Earth leading to "socialism in space" could be tacitly assumed without requiring description. The admirable individuals and projects described in SF both exemplified and encouraged intelligentsia ideals of cultivation, social and scientific progress, and passionate devotion to moral standards. They showed what it should mean to be Soviet (or, sometimes, more specifically Russian) and granted every good person a place in this meritocratic future where the world has not ended in nuclear

---

session, held in late March 1963 for science fiction writers. One well-known writer, Aleksandr Kazantsev, began to denounce his colleague as 'abstractionist' and attributed fascist ideas to him. Nobody dared to protest, and Arkady Strugatsky realized, cold perspiration beading his forehead, that he too was paralyzed by fear. Here was 'his majesty Idiot in search of revenge,' but what if Kazantsev's attack was approved by the party organization? As shame and rage overwhelmed him, Strugatsky stood up and challenged the raving denouncer. His passion broke the ice of common fear, and everybody began to speak and shout. From the meeting Strugatsky went straight to a bar to calm his nerves with a strong drink" (Zubok, *Zhivago's Children*, 218).

30 Elana Gomel, "The Poetics of Censorship: Allegory as Form and Ideology in the Novels of Arkady and Boris Strugatsky," *Science Fiction Studies* 22, no. 1 (1995): 87–105.

war. Moreover, in the Thaw period—unlike the era of Stagnation that followed under Leonid Brezhnev—most members of the technical intelligentsia were, perhaps for the last time, persuaded of the potential reality of the Soviet Union's science fictional dreams (to make *fantastika* into reality!).

It makes sense, given the state's huge investment in education and in scientific research (culminating, again, in Sputnik and the flights of Gagarin and others), that SF authors would form part of the collaboration between the intelligentsia and the state and be drawn into its various organs and literary institutions. Joining the Writers' Union, for the most successful authors, meant now both the need and the opportunity to make a living doing what writers do. When the Strugatsky brothers' manuscripts were subjected to censorship, often with results they disliked, they had little choice if they wanted to see publication: they were no longer amateurs, but authors who craved the experience of writing and publishing, and the various perks that came with literary careers: not even necessarily the "bribery" of dachas and nice vacations available to Writers' Union members, but pride in their published works and access to laudable tasks, such as mentoring younger writers. Still, whether they meant it to or not, their 1974 novel *A Billion Years before the End of the World* (Za milliard let do kontsa sveta, published in English in 1978 as *Definitely Maybe*) can be read as showing the ways a hostile system could pressure a writer or scientist who was working on an *undesirable* project.[31] The push to cooperate with the Soviet literary bureaucracy was tacitly backed by knowledge of what happened to cultural figures who refused to play along (poet Joseph Brodsky was arrested and tried in 1964 for "being a drone" [*tuneiadstvo*]), and it meant that in the case of SF the intelligentsia could stand only so far from the center of power while continuing to create and disseminate their narratives. (Underground samizdat translations of Western SF let a writer be dissident without actually dissenting, but most of the truly dissident authors were not writing SF; Abram Tertz [Andrei Sinyavsky], in a few of his works, was an exception.) Western translations, especially in the US, tended to highlight evidence of dissident content in works that might be more complexly critical, which could get authors into trouble too (as when the Strugatskys refused to let the Bantam paperback edition of *Snail on the Slope* be presented as a dissident work).[32]

---

31 Yvonne Howell disagrees, stressing the idea of the homeostatic universe. See Yvonne Howell, "Arkady and Boris Strugatsky: The Science-Fictionality of Russian Culture," in *Lingua Cosmica: Science Fiction from Around the World*, ed. Dale Knickerbocker (Champaign: U of Illinois Press, 2018), 214–215.

32 See Petri Liukkonen and Ari Pesonen, "Arkady Strugatsky (1925–1991)" and "Boris Strugatsky (1933–2012)," Authors Calendar, accessed March 30, 2022, http://authorscalendar.info/strugats.htm.

Dmitry Zanerv's 2015 article, "Legko byt' inelligentom,"[33] obviously plays off the title of the Strugatskys' 1964 novel *Hard to Be a God* (Trudno byt' bogom),[34] a novel that was obligatory reading for Soviet *intelligenty* even if they were not particular fans of SF. Zanerv critiques the Strugatsky brothers, the best-known and best-loved Russophone SF authors of the Soviet period, as typical *intelligenty*, limited as much as enhanced by their own educations (Arkady in linguistics and Boris in astronomy) and marked by the intelligentsia's dual devotion to enlightenment and to a code of human honor and decency. Zanerv criticizes their attempts to be philosophers, which he feels were stunted by the limits of Soviet-era education; he sees their philosophical achievements in literature lagging far behind those of Stanisław Lem, who was copiously translated into Russian and widely admired by Soviet readers. This critique, like the shift of much of the best Soviet SF toward more pessimistic themes after the mid-1960s, shows how the genre was conditioned by its time, particularly as encouragement for the projects and ambitions of the Thaw era, space race and all, came to feel hollow in the years of "stagnation" that followed. The Thaw was a brief golden age for SF, and though some successful authors continued to write and publish it grew harder to make it through the editorial process into print; many other writers decided to give up.[35] Some works by Thaw-era SF writers were not published until the years of glasnost' and perestroika, when Soviet editorial policies opened up once again.

Post-Stalin Soviet SF may be helpfully contrasted with another divergent genre of the time, Village Prose, which explored the legacy of specifically ethnic Russian traditions, especially those of the Russian village, mourning what had been lost and destroyed by Soviet modernity, forced industrialization and the environmental damage and dispropriation caused by projects like hydroelectric dams. Village Prose too was written in realistic style, and it surely appealed to readers who were acquiring the logocentric intelligentsia behaviors that their non-intelligentsia upbringing had not provided, while pointing toward the country's past. SF authors were future-oriented, dedicated to technological progress that would enable exploration of the cosmos while also liberating human

---

33 *Oktiabr'* 7 (2015): 157–169 (see also the same work in translation "It's Easy to Be One of the Intelligentsia," *Russian Studies in Literature* 52, nos. 3–4 [2016]: 282–302).
34 The Strugatskys' 1964 novel *Trudno byt' bogom* has appeared in English twice as *Hard to Be a God*: in Wendayne Ackerman's version, made from the German translation (New York: DAW Books, 1973), and a version translated directly from the Russian by Olena Bormashenko (Chicago, IL: Chicago Review Press, 2012).
35 Rafail Nudelman, "Soviet Science Fiction and the Ideology of Soviet Society," *Science-Fiction Studies* 16 (1989): 52–53.

beings for moral and intellectual development. Thus SF authors were typically more cosmopolitan (and fairly often were not ethnically Russian; indeed, nine of the forty-seven authors in Britikov were "cosmopolitan" in the later Soviet sense of being Jews). The lines are not as clean as they might be: Vladimir Soloukhin, in a late talk on ecology, referred to the earth as a spaceship on which we are all cosmonauts,[36] while Chingiz Aitmatov's 1980 novel... *The Day Lasts Longer than a Hundred Years* (*I dol'she veka dlitsia den'*...: the title is a citation of a poem from Pasternak; the English translation missed that) braids traits of Village Prose together with a thread of SF narrative.[37] On the other hand, works of SF often lovingly depict the home planet, its nature and culture(s), so unlike the hostile environments of space and of other planets, and so potentially fragile when faced with crisis. Some SF shows the planet under benign human control, with weather tamed and agriculture and industry laid out as sensibly as in Vera Pavlovna's Fourth Dream, other narratives were blindingly ignorant about the potential social and environmental impacts of changes they imagined (such as melting the polar icecaps).

This examination of the Soviet intelligentsia's connections with science fiction suggests significant overlaps and commonalities, and it is not surprising that Zanerv would point to the best-known Soviet SF authors as *imperfect* members of the intelligentsia, itself necessarily an imperfect social group. Whether and to what extent the Thaw-era SF writers succeeded, and even could have succeeded, in their intelligentsia mission is another question. What is clear is that the best of them continue to appeal to readers: the Strugatskys are regularly reprinted; Efremov still has lots of fans and is still appreciated. Later Soviet SF was slowed by general stagnation, with some of its most lasting achievements appearing in children's stories (like Kir Bulychyov's "Alisa" tales), but, as Sofya Khagi shows, interpreting post-Soviet SF, even the most deeply dystopian works, requires knowing the Strugatskys' more optimistic work as well.[38] Once the SF avant-garde, Thaw authors have now become classics and part of the essential background for reading more recent works.

---

36 Vadimir Soloukhin, *Kameshki na ladoni* (Moscow: Sovetskaia Rossiia, 1977), accessed March 2, 2022, https://litlife.club/books/25419/read?page=21.
37 Aitmatov, *The Day Lasts Longer than a Hundred Years*, trans. F. J. French (Bloomington: Indiana UP, 1983).
38 Khagi, "One Billion Years after the End of the World: Historical Deadlock, Contemporary Dystopia, and the Continuing Legacy of the Strugatskii Brothers," *Slavic Review* 72, no. 2 (2013): 267–286.

Bibliography

Arbitman, Roman. "Back in the 1960s: Notes by a Man Who Wasn't There." *Science Fiction Studies* 31, no. 3 (2004): 407–414.

Bailes, Kendall. *Technology and Society under Lenin and Stalin: Origins of the Soviet Technical Intelligentsia, 1917–1941*. Princeton, NJ: Princeton UP, 1978.

Chernyshova, Tatiana. "Science Fiction and Myth Creation in Our Age." *Science Fiction Studies* 31, no. 3 (2004): 345–357.

Csicsery-Ronay, István, Jr. "Soviet Science Fiction: The Thaw and After." *Science Fiction Studies* 31, no. 3 (2004): 337–344.

Gerovitch, Slava. "Stalin's Rocket Designers' Leap into Space: The Technical Intelligentsia Faces the Thaw." *OSIRIS* 23 (2008): 189–209.

Gomel, Elena. "Gods like Men: Soviet Science Fiction and the Utopian Self." *Science Fiction Studies* 31, no. 3 (2004): 358–377.

Hellman, Ben. "Paradise Lost: The Literary Development of Arkadii and Boris Strugatskii." *Russian History* 11 (1984): 311–19.

Howell, Yvonne. *Apocalyptic Realism: The Science Fiction of Arkady and Boris Strugatsky*. New York: Peter Lang, 1994.

———. "Arkady and Boris Strugatsky: The Science-Fictionality of Russian Culture." In *Lingua Cosmica: Science Fiction from Around the World*, edited by Dale Knickerbocker, 201–220. Champaign: U of Illinois Press, 2018.

Kluger, Daniel. "Fables of Desire." *Science Fiction Studies* 31, no. 3 (2004): 415–417.

Kukulin, Il'ia. "Periodika dlia ITR: Sovetskie nauchno-populiarnye zhurnaly i modelirovanie interesov pozdnesovetskoi nauchno-tekhnicheskoi intelligentsii." Периодика для ИТР: советские научно-популярные журналы и моделирование интересов позднесоветской научно-технической интеллигенции." *Novoe literaturnoe obozrenie* 3 (2017): 61–85.

Major, Patrick. "Future Perfect? Communist Science Fiction in the Cold War." *Cold War History* 4, no. 1 (2003): 71–96.

Nudelman, Rafail. "Soviet Science Fiction and the Ideology of Soviet Society." *Science-Fiction Studies* 16 (1989): 38–66.

Tucker, Frank H. "Soviet Science Fiction: Recent Development and Outlook." *Russian Review* 33 (1974): 189–200.

Zubok, Vladislav. *Zhivago's Children: The Last Russian Intelligentsia*. Cambridge, MA: Harvard UP, 2011.

The Intelligentsia and the "Thick Journal"

Marina Adamovich

The thick journal (TJ) is a specific type of intellectual literary publication in Russian culture. In the history of Russian journalism, TJ was traditionally a periodical that presented current literature and thoughts. TJ combines literary publications (short stories, novels, drama, and poetry) with journalism (articles and bibliography—criticism of literature, arts, music, political and social reviews, essays, etc.) The Russian TJ is a specifically presented type of "encyclopedia of contemporary thoughts."[1] As a unique cultural phenomenon, its mission is to express the epoch's main humanitarian values and cultural tendencies. Traditionally TJ has been a tribune for self-expression of the national intelligentsia.

This phenomenon could be analyzed from the standpoint of journalism, literary criticism, or culturology; it could be studied as a projection of ideological tendencies in the context of general social problems or of the main conflicts of the epoch, as a replication of the literary process, or, lastly, as a mirror of national discourse, the self-consciousness of the intellectual and spiritual elite. In the

---

1 Valeriia Pustovaia, "Diskussiia ob intelligentsii v literaturnykh zhurnalakh postsovetskoi epokhi: logika transformatsii poniatiia" (PhD diss., MSU School of Journalism, Moscow, 2008), www.dissercat.com/content/diskussiya-ob-intelligentsii-v-literaturnykh-zhurnalakh-postsovetskoi-epokhi-logika-transfor.

context of the topic "The Intelligentsia and the Thick Journal," this chapter will analyze the TJ as a reflection of self-consciousness of the intellectual elite, alternating consideration of examples of TJ and then their connection with the mission and history of the Russophone intelligentsia, with special attention to *The New Review* (Novyi Zhurnal, or NR).

But first, a short observation on the history of the Russian TJ. Establishment of the TJ used to be linked to the epoch of Elizaveta Petrovna, Empress of Russia (1709–1762), when the newspaper the *Moscow Review* (Moskovskie vedomosti, 1756–1917) was founded at Moscow University. The magazines *Economic Journal* (Ekonomicheskii magazin, 1780–1789), *Political Journal* (Politicheskii zhurnal, 1790–1810), *Hippocrene or the Pleasures of Logophilia* (Ippokrena, ili utekhi liubosloviia, 1799–1801), and others served as supplements of this newspaper. We cannot classify these publications as typical TJ, but their establishment shows the Russian elite's first efforts to create a platform for itself with the general purposes of enlightenment, a platform for cultural and spiritual dialogue between intellectuals and the state. It is very important that these efforts appeared at the university: there was a real attempt to recreate the European experience of forming the phenomenon of the "intellectual" as a critical thinker who offered ethical solutions and moral rules—a public spiritual leader.

TJ in its classic format emerged in the era of Empress Catherine the Great with her magazine *All Kinds of Things* (Vsiakaia vsiachina, 1769–1770) and the private journals the *Drone* (Truten', 1769–1770) and the *Painter* (Zhivopisets, 1772–1773), published by Nikolai Novikov. Traditionally, these journals have been analyzed in the context of their antagonism: "Novikov's journals argued with the governmental press. . . . [The journals presented] opposing views of the progressive part of society" and reflected a conflict with the official journal published by the Empress, who criticized only "general human vices."[2]

The roots of TJ as a place for intellectual discussion formed in that epoch: a new progressive social class of nobility was born. The Russian nobility had to play the role of the spiritual elite of an enlightened state. The new social class needed self-expression and self-consciousness to create its own moral code for social practices. Novikov's intentions were more radical: bringing up an *independent*, active spiritual national elite. The original, official cultural institutions, conservative and patriarchal, pushed the intellectual elite to a self-governing private platform. TJ had become the only place for intellectual discussions in literary-centripetal Russian culture.

---

2 Tat'iana Snigireva and Aleksei Podchinenov, "Tolstyi zhurnal v Rossii kak tekst i gipertekst," *Izvestiia Ural'skogo gosudarstvennogo universiteta* 13 (1999): 5–13.

"Culturological analysis of the 'TJ' phenomenon includes the important aspect of the relationship between TJ and national self-consciousness," write Russian researchers T. Snigireva and A. Podchinenov. They quote V. Lakshin, who described the role of newspapers as the "official voice" of government and the role of magazines as an "informal voice of society": "We could say that a unique social-moral phenomenon like the Russian intelligentsia—with all its dignities and weaknesses—is a direct result of the practices of Russian literature and journalism in their thick journals."[3]

From the very beginning all known "thick journals"—as described in the chapter by Marcus Levitt—played the role not only of "literary reading" but also of "intellectual message" and of a center for forming intellectual discourse for all types of intelligentsias—conservative, liberal, democratic or revolutionary.

TJ represents a unique *text*. Yury Tynyanov wrote about TJ as a "special original literary text."[4] N. Eidelman has analyzed Herzen's *Kolokol* as a text with formal-semantic unity in which all elements are important—from fonts to tables of contents and even circulation numbers. Remarkably, all new journals would state their credo. For example, Dostoevsky's *Time* (Vremia, 1861–1863) declared: "[T]he journal's goal is the unity of knowledge with the people's roots."[5] The lodestar of the famous Soviet liberal magazine *New World* (Novyi mir) under the leadership of Aleksandr Tvardovsky was "The ideological views of *novomirovtsy* [the journal's editorial staff] with their dream of 'socialism with a human face.'"[6]

However, TJ is not only *text*—this phenomenon is at the same time a unique *hypertext*. This hypertext plays an important role as a center for forming the reader's discourse, its moral and behavioral codes, being a tribune of the intellectual elite's self-consciousness. The hypertext of TJ is the aggregate of texts by writers, the magazine, and readers that are interconnected, in associative ways, with references to each other; this "interconnection" creates a hyper-semantic (V. Toporov) linguo-conceptual impact, actual or potential, in the field of culture.[7] It manifests itself as a "specific text whose quality is exclusively functional: it operates not as a message" (each element and the relationship of

---

3 Vladimir Lakshin, "'Phenomen 'tolstyi zhurnal' v Rossii kak iavlenie natsional'noi kul'tury," in idem, *Berega kul'tury*, ed. Svetlana Lakshina (Moscow: MIROS, 1994): 24.
4 Iurii Tynianov, "Zhurnal, kritik, chitatel' i pisatel'," in idem, *Poetika. Istoriia literatury. Kino* (Moscow: Nauka, 1977), 148.
5 Fedor Dostoevskii, "Ob"iavlenie o podpiske na zhurnal 'Vremia' na 1861 g.," in idem, *Sobranie sochinenii v tridtsati tomakh*, vol. 18 (Leningrad: Nauka, 1978), 35.
6 Snigireva and Podchinenov, "Tolstyi zhurnal v Rossii," 8.
7 On the definition of hypertext see Vladimir Toporov, *Peterburgskii tekst russkoi literatury* (St. Petersburg: Iskusstvo, 2003); Martin Wallace, *Recent Theories of Narrative* (Ithaca, NY:

elements comprise a *message*), but rather as "a code encompassing information about the very type of language," as informational hyper-semantic units.[8] The constitutional component of hypertext (also known as super-text) "organizes its conceptual-semantic interactivity and communicative-semantic integrity."[9] TJ might be analyzed as hypertext of an open type. Any individual issue of a TJ also retains all the functions of the whole publication as a hypertext.

Novikov, of course, is known as one of the first representatives of the so-called "Russian intelligentsia." Dmitry Likhachev, in his famous essay "About the Russian Intelligentsia: Letter to the Editorial Team," wrote: "The first real typical representatives of the Russian intelligentsia appeared at the end of the eighteenth and the beginning of the nineteenth century: Sumarokov, Novikov, Radishchev, Karamzin" (see Marcus Levitt's chapter for more details).[10]

From the very beginning, attempts to define the phenomenon of the "intelligentsia," or the *intelligent* as a representative of the intelligentsia, have faced the problem of recognition in the context of Hegel's theory of intersubjective recognition: the phenomenon is explored by someone who represents the phenomenon; the researcher is an object and a subject of study at the same time. This paradox causes the loss of an academically clear definition. There are some traditional definitions from different dictionaries, for example, from the Oxford Dictionary: "Intellectuals or highly educated people as a group, especially when regarded as possessing culture and political influence" (Oxford Dictionary), and from *Dictionary of the Russian Language* (Ozhegov): "Intelligentsia is a definition of people engaged in intellectual work, educated, with special knowledge in different spheres of science, technology and culture; a social group of people engaged in such types of work."

The critic and journalist Razumnik Ivanov-Razumnik, in "What Is the Intelligentsia?" writes: "The history of the Russian intelligentsia is precisely the history of the Russian consciousness because the Russian intelligentsia is the holder of Russian consciousness."[11] Classifying the intelligentsia as "people of self-consciousness," he points out that "they are not a social group, or workshop,

---

Cornell UP, 1986); Paul Crosthwaite, ed., *Criticism, Crisis, and Contemporary Narrative: Textual Horizons in an Age of Global Risk* (New York: Routledge, 2011).

8   A. G. Loshakov, "Sverkhtext: problema tselostnosti, printsipy modelirovaniia," *Izvestiia Rossiiskogo gosudarstvennogo pedagogicheskogo universiteta* 66 (2008): 102.

9   Vytautas Petrušonis, *Respect of the Locus' Cultural Identity in Architectural Design* (Vilnius: Tekhnika, 2004).

10 Dmitrii Likhachev, "O russkoi intelligentsii. Pis′mo v redaktsiiu," *Novyi mir* 2 (1993): 3–9.

11 Razumnik Ivanov-Razumnik, "Chto takoe 'intelligentsiia'?," in *Intelligentsiia—vlast′—narod. Russkie istochniki sovremennoi sotsial′noi mysli: Antologiia*, ed. L. Novikova and I. Sizemskaia (Moscow: Nauka, 1992), 74.

not a corporation, not a circle . . . but a complex of vital forces of the nation." Separate *intelligenty* have existed for all time; the "intelligentsia was born only when separate *intelligenty* organically gathered into a strong unit." Ivanov-Razumnik points out that first, the "intelligentsia" is not limited to particular occupations; second, "the main quality of the intelligentsia is its ongoing tradition; . . . mathematically—[it] is a continuous function;" "this group was united by the energy of struggle for liberation"; "this epic struggle grouped the Russian intelligentsia into a solid immense energy of resistance." As we see, Ivanov-Razumnik highlighted the moment of "resistance." More accurate words might be "independent thoughts" and "independent actions" as the basis of this phenomenon.

Describing the history of the intelligentsia as an opposition, Ivanov-Razumnik points out the main milestones of its spiritual evolution: from private antagonism and opposition in the mid-18th-19th centuries to the "mass of *raznochintsy*,"[12] since at that time the intelligentsia had become a group outside the usual divisions of social class. Thus the definition Ivanov-Razumnik proposes: "'Intelligentsia' means ethically—anti-bourgeois; sociologically—out-of-class, the group of succession creates new forms and ideals, and realization of them with the goal of intellectual and physical, social and personal liberation of individuals."[13]

Likhachev in his "Letter . . ." stresses "the most associated-emotional character" of this phenomenon: "The main principle of the *intelligent* is his intellectual freedom—freedom as an ethical category. The intelligent is not free only due to his moral consciousness and his thought."[14] As mentioned before, "the main disadvantage of most definitions of the intelligentsia . . . is not their unclearness but simplicity and uncomplicatedness," because this "clearness" distorts the "real amorphousness and ambivalence of the intelligentsia."[15]

A very strong myth of the intelligentsia in Russian culture has been adopted by other world cultures. We interpret the myth not as a legend but as reality—in Aleksei Losev's definition: myth represents the highest concrete intensive

---

12 In nineteenth- and early twentieth-century Russia, the name *raznochintsy* was used for a category of people of various ranks, belonged to no particular social class or group, who received an education and left their former class. The word *raznochintsy* means "different social ranks" (*raznye chiny*). For more details, see earlier articles in this collection.
13 Ivanov-Razumnik, "Chto takoe 'intelligentsiia'?," 86.
14 Dmitrii Likhachev, "O russkoi intelligentsii: pis'mo v redaktsiu," 3.
15 Mikhail Lotman, "Intelligentsiia i svoboda (k analizu intelligentskogo diskursa)," in *Russkaia intelligentsiia i zapadnyi intellektualizm: Istoriia i tipologiia*, ed. B. A. Uspenskii (Moscow: O.G.I., 1999), 123; see also M. Gasparov, "Russkaia intelligentsiia kak otvodok evropeiskoi kul'tury," in *Russkaia intelligentsiia i zapadnyi intellektualizm: Istoriia i tipologiia*, ed. B. A. Uspenskii (Moscow: O.G.I., 1999), 20–27.

reality. Myth presents a "coherence of subject and object," a "harmony of idea and life" combining personal and social levels of existence.[16] The myth of the intelligentsia has a high-level axiology. Inside the cultural myth, the antagonism between "doctrinaire" and "descriptive" in dialogues about the intelligentsia dissolves. The ideal image of the *intelligent* and his ideal images of society are connected; the combination of a personal image of the world and a real matrix of the Russian culture is formed, as well as values and actions. Lotman writes:

> Intelligentsia discourse is a kind of meta-language of Russian culture, engendered by it, isomorphic to it and semantically dependent on it. . . . Intelligentsia discourse is a function of Russian culture, whereas the intelligentsia itself is the voice of this discourse, and it will exist as long as the demand for self-expression is preserved in Russian culture.[17]

Thus, the role of the *intelligent* highlights a strong metaphysical/irrational moral-ethical codex and action—social and creative.

Researchers note one more important characteristic of this discourse—the intelligentsia's intent to be influential, the energy to create leadership. The opposition, as a complex of unauthorized independent thoughts, ideas, and social behavior, always has a zest for power and spiritual leadership. All these traits—membership in the intellectual elite, creation of ideologemes in society, mass consciousness and national logistics, spiritual leadership of the nation—indicate "power-philia" and point to the role of power in the intelligentsia narrative. This has resulted in various relationships with authorities. For European intellectuals, often involved in society through academic institutions, connections with authorities were legitimated, whereas the Russian intelligentsia was pushed aside from contributing to government from the very beginning.

The epoch of the *raznochintsy* produced new political, social, ethical, and cultural layers of the intelligentsia narrative. The *intelligent*'s self-expression as a spiritual leader of the nation with hyper-responsibility and a strong moral code—legitimated or not—appeared on the pages of TJ in its own text. On the other hand, the narrative of the *intelligent* became more and more radical, rebellious, and concentrated on the concrete task of power. This process was clearly analyzed by the authors in *Landmarks* (Vekhi, 1909), as described in Olga Sobolev's chapter.

---

16 Aleksei Losev, *Dialektika mifa* (Moscow: Mysl', 2001).
17 Lotman, "Intelligentsiia i svoboda," 149; see also Gasparov, "Russkaia intelligentsiia," 20–27.

After October 1917 the Russian intelligentsia's development and its relationship with TJ split into two different paths: Soviet and foreign.

During the first post-revolutionary years, all traditional TJs of the Russian Empire—both conservative and liberal—were closed. The first Soviet decade saw the creation of the so-called "proletarian intelligentsia" and its press. Newspapers—as a wide-open resource of propaganda—were the most popular format for Soviet media. This was a period when the role of spiritual elite was played by Lenin's old radical intelligentsia. The new rulers faced the task of creating a new "Soviet class" of professionals, European-style specialists, "intellectuals"—a crucial process for all types of ideocracy.

New Soviet TJs—such as *New World* (Novyi mir, 1925-), *Star* (Zvezda, 1924-), and *Banner* (Znamia, 1931-)—became the main platforms of "correct" discourse for the Soviet intelligentsia. But the most important role was played by the magazine *Literary Critic* (Literaturnyi kritik, 1933–1940). *Literaturnyi kritik* was founded as a special TJ for intellectuals by the best thinkers of the Soviet Union: Pavel Yudin, director of the Institute of Philosophy; Elena Usievich, a close associate of Lenin; György Lukács; and others from Lunacharsky's circle in the Institute of Literature and Art of the Communist Academy. *Literaturnyi kritik* presented a contradictory type of TJ tasked with expressing the self-consciousness of intellectuals and, at the same time, providing official propaganda. The journal became a special platform for formulating the specific narrative of the *Soviet* intelligentsia, including its aesthetics of Socialist realism.

The text of *Literaturnyi kritik* was based on German classic philosophy, especially Hegel's philosophy of right, state, and rationality. The magazine analyzed the works of Kant and Hume and Russian classic literature, combining this with Marxism-Leninism. Lukács, an apologist of European Marxism, became one of the journal's primary essayists. Among his topics was a comparative analysis of Marxism and Nazism as incarnations of two antagonistic principles—the rational and the irrational. Mark Lipovetsky writes: "[T]he journal was in the mainstream of Stalin's transformation of Soviet ideology."[18] We can say that *Literaturnyi kritik* was one of the creators of the hypertext of the Soviet totalitarian state's new intellectual elite. Under censorship and ideological self-control, it presented the hypertext of the Soviet intelligentsia.

In this context, Walter Benjamin (1892–1940) offers interesting notes on the Soviet intelligentsia. His *Moscow Diary* describes the role of intellectuals in the

---

18 Mark Lipovetskii, "Zhurnal 'Literaturnyi kritik': Lukach i Lifshits. IFLI," in *Istoriia russkoi literaturnoi kritiki: Sovetskaia i postsovetskaia epokhi*, ed. E. Dobrenko and G. Tikhanov (Moscow: Novoe literaturnoe obozrenie, 2011), 280.

social process of Soviet totalitarianism: "The intellectual [in the Soviet Union] is, first, a functionary working in a censored, juridical or financial institute where he is fated to die; . . . he is involved in power. He represents the ruling class. Among the different organizations of these rulers, the Association of Proletarian Writers of the Soviet Union is the most powerful literary organization. It supports the idea of dictatorship in the sphere of creating art."[19] Benjamin accused the USSR of being a "restoration" regime, "promoting cultural values of the bourgeoisie in distorted primitive forms of imperialism."

The process of forming the new Soviet elite as a neo-bourgeoisie is described by Prof. Nicholas Timasheff, a famous American sociologist, in his book *The Great Retreat: The Growth and Decline of Communism in Russia* (1946).[20] He notes the process of forming a new Soviet bourgeoisie in the USSR in the 1930s. By separating the "proletarians of brainwork" from the mass working class, creating a special spiritual elite—with all financial and social benefits—this practice was part of the official policy of an ideological state. It was a paradoxical "incarnation" of one element of intelligentsia discourse—being "a spiritual leader."

But the structure of the "Soviet *intelligent*/Soviet TJ" consists of an explosive mechanism that leads us to the emergence of the spiritual elite's self-awareness. Having created TJ as a platform for intelligentsia self-expression, the authorities lost control over development of the narrative *intelligent* on its pages. The immanent character of the process of self-construction of narratives and formation of its own hypertexts—based on the principal of Absolute Freedom (freedom as free will, but not determined will)—allows the hypertext of TJ to escape total official control. The intelligentsia and its TJ operate as beholders of metaphysical freedom and inner moral ideals.

In the memoirs of Soviet dissidents we note: most of them do not describe dissidence as a political movement, but all of them write about *conscience*—a moral sense: "I can formulate my personal goal in a very simple way: to live in accordance with my conscience" (V. Voinovich); "we all were obedient to our conscience" (N. Gorbanevskaya); "the dissident movement was an absolutely spiritual affair and intertwined with our conscience" (Yu. Kim); "being an honest man" (S. Kovalev); and Andrei Sakharov: "What is the intelligentsia able to do? Nothing—except create an Ideal."[21] We see that the Russian intelligentsia credo is a strong *internal ethical rightness*.

---

19 Walter Benjamin, *Moskovskii dnevnik* (Moscow: Ad Marginem, 1997), 15.
20 Nicholas Timasheff, *The Great Retreat: The Growth and Decline of Communism in Russia* (New York: E. P. Dutton & Company, 1946).
21 Aleksandr Arkhangel'skii, ed., *Svobodnye liudi: Dissidentskoe dvizhenie v rasskazakh uchastnikov* (Moscow: Vremia, 2018), 16, 20, 27, 30.

"Moral honesty" and "conscience" become key words for the text of the late Soviet intelligentsia. Though under the Soviet regime the text of TJ partly provided an official ideology (including the aesthetics of socialist realism), journals delivered the text of independent thoughts and self-expression—and functioned as an open hypertext of classic TJ.

During the Thaw the pages of *Novyi mir* revealed changes. The liberal editorial board, led by Tvardovsky (1950–1954; 1958–1970), played a great role in the process of configuring the TJ's hypertext; the magazine gathered a circle of independent authors: Anna Akhmatova, Viktor Astafyev, Fyodor Abramov, and other "writer-environmentalists," Vasily Grossman, Vasyl Bykov, Fazil Iskander, Boris Pasternak, David Samoilov, Aleksandr Solzhenitsyn, Yury Trifonov, Nikolai Zabolotsky, Vladimir Voinovich, critics Vladimir Lakshin, Andrei Sinyavsky, Igor Vinogradov, and others. In literary circles of the time "one *tvard*" (from Tvard-ovsky) was used as a measure of moral courage. All aspects of intellectual context in politics, culture and literature were reflected on the pages of *Novyi mir*. Some members of this editorial board were fired after expressing support for the Prague Spring in 1968. At that time "the road map of the Soviet journal's world had been created," "the world of journals became multi-polar—as the national tradition demanded"—from conservative-official to liberal-oppositional, notes Sergei Chuprinin in his article "From Ideological NEP to the Great Schism."[22]

Znamia was another liberal Soviet journal. Founded as a publication of the Literary Association of the Red Army and Navy, it became a leading liberal TJ in the 1990s. Lev Losev noted that these "high-brow literary publications . . . are real defenders of culture from raging vulgarity."[23] Losev mentions that the narrative of the modern Russian TJ is marginal, independent not only from the narrative of official circles but also from the discourse of mass culture.

During the 1990s many discussions about the Russian intelligentsia took place on the uncensored pages of TJ. The intellectual elite tried to find new logistics for development of a free Russia, its path to democracy and the role of the intelligentsia in this democratic state—presumably a powerful and influential role. The narrative of TJ encompasses an immense number of political and economic issues. The hypertext of TJ becomes more open, including narratives from newspapers and *samizdat*. During perestroika *Novyi mir*'s circulation rose to 2,660,000 copies—an enormous amount even for newspapers, never mind thick journals.[24]

---

22 Sergei Chuprinin, "Ot 'ideologicheskogo nepa' k 'velikomu raskolu,'" in idem, *Ottepel' kak nepovinovenie* (Moscow: Novoe literaturnoe obozrenie, 2023), 16.
23 See Lev Losev's article, in *Nashe znamia: 1931–2001* (Moscow: Znamia, 2001), 581.
24 "Novyi Mir," Wikipedia, https://en.wikipedia.org/wiki/Novy_Mir.

At the beginning of the 2000s, as a new Russian elite with a clear narrative of consumerism was forming, the situation for TJ as intellectual publications became difficult.[25] Statements like "TJ is dead" became popular—as well as the declaration that the intelligentsia itself was dead. Sergei Chuprinin noted:

> In the 2000s all discussions about the past, present, and future of our Fatherland moved to the Internet, social networks, and the city streets . . . we want to be the Exhibition—keeping all the quality of a universal *magazine* of contemporary Russian literature and public thoughts . . . today they seem to be in need of our support, analysis, and protection.[26]

In the political context of the increasing power of authoritarianism in Russia, Natalia Ivanova wrote about *déjà vu* in modern Russia:

> When the country was literary-centripetal we knew that if *Znamia* published *Heart of a Dog,* . . . and *Novyi mir* published *Doctor Zhivago,* and 'reading Russia' read these texts—everything had changed. . . . [Today] . . . billionaires sing Soviet songs with nostalgia and satisfaction . . . 'Stalinist' modern style is in demand . . . a reverse mechanism has been pushed . . . the situation for the *intelligent* part of society has worsened.[27]

The theme of "the forbidden intelligentsia" has become especially important for present-day Russia. There are two possible interpretations: the insolvency of the whole intelligentsia text and its "artificial" discourse, or isolation because of important changes in society. In the first case, the death of the intelligentsia is inevitable; in the second—the intelligentsia becomes marginal. There were numerous articles revising this narrative on the pages of *Znamia* during the 2000s. For example, Aleksandr Podrabinek's "Dissidenty" gave a final verdict: go "from clear active opposition to stoicism and inner spiritual resistance."[28]

---

25 Margarita Novak, "Ideologiia konsumerizma v massovoi kul'ture sovremennoi Rossii: filosofsko-kul'turologicheskii analiz" (PhD diss., Belgorod State University, Belgorod, 2012), 166.
26 Chuprinin uses the English word "magazine," which gives rise to a play on words: "the Exhibition" is "the State Exhibition of Achievements of the National Economy," "magazine" (*magazin*) in Russian means "a store"; thus *Znamia* is a magazine that functions as an exhibition/storefront presenting the best achievements in literature. S. Chuprinin, "'Znamia' v 2014 g.: Deklaratsiia o namereniiakh," *Znamia* 1 (2014): 3.
27 Natal'ia Ivanova, "Drugaia zhizn' v SSSR," *Znamia* 11 (2013): 4.
28 Aleksandr Podrabinek, "Dissidenty," *Znamia* 11 (2014): 5.

Sergei Erlikh analyzed fundamental changes in Russian society in the mid-2000s in his philosophical essay "Russian Memory," about the legitimacy of newly elected authorities in the context of metaphysical aspects of the phenomenon of memory.[29] He wrote about "the master-class of memory work from the Kremlin," and "the conspiratorial version of patriotism" after the "uncultured shock" of the 1990s: "To strengthen its power a political regime tries to create a picture of the past that defends the present. . . . Control over memory is a guarantor of the stability of government in the epoch of communicative civilization"; the text of the intelligentsia must achieve marginality in modern Russian society. Thus, the text of TJ also becomes marginal.

At the same time, comparative analysis of the texts of *intelligent* and intellectual began to be published on the pages of TJ. In Likhachev's "Letter . . .": "Is the intelligentsia a phenomenon of West or East? The answer is in whether we see Russia as a Western county or an Eastern one. Without a doubt Russia is a part of Europe in its religion and culture." Vittorio Strada, an Italian intellectual, wrote: "The Russian intelligentsia and European intellectual had parallel but differentiated development."[30] The so-called "Russian intelligentsia" was a child of the European Enlightenment.

We have already seen that these two hypertexts are almost identical. Numerous definitions of the intellectual can be found in dictionaries, for example: "An intellectual is a person who engages in critical thinking, research, and reflection about the reality of society, who may also propose solutions for the normative problems of society, and thus gains authority as a public intellectual" (Wikipedia); "[a person] relating to ability to think and understand things, especially complicated ideas" (Cambridge).

In the TJ *Iron Ration* (Neprikosnovennyi zapas),[31] Jürgen Habermas wrote: "The modern type of the *intellectual* (person) is quite different from the previous ones that drown in the past. After 1945, intellectuals—Camus and Sartre, Adorno and Marcuse, Max Frisch and Heinrich Böll— . . . all respond to events on their own initiatives—without any orders from party or collective decision; they use their own professional knowledge openly and outside the sphere of their affiliation;" "They do not pretend to have the status of an elite; they have no other legitimations except the role of a citizen of the democratic state."[32]

---

29 Sergei Erlikh, "Russian Memory," *Znamia* 1 (2015): 140.
30 Vittorio Strada, "V svete kontsa, v preddvestii nachala," *Kontinent* 72 (1992): 213, 217.
31 *Neprikosnovennyi zapas* is a publication of Novoe literaturnoe obozrenie publishing house. The magazine was founded in 1998.
32 Iu. Khabermas, "Pervym pochuiat' vazhnoe. Chto otlichaet intellektuala," *Neprikosnovennyi zapas* 47 (2006): 7.

In modern communicative society the traditional type of an *intellectual* was transformed. Habermas connects these metamorphoses to general changes in the communicative society: the collapsed "grand narrative" and "language games": "The public sphere became less formalized and its traditional social roles more differentiated." Old-style intellectuals went out into the wide-open space of democracy; the new postmodern society would be a collaboration of different smaller communities; these communities would not suppress one another, and their narratives would not pretend to universal, powerful legitimacy.[33] Thus the pretensions of logocentric narrative as the universal will come to an end; "language games" will neutralize the "power" component of the hypertext of intellectuals and become the general structuring principle.

The revolutionary changes in contemporary civilization ratified the marginal role of intellectuals:

> Under these conditions intellectuals' statements have lost the ability to motivate public attention . . . though we cannot say that the electronic revolution in mass media has destroyed the stage for elite performances of conceited intellectuals. . . . [The audience] no longer consists of 'viewers'—it consists of potential participants of this dialogue in which everyone is able to speak and listen to others. The ideal type of such a discussion is the exchange of arguments.[34]

At the beginning of the twenty-first century the Russian TJs clearly transcend the limits of traditional studies that place the phenomenon of the intelligentsia inside the context of wide-ranging trends in modern civilization. TJs have initiated the comparative analysis of the text of "the Russian intelligentsia" and "Western intellectuals." In this context the journal *Continent* (Kontinent) plays an important role.

Created in France in 1974 by the dissident writer Vladimir Maksimov, *Kontinent* declared the theme of the intelligentsia its key subject. The journal made no distinction between the Russian intelligentsia and Western intellectuals: "We speak in the name of the continent of culture of all countries of Eastern

---

33 Referring to Lyotard, metanarratives have lost their force of legitimization after catastrophes (the Holocaust, etc.) in the twentieth century. See: J. Lyotard, *La condition postmoderne* (Paris: Minuit, 1979); cf. the Russian translation: Zh.-F. Liotard, *Sostoianiie postmoderna*, trans. N. A. Shmatko (St. Petersburg: Aleteiia, 1998), 160; J. Lyotard, *Tombeau de l'intellectuel et autres papiers* (Paris: Galilée, 1984).
34 Khabermas, "Pervym pochuiat' vazhnoe," 9.

Europe. . . . Eastern and Western Europe present two halves of the continent, and we have to hear and understand each other before it is too late."[35]

In the 1990s *Kontinent* was published in post-Soviet Russia; the magazine occupied the special niche of an intellectual center for studying general problems of democracy in Eastern Europe: "*Kontinent*, the journal of the Opposition and anti-communist Resistance, will be a publication of the spiritual Renaissance and Creation of New Russia," a journal of "wide and free discussions on all the main problems . . . of our civil society and our Church, on power structures and the deepest layers of social-economic life and the spheres of spiritual aspirations," studying questions of "the national consciousness of all nations."[36]

The journal's strategy included analysis of the relationship between the West and Russia: "It is impossible to understand the cultural and political history of the new Russia without Western contributions and exchange on both sides." The journal planned to "move out from the binomial opposition of Russia–Europe" in the modern global world. The circle of *Kontinent* outlined two tasks for the Russian intelligentsia: "renationalization and re-Europeanization" and "liberation from Russian-centripetal and Intelligentsia-centripetal ideology."[37]

There were numerous discussions on this topic; for example, a conversation between Igor Vinogradov, the editor in chief, and Vyacheslav Ivanov (Stanford University). Ivanov's idea of forming a new spiritual elite—"The intelligentsia is a stalker in the noosphere (the sphere of human consciousness and mental activity in relation to evolution)"—gained Vinogradov's support: "The real function and devotion of this . . . 'little nation' inside the big nation—is creating the highest spiritual-ethical national standards and a criterion of the historical national existence and transforming it to the consciousness of society."[38]

Political opposition to the journal was growing in the context of the developing authoritarian regime in present-day Russia. The magazine was one of the first Russian publications to formulate the main threats of the 2000s: authoritarianism, "Soviet" tendencies in domestic policy, and creation of a new "Putin-style" political and cultural elite.[39] *Kontinent* turns us to analysis of the TJ

---

35 "Ot redaktsii," *Kontinent* 1 (1974): 6.
36 I. Vinogradov, "K chitateliam 'Kontinenta,'" *Kontinent* 72 (1992): 9.
37 Strada, "V svete kontsa," 212.
38 Viacheslav Ivanov, "'U menia net segodnia osobykh strakhov po povodu budushchego Rossii v XXI veke," conversation with Igor' Vinogradov, *Kontinent* 106 (2000): 267, 269.
39 See Larisa Piiasheva, "Nachinaia s avgusta 1998 goda v Rossii proizoshel perekhod vlasti v ruki spetssluzhb," *Kontinent* 147 (2011): 216–226; Igor' Kliamkin and Tat'iana Kutkovets, "Kremlevskaia shkola politologii," *Kontinent* 131 (2007): 144–175; Andrei Illarionov, "Slovo i delo," *Kontinent* 134 (2007): 83–147, 136 (2008): 159–215; Aleksandr Pumpianskii, "Delo Khodorkovskogo," *Kontinent* 146 (2010): 70–115.

in exile, to the hypertext of TJ in the Russian diaspora as the clearest sample of the traditional classic narrative of TJ in modern times, as a text of independent thoughts and uncensored literature.

There were numerous journals in exile in the twentieth century: *Contemporary Notes* (Sovremennye zapiski, 1920–1940), *Renaissance* (Vozrozhdenie, 1925–1940; 1949–1974), *New City* (Novyi grad, 1931–1939), *Herald of the Russian Christian Movement* (Vestnik RSKhD, 1925–1994), *Facets* (Grani, 1946–1991), *The New Review* (Novyi zhurnal, 1942-), *Gnosis* (1978–2006), *22* (1978–2017), *Sintaksis* (1978–2001), and others.

During World War II all Russophone TJ in Europe were closed. But new publications appeared in the first post-war years, in the DP camps. For example, in the Schleißheim DP camp the magazine *New World: Magazine of International Journalism, Literature, and Humor* (Novyi mir: zhurnal inostrannoi publitsistiki, khudozhestvennoi literatury i iumora) was printed. *Sowing* (Posev, circulation of 1200) was published in November 1945, in the Mönchehof DP camp.[40] Aleksandr Kornilov wrote:

> The best of [the intelligentsia's] representatives could give hundreds of refugees 1) political thought alternative to that of the Soviet regime in the USSR; 2) systems—educational and national upbringing; 3) striking artistic events; 4) a publishing network; 5) new literature.... The history of the influence of the post-war Russian intelligentsia on the "titular society" of its new homeland has not yet been systematized... without a doubt we have to admit that the DP period was an important phase in the process of consolidation of the Russian immigration—as well as in forming the Russian intelligentsia abroad.[41]

The creation of TJs in exile resulted from the efforts of many multi-ethnic Russophone émigrés—the spiritual elite of the Diaspora. Though "Russia Abroad" was actualized as an object of ethnic culture, this is a sample of the free evolution of the classic "Russian text," including "the Russian intelligentsia," in the intercultural context of the European parent-text. The phenomenon of the "émigré-intelligent" has not been studied, though TJs outside Russia reflect the whole spectrum of this discourse.

---

[40] "DP" refers to "displaced persons." See Emmanuil Shtein, *Russkaia pechat' lagerei 'Di-Pi'* (Orange: Antiquary, 1993), 137.

[41] Aleksandr Kornilov, "Rossiiskaia intelligentsiia i mir peremeshchennykh lits stran Europy," *Intelligentsia i mir* 1 (2011): 15.

The New Review (Novyi zhurnal) was founded by Mark Aldanov and Mikhail Tsetlin, writers from the "first wave" of Russian emigration, in New York in 1942. It was Ivan Bunin's idea to recreate the Parisian *Sovremennye zapiski* (1920–1940). In the most dramatic war years without European Russian journals, the editors wrote: "This fact increases our responsibility and imposes a duty that previous magazines never had: . . . to open the pages of *Novyi Zhurnal* to writers of all styles and opinions."[42] This fundamental pluralism was the key to the journal's longevity. Among its authors were Ivan Bunin, Aleksandra Tolstaya, Vladimir Nabokov, Georgy Adamovich, Georgy Ivanov, and other writers, political activists, philosophers, and historians. The Russian DP intelligentsia presented a whole spectrum of creative inhabitants: novelists, poets, essayists, thinkers—Sergei Maksimov, Nikolai Ulyanov, Boris Filippov, Olga Anstei, Ivan Elagin, and others. Almost all Russian laureates of the Nobel Prize in Literature have been among the magazine's authors: Ivan Bunin, Boris Pasternak, Aleksandr Solzhenitsyn, Joseph Brodsky, and Svetlana Alexievich.

The narrative of *Novyi Zhurnal* could be described as: Literature—Russia—Freedom—Emigration. The liberation of Russia was declaimed as the mission of the multi-ethnic Russophone émigrés. "Freedom" was perceived as a person's immanent right and the basic component of the text "intelligent." "Immigration" was interpreted as the realization of freedom. Roman Gul, then editor in chief of *Novyi Zhurnal*, writer and political activist, wrote in his three-volume memoirs of emigration: "Without any doubts I choose freedom because the Motherland without freedom is not the Motherland; whereas freedom without the Motherland—though very hard, maybe even dreadful—is still *My Freedom.*"[43]

The main task of *Novyi Zhurnal* was to give its readers new conceptions and new models of intellectual community and to uphold the mission of the émigré community: to preserve and develop the best Russian cultural traditions in order to bring them back to liberated Russia.

Most DPs—the magazine's readers and writers—presented a discourse of the so-called "Soviet man." Thus, the pages of NR reflected the complicated process of converting the "Soviet" narrative into a new text. The difference of the two narratives—"Soviet intelligentsia" and "Old Russian intelligentsia"—appeared on all levels, starting with language as one component of mentality. Linguistic discussions were important for literary-centripetal Russian cultural discourse. Other themes reflected on the pages of the journal were education, the relationship between the Diaspora and the "titular nation" of the new homeland, Soviet aggression, literature and ethnic culture, preservation of national legacy, religion, and so on.

---

42 "Ot redaktsionnoi gruppy," *Novyi zhurnal* 1 (1942).
43 Roman Gul', *Ia unes Rossiiu*, vol. 1, *Rossiia v Germanii* (New York: Most, 1981), 184.

From the very beginning *Novyi Zhurnal* interacted with Western intellectuals—writers, journalists and thinkers—including émigré-representatives of academia: Professors Mikhail Karpovich (Harvard), Nicholas Timasheff (Fordham University), Pitirim Sorokin (Harvard), Igor Chinnov (University of Pittsburgh), Yury Ivask (University of Massachusetts and others), Leonid Rzhevsky (NYU), Boris Filippov (American University), Nikolai Ulyanov (Yale), and others. There were also American and European intellectuals among the authors—George Kennan, Thomas Whitney, John Glad, Rene Guerra, and others.

Many of *Novyi Zhurnal*'s texts treat problems of dictatorship, ideocracy, and general ideas of socialism. The intelligentsia of the Diaspora was one of the greatest contributors to the international anti-communist and anti-Soviet struggle. In the Diaspora the traditional oppositional hypertext of the intelligentsia was transformed into political resistance to the Soviet regime—paradoxically, the intelligentsia-émigrés turned into strong supporters of the governments and the official policies of their new homelands.

Based on the conception of integrated Russian culture inside and outside Russia, *Novyi Zhurnal* published uncensored literature from the USSR: chapters from *Doctor Zhivago* by Boris Pasternak, poems by Maximilian Voloshin, novels by Lidiya Chukovskaya, and others. The name of Varlam Shalamov came to world literature from the pages of *Novyi Zhurnal*. The theme of the GULag appeared in the magazine with the post-war immigration. Sergei Maksimov was one of the first writers to describe the Soviet GULag in his novels.

Nikolai Ulyanov, a post-war émigré, noted in 1951:

> The immigration had all legal grounds to think that it had a monopoly on Russian culture. . . . For three decades Russian professors have contributed their brilliant papers to Western universities. . . . In Soviet Russia, a hidden, unspoken but very clear feeling was alive: the center of Russian culture is abroad. . . . The whole civilized world understood the mission of the emigration as a struggle of culture against chaos.[44]

We see that the questions of freedom as the inner substance of culture and preservation of highbrow spiritual traditions were vital for émigré-*intelligenty* with their dramatic Soviet past.[45]

---

44 Nikolai Ul'ianov, "Kul'tura i emigratsiia," *Novyi zhurnal* 28 (1952): 261–272.
45 *Novyi Zhurnal* presented numerous opinions about the *intelligent*-émigré. For example, Gennadii Eikalovich, "Fenomen intelligentsii," *Novyi Zhurnal* 155 (1984); Naum Korzhavin,

Novyi Zhurnal's "Online Social Supplement" (2017–2018) was the journal's response to changes in modern society.[46] Its main theme was "the intelligentsia in communicative society." On this topic, independent Russian and Western intellectuals—writers, journalists—created important original inter-hypertext with a wide-open structure. The pages of NR—"physical" or "virtual"—present a history of the self-consciousness of the *intelligent* in his or her self-developing narrative.

The logo-centripetal (word-based) text of modern culture is impulsively shifting into image-centripetal narrative in the twenty-first century. Modern society uses an "external" virtual narrative in reality; both texts—"physical" and "virtual"—are mixed and interacting. This new unexplored process must be adopted by the texts of the intelligentsia and TJ.

The phenomenon "TJ in emigration" proves that the universal nature of the "intelligentsia" text can reproduce itself in an external, nonnative context. The marginality of intelligenty reflects the immanent freedom that allows them to survive and realize the text in different cultural systems. Some components of this text—love of power and strong ethics—mutually compensate for each other.

This allows us to speak of the intelligentsia's ability to reproduce its text under any circumstances of mass culture. A spiritual elite is always small, always marginal, but constantly the main creator of culture. The *intelligent*'s narrative demands the text of TJ as an adequate form for its self-expression, self-consciousness, and self-development. In a new communicative civilization TJ's own text could be presented in traditional, "paper" formats, or in "virtual"—or in any other forms in the future, but the text "TJ" will continue to be upheld by the hypertext of the "intelligentsia."

Bibliography

Arkhangel'skii, Aleksandr. *Svobodnye liudi. Dissidentskoe dvizhenie v rasskazakh uchastnikov*. Moscow: Vremia, 2018.

Benjamin, Walter. *Moskovskii dnevnik*. Moscow: Ad Marginem, 1997.

Chuprinin, Sergei. "Ot 'ideologicheskogo nepa' k 'velikomu raskolu.'" In idem, *Ottepel' kak nepovinovenie*, 9–18. Moscow: Novoe literaturnoe obozrenie, 2023.

"Epokha dlinoiu v zhizn'," *Novyi Zhurnal* 240 (2005); Ernst Neizvestnyi, "Shest' monologov," *Novyi Zhurnal* 249 (2007); Mikhail Epstein, "Russkii iazyk: Sistema i svoboda," *Novyi zhurnal* 250 (2008); Andrei Ivanov, "Pisatel' i tolpa," *Novyi zhurnal* 277 (2014).

46 See the journal's website at www.newreviewworld.com

Crosthwaite, Paul, ed. *Criticism, Crisis, and Contemporary Narrative: Textual Horizons in an Age of Global Risk.* New York: Routledge, 2011.

Dostoevskii, Fedor. "Ob"iavlenie o podpiske na zhurnal 'Vremia' na 1861 g." In idem, *Sobranie sochinenii v tridtsati tomakh*, vol. 18, 35–40. Leningrad: Nauka, 1978.

Gasparov, Mikhail. "Russkaia intelligentsiia kak otvodok evropeiskoi kul'tury." In *Russkaia intelligentsiia i zapadnyi intellektualizm: Istoriia i tipologiia*, edited by B. A. Uspenskii, 20–27. Moscow: O.G.I., 1999.

Gul', Roman. *Ia unes Rossiiu. Apologiia russkoi emigratsii.* Volume 1: *Rossiia v Germanii.* New York: Most, 1981.

Ivanov, Viacheslav. "'U menia net segodnia osobykh strakhov po povodu budushchego Rossii v XXI veke." Conversation with Igor' Vinogradov." *Kontinent* 106 (2000): 254–270.

Ivanov-Razumnik, Razumnik. "Chto takoe 'intelligentsiia'?" In *Intelligentsiia—vlast'—narod. Russkie istochniki sovremennoi sotsial'noi mysli: Antologiia*, edited by L. Novikova and I. Sizemskaia, 73–80. Moscow: Nauka, 1992.

Kornilov, Aleksandr. "Rossiiskaia intelligentsiia i mir peremeshchennych lits stran Evropy." *Intelligentsiia i mir* 1 (2011): 19–36.

Lakshin, Vladimir. "Phenomen 'tolstyi zhurnal' v Rossii kak iavlenie natsional'noi kul'tury." In idem, *Berega kul'tury*, edited by Svetlana Lakshina, 23–25. Moscow: MIROS, 1994.

Likhachev, Dmitrii. "O russkoi intelligentsii: pis'mo v redaktsiiu." *Novyi mir* 2 (1993): 3–9.

Lipovetskii, Mark. "Journal 'Literaturnyi kritik': Lukach i Lifshits. IFLI." *Istoriia russkoi literaturnoi kritiki: sovetskaia i postsovetskaia epokhi*, edited by E. Dobrenko and G. Tikhanov, 212–214. Moscow: NLO, 2011.

Losev, Aleksei. *Dialektika mifa.* Moscow: Mysl', 2001.

Loshakov, Aleksandr. "Sverkhtext: problema tselostnosti, printsipy modelirovaniia." *Izvestiia Rossiiskogo gosudarstvennogo pedagogicheskogo universiteta* 66 (2008): 100–109.

Lotman, Mikhail. "Intelligentsiia i svoboda (k analizu intelligentskogo diskursa)." In *Russkaia intelligentsiia i zapadnyi intellektualizm: Istoriia i tipologiia*, edited by B. A. Uspenskii, 122–149. Moscow: O.G.I., 1999.

Lyotard, Jean-François. *La condition postmoderne.* Paris: Les éditions de minuit, 1979.

———. *Tombeau de l'intellectuel et autres papiers.* Paris: Galilée, 1984.

——— [Liotar, Zhan-Fransua]. *Sostoianie postmoderna*, translated by N. A. Shmatko. St. Petersburg: Aleteiia, 1998.

Martin, Wallace. *Recent Theories of Narrative*. Ithaka, NY: Cornell UP, 1986.

Novak, Margarita. *Ideologiia konsumerizma v massovoi kul'ture sovremennoi Rossii: filosofsko-kul'turologicheskii analiz*. PhD diss., Belgorod State University, Belgorod, 2012.

Petrušonis, Vytautas. *Respectation of the Locus' Cultural Identity in Architectural Design*. Vilnius: Tekhnika, 2004.

Pozin, Mikhail, and Emmanuil Shtein. *Russkaia pechat' lagerei "Di-Pi."* Orange: Antiquary, 1993.

Pustovaia, V. *Diskussia ob intelligentsii v literaturnykh zhurnalakh postsovetskoi epokhi: logika transformatsii poniatia*. PhD diss., MSU School of Journalism, Moscow, 2008.

Raeff, Marc. *Russia Abroad: A Cultural History of the Russian Emigration, 1919–1939*. Oxford: Oxford UP, 1990.

Snigireva, Tatiana, and Aleksei Podchinenov. "Tolstyi zhurnal v Rossii kak tekst i gipertekst." *Izvestiia Ural'skogo gosudarstvennogo universiteta* 13 (1999): 5–13.

Strada, Vittorio. "V svete kontsa, v preddvestii nachala." *Kontinent* 72 (1992): 210–226.

Timasheff, Nicholas. *The Great Retreat: The Growth and Decline of Communism in Russia*. New York: E. P. Dutton & Company, 1946.

Toporov, Vladimir. *Peterburgskii tekst russkoi literatury*. St. Petersburg: Iskusstvo, 2003.

Tynianov, Iurii. "Zhurnal, kritik, chitatel' i pisatel'." In idem, *Poetika. Istoriia literatury, kino*, 147–149. Moscow: Nauka, 1977.

A Romantic Ironist or a New Intellectual? Tatyana Tolstaya and Her Critique of the Russian Intelligentsia

Alexandra Smith

Introduction

Following the collapse of the Soviet Union, the legacy of Marxist utopianism has become a debated subject among Russian intellectuals. With the post-Soviet revival of interest in Russian Orthodoxy and Russian religious philosophy of the 1880s-1930s, the Russian intelligentsia's image became tarnished. Many Russians grew scornful of the intelligentsia's radical ideological beliefs, which had laid the ground for establishment of the Bolshevik government in Russia in 1917. Indeed, the Russian intelligentsia is generally associated with utopian thinking. Katerina Clark defines it as "a self-proclaimed interest group that . . . always considered themselves a unique and indigenous body with privileged access to truth."[1] Richard Pipes describes this group as "intellectuals craving

---

1 Katerina Clark, "The King is Dead, Long Live the King: Intelligentsia Ideology in Transition," paper presented at the conference "Russia at the End of the Twentieth Century: Culture and Its Horizons in Politics and Society," Stanford University, October 1998, 1–31, here 3; accessed July 11, 2017, https://web.stanford.edu/group/Russia20/volumepdf/clark_fin99.pdf

for political power"[2] and radical advocates of the enlightenment who criticised views about the accidental nature of history and "transcendental moral values."[3]

Caryl Emerson affirms that many famous populists and anarchists came from the ranks of the Russian intelligentsia. The kind of "quirky loners like Leo Tolstoy" and "intuitive liberals like Anton Chekhov," maintains Emerson, were outside their ranks.[4] Emerson welcomes the critical evaluation of the intelligentsia by post-Soviet intellectuals who find "pre-visions of totalitarianism and surrealism" in the works of the intelligentsia.[5] She also describes "concerned Russian social thinkers" in the early 1990s as "radical ironists."[6] In Emerson's view, such an ironic vision, mixed with "a surprising fatalism, superstition, a willingness to integrate the eclectic," is rooted in the rich intellectual tradition advocated by many Russian writers and thinkers.[7] Vadim Shkolnikov, furthermore, links the emergence of Russian intelligentsia to the development of realism. Shkolnikov aptly points out that the notion of intelligentsia does not have specific temporal boundaries and that Russian nineteenth-century intelligentsia acquired a mythic image due to specific social and historical factors. He writes: "[I]n Russia, in the absence of a politically and economically powerful bourgeoisie, realism evolved as the self-reflection and tragic drama of *the intelligentsia as subject*." Shkolnikov notes that, "within the context of Russian cultural history, the very concept of 'reality' and the mentality of a 'realist' took on additional social significance, as key mythologemes in the discourse and mythical narrative of the intelligentsia."[8] Inna Kochetkova suggests that the intelligentsia myth has been significantly transformed since the 1860s. She describes the core element of the intelligentsia myth as "a belief in the possibility of human perfection." While the intelligentsia myth was often used to secure "the dominance of some groups over others," it continues to influence many "identity projects of Russian intellectuals" today.[9]

Zygmunt Bauman's examination of the role of intellectuals in modern and postmodern societies links the term "intellectual" to the legacy of the

---

2 Richard Pipes, *The Russian Revolution* (New York: Knopf Doubleday Publishing Group, 1991), 126.
3 Ibid., 140.
4 Caryl Emerson, "*And the Demons Entered into the Swine*: The Russian Intelligentsia and Post-Soviet Religious Thought," *Cross Currents* 43, no. 2 (1993): 184–202, here 185.
5 Ibid., 199.
6 Ibid.
7 Ibid., 200.
8 Vadim Shkolnikov, "Sociality—or Death: Belinskii's Phenomenological Realism and the Emergence of Russian Intelligentsia," *The Russian Review* 81 (2022): 683–704, here 684.
9 Inna Kochetkova, *The Myth of the Russian Intelligentsia: Old Intellectuals in the New Russia* (London: Routledge, 2009), 164.

Enlightenment. According to Bauman, this term was coined at the beginning of the twentieth century with the view to recapture and reassert the function of the values rooted in the Enlightenment in the production and dissemination of knowledge in the global context. Bauman explains that the term was applied to journalists, writers, artists, and public figures who felt that "it was their moral responsibility . . . to interfere directly with the political processes through influencing the minds of the nation and moulding the actions of its political leaders."[10] He distinguishes between the two different contexts in which modern intellectuals operate. While "the typically modern view of the world is one of essentially ordered totality," Bauman affirms, "the typically post-modern view of the world is . . . one of unlimited number of models of order." As Bauman points out, in the postmodern context, each model is "generated by a relatively autonomous set of practices."[11]

Ludmilla Ulitskaya, one of the most significant Russian writers today, exemplifies Bauman's vision of postmodern intellectuals well because she is concerned with the notion of diversity and the deconstruction of metanarratives. Elizabeth Skomp and Benjamin Sutcliffe locate the popularity of Ulitskaya's work as her strongly pronounced compassion towards her characters. They explain: "Ulitskaya's status as author, *intelligentka*, and enemy of Putin permits her to introduce both a serious critique of the past and the need for tolerance in the present."[12] In her essay "Reading as a Heroic Feat," published in English in 2018, Ulitskaya describes the death of her friend who wanted to understand during her final hours of life what the term "intelligentsia" signified to Ulitskaya. In reply to this conversation, Ulitskaya writes:

> This vanishing breed is hard to pin down. The intelligentsia has included those leaning toward Europe and enamored with the East, liberals and conservatives, believers and atheists, workaholics and idlers, yet always humanists, the kind we meet on the pages of our beloved classics. Which suggests another trait common to the Russia intelligentsia—reading as an absolute necessity.[13]

---

10 Zygmunt Bauman, *Legislators and Interpreters: On Modernity, Post-modernity and Intellectuals* (Cambridge: Polity Press, 1987), 1.
11 Ibid., 3–4.
12 Elizabeth A. Skomp and Benjamin M. Sutcliffe, *Ludmila Ulitskaya and the Art of Tolerance* (Madison: U of Wisconsin Press, 2015), 171.
13 Lyudmila Ulitskaya, "Reading as a Heroic Feat: The Intelligentsia and The Uncensored Literature," *Russian Journal of Communication* 10, nos. 2–3 (2018): 262–272, here 262.

Ulitskaya's essay exemplifies Shkolnikov's belief in the intricate link between Russian intelligentsia and realism. As Shkolnikov maintains, "Belinskii's realist agenda was always focused on fostering the development of a distinct type of reading public—which can be conceived as an 'imagined community.'" Belinsky's vision of educated readers presupposes "a sense of unity beyond the sphere of actual personal interaction."[14]

In her essay on Russian intellectuals, Ulitskaya talks about many Soviet readers who were able to read forbidden books, including some poems by Mandelshtam. She defines their mode of reading as "a risky endeavour" and "a heroic deed," because "it required courage, or at least willingness to keep at bay one's fear."[15] She writes about her experience of reading Mandelshtam's poetry thus: "I gasped when I read that passage, for neither I nor my friends suspected that fear and writing were so closely connected in Mandelshtam. We, the Soviet readers, felt the shadow of that fear fall over us as well."[16] Similarly, Tatyana Tolstaya, another famous contemporary writer, advocates the importance of reading as a tool of developing one's critical thinking. The present chapter will analyze Tolstaya's ongoing reassessment of the image of the Russian intelligentsia. Considering Emerson's suggestion that using romantic irony offers artists the possibility of replacing the intelligentsia's teleological vision of history with the creative exploration of an unpredictable present, I will examine Tolstaya's interest in new reading communities.

Tatyana Tolstaya (born 1951) had her literary debut in 1983. In 1987 she published her collection of stories *On the Golden Porch* (Na zolotom kryl′tse sideli). Tolstaya's playful mix of the fantastic and the real in her early stories was welcomed by critics as an innovative writing mode. As Norman Shneidman notes, her stories from the 1980s are full of "disillusioned dreamers" and "social misfits." In Shneidman's view, while Tolstaya's fiction is free from ideological messages, it expresses "a social concern for the underdog and for those who are abused by nature and life."[17] In the 1990s Tolstaya became more preoccupied with the historical past. Many of her characters set in the 2000s were modelled on "real-life prototypes."[18] Yet Tolstaya's novel *The Slynx* (Kys′, 2000) is of hybrid genre: it combines elements of science fiction, dystopia, Russian folklore and *skaz*. *The Slynx* has similarities with Vladimir Sorokin's dystopian *Blue Lard*

---

14 Shkolnikov, "Sociality or—Death," 686.
15 Ulitskaya, "Reading as a Heroic Feat," 263.
16 Ibid., 263.
17 Norman N. Shneidman, *Russian Literature, 1995–2002: On the Threshold of a New Millennium* (Toronto: U of Toronto Press, 2004), 124.
18 Ibid., 124.

(Goluboe salo, 1999), which distorts the images of Russian writers in a distant future. Both narratives express a sense of anxiety about the survival of Russian literature going forward. "The conclusion of the narrative," writes Shneidman about *The Slynx*, "points to the fact that major natural disasters, as well as dictatorial oppression, usually create havoc in the personal lives of the people, but rarely eliminate their thirst for knowledge, enlightenment, and freedom."[19] Yet the novel depicts Kudeyar Kudeyarych's totalitarian behaviour in a pessimistic way: he assumes power by pretending to be a democrat, but later he becomes a dictator. Shneidman sees the novel as an important contribution to contemporary debates about totalitarianism.

In the 2000s-2020s Tolstaya moved from using fantasy and folklore in her stories to discussing present-day concerns. She has become increasingly interested in autobiographical writing, too. The present chapter will focus on the representation of Russian intellectuals in her works. It will also examine Tolstaya's self-representation as a public intellectual in her stories and in media of the 2010s-2020s.

According to John Givens, Tolstaya's evolution as a writer can be divided into three periods. He describes the 1980s as the "meteoric rise" of Tolstaya as a writer. That decade is followed by a decade of creative silence and residence abroad, where she taught at American universities and worked on her novel *The Slynx*. Givens identifies a third period with Tolstaya co-hosting the Russian talk show *The School of Malicious Gossip* (Shkola zlosloviia).[20] In the last twenty years Tolstaya has also written many stories and essays based on personal experiences.[21] Today Tolstaya acts as a public intellectual and ironist who keeps a safe distance from the image of the Russian intelligentsia shaped during the Thaw period. She also uses social media for self-promotion.

The Image of the Russian Intelligentsia in Tolstaya's Fiction

Despite Tolstaya's extensive criticism of the Russian intelligentsia in her works, some critics think that her rebellious mindset recalls the characteristics of the liberal intelligentsia as it emerged in the post-Stalin period. Helena Goscilo

---

19 Ibid., 125.
20 John Givens, "Tatyana Tolstaya, Mikhail Bulgakov," *Russian Studies in Literature* 51, no. 3 (2015): 1–4, here 1.
21 See, for example: Tat'iana Tolstaia, *Legkie miry: Povesti, rasskazy, esse* (Moscow: Ast, 2014); eadem, *Voilochnyi vek* (Moscow: Ast, 2015).

describes Tolstaya as a typical representative of "the middle-aged Russian intelligentsia."[22] Vladislav Zubok labels the group of Russians who were active in the 1960s-1970s as "Zhivago's children." In his opinion, the idea of an intelligentsia linked to the goal of national self-determination was alien to them because they lived "in constant fear of resurgent Russian nationalism."[23]

According to Zubok, "the centrality of culture and art in the social life of their people" was one of the main concerns of "Zhivago's children." They dreamed of building a fairer society "based on noncapitalist foundations," so that the drive for material goods could be overcome.[24] Tolstaya's story "Okkervil River" (Reka Okkervil', 1999) re-evaluates this trend. It humorously depicts an eccentric collector of old records who promotes the cult of one former diva in a quasi-religious manner. As Deming Brown notes, Tolstaya's short fiction often portrays eccentric and lonely people "presented in a humorous, if sympathetic, light."[25] Her tendency to focus on eccentric individuals rather than on a collective identity might reflect the way many people of Tolstaya's generation "lashed out at the *shestidesiatniki* from a postmodernist position."[26]

Criticism of "Zhivago's children" is also felt strongly in Tolstaya's collection of stories *Okkervil River* (2005), which contains many mythologized images of representatives of the Russian intelligentsia of the 1980s-1990s. The book foregrounds the decay of the Russian intelligentsia's values. Several protagonists described in the book, including characters in the stories "Fakir" and "The Blank Page" (S chistogo lista), are portrayed as disillusioned dreamers. Elena Sergeeva asserts that these stories deconstruct the sacred image of the intelligentsia forged in the Thaw period by creating an ironic distance from it.[27]

Similarly, Tolstaya's *Slynx* contains parodic touches related to the intelligentsia's failure to act as a moral authority. The novel makes semi-veiled allusions to the shortcomings of contemporary life in Russia including spiritual and cultural degradation, the lack of personal responsibility, and the childlike worldview of many prominent intellectuals. Andrei Ashkerov suggests that Tolstaya's portrayal of the inner conflicts and failures of the intelligentsia might be viewed

---

22 Helena Goscilo, *The Explosive World of Tatyana N. Tolstaya's Fiction* (London and New York: Routledge, 1996), 3.
23 Vladislav Zubok, *Zhivago's Children: The Last Russian Intelligentsia* (Cambridge, MA: Harvard UP, 2009), 357–358.
24 Ibid., 358.
25 Deming Brown, *The Last Years of Soviet Russian Literature: Prose Fiction 1975–1991* (Cambridge: Cambridge UP, 1993), 128.
26 Zubok, *Zhivago's Children*, 360.
27 E. A. Sergeeva, "Mifologizatsiia sovetskoi intelligentsii v rasskazakh T. Tolstoi," *Izvestiia Saratovskogo universiteta* 13, no. 2 (2013): 98–101, here 101.

as a spectacle created by an intellectual fashion trendsetter.[28] Yet he overlooks Tolstaya's ironic deconstruction of the bookish mindset in *The Slynx*. Here is one example: following establishment of a new order in a country that has survived an explosion, Benedict is keen to consult poetic collections from the past and look for useful prophecies. A passage from Pushkin's poem "To Vyazemsky" strikes him as important. It states pessimistically: "Man suits all elements, every season / Tyrant, traitor, or the prison."[29] After reading several quotes from different collections of poetry, Benedict concludes that all the books he read so far are talking about the same things. He even suspects that his father in-law, the tyrant, must "have been putting a little collection together"[30] with a view to validating his own autocratic behaviour. Such a selective reading of Russian poetry gives the impression that authoritarian rule had always existed in Russia and that tyranny was congruent with Russian values. Benedict's reductionist manner of reading Pushkin's texts also invokes Russian and Soviet educationalists, who were eager to appropriate Russian literature for ideologically driven policies.

In *The Slynx* Tolstaya also makes fun of the prestige that Russian poetry featuring fighters of oppression has enjoyed in Russia and abroad. As Clare Cavanagh convincingly argues, Russian poets' lives were ascribed with symbolic meaning seen as "an analogue for the life of the people."[31] Similarly, in her story "The Poet and the Muse" (Poet i muza) Tolstaya laughs away the traditional dichotomy, rooted in European Romanticism, that features the poet and his muse. In this story the poet Grisha decides to sell his skeleton to the Academy of Sciences for sixty rubles for the use of medical students. His decision to become immortal is inspired by Pushkin's poem "Monument" (Pamiatnik), in which the lyric hero dreams of escaping decay. It is obvious from this example that one concern in Tolstaya's fiction is related to different modes of reading. Both Benedict and Grisha are presented as naïve readers who equate life with art and ignore the complexities of human nature. Both narratives point to the repetitive nature of Russian culture, which promotes the established literary canon as sacred. Tolstaya considers this reliance on the canon damaging for the survival of Russian culture. The decaying phase of the Russian intelligentsia's ideals and its stagnation are also criticized in *The Slynx*: the novel portrays Moscow not as a center of economic development but as a dystopian world full of amnesia.

---

28 Andrei Ashkerov, "Tat'iana Tolstaia i vlast' intelligentsii," *Russkii zhurnal*, March 11, 2002, http://old.russ.ru/krug/20020311_ashk.html.
29 Tatyana Tolstaya, *The Slynx*, trans. Jamey Gambrell (New York: NYRB Classics, 2007), 274.
30 Ibid., 274.
31 Clare Cavanagh, *Lyric Poetry and Modern Politics: Russia, Poland, and the West* (New Haven, CT: Yale UP, 2009), 267.

Danica Jenkins identifies in the novel Tolstaya's desire to reflect on the mindset of Russian intellectuals. Jenkins suggests that Tolstaya's intent is not to highlight the flaws of the intelligentsia's utopian aspirations but to use the fantastic for creating "an alternate dimension from which one can critically examine the historical patterns of Russia."[32] Using the fantastic enables Tolstaya to voice her concerns not only about the cyclical vision of history popular among many Russian intellectuals but also to pose a question about the future direction of Russian cultural life. According to Jenkins, Tolstaya uses fiction "as a way to meditate upon the . . . degeneration that has plagued Russian history."[33] Commenting on Benedict's submissive behavior and non-critical acceptance of the new social order, Jenkins suggests that Benedict represents 1990s Russian intellectuals who are happy "to tolerate without question the increasingly bureaucratic and unjust nature of Russian politics and culture."[34] She rightly argues that Tolstaya criticizes the routinised behavior of many Russians who are reluctant to change.

Tolstaya's criticism of the ahistorical nature of totalitarian leadership in Russia also exposes the mimicry of the Russian intelligentsia. Serguei Oushakine's article on Russian dissidents of the 1970s-1980s asserts that the construction of their identity as martyrs of the existing oppressive order paradoxically reinforced the existing power structure in Russia. Consequently, their role in Soviet society was limited.[35] Oushakine proposes seeing Soviet dissidents as a neo-intelligentsia that, unlike the old intelligentsia, did not develop an alternative view of historical development.[36] His observations can be used as a key to unlock the political message embedded in Tolstaya's *Slynx*, which criticizes the inability of the post-Soviet intelligentsia to offer an alternative political model. This is exemplified by Benedict's successful overthrow of Kuzmich, which results in perpetuation of totalitarian rule. Tolstaya links the success of totalitarian ideology to the Russian intelligentsia's inertia.

According to Alla Latynina, Tolstaya's subversion of the dystopian genre implies a critical view of Russian literature's role in the post-Soviet period. She feels that Benedict's obsession with books does not help him change anything in

---

32 Danica Jenkins, "Stepping through the Mirror: A Dystopian Vision of Regression and Stagnation in Tatyana Tolstaya's *The Slynx*," *Australian & New Zealand Journal of European Studies* 2, no. 2 (2010): 92–99, here 92.
33 Ibid., 92.
34 Ibid., 94.
35 Serguei Alex Oushakine, "The Terrifying Mimicry of Samizdat," *Public Culture* 13, no. 2 (2001): 191–214, here 204.
36 Ibid., 198.

his life and that the novel's hybrid genre enables the reader to move away from reliance on utopian literature. In Latynina's opinion, *The Slynx* can be effectively read as "an expertly blended cocktail of dystopia, satire, and the clichés of science fiction."[37] It demonstrates Tolstaya's departure from the utopian model of social engineering found in the literary works of her predecessors. Furthermore, Tolstaya's ironic distance from the utopian and anti-utopian traditions, as manifested in *The Slynx*, makes her an eccentric writer with an interest in remolding Russian canonical themes and in advocating indeterminacy rather than a teleological vision of history.

By demonstrating in *The Slynx* that the intelligentsia has become morally bankrupt, Tolstaya questions the validity of the Russian moral project created by many progressive writers and thinkers. Their promotion of the noble image of individuals who work for the moral progress of society is scrutinized in *The Slynx* in order to question the usefulness of the vision of the official canon created during Soviet times for construction of a new Russian identity.

Images of the Intelligentsia in Tolstaya's Essays, Social Media, and Interviews

While Tolstaya's public persona does not align with the intelligentsia myth, it would be wrong to overlook Tolstaya's desire to influence public opinion by promoting certain debates and controversial views. In her 1989 interview in the Canadian cultural magazine *Border/Lines* Tolstaya presents herself as a writer concerned with eternal questions and human psychology. She states that neither social problems nor progress interest her.[38]

The interview illustrates Tolstaya's aversion to history and her interest in human beings per se. She thinks that in every country "the same human being"[39] chooses to believe in God or not to believe in God. Yet her early fiction features characters were shaped by everyday life in the 1980s Soviet Union, which she describes as crazy and horrible. Tolstaya claims that developing a certain sense of humor enabled her to survive in such a life.

---

37 Alla Latynina, "'There's Your Spiritual Renaissance for You': On Tatyana Tolstaya's *The Slynx*," *Russian Studies in Literature* 39, no. 4 (2003): 66–71, here 71.
38 Ioan Davies, "An Interview with Tatyana Tolstaya," *Border/Lines* 20/21 (1990–1991): 26–29, here 26.
39 Ibid.

In her view, those who lack a sense of humor are doomed as human beings to become half-animals.[40] In this interview, Tolstaya appears self-critical, humble, and satirically minded—strikingly different from Russian intellectuals of the Thaw period. According to Vladislav Zubok, writers such as Andrei Sinyavsky and Aleksandr Solzhenitsyn attempted to recapture the "intellectual and spiritual exaltation"[41] of the old intelligentsia. Their desire to influence Russian readers was linked to the creation of new public spaces and discussions.

It would be difficult to align Tolstaya's pronouncements with the romanticized vision of the Russian intelligentsia typically described as a group of people "with privileged access to truth."[42] In contrast, Tolstaya's views appear idiosyncratic and individualistic. By promoting comedy as a social corrective, she aspires to reduce conventional beliefs to the ridiculous. Her strong interest in laughter suggests that in satire, as in drama in general, language becomes entwined with symbolic action that makes supporters of normative conventions look hypocritical and absurd. She sees herself as a performer who exposes the falsity of desires for a privileged position and prominence as a public figure. While she accuses elderly people of creating false memories about the past, she warns young people not to be seduced by utopian ideology. Her explanation of the empty spaces that derive from crushed illusions sounds remarkably post-utopian. The interview was given to a journalist in Toronto in 1989, and it sounds rather prophetic in anticipating the Russian memory wars of the 2000s.

Tolstaya's desire to communicate the truth to her readers in a satirical way exemplifies Kenneth Burke's understanding of comedy as social corrective and purposeful communication. Burke maintains that, in addition to triggering laughter, comedy has a persuasive potential to promote different worldviews and alter existing conventional assumptions. Burke's notion of corrective laughter presupposes a different way to view the world with the help of humor and incongruity. He elucidates: "Seeing the world from its opposite, from incongruity is not a literary conceit.... Comedy is precisely that—holding the conventional up to its opposite, to irony and satire."[43] In her 1989 interview, Tolstaya performs the role of a social critic by transcending the situation and advocating comedy as a tool that lets the reader overcome the limitations of systems of thought such as labelling and conformity. Both humor and laughter offer a more compassionate point of view to overcome disagreements. They also relieve tensions arising from conflict.

---

40 Ibid.
41 Vladislav Zubok, *Zhivago's Children*, 161.
42 Clark, "The King is Dead," 3.
43 Kenneth Burke, *Language as Symbolic Action* (Berkeley: U of California Press, 1966), 45.

As a specialist in Classical Studies, Tolstaya would know that comic corrective was practiced in early times, notably in Ancient Greece. Diogenes of Sinope, for example, was well known for his eccentric behavior, anecdotes, and humorous performances. Philip Bosman sees Diogenes's performances as part of Cynic philosophy and its program of social criticism. Diogenes aspired to encourage the audience to question the ethics on which existing norms and conventions were founded. Bosman writes: "Working within the broad Socratic and, more particularly, Antisthenic legacy, Diogenes used both conventional and unconventional methods to get his message across."[44] Antisthenes, the founder of Cynic philosophy and student of Socrates, promoted ascetic practices and the use of spectacle as social protest. Cynic philosophers were known for their performances and witty comments aimed at subverting social conventions. Similarly, Tolstaya has evolved as a writer, food critic, performer, TV host, and public figure who uses blogs and social media to promote herself as an eccentric philosopher in the style of Diogenes. According to Andreas Huyssen, since the 1970s the "return of Diogenes as postmodern intellectual"[45] has become a visible phenomenon in the West. It can be explained by the emergence of "a new type of postenlightened schizocynicism that remains immune to traditional forms of ideology critique."[46] In his forward to Peter Sloterdijk's book on cynical reason, Huyssen states:

> Sloterdijk sees cynicism as the dominant operating mode in contemporary culture, both on the personal and institutional levels, and he suggests reviving the tradition of kynicism, from Diogenes to Schweik, as a counterstrategy, as the only form of subversive reason left after the failures and broken promises of ideology critique in the tradition of Western Marxism. By focusing on cynicism as a central feature of the postmodern condition in the 1970s and 1980s . . . , Sloterdijk attempts to theorize that which has often remained submerged in the recent debate about modernity and postmodernity: the pervasive sense of political disillusionment in the wake of the 1960s and the pained feeling of a lack of political and social alternatives in Western societies today.[47]

---

44 Philip Bosman, "Selling Cynicism: The Pragmatics of Diogenes' Comic Performances," *Classical Quarterly* 56 (2006): 93–104, here 93.
45 Andreas Huyssen, "The Return of Diogenes as Postmodern Intellectual," in idem, *Critique of Cynical Reason*, ed. P. Sloterdijk (Minneapolis: U of Minnesota Press, 1987), ix-xxv, here ix.
46 Ibid., x.
47 Ibid., xi.

Similarly, Tolstaya expresses her sceptical views about any attempts either to revive utopian ideologies from the past or to create new ones. In her 1989 interview, the Diogenes-like persona is strongly felt in Tolstaya's pronouncements about the futility of using gender studies and feminist theory in literary criticism. Responding to a question about contemporary women writers in Russia, she says: "I don't believe in women's literature. I think there are just writers. Good writers, bad writers."[48] By referring in her answer to human beings who happen to write, Tolstaya intentionally questions the limitations of modes of thinking pertaining to the construction of one's identity in accordance with ideological beliefs.

Tolstaya's strategy of using rhetorical devices to question popular stereotypes and existing social norms is not limited to her fiction. It is also embedded in her essays, television talks and interviews. As Olga Osmukhina asserts, Tolstaya's use of metaphor enables her to portray familiar things and everyday day life in Russia "from an unexpected angle."[49]

One could add that sometimes Tolstaya creates metaphors as a social spectacle, in order to shock her reader. This is especially true of her article on the Russian intelligentsia under communism and perestroika, boldly titled "The Perils of Utopia." Tolstaya thinks that the innate idealism of the Russian intelligentsia and its faith "in such abstractions as 'the people' and 'the beloved foreigners' have made it ill prepared it to deal with harsh and complex realities."[50] She criticizes the intelligentsia's belief in the existence of the people as "as a mythological, indivisible whole" and its self-representation as a group of morally minded individuals as fallacious arguments.[51] Tolstaya claims that, at the beginning of perestroika, the intelligentsia's romantic idealization of the people began withering away. Implicitly, she sees the intelligentsia's inability to solve practical problems as one of the factors that contributed to the collapse of the Soviet Union. In her view, while the Russian intelligentsia is good at talking, writing, and dreaming, it is not capable of resolving concrete problems due to its infantilism. She states:

> When dreaminess and idealism run into the crude prose of life, the intelligentsia is shocked. In this new historical phase, one

---

48 Davies, "An Interview with Tatyana Tolstaya," 27.
49 Olga Osmukhina, "Literature as Technique: Tatyana Tolstaya," *Russian Studies in Literature* 48, no. 4 (Fall 2012): 7–17, 8.
50 Tatyana Tolstaya, "The Perils of Utopia: The Russian Intelligentsia under Communism and Perestroika," trans. Jamey Gambrell, *Development and Change* 27 (1996): 315–329, here 316.
51 Ibid., 321.

of the worst problems has become the issue of ethnic conflict and ethnic and national identity. Here again, the tendency of the intelligentsia to romanticize other groups ... has not helped it to understand what must be faced today.[52]

Tolstaya's statement about Russians' love for other nations parodies the idealized image of Pushkin found in Dostoevsky's 1880 Pushkin speech, which praises Pushkin's ability to absorb foreign traditions. Tolstaya distances herself from those Russian intellectuals who slavishly follow western models of behavior. "Russians, more than any other people I know," she muses, "are periodically seized by a passionate love for other peoples, nations, cultures, customs and languages—a passion which goes absolutely unrequited."[53] She also notes that the Russian intelligentsia's passion for the exotic other is selective, because it excludes many countries, including China, Portugal, and Iran. Tolstaya publicly performs the role of a sinner and subjects herself to flogging. She admits that her own shock at the war in Chechnya resulted in escapist behavior. She advises her fellow writers to embrace art as "the only thing that truly belongs to the intelligentsia."[54] In her view, all other methods of influencing readers have failed.

Tolstaya's vision of the Russian intelligentsia's failure aptly matches her culinary metaphor suggesting that the intelligentsia should be considered not a layer in the cake of society but "the rum that soaks the cake of society."[55] Tolstaya believes that the spirit of the old intelligentsia was destroyed by the Bolshevik government. She labels the Russian intelligentsia's enthusiasm for the revolution as paradoxical. Her redefinition of art as a sphere of activity that could prevent the intelligentsia from sliding into the perils of utopia seems to be linked to the notion of art as device. Her article on the intelligentsia concludes with this pronouncement: "[N]either prison, nor freedom can prevent the artist from creating.... Now, when no one needs the artist, he is truly alone with himself and his own judge for the first time in Russian history."[56] Yet her statement that the time of the political has passed and that only art could attract faithful adherents now seems problematic.

At the same time, Tolstaya appears comfortable with the image of the intellectual who writes for a wide range of middle-class readers. She appears to have flourished amid the mass culture of the 1990s-2020s. Her essays and

---

52 Ibid., 323.
53 Ibid., 323.
54 Ibid., 328.
55 Ibid., 318.
56 Ibid., 329.

programs like *The School of Malicious Gossip* (2002–2014) and the YouTube series *White Noise* (Belyi shum) have the important function of overcoming the fear of anonymity with which the urban mass is associated. Like a detective, she introduces her readers and viewers to a variety of individuals, rescuing them from abstract collective identity. Such a desire to rescue individuals from the mass invokes the religious act of redemption. By singling out an individual's soul she shows redemption from mass culture. Both programs comprise interviews with interesting critics, writers, economists, poets, and historians, who do not belong to the mainstream of Russian contemporary culture.

With her programs and social media posts Tolstaya plays a useful role in binding society into a reading group and combating the isolation of individuals. According to an interview of July 22, 2020, Tolstaya is not opposed to modern technology and is happy to use YouTube to discuss Russian literature and culture. Furthermore, she sees herself and her co-presenters of the YouTube program *White Noise* as "keepers of Russian culture."[57] In the same interview, she refers to herself as a missionary who helps Russian non-commercial culture survive during a time of fake news and rapid commercialization of state media. Tolstaya is keen to promote debates about the past through social media, overcoming thereby the lack of spaces where public knowledge about Russian culture can be evaluated critically. For example, one program was dedicated to the Russian Symbolist poet Aleksandr Blok. Tolstaya invited Professor Dina Magomedova to discuss Blok's controversial long poem "The Twelve" in the context of Blok's responses to revolutionary violence and chaos. Their discussion ranged from Blok's representation of evil in the poem as inspired by Dostoevsky's novel *The Demons* to Blok's appearance, his voice, and his love life.[58] The program deconstructs the myth of the poet-martyr and draws the audience's attention to examining poets as interesting people with their own anxieties. The program also calls on collectors and poetry lovers to locate vinyl records featuring the voice of Russian opera singer Lyubov Andreevna Delmas (1884–1969), one of Blok's muses. The program attracted more than 10,000 viewers within two days of its release. One comment (signed by a Dr. Hatter) expresses gratitude to Tolstaya for bringing a sense of meaning to the YouTube space often filled with "interviews with people who are of no interest to others." Several comments suggest that the new project *White Noise* should help to restore "the Russian

---

57 Tat'iana Tolstaia, "O 'Belom shume,' Sobchak i feminitivakh," YouTube, July 22, 2020, https://www.youtube.com/watch?v=fbgDPu6LgIU.
58 Tat'iana Tolstaia, "Blok," YouTube, August 18, 2020, https://www.youtube.com/watch?v=gWP95mgiPPA.

genetic code." Given the rise of nationalism in Russia in the post-Soviet period, such a comment is hardly surprising.

Paradoxically, by presenting herself as an heiress of Lev Tolstoy, Natalia Krandievskaya, and Aleksei N. Tolstoy, Tolstaya creates a linguistic identity that highlights her sensitivity to the creative potential of the Russian language. Several contemporary scholars have pointed out that Tolstaya displays "the elite linguistic identity" of a Russian native speaker with the well-developed ability to speak well in a variety of communicative situations. Tatyana Ostrovskaya, for example, defines Tolstaya "as a connoisseur of words" who fights against the "total corruption of language."[59] Ostrovskaya sees Tolstaya not as a representative of the intelligentsia but as a member of the post-Soviet elite. Ostrovskaya explains: "Not in vain is T. Tolstaya called the Ksenia Sobchak of Russian literature in some publications. Behavioral patterns of scandal, cynicism, scandalous value in the presence of a strong personality, charisma . . . contribute to the fact that these discursive identities arouse admiration and a desire to imitate in some and in others complete rejection of their behavioral discourse."[60] Similarly, Ashkerov suggests that Tolstaya has transformed the inferiority complex and anxieties of the Russian intelligentsia into a successful commercial product.[61]

In sum, several contemporary critics consider Russian literary culture today inseparable from the pressures of a commercial market. In this context, Tolstaya's interpretation of the notion of Russian messianism, which became popular among Russian nationalists at the end of the 1990s, is especially insightful. In her essay "The Russian World" (Russkii mir), Tolstaya condemns the idea as an outmoded fantasy: "Russians for some reason assume that they are a God-bearing people. . . . But Russians have at least one sin on their conscience, which is that Russians do not love their neighbour."[62] Such a comment reveals Tolstaya's preference to talk about the Russian people rather than on behalf of the Russian people. The essay is full of ironic remarks, creating thereby a sense of critical distance between the narrator and the object of her essay.

Commenting on Tolstaya's works of the 2010s, Irina Surat maintains that Tolstaya has moved away from her mythopoeic image of a Russian world to a semi-autobiographical portrayal of Russian life observed from the margins.

---

59 Tatyana A. Ostrovskaya, Irina S. Karabulatova, Zaineta R. Khachmafova, Svetlana A. Lyasheva, Gennady Vassil'evich Osipov, "The Discourse of the Russian Elite in the Era of 'Liquid' Modernity as a Problem of Ethnic, Social and Cultural Security," *Mediterranean Journal of Social Sciences* 6, no. 3 (2015): 147–153, here 149.
60 Ibid., 152.
61 Ashkerov, "Tat'iana Tolstaia i vlast' intelligentsii."
62 Tat'iana Tolstaia, "Russkii mir," in eadem, *Den': Lichnoe* (Moscow: Astrel', 2002), 454.

Surat considers Tolstaya's new kind of prose more engaging. In her opinion, Tolstaya has become interested in fiction that is rooted in personal experience and "presented directly... in the first person."[63] Yet, despite Tolstaya's insistence on the importance of culture to the formation of personal identity, Tolstaya is not completely oblivious to the diversity of political views in contemporary Russia. Her nostalgic views on Russian traditional food and on the negative effect of globalization on food consumption in Russia invoke many Russian nationalists, including Nikita Mikhalkov, who wanted to create his own food chain *Let's Eat as if We Are at Home* (Edim kak doma). Curiously, as Mellissa Caldwell notes, "Russian consumers who are participating in nationalist-oriented consumer campaigns" have started discussing foreign fast food, including McDonald's, as authentically Russian products.[64] She notes that through the process of domestication "McDonald's has become localized."[65] In her essay "The Golden Age" (Zolotoi vek, 1992), Tolstaya laments the disappearance of many traditional culinary traditions in contemporary Russia and calls for their revival. She states, for example, that some traditional Russian desserts and drinks outlived many Russian leaders, including Lenin and Gorbachev. She praises Elena Molokhovets's 1861 book of Russian recipes as a manifestation of the Golden Age of Russian culture, especially because it includes some 1,500 recipes. Tolstaya calls for the revival of Russian traditional food. She suggests that the main dishes and ingredients to be remembered most of all in contemporary Russia should include fish, mushrooms, pies, aspic, cabbage soup, pancakes, and buckwheat porridge.[66] Her cabbage pie has been advertised recently on Jenny Smile's prestigious webpage that features exclusive cuisine.[67]

Tolstaya's campaign for the revival of Russian traditional culinary art can be seen as a manifestation of ethnocentric nationalism. This nationalistic trend affects contemporary memory wars and threatens the sustainability of liberal values in Putin's Russia. Tolstaya's initial career as a writer coincided with the memory boom that took place in the late 1980s. Nikolay Koposov characterizes the growth of historiographic interest in personal experiences as an "attempt to restore subjectivity to history's rank-and-file actors."[68] He claims that Russian

---

63 Irina Surat, "Sometimes Love: The New Prose of Tatyana Tolstaya," *Russian Studies in Literature* 51, no. 3 (2015): 5–30, here 10.
64 Melissa L. Caldwell, "Domesticating the French Fry: McDonald's and Consumerism in Moscow," *Journal of Consumer Culture* 4, no. 1 (2004): 5–26, here 5.
65 Ibid., 6.
66 Tat'iana Tolstaia, "Zolotoi vek," club366.ru, accessed February 9, 2023, http://www.club366.ru/articles/121439.shtml.
67 Jenny Smile, "Pirog s kapustoi ot T.Tolstoi," Jenny Smile's Cuisine, October 29, 2021, https://jennysmile83.wordpress.com/2021/10/29/пирог-с-капустой-от-т-толстой/.
68 Nikolay Koposov, *Memory Laws, Memory Wars* (Cambridge: Cambridge UP, 2017), 43.

culture has become a depository of collective memory and that, in the eyes of many Russians today, "memory forms the core of personal (and collective) identity."[69] In the context of this postmodernist tendency to produce counter-memories to those that were linked to master narratives, Tolstaya's career as an autobiographer, chef and writer is inseparable from ongoing reassessment of the Soviet legacy. In her comments as a presenter of the program *White Noise*, Tolstaya inserts her own recollections of the past. In a program on Tsvetaeva, for example, she reads a poem in memory of Tsvetaeva written by her grandmother Natalia Krandievskaya, and in a program on Blok she talks about Voloshin's wife and the circle of Voloshin's friends whom she met. In sum, her personal stories about the past establish a sense of authenticity and present her as a living link between the past and the present. Tolstaya's YouTube career manifests her desire to gather Russian intellectuals into a new reading group.

Tolstaya's Self-Representation in Russian Social Media

By adopting social media as an ally, Tolstaya aspires to overcome the gulf between elitist and mass culture. Despite Tolstaya's success as a writer and a public intellectual, Osmukhina thinks that Tolstaya's preoccupation with commercially successful projects prevents her from writing new stories. She sees Tolstaya's former role as a co-presenter of the controversial TV show *School of Malicious Gossip* and her appearance as a guest on various entertainment programs, including *A Moment of Fame*, as a distraction from her work as a writer. As Osmukhina suggests, the endeavor to link creativity to market demands reveals the desire of writers to influence their readers by pretending that "the show goes on" despite the growing popularity of visual culture.[70]

It can be argued that Tolstaya's multi-faceted public persona has been shaped by post-Soviet and western cultural trends of the 1990s-2020s oriented towards glamour and the use of affect in contemporary art through such practices as installations, site-specific performances, conversational and participatory art, including happenings, and other post-dramatic forms of performance. As Nigel Thrift points out, glamour serves "as a secular magic" and offers "enough familiarity to engage the imagination."[71] Similarly, in his book on tricksters in Soviet

---

69 Ibid., 43.
70 Osmukhina, "Literature as Technique," 15.
71 Nigel Thrift, "Understanding the Material Practices of Glamour," in *The Affect Theory Reader*, ed. Melissa Gregg and Gregory J. Seigworth (Durham, NC: Duke UP, 2010), 289–308, 297.

and post-Soviet culture, Mark Lipovetsky talks about the spread of cynical reason and the demise of the Russian intelligentsia. He concludes his study with this pessimistic statement:

> In fact, there is no exaggeration in saying that the collapse of late Soviet culture can be interpreted as the result of a quiet cynical revolution, during which 'cynical reason' infiltrated all spheres and institutions of social life and eroded them from the inside to the point of their collapse. In this perspective, the post-Soviet society should be interpreted as the triumph of the former Soviet 'cynical reason,' which acquires the functions of the official mainstream in cultural, social, ideological, and economic spheres.[72]

Bearing in mind Tolstaya's interest in mixing the fantastic with the real, as well as in contemporary urban tales and literary anecdotes, her current interest in performance as an extension of writing appears logical: it goes beyond her desire to be commercially successful. The interest in glamour as a special form of excitement and as a form of secular magic derives from Tolstaya's preoccupation with boredom in everyday life and disillusionment. "As sources of identity and hope," maintains Thrift, "every culture displays ideals that cannot be fully realised in everyday life."[73] These ideals can be experienced as fleeting fantasies, utopias, daydreams, and heterotopias that envisage different worlds to come. Once these ideals are transposed in one's imagination to a distant cultural domain, they could be envisaged as practical realities. According to Thrift, the process of engaging alternative versions of the self comprises "knowingly engaging in self-representation and receiving affirmation from an audience."[74] In other words, the creation of worlds of self-difference enables one's extra selves to thrive because they serve as subject and object simultaneously.

The above model of self-creation through art, comparable to the use of laughter in everyday life, resembles Tolstaya's vision of humor as a tool of survival in a world full of rapid changes and anxieties. Bearing in mind that glamour has a dual function as an economic and an imaginary force, it appears that Tolstaya creates her own bewitching beauty through her creative outputs as an antidote to metanarratives. By generating enchantment without

---

72 Mark Lipovetsky, *Charms of the Cynical Reason: The Trickster's Transformations in Soviet and Post-Soviet Cultures* (Boston, MA: Academic Studies Press, 2010), 271.
73 Thrift, "Understanding the Material Practices of Glamour," 298.
74 Ibid.

supernaturalism through her storytelling, performing and writing, Tolstaya creates a more magical world than the Soviet and Russian intelligentsia have envisaged. However, the sober view of reality expressed in her essays and interviews suggests that her effort to allure the audience into her alternative reality/heterotopia is highly calculated.

Tolstaya's comic intervention in the process of rewriting cultural history by the members of Soviet intelligentsia who are usually called *shestidesiatniki* might appear to be a more individualistic form of social protest than the one undertaken by the aforementioned Cynics. Yet her portrayal of the intellectuals of the 1960s as delusional and idealistically minded undermines their own story based on the mythologized image of the intelligentsia, in accordance with which they have recovered from their misplaced faith in socialism. According to Kochetkova, one of the memory wars in Putin's Russia pertains to a conflict between the *shestidesiatniki* and *semidesiatniki*. She states: "The subsequent generation of intelligentsia (the *semidesiatniki*) have tried to silence the *shestidesiatniki* and what they stand for by practicing a form of intellectual cleansing."[75] She explains that the emergence of a new power narrative of the moral self aspires to overshadow the narrative plot of *shestidesiatniki* by displacing romanticism as something shameful.

The set of values advocated by *semidesiatniki* revolves around the notions of realism and pragmatism. The latter is promoted by *Independent Newspaper* (Nezavisimaia gazeta) as a new image for the Russian intelligentsia. Kochetkova herself is scornful of the attempt of *shestidesiatniki* to apply the intelligentsia myth to their autobiographical narratives because their newly created versions of the myth promote unrealistic expectations. By anchoring Tolstaya's ongoing critique of the *shestidesiatniki* in the space of the memory wars described in Kochetkova's study, we see that Tolstaya's use of humor in everyday life as a survival tool enables her to overcome her Soviet self. It also enables her to move from the margins of Russian culture into its mainstream and to celebrate creativity in all spheres of life.

Conclusion

As the present chapter has demonstrated, it would be difficult to label Tolstaya and other contemporary writers of her generation as representatives of the

---

[75] Inna Kochetkova, *The Myth of the Russian Intelligentsia: Old Intellectuals in the New Russia* (Abington: Routledge, 2010), 71.

intelligentsia, if that is seen as the avant-garde of social transformations. Yet the intelligentsia myth as a point of reference has not disappeared in Putin's Russia. Following the collapse of the Soviet Union in 1991, the dichotomy of the periphery and the centre has changed dramatically, too. Many cultural centres in contemporary Russia offer their own vision of an intelligentsia that suits their political interests. The internet journal *Intelligentsia and Peace* (Intelligentsia i mir), founded by Ivanovo State University in 2001, describes itself as a Russian interdisciplinary journal of the humanities. It offers a wide range of topics, discussing state pensions, Russian-German cultural relations, charity work, and psychology. One issue contains an article on the post-Soviet intelligentsia that describes doctors, teachers, and artists who share beliefs in selfless behaviour. The article presents altruistic behaviour as a common trait of representatives of the intelligentsia.[76] In contrast to the article on psychological peculiarities of the intelligentsia, the website of the popular radio programme *Echo of Moscow* (Ekho Moskvy) forges a clearly political role for the modern Russian intelligentsia. In June 2020 it published an open letter urging citizens of Russia to oppose the proposed corrections to the Constitution, signed by many intellectuals who define themselves as "the Congress of the intelligentsia."[77] The signatories include such prominent writers as Dmitry Bykov and Liudmila Ulitskaya. Yet the name of Tatyana Tolstaya is absent from this letter. It appears that she would rather see herself as an eccentric intellectual who has warned her fellow writers about the perils of utopia.

Bibliography

Ashkerov, Andrei. "Tat'iana Tolstaia i vlast' intelligentsii." *Russkii zhurnal*, March 11, 2002. http://old.russ.ru/krug/20020311_ashk.html

Bauman, Zygmunt. *Legislators and Interpreters: On Modernity, Post-Modernity and Intellectuals*. Cambridge: Polity Press, 1987.

Brown, Deming. *The Last Years of Soviet Russian Literature: Prose Fiction 1975–1991*. Cambridge: Cambridge UP, 1993.

Bosman, Philip. "Selling Cynicism: The Pragmatics of Diogenes' Comic Performances." *Classical Quarterly* 56 (2006): 93–104.

---

76 I. N. Kuleshova, V. K. Minnikov, and E. V. Skryabina, "Social and Psychological Features of Altruistic Motivation of Modern Intelligentsia," *Intelligentsia i mir* 2 (2020): 40–44, here 41.
77 EkhoMSK, "Obrashchenie Kongressa intelligentsii k grazhdanam Rossii," *Ekho Moskvy*, June 10, 2020, https://echo.msk.ru/blog/echomsk/2657940-echo/.

Burke, Kenneth. *Language as Symbolic Action*. Berkeley: U of California Press, 1966.

Caldwell, Melissa L. "Domesticating the French Fry: McDonald's and Consumerism in Moscow." *Journal of Consumer Culture* 4, no. 1 (2004): 5–26.

Cavanagh, Clare. *Lyric Poetry and Modern Politics: Russia, Poland, and the West*. New Haven, CT: Yale UP, 2009.

Clark, Katerina. "The King is Dead, Long Live the King: Intelligentsia Ideology in Transition." Paper presented at the conference "Russia at the End of the Twentieth Century: Culture and Its Horizons in Politics and Society." Stanford University, October 1998, 1–31. Accessed November 7, 2017. https://web.stanford.edu/group/Russia20/volumepdf/clark_fin99.pdf

Davies, Ioan. "An Interview with Tatyana Tolstaya." *Border/Lines* 20/21 (1990–1991): 26–29.

Emerson, Caryl. "*And the Demons Entered into the Swine*: The Russian Intelligentsia and Post-Soviet Religious Thought." *Cross Currents* 43, no. 2 (1993): 184–202.

EkhoMSK. "Obrashchenie Kongressa intelligentsii k grazhdanam Rossii." *Ekho Moskvy*, June 10, 2020. https://echo.msk.ru/blog/echomsk/2657940-echo/.

Givens, John. "Tatyana Tolstaya, Mikhail Bulgakov." *Russian Studies in Literature* 51, no. 3 (2015): 1–4.

Goscilo, Helena. *The Explosive World of Tatyana N. Tolstaya's Fiction*. London: Routledge, 1996.

Huyssen, Andreas. "The Return of Diogenes as Postmodern Intellectual." In idem, *Critique of Cynical Reason*, edited by P. Sloterdijk, ix-xxv. Minneapolis: U of Minnesota Press, 1987.

Jenkins, Danica. "Stepping through the Mirror: A Dystopian Vision of Regression and Stagnation in Tatyana Tolstaya's *The Slynx*." *Australian & New Zealand Journal of European Studies* 2, no. 2 (2010): 92–99.

Kochetkova, Inna. *The Myth of the Russian Intelligentsia: Old Intellectuals in the New Russia*. London: Routledge, 2009.

Koposov, Nikolay. *Memory Laws, Memory Wars*. Cambridge: Cambridge UP, 2017.

Kuleshova I. N., V. K. Minnikov, and E. V. Skriabina. "Sotsial'no-psikhologicheskie osobennosti al'truisticheskoi motivatsii sovremennoi intelligentsii." *Intelligentsia i mir* 2 (2020): 40–44.

Latynina, Alla. "'There's Your Spiritual Renaissance for You': On Tatyana Tolstaya's *The Slynx*." *Russian Studies in Literature* 39, no. 4 (2003): 66–71.

Lipovetsky, Mark. *Charms of the Cynical Reason: The Trickster's Transformations in Soviet and Post-Soviet Cultures.* Boston, MA: Academic Studies Press, 2010.

Osmukhina, Olga. "Literature as Technique: Tatyana Tolstaya." *Russian Studies in Literature* 48, no. 4 (2012): 7–17.

Ostrovskaya, Tatyana A., Irina S. Karabulatova, Zaineta R. Khachmafova, Svetlana A. Lyasheva, and Gennady Vassil'evich Osipov. "The Discourse of the Russian Elite in the Era of 'Liquid' Modernity as a Problem of Ethnic, Social and Cultural Security." *Mediterranean Journal of Social Sciences* 6, no. 3 (2015): 147–153.

Oushakine, Serguei Alex. "The Terrifying Mimicry of Samizdat." *Public Culture* 13, no. 2 (2001): 191–214.

Pipes, Richard. *The Russian Revolution.* New York: Knopf Doubleday Publishing Group, 1991.

Sergeeva, E. A. "Mifologizatsiia sovetskoi intelligentsii v rasskazakh T. Tolstoi." *Izvestiia Saratovskogo universiteta* 13, no. 2 (2013): 98–101.

Shneidman, Norman N. *Russian Literature, 1995–2002: On the Threshold of a New Millennium.* Toronto: U of Toronto Press, 2004.

Shkolnikov, Vadim. "Sociality—or Death: Belinskii's Phenomenological Realism and the Emergence of Russian Intelligentsia." *The Russian Review* 81 (2022): 683–704.

Skomp, Elizabeth A., and Benjamin M. Sutcliffe. *Ludmila Ulitskaya and the Art of Tolerance.* Madison: U of Wisconsin Press, 2015.

Smile, Jenny. "Pirog s kapustoi ot T.Tolstoi." *Jenny Smile's Cuisine.* October 29, 2021. https://jennysmile83.wordpress.com/2021/10/29/пирог-с-капустой-от-т-толстой/

Surat, Irina. "Sometimes Love: The New Prose of Tatyana Tolstaya." *Russian Studies in Literature* 51, no. 3 (2015): 5–30.

Thrift, Nigel. "Understanding the Material Practices of Glamour." In *The Affect Theory Reader*, edited by Melissa Gregg and Gregory J. Seigworth, 289–308. Durham and London: Duke UP, 2010.

Tolstaia, Tat'iana [Tolstaya, Tatyana]. "The Perils of Utopia: The Russian Intelligentsia under Communism and Perestroika." Translated by Jamey Gambrell. *Development and Change* 27 (1996): 315–329.

———. "Russkii mir." In eadem, *Den': Lichnoe.* Moscow: Astrel', 2002.

——— [Tolstaya, Tatyana]. *The Slynx.* Translated by Jamey Gambrell. New York: NYRB Classics, 2007.

———. *Legkie miry: Povesti, rasskazy, esse.* Moscow: Ast, 2014.

———. *Voilochnyi vek*. Moscow: Ast, 2015.

———. "Blok." YouTube. August 18, 2020. https://www.youtube.com/watch?v=gWP95mgiPPA

———. "O 'Belom shume,' Sobchak i feminitivakh." YouTube. July 22, 2020. https://www.youtube.com/watch?v=fbgDPu6LgIU

———. "Zolotoi vek." YouTube. Accessed February 9, 2023. http://www.club366.ru/articles/121439.shtml

Ulitskaya, Lyudmila. "Reading as a Heroic Feat: The Intelligentsia and The Uncensored Literature." *Russian Journal of Communication* 10, nos. 2–3 (2018): 262–272.

Zubok, Vladislav. *Zhivago's Children: The Last Russian Intelligentsia*. Cambridge, MA: Harvard UP, 2009.

Part 4

THE TWENTY-FIRST CENTURY

Ulitskaya and Pelevin on the *Shestidesiatniki*

Sofya Khagi

The liberal intelligentsia of the 1960s—the famous and influential generation known as the *shestidesiatniki*—looms large in the post-Soviet cultural imagination.[1] They figure in works in a range of genres by numerous authors, such as Aleksandr Genis and Pyotr Vail, Vasily Aksyonov, Boris Strugatsky, Lyudmila Ulitskaya, and Dmitry Bykov.[2] Russia's publishing giant AST, in the division run by Elena Shubina, has produced an entire series under the rubric *The Great Shestidesiatniki* (Velikie shestidesiatniki). Scholarly monographs by Inna Kochetkova and Vladislav Zubok, as well as articles by Mark Lipovetsky and Ilya Kukulin, have likewise examined the legacy of this generation of public intellectuals.[3]

---

1 The 1960s largely overlapped with the period of Nikita Khrushchev's reforms, dubbed the Thaw after Ilya Ehrenburg's novel of the same name (*Ottepel'*, 1954), published a year after Stalin's death.
2 See, e.g., Aleksandr Genis and Petr Vail', *Shestidesiatye: mir sovetskogo cheloveka* (Ann Arbor, MI: Ardis, 1989); Vasilii Aksenov, *Tainstvennaia strast': roman o shestidesiatnikakh* (Moscow: Sem' dnei, 2009); Liudmila Ulitskaia, *Zelenyi shater* (Moscow: Eksmo, 2011); Sergei Vititskii, *Bessil'nye mira sego* (Donetsk: Stalker, 2003); Dmitry Bykov's biography of Bulat Okudzhava (Moscow: Molodaia gvardiia, 2009); and his collections of essays: Dmitrii Bykov, *Obrechennye pobediteli: Shestidesiatniki* (Moscow: Molodaia gvardiia, 2018); and idem, *Sentimental'nyi marsh: Shestidesiatniki* (Moscow: Molodaia Gvardiia, 2019).
3 See Inna Kochetkova, *The Myth of the Russian Intelligentsia: Old Intellectuals in the New Russia* (London and New York: Routledge, 2010); Vladislav Zubok, *Zhivago's Children: The Last Russian Intelligentsia* (Cambridge, MA: Harvard UP, 2009); Mark Lipovetskii, "Traektorii

In his monograph, *Zhivago's Children: The Last Russian Intelligentsia* (2009), Zubok describes the *shestidesiatniki* as follows:

> They were the graduates of the best universities ... and were destined to become the highly educated group that Stalin cynically called the Soviet intelligentsia.... The educated cadres trained for Stalinist service turned out to be a vibrant and diverse tribe, with intellectual curiosity, artistic yearnings, and a passion for high culture. They identified not only with the Soviet collectivity, but also with humanist individualism.... Zhivago's children ... rekindled the intelligentsia's dream of a just and humane Russian society.[4]

Zubok's study begins with an account of Boris Pasternak's life and oeuvre, recounting the poet's persecution after his novel *Doctor Zhivago* was published in Italy (1957) and Pasternak was awarded a Nobel Prize for literature. Zubok envisions the poet's funeral as an event that (re)-awakened the ideal of civic solidarity among the new generation of the Soviet intelligentsia. He goes on to narrate the engrossing journey, with its highs and lows, of the generation of the 1960s, from the Twentieth Party Congress, made famous by Khrushchev's denunciation of the cult of personality, all the way to the decline of the 1960s intelligentsia and the intelligentsia at large after the traumatic breakdown of the Soviet Union. Zubok concludes by affirming the ethos of educated civic participation and the belief in humane socialism embodied by "Zhivago's children."

Why do the history and legacy of the 1960s intelligentsia figure so prominently in post-Soviet cultural and political discourse? The *shestidesiatniki* manifested the historically deep ethos of an enlightened, free-minded, and

---

ITR-diskursa: razroznennye zametki," *Neprikosnovennyi zapas* 74, no. 6 (2010): 213–230, and that essay's English-language version, Mark Lipovetsky, "The Poetics of the ITR Discourse: In the 1960s and Today," in idem, *Postmodern Crises: From Lolita to Pussy Riot* (Boston, MA: Academic Studies Press, 2017), 33–52; Il'ia Kukulin, "Al'ternativnoe sotsial'noe proektirovanie v sovetskom obshchestve 1960kh-1970kh godov, ili Pochemu v sovremennoi Rossii ne prizhilis' levye politicheskie praktiki," *Novoe literaturnoe obozrenie* 88, no. 6 (2007): 169–201; and idem, "Sentimental'naia tekhnologiia: Pamiat' o 1960-kh v diskussiiakh o modernizatsii 2009–2010 godov," *Neprikosnovennyi zapas* 74, no. 6 (2010): 277–301.

4   Zubok, *Zhivago's Children*, 21–22. Cf. Gessen: "In 1958 the world watched with horror as the Soviet government shepherded a mob that verbally trampled the poet Boris Pasternak.... Still, a certain reprieve from the paralyzing fear of the Stalin years ... produced an atmosphere that shaped one of the most important generations in Soviet history, the shestidesiatniki." See Masha Gessen, *Dead Again: The Russian Intelligentsia after Communism* (New York: Verso, 1997), 10.

ethical elite guiding the people, which was advanced from the eighteenth century onward and articulated most forcefully in the nineteenth-century Russian literary classics. In this influential paradigm, moral (self)-betterment is primary and enables social improvement. Hopes are staked "not on new projects of a future society but on projects for the transformation of human nature, myths about the self-determination of man in a totalitarian society and about [that society's] gradual transformation."[5] As such, the generation of the 1960s stands in for the aspirations of the Russian/Soviet intelligentsia at large, and the controversy around whether they proved successful (or, in the more widespread view, have failed) reflects on the generic intelligentsia project.

As Kochetkova observes in her book, *The Myth of the Russian Intelligentsia: Old Intellectuals in the New Russia* (2010), debates about who is and is not a member of the intelligentsia, and whether the intelligentsia is extinct or alive, became prominent after the Soviet Union disintegrated. The generation of the 1960s stood at the very center of those debates:

> These were the children of Khrushchev's Thaw, many of whom became Gorbachev's companions-in-arms. They are often referred to as simultaneously the reincarnation of the classical intelligentsia tradition and its last embodiment. After Perestroika failed, . . . the *shestidesiatniki* became demonized as the generation of failed intelligentsia; the integrity and value of their authority was severely challenged.[6]

Since the *shestidesiatniki* embody the prestige and responsibility of the intelligentsia, they are held accountable for the "people and country," from the charged vantage of the fall of the Soviet Union and the attendant crisis, the alleged demise of the intelligentsia as a uniquely Russian phenomenon.[7]

Whether critical or nostalgic, post-Soviet appraisals of the *shestidesiatniki* tend to envision them as key players and central reference points across twentieth-century history. They point back to the original Socialist/revolutionary promise via de-Stalinization, the twentieth Party Congress, and the ensuing high-spirited era of the Thaw.[8] Where socialism, even "with a human face," has no

---

5 Kukulin, "Al'ternativnoe sotsial'noe proektirovanie," 171.
6 Kochetkova, *The Myth of the Russian Intelligentsia*, xiii.
7 On the post-Soviet crisis of the intelligentsia, see also Zubok, *Zhivago's Children*, 335–362; Gessen, *Dead Again*; and Dmitri Shalin, ed., *Russian Intelligentsia in the Age of Counterperestroika: Political Agendas, Rhetorical Strategies, Personal Choices* (New York: Routledge, 2019).
8 Post-Soviet nostalgia "is the longing for the very real humane values, ethics, friendships, and creative possibilities that the reality of socialism afforded—often in spite of the state's

appeal, Zhivago's children are seen to revive the mores of the pre-revolutionary intelligentsia and hearken back to the cultural riches of the nineteenth century and the Silver Age. At the same time, they are seen to look forward to perestroika, the traumatic disintegration of the USSR and the troubled post-Soviet decades. With so much history converging on the shoulders of the *shestidesiatniki*, they carry, justifiably or not, high explanatory valence. And, since predicaments seem to outnumber achievements in much of modern Russian history, their opponents dispense blame much more readily than praise.

The charges against them advanced from opposite sides of the political spectrum, conservative and liberal, are divergent though often equally harsh. From the former perspective, they are deemed traitors who undermined the foundations of Soviet society for decades through dissident efforts, until they finally authored perestroika and brought the country to a sudden and disastrous collapse.[9] Yet their natural heirs, the post-Soviet liberal camp, have advanced critiques no less charged, whether decrying the *shestidesiatniki*'s naivety and lack of practical verve or castigating them for alleged elitism or adherence to "obsolete" mental frameworks such as essentialist or binary thinking.[10] That said, the generation of the 1960s is perceived as a source of discredited yet not forgotten social romanticism—"that is, of actions founded on faith in the productivity of a selfless personal effort."[11]

In this essay, I will explore the portrayal of the *shestidesiatniki* by two major post-Soviet writers: Lyudmila Ulitskaya in *The Big Green Tent* (Zelenyi shater, 2010), and Victor Pelevin in *Generation "П"* (1999). These novels present a spectrum of post-Soviet responses to the myth of the *shestidesiatniki*: an earnest, if tempered, tribute (Ulitskaya) contrasts with a satirical interrogation of their political and ethical principles (Pelevin). Notwithstanding the obvious divergences—Ulitskaya is speaking about her own cohort and stresses generational promise and honorable intent—the younger writer, Pelevin, who zeroes in on their ephemeral or, worse, deleterious practical results, in fact condemns them far less harshly than his own peers.

---

proclaimed goals" (Alexei Yurchak, *Everything Was Forever Until It Was No More: The Last Soviet Generation* [Princeton, NJ: Princeton UP, 2006], 8).

9 For a survey of the *shestidesiatniki*'s criticisms in the 1990s by nationalists, see Kochetkova, *The Myth of the Russian Intelligentsia*, 63–70.

10 See, e.g., Lipovetsky, "The Poetics of the ITR Discourse." For the Russian intelligentsia's belief in objective truth, see Isaiah Berlin, introduction to *Russian Intellectual History: An Anthology*, ed. Marc Raeff (New York: Harcourt, Brace, and World, 1966), 6.

11 Kukulin, "Sentimental'naia tekhnologiia," 301.

So We Won't Perish One by One

The Big Green Tent paints a sweeping historical canvas, spanning over four decades of Soviet history between the deaths of two Josephs, Stalin (in 1953) and Brodsky (in 1996). It begins as the coming-of-age story of three schoolmates, Sanya Steklov, Mikha Melamid, and Ilya Bryansky, who grow up in the impoverished yet culturally vibrant post-World War II Moscow. The boys are ostracized by their schoolmates for lacking an instinct for aggression and not participating in school fights. A gifted teacher of literature, Victor Yulievich Shengeli, inculcates in them a passion for reading and high culture.[12]

In *The Big Green Tent*, Ulitskaya defines the intelligentsia of the 1960s as "impractical people with spiritual needs":

> They did not constitute a party, a social circle, a secret society; they were not even a cohort of like-minded people. Perhaps the only thing that united all of them was a mutual hatred of Stalinism. And, of course, reading. Hungry, unrestrained, obsessive reading. Reading was a passion, a neurosis, a narcotic. For many, books became surrogates for life rather than mere teachers of life.[13]

> Это была не партия, не кружок, не тайное общество, даже не собрание единомышленников. Пожалуй, единственным общим знаменателем было их отвращение к сталинизму. И, конечно, чтение. Жадное, безудержное, маниакальное чтение—хобби, невроз, наркотик. Для многих книга из учителя жизни превращалась в ее заменитель.[14]

---

12 Ulitskaya has a specific definition of *intelligenty*: "Such characters model sincerity and Western, liberal mores, signaling that this group is well-educated, shaped by prerevolutionary values that preclude totalitarianism and instead reflect ethical behavior." See Elizabeth A. Skomp and Benjamin M. Sutcliffe, *Ludmila Ulitskaya and the Art of Tolerance*, foreword Helena Goscilo (Madison: U of Wisconsin Press, 2015), 102. Ulitskaya wrote *The Big Green Tent* "in great part to rehabilitate this generation, whose opposition to the government is often faulted for post-Soviet chaos" (ibid., 106).

13 Ludmila Ulitskaya, *The Big Green Tent*, trans. Polly Gannon (New York: Farrar, Straus, and Giroux, 2015), 232.

14 Ulitskaia, *Zelenyi shater*, 240.

Under Shengeli's dedicated mentorship, the boys receive training in literature and history and, no less centrally, moral education.[15] The trio and their pedagogue form a life-long bond.

The *shestidesiatniki* are often depicted as "children of the Commissars," who developed in opposition to the generation of their parents, who were firmly in the grip of Stalinist ideology. Importantly, Ulitskaya's boys are all raised fatherless: Sanya grows up with two refined old-school women, Mikha—with an obnoxious aunt, and Ilya—with a working-class single mother. Shengeli becomes their surrogate father, and the tours he leads around Moscow expose the boys to the capital's cultural riches and connect them—over the heads of their parents—to the earlier, aesthetically rich and morally ethical pre-revolutionary tradition.[16]

Ulitskaya defines herself as belonging to a junior branch of the 1960s generation (she was born in 1943), like her protagonists, born circa 1940.[17] On this basis, she demarcates herself and her heroes from the older cohort of *shestidesiatniki* born in the late 1920s and 1930s, and she is able to fend off a critique often leveled against them: that they did not altogether free themselves from the clutches of Soviet ideology. If the older *shestidesiatniki* experienced the dismantling of their proper Soviet Weltanschauung as adults yet retained their faith in a "socialism with a human face," the younger ones, Ulitskaya claims, harbored no such illusions.

The teenaged Sanya, Mikha, and Ilya indeed grow perpendicular to their parents, developing a strong oppositional stance toward the Soviet status quo. The rift between generations, à la Ivan Turgenev's classic model of intergenerational conflict in *Fathers and Children* (Ottsy i deti, 1862), is also demonstrated in the story of Olya, Ilya's future wife and initially a proper Soviet girl, daughter of a woman from the Soviet "nomenclature." If Olya's mother readily takes advantage of her privileges, exhibiting the compromised integrity of the Soviet intelligentsia, Olya, along with a group of other students, supports a professor

---

15 The *intelligenty* "are a special family of affinity, joined by ethics, education, and moral behavior in difficult times." See Skomp and Sutcliffe, *Ludmila Ulitskaya and The Art of Tolerance*, 109.
16 Along with Shengeli, Sanya's aristocratic grandmother provides a connection to pre-revolutionary culture. "The generation . . . found its moral authorities not among the previous generation, . . . but among the generation before that, which had been shaped during that other life." See Alla Latynina, "Soviet Power Has Killed Them All . . . Liudmila Ulitskaia's *The Green Tent*," *Russian Studies in Literature* 49, no. 1 (2012): 11. The original Russian version of this article is Alla Latynina, "Vsekh sovetskaia vlast' ubila . . . 'Zelenyi shater' Liudmily Ulitskoi," *Novyi mir* 6 (2011): 169–177.
17 "I am not quite an authentic *shestidesiatnik* because I belong to their junior wing" (Liudmila Ulitskaia, "Razgovor pod zelenym shatrom. Stenogramma vstrechi iz tsikla 'vazhnee chem politika,'" February 15, 2011, https://www.hse.ru/data/2011/09/02/1268300018/Ulitskaya_Razgovor_pod_zelenym_chatrom_15022011.pdf).

imprisoned for publishing abroad (an allusion to the Sinyavsky-Daniel trial). She signs a petition in his defense and then is expelled from the university, a shock to her self-satisfied mother. As Ilya and Olya marry, they get involved in *samizdat* (underground publications) and *tamizdat* (literature smuggled abroad for publication) activities, trafficking works like Aleksandr Solzhenitsyn's *The Gulag Archipelago* (Arkhipelag Gulag, 1958–1968).[18]

The Big Green Tent conveys the exhilarating atmosphere of the dissident community in the 1960s and 1970s, and zeroes in on the high points of Khrushchev's Thaw and the later Brezhnev era, including the 1957 Youth Festival in Moscow, the 1965 Sinyavsky-Daniel trial, and the Prague Spring of 1968.[19] It is the dissident Muscovites' support of the Prague Spring that is emblematic in the narrative as an expression of a newly found or recovered spirit of civic protest and freedom that animates Ulitskaya's protagonists:

> On the night of August 21, 1968, an event took place that would change everything: Soviet troops entered Czechoslovakia. . . . On Red Square, next to Lobnoe Mesto, also known as the Place of Skulls, there had been a demonstration against the invasion of Czechoslovakia. The names of seven people who went out onto the square were already known. All the demonstrators but one . . . had been arrested.[20]

> В ночь на двадцать первое августа 1968 года произошло событие, которое совершенно все изменило: советские войска вошли в Чехословакию. . . . На Красной площади возле Лобного места прошла демонстрация против ввода войск в Чехословакию. Имена семерых человек, вышедших на площадь, были известны. Все, кроме одной участницы, . . . были уже арестованы.[21]

It is the advance of Soviet tanks into Prague that destroys Mikha's remaining illusions about the Soviet system. A student of Marxism, he was trying to work

---

18 "At different times, a word written, a poem recited, a book owned could lead to grave consequences for the transgressor, from loss of social standing, to prison, to death. The more the Word was pushed underground, the more it became imbued with mythical, possibly lethal power" (Gessen, *Dead Again*, 10).
19 The only brief allusion to Sputnik and Gagarin occurs at the end of the long list of Khrushchev's chaotic activities.
20 Ulitskaya, *The Big Green Tent*, 452–453.
21 Ulitskaia, *Zelenyi shater*, 466.

out "how such wonderful ideas about justice could become so misshapen, so distorted, in their implementation" ("pochemu prekrasnye idei sotsial'noi spravedlivosti tak krivo voploshchaiutsia"). Now "the truth was laid bare—it was a grandiose lie, cynicism, inconceivable cruelty, shameless manipulations of people who had lost their humanity . . . out of fear" ("tut stalo iasno i kholodno—grandioznaia lozh', tsinizm, nepostizhimaia zhestokost', besstydnaia manipuliatsiia liud'mi, teriaiushchimi chelovecheskii oblik i dostoinstvo . . . ot strakha").[22] The mention of fear is important—per Ulitskaya, her *shestidesiatniki* heroes are different from the previous generation, whose sense of dignity and self-worth had been crushed by Stalinist terror.[23] The new intelligentsia are not intimidated or, at any rate, less intimidated than their parents, and prepared to stand up for their convictions.

Ulitskaya's admiration of the dissident circle, however earnest, at times displays a tinge of irony. As she describes dissident discussions, "tea and vodka poured in rivers, kitchens basked in the fervent steam of political dispute, so that the dampness crept up the walls to the hidden microphones behind the tiles at the level of the ceiling" ("chai i vodka lilis' rekoi, kukhni puzyrilis' parom politicheskikh diskussii, tak chto syrost' polzla ot steny vozle plity vverkh, k zapriatannym mikrofonam").[24] This characterization suggests a somewhat overblown perception of self-worth on the part of the oppositional intelligentsia. Some are genuine dissenters, while many are mere pretender dissidents.[25]

As Ilya expostulates on his *samizdat* and *tamizdat* activities to his friend Mikha, he displays a degree of similar self-indulgence:

> The phenomenon itself is remarkable and unprecedented. It's vital energy that is spread from source to source, establishing threads, forming a sort of spider web that links many people. . . . Mikha sat rapt and openmouthed, quite literally. A small trace of saliva had even gathered in the corner of his mouth, as happens with a sleeping child. . . . At that moment Ilya was himself

---

22 Ulitskaya, *The Big Green Tent*, 452; eadem, *Zelenyi shater*, 467.
23 "The older generation had been intimidated, deluded, or, worse still, molded by Stalin. The 'sons' were therefore exceptionally raucous in their rejection of at least the externals of the preceding era." See Geoffrey Hosking, "The Twentieth Century: In Search of New Ways, 1953–80," in *The Cambridge History of Russian Literature*, ed. Charles A. Moser (Cambridge: Cambridge UP, 1989), 552.
24 Ulitskaya, *The Big Green Tent*, 265; eadem, *Zelenyi shater*, 274.
25 "The hosts would press a telling finger to their lips if the conversation took too dangerous a turn, because they too wanted to be part of the great face-off between the intelligentsia and the power structure" (Latynina, "Soviet Power Has Killed Them All," 19).

enamored of his role in furthering world progress. The grandiose picture he painted did not entirely jibe with reality, but it wasn't pure invention, either. The petty demons of the Russian revolution, the very ones Dostoevsky described, haunted the darkening recesses of the forlorn, overgrown garden. . . . The long shadow of the completely ingenuous Chekhov was moving in the direction of Immer's garden store. . . . But, on the whole, progress was on the march.[26]

Явление это само по себе потрясающее и небывалое. Это живая энергия, которая распространяется от источника к источнику, и протягиваются нити, и образовывается своего рода паутина между людьми. . . . Миха сидел, разинув рот в прямом смысле слова. Даже легкая слюнка набегала в углах губ, как у спящего ребенка. . . . Илья и сам в этот момент наслаждался собственной ролью в мировом прогрессе. Нарисованная им величественная картина не вполне соответствовала действительности, но она и не была чистым вымыслом. Мелкие бесы русской революции—те самые, Достоевские—клубились в темнеющих углах оскудевшего сада. Длинная тень не повинного ни в чем Чехова двигалась в направлении огородного магазина Иммера. . . . Но в целом прогресс куда-то двигался, несомненно![27]

For most of the story the narrator identifies with her heroes, but here an ironic distance can be felt. The passageways of *samizdat* conducting vital living energy, as Ilya melodramatically claims, recall the current of dampness creeping up the kitchen walls, as the intelligentsia delights in its attestations of dissent. Mikha, enthralled by his friend's work, is salivating like a sleeping child. What he sees as a sacred mission carried out in the decaying Chekhovian orchard (*Vishnevyi sad*, 1903) is, moreover, plagued by "demons"—traitors and provocateurs, as in Fyodor Dostoevsky's *Demons* (*Besy*, 1871–1872).

The Big Green Tent revolves around the central metaphor of the imago, an insect's mature developmental stage that the novel's protagonists fail to reach: "The insect does not pupate, does not reach the imagal stage (when it frees its wings from the pupal envelope) but remains a larva, although one capable of

---

26 Ulitskaya, *The Big Green Tent*, 433–434.
27 Ulitskaia, *Zelenyi shater*, 448.

reproduction."[28] Ulitskaya diagnoses the Soviet society of the time as infantile. Alla Latynina, for one, finds the logic of this metaphor questionable: "What is the implication of that? That protest is a consequence of childishness? Which means that conformism is a sign of maturity?"[29] What Ulitskaya seems to say, however, is different. In Shengeli's understanding, the boys' initiation into adulthood, likened to insect metamorphosis, means the awakening of a moral responsibility: "through orphanhood, humiliation, cruelty, and loneliness, to . . . the sense of good and evil, and the understanding that love is the supreme value" ("cherez sirotstvo, obidy, zhestokost' i odinochestvo k . . . osoznaniiu dobra i zla, k ponimaniiu liubvi kak vysshei tsennosti").[30] An educated former prison convict, Vinberg, estimates the Soviet Union to be a land of children: "Culture blocks the natural impulses of adults; but not of children. And where there is no culture, blocking is absent. There is a cult of the father, of obedience, and at the same time an unmanageable childish aggression" ("Kul'tura blokiruet prirodnye reaktsii u vzroslykh, no ne u detei. A kogda kul'tury net, blokirovka otsutstvuet. Est' kul't ottsa, poslushanie, i odnovremenno neupravliaemaia detskaia agressiia").[31] The children—the generation of the 1960s—have the potential to overcome ingrained fear and break through into adulthood—understood as possessing an active ethical sense.

As their fates unfold over the course of decades, it becomes clear that none of the novel's main characters succeed in their aspirations. Sanya's prospects as a gifted musician are cut short early on when a school bully injures his hand, permanently disabling two of his fingers. The bright and handsome Ilya falls into a trap set by the KGB, becomes their agent, emigrates, and dies prematurely of a terminal illness. Mikha, the most empathetic and creative of the trio, witnesses, in one more evocation of Dostoevsky's *Demons*, the betrayal of the dissident circle by his father-in-law, a respected old-school dissident. Tellingly, the traitor belongs to the older generation. Mikha ends up committing suicide at the age of thirty-three, with obvious Christological references, because, he feels, his poetry remains as infantile as ever, and it is time to liberate himself and his close friends "from the utter failure of his existence, from his inability to live like a normal, fully grown man" ("ot bezdarnosti svoego sushchestvovaniia, ot

---

28 Latynina, "Soviet Power Has Killed Them All," 22. "'The world of larvae negates a sense of responsibility, it lives by this moment's needs, values pleasures more than anything else in life.' Anastasiia Gosteva, "Lichinki, deti lichinok. Interv'iu s Liudmiloi Ulitskoi," Gazeta.ru, December 21, 2010, https://www.gazeta.ru/culture/2010/12/21/a_3472805.shtml.
29 Latynina, "Soviet Power Has Killed Them All," 23.
30 Ulitskaya, *The Big Green Tent*, 75–77; eadem, *Zelenyi shater*, 82.
31 Ulitskaya, *The Big Green Tent*, 377; eadem, *Zelenyi shater*, 390.

polneishei nevozmozhnosti zhit′ normal′noi i polnotsennoi zhizn′iu vzroslogo cheloveka").[32] He mutters, "Imago," and throws himself out a window.

Ilya senses acutely during a late visit to his former teacher Shengeli that they are all losers, redeemed only by the sentiment of mutual empathy:

> Mikha is a mediocre poet, an idealist. Sanya is a musician manqué. And now I've become a stool pigeon.... Maybe it was true that only beauty would save the world, or truth, or some other high-flown garbage; but fear was still more powerful than anything else.... It was not Pasternak who would remain, but Mandelstam, because his poetry expresses the full horror of his time and recoils from it. But Pasternak always wanted to reconcile himself to it.... What did he want to tell him? Nothing. This was just what he wanted: to sit down and drink a glass together, to commiserate with each other.[33]

> Миха—бесталанный поэт, идеалист. Саня—несостоявшийся музыкант. А я теперь стукач. . . . Может, мир спасет красота, или истина, или еще какая-нибудь прекрасная хрень, но страх все равно всего сильней. . . . Не Пастернак, а Мандельштам останется, потому что у него больше ужаса времени. А Пастернак все хотел со временем примириться. . . . А что он . . . хотел сказать? Да ничего. Вот именно этого хотелось: сидеть, выпивать, испытывать друг к другу сострадание.[34]

Ilya wonders how his well-intentioned and brilliant friends have, like himself, fared so miserably. He is still more shocked by what has happened to their teacher. Why is he lying all alone, drunk, surrounded by the finest works of Russian literature? Ulitskaya's answer, predictably, is that fear (the totalitarian machine) has aborted their high-minded yearnings. All that remains is their feeling of mutual sympathy, compassion, and love.

The unusual architectonics of *The Big Green Tent* realizes the leitmotif of inter-connectedness, which was a core value for the generation of the 1960s. The novel's structure is also reminiscent of *Doctor Zhivago*'s poetics of the

---

32 Ulitskaya, *The Big Green Tent*, 525; eadem, *Zelenyi shater*, 541.
33 Ulitskaya, *The Big Green Tent*, 296–97.
34 Ulitskaia, *Zelenyi shater*, 306–307.

"crossings of fates."[35] One story "hangs on a hook left from the previous story; the action develops not in linear style but moves in a spiral, twining events into a skein, braiding and weaving together the characters' fates."[36] Ulitskaya reifies the metaphor of "the common circle" and thereby dramatizes the *shestidesiatniki*'s yearning, in the words of a popular song by Bulat Okudzhava, to "hold onto each other's hands so as not to perish one by one" (Voz'memsia za ruki, druz'ia, 1967). The dying Olga's Isaiah-inspired prelapsarian dream of a green tent providing a final dwelling for, and reconciliation to, everyone in her circle, realizes the same notion.[37] The heroes of Ulitskaya's novel do in fact perish one by one, but their striving may be as uplifting as it is ephemeral.

Fathers and Demons

As early as his essay of 1993, "John Fowles and the Tragedy of Russian Liberalism" (Dzhon Faulz i tragediia russkogo liberalizma), Viktor Pelevin draws, like Ulitskaya, on the Chekhovian motif of the cherry orchard to reflect on the late Soviet intelligentsia ousted by *pupki* ("navels"), post-Soviet power- and wealth-grabbing New Russians:

> Chekhov's cherry orchard mutated but nevertheless survived behind the Gulag wire.... But now the very climate has changed. It looks like cherries will no longer grow in Russia.... "Freed from the laws of the market..., members of the intelligentsia lived in an imaginary, illusory world. External reality in the form of the cop only now and then would wander into their editorial office lived according to the laws of *The Glass Bead Game*. Strange, transient, esoteric phenomena with no counterparts in the other, real world were born here."... The[ir] replacements are the dark, criminal *pupki* who can be taken for middle class only after a fifth shot of vodka.
>
> Чеховский вишневый сад мутировал, но все-таки выжил за гулаговским забором.... А сейчас меняется сам климат.

---

35 "*Doctor Zhivago*, itself a novel about the tragedy of intellectuals, is the most significant intertext in *The Big Green Tent*" (Skomp and Sutcliffe, *Ludmila Ulitskaya and The Art of Tolerance*, 125).
36 Latynina, "Soviet Power Has Killed Them All," 15.
37 "Perhaps in the present we in our country need the elimination of aggression and animosity that eats up generations more than intellectual tension" (Gosteva, "Lichinki, deti lichinok. Interv'iu s Liudmiloi Ulitskoi").

Вишня в России, похоже, больше не будет расти. . . .
"Освобожденные от законов рынка . . . , интеллигенты жили
в вымышленном, иллюзорном мире. Внешняя реальность,
принимая облик постового, лишь изредка забредала в
эту редакцию, жившую по законам "Игры в бисер". Здесь
рождались странные, зыбкие, эзотерические феномены, не
имеющие аналогов в другом, настоящем мире". . . . На [это]
место приход[ят] темные уголовные пупки, которых можно
принять за средний класс только после пятого стакана
водки.[38]

Pelevin cites an essay by Genis from *Independent Newspaper* (Nezavisimaia gazeta) that uses expressions such as "real life" (*podlinnaia zhizn'*) and "real world" (*nastoiashchii mir*), before wryly remarking that the author differs from the Soviet intelligentsia "merely by the assemblage of hallucinations that he takes for reality himself" ("tol'ko tem naborom galliutsinatsii, kotorye prinimaet za real'nost' sam").[39] By implication, *shestidesiatniki* such as Genis seamlessly turn into post-Soviet cogs in the machine of market capitalism because for them it represents the move from illusory to real existence. If fear plays the role of ultimate reality in Ulitskaya, the cynicism of Pelevin's post-Soviet players is driven by their belief—however misguided—in the ultimate reality of the consumer world unfolding around them.[40]

Pelevin's novel *Generation "П"* elaborates on the theme of the downfall of the intelligentsia in early post-Soviet Russia in a way that is at once comical and unforgiving. Vavilen Tatarsky, the hero, comes of age as the Soviet Union disintegrates. As a youngster, he was an aspiring poet and studied at the Moscow Literary Institute. With the country's collapse, he becomes an advertising copywriter, concocting Russian ads patterned on American techniques. By the novel's end, he is the symbolic husband of the goddess of money, Ishtar of the Sumerian pantheon, and presides over Russian advertising as a media divinity.

Generation "П" begins with a mockingly nostalgic evocation of the last Soviet generation: "Once upon a time in Russia there really was a carefree, joyful generation that smiled in joy at the summer, the sea, and the sun, and chose Pepsi" ("Kogda-to v Rossii i pravda zhilo bespechal'noe iunoe pokolenie, kotoroe

---

38 Viktor Pelevin, *Vse povesti i esse* (Moscow: Eksmo, 2005), 393–397.
39 Ibid., 393–394. I was unable to locate Genis's essay.
40 I would like to thank my anonymous reviewer for drawing my attention to the relevance of Pelevin's essay for this discussion.

ulybnulos' letu, moriu i solntsu—i vybralo 'Pepsi'").[41] The lines may prompt the reader to recall Khrushchev's famous tasting of Pepsi at the 1959 American exhibition in Moscow, under Richard Nixon's wary gaze. Just as Ulitskaya's *Big Green Tent* highlights the Sixth World Festival of Youth and Students in 1957 Moscow, the 1959 American national exhibition figures as another major event of the Thaw. Here, the "prelapsarian" condition of Homo Sovieticus is swiftly disrupted by a sampling of the iconic Western soft drink—as a prelude to, and emblem of, falling for the allure of the world beyond the Iron Curtain just a few decades thereafter.

Along with love of Pepsi, "Generation P"—the children of the *shestidesiatniki*, as we learn at the novel's outset—harbors a passion for poetry, and Pasternak's poetry in particular, all conveniently beginning with a 'П'. Vavilen Tatarsky, an average, even mediocre, representative of that generation, develops a taste for versification "out in the countryside during summer [when] he read a small volume of Boris Pasternak" ("letom, v derevne, [kogda] on prochital malen'kii tomik Borisa Pasternaka"). The poems, "which had previously left him entirely cold, had such a profound impact that for several weeks he could think of nothing else—and then began writing verse himself" ("Stikhi, k kotorym on ran'she ne pital nikakoi sklonnosti, do takoi stepeni potriasli ego, chto neskol'ko nedel' on ne mog dumat' ni o chem drugom, a potom nachal pisat' ikh sam").[42]

If Ulitskaya, in an intelligentsia cliché, portrays a passion for literature as instrumental to, and a sign of, a strong ethical stance in her protagonists, Pelevin precludes any assumptions of intellectual, aesthetic, or moral superiority in Tatarsky, regardless of his cultural leanings. Pelevin's protagonist is a poor poet—the first line of verse he composes, "The sardine-clouds swim onwards to the south" ("Sardiny oblakov plyvut na iug"), has, as he himself realizes, "a fishy odor" ("pakhnet ryboi"). His fondness for poetry is trite, merely following the trend of the late Soviet intelligentsia: "His was an absolutely typical case, which ended in typical fashion when Tatarsky entered the Literary Institute" ("Sluchai byl sovershenno tipichnym i tipichno zakonchilsia—Tatarskii postupil v Literaturnyi Institut").[43]

Along with problematizing the link between culture and ethics, Pelevin subverts the intelligentsia's comfortable and hackneyed sense of self-worth, as derived from its opposition to the status quo:

---

41 Victor Pelevin, *Homo Zapiens*, trans. Andrew Bromfield (New York: Penguin, 2002). Idem, *Generation "П"* (Moscow: Vagrius, 1999), 9.
42 Pelevin, *Homo Zapiens*, 3; idem, *Generation "П,"* 13.
43 Ibid.

Something began happening to the very eternity to which he decided to devote his labors and his days. . . . It turned out that eternity only existed for as long as Tatarsky sincerely believed in it and was actually nowhere to be found beyond the bounds of that belief. In order for him to believe sincerely in eternity, others had to share in this belief, because a belief no one else shares is called schizophrenia. . . . And he realized something else too: the eternity he used to believe in could only exist on state subsidies, or else—which is just the same thing—as something forbidden by the state.[44]

С вечностью, которой Татарский решил посвятить свои труды и дни, тоже стало что-то происходить. . . . Оказалось, что вечность существовала только до тех пор, пока Татарский искренне в нее верил, и нигде за пределами этой веры ее, в сущности, не было. Для того чтобы искренне верить в вечность, надо было, чтобы эту веру разделяли другие—потому что вера, которую не разделяет никто, называется шизофренией. . . . Кроме того, он понял еще одно: вечность, в которую он раньше верил, могла существовать только на государственных дотациях—или, что то же самое, как нечто запрещенное государством.[45]

In one of the thought-provoking paradoxes that are a hallmark of his writing, Pelevin claims that eternity—the metaphysical stronghold of the intelligentsia—and the intelligentsia themselves—have been nurtured by autocracy. That the Russian intelligentsia has historically derived its moral authority from opposing the ignominy of the state is well-known.[46] But Pelevin pushes this line of thought to an unexpected subversive conclusion. The intelligentsia and the state exist in symbiosis; they are like a weight and a counterweight; or, if one employs a financial metaphor, the intelligentsia is backed up by tyranny, the way gold or silver back up a paper currency. And so, while the compromised Soviet intelligentsia exists on state subsidies, like Olya's mother in Ulitskaya's novel, its dissenting segment needs the state no less, and perhaps more—to back up

---

44 Pelevin, *Homo Zapiens*, 3–5.
45 Pelevin, *Generation "П,"* 13–15.
46 On the intelligentsia's valor in the face of governmental prosecution, see Dmitrii Likhachev, "O russkoi intelligentsii," in idem, *Vospominan'ia, razdum'ia, raboty raznykh let*, ed. O. V. Panchenko et al. (St. Petersburg: ARS, 2006), 389.

its symbolic capital. In this light, the microphones installed by the KGB, or imagined to be installed, in the apartments of Ulitskaya's dissidents are a requisite part of the entire histrionic set-up, affirming their self-idealization.[47]

Like Ulitskaya's boys and their teacher, Tatarsky is inspired by Pasternak. In the case of Pelevin's protagonist, what Ulitskaya cautiously terms Pasternak's desire "to reconcile with the times" grows into full-blown Social Darwinism, the adaptation and survival of the fittest in the rough-and-tumble post-Soviet milieu. The banal Tatarsky, the "hero of the time," possesses perhaps one forte, a high adaptability to the dominant behavioral trends, whether late Soviet (culture, idealism) or post-Soviet (marketability, cynicism). His very mediocrity, his lack of a firm interiority, enables an efficient mimicry that meets novel external pressures, not only "reconciling" with the post-Soviet environment but prospering in it.

Pelevin's biological metaphor of Oranus (*rotozhopa*, in colloquial Russian) conveys a problematic similar to Ulitskaya's imago. If *The Big Green Tent* likens immature individuals to the larval stage of insect development, with an ability to consume and reproduce without developing into full-grown specimens, *Generation "П"* imagines Oranus as a bio-aggregate that imprisons post-Soviet humans and limits their cognitive and emotional processes to the digestion and elimination of money. Each human is trapped in a cycle of consumption-excretion, a *Perpetuum mobile* of consumer culture. They are efficient biological specimens in the sense of survival and reproduction, but they lack human traits such as free will, responsibility, and ethics. The ethical norms of the intelligentsia do not foster post-Soviet survival and are therefore quickly discarded.

In Pelevin's satire, the former devotees of the spirit, the mythologized Russian intelligentsia, or more precisely its Soviet heirs, readily succumb to post-Soviet market realities.[48] The death of the intelligentsia and the death of the autocratic

---

47 Cf. Katerina Clark: "Under a powerful state, they may function either as promulgators of the official ideology, or as staunch opponents of it. In either case, their power (whether symbolic or actual) derives from the power of the state." See Katerina Clark, "The King is Dead, Long Live the King: Intelligentsia Ideology in Transition," in *Conference on Russia at the End of the Twentieth Century: Culture and Its Horizons in Politics and Society*, Stanford University, October 1998, accessed June 15, 2022, https://web.stanford.edu/group/Russia20/volumepdf/clark_fin99.pdf. Cf. Oushakine: "The oppositional discourse in a sense shared the symbolic field with the dominant discourse: it echoed and amplified the rhetoric of the regime, rather than positioning itself outside of or underneath it." See Serguei Oushakine, "The Terrifying Mimicry of Samizdat," *Public Culture* 13, no. 2 (2001): 192.
48 "The career of a poet turned advertising writer—copywriter—parallels the post-Perestroika cultural crisis in Russia and the degradation of the Word, which, in turn, symbolizes the demise of the intelligentsia." See Lyudmila Parts, "Degradation of the Word or the Adventures of the Intelligent in Viktor Pelevin's *Generation 'П*,'" *Canadian Slavonic Papers* 46, nos. 3–4

Soviet system prove to be two sides of the same coin: The intelligentsia expires just as "the Soviet Union improved so much it has ceased to exist" ("SSSR... uluchshilsia nastol′ko, chto perestal sushchestvovat′").[49] The novel's dedication, "to the memory of the middle class" ("pamiati srednego klassa"), refers to the degraded version of the intelligentsia under the new conditions. This is the intelligentsia that "ceased thinking nationally and turned to the question of where it can get money" ("perestavsh[aia] myslit′ natsional′no i zadumavsh[aiasia] o tom, gde vziat′ deneg").[50] This leads one to wonder whether intelligentsia mores are *a priori* suspect or the market is irresistibly enticing (perhaps both).

Importantly for this analysis, Pelevin's narrative illumines how "the Soviet Union improved so much it has ceased to exist" by interrogating the *shestidesiatniki* ethos—and the relationship between fathers, the liberal intelligentsia of the 1960s, and children, Generation P:

> Take the very name Vavilen, which was conferred on Tatarsky by his father, who managed to combine in his heart a faith in communism with the ideals of the sixties generation. . . . Tatarsky's father clearly found it easy to imagine a faithful disciple of Lenin gratefully learning from Aksyonov's liberated page that Marxism originally stood for free love, or a jazz-crazy aesthete suddenly convinced by an elaborately protracted saxophone riff that communism would inevitably triumph. It was not only Tatarsky's father who was like that—the entire Soviet generation of the fifties and sixties was the same.[51]
>
> Взять хотя бы само имя "Вавилен", которым Татарского наградил отец, соединявший в своей душе веру в коммунизм и идеалы шестидесятничества. . . Оно было составлено из слов "Василий Аксенов" и "Владимир Ильич Ленин". Отец Татарского, видимо, легко мог представить себе верного ленинца, благодарно постигающего над вольной

(2004): 441. Similarly, Tatarsky "embodies the fate of the intelligentsia, killed dead by the dollar, Dallas and digital images." See Stephen Hutchings, *Russian Literary Culture in the Camera Age: The Word as Image* (London: Routledge, 2004), 177.

49 Pelevin, *Homo Zapiens*, 3; idem, *Generation "П,"* 13.
50 Pelevin, *Homo Zapiens*, 208; idem, *Generation "П,"* 255. Pelevin comes up with the term "lumpen intelligentsia," after Karl Marx's *lumpenproletariat*, suggesting an intelligentsia devoid of its traditional mores.
51 Pelevin, *Generation "П,"* 12. Here I cite from Pelevin's original rather that Bromfield's translation because Bromfield departs significantly from the original text.

аксеновской страницей, что марксизм изначально стоял за свободную любовь, или помешанного на джазе эстета, которого особо протяжная рулада саксофона заставит вдруг понять, что коммунизм победит. Но таков был не только отец Татарского,—таким было все советское поколение пятидесятых и шестидесятых.[52]

From the perspective of Pelevin's novel, the liberalizing *shestidesiatniki* project was untenable. Tatarsky's name, Vavilen, a combination of Vasily Aksyonov, a popular writer associated with the youth prose during the Thaw, and the Bolshevik leader V. I. Lenin, given by his father, is as inept stylistically as it is misguided ideologically. Given our knowledge of subsequent history, the *shestidesiatniki*'s strivings to reconcile original communist ideals and Western liberal culture, with a generous icing of imported consumer goods and pop entertainment, was bound to fail. Against their better hopes, the Soviet Union would not be reformed—rather, its "improvement" would entail its destruction.

If one applies Ulitskaya's central metaphor of the imago to Pelevin's narrative, the *shestidesiatniki* have failed here too to develop into responsible adults. Yet in Pelevin's case the diagnosis of infantilism is more emphatic. This applies equally to the Soviet youth of the Thaw and the Western youth culture of the sixties. Both engaged in frivolous opposition to government because the overflowing of youthful vitality sought some kind of outlet on both sides of the Iron Curtain. What links the Soviet *shestidesiatniki* and Western flower children is a belief that rebellion spiced up with sex, rock, and marijuana can offer a serious challenge to the system. It cannot—because a personal letting go merely reinforces societal mechanisms of repression, venting youthful energies in a mock rebellion. A serious collective opposition to the status quo would have to go beyond Aksyonov's youths discussing jazz and Lenin, or the campus-based Beatles- and Bob Dylan-accompanied play of flower children, however appealing such frolicking may have been.[53]

As Pelevin bleakly jokes, the generation of the 1960s "gave the world the amateur song and ejaculated the first sputnik—that four-tailed spermatozoon of the future that never began—into the dark void of cosmic space" ("podari[lo] miru samodeiatel'nuiu pesniu i konchi[lo] v chernuiu pustotu kosmosa pervym

---

52 Pelevin, *Generation "П,"* 12.
53 "Aksyonov's heroes might renew themselves in the Baltic provinces, where they could pick up the latest western fashions and ideas, but they finished by heading for Siberia and honest labor on the virgin lands" (Hosking, "The Twentieth Century," 553).

sputnikom—chetyrekhvostym spermatozoidom tak i ne nastavshego budush-chego").[54] The double entendre of *konchili*, in its senses of "finished" and "ejaculated," dramatizes the ironic bond between youthful sexual and revolutionary drives. It offers an epitaph to the idealism-of-space promise, a staple of the Thaw and the Soviet myth at large. The launch of Sputnik (1957) is presented as the Soviet body-politic's last vital deed, followed by a descent into impotence.

Pelevin's novel emerged out of a historical moment that demonstrated the failure of *shestidesiatniki* aspirations: the communism-plus-liberalism hybrid did not work out, and neither did hopes for modernization, historical progress, and social improvement under intelligentsia progressorism. Perhaps most detrimentally to the morale of the intelligentsia, their moral code has been trashed as well. What happened, as *Generation "П"* demonstrates with mixed laughter and bitterness, was the transformation of the 1960s leftist scenario into a brand in the universe of brands—along with the Soviet space program, the Soviet Union at large, the *shestidesiatniki*, the Russian intelligentsia at large, and so on. In short, as Pelevin quips, "that which is most sacred and exalted should be sold at the highest price possible because afterwards there will be nothing to sell" ("prodavat' samoe sviatoe i vysokoe nado kak mozhno dorozhe, potomu chto potom torgovat' budet uzhe nechem").[55]

Generation "П" takes issue with the Russian liberal intelligentsia's vision of social improvement through education, technological progress, and a personal code of honor. Just as Pelevin denies any correlation between the love of poetry and ethical behavior, he demonstrates that no correlation obtains between knowledge and ethics. The regime of the Chaldeans, elite human servants of Ishtar, the goddess of money, is based on sophisticated esoteric insights into social mechanisms. Knowledge, if any is to be gained, only serves the purposes of personal promotion. As a member of the failed (dead) intelligentsia, Tatarsky is co-opted by the establishment and becomes increasingly complicit as he gains more insight into the workings of power and attains a commanding position within it.

How does Pelevin envision the relationship between the generation of the 1960s and their children, Generation P, young and active during perestroika and the disintegration of the USSR? In the protagonist's realization, it is his peers, fallen into unbridled cynicism and greed, who are the apocalyptic, all-destroying Beast, the novel's Pizdets, advancing on the world. How does it turn out that Vavilen Tatarsky, conceived by his father as a utopian Aksyonov-Lenin hybrid,

---

54 Pelevin, *Homo Zapiens*, 2; idem, *Generation "П,"* 12.
55 Pelevin, *Homo Zapiens*, 17; idem, *Generation "П,"* 30.

ends up as the demonic Vavilon (Babylon) from the Bible who presides over post-Soviet Russia's Witches' Sabbath?

If Ulitskaya echoes Turgenev's classical model of generational change, with the *shestidesiatniki* children perpendicular to their Stalinist parents, Pelevin's vision resembles Dostoevsky's contrasting, itself polemical to Turgenev, model from *The Demons*. Inasmuch as the materialistic and demonic Generation P(izdets) seems at cross purposes with their idealistic fathers, they supplant the *shestidesiatniki* with the same kind of inevitability demonstrated in the fathers/children intergenerational dynamic in Dostoevsky's novel. The high-minded Western-influenced fathers, whether of the 1840s or the 1960s, are shown as hapless yet logical progenitors of their nihilistic children. Just as the histrionic phrasemonger Stepan Trofimovich Verkhovensky, Dostoevsky's parody of Turgenev, makes way for the dastardly and super-practical Pyotr Stepanovich, Pelevin's admirer of Lenin and jazz (and Pepsi, too) sires Vavilen Tatarsky, the future petty demon and consort of the goddess of money.

As Tatarsky is pettily demonic, so is his mentor and predecessor in the media business, Azadovsky, named Legion by his father:

> "You're no Vladimir; you are called Vavilen. . . . My old man was a wanker, too. Know what he called me? Legion. He probably did not even know what the word means. It used to make me miserable too, at first. Then I found out there was something about me in the Bible, so I felt better about it."[56]

> Ты не Владимир, а Вавилен—сказал Азадовский. . . У меня папаша тоже мудак был. Он меня знаешь как назвал? Легионом. Даже не знал, наверно, что это слово значит. Сначала я тоже горевал. Зато потом выяснил, что про меня в Библии написано, и успокоился.[57]

Azadovsky's name evokes "My name is Legion" (Luke 8:27–37), a group of demons in the New Testament, in the episode known as "Exorcism of the Gerasene Demoniac." Dostoevsky chose this episode, in which Jesus heals a man of Gadarenes who is possessed by demons, as the epigraph to *The Demons*. Azadovsky's father, of the same generation as Tatarsky's, is prophetic despite

---

56 Pelevin, *Homo Zapiens*, 186.
57 Pelevin, *Generation "П,"* 152–153.

himself: his offspring is another opportunistic member of Generation P. In a satirical touch, Azadovsky amuses himself by awarding toy medals of honor to his pet hamster Rostropovich, named for the renowned cellist and dissident from the *shestidesiatniki* generation—until he is killed by his associates and replaced by the next media godhead, Tatarsky.

The *shestidesiatniki*-parents' naivety and unreflective Western consumerist and pop-cultural leanings are a source of unforeseen transformation in Generation P, yet Pelevin appears less prepared to dispense unequivocal condemnation of the older generation. He certainly takes satirical freedoms with them and suggests a natural lineage between them and Generation P(izdets)—yet he directs his sharpest critique not at the fathers, however misguided their love of Aksyonov-Lenin-jeans-jazz, but rather at Tatarsky's and his own generation, which has betrayed the humanistic ideals of the 1960s. However untenable, such ideals are still not without appeal. Pelevin's diagnosis of infantilism, unlike Ulitskaya's, pinpoints idealism, not a lack of ethics, on the part of the *shestidesiatniki*; it is their children who are in the larval condition of mere consumption. The fathers may have been juvenile and shortsighted, but the children, aged and hardened under duress, are neither. The latter are also anything but virile, unable "to ejaculate Sputnik" or indeed much of anything, only to copulate with money or money surrogates, as Tatarsky does with Ishtar's golden idol. Perpendicular to the *shestidesiatniki*'s aspirations to help society progress, Generation P controls and creates reality through technological devices and manipulates people to gain maximal money and power. One might say that they continue the "guiding mission" of the intelligentsia—but in a thoroughly cynical and perverted manner.[58]

Conclusion

Debates around the generation of the 1960s illuminate the major developments of twentieth-century history, appraise the fate of the educated—scientists, artists, intellectuals—in post-Soviet Russia, and, in a longer perspective, contribute to the understanding and evaluation of the intelligentsia project over the course of modern Russian history. Ulitskaya offers an inspired, if not unequivocal, homage to her generation and insists on their moral righteousness in the face of oppression. Typical of her oeuvre overall, she embraces a conciliatory approach. Pelevin's take on the 1960s intelligentsia and the intelligentsia phenomenon as

---

58 The tendency to eulogize the era of the 1960s, even if ironically, increases in Pelevin's later works.

such, also characteristic of his general mindset, is satirical and polemical. The dreams of the *shestidesiatniki* have never been fulfilled. Are these dreams, then, a sign of sheer infantilism or "a deception that uplifts us dearer than a host of bitter truths"?[59]

Bibliography

Aksenov, Vasilii. *Tainstvennaia strast': roman o shestidesiatnikakh*. Moscow: Sem' dnei, 2009.

Bykov, Dmitrii. *Bulat Okudzhava*. Moscow: Molodaia gvardiia, 2009.

———. *Obrechennye pobediteli: Shestidesiatniki*. Moscow: Molodaia gvardiia, 2018.

———. *Sentimental'nyi marsh: Shestidesiatniki*. Moscow: Molodaia gvardiia, 2019.

Clark, Katerina. "The King is Dead, Long Live the King: Intelligentsia Ideology in Transition." In *Conference on Russia at the End of the Twentieth Century: Culture and Its Horizons in Politics and Society*. Stanford University. October 1998. https://web.stanford.edu/group/Russia20/volumepdf/clark_fin99.pdf.

Genis, Aleksandr, and Petr Vail'. *Shestidesiatye: mir sovetskogo cheloveka*. Ann Arbor, MI: Ardis, 1989.

Gessen, Masha. *Dead Again: The Russian Intelligentsia after Communism*. New York: Verso, 1997.

Gosteva, Anastasiia. "Lichinki, deti lichinok. Interv'iu s Liudmiloi Ulitskoi." Gazeta.ru. December 21, 2010. https://www.gazeta.ru/culture/2010/12/21/a_3472805.shtml.

Hosking, Geoffrey. "The Twentieth Century: In Search of New Ways, 1953–80." In *The Cambridge History of Russian Literature*, ed. Charles A. Moser, 520–94. Cambridge: Cambridge UP, 1989.

Hutchings, Stephen. *Russian Literary Culture in the Camera Age: The Word as Image*. London: Routledge, 2004.

Kochetkova, Inna. *The Myth of the Russian Intelligentsia: Old Intellectuals in the New Russia*. London and New York: Routledge, 2010.

---

[59] Aleksandr Pushkin, *Polnoe sobranie sochinenii v shestnadtsati tomakh*, ed. Maksim Gor'kii et al. (Moscow: Izdatel'stvo Akademii Nauk SSSR, 1937–1959), vol. 3, 251.

Kukulin, Il'ia. "Al'ternativnoe sotsial'noe proektirovanie v sovetskom obshchestve 1960kh-1970kh godov, ili Pochemu v sovremennoi Rossii ne prizhilis' levye politicheskie praktiki." *Novoe literaturnoe obozrenie* 88, no. 6 (2007): 169–201.

———. "Sentimental'naia tekhnologiia: pamiat' o 1960-kh v diskussiiakh o modernizatsii 2009–2010 godov." *Neprikosnovennyi zapas* 74, no. 6 (2010): 277–301.

Latynina, Alla. "Vsekh sovetskaia vlast' ubila... *Zelenyi shater* Liudmily Ulitskoi." *Novyi Mir* 6 (2011): 169–77. [In English: Alla Latynina. "Soviet Power Has Killed Them All... Liudmila Ulitskaia's *The Green Tent*." *Russian Studies in Literature* 49, no. 1 (2012), 68–84.]

Likhachev, Dmitrii. "O russkoi intelligentsii." In idem, *Vospominan'ia, razdum'ia, raboty raznykh let*, ed. O. V. Panchenko et al. St. Petersburg: ARS, 2006.

Lipovetskii, Mark. "Traektorii ITR-diskursa: razroznennye zametki." *Neprikosnovennyi zapas* 74, no. 6 (2010). [In English: Mark Lipovetsky. "The Poetics of the ITR Discourse: In the 1960s and Today." In idem, *Postmodern Crises: From Lolita to Pussy Riot*, 33–52. Boston, MA: Academic Studies Press, 2017.]

Oushakine, Serguei. "The Terrifying Mimicry of Samizdat." *Public Culture* 13, no. 2 (2001): 191–214.

Parts, Lyudmila. "Degradation of the Word or the Adventures of the Intelligent in Viktor Pelevin's *Generation 'П.'*" *Canadian Slavonic Papers* 46, nos. 3–4 (2004): 435–449.

Pelevin, Viktor. *Generation "П."* Moscow: Vagrius, 1999. [In English: Victor Pelevin. *Homo Zapiens*, trans. Andrew Bromfield. New York: Penguin, 2002.]

———. *Vse povesti i esse*. Moscow: Eksmo, 2005.

Raeff, Marc, ed. *Russian Intellectual History: An Anthology*. New York: Harcourt, Brace, and World, 1966.

Shalin, Dmitri, ed. *Russian Intelligentsia in the Age of Counterperestroika: Political Agendas, Rhetorical Strategies, Personal Choices*. New York: Routledge, 2019.

Skomp, Elizabeth A., and Benjamin M. Sutcliffe. *Ludmila Ulitskaya and the Art of Tolerance*. Madison: U of Wisconsin Press, 2015.

Ulitskaia, Liudmila. "Razgovor pod zelenym shatrom. Stenogramma vstrechi iz tsikla 'vazhnee chem politika.'" February 15, 2011. https://www.hse.ru/data/2011/09/02/1268300018/Ulitskaya_Razgovor_pod_zelenym_chatrom_15022011.pdf.

———. *Zelenyi shater*. Moscow: Eksmo, 2011. [In English: Ludmila Ulitskaya. *The Big Green Tent*, trans. Polly Gannon. New York: Farrar, Straus, and Giroux, 2015.]

Vititskii, Sergei. *Bessil'nye mira sego*. Donetsk: Stalker, 2003.

Yurchak, Alexei. *Everything Was Forever Until It Was No More: The Last Soviet Generation*. Princeton, NJ: Princeton UP, 2006.

Zubok, Vladislav. *Zhivago's Children: The Last Russian Intelligentsia*. Cambridge, MA: Harvard UP, 2009.

The Intelligentsia and the Intellectuals: A History of Two Terms in Russian Philosophical Discourse

Alyssa DeBlasio

Early in Viktor Pelevin's 2004 novel, *The Sacred Book of the Werewolf* (Sviashchennaia kniga oborotnia), the reader is presented with a story of how the Russian intelligentsia came to be replaced by intellectuals. It used to be the case, the story goes, that the intelligentsia were those 100,000 citizens who received a low salary for performing an "entry-level" sex act on the red dragon who once ruled the city. Eventually the intelligentsia staged a coup, banished the red dragon, and installed the green toad on the throne. "At first they thought that under the toad they would do exactly the same thing, only now for ten times more money."[1] However, with the ascension of the green toad, the legend continues, the job of the intelligentsia was replaced by a group of just three intellectuals who performed the work of all 100,000 and for ten times the pay. Only now, these three intellectuals were required perform a much more involved sex act on the toad, perform it continuously, and, in the modern capitalist mode, do so "with the highest professional quality and the ability to smile optimistically from the corners of their mouths while they work."[2] "Here is the main idea," the

---

1 An earlier version of some sections of this work appeared as part of chapter six in Alyssa DeBlasio, *The End of Russian Philosophy: Tradition and Transition at the Turn of the 21st Century* (London: Palgrave MacMillan, 2014). Viktor Pelevin, *Sviashchennaia kniga oborotnia*, accessed April 8, 2020, http://pelevin.nov.ru/romans/pe-SKO/.
2 Pelevin, *Sviashchennaia*.

story concludes: "Those 100,000 were called the intelligentsia. And these three are called intellectuals."[3]

Pelevin's salacious account in *The Sacred Book of the Werewolf* serves as a pointed allegory for the emergence of the modern Russian state and the deferential relationship of the Russian creative class to power. Yet, the novel takes for granted that readers all agree on the concepts at play. In fact, since its entrance into popular vernacular in the middle of the nineteenth century, the term "intelligentsia" has been shrouded in a contentious cloud, used for the purposes of adulation and insult, and applied to philosophers, writers, scientists, and ordinary people in both a positive and a pejorative light. The term "intellectual," on the contrary, is a comparatively new addition to this debate, entering popular use in Russian in the first decade of the twenty-first century.

This chapter will trace the history of these two concepts in Russian philosophical thought, from the late 1800s through their renewed debate in the early 2000s. I argue that, within this history, two defining themes emerge. The first is an acute lack of consensus over what the intelligentsia actually *is*. The second is the way the intelligentsia resists categorization as a class and is better described either in terms of its cultural mythology, as in the title of the present volume, or (to borrow from music theory) as a "mode" that unites according to reliable thematic behaviors. I conclude by examining the post-Soviet confrontation of these two categories in the 2000s and 2010s, when use of the term "intellectual" peaks and replaces the intelligentsia as the guiding model for philosophical production. Today, other pressing philosophical matters—most notably, the ongoing ideological consolidation in higher education and a new wave of institutional repressions following Russia's 2022 invasion of Ukraine—have all but eclipsed any discussion of the roles of the intelligentsia and the intellectuals in Russia. And yet, as Pelevin described, these terms remain in dialogic opposition, retaining their ambiguous relationship to each other and to the structures of power.

The discipline of philosophy can provide distinctive insights into the debate between the intelligentsia and intellectuals. Philosophers have historically served as the vanguard of the intelligentsia, both in the early twentieth century and certainly in the Soviet period, where departments of the history of Russian philosophy were transformed into departments of Marxism-Leninism, with their members called upon to answer the pressing ideological questions facing Soviet ideologs of the day. In Russia, as across Europe, philosophy was the

---

3 Ibid. Vitalii Kurennoi also addresses this passage by Pelevin in his "Intellektualy," in *Mysliashchaia Rossiia. Kartografiia sovremennykh intellektual'nykh napravlenii*, ed. Vitalii Kurennoi (Moscow: Nasledie Evrazii, 2006), 7–8.

birthplace of the idea of the intellectual, stretching from Immanuel Kant through Antonio Gramsci and then to post-World War II intellectuals like Jacques Derrida, Emmanuel Levinas, and Michel Foucault, for whom philosophy was often intertwined with, if not inseparable from, politics. In contemporary Russia, the debate over the intelligentsia and the intellectuals arose most acutely in the discipline of philosophy, where in the 2000s and 2010s these categories became essential to how the discipline conceived of its changing role. By casting the model of the intelligentsia aside, Russia's philosophers, in essence, enacted a process of breaking with the past of their own discipline—with the transcendentally oriented, internally validated, and "nationally distinctive" tradition of philosophizing in Russia that, at least until Russia's 2022 invasion of Ukraine, was generally accepted as having outlived its usefulness in a contemporary landscape of academic reform and quantitative assessment. Philosopher Dmitry Uzlaner summarized this shift when in 2010 he wrote: "It's not fashionable to be a member of the intelligentsia these days. . . . Being an intellectual, now that's a different story."[4]

The word *intelligentsiia* (from the Polish *inteligencja*) entered regular use in the Russian language at the end of the 1800s as a way of referring to the social group that had emerged in the 1850s and 1860s and included Fedor Dostoevsky, Mikhail Katkov, Nikolai Mikhailovsky and, later, Vasily Rozanov and Anatoly Lunacharsky.[5] With a few exceptions, these thinkers came from the land-owning classes but not from the gentry; they were the product of the formation of educated *raznochintsy* (of various ranks) in the 1840s who became *déclassé* as they emerged from the universities highly educated and, as Hugh Seton-Watson writes, "profoundly alienated from the political and social regime."[6] Rose Glickman adds that these *raznochintsy*, including writers from mixed class backgrounds or uneducated families who made names for themselves in the 1860s (e.g., Fedor Reshetnikov, Nikolai Uspensky, Aleksandr Levitov), "were really the

---

4 Dmitrii Uzlaner, "Tragediia intellektualov," *Russkii zhurnal*, October 20, 2010, http://www.russ.ru/pole/Tragediya-intellektualov.

5 The term *inteligencja* was already present in a Polish encyclopedia by 1863, referring to "all people who applied education and knowledge to their activities." See Jan Szczepański, "The Polish Intelligentsia: Past and Present," *World Politics* 14, no. 3 (1962): 408. For a detailed history of the development of the word "intelligentsia" in Russia, see S. O. Shmidt, *Obshchestvennoe samosoznanie rossiiskogo blagorodnogo sosloviia: XVI-pervaia tret' XIX veka* (Moscow: Nauka, 2002); Sergei Sergeev, "Dosovetskaia Rossiia (XVIII–do nachala XX veka)," in *Mysliashchaia Rossiia. Istoriia i teoriia intelligentsii i intellektualov*, ed. Vitalii Kurennoi (Moscow: Nasledie Evropy, 2009), 15–53.

6 Hugh Seton-Watson, "The Russian Intellectuals," in *The Intellectuals: A Controversial Portrait*, ed. George Bernard de Huszar (New York: Free Press, 1960), 43. See also Martin Malia, "What Is the Intelligentsia?," *Daedalus* 89, no. 3 (1960): 446.

first generation of Russian writers to depend on literature for their livelihood" and were regular contributors to journals like the *Contemporary* (Sovremennik) and the *Russian Word* (Russkoe slovo).[7]

Until the mid-1800s, *raznochintsy* was a formal, taxable estate/class that included primarily discharged soldiers and their families, but also served as a temporary designator for individuals with no social status or material means who were not otherwise affiliated with a peasant commune. By the 1860s–70s, however, a new group of *raznochintsy* was taking shape. It came to comprise writers, social commentators, and thinkers from a variety of class backgrounds (e.g., petit bourgeois, peasant) and with liberal, democratic, or revolutionary leanings, to the point where the term eventually began to signal not just class status but also political views.[8] Importantly, the new *raznochintsy* held "a university or secondary education and were *engaged in intellectual work as a profession*," thereby laying the ground for the popular emergence of the term "intelligentsia" in the late 1800s.[9] In fact, A. Yu. Prokofyeva asserts that the terms *intelligentsiia* and *raznochintsy* were often used synonymously in the late nineteenth century, forming "a historical line from the *raznochintsy* to the Soviet intelligentsia," in Viktor Martyanov's words.[10] By the early twentieth century, thus, the Russian noun *intelligent* had come to refer to an educated member of the cultural vanguard with strong humanistic leanings but weak class ties; it signaled those members of the educated elite who were engaged in intellectual labor, spoke out in the name of injustice, and were tasked with preserving cultural and intellectual values for posterity.

For philosophers and cultural critics of the early twentieth century, it was this humanistic component that most clearly characterized the intelligentsia—what in 1907 R. V. Ivanov-Razumnik called the tendency of the intelligentsia "toward physical and intellectual, societal, and personal liberation of the individual."[11]

---

7 Glickman separates the *raznochintsy* from the *intelligentsiia*, noting that works by the former were well received among the latter. Rose Glickman, "An Alternative View of the Peasantry: The Raznochintsy Writers of the 1860s," *Slavic Review* 32, no. 4 (1973): 693.
8 A. Iu. Prokof'eva, "Raznochintsy," *Bol'shaia rossiiskaia entsiklopediia*, accessed May 10, 2021, https://bigenc.ru/domestic_history/text/3490843.
9 Ibid. Emphasis mine.
10 Ibid.; Viktor Mart'ianov, "Postsovetskaia Rossiia: Sotsial'no-teoreticheskie razmyshleniia," in *Mysliashchaia Rossiia. Istoriia i teoriia intelligentsii i intellektualov*, ed. Vitalii Kurennoi (Moscow: Nasledie Evropy, 2009), 76. It is also not uncommon to see the two terms together, for instance, in the phrase "raznochinskaia intelligentsiia." Sergei Sergeev talks about the *intelligentsiia-razochintsy* of the mid-nineteenth century, combining both words into a single term. See Sergeev, "Dosovetskaia Rossiia (XVIII–do nachala XX veka)," 25.
11 Razumnik Ivanov-Razumnik, "Chto takoe intelligentsia," in *Intelligentsiia—vlast'—narod*, ed. L. I. Novikova and I. N. Sizemskaia (Moscow: Nauka, 1993), 73–80.

For Maksim Slavinsky, journalist and editor of several influential political and economic journals including *Russian Thought* (Russkaia mysl') and *Herald of Europe* (Vestnik Evropy), "the intelligentsia is not just the creator of all immaterial values, ... but is the permanent distributor of [those values]."[12] On this view, progress would be impossible without the intelligentsia. It is no surprise, then, that for Slavinsky "it is the intelligentsia [that] stands guard for all elements of the national consciousness of its people."[13]

At the same time, literary scholar Dmitry Ovsyaniko-Kulikovsky tried to forge his own, broader definition, whereby the intelligentsia refers to all of educated society. In "Psychology of the Russian Intelligentsia" (Psikhologiia russkoi intelligentsii, 1910), he wrote: "[The intelligentsia] includes everyone who one way or another, directly or indirectly, actively or passively takes part in the intellectual life of the country."[14] In the Soviet period, however, where the literacy rate had reached nearly 100% by the 1970s, this diluted definition risked becoming all-inclusive, so that anybody with a university degree or classic works of literature on their bookshelves would have been included among the ranks of the intelligentsia.

While the above definitions all hold positive weight, "intelligentsia" has been equally employed as a term of abuse. In particular, it took on a negative connotation in the 1909 collection *Landmarks* (Vekhi), edited by political philosopher and future government functionary Mikhail Gershenzon. While the authors of *Vekhi* (including philosophers Nikolai Berdyaev, Sergei Bulgakov, and Pyotr Struve) would have certainly considered themselves the vanguard that, in Slavinsky's 1910 definition, "stands guard for all elements of the national consciousness of its people," they used *intelligentsiia* as a pejorative term.[15] In particular, they used it to refer to the positivists who had emerged in Russia in the 1870s (e.g., Mikhailovsky and Lavrov) and the Marxist materialists who followed in the 1890s (e.g., Bogdanov and Lunacharsky).

As Berdyaev wrote in *Vekhi*, the materialistic hegemony that had taken hold of Russia's intellectual and political life "combined a rational consciousness with extreme emotionalism and with a weak appreciation of intellectual life as an autonomous value."[16] The intelligentsia was demagogic, averse to universalism,

---

12 Maksim Slavinskii, "Russkaia intelligentsia i natsional'nyi vopros," in *Intelligentsiia v Rossii* (Moscow: Mysl', 1971), 231.
13 Ibid., 231.
14 Dmitrii Ovsianiko-Kulikovskii, "Psikhologiia russkoi intelligentsii," in *Intelligentsiia v Rossii* (Moscow: Mysl', 1971), 192.
15 Slavinskii, "Russkaia intelligentsia i natsional'nyi vopros," 231.
16 Nikolai Berdiaev, "Filosofskaia istina i intelligentskaia pravda," in *Vekhi* (Moscow: n.p., 1909), 9.

and maintained a dangerous reverence for science, he continued.[17] It is because of this materialist intelligentsia, the *Vekhi* authors claimed, that Russia had been unable to form a "national philosophical tradition."[18] For Berdyaev in particular, the intelligentsia's primary transgression was its atheism: "Its atheism is the fault of its will, for it freely chose the path of worshipping man and thereby crippled its soul and deadened within itself the instinct for truth."[19] Berdiaev's view was shared by Ivan Petrunkevich, who claimed in 1910 that "the Russian intelligentsia, having adopted an atheist worldview, took up a false place in its relationship to the people."[20] For Struve, the conceptual form of the Russian intelligentsia was its apostasy: that is, the formal disaffiliation of its members from institutions of religion and government, as well as its open hostility towards those institutions. In its absolute form, the apostasy of the intelligentsia led to anarchism, as in the cases of Bakunin and Kropotkin; in its relative form, it led to revolutionary radicalism and the Bolshevism of the Russian revolution.

Whereas the authors behind *Vekhi* had the future Bolsheviks in mind when they attacked the intelligentsia for being a false, atheist vanguard, Lenin was using the same argument and the very same word as justification to scatter them across Europe. When Lenin expelled many of Russia's philosophers in 1922 on the voyages of the Philosophy Steamer, whose passengers included some of the same *Vekhi* authors, he sentenced them on that exact charge—of being members of a destructive, backwards intelligentsia. On August 31, 1922, the front-page headline in *Pravda* read "The First Warning" (Pervoe predosterezhenie), announcing the impending expulsion of the Kadet Party, White Guard "intelligentsia" on which the government had "already wasted enough effort."[21]

Given the myriad of definitions and meanings ascribed to the intelligentsia, by the early twentieth century the term had already become a space easily filled with meaning, employed equally in praise and insult. Like the title "philosopher," which was for Plato the highest status an individual could attain and for Dostoevsky (and many of his literary characters) "a term of abuse, meaning 'fool,'" the meaning of *intelligentsiia* was supplied by the intention of the user.[22] The semantic opacity surrounding the word continued into the Soviet period and,

---

17 Ibid., 7–8.
18 Ibid., 13.
19 Ibid., 22.
20 Ivan Petrunkevich, "Intelligentsiia i 'Vekhi,'" in *Intelligentsiia v Rossii* (Moscow: Mysl', 1971), viii.
21 "Pervoe predosterezhenie," *Pravda*, August 31, 1922, 1.
22 Fedor Dostoevskii, "Ob"iavlenie o podpiske na zhurnal 'Vremia' na 1861 g.," in idem, *Polnoe sobranie sochinenii*, ed. V. G. Bazanov (St. Petersburg: Nauka, 1911), 329.

as Aleksandr Kustaryov argues, during the second half of the twentieth century the intelligentsia was understood through the lens of two dominating myths: 1) as superior, because of its unparalleled spirituality (*dukhovnost'*); and 2) as fraudulent, having retarded Russia's intellectual and political development with its claims to spiritual insight.[23] Equally important for our purposes here is Kustaryov's observation that, in Soviet-era speculation on the meaning and function of the intelligentsia, one of the few constants on both sides of the debate is the assumption that there is no intelligentsia in the West, while in Russia there are no intellectuals.[24]

While the intelligentsia emerged from the overcoat of Russian philosophical history, the concept of the intellectual was born of European debates over similar concerns. In Europe, as Svetlana Evdokimova's chapter in this volume describes, the term "intellectual" gained public notoriety in the response surrounding Émile Zola's "J'Accuse!" in the winter of 1898, which was followed less than a month later by Maurice Barrès's "Protest of the Intellectuals" in *Le Journal*. These letters, colored by the public and political drama that surrounded their publication, were seen as the pioneering effort on the part of French intellectuals to influence public opinion on political affairs—or, as Zola put it: "to enlighten those who have been kept in the dark."[25]

Yet, if we turn backwards in time to Kant's essay "An Answer to the Question: What is Enlightenment?" (1784) and, later, *The Conflict of the Faculties* (1798), we see that the expectation of a civic function from the intellectual was not specific to the late nineteenth century. Kant had already speculated on the public dimension of intellectual life in his discussions of the *Gelehrter*. Although translated most often as "scholar," *Gelehrter* does not mean for Kant a scholar in the pedagogical sense of the word, nor is he referring to a well-rounded *homme de lettres*. Instead, with *Gelehrten* he is indicating a particular group of public intellectuals whose duty it was to address society on issues of expertise: one *Gelehrter* might investigate the injustice of taxes, he notes, while another might be obliged to lay bare the mistaken aspects of Church symbolism.[26] This necessary public function is what Kant called the "public use of reason": that is, "the

---

23 Aleksandr Kustarev, "Sovetskaia Rossiia: samoopredelitel'nye praktiki sovetskoi intelligentsii," in *Mysliashchaia Rossiia. Istoriia i teoriia intelligentsii i intellektualov*, ed. Vitalii Kurennoi (Moscow: Nasledie Evropy, 2009), 69–70.
24 Ibid., 69. For more on the intelligentsia and intellectuals, see Aleksandr Kustarev, *Nervnye liudi. Ocherki ob intelligentsii* (Moscow: Tovarishchestvo nauchnykh izdanii KMK, 2006).
25 Émile Zola, "J'accuse!," *L'Aurore* 87, no. 13 (January 1898): 2.
26 Immanuel Kant, *Beantwortung der Frage: Was ist Aufklärung?*, ed. Jean Mondot (Saint-Étienne: P de l'Université de Saint-Étienne, 1991), 76.

use that anyone as a scholar makes of reason before the entire literate world."[27] In this way, Kant's intellectuals are responsible not only to their own faculty of reason but to the public they address, whereby they have a civic duty to impart to the public only "carefully considered and well-intentioned thoughts."[28]

While the Dreyfus affair thrust the category on which Kant had already speculated into the public eye, by the twentieth century it had become common to speak of intellectuals not only as a social category, but as intimately connected with both the public and political spheres. Not surprisingly, for Gramsci, intellectuals were necessarily political beings, given that their social functions were bound in class roots. It is along these lines that Gramsci famously distinguished two kinds of intellectuals: organic intellectuals, who are identified first and foremost with the class to which they organically belong; and traditional intellectuals, who are trained in their disciplines and serve the social function of their profession. While traditional intellectuals are likely to conceal their attachment to their class in order to claim that their social function (i.e. the fruits of their particular vocation) is somehow independent of class ties, Gramsci continues, they too are guided by concrete historical processes and social developments."[29] We see these same sentiments in Pascal Ory and Jean-François Sirinelli's claim at the end of the twentieth century, where they argue that intellectuals are always connected to the political process, in that they are either creators or employers of ideology.[30]

By the end of the twentieth century, the public function about which Kant had spoken had become a near prerequisite for one to be granted the title of "intellectual." Richard A. Posner's table of the top 600 intellectuals, which includes such well-known figures as Hannah Arendt, Roland Barthes, Isaiah Berlin, Jacques Derrida, Michel Foucault, George Orwell, and Edward Said, was compiled based solely on quantitative measures of public notoriety: media mentions, web hits, and scholarly citations.[31] Indeed, according to Neil Jumonville, the intellectual is "a generalist knowledgeable about cultural and political matters . . . whose ideas reach a substantial public."[32] For Stefan Collini, the intellectual's creative, analytical, and scholarly capacities are almost

---

27 Ibid.
28 Ibid.
29 Antonio Gramsci, "The Intellectuals," in idem, *Selections from the Prison Notebooks*, ed. and trans. Quinton Hoare and Geoffrey Nowell Smith (New York: L International P, 1971), 3–23.
30 Pascal Ory and Jean-François Sirinelli, *Les intellectuels en France de l'affaire Dreyfus à nos jours* (Paris: Armand Colin, 1986), 10.
31 Richard Posner, *Public Intellectuals: A Study of Decline* (Cambridge, MA: Harvard UP, 2001), 194–206.
32 Neil Jumonville, ed, *The New York Intellectuals Reader* (New York: Routledge, 2007), 1.

secondary to his public function. The intellectual must: 1) reach a wide (often unintended) public; 2) successfully articulate some concerns of that public; and 3) establish a positive reputation for these articulations.[33] Like Kant before him, Noam Chomsky adds to the intellectual's public responsibility the duty "to speak the truth and to expose lies," particularly where "the creation and analysis of ideology" is concerned.[34]

Yet, alongside the crystallization of the intellectual as a necessarily public being, beginning in the 1980s, surrounding Russell Jacoby's *The Last Intellectuals: American Culture in the Age of Academe* (1987), we see the emergence of studies that posit the "death" of intellectuals in the face of their failure to live up to their communal duty. Foucault laments that "[if] this category exists, which is not certain nor perhaps even desirable—[they] are abandoning their old prophetic function."[35] For John Gross, the death of the intellectual may not necessarily be due to shortcomings within the profession, but is perhaps indicative of a shift in intellectual culture more broadly conceived, whereby the written genre no longer holds the esteemed position it did during an earlier stage of modernity.[36] More specifically, for Daniel Bell this shift was made possible by the rise of the sciences in the 1920s–1940s, in particular the development of the atomic bomb, during which theoretical knowledge came to the forefront as the determining factor in new directions in research and scholarly inquiry.[37] We could add to this list of factors the rise of specialization in academia, whereby the *homme de lettres* is often viewed as having been replaced by specialized academics who cater to the university market and *not* the public. The main takeaway here is that, as with the intelligentsia, there is an acute lack of clarity in the history of philosophy over what intellectuals *are* and whether they have a responsibility to the public.

These two categories—the intelligentsia and the intellectuals—meet most acutely in Russian philosophical discourse in the first decade of the twentieth century. A small number of Russian-language articles take up this dichotomy earlier, in the late 1990s and very early 2000s, including Serguei Oushakine's "Functional Intelligentsia-ness" (Funktsional'naia intelligentnost', 1998), Boris Uspensky's *The Russian Intelligentsia and Western Intellectualism*

---

33 Stefan Collini, *Absent Minds: Intellectuals in Britain* (Oxford: Oxford UP, 2006), 52.
34 Noam Chomsky, "The Responsibility of Intellectuals," *The New York Review of Books*, February 23, 1967, accessed May 10, 2020, http://www.nybooks.com/articles/12172.
35 Qtd. in Paul Bové, *Intellectuals in Power: A Genealogy of Critical Humanism* (New York: Columbia UP, 1986), 20.
36 John Gross, *The Rise and Fall of the Man of Letters: A Study of the Idiosyncratic and the Humane in Modern Literature* (New York: Macmillan, 1969), 285.
37 Daniel Bell, *The Intellectual and the University* (New York: The City College, 1966), 3.

(Russkaia intelligentsiia i zapadnyi intellektualizm, 1999), and Boris Firsov's "The Intelligentsia and the Intellectuals at the End of the Twentieth Century" (Intelligentsiia i intellektualy v kontse XX veka, 2001).[38] Among those histories explaining the emergence of this term in Russia is an account by Mischa Gabowitsch, which projects the introduction of intellectuals in Russia back to the 1997 founding of the journal *Iron Ration* (Neprikosnovennyi zapas). According to Gabowitsch, the journal was initially planned as a critical literary supplement but soon began to print content addressing political and social issues, thereby including on its pages "the basics of the self-understanding of the new, independent cultural elite in Russia, which was on its way from the homogenous class of the Russian intelligentsia to diversified intellectuals."[39]

In cultural texts from the early twenty-first century, the intelligentsia is often represented as a romanticized collection of educated and disaffected workers of the "mental" professions or creative class, defined by cultural literacy, a retreat from the public and political spheres, and stereotypically "intellectual" behaviors ranging from reading literary journals to blogging about culture and current events. Vitaly Kurennoi has explained these and other traits as comprising the "integral" quality of the intelligentsia, meaning that it is defined according to specific expectations of "behavior, a specific way of life (*obraz zhizni*)."[40] Aleksandr Kustaryov describes the intelligentsia as the collective "'intellect' and 'conscience' of society" (*um i sovest' obshchestva*).[41] In their more recent study, Olga Zdravomyslova and Natalia Kutukova write that the intelligentsia "is always an address to cultural memory, an establishment of an affinity with it."[42]

These and other definitions do not shed light on what the intelligentsia *is* so much as they highlight the way it functions as a mode that transcends historical, economic, political, and class divides. In music theory, a mode unites a composition according to predictable melodic behaviors and patterns. It can be aligned with emotion or intention; it lends unity to a single piece of music while also uniting disparate bodies of work across space and time. Philosophically, the

---

38 Serguei Oushakine, "Funktsional'naia intelligentnost'," *Polis* 1 (1998): 8–22; Boris Uspenskii, ed., *Russkaia intelligentsiia i zapadnyi intellektualizm: Istoriia i tipologiia* (Moscow: O.G.I., 1999); Boris Firsov, "Intelligentsiia i intellektualy v kontse XX veka," *Zvezda* 8 (2001), accessed May 12, 2020, https://magazines.gorky.media/zvezda/2001/8/intelligenciya-i-intellektualy-v-koncze-hh-veka.html.
39 Mischa Gabowitsch, "NZ—die Eiserne Ration einer neuen russländischen Öffentlichkeit," *Osteuropa* 9–10 (2003): 1437.
40 Kurennoi, "Intellektualy," 8.
41 Kustarev, "Sovetskaia Rossiia," 76.
42 Ol'ga Zdravomyslova and Natal'ia Kutukova, "Intelligentsiia kak vyzov: identichnost' rossiiskoi intelligentsii v XXI veke," *Kontsept: filosofiia, religiia, kul'tura* 4, no. 1.13 (2020): 8.

idea of mode also contains an ethical potential, as Greek philosophers, most notably Plato in *The Republic*, aligned musical modes with ethical imperatives for the proper formation of the soul.[43] Much like the concept of the *narod*, which too is best described as a mode rather than a category or class, members of the intelligentsia are united in their participation in the myth of the intelligentsia, in the way a mode unites a piece of music in accordance with the boundaries of its formula.[44] The intelligentsia can include high-earning actors, middle-class university professors, and low-paid museum workers; we can find its markers seemingly everywhere in Russian culture, from metro attendants reading novels in their booths to appeals by the very wealthy on behalf of the Russia-K (Kul'tura) channel. Among the most striking contemporary examples of the intelligentsia's classless dimension and its enduring mythical modality is the 2010 trial of oligarch Mikhail Khodorkovsky, where individuals from nearly every level of the pay scale—from public-school teachers to celebrities—protested in defense of a man who was once the wealthiest oligarch in Russia.[45]

We find a particularly telling portrait of the intelligentsia mode in Avdot'ia (Dunia) Smirnova's film *Two Days* (*Dva dnia*, 2011). The film's narrative hinges on the unlikely romance of Masha, a provincial museum curator who has dedicated her life to preserving the legacy of a forgotten nineteenth-century writer, and Pyotr, a deputy minister from Moscow tasked with seizing the museum's land for redevelopment. They represent two very different kinds of *intelligenty*, each existing in a Russia unknown to the other. In Smirnova's comedic style, both protagonists are initially portrayed as caricatures of their respective class identities: Masha lives in a dilapidated *izba* while Pyotr travels everywhere in a bespoke suit. What brings them together is not any shared social or economic reality, but their commitment to the intelligentsia mode, which unites them in their growing appreciation for each other and the different worlds they represent.

Reflection on the intelligentsia and the "intellectual elite" has become a defining theme of Smirnova's career. Over the decades she has worked to make "highbrow" filmmaking marketable for Russian audiences, which often includes blending genre conventions with Russian cultural themes, featuring characters rooted in the Russian literary and cultural elite, and choosing to shoot at locations of cultural significance, including the Spasskoe-Lutovinovo

---

43 Plato, *The Republic*, ed. G. R. F. Ferrari, trans. Tom Griffith (Cambridge: Cambridge UP, 2000), 397a–400e.
44 On the disparate social and philosophical ideas included within the categories of *narod* and *narodnost'*, see Mikhail Epshtein, "Zagadka naroda," InteLnet, May 1992, accessed April 8, 2020, http://www.emory.edu/INTELNET/esse_narod.html.
45 I am grateful to Rossen Djagalov for this example.

estate and the Kuntskamera Museum. In a controversial interview from 2021, Smirnova argued that Russia's social problems were rooted in the lack of a properly educated "intellectual elite," and that "in order to rule Russia effectively, one must have a significant knowledge of history . . . and also Russian philosophy."[46] Among those she identified as members of Russia's intellectual elite was Vladislav Surkov, former aide to Putin and one of the architects of the idea of the "Russian world," which fueled support for the war in Ukraine following the 2022 invasion.[47] Thus, we might read the collision between Masha's and Pyotr's worlds in *Two Days* (she nurtures in him an appreciation for "Russian culture," while he helps her see that politics can operate with a conscience) as an encounter between the intelligentsia and the intellectuals, at least in Smirnova's understanding of the terms.[48] The closing scene of *Two Days*, where the couple argue about how they will blend Masha's cultural work with Pyotr's new role as the governor of the region, serves as a metaphor for the intelligentsia's and the intellectuals' never-ending process of defining themselves in relation to each other and to structures of power.[49]

Perhaps the most important contribution to the intelligentsia-intellectuals debate is the two-volume collection *Thinking Russia* (Mysliashchaia Rossiia, 2006 and 2009), edited by Vitaly Kurennoi. One the one hand, both volumes replicate the contradictory application of these two terms and the varied methodological and conceptual approaches at play in their interpretation. For Sergei Sergeev, for instance, the distinction between the two can be summarized in a *reversal* of Pelevin's allegory: "And thus," Sergeev writes, "'ideologues' and 'humanists' are intellectuals; professional 'ideologues' and 'humanists' are members of the intelligentsia."[50] On the other hand, the very emergence of this term—*intellektual*—seems to indicate a demand for an alternative to the traditional intelligentsia model on which Russian culture has long relied.

---

46 Avdot'ia Smirnova, "Shkola zlosloviia s Sobchak: Kirienko, Nemtsov, Naval'nyi i, konechno zhe, Chubais," interview by Kseniia Sobchak, Ostorozhno: Sobchak, November 29, 2021, accessed July 11, 2023, https://www.youtube.com/watch?v=3deY1Q9ThMs, 18:37–18:53.
47 Ibid., 24:12.
48 While the Russian term *intellektualy* is most commonly employed to set Western/non-Russian thinkers and approaches apart from Russian thinkers, Smirnova uses the phrase "intellectual elite" to refer to Russian politicians, thinkers, ideologues, etc., whom she values for what she sees as their intellectual contributions and service to the state. See ibid.
49 For more on the representation of the intelligentsia in *Two Days* see Stephen M. Norris, "Avdot'ia Smirnova: *Two Days* (*2 dnia*, 2011)," *KinoKultura* 36 (2012), accessed July 10, 2023, http://www.kinokultura.com/2012/36r-dvadnia.shtml.
50 Sergeev, "Dosovetskaia Rossiia (XVIII—do nachala XX veka)," 20.

An analysis of the Russian book corpus on Google Ngram Viewer offers a visualization of how the words *intellektual* (green line) and *intellektualy* (red line) came into popular use in the 1990s and peaked around 2010 (Fig. 1). The emergence of these terms coincided with the peak of *intelligentsiia* (blue line), usage of which fell significantly in the twenty-first century, perhaps a result of the very debates addressed in this chapter.

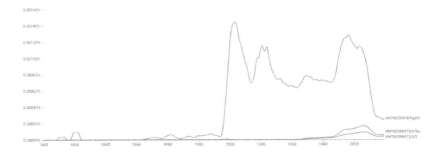

Figure 1: Comparative bibliometric data from Google Ngram Viewer on the use of the terms *intelligentsiia* and *intellektual/y* in the Russian book corpus: 1800–2019.

This data supports one of the few ideas on which philosophers seem to agree: that regardless of the intelligentsia's history or function, it reached a new crisis point in the twenty-first century. And indeed, the attack on the intelligentsia came at an especially trying time for the Russian academy. Russian universities were under pressure to reform and align themselves with Western standards of success, in particular by increasing their presence in international journals. Research by Natalia Kovalyova revealed that, in 2010, Russian scholars were citing more books and fewer articles than their Western counterparts, and that Russian scholars lagged behind their colleagues abroad by a citation gap of about fifteen years.[51] That same year, Minister of Education and Sciences Dmitry Livanov reported that the average age of university level instructors was somewhere in the fifties or sixties, meaning that most professors in the Russian Federation were trained in their professions in the mid-1970s or earlier, during the years of a closed Soviet intellectual community where research opportunities and expectations for international proficiency and collaboration were significantly different.[52]

---

51 Natalia Kovalyova, "The Interplay of the Material and the Discursive in Russian Academic Prose (1980–2010)," *Russian Journal of Communication* 6, no. 1 (2014): 6–19.
52 "Professional'noe obrazovanie Rossii: Kakim ono dolzhno byt'?," guests Dmitrii Livanov and Andrei Volkov, "Goriachie interv'iu," *Ekho Moskvy*, September 3, 2010. By way of comparison, the 2008 "National Study of Postsecondary Faculty" showed that the number of professors

For Vadim Radaev, the longtime first vice-rector at the Higher School of Economics in Moscow, a main obstacle in Russia's path towards international scholarly integration in the first decade of the twenty-first century was "the inertia of the Soviet period," where insular practices like lack of mobility continue to retard progress.[53] Philosopher Vasily Vanchugov describes his own discipline as follows: "Our [Russian] philosophers know foreign languages well enough to familiarize themselves with the work of foreign colleagues, but not well enough to make a serious (and not farcical) mark at the international level."[54] In 2009, chemist Artyom Oranov remarked that "Russian scholars publish [in Russian] in journals that nobody reads," and "very often people are chosen entirely randomly for high-ranking positions."[55] He concluded with a devastating metaphor: "Russian academia is stewing in its own juice."[56]

One explanation for these and other challenges is the fact that very few academics were replaced in the immediate years following the collapse of the Soviet system. Although Marxist-Leninist philosophy was radically and immediately delegitimized in East Germany and the Czech and Slovak Republics through staffing changes and restructuring in philosophy departments, the Russian professoriate did not undergo such shifts. After 1991, most philosophy departments were merely renamed to reflect the political evolution: departments of dialectical materialism became departments of theoretical philosophy; departments of historical materialism became departments of social philosophy; and, most controversially, departments of scientific atheism often resurfaced as departments of religious philosophy (as was the case at Moscow State University). Nikolai Plotnikov's work on intellectual networks articulates how, in the 1990s, "absolutely no de-Sovietizing took place in philosophy [in Russia]: neither institutionally nor conceptually."[57] For Vladimir Salnikov, the

---

aged sixty-five and older in the United States had held steady at around four percent since the 1990s. Faculty members aged sixty-one or older represented twelve percent of the professoriate. Susan Kemper, "Older Professors: Fewer, and Better, than You Think," *The Chronicle of Higher Education*, November 14, 2010, accessed May 10, 2020, http://chronicle.com/article/Older-Professors-Fewer-and/125347/.

53 Vadim Radaev, "Issledovatel'skie instituty: sostoianie i problemy. Beseda s Vadimom Radaevym," in *Mysliashchaia Rossiia. Kartografiia sovremennykh intellektual'nykh napravlenii*, ed. Vitalii Kurennoi (Moscow: Nasledie Evrazii, 2006), 41.

54 Vasilii Vanchugov, "Umnym filosofiia v pomoshch', drugim—v nakazanie," interview with Aleksei Nilogov, *NG—Ex libris*, August 5, 2010, accessed June 7, 2021, http://www.alex-nilogov.narod.ru/sofr_rus_fil/vanchugov_umnym-filosofiya.html.

55 Artem Oganov, "Kak ostanovit' 'utechku mozgov' iz Rossii?," Lenta.ru, accessed May 10, 2020, http://lenta.ru/conf/oganov/.

56 Ibid.

57 Nikolai Plotnikov, "Filosofii v Rossii prosto ne sushchestvuet," interview with Aleksei Nilogov, *Russkii zhurnal*, January 18, 2008, accessed December 2, 2018, http://www.russ.ru/Mirovayapovestka/Filosofii-v-Rossii-prosto-ne-suschestvuet.

problems of Russia's universities are rooted in the "post-Soviet behavior of the former Soviet intelligentsia" during the period immediately following the collapse of the Soviet Union, during which the intelligentsia had already lost its cultural capital but nonetheless remained in positions of intellectual power.[58]

Thus, when higher education administrators and officials set about reforming the Russian university system, they set their sights on quantitative metrics of "professionalization"—a concept which, as both Kurennoi and Radaev argue, was absent from the Soviet educational structure.[59] The first institution to enact a system to measure "professionalism" among faculty was the Higher School of Economics in Moscow, which as early as 2005 began assigning points and awarding academic bonuses (*akademicheskie nadbavki*) for number of publications, for publications in international, peer-reviewed journals, and later, for "contributing to the scholarly reputation of [the university]."[60] (These practices have since become mainstream across Russia.) No longer could cerebral or artistic labor sustain the intelligentsia as both a "way of life" and a source of income, as it did for Belinsky, Dostoevsky, Mikhailovsky, Rozanov, and others whose careers took shape at that historical moment when the *intelligentsiia* and the *raznochintsy* merged.[61] For Russian universities seeking to assimilate the Soviet intelligentsia into the capitalist mode, the idea of professionalization must have seemed like a promising middle ground between the Soviet past and the globalized academic market, since the idea of professions could be conceived as "neutral vis-à-vis the class structure and could therefore act to salve the wounds of the modern capitalist order."[62] Unsurprisingly, while philosophers in Europe often include the requirement that intellectuals speak truth to power and uphold democratic values, that responsibility has not found its way into analogous Russian debates.[63]

---

58 Vladimir Sal'nikov, "Moi frustratsii v 90-kh," *Logos* 5/6 (2000), accessed May 10, 2020, http://www.ruthenia.ru/logos/number/2000_5_6/2000_5-6_08.htm.
59 Kurennoi, "Intellektualy," 9; Radaev, "Issledovatel'skie instituty," 42–3.
60 Vadim Radaev, "Realizatsiia effektivnogo kontrakta s PPS v forme akademicheskikh nadbavok," Vysshaia shkola ekonomiki, Moscow, 2013, accessed April 1, 2020, https://kpfu.ru/portal/docs/F1928560607/Effektivnyj.kontrakt_NIU_VShE.pdf. This question was taken up as recently as October 2020 at the Institute of Philosophy, as part of a roundtable dedicated to "Philosophy as Profession and Calling." See Institut filosofii RAN, "Kruglyi stol k 100-letnemu iubileiu Instituta na temu 'Filosofiia kak professiia i prizvanie,'" October 6, 2020, accessed October 7, 2020, https://www.youtube.com/watch?v=xwBqmKFOVbM.
61 For more on these thinkers in relation to the intelligentsia/intellectuals debate, see Sergeev, "Dosovetskaia Rossiia (XVIII–do nachala XX veka)," 19–20.
62 Terrence Halliday, "Professions, Class, and Capitalism," *European Journal of Sociology* 24, no. 2 (1983): 321–346.
63 This process of "professionalization" was taking place at the same time as Russia's younger generation began experiencing significant attitudinal shifts in their generational relationships to the intelligentsia paradigm, as Zdravomyslova and Kutukova have shown.

The *Thinking Russia* collection and other recent debates on the categories of the intelligentsia and intellectuals serve as a mirror for a much broader conversation over the trajectory of the discipline of philosophy in the twenty-first century. Russia's Western-oriented generation of philosophers see themselves as global intellectuals and not as members of the Russia-based intelligentsia; they associate their work with the professional stamps of their discipline and with the interests of the creative class and/or middle class, and not with the traditional vision of the intelligentsia as a mode that transcends historical, economic, political, and class divides. They are also, often much more than their Western counterparts, subject to strict metrics as to what defines their professionalism where, ironically, the concept of "professionalism" functions as both the liberating force from the historical opacity of the intelligentsia and also the remaining vestiges of its presence.

Russia's war in Ukraine has, once again, put these two terms to the test. Debates over the intelligentsia and the intellectuals are increasingly mapped onto views about the war, where the intelligentsia has regained some of its social power to influence and transform, and where its collective voice is employed in the service of the state or the opposition, depending on the positionality of the author.[64] Intellectuals, conversely, are often treated as representatives of "Western thinking," and efforts to "professionalize" the Russian academy have slowed or stalled in the face of a new wave of academic repressions and a "brain drain" that, in some cases, has diminished departments by fifty percent or more.[65] As early as 2013, in an interview with Channel One, Vladimir Putin singled out the intelligentsia for preventing revolution, with preventing things in Russia from "getting worse, much worse."[66] And yet, historically, members of the intelligentsia have both aligned themselves with power and also opposed it: some have found "a spiritual and moral meaning in war," to quote philosopher Natalia Balakleets, while others have worked "to expose its inhumane nature

---

64 For one of many post-February-2022 examples of texts that divide the intelligentsia based on whether they support the war, see Liubov' Chizhova, "'Ne mogu molchat'!' Intelligentsiia za voinu i protiv nee," Svoboda, March 2, 2022, accessed July 10, 2023, https://www.svoboda.org/a/ne-mogu-molchatj-intelligentsiya-za-voynu-i-protiv-nee/31730348.html.
65 On the 2022–2023 "brain drain" in the Russian academy, see Iuliia Balakhonova, "Utek mozga: Rasskaz o tom, kak uchenye opiat' uezzhaiut iz Rossii," Proekt, March 27, 2023, accessed July 10, 2023, https://www.proekt.media/guide/uchenye-uezzhayut/.
66 "V. Putin: Intelligentsiia dolzhna predokhraniat' obshchestvo ot revoliutsii," RBC, September 4, 2013, https://www.rbc.ru/society/04/09/2013/57040ef09a794761c0ce1507, accessed July 6, 2023; Vladimir Sal'nikov, "Moi frustratsii v 90-kh."

and do not distinguish between acts of aggression and of defense."[67] The cultural and philosophical weight of the term "intelligentsia," as well as the debates it raises, all suggest that the term is unlikely to disappear anytime soon. However, the arrival of the concept of the "intellectuals," and its assimilation as a challenge to the intelligentsia mode, signals that these terms will continue to serve as key counterpoles in the decades to come.

Bibliography

Balakhonova, Iuliia. "Utek mozga: Rasskaz o tom, kak uchenye opiat' uezzhaiut iz Rossii." *Proekt*, March 27, 2023. Accessed July 10, 2023. https://www.proekt.media/guide/uchenye-uezzhayut/.

Balakleets, Natal'ia. "Intellektualy kak sozdateli narrativov o voine." *Vestnik Samarskogo gosudarstvennogo tekhnicheskogo universiteta* 4, no. 2 (2022): 5–16.

Bell, Daniel. *The Intellectual and the University*. New York: The City College, 1966.

Berdiaev, Nikolai. "Filosofskaia istina i intelligentskaia pravda." In *Vekhi*, 1–22. Moscow: n.p., 1901.

Bové, Paul. *Intellectuals in Power: A Genealogy of Critical Humanism*. New York: Columbia UP, 1986.

Chizhova, Liubov'. "'Ne mogu molchat'!' Intelligentsiia za voinu i protiv nee." *Svoboda*, March 2, 2022. Accessed July 10, 2023. https://www.svoboda.org/a/ne-mogu-molchatj-intelligentsiya-za-voynu-i-protiv-nee/31730348.html.

Chomsky, Noam. "The Responsibility of Intellectuals." *The New York Review of Books*, February 23, 1967. Accessed July 10, 2023. http://www.nybooks.com/articles/12172.

Collini, Stefan. *Absent Minds. Intellectuals in Britain*. Oxford: Oxford UP, 2006.

DeBlasio, Alyssa. *The End of Russian Philosophy. Tradition and Transition at the Turn of the 21st Century*. London: Palgrave MacMillan, 2014.

Dostoevskii, Fedor. "Ob"iavlenie o podpiske na zhurnal 'Vremia' na 1861 g." In idem, *Polnoe sobranie sochinenii*, edited by V. G. Bazanov. St. Petersburg: Nauka, 1911.

---

67 Natal'ia Balakleets, "Intellektualy kak sozdateli narrativov o voine," *Vestnik Samarskogo gosudarstvennogo tekhnicheskogo universiteta* 4, no. 2 (2022): 13. Balakleets begins her article by distinguishing the intelligentsia from intellectuals (ibid., 6).

Epshtein, Mikhail. "Zagadka naroda." InteLnet. May 1992. Accessed July 10, 2023. http://www.emory.edu/INTELNET/esse_narod.html.

Firsov, Boris. "Intelligentsiia i intellektualy v kontse XX veka." *Zvezda* 8 (2001). Accessed May 12, 2020. https://magazines.gorky.media/zvezda/2001/8/intelligencziya-i-intellektualy-v-koncze-hh-veka.html.

Gabowitsch, Mischa. "NZ—die Eiserne Ration einer neuen russländischen Öffentlichkeit." *Osteuropa* 9–10 (2003): 1437–1438.

Glickman, Rose. "An Alternative View of the Peasantry: The Raznochintsy Writers of the 1860s." *Slavic Review* 32, no. 4 (1973): 693–704.

Gramsci, Antonio. "The Intellectuals." In idem, *Selections from the Prison Notebooks*, edited and translated by Quinton Hoare and Geoffrey Nowell Smith, 3–23. New York: L International P, 1971.

Gross, John. *The Rise and Fall of the Man of Letters: A Study of the Idiosyncratic and the Humane in Modern Literature.* New York: Macmillan, 1969.

Halliday, Terrence. "Professions, Class, and Capitalism." *European Journal of Sociology* 24, no. 2 (1983): 321–346.

Institut filosofii RAN. "Kruglyi stol k 100-letnemu iubileiu Instituta na temu 'Filosofiia kak professiia i prizvanie." YouTube. October 6, 2020. https://www.youtube.com/watch?v=xwBqmKFOVbM.

Ivanov-Razumnik, Razumnik. "Chto takoe intelligentsia." In *Intelligentsiia—vlast'—narod*, edited by L. I. Novikova and I. N. Sizemskaia, 73–80. Moscow: Nauka, 1993.

Jumonville, Neil, ed. *The New York Intellectuals Reader.* New York: Routledge, 2007.

Kant, Immanuel. *Beantwortung der Frage: Was ist Aufklärung?* Edited by Jean Mondot. Saint-Étienne: P de l'Université de Saint-Étienne, 1991.

Kemper, Susan. "Older Professors: Fewer, and Better, Than You Think." *The Chronicle of Higher Education*, November 14, 2010. http://chronicle.com/article/Older-Professors-Fewer-and/125347/.

Kovalyova, Natalia. "The Interplay of the Material and the Discursive in Russian Academic Prose (1980–2010)." *Russian Journal of Communication* 6, no. 1 (2014): 6–19.

Kurennoi, Vitalii. "Intellektualy." In *Mysliashchaia Rossiia. Istoriia i teoriia intelligentsii i intellektualov*, edited by Vitalii Kurennoi, 5–27. Moscow: Nasledie Evrazii, 2006.

Kustarev, Aleksandr. *Nervnye liudi. Ocherki ob intelligentsii.* Moscow: Tovarishchestvo nauchnykh izdanii KMK, 2006.

———. "Sovetskaia Rossiia: samoopredelitel'nye praktiki sovetskoi intelligentsii." In *Mysliashchaia Rossiia. Istoriia i teoriia intelligentsii i intellektualov*, edited by Vitalii Kurennoi, 54–71. Moscow: Nasledie Evropy, 2009.

Malia, Martin. "What Is the Intelligentsia?" *Daedalus* 89, no. 3 (1960): 441–458.

Mart'ianov, Viktor. "Postsovetskaia Rossiia. Sotsial'no-teoreticheskie razmyshleniia." In *Mysliashchaia Rossiia. Istoriia i teoriia intelligentsii i intellektualov*, edited by Vitalii Kurennoi, 72–95. Moscow: Nasledie Evropy, 2009.

Norris, Stephen M. "Avdot'ia Smirnova: *Two Days* (*2 dnia*, 2011)." *KinoKultura* 36 (2012). Accessed July 10, 2023. http://www.kinokultura.com/2012/36r-dvadnia.shtml.

Oganov, Artem. "Kak ostanovit' 'utechku mozgov' iz Rossii?" Lenta.ru. Accessed May 10, 2020. http://lenta.ru/conf/oganov/.

Ory, Pascal, and Jean-François Sirinelli. *Les intellectuels en France de l'affaire Dreyfus à nos jours*. Paris: Armand Colin, 1986.

Plotnikov, Nikolai. "Filosofii v Rossii prosto ne sushchestvuet." Interview with Aleksei Nilogov. *Russkii zhurnal*, January 18, 2008. http://www.russ.ru/Mirovayapovestka/Filosofii-v-Rossii-prosto-ne-suschestvuet.

Posner, Richard. *Public Intellectuals: A Study of Decline*. Cambridge, MA: Harvard UP, 2001.

Oushakine, Serguei. "Funktsional'naia intelligentnost'." *Polis* 1 (1998): 8–22.

Ovsianiko-Kulikovskii, Dmitrii. *Psikhologiia russkoi intelligentsii*. Moscow: Mysl', 1971.

Pelevin, Viktor. *Sviashchennaia kniga oborotnia*. Pelevin.nov.ru. Accessed April 8, 2020, http://pelevin.nov.ru/romans/pe-SKO/.

"Pervoe predosterezhenie." *Pravda*, August 31, 1922.

Plato. *The Republic*. Edited by G. R. F. Ferrari, translated by Tom Griffith. Cambridge: Cambridge UP, 2000.

"Professional'noe obrazovanie Rossii: Kakim ono dolzhno byt'?" Guests Dmitrii Livanov and Andrei Volkov. "Goriachie interv'iu." *Ekho Moskvy*, September 3, 2010.

Prokof'eva, A. Iu. "Raznochintsy." *Bol'shaia rossiiskaia entsiklopediia*. Accessed May 10, 2021. https://bigenc.ru/domestic_history/text/3490843.

Radaev, Vadim. "Issledovatel'skie instituty: sostoianie i problemy. Beseda s Vadimom Radaevym." In *Mysliashchaia Rossiia. Kartografiia sovremennykh* intellektual′nykh napravlenii, edited by Vitalii Kurennoi, 35–49. Moscow: Nasledie Evrazii, 2006.

Radaev, Vadim. "Realizatsiia effektivnogo kontrakta s PPS v forme akademicheskikh nadbavok." Vysshaia shkola ekonomiki, Moscow, 2013. Accessed April 1, 2020. https://kpfu.ru/portal/docs/F1928560607/Effektivnyj.kontrakt_NIU_VShE.pdf.

Sal′nikov, Vladimir. "Moi frustratsii v 90-kh." *Logos* 5/6 (2000). Accessed May 10, 2020. http://www.ruthenia.ru/logos/number/2000_5_6/2000_5-6_08.htm.

Sergeev, Sergei. "Dosovetskaia Rossiia (XVIII–do nachala XX veka)." In *Mysliashchaia Rossiia. Istoriia i teoriia intelligentsii i intellektualov*, edited by Vitalii Kurennoi, 15–53. Moscow: Nasledie Evropy, 2009.

Seton-Watson, Hugh. "The Russian Intellectuals." In *The Intellectuals: A Controversial Portrait*, edited by George Bernard de Huszar, 41–52. New York: Free Press, 1960.

Shmidt, S. O. *Obshchestvennoe samosoznanie rossiiskogo blagorodnogo sosloviia: XVI-pervaia tret′ XIX veka*. Moscow: Nauka, 2002.

Slavinskii, Maksim. *Russkaia intelligentsiia i natsional′nyi vopros*. Moscow: Mysl′, 1971.

Smirnova, Avdot′ia. "Shkola zlosloviia s Sobchak: Kirienko, Nemtsov, Naval′nyi i, konechno zhe, Chubais." YouTube, November 29, 2021. https://www.youtube.com/watch?v=3deY1Q9ThMs.

Szczepański, Jan. "The Polish Intelligentsia: Past and Present." *World Politics* 14, no. 3 (April 1962): 406–420.

Uspenskii, Boris, ed. *Russkaia intelligentsiia i zapadnyi intellektualizm: Istoriia i tipologiia*. Moscow: O.G.I., 1999.

Uzlaner, Dmitrii. "Tragediia intellektualov." *Russkii zhurnal*, October 20, 2010. Accessed June 7, 2021. http://www.russ.ru/pole/Tragediya-intellektualov.

"V. Putin: Intelligentsiia dolzhna predokhraniat′ obshchestvo ot revoliutsii." RBC, September 4, 2013. https://www.rbc.ru/society/04/09/2013/57040ef09a794761c0ce1507.

Vanchugov, Vasilii. "Umnym filosofiiav pomoshch′, drugim—v nakazanie." Interview with Aleksei Nilogov. *NG—Ex libris*, August 5, 2010. Accessed June 7, 2021. http://www.alexnilogov.narod.ru/sofr_rus_fil/vanchugov_umnym-filosofiya.html.

Zdravomyslova, Ol′ga, and Natal′ia Kutukova. "Intelligentsiia kak vyzov: identichnost′ rossiiskoi intelligentsii v XXI veke." *Kontsept: filosofiia, religiia, kul′tura* 4, no. 1.13 (2020): 7–20.

Zola, Émile. "J'accuse!" *L'Aurore* 87, no. 13 (January 1898): 1–2.

Legacy and Denial: Russian Intelligentsia on Screen and Online in the First Two Decades of the Twenty-First Century

Tatiana Smorodinska

In the history of Russian intelligentsia there was a short-lived but important period, which lasted roughly for the first two decades of the twenty-first century and ended abruptly with the Russian invasion of Ukraine on February 24, 2022. It was the time when a new generation of Russians, born a decade before and after the collapse of the Soviet Union, attempted to play an active role in public life and ensure social progress. The paper will analyze that endeavor, as presented in various digital media projects and contemporary cinema. Since the beginning of the war some projects mentioned in this paper have been closed or banned; some people were labeled "foreign agents" (*inostrannye agenty*), and some emigrated.

In 2013 the *Moscow News* (Moskovskie novosti) newspaper launched the *New Intelligentsia* (Novaia intelligentsiia) project.[1] It included interviews, short video polls, and an award ceremony. The timing was clearly linked to the 2011–2012 protests, perceived as a political awakening of the new generation of Russian intellectuals in hope of the return of the glorified Russian intelligentsia to social and political life. However, in the atmosphere that followed Russia's annexation of Crimea all hopes vanished, and the project was abandoned. Various

---

1 "Novaia intelligentsiia," *Moskovskie novosti*, accessed May 6, 2024, https://www.mn.ru/trend_25.

discussions, books, articles, debates, conferences on the fate and future of the Russian intelligentsia continued to appear in the media and academia, reaching sad conclusions about its final demise or uncertain and negligible future. Most scholars, writers, or journalists involved in those discussions belonged to the last generation of the Soviet intelligentsia and lamented the impotence, failure, and irrelevance of that social group in contemporary Russia. However, the new generation of Russian intellectuals, who denied and discredited the old Russian intelligentsia myth and refused to self-identify as "intelligentsia," in fact tried to build on it and to continue its legacy. Even though the war destroyed a lot of aspirations and erased their achievements, they dared to try, and the effort deserves to be recognized.

Compared to late Soviet cinema, post-Soviet filmmakers demonstrated less interest in intelligentsia characters. The younger generation of Russian filmmakers, born in the late 1970s and the 1980s, had witnessed the process of the intelligentsia's degradation and either preferred to go sentimentally back to times when the intelligentsia was socially relevant (the 1960s and 1970s),[2] or celebrated the elderly survivors of the once-respected group in the Soviet society, which was quickly fading away in Post-Soviet Russia.[3] Cinematic portrayals of the contemporary intelligentsia were rare and ranged from mockery and repudiation to lamenting an inevitably tragic destiny and human and professional failure. Once admired and honored keepers of Russia's cultural heritage, guardians of the national moral code and ethical conduct, museum curators, librarians, teachers, scholars, and doctors were depicted as discredited, impoverished, and demoralized.

In contemporary Russian cinema a schoolteacher, the classical representative of intelligentsia, was mercilessly removed from any pedestal. The award-winning film *The Geographer Drank His Globe Away* (Geograf globus propil, 2013, dir. A. Veledinsky) portrayed the tragic figure of a teacher, a "superfluous man," an outsider among his colleagues, who had failed in his mission and was doomed to obliteration. Another disillusioned provincial teacher, in *The Pencil* (Prostoi karandash, 2019, dir. N. Nazarova), tells an idealistic new hire: "We teachers

---

2 E.g., see *The Thaw* (Ottepel', 2013, dir. V. Todorovsky); *Odesa* (Odessa, 2019, dir. V. Todorovsky); *Paper Soldier* (Bumazhnyi soldat, 2008, dir. A. German, Jr.); *Dovlatov* (2018, dir. A. German, Jr.); *Mysterious Passion* (Tainstvennaia strast', 2016, dir. V. Furman); *A Film about Alekseev* (Kino pro Alekseeva, 2014, dir. M. Segal), to name a few.

3 See *Come Look at Me* (Prikhodi na menia posmostret', 2000, dir. M. Agranovich); *From Nowhere with Love or Merry Funerals* (Niotkuda s liubov'iu ili veselye pokhorony, 2007, dir. V. Fokin); *Van Goghs* (Van Gogi, 2018, dir. S. Livnev); *Carp Frozen* (Karp otmorozhennyi, 2017, dir. V. Kott); *On Upper Maslovka* (Na Verkhnei Maslovke, 2004, dir. K. Khudyakov); *The Actress* (Artistka, 2007, dir. S. Govorukhin); *Bolshoi* (Bol'shoi, 2016, dir. V. Todorovsky).

haven't been intelligentsia for a long time, it's time to admit it!" ("My, uchitelia, davno ne intelligentsiia, pora eto priznat'!"), denying any obligation to sacrifice one's livelihood for the sake of an ethical mission, as prescribed for the old-school intelligentsia. However, Antonina, the main character in *The Pencil*, was not a seasoned professional teacher; she was an artist from St. Petersburg who took an art teaching position at a provincial school to support her husband, a political prisoner, who was serving his sentence in the area. She refused to deny her intelligentsia roots and convictions and was killed for taking a stand. Living up to the expected high moral bar in post-Soviet Russia was a challenge, and very few were able to withstand the pressure, as depicted in *Tambourine, Drum* (Buben, baraban, 2009, dir. A. Mizgirev). The main character Katya, a librarian, enjoyed the reputation of a local *intelligent*, but poverty and a miserable existence led her to a total moral downfall when she hired an assassin to murder a rival in her unhappy romance. A collection of cinematic novellas, *The Stories* (Rasskazy, 2012, dir. M. Segal), declared the metaphorical death of one of the most upstanding Russian cultural myths: "the literary nature of its [Russia's] spirituality,"[4] as well as the physical death of the bearer of that myth, a mysterious librarian who used the extrasensory powers of Russian poetry to search for missing children. In that absurdist episode, the librarian perished the moment a book (a volume from Pushkin's collected works) was set on fire, symbolizing the end of the epoch.[5]

However, there was a noticeable yearning in Russian society for artistic assurance that the intelligentsia legacy endured. Medical professionals seemed to be filmmakers' last resort to represent a group still upholding intelligentsia values, which might explain the success of *Arrhythmia* (Aritmiia, 2017, dir. B. Khlebnikov). Professional challenges and personal drama didn't undermine the integrity and values of Oleg, an emergency doctor, played by Aleksandr Yatsenko. His character fascinated both the audience and the critics, as an endorsement of the legendary noble and selfless image of the intelligentsia. Two years later, the same actor's performance as a heroic emergency doctor in TV series *The Outbreak* (Epidemiia, 2019, dir. P. Kostomarov), released on Netflix as *To the Lake*, reinforced the desire to see an affirming intelligentsia image on the screen. Another example was the biopic *Doctor Liza* (Doktor Liza, 2020, dir. O. Karas), a tribute to Elizaveta Glinka, a humanitarian worker and doctor of palliative medicine who played a significant role in charity promotion in

---

4 As defined by Boris Paramonov in his 2012 article "Russian Literature in the Christian Context," in Digital Scholarship @ UNLV, Center for Democratic Culture, Russian Culture, ed. Dmitrii Shalin (Las Vegas: U of Nevada, 2012), 1–29, https://digitalscholarship.unlv.edu/russian_culture/20.

5 Novella "Energy Crisis" (Energeticheskii krizis).

Russia. The film revealed serious problems with the current state of medicine, government neglect of homelessness and extreme poverty, but at the same time depicted doctor Liza as almost a saint, able in one day to help dozens of people and effortlessly reform a ruthless policeman assigned to investigate and arrest her. That miraculous transformation of the fictional policeman inserted in the biopic unfortunately contributed to Glinka's "canonization" rather than to a candid appreciation of her humanitarian work. The film received mixed reactions, primarily because of the politically controversial, pro-regime actions of Elizaveta Glinka during the military conflicts in Ukraine and Syria. Nevertheless, the idealized screen appearance of Doctor Liza propagated the role the intelligentsia could and should play in contemporary Russian society.

Apart from doctors, any attempt to create an image of a righteous, selfless Russian *intelligent* in film was often viewed as fake, unrealistic. A perfect example was *Two Days* (Dva dnia, 2011, dir. A. Smirnova), a sentimental portrayal of a provincial museum curator who tirelessly defended the very core of Russian culture, Russian classical literature, against the ruthless advances of modern bureaucracy and mercantilism. In that romantic comedy Masha, a passionate and principled art historian, reformed the greedy, powerful bureaucrat Pyotr. The film failed in theaters but got some favorable reviews from viewers, who described it as a "fairy tale for adults" (*skazka dlia vzroslykh*), "a light, nice, positive film" (*svetlyi, dobryi, pozitivnyi fil'm*). Yet, the most often used title in online viewers' comments was "I don't believe it!" (*Ne veriu!*).[6] Smirnova's previous work, a 2008 film adaptation of Ivan Turgenev's *Fathers and Sons* (Ottsy i deti), might explain her ongoing fascination with the nineteenth-century image of the Russian intelligentsia, but her pursuit to project that myth into modern reality unfortunately made her character look like a relic or a misplaced museum exhibit.

In 2018 intelligentsia characters were featured in two popular comedies, both produced by Comedy Club: *The Year of Culture* (God kul'tury, dir. T. Kalatozishvili) and *House Arrest* (Domashnii arest, dir. P. Buslov). *The Year of Culture* was a classical sitcom, a humorous take on Smirnova's *Two Days*, with the same actor, Fedor Bondarchuk, fittingly cast in the role of a corrupt official sent from Moscow to a provincial university. The story of the reeducation of Moscow bureaucrat and his conversion into a passionate defender of cultural and educational values was told as a series of episodes full of slapstick comedy and buffoonery. The Russian intelligentsia (university faculty in the series) was also mocked as a group of cowards, degraded alcoholics, and people who

---

6 "Retsenzii/ 2 dnia (2011)," Kinopoisk, accessed May 6, 2024, https://www.kinopoisk.ru/film/494741/reviews/.

have lost their moral compass. That included the main protagonist Sophia Belozerova, who gladly agreed to commit a crime in the name of a higher goal. *House Arrest* became a major statement for Semyon Slepakov, producer and scriptwriter for the series, in which he created a gallery of characters some critics compared to those of Nikolai Gogol or Mikhail Saltykov-Shchedrin. As far as representation of the intelligentsia, it was far from favorable. Marina Bylinkina, a university professor, a single mother and passionate defender of a local historical site, readily became an informant for the FSB, and by the end of the series successfully turned into a city bureaucrat herself. Eduard Kargapolov, university president and Marina's lover, personified a full range of accusations against the Soviet intelligentsia: weakness, cowardice, conformism, impotence (both physical and mental). Slepakov was pitiless to the myth, mocking in cold blood even the cinematographic remnants of affection for the intelligentsia, as in a shower scene that derided a beloved episode from Eldar Ryazanov's 1976 comedy *The Irony of Fate, or Enjoy Your Bath* (Ironiia sud′by, ili, S legkim parom).

Popular web productions offered mostly harsh portrayal of the intelligentsia as well. The web series *The "On the Chest" Bar* (Bar "Na grud′," 2018, dir. I. Vilkova) depicted the Russian *intelligent* as a self-absorbed, vindictive, and ridiculous narcissist (in the episodes "The Extremist" [Ekstremistskaia] and "The City-Defending" [Gradozashchitnaia]). Art director Vladlen, an activist fighting for the historical preservation of St. Petersburg, offered his sperm to populate the city with intelligent people, and literally defecated on his opponent's car as revenge. His friend and partner Vera, hopelessly in love with him, cried in a bar and complained to a stranger: "He doesn't drink [alcohol]. [He's an] *intelligent*, dammit. I want kids by him, he's a third-generation Petersburg native" ("Ne p′et. Intelligent, suka. Detei ot nego khochu, on peterburzhets v tret′em pokolenii"). Anton Lapenko, in his absurdist humorous YouTube series *Inside Lapenko* (Vnutri Lapenko), which became one of the most successful web projects of 2019, created several characters representing the intelligentsia: self-doubting, naïve, and good-for-nothing engineer Lapenko; corrupt and arrogant TV channel director and former English teacher Richard Sapogov; and Russian nationalist, artist, cosmist, and healer Gvidon Vishnevsky. Although those characters ridiculed and mocked the pretentiousness and failed mission of the Russian intelligentsia in the 1990s, the fact that the series gained such popularity in 2019 is telling.[7]

Contemporary cinematic portrayals of the intelligentsia obviously contributed to the demise of the intelligentsia myth. Such sarcastic, slashing

---

7 V. Karpova, "Vnutri Lapenko: Fenomen novoi komedii," *Kinoteksty*, February 9, 2020, https://cinetexts.ru.

representations resonated perfectly with the new generation of Russians, for whom the term "intelligentsia" was either used ironically, due to the compromised integrity of the Soviet intelligentsia, or was applied to describe saintly heroes of the past, especially the nineteenth century, whose high moral ground was out of reach to cynical and self-absorbed contemporaries. Most young Russian intellectuals did not identify themselves as "intelligentsia;" instead they used various definitions, such as "millennials," "cosmopolitans," "liberals," and so on. A survey by the *Moscow News* project, *New Intelligentsia* (Novaia intelligentsiia, 2013), revealed that most young Russians define *intelligent* as "educated, cultured, good-mannered" (*obrazovannyi, kul'turnyi i vospitannyi*). One of the creators of the project, Elena Barysheva, explained:

> In that project we tried to reconsider the Soviet notion of *intelligent,* wanted to demonstrate that *intelligenty* exist, but they are "new," active. Such a synthesis of soul, mind, and action. It seems to me that now the notion *intelligentsiia* sounds rather strange among people younger than thirty [years old]. What's left is the description "a person of intelligent appearance," which means he is decently dressed, perhaps wears glasses, quiet, talks politely. People are unlikely to call themselves *intelligenty*—that was [true] in 2012 and it is now. Someone else can call you that [*intelligent*] or describe the social group you belong to, but you yourself would be unlikely to call yourself that. It is not modest, and the essence of the notion is diluted.

> Мы в том проекте пытались переосмыслить советское понятие «интеллигент», хотели показать, что интеллигенты есть, но они «новые», деятельные. Такой вот синтез души, ума и действия. Мне кажется, что сейчас понятие «интеллигенция» звучит довольно странно среди людей младше тридцати лет. Осталось разве что описательное «человек интеллигентной наружности», то есть он нормально одет. Возможно есть очки, тихий, разговаривает вежливо. Сами люди себя—это было и в 2012 году, и сейчас—едва ли назовут интеллигентами. Так могут тебя назвать или описать среду к которой принадлежишь, но сам едва ли так о себе скажешь. Не скромно, да и суть понятия размытая.[8]

---

8 Elena Barysheva, Facebook text message, November 1, 2019.

Part of the *Moscow News* project was an award ceremony. The overwhelming majority of prizes were awarded to charity projects. The number of young intellectuals concerned about education, social development, volunteerism, the environment, and charity was constantly growing in pre-war Russia. Crowdfunding, non-governmental charity organizations, and volunteer groups were managed by young Russian intellectuals who might not have identified themselves as intelligentsia, but their work fitted precisely into the definition of the traditional intelligentsia mission: to serve society, to enlighten, to help the needy. Many young respondents, interviewed informally, identified as intelligentsia people who created various educational and charity websites, such as Arzamas (www.arzamas.ru), PostNauka (www.postnauka.ru), and Takie dela (www.takiedela.ru), as well as people who established funds or organized crowdfunding, social, or environmental grassroot movements. Arzamas Academy was a non-profit organization, founded in 2015 by Philipp Dzyadko, Anastasia Chukhrai, and Daniil Perushev. It offered online courses on history and culture and ran podcasts from Arzamas Radio. Hundreds of enthusiasts and experts created innovative academic materials, technologically advanced and of excellent quality, which made it very appealing to young Russians. In 2012 Ivar Maksutov launched the online educational portal PostNauka, which after nine years developed into a company with offices in Moscow and London, a publishing house, an educational institution, and a YouTube channel, in partnership with major Russian industrial companies, universities and foundations. So It Goes (Takie dela) was an informational portal for the charity fund Help Needed (Nuzhna pomoshch'), working tirelessly since 2012 to increase awareness of social problems and to help fundraising and volunteer efforts.

The project So It Goes made serious efforts to encourage socially responsible business models and to promote non-profit organizations. The role of business in supporting enlightenment, education, and environmental missions in the Russian provinces was also growing before the war. The Luminary Center for talented and gifted children in a small village in Dagestan, which had an observatory, robotics, VR laboratories, and an art workshop, was founded by a retired teacher, Makhmud Abdulkerimov, but financed by his son Abdul, the founder of Digital Space Venture.[9] Collaboration of the canned vegetable producer Uncle Vanya (Diadia Vania) with the Red Pepper Creative Agency resulted in production of short inspirational feature films, which combined product placement with a strong message of environmental awareness, social responsibility, empathy, and love for one's native land and people. One of the Uncle Vanya

---

9   See the center's website at http://luminarycenter.ru.

short films, *An Ecology Lesson* (Urok ekologii, 2019, dir. I. Sosnin), featured a teacher in a provincial school who not only succeeded in defending a local park from destruction, but managed to convert his students and other teachers into active citizens and environmental activists.

Young professionals and intellectuals in the Russian capitals favored the idea of giving back to the people and the place one came from. In 2017 a group of young programmers from Moscow started a venture called Little Club (Kruzhok). Several times a year they went to remote villages and taught children coding and web design *pro bono*. The support of So It Goes, various YouTube influencers, and social media amplified their message: the Little Club project went viral and attracted musicians, architects, artists, astronomers, and journalists from major cities, who joined to volunteer their time and resources to make a real change in the lives of provincial youth. In March of 2022, after the Russian invasion of Ukraine, the project announced that they would put their activity on hold, but in 2023 the operation was closed for good. The organizers stated on their Telegram channel:

> We couldn't find the resources needed for long-term and independent development without unpleasant compromises. We didn't see a way to engage in true scaling of our project in the regions, while adhering to the important values and views on what is happening with the life of people and [life] of the country—cultural, social, economic, and moral. We found it impossible to develop the project without putting its participants at risk.
>
> Мы не смогли найти нужные нам ресурсы на долгосрочное и независимое развитие, не идя на неприятные компромиссы. Не увидели способа заниматься настоящим масштабированием проекта в регионах, придерживаясь важных для нас ценностей и взглядов на то, что происходит с жизнью людей и страны—жизнью культурной, социальной, экономической и нравственной. Не нашли возможности развивать проект, не создавая рисков для его участников.[10]

In 2010s documentary films and projects became the most important venue for political and social commentary in Russia. Political hits, like the 2017 YouTube documentary *He's Not Dimon to You* (On vam ne Dimon) and 2020's *A Palace*

---

10 "Kruzhok ukhodit," Kruzhok, Telegram, June 16, 2023, 9:03 a.m., https://t.me/kruzhokio/71.

for Putin (Dvorets dlia Putina) by Aleksei Navalny surpassed any of the feature films produced in Russia in popularity, particularly among young Russians. As of March 6, 2021 *A Palace for Putin* had 117,012,004 views on YouTube. The documentary, as well as attempted murder and arrest of Navalny himself, triggered a new round of protests, which were mercilessly and violently suppressed, but the demographic of these protests was much younger than in 2011–2012.

Protests and any kind of oppositional activism became dangerous activity in Putin's Russia, particularly since the beginning of the war, as political repressions intensified, yet the geography and demographics of the opposition movement and civil activism proved that educated young Russians in the provinces were emerging as worthy heirs to the intelligentsia in the darkest times of Russian history. The YouTube channel Sobchak.doc produced a 2021 documentary, *Protests: What's next?* (Protesty. Chto dal'she?), which analyzed the pre-war protest movement in Russia and included interviews with participants. Among the interviewees were two provincial schoolteachers, both under thirty, both considering participation in the protests their mission, both wanting to set an example for their students. Back in 2014, Andrei Loshak, a TV journalist and documentary filmmaker (and a founder of So It Goes), produced a documentary series for the TV channel Dozhd' called *A Journey from Petersburg to Moscow* (Puteshestvie iz Peterburga v Moskvu), obviously alluding to the famous 1790 work by Aleksandr Radishchev. It was a six-part series that followed the same route, and every stop was accompanied by a direct quote from Radishchev. Along with miserable, depressed people, Loshak talked to quite a few museum curators, librarians, and teachers (most of them young women) who projected amazing dignity, integrity, and devotion to their professional duty. Unlike feature films, documentary online projects have presented a different picture: a revival of the Russian intelligentsia, particularly in the provinces.

History has always been one of the most heated and ideologically biased topics in Russian intellectual discourse. New evolving digital formats and the involvement of the most popular influencers and videobloggers made historical documentaries very popular among younger audiences. State propaganda and alternative critical views on history were competing for the new generation's attention, and the episode length and format played a crucial role. For example, digital documentary projects by Mikhail Zygar attempted to change the approach to documentary filmmaking, and to appeal to an audience that preferred social networks to TV, lengthy videos, and books. *1917: Free History* (1917. Svobodnaia istoriia) was a documentary project produced in a new format, as a social network for the most prominent people of the 1917 Russian revolution. The project existed live on the web throughout 2017. According to

Zygar, "The social network format is simply an excellent way of translating that epoch into contemporary language."[11] More than a thousand historical figures "posted" daily on the website. Users could follow them, friend them, comment, like and share their posts. The team used hundreds of volunteer researchers, who spent a lot of time in the archives. In the production they used archival footage, photographs, excerpts from diaries and memoirs, letters, and newspaper articles of the time. The Creative Studio Future History (Istoriia budushchego), founded by Mikhail Zygar and Karen Shainian, developed several digital documentary projects: one of them was an online history game, *The Map of History* (Karta istorii). Each major event in Soviet history was represented by a historical figure, and by making life choices for that person gamers educated themselves about various controversial moments in history. In the annotation for the game the producers announced that they wanted to refocus the historical narrative from the state and its rulers onto civil society. Such multimedia, interactive, non-linear storytelling was more expensive to make than a traditional documentary series. Collaboration with Timur Bekmambetov helped Zygar to produce a new award-winning documentary series, *1968. Digital*, a web series for the smartphone screen. For several minutes a phone screen was turned into the imaginary smart phone of a key historical persona of 1968: Andy Warhol, John Lennon, Jacqueline Kennedy, Vladimir Vysotsky, and others. The 2019 project *Mobile Art Theater* (Mobil'nyi khudozhestvennyi teatr) by Zygar was an audio production that used a smartphone application; it won several awards and was nominated for the Golden Mask (Zolotaia maska) award. The first episode, "1000 steps with Kirill Serebrennikov" (1000 shagov s Kirillom Serebrennikovym), followed the same route along Moscow streets that Serebrennikov walked while he was under house arrest, and recorded conversations between Zygar and Serebrennikov on the way.

Interactive documentary projects such as *1917: Free History* and *1968: Digital* offered users a completely different nature of experience: historical events were presented in the form of social media feeds. Such an approach drifts rather far from traditional documentary filmmaking. Nevertheless, since 2019 the International Documentary Film Festival (ArtDocFest) has begun to include online documentaries (films, projects, web series) in their competition program. Most documentary films, including web docs, still follow the traditional model of linear narration. As some filmmakers admitted, they turned

---

11 Andrei Muchnik, "New Website Lets Users Relive Russian History One Day at a Time," *Moscow Times*, December 1, 2016, accessed July 23, 2023, https://www.themoscowtimes.com/2016/12/01/new-website-allows-users-to-relive-history-one-day-at-a-time-a56376.

to making web doc series because they were cheaper to make (compared to multimedia storytelling), did not need anybody's approval, and provided direct access to the audience. One could make a film or series with a small budget, and no sponsors (crowdfunding was the most popular financial solution). The web doc reached viewers directly—no distributors, censorship, or permissions. The other distinctive feature of web series was time. Not only had production and post-production time substantially decreased, but the average running time of each episode was from ten to fifteen minutes. Documentary films made for TV or the big screen seldom run less than forty minutes. According to Arseny Gonchukov, a web series director, people do not want to watch online video segments longer than ten minutes. His 2015 historical documentary web series *Russia on the Blood: The History They Want to Forget* (Rossiia na krovi. Istoriia, kotoruiu khotiat zabyt') was produced by Oleg Berkovich and Valder Studio; it was geared specifically towards a younger audience, and it told the story of political violence in Russia from the murder of Aleksandr II to Stalin's death. The documentary series consisted of ten short infographic videos per season, six to eight minutes each. The first season on YouTube generated 750,000 views, with comments that demonstrated a wide range of reactions, and it initiated serious discussions on other internet platforms.

Internet technologies were rapidly changing society, helping young Russian intellectuals to get involved in various activities traditionally perceived as the "intelligentsia mission." Enlightenment, asserting a message of kindness, empathy, tolerance, social and political engagement seemed to be a prime concern for the new generation of intellectuals. The fund in support of deaf-blind people Co-Unity (Fond podderzhki slepoglukhikh "So-edinenie") together with the web publication *Afisha Daily* launched a special online project, *Exchange of Lives* (Obmen zhizniami), in which famous bloggers (regardless of the theme of their blogs and interests) demonstrated daily life challenges for deaf-blind persons. The So It Goes interactive project *Everything is Complicated* (Vse slozhno) followed the life of an HIV-positive girl and aimed at dismantling numerous myths around AIDS in Russia. In that project the viewer could make choices for the character and observe the consequences. The animated web project *Trust* (Doverie), produced by Valeria Gai-Germanika, told real stories of trust and kindness in society. The experimental documentary web-series *Life of a Man* (Zhizn' cheloveka), directed by Kristina Kuzhakhmetova, a joint project with So It Goes, addressed issues of critical illness, medical ordeals, and spiritual support. Both *Trust* and the *Life of a Man* series were selected in 2018 for RealistFest (the first international web series festival), ArtDocFest, and nominated for the first Russian award in the field of web industry.

It is arguable, though, whether the length of episodes or technological innovations can significantly increase a project's popularity. The phenomenon of Yury Dud proved otherwise. A videoblogger who gained his fame and nineteen million subscribers by interviewing rap musicians, internet celebrities, and actors, began producing documentary films that generated millions of views. Leonid Parfenov's professional and sophisticated *Parfenon* (a YouTube series started in 2018) seldom hit one million views per episode, yet the three-hour long 2019 documentary by Dud, *Beslan: Remember* (Beslan. Pomni), had fourteen million views in the first ten days, and his two-hour *Kolyma—Birthplace of Our Fear* (Kolyma—rodina nashego strakha) generated 25,342,773 views (as of March 6, 2021). In the *Beslan* film Yury Dud incorporated a fundraising feature to help victims and raised a significant sum of money. In March 2021 Dud released a new film on his YouTube channel, *How Enlightenment Can Change the Provinces* (Kak prosveshchenie mozhet meniat' provintsiiu), which presented the work of the educational venture Little Club (mentioned above). He announced two reasons for his choice of topic: to promote educational projects in the Russian provinces and to attract attention to the new repressive law adopted by the government regulating educational activity.[12] He raised over a million rubles in a week to support Little Club and unequivocally denounced the political and ideological control the state was attempting to extend over independent educational projects.

Dud's empathy and desire to educate and enlighten his audience might suggest that he fitted the definition of an *intelligent*, but very few would call him that. He was reproached for using obscenities, asking indecent questions, making factual mistakes, lacking in-depth understanding of historical processes, and so on. Would Dud be upset that he was not considered part of the intelligentsia? Most likely not. Some Russian intellectuals, such as Aleksandr Nevzorov, deliberately refused to be called *intelligent*, and those born less than thirty years ago were not concerned with that attribution at all. However, the new generation of Russian intellectuals, while rejecting the eminence, social stature, some of the canonical distinctive features, and the name "intelligentsia" itself, demonstrated self-evident adherence to the ideals, mission, and traditions of the Russian intelligentsia.

---

12 Russian Federal law No. 85-FZ "O vnesenii izmenenii v Federal'nyi zakon 'Ob obrazovanii v Rossiiskoi Federatsii'" [On changes in the federal law "On education in the Russian Federation"], April 05, 2021, Ofitsial'noe opublikovanie pravovykh actov [Official publication of legal acts], accessed May 6, 2024, http://publication.pravo.gov.ru/Document/View/0001202104050036.

In his 2018 essay "Intelligentsia, Intellectuals, and the Social Functions of Social Intelligence," Mikhail Epstein wrote that the purpose in life should be *humanification* (*vochelovechivanie*). He described it as an "intellectual and existential process," which will bring "the reunification of the individual with humanity," the process in which the intelligentsia, according to Epstein, plays a vital and instrumental role.[13] Before the war many young Russian intellectuals were actively involved in the process of humanification, though rejecting the "intelligentsia" self-definition. The head of the *Moscow News* editorial board, Rostislav Vylegzhanin, stated in the introduction to the 2013 *New Intelligentsia* project:

> You do not consider yourselves to be intelligentsia—and you shouldn't. But that doesn't stop us from considering you to be intelligentsia. After all, as one interviewee said, an *intelligent* is someone who would never call himself an *intelligent*.
>
> Не считаете себя интеллигенцией—не надо. Но это совсем не мешает нам считать вас таковой. В конце концов, как сказал один из наших героев в интервью, интеллигент—это тот, кто сам себя интеллигентом никогда не назовет.

Every page in the special edition devoted to the project had the subtitle "I am a Human Being" (Ia chelovek), affirming participation in the process of humanification described by Epstein.[14]

Political activity in Putin's Russia always required courage, self-sacrifice, and fearlessness, and was feasible for singular and extraordinary heroes, but it was empathy and benevolence among young Russian intellectuals that galvanized the new intelligentsia mission in the first two decades of the twenty-first century. Epstein in his article characterized the contemporary Russian intelligentsia as "pressed between the hammer of the state and the anvil of the people," as "sparks of reason fading in the cold wind of cosmic and political entropy." "Cold winds of entropy" described the atmosphere created by Aleksei German, Jr., in his 2015 film *Under Electric Clouds* (Pod elektricheskimi oblakami), an elusive vision of Russia's near future. Episodes featuring various "superfluous men" characters were centered around an abandoned tower built on grounds seized

---

13 Mikhail Epstein, "Intelligentsia, Intellectuals, and the Social Functions of Intelligence," *Russian Journal of Communication* 10, nos. 2–3 (2018): 176–178.

14 *Novaia intelligentsiia 2013*, The Moscow News, accessed May 6, 2024. https://issuu.com/moscownews/docs/131208233018-7b2eaa3d92b24685ab489e388d94ffbd.

from a museum. The disillusionment and despair of the characters might seem depressive and hopeless, but at the end of the film they demonstrated, as Sergei Toymentsev put it in his review, a "resolute and unbending commitment to the basic human values in acts of self-sacrifice or mere kindness towards the other."[15] German in his previous works portrayed the intelligentsia of the past; *Under Electric Clouds* is the first film about his own generation:

> Through our impressions of time and the country we tried to tell about the people, who even in the current situation still want something—for example, to defend a museum where they work, or despite everything to build a beautiful building, and in the meantime when facing the choice between indecent and decent decisions, choose the decent one. They don't talk about that much now, but I've seen people like that and I know them.[16]

> Через свои ощущения от страны и времени мы попытались рассказать о людях, которые в нынешних условиях еще что-то хотят—например, хотят защитить музей, в котором работают, или, несмотря ни на что, выстроить красивое здание, и при этом, выбирая между порядочным и непорядочным решением, выбирают порядочное. Про это мало говорят сейчас, но я таких людей видел и знаю.

German did not call his characters "intelligentsia," but that's exactly who those people were, along with the creators of Arzamas Academy and So It Goes, charity workers, grassroot activists, human rights advocates, the thousands of young Russians who took on the intelligentsia mission and faithfully continued its legacy in the pre-war years.

The exodus of the young generation from traditional media into online communication and social networks triggered the rise of YouTube influencers, popular videobloggers, and online communities. The popularity of web series, web documentaries, and educational web sites was evolving with unprecedented speed, particularly in Russia, where resources and support for young

---

15 Sergei Toymentsev, "Review of *Under Electric Clouds* (*Pod elektricheskimi oblakami*) by Aleksei German Jr.," *KinoKultura* 50 (2015), accessed July 23, 2023, http://www.kinokultura.com/2015/50/50r-pod-elektricheskimi-oblakami.shtml.

16 "German-mladshii nazval svoi novyi fil'm antiglobalistskim," interview with Aleksei German Jr., Lenta.ru, February 9, 2015, accessed July 23, 2023, https://lenta.ru/news/2015/02/09/german/.

filmmakers, independent journalists, and educators were limited, along with increased censorship and political pressures. It is fascinating that the traditional film industry continued to record and testify to the downfall of the Russian intelligentsia, while alternative digital media, web projects and documentaries manifested the opposite—the birth of a new generation of educated and socially engaged Russians who took on responsibility to influence, guide, educate and lead their communities and society at large, which in fact is the mission of the traditionally defined intelligentsia.

Unfortunately, the Russian invasion of Ukraine changed everything. The brutal and unprovoked attack was a shock to many Russians, particularly to the Russian intelligentsia. Economic and financial sanctions, total censorship, harsh political repressions, and broad crushing of any dissent had followed immediately and caused a consequential flight of many Russian intellectuals abroad. Those who stayed had to adapt to the country's dramatically changed political and social atmosphere, leaving behind any hopes and aspirations for the new Russian intelligentsia in the pre-war years. Though the period described in this article was abruptly cut short, the efforts to make a difference became an important page the history of the Russian intelligentsia, which is not over yet.

Bibliography

Arkhangel'skii, Aleksandr. "Intelligentsiia—eto cool." Colta.ru. February 8, 2017. https://www.colta.ru/articles/society/13865-intelligentsiya-eto-cool.

Baker, Maxine, and Michael Darlow. *Documentary in the Digital Age*. Oxford: Focal, 2006.

Dubin, Boris, and Lev Gudkov. *Intelligentsiia. Zametki o literaturno-politicheskikh illiuziiakh*. St. Petersburg: Izdatel'skii dom Ivana Limbakha, 2009.

Epstein, Mikhail. "Intelligentsia, Intellectuals, and the Social Functions of Intelligence." *Russian Journal of Communication* 10, nos. 2–3 (2018): 165–181.

Gudkov, Lev. "'Intelligentsia': The Vanished Concept and Its Aftermath." *Russian Journal of Communication* 10, nos. 2–3 (2018): 147–164.

Kochetkova, Inna. *The Myth of the Russian Intelligentsia. Old Intellectuals in the New Russia*. New York: Routledge, 2010.

Ling, Viktoriya, Lyudmila Sotnikova, Irina Rodionova, Irina Vasilets, Olga Zavjalova, Victoria Fedorovskaya, and Ekaterina Datkova . "Online Educational Resources for Students and Digital Barrier." *TEM Journal* 9, no. 1 (2020): 373-379.

Losev, Aleksei. *Derzanie dukha*. Moscow: Izdatel'stvo politicheskoi literatury, 1988.

Shalin, Dmitrii. "Intellectual Culture." In *Russian Culture at the Crossroads: Paradoxes of Postcommunist Consciousness*, edited by Dmitrii Shalin, 41–97. Boulder, CO: Westview Press, 1996.

———. "Intellectual Culture: The End of Russian Intelligentsia." In Digital Scholarship@UNLV. Center for Democratic Culture. Russian Culture, edited by Dmitri N. Shalin, 1–68. Las Vegas: U of Nevada Press, 2012.

Sibiriakov, Igor'. "Novaia rossiiskaia intelligentsia: Problemy samoidentifikatsii." *Vesnik Iuzhno-Ural'skogo gosudarstvennogo universiteta* 13, no. 1 (2013): 57–62.

Zanerv, Dmitrii. "It's Easy to Be One of the Intelligentsia." *Russian Studies in Literature* 52, nos. 3–4 (2016): 282–302.

Zubok, Vladislav. *Zhivago's Children: The Last Russian Intelligentsia*. Cambridge, MA: The Belknap Press, 2009.

Contributors

Marina Adamovich is Editor-in-Chief of *Novyi Zhurnal* (*The New Review*).

Carol Any is Professor of Language and Cultural Studies and Russian Section Head at Trinity College in Hartford, Connecticut.

Alexander Burry is Professor of Slavic and East European Languages and Cultures at the Ohio State University in Columbus, Ohio, and Co-Editor of the Slavic and East European Journal.

Alyssa DeBlasio is Professor of Russian and John B. Parsons Chair in the Liberal Arts and Sciences at Dickinson College in Carlisle, Pennsylvania.

Michael Denner is Professor of Russian, East European, and Eurasian Studies at Stetson University in DeLand, Florida.

Svetlana Evdokimova is Professor of Slavic Studies and Comparative Literature and Chair of Slavic Studies at Brown University in Providence, Rhode Island.

Sibelan Forrester is Susan W. Lippincott Professor of Modern and Classical Languages and Russian at Swarthmore College in Swarthmore, Pennsylvania.

Gary Hamburg is the Otho M. Behr Professor of the History of Ideas in the Department of History at Claremont-McKenna College in Claremont, California.

Maria Ignatieva is Martha W. Farmer Endowed Professor in the Department of Theatre, Film and Media Arts at the Ohio State University, Lima Campus, and

Affiliated Member of the Department of Slavic, East European, and Eurasian Languages and Cultures at the Ohio State University in Columbus, Ohio.

Sofya Khagi is Professor of Slavic Languages and Literatures at the University of Michigan in Ann Arbor, Michigan.

Konstantine Klioutchkine is Associate Professor of German and Russian and Chair of the Department of German and Russian at Pomona College in Claremont, California.

Marcus Levitt is Professor Emeritus of Slavic Languages and Literatures at the University of Southern California in Los Angeles, California.

Irene Masing-Delic is Professor Emerita of Slavic Languages and Literatures at the Ohio State University and Research Professor at The University of North Carolina at Chapel Hill.

Olga Partan is Associate Professor and Program Coordinator of Russian Studies in the Department of World Languages, Literatures and Cultures at the College of the Holy Cross in Worcester, Massachusetts.

Alexandra Smith is a Reader in Russian Studies in the Russian Section of the Department of European Languages and Cultures at the University of Edinburgh, Scotland.

Tatiana Smorodinska is C.V. Starr Professor of Russian and East European Studies, Chair of the Russian Department and Director of the Kathryn Wasserman Davis School of Russian at Middlebury College in Vermont.

Olga Sobolev is Director of the Language, Culture and Society Program at the London School of Economics and Political Science.

Index

Abdulkerimov, Makhmud: 340
Abramov, Fyodor: 253
Absaliamov, Abdurakhman: 217n24, 217n28
Adamovich, Georgy: 259
Adamovich, Marina: xxxi, 245–263
Addison, Joseph: 6
Agranov, Yakov S.: 176
Agranovich, M., *Come Look at Me*: 335n3
AIDS in Russia: 344
Aitmatov, Chingiz, *The Day Lasts Longer than a Hundred Years*: 342
Akhedzhakova, Liya: XVI
Akhmatova, Anna: 253
Aksakov, Ivan: 48, 59
Aksakov, Konstantin: 161n35
Aksyonov, Vasily: 289, 305, 306, 307, 309
Aldanov, Mark: 259
Alekseev, Konstantin, *see*: Stanislavsky
Alexander I, Tsar: xiii, 169
Alexander II, Tsar: xiii, 31, 47, 48, 50, 53, 58, 60, 140, 344
Alexander III, Tsar: 75
Alexievich, Svetlana: xxi, 259
Aliger, Margarita: 214n9, 214n13, 216
Almazov, Boris: 161n35
Altruism: 33
Altstadt, Audrey L.: 222n49
Anarchism, Anarchist: 67, 70, 265, 318; mystical anarchism: 192, 195
Andreev, Leonid: 105
Annenkov, Pavel: 41–42, 51; *A Remarkable Decade, 1838–1848*: 41
Annenskii, Nikolai F.: 170n22
Anstei, Olga: 259
Antisthenes (the Cynic): 274
Antokolsky, Pavel: 194, 200, 201
Antonov, Oleg: 237
Antonovich, M.A.: 59
Any, Carol: xxx, 211–228
Arendt, Hannah: 320
Arensky, Pavel: 194
Aristocracy, Aristocrats, Gentry: xi, xiii, 31, 33, 39, 84, 88, 107, 109, 110, 118, 119, 153, 154, 166, 168, 201, 315

Arkhangel'skii, Aleksandr: 252n21
Arkhangel'skii, Andrei: xvn14
Artizov, Andrei: 213n7
Arzamas Academy: 340, 347
Ascetic(ism): 62, 128, 129n20, 130, 132, 274
Ashkerov, Andrei: 269–270, 278
Askol'dov, Sergei A.: 123, 126, 139–141
Astafyev, Viktor: 253
Atheism, Atheist: 46, 55, 57, 124, 126, 130, 136, 139, 140, 159, 160, 266, 318, 326
Autant-Mathieu, Marie-Christine: 203n42
Authoritarian(ism): 257
Autocracy: 4, 15, 16, 17, 18, 58, 158, 172, 174, 194, 303
Avdeev, Viktor: 215
Avenarius, Richard: 138
Averbakh, Leopold: 212, 219

Babaevsky, Semën: 215, 217n29
Babichenko, D.I.: 222n48, 223n51, 223n52
Babkin, D.S.: 17n51, 18n54, 19n59
Bailes, Kendall: 229n1
Bakhov, Vladlen: 236
Bakhrushin, Aleksei: 107, 111; Bakhrushin Theater Museum: 108
Bakunin, Mikhail A.: 173, 318
Balakhanova, Iuliia: 328n65
Balakleets, Natalia: 328
Baluev, Boris P.: 168n17, 169n18, 170n25
Banerjee, Anindita: 230
Banner (Znamya): 251, 253, 254
Barrès, Maurice: 96, 319
Barthes, Roland: 320
Barysheva, Elena: xvn14, 339
Baryshnikov, Mikhail: XXI
Batkin, Leonid: 224
Bauman, Zygmunt: 265–266
Beccaria, Cesare: 6
Beethoven, Ludwig von, *Ninth Symphony*: 137
Beketov, Aleksei: 46
Bekmambetov, Timur: 343
Belinkov, Arkady: 225
Belinsky, Vissarion: 34, 45, 57, 156, 267, 327
Bell, Daniel: 321

Bely, Anatoly: XXII
Belyaev, Aleksandr: 231
Belyaev, Ivan D., *Peasants in Old Russia*: 167
Benda, Julien: 97–98, 99
Benjamin, Walter, *Moscow Diary*: 251–252
Berdyaev [Berdiaev], Nikolai A.: 85n12, 126, 132–135, 138, 141, 145, 149, 150, 155n18, 158, 159, 317
Berezhanskaia, I. Iu.: 176n52
Berkov, P. N.: 9n19
Berkovich, Evgeniya: xx
Berkovich, Oleg: 344
Berlin: 182
Berlin, Isaiah: x, xi, xxiv, xxvi, 73, 94, 292n10, 320
Beslan: 345
Bestuzhev-Riumin, Konstantin N.: 168–169
Blagoi, Dmitry: 195
Blok, Aleksandr: 277, 280
Boborykin, Piotr: xi, 83, 84, 90, 96
Boer, Roland: 136
Bogaebskaia, Kseniia P.: 178n63
Bogdanov, Aleksandr: 66, 138, 317; *Red Star*: 230, 240
Bogucharsky, Vasily Ya.: 173
Bolsheviks: xiii, 106, 121, 142, 144, 160, 175, 177, 179, 181, 193, 205, 211, 230, 264, 276, 306; Bolshevism: 63, 141, 219, 318
Bondarchuk, Fedor: 337
Bondi, Sergei M.: 178
Bosman, Philip: 274
Botkin, Vasily: 51
Bourgeois society: 54, 125, 176
Bourgeoisie: XIII, 130, 154, 177, 252
Boym, Svetlana: 150
Bradley, Joseph: 9n21
Brave New World: 231
Breitburg, S.M.: 218
Brezhnev, Leonid: 151, 239, 241, 295
Britikov, Anatoly: 231, 233, 234, 235, 236, 237, 243
Brodskaya, Galina: 106
Brodsky, Joseph: 241, 259, 293
Brooks, Jeffrey: 219n38
Brower, Daniel: 34n5
Brown, Deming: 269
Brusser, Anna: 207
Bukharin, Nikolai: 212
Bulgakov, Mikhail A.: 230; *Heart of a Dog*: 254
Bulgakov, Sergei N.: 125n6, 126, 128–130, 131, 135, 142–143, 144, 149, 150, 158–159, 160–161, 317
Bulychyov, Kir (Igor Mozheiko): 235n18, 243
Bunin, Ivan: 218, 259
Bureaucrats: 39, 94n33, 271, 337, 338

Burke, Kenneth: 273
Burmistrov, Konstantin: 198
Burry, Alexander: xxviii, 44–61
Burtsev, Vladimir L.: 173
Buslov, P., *House Arrest*: 337
Butashevich-Petrashevky, Mikhail: 46
Bykov, Dmitry: 283, 289
Bykov, Vasyl: 253
Byron, Lord (George Gordon): 134

Caldwell, Mellissa: 279
Čapek, Karel: 230
Capitalism: 30, 36, 38n12, 52, 106, 132n48, 301; (non-)capitalist: 55, 106, 137n69, 162, 236, 269, 315, 327
Catherine II, "the Great": xii, xiii, xxvii–xxviii, 3–21, 167, 168, 169, 180, 246; *Vsiakaia vsiachina* (journal): 7, 246
The Cause (progressive journal): 29, 31
Cavanagh, Clare: 270
Censor(ship): x, xxii, xxiii, xxvii, xxx, 7, 12, 16n48, 19, 20n63, 37, 46, 52, 59, 116, 162, 174, 180, 220, 226, 230n4, 232n11, 233, 236, 239, 240, 241, 251, 252, 253, 258, 260, 344, 348
Chaliapin, Feodor: 110
Change of Landmarks (Smena vekh): 151
Charity: 10, 340
Charles, Christophe: 95
Chechnya: 276
Cheka: 176, 204m45; FSB: 338; KGB: 206, 298, 304; NKGB: 189; NKVD: 189, 213n7, 225; OGPU: 189, 204, 21n7
Chekhov, Anton: xxviii, xxix, 41, 80–101, 105, 112, 115, 116, 265, 297; *The Cherry Orchard*: 113, 119, 297, 300; *Ivanov*: 119–120; *Three Sisters*, 113; *Three Years*: 87n18; *Uncle Vanya*: 41n21, 87n17, 113
Chekhov, Mikhail: 194, 203, 204
Chernyshevsky, Nikolai: 33–34, 37, 44, 47, 48, 49, 50, 52–53, 55, 56, 86, 87, 88, 156, 167; *What Is to Be Done?*: 33, 52–53, 230, 243
Chizhova, Liubov': 328n64
Christ(ian), Christianity: xx, 32, 45, 46, 47, 49n8, 52, 55–58, 60, 65, 74, 99n43, 109, 114, 131, 132, 133, 136, 137, 138, 140, 143, 158, 159, 161, 194, 195, 258, 298, 336n4
Chomsky, Noam: 321
Chubais, Anatoly: 162
Chukhrai, Anastasia: 340
Chukovskaya, Lidiya K.: 260
Chuprinin, Sergei: 253, 254
Civil War (Russian): xxi, 125, 181, 195, 199
de Clairvaux, St. Bernard: 190

Clark, Katerina: 224, 264, 273n42, 304n47
Clausewitz, Carl von: 68
Clemenceau, George: 96
Clement V, Pope: 191
Clergy: xiii, xxvn40, 7n14, 11, 31, 39
Collini, Stefan: 320–321
Communism, Communist: xxxi, 34, 46, 145, 305
Communist Party: xiv, xx, 198, 212, 213, 214, 217, 220, 225
Conservative(s): 39, 44, 48, 56, 84, 94n35, 96, 99, 168, 246, 251, 292
Constantinople (Istanbul): 144
Constitutional Democrats (Kadets): 143, 144, 152, 153n10, 162, 172, 175, 318
The Contemporary (Sovremennik): 29, 31, 34, 35, 38n14, 49, 53, 88, 316
Continent (Kontinent): 256
Craven, Kenneth: 6n9, 9n20, 11n31, 13n41
Crimea: xv, 47, 73, 76, 334
Crone, Anna Lisa: 19n61
Crosthwaite, Paul: 248n7
Crowdfunding: 344
Csichery-Ronay, István: 235n20
Cynics: 274, 282
Czechs: 39, 40, 326

Dagestan: 340
Daniel, Yuli: xxvi, 295
Danilevsky, N. Ia.: 39n18, 54
Davies, Ioan: 272n38
Day (journal): 48
DeBlasio, Alyssa: xxxi–xxxii, 313–333
Decembrists: xii–xiii, 169, 171, 173, 193–194
Deliagin, Mikhail: xvn14
Delmas, Lyubov A.: 277
de Madariaga, Isabel: 13n41, 18n52
Democratic: xxxi, 88, 143, 154, 174, 175, 176, 247, 253, 255, 316, 327, 336n4
Denner, Michael: xxvii–xxix, 62–79
Derrida, Jacques: 315, 320
Derzhavin, Gavriil: 19n61
De-Stalinization: 291
Dictator(ship): xvii, xviii, 17, 174, 177, 252, 260, 268
Diderot, Denis: 18
Digital Space Venture: 340
Diogenes of Sinope: 274, 275
Dissident(s): xiv, xviii, 181, 241, 252, 254, 256, 271, 296, 298
Djagalov, Rossen: 323n45
Dmitriev-Mamonov, Matvei: 193
Dobrenko, Evgeny: 212n3, 213n4
Dobrolyubov, Nikolai: 34, 44, 49, 50, 51, 55, 87, 88, 108–109

Documentary film: 343–344
Dolmatovsky, Evgeny: 216
Domostroi: 108
Dorogova, Maria: 207
Doroshevich, Vlas: 112, 118
Dostoevsky, Fyodor: xxviii, 20, 35, 37, 40, 44–61, 88, 106, 124, 139, 141, 142, 144, 219, 297, 308, 315, 318, 327; *The Adolescent* (*The Raw Youth*): 37n11, 55–56; *The Brothers Karamazov*: 57–58, 125n7, 130, 133, 134, 158; *Crime and Punishment*: 37, 49, 52–53; *Demons*: 49, 54, 141, 277, 297, 298, 308; *Diary of a Writer* or *A Writer's Diary*: 40, 45, 48n7, 59; *The Double*: 45n2; *Epoch* (journal): 52; *The Idiot*: 53; *Notes from the House of the Dead*: 47, 49; *Notes from Underground*: 37, 49, 52; *Poor Folk*: 45; "Pushkin Speech": 59, 60, 124n5, 276; *Time* (journal): 49, 51, 52, 247; *Winter Notes on Summer Impressions*: 51, 52
Dostoevsky, Mikhail: 48
Dowler, Wayne: 50
Doyle, William: 15n45
Dozhd', see: *TV Rain*
Dreyfus affair: 92, 93, 95, 96, 98, 99, 319–320
Druzhinin, Aleksandr: 51
Dud, Yuri: xxii, xxiii, 345
Duma: 153n10, 157, 162, 173
Dylan, Bob: 306
Dzhivelegov, Aleksei K.: xxx, 1, 165, 172
Dzyadko, Philipp: 340

Echo of Moscow (radio station): xxii–xxiii, 283
Educated: ix, xviii, xx, xxi, xxvi, 7, 30, 35, 37, 39, 40, 42, 48, 63, 84, 90, 93, 95, 108, 153, 167, 174, 176, 215, 229, 231, 236, 240, 267, 293n12, 316, 322
Efremov, Ivan: 234, 238–239; *The Andromeda Nebula*: 231, 237, 240; *Hour of the Bull*: 239
Efron, Ariadna: 200
Ehrenburg, Ilya, *The Thaw*: 289n1
Eidelman, N.: 247
Eikalovich, Gennadii: 260n45
Elagin, Ivan: 259
Electrotechnical Institute: 153
Elizaveta Petrovna (Empress): 246
Elshtein, Genrikh: 225
Emel'ianov, Iurii N.: 171n28, 175, 179
Emerson, Caryl: 151n5, 265
Emigration, Émigrés: xvii, xxi, xxii, xxiv, 145, 192, 200, 251, 259; list of émigré journals: 258; émigré professors: 260

Emtsev, Mikhail and Eremei Parnov: 239n27
Engel, Barbara: xxiv
Engels, Friedrich: 126, 127, 136
England: xii, 10; English: 5, 6, 232
Enlightenment: 4, 5, 9, 12, 14, 16, 17, 98, 155, 159, 255, 265, 266
Epstein, Mikhail: xviii, 323n44, 346
Erlikh, Sergei: 255
Europe, European: xxiii, xv, 10, 12, 92, 140, 143, 144, 160; imperialism: 176; intellectuals: xxix, 83, 92, 94, 99, 246, 250, 255, 260; literature: 167
Evdokimova, Svetlana: xxix, 80–101, 319
Evstratov, Alexei: xxv

Fadeev, Aleksandr: 225
Faggionato, Raffaella: 11n29, 12n34, 12n35, 12n36, 13n39, 13n41
Fascism: 145; fascist: 239, 240n29
Fazin, Zinovy: 214–215, 217n25
Fedin, Konstantin: 217, 218, 225
Fedorets, Anna: 110n7
Fedoseev, Gavriil S.: 214, 215
Fedotov, A: 89n19, 111
Fedotov, Georgy: 189
Feuerbach, Ludwig: 45, 139
Fifth Wave (literary journal and publisher): xxiii
Figner, Vera: 55, 175
Filippov, Boris: 259, 260
Film: xxi, xxii, 206, 236n21, 239n28, 323, 334–348
Finkel, Stuart: 177
Firsov, Boris: 322
Flame (Ogonyok): 218
Fokin, V., *From Nowhere with Love or Merry Funerals*: 335n3
Folk: see *Narod*
Foreign agent (*Inoagent*): xv, xvi, 334
Forrester, Sibelan: xxx, 229–244
Fortinskii, Fedor: 191n7
Foucault, Michel: 67, 72, 315, 320, 321
Fourier, Charles: 46
Frank, Joseph: 45, 47, 51, 55, 56
Frank, Semyon L.: 62, 64, 149, 150, 153, 155, 156, 157n23, 160
Freedom Letters (publisher): xxiii
Freemasonry: 10, 11, 14, 191, 192, 196
French: 45, 68, 92, 95, 96n38, 112, 181
From Under the Rubble (Iz-pod glyb): 151
FSB, *see*: Cheka, etc.
Furman, V.: 335n2
Fyodorovism: 135n61, 138

Gabowitsch, Mischa: 322
Gagarin, Yuri: 241, 295n19

Gai-Germanika, Valeria: 344
Gaidar, Egor: 162
Galkin, Maxim: xxii
Gandhi, Mahatma: 77, 157n20
Garrard, Carol: 222n49
Garrard, John: 222n49
Gasparov, Mikhail: 250n7
Gavrilova, Irina A.: 174
Gavrilov, Sergei V.: 167n8, 174
Gay, Peter: 4n2
Gelman, Marat: xxiv
Genis, Aleksandr: 289, 301
Gentry, *see*: Aristocrats
German: xi, xiii, 54, 112, 232, 283
German, Aleksei, Jr.: 335n2, 347n16; *Under Electric Clouds*: 346–347
Germany: 14, 154, 166; East Germany: 326
Gerovitch, Slava: 238
Gerschkovich, Evgeniia: 107n5
Gershenzon, Mikhail: 149, 150, 157, 159n30, 317
Gessen, Masha: xivn13, xxv, 290n4, 295n18; *Dead Again*, 291n7
Givens, John: 268
Gladkov, Fyodor, *Cement*: 231n5
Glickman, Rose: 315
Glinka, Elizaveta: 336–337
God-builders, God-building: 125–126, 135–139
Goethe, Wilhelm von, *Faust*: 218
Gogol, Nikolai: 21n68, 47, 50, 81n3, 151, 178, 217, 358; *Dead Souls*: 141; *Passages from Correspondence with Friends*: 47
Golos minuvshago: xx, 165, 172–182
Gomel, Elana: 240
Goncharov, Ivan: 37, 51; *Oblomov*: 51; *The Precipice*: 37
Gonchukov, Arseny: 344
Goodman, Dena: 7n13, 10n27
Gorbachev, Mikhail: xiv, 279, 291
Gorbanevskaya, Natalia: 252
Gordon, Colin: 67, 72, 77
Goriaeva, T.M.: 212n2, 222n49
Gorky, Maxim: xiii, 72–73, 82, 105, 116, 120, 126, 128, 135, 138, 212, 213, 214, 215, 216, 217, 219, 221, 222, 226; *Confession*: 136; *The Lower Depths*: 120; *Mother*: 231n5; *The Summer Folks*: 120
Goscilo, Helena: 268–269
Gosteva, Anastasiia: 298n28, 300n37
Govorukhin, Stanislav: 162, 335n3
Gozzi, Carlo, *Princess Turandot*: 204
Gradovsky, Aleksandr: 59
Gramsci, Antonio: 315, 320
Granin, Daniil: 239n27

Granovsky, Timofey: 156
Great Reforms (1861): 166, 171n33
Grebenshchikov, Boris: xxii
Grekova, I. (Elena Ventsel): 232n10
Griboedov, Aleksandr: 81n3, 105
Grigorovich, Dmitry: 84n10, 86, 88
Grigoryev, Apollon: 48, 49
Gromov, N.I.: 19n60
Gross, John: 321
Grossman, Vasily: 253
Gul, Roman: 259
GULag: 189, 206, 223, 234, 260, 295, 300
Gurevich, Georgy: 234n15
Gusev, Nikolai N.: 180n75
Gustafson, Richard: 72

Haass, Dr. Friedrich: 92, 93, 98
Habermas, Jürgen: 4, 17, 255–256
Halliday, Terence: 327n62
Hamburg, Gary M.: xxv, xxx, 165–187
Hauptmann, Gerhart: 117
Hegel, Georg Friedrich: 57, 72, 248, 251; Hegelian: 45, 46, 72
Helvétius, Claude Adrien: 14, 15
Herald of Europe (Vestnik Evropy): 39n16, 317
Herzen, Aleksandr: xxvii, 50n10, 51, 92, 161n35; *Kolokol*: 247
Higher School of Economics (Moscow): 326, 327
Homer: 51
Hosking, Geoffrey: 296n23, 306n53
Howell, Yvonne: 241n31
Hume, David: 251
Hutchings, Stephen: 305n48
Huyssen, Andreas: 274

Ibsen, Henrik: 117
Ignatieva, Maria: xxix, 105–122, 203
Illarionov, Andrei: 257
Imperialism: 176, 252
Independent Newspaper (Nezavisimaia Gazeta): 282, 301
Inoagent, see Foreign agent
Intellectual(s): ix, xxxi–xxxii, 31, 88, 92, 94, 95, 96, 151, 162, 251, 255, 261, 264, 266, 268, 289, 313–329, 336, 340, 344, 345, 348
Intelligentsia and Peace (Intelligentsia i mir): 283
Internet: xxii, xxvii, 254, 344
Iron Ration (Neprikosnovennyi zapas): 255, 322
Iskander, Fazil: 253
Ivanov, A.E.: 154n11

Ivanov, Georgy: 259
Ivanov, Viacheslav V.: 257
Ivanov, Vsevolod: 217
Ivanov-Razumnik, Razumnik: 193n13, 248–249, 316
Ivanova, Natalia: 254
Izgoev, Aleksandr: 150, 161–162

Jacoby, Russell: 321
Jaurès, Jean: 97
Jenkins, Danica: 271
Jones, Dan: 191n7
Jones, W. Gareth: 5n6, 5n7, 6, 8, 9n19, 10n24, 10n25, 10n26, 11n28, 12n36, 13n38, 13n39, 13n41
Jumonville, Neil: 320

Kalatozishvili, T., *House Arrest*: 337–338; *The Year of Culture*: 337
Kalugin, Dmitry: 5n4, 6n8, 8n16, 8n17, 9n22
Kant, Immanuel: 127, 251, 315, 319–320, 321; neo-Kantians: 124, 157
Kaplan, Fanya: 175
Kaplan, Vera: 9n21, 10n26
Kara-Murza, Vladimir: xx
Karakozov, Nikolai: 31, 53
Karamzin, Nikolai M.: 11, 12n33, 248
Karas, O.: *Doctor Liza*: 336
Karelin, Apollon: 189, 192, 196, 200, 204, 207
Karlinsky, Simon: 87
Karpova, V.: 338n7
Kataev, Valentin: 225; *Time, Forward!*: 231n5
Kataev, Vladimir: 81n2, 81n4
Katkov, Mikhail: 315
Kaverin, Veniamin: 217, 218
Kazantsev, Aleksandr: 231n7, 239n28, 239–240n29
Kemper, Susan: 326n52
Ketcham, Michael G.: 7n13
KGB, see: Cheka etc.
Khagi, Sofya: xxxi, 243, 289–312
Khamatova, Chulpan: xxii
Khazanov, Pavel: xiv
Khlebnikov, B., *Arrhythmia*: 336
Khodorkovsky, Mikhail: 323
Khomyakov, Aleksei: 50, 52
Khrapovitsky, Metropolitan Antony: 152n9
Khristoforov, V. S.: 176n52, 211n1
Khrushchev, Nikita: 230, 232, 238, 239, 289n1, 290, 291, 295, 302
Khudyakov, K., *On Upper Maslovka*: 335n3
Kim, Yuli: 252
Kireevsky, Ivan V.: 52, 181
Kirpichnikov, Aleksandr I.: 178
Kiseleva, Mariia: xxin28

Kistyakovsky, Bogdan: 150, 161
Kizevetter, Aleksandr A.: 167, 168, 173, 180
Klevantseva, Tatyana: 105n2
Kliamkin, Igor: 257n39
Klioutchkine, Konstantine: xxviii, 29–43
Kluchevsky (Klyuchevsky), Vasily O.: 11, 171
Knight, Nathaniel: 39n19
Knights Templar: xx, 188–208
Knipper, Olga: 113, 117, 119–120
Kochetkova, Inna: xxv, 265, 282, 289, 291, 292n9
Kokh, Ol'ga B.: 167n9
Kolchak, Admiral Aleksandr V.: 175
Kolonitskii, Boris: 39n19
Kondratyev, Sergei: 194
Koposov, Nikolay: 279
Koptiaeva, Antonina: 216
Kornilov, Aleksandr A.: 174, 258
Korolenko, Vladimir: 92, 98, 176
Korzhavin, Naum: 260n45
Koselleck, Reinhart: 13n37, 17
Kostomarov, P.: *Epidemiia*, 336
Kostyuchenko, Gennadii: 224n61
Kott, V.: *Carp Frozen*: 335n3
Kovalev, Sergei: 252
Kovalyova, Natalia: 325
Kozitsky, G.V.: 7n15, 9n19, 10
Kropotkin, Pyotr A.: 55, 73, 90, 175, 192, 318
Krandievskaya, Natalia: 278, 280
Kritsky, Yury M. 173, 179
Krylenko, Nikolai V.: 176
Krymov, Dmitrii: xxi
Kudrin, Aleksei: 162
Kukulin, Ilya: 237n22, 291n3, 292n11
Kulak(s): 107
Kulakova, L.I.: 21n69
Kurennoi, Vitalii: 314n3, 322, 324, 327
Kurilov, A. S.: 213n5, 213n6, 214n9
Kustaryov, Aleksandr: 319, 322
Kutkovets, Tat'tana: 257n39
Kutukova, Natalia: 322, 327n63
Kutuzov, A.M.: 15n46
Kuzhakhmetova, Kristina: 344
Kuzmin, Dmitri: xxii

La Vopa, Anthony J.: 17n49, 17n50
Labor: ix, 33, 35, 36, 55, 93, 127, 128, 137, 155n16, 180, 237, 238, 306n53, 316, 327; forced labor: 169, 179, 189
Lakshin, Vladimir: 247, 253
Lamanova, Nadezhda: 117n26
Landmarks (*Vekhi*): xxix, 62, 64, 67, 81, 82, 83, 95, 124, 126, 130–132, 134, 138, 139, 149–162, 250, 317
Lapenko, Anton: 338

Lappo-Danilevsky, K.Iu.: 19n56
Larina, Ksenia: xxii, xxiii
Latsky, Evgeny A.: 182
Latynina, Alla: 271, 294n16, 296n25, 298, 300n36
Lavrov, Pyotr: 34, 36, 55, 56, 87n18, 131, 167, 173, 317; *Historical Letters*: 55
Leatherbarrow, William J.: xxv
Leckey, Colum: 4–5, 9n21, 9n22
Leikina-Svirskaia, V.R.: 30n1
Lem, Stanisław: 242
Lenin, Vladimir: xiii, 66, 120, 127, 135, 139, 152, 175, 230, 251, 279, 305, 307, 309, 318; Leninism: 314; Leninist: 125, 326; *Materialism and Empiriocriticism*: 127
Leontiev, Konstantin: 60
Lermontov, Mikhail Iu.: 192; *The Novice* (Mtsyri): 218
Leskov, Nikolai: 37, 39; *No Way Out*: 37
Levinas, Emmanuel: 315
Levitov, Aleksandr: 315
Levitt, Marcus: xxvii–xxviii, 3–21, 247, 248
Liberal(s): xxxi, 4, 18, 31, 32, 38n12, 39, 46, 48, 54, 57, 59, 76, 84, 85, 87–90, 94, 96–97n40, 143, 144, 150–151, 153, 157, 162, 166, 170, 171, 172, 174, 175, 181, 224, 247, 251, 253, 265, 266, 268, 279, 289, 292, 293n12, 300, 305–307, 316, 339
Lidin, Vladimir: 216
Likhachev, Dmitry: 248, 249, 255, 303n46
Lipovetsky, Mark: xiv, xxv, 251, 281, 289, 292n10
Literary Critic (Literaturnyi kritik): 251
Literary Gazette (Literaturnaia gazeta): 213
Literary Institute: 213, 214, 222n49, 224, 225, 234, 236n21, 301, 302
Litvinova, Renata: xxii
Liukonnen, Petri: 241n32
Livanov, Dmitry: 325
Livnev, S.: *Van Goghs*: 335
Logocentric: x, xxvi, xxvii, 256; logo-centripetal: 261
Lomonosov, Mikhail: 19–21
Longinov, M.N.: 8n18
Loris-Melikov, Mikhail: 59, 174
Losev, Aleksei: 249
Losev, Lev: 253
Loshak, Andrei: 342
Loshakov, A.G.: 248n8
Losskaia, Veronika: 200n33
Lotman, Mikhail: 80–81n2, 82, 249n15, 250n17
Lotman, Yury: 121, 193
Lubyanka Prison: 176

Lukács, György: 251
Lunacharsky, Anatoly: 123, 126, 135, 136, 137, 138, 139, 212, 251, 315, 317
Lvova, Vera: 194, 207
Lyotard, J.: 256n33

Mably, Gabriel Bonnot de: 14, 16
Mach, Ernst: 138
Maggs, Barbara: 5n5
Magomedova, Dina: 277
Maikov, Apollon: 56
Major, Patrick: 239n28
Makagonenko G.P.: 13n39
Makarevich, Andrei: xxii
Makarov, V.G.: 211n1
Makeev, Mikhail: 34n8
Makovitsky, Dushan P.: 180
Maksimov, Sergei: 259
Maksimov, Vladimir: 256–257
Maksutov, Ivar: 340
Malia, Martin: xi, xin1, xiiin10, 195
Mamontov, Savva: 107, 116; Mamontov Opera: 108
Manchester, Laurie: xxv
Mandelstam, Osip: 267, 299
Marchenko, I.: 222
Marker, Gary: 7n13, 9n21, 11n28, 11n32, 12n34
Martyanov, Viktor: 316
Martynov, Georgy: 237n22
Marx, Karl: 34, 126, 134, 136, 305
Marxism: 124, 30, 132, 133, 135, 136, 166, 173, 179, 251, 274, 295, 305, 314
Marxist: 31, 34, 72, 125, 128, 129, 132, 134, 138, 193, 220, 236, 264, 317, 326
Masing-Delic, Irene: xxix, 123–148
Materialism, Materialists: xiii, xxix, 19, 126, 131, 135, 139, 141, 145, 193, 216–217, 232, 236, 308, 317, 318, 326
Maupassant, Guy de: 96n38
Maurras, Charles: 94n35
McArthur, Gilbert H.: 13n41
McClellan, David: 127n14
McConnell, Allen: 14n43, 15n45, 16n48, 18
Medicine: 99, 167, 235, 336–337
Mednikov, Anatolii: 216n21, 217n30
Medvedev, R.A.: 222n49
Meersoon, Yana: 203n42
Melgunov, Sergei P.: xxx, 165, 166, 171–178, 179, 181–182
Mel'nikova, Anna S.: 170n21, 170nn26–27
Memorial: xix, xixn24
Menzel, Birgit: 189n4
Merchants: xiii, xxix, 31, 86, 105–122
Merezhkovsky, Dmitry: 81, 82n5, 152
Messenger of Europe: 39

Meyerhold, Vsevolod: 118
Mikhailovsky, Nikolai: 32, 36, 40, 55, 56, 60, 131, 167, 173, 315, 317, 327; *What Is Progress?*: 55
Mikhalkov, Nikita: 162, 279
Miller, Orest: 46
Milyukov, Pavel N.: 63, 67, 152, 155n18
Mizgirev, A.: *Tambourine, Drum*: 336
Mlodetsky, Ippolit: 59
Modernity: 11n29, 30, 69, 242, 274, 321
Montesquieu: 6
Moravskii, Evgenii: 193n15
Morning light (*Utrennii svet*, Masonic journal): 10
Morozov, Savva: xxix, 105, 106, 107, 109–112, 114–121
Morson, Gary Saul: xxvi, 75, 82–83
Moscow: xixn24, xxi, 5, 11, 12n36, 14, 30, 50, 75, 90, 91, 92, 108, 111, 166, 169, 171, 174, 176, 178, 194, 198, 199, 200, 205, 206, 214, 215, 218, 220, 223n52, 225, 270, 293–295, 302, 323, 326, 337, 340, 341, 343; Third Rome: 145; Moscow (State) University: 12, 165, 166, 169, 171, 178, 246, 326
Moscow Art Theatre (MAT): xxix, 80, 105–121, 190, 194, 198, 200, 203
Moscow News (Moskovskie novosti): 334, 339–340, 346
Moscow Review (Moskovskie vedomosti): 246
Muchnik, Andrei: 343n11
Müller, Otto Wilhelm: 39n19
Muratov, Dmitrii: xviii, xviiin22, xx, xxn26, xxi
Myakotin, Venedikt A.: 170
Myth(ology): ix, 249–250, 283, 304, 314, 337

Nabokov, Vladimir: 123, 127, 259
Nahirny, Vladimir: xxv
Napoleon(ic): 77, 166
Narod (folk, the People): 47, 48, 52, 57, 62, 65, 124, 130, 136, 139, 140, 155, 167, 323
Narovchatov, Sergei: 218
Natural science: ixn1, xxvi, 32, 33, 35, 167, 230, 234, 235, 238, 239, 248, 318, 321
Navalny, Aleksei: xx–xxi, 341–342
Nazarova, N., *The Pencil*: 335–336
Nazarova, Yulia: 196
Nazism: 251
Nechaev, Sergei: 54, 55
Nechepurenko, Ivan: xviiin19
Nekrasov, Nikolai: 49, 55, 88, 180
Nemirovich-Danchenko, Vladimir: 106, 111, 112, 113, 115–118
Nevelev, Gennadii A.: 170n23
Nevzorov, Aleksandr: 345

New Intelligentsia: 334
New Times: 99
New World (Novy Mir): 218, 247, 251, 253
Nicholas I, Tsar: 31, 47, 48, 169
Nicholas II, Tsar: 75
Nietzsche, Friedrich: 134, 135n61, 136
Nihilism: 62, 141, 160
Nihilists: 33, 49, 50, 51, 53
Nikitin, Andrei: 189, 195n21, 197, 202n39, 204n44, 204n46, 205n47, 206n50, 206n51, 207
Nikitin, Leonid: 189
Nikolaev, S.I.: 9n22
Nizhny Novgorod: 199
NKVD: see Cheka, etc.
Norris, Stephen M.: 324n49
Nostalgia: 254, 291n8
Notes of the Fatherland: 29, 31, 37n11, 55
Novak, Margarita: 254n25
Novikov, Nikolai: xii, xxvii–xxviii, 3–14, 16, 21, 246, 248; *The Library for Reading*: 29
Novyi Zhurnal (*The New Review*): 246, 259–261
Nudelman, Rafail: 242n35

October (journal): 218
Odoevsky, Vladimir: 165
Offord, Derek: xxv, 44
Ogryzko, Viacheslav: 214n8, 215n15
Okudzhava, Bulat: 289n2, 300
Old Believers: 109, 171
Olsen, Niklas: 17n49
O'Malley, Laura Donnels: 13n40
On a Foreign Shore (journal): 182
Oranov, Atryom: 326
Orlov, Mikhail: 193n17
Orlov, Iurii: 112n12, 117n27
Orochko, Anna: 194
Orwell, George, *1984*: 231, 320
Ory, Pascal: 95, 320
Oshanin, Lev: 215n16, 217n24
Osipov, Maxim: xxiii, xxiiin36
Osmukhina, Olga: 275, 280
Ostrovskaya, Tatyana: 278
Ostrovsky, Aleksandr: 51, 81, 108, 109, 118; plays: 108; *The Snow Maiden*, 113, 116–117; *The Storm*: 51, 108; *Without a Dowry*, 114
Oushakine, Serguei: 271, 304n47, 321
Out of the Depth: 126, 139, 145, 151
Ovsyaniko-Kulikovsky, Dmitry: 317

Pachmuss, Temira: 54
Page, Tanya: 19n57
Pan-Slavism: 54

Panaev, Ivan: 49
Paperno, Irina: 34n6
Papmehl, K.A.: 6n9, 13n41
Paramonov, Boris: 336n4
Parfenov, Leonid: 345
Paris: 182, 191, 192, 201
Partan, Olga: xxx, 188–210
Parts, Lyudmila: 304n48
Pask, Kevin: 4n1
Pasternak, Boris: 253, 259, 290, 299, 302, 304; *Doctor Zhivago*: 254, 260, 290, 299, 301n35
Paul, Aleksandr: 206, 207
Paustovsky, Konstantin: 216, 217–218
Pavel Petrovich (Pavel I, son of Catherine II): 12, 169
Pavlenko, Pyotr: 225
Peasants: xiii, 39, 45, 48, 51, 55, 88, 94n33, 116, 139, 140, 155, 167–169, 172; Peasant commune: 168, 170, 316
Pecheta, Vladimir I.: 166, 172
Pekarsky, P.: 7n15
Pelevin, Victor: xxxi, 292, 300–310, 324; *Generation "П"*: 301–309; *Sacred Book of the Werewolf*: 313–314
People's Will: 58
Perestroika: xxiv, xxxi, 242, 253, 275, 292
Pesonen, Ari: 242
Perushev, Daniil: 340
Peter I, "the Great": xi, 49, 169
Petersburg, *see*: Saint Petersburg
Petrashevsky Circle: 46, 171, 173
Petriichuk, Svetlana: xx
Petrunkevich, Ivan: 318
Petrušonis, Vytautas: 248n9
Philippe IV, French King: 191
"Philosophers' [Steam]Ships": 125, 151, 177, 211, 318
Philosophers: 314–315, 318, 325; Philosophy: ix, xiii, xxix, 7, 53, 54, 99, 130, 134, 135, 136, 138, 158, 192, 193, 199, 216, 251, 264, 274, 314, 315, 321, 324, 326, 328
Piiasheva, Larisa: 257n39
Pimenov, V.F.: 214n9, 214n11, 217n24
Pinkham, Sophie: xviin21
Pipes, Richard: xxiv, xxv, 30n1, 39n19, 84, 264–265
Pisarev, Dmitry: 33, 34, 35, 37, 44, 53, 55, 87, 156
Plato: 318, 323
Platonov, Andrei: 230
Plekhanov, Georgy: 125, 126, 127, 134, 136, 138, 139
Plotnikov, Nikolai: 326

Pobedonostsev, Konstantin: 60, 134
Podrabinek, Aleksandr: 254
Pogroms: 175
Pokrovsky, Mikhail N.: 173, 175, 177
Polchinenov, Aleksei: 246n2, 247
Poles: 39, 40; Polish: 33, 39, 154n14, 315
Poliakov, Iu.A.: 223n53
Ponomariov, Lev: xix
Poole, Randall: 128n18, 144n105
Popular Socialists: 170, 171, 172, 175
Populism, Populist: 32, 55, 56, 132, 167, 170, 173, 181
Posner, Richard A.: 320
Post-Soviet: viii, xiv, xviii, xxxi, xxxii, 162, 189n4, 240, 243, 257, 264, 265, 271, 278, 280, 281, 283, 290, 291, 292, 300, 301, 304, 308, 309, 314, 327, 335, 336,
Postmodern(ity): ???, 274
Power: xxii, xxvii, xxviii, xxx, 4, 5, 8, 15, 16, 17, 18, 20, 54, 64, 65, 66, 69, 70, 85, 90, 97n40, 108, 115, 131, 136, 149, 154, 155, 165, 173, 174, 175, 176, 177, 190, 192, 196, 199, 212, 213, 217, 241, 250, 252, 253, 255, 256, 257, 261, 265, 268, 271, 282, 295n18, 296n25, 300, 304n47, 307, 309, 314, 324, 327, 328
Pozner, Vladimir: xvn14
Prague Spring: 295
Problems of Idealism: 126, 128
Progressive: xi, xv, xxviii, 29–40, 41, 45, 49, 55, 83, 125n8, 156, 173, 230, 242, 246, 272
Prokofyeva, A.Yu.: 316
Proletarian(s): 37, 212, 251, 252
Proletariat: xiii, 126, 130, 132
Propaganda: xvii, xviii, xxii, xxiii, 36, 155n16, 239, 251, 342
Protest: xvii, xviii, 166, 342
Protopopov, Mikhail: 154n12
Pugacheva, Alla: xxii
Pumpianskii, Aleksandr: 257n33
Purges: xxx, 160, 211, 220, 225, 226; the Great Purge, 220, 222–224
Pushkin, Aleksandr: 20n63, 46, 50, 88, 105, 177, 178, 180, 181, 219, 270, 336; *The Bronze Horseman*: 218; *Eugene Onegin*: 218
Pustovaia, Valeriia: 247n1
Putin, Vladimir: xiv, xvi, xvii, xviii, 162, 257, 266, 279, 282, 283, 324, 328, 342

Radaev, Vadim: 326, 327
Radicalism: 36
Radical(s): 4, 15n45, 18, 33, 35, 36, 37, 44, 45n3, 47–60, 77, 83, 84, 86–90, 99, 130, 131, 143, 156, 162, 170, 171, 246, 250, 251, 264, 265, 318

Radishchev, Aleksandr: xii, xxvii–xxviii, 3–4, 14–21, 173, 248; *Journey from St. Petersburg to Moscow*: 6n9, 14, 16, 19, 342
Radishcheva, Olga: 106, 112n14, 113n15, 117n23–25, 117n28, 118n31, 119n34
Raeff, Mark: xxiv, 6n8, 30n1, 292n10
Ralls, Karen: 191
RAPP (Russian Association of Proletarian Writers): 212, 213, 214, 219, 221, 252
Raspe, R.E., Baron von Münchhausen: 129
Raznochintsy: xiii, 31, 47, 84, 88, 89, 249, 250, 315, 316, 327
Read, Christopher: 124n4
Religion: xixn24, xxix, 99, 109, 114, 124, 126, 127, 129, 130, 132–134, 136–139, 141, 142, 144, 154, 158, 160n31, 199, 255, 259, 318
Reshetnikov, Fedor: 315
Revolution, of 1848: 154; French: xxviii, 4, 14, 94, 194; Russian: 156; *1905*: 62, 142, 149, 154, 157, 162, 180, 318; 1917, *February*: 174; *October*: xiii, xxi, 121, 123, 139, 141, 143, 151, 195, 199, 251
Revolutionary: xi, xiii, xxviii, xxx, 3, 14, 16, 17, 19, 33, 37, 45, 46, 50, 53, 54, 55, 57, 85, 88, 131–132, 140–142, 150, 153n10, 156, 157, 170, 173, 174, 188, 190, 192, 193, 247, 256, 277, 291, 293n12, 307, 316, 318
Reyfman, Irina: 16n47
Rieber, Alfred: 108n6, 110
Rogacheva, Sofiia: xvin16
Romanovich-Slavatinsky, Aleksandr V.: 16, 168n137
Romanticism: xxvi, 94, 131, 270
Rosicrucianism: 12, 17
Rostropovich, Mstislav: 309
Rousseau, Jean-Jacques: 14, 73
Rozanov, Vasily: 152n9, 315, 327
Russian Empire: 11, 63, 66, 69, 92, 154, 251
Russian Orthodoxy: xviii, 13, 48, 50, 51, 52, 109, 125, 131, 138, 141, 144, 151, 154, 162, 264
The Russian Messenger (Russkii vestnik): 39, 55
Russian Thought (Russkaia mysl'): 85, 99, 317
The Russian Word (Russkoe slovo): 31, 35, 48, 49, 112, 316
Ryazanov, Eldar, *The Irony of Fate*: 338
Ryu, In-ho L: 12n36, 13n39

Safronova, Viktoriia: xxin28
Saddiqi, Asif: 231n6
Said, Edward: 320
Saint Petersburg: xi, xii, 11, 14, 18, 30, 45, 47, 50, 94n33, 118, 166, 338; Leningrad: 213; Saint Petersburg University: 49, 154n12

Saint-Simon, Henri: 96n38
Sanin, Aleksandr: 118
Sakharov, Andrei: xix, 238, 252
Sakulin, Pavel N.: xxx, 165–166, 172
Salnikov, Vladimir: 326–327, 328n66
Saltykov-Shchedrin, Mikhail: 37n11, 49, 53, 54, 60, 86, 87, 88, 338
Samizdat: xxiiin34, 198, 241, 253, 271n35, 295, 296, 297, 304n47
Samoilov, David: 253
Schiller, Friedrich, *Ode to Joy*: 237
Schönle, Andreas: xxv
Schweik (the Good Soldier): 77, 274
Science, *see*: Natural sciences
Science fiction: 229–243, 267, 272; authors listed: 233n12
Sdvizhkov, Denis: xxv
Segal, M., *Kino pro Alekseeva*: 335n2; *Rasskazy*, 336
Selvinsky, Ilya: 217, 218, 225
Semennikov, V.P: 7n14
Semevsky, Vasily I.: xxx, 165, 166–170, 171, 172
Semidesiatniki (people of the seventies): 282
Sentimentalism: 19, 142
Serebrianikov, OR IS IT SEREBRENNIKOV??? Kirill: xxii, 343
Serebrov, A.: 105n1
Serfdom: xxvii, 4, 7, 16, 19, 46, 50, 140, 167–169; emancipation: 171
Sergeev, Sergei: 315n5, 316n10, 324
Sergeeva, Elena A.: 269
Serman, I.Z.: 14n42
Seshukov, S.I.: 212n2
Seton-Watson, Hugh: 315
Shaginian, Marietta: 220–221, 226
Shainian, Karen: 343
Shalamov, Varlam: 260
Shalin, Dmitri: xxv, 291n7
Shapiro, Leonard: 151n5, 151n6
Shatz, Marshall: xxiv
Shchepkina-Kupernik, Tatiana: 219n37
Shcherbakov, Aleksandr: 220
Shchukin Theater Institute: 109, 206, 207
Shchyogolev, Pavel E.: 173
Shelgunov, Nikolai: 31, 36
Shenderovich, Viktor: xv, xvi
Shentalinsky, Vitaly: 223
Shestidesiatniki (people of the sixties): xiv, xxxi, 233, 269, 282, 289–310
Shingareva, Ekaterina: 112n14, 117n28, 118n31, 119n34
Shishkin, Mikhail: xv, xvii, xxii
Shklovsky, Viktor: 225
Shkolnikov, Vadim: 265, 267
Shmidt, S.O.: 315n5

Shneidman, Norman: 267, 268
Sholokhov, Mikhail: xxvi
Shtein, Emmanuil: 258n41
Shtut, Sarra M.: 218
Shubina, Elena: 289
Siberia: 48
Sidorenko, Oleg V.: 170n24
Sidorov, Aleksei: 195
Silver Age: xxix, 81n3, 144, 236, 292
Simonov, Konstantin: 216, 224, 225
Simonov, Ruben: 194, 204, 206
Sinyavsky, Andrei D.: xviii–xix, xxiv, xxvi, 181, 253, 273, 295; as Abram Tertz: 241
Sirinelli, Jean-François: 95, 320
Sizov, Mikhail: 206
Skabichevsky, A.M.: 38n11, 54
Skomp, Elizabeth: 266, 293n12, 294n15
Slavinsky, Maksim: 317
Slavophiles: 44, 48, 49, 50, 52, 60, 161n35
Slepakov, Semyon: 338
Sloterdijk, Peter: 274
Smile, Jenny: 279
Smirnov, Evgeny: 195
Smirnova, Avdot'ia (Dunia): 323–324; *Two Days*: 323, 337
Smith, Alexandra: xxxi, 264–286
Smith, Douglas: 4n3, 5, 6n9, 11n29
Smorodinska, Tatiana: xxxii, 334–349
Smyshlyaev, Valentin: 194
Snigireva, Tatiana: 246n2, 247
Sobchak, Ksenia: 278
Sobolev, Leonid: 221
Sobolev, Olga: xxix, 149–164, 250
Social media: 268, 272, 277, 280
Social sciences: 32
Socialism: 45n3, 55, 124–145, 240, 247, 260
Socialist: 46, 51, 58, 121, 128, 130, 132, 135, 139, 155, 171
Socialist Realism: 224, 225, 230, 231n5, 232, 235, 251, 253
Socialist Revolutionaries: 175, 178
Solonovich, Aleksei: 193n16
Soloukhin, Vladimir: 243
Solovyov, Vladimir: 142n96
Solzhenitsyn, Aleksandr: xxvi, 67, 77, 253, 259, 273; *The Gulag Archipelago*, 295
Son of the Fatherland: 170
Sorokin, Vladimir: xxi, 267
Sosnin, I., *An Ecology Lesson*: 341
Soviet: xiv, xviii, xxiv, xxv, xxx, 41, 63, 107, 138, 151, 160, 161, 165, 173, 177, 188, 189, 196, 207, 211, 217n28, 230n4, 241, 251, 252, 254, 257, 259, 267, 280, 281, 292, 298, 300, 304, 307, 314, 317, 326, 327, 335; literature: 236, 242

Soviet Union: viii, x, xxxii, 63, 66, 106, 107, 182, 204n45, 212, 232n11, 241, 251, 252, 264, 272, 275, 283, 290, 291, 298, 301, 305–307, 327, 334
Sovremennik, see: *The Contemporary*
Sovremennye zapiski (Contemporary Notes): 258, 259
Speshnev, Nikolai: 46
Spirkin, Alexander: 129n21
Sputnik: 241, 295n19, 306, 307, 309
Stagnation: xxx, 151, 239, 241, 242, 243, 270
Stalin, Joseph: 107, 160, 211, 212, 219, 223–224, 225, 226, 229n1, 231, 234, 238, 251, 290, 293, 296, 344; Prize: 215; terror: 189; Stalinist: 191, 237, 254, 294
Stanislavsky, Konstantin: xxix, 73, 105–121, 203, 204, 205; *My Life in Art*: 107, 110
Star (*Zvezda*): 251
Stavsky, Vladimir: 214
Stolipyn, Pyotr: 154n12, 162
Strada, Vittorio: 255
Strakhov, Nikolai: 48, 49, 56, 60
Strindberg, August: 117
Strugatsky, Arkady: 232, 239n29
Strugatsky, Arkady and Boris: 239, 240n30, 241, 243; *Definitely Maybe* (*Za milliard let do kontsa sveta*): 241; *Far Rainbow*: 236; *Hard to Be a God*: 242; *Roadside Picnic*: 239n28; *Snail on the Slope*: 241
Strugatsky, Boris: 234, 240, 289
Struve, Nikita: 139n82
Struve, Pyotr: 150, 157n23, 160, 162, 317, 318
Students: xxvii, 11, 14, 15n45, 33, 49, 80, 86, 87, 88, 96, 153, 167, 169, 192, 194, 201, 206, 207, 214–218, 222n49, 224–225, 235n19, 270, 294, 302, 341, 342
Subotskii, L.: 213n6, 221n43
Suicide: 38, 56, 120, 121, 132, 133n47, 298
Sulerzhitsky, Leopold: 73
Sumarokov, Aleksandr: 248
Surat, Irina: 278–279
Surkov, Aleksei: 221, 225
Surkov, Vladislav: 324
Sutcliffe, Benjamin: 266, 293n12, 294n15
Suvin, Darko: 233
Suvorin, Aleksei: 58, 99
Svirsky, Aleksei I: 216

Tamizdat: xxiii, 295, 296
Tarasov, Nikolai: xxix, 121
Tarkovsky, Andrei, *Stalker*: 239n28
Telegram (messaging app): 341
Thaw: xiv, xxx, 229, 230–233, 234n15, 235–237, 241–243, 253, 268, 269, 273, 289n1, 291, 295, 302, 306, 307, 335n2

"Thick" (Fat) journals: xx, xxxi, 29, 30, 37, 40, 165, 245–261
Thrift, Nigel: 280, 281
Tikhonov, Nikolai: 225
Timasheff, Nicholas: 252, 260
Timofeev, Leonid I.: 215–216
Tkachyov, Pyotr: 31, 34, 36, 55
Todorovsky, V., *Bolshoi*: 335n3 *Odesa*: 335n2; *The Thaw*: 335n2
Tolstaya, Aleksandra: 259
Tolstaya, Tatyana: xxxi, 267–283; *Okkervil River*: 269 *On the Golden Porch*: 267; *The School of Malicious Gossip*: 268, 277, 280; *The Slynx* (*Kys'*): 267–268, 270, 271–272; *White Noise*: 277, 280
Tolstoy, Aleksei K.: 105, 112, 113, 117
Tolstoy, Aleksei N.: 230, 278
Tolstoy, Lev: xxviii–xxix, 20, 39, 44, 64–79, 86, 87, 88, 105, 180, 181, 219, 265, 278; the anarchist: 70; *Anna Karenina*: 87n18; *The Death of Ivan Ilyich*: 74; *The Kingdom of God is Within You*: 66, 69, 75, 78; *War and Peace*: 39, 64, 65, 67–68, 72, 76, 78; *What Is Art?*: 70; *What, Then, Shall We Do?*: 66, 68
Toporov, Vladimir: 247
Totalitarian(ism): xxiii, xxx, 17, 85, 188, 251, 252, 265, 268, 271, 291, 293n12, 299
Toymentsev, Sergei: 347
Translation: 167, 217n28, 232, 241, 242
Tredyakovsky, Vasily: x
Tretyakov, Pavel: 107, 111; Tretyakov Gallery: 108
Trifonov, Iurii: 218n33, 253
Tromly, Benjamin: 238
Trotsky, Leon: 212
Trubetskoi, Prince Evgenii: 152n9
Tsetlin, Mihail: 259
Tsvetaeva, Marina: xxvii, 188, 189, 194, 200–203, 280; *Snowstorm*: 200–203
Tsyavlovsky, Mstislav A.: 177–182
Turgenev, Ivan: xiii; 33, 34, 35, 36, 38n12, 39, 50, 51, 53, 54, 59, 81n3, 86, 87, 88, 308; Bazarov as model nihilist: ???, 134: *Fathers and Children* or *Fathers and Sons*: viii, 33, 36, 294, 337; *On the Eve*: 51; *Virgin Soil*: 38n12
TV Rain (*Dozhd'*): xxiii, 342
Tvardovsky, Alexander: xxvi, 247, 253
Tynyanov, Yuri: 247
Tyutchev, Fyodor, "Cicero": 143

Uittenkhoven, Aleksandr: 197n27
Ukraine: xiv, xv, xvi, xix, xxii, xxiv, 314, 315, 328, 334, 337, 341, 348; "de-Nazification" of: xvii

Ulitskaya, Liudmila: xiv, xvii, xxi, xxxi, 266–267, 283, 289; *The Big Green Tent*, 292, 293–300, 301, 303, 308
Ulyanov, Nikolai: 259, 260
Universities, university: xi, xiv, 11–13, 14, 49, 110, 155, 165–167, 169, 171, 178, 192, 213–215, 231, 246, 260, 283, 290, 295, 316, 317, 321, 323, 325–327, 337–338
Urushadze, Georgy: xxiii
Usievich, Elena: 251
Usitalo, Steven A.: 19n62
Uspensky, Boris: 321–322
Uspensky, Gleb: 59, 86, 87, 88
Uspensky, Nikolai: 315
Utopian(ism): 17, 45, 46, 51, 52, 57, 107, 125, 136, 138, 144, 230, 240, 264, 271–273, 275, 276, 283, 307
Uzlaner, Dmitry: 315

Vail, Pyotr: 289
Vakhtangov, Evgeny: 189, 201, 203–207
Valder Studio: 344
Valk, Sigismund N.: 174
Vanchugov, Vasily: 326
Varshavsky, Ilya: 234n16
Vdovin, Aleksei: 34–35n8
Vekhi, see: Landmarks
Veledinsky, A., *The Geographer Drank His Globe Away*: 335
Venediktov, Aleksei: xxiii
Verne, Jules: 230, 235
Vilkova, I.: *The "On the Chest" Bar*: 338
Village Prose: 242, 243
Vinogradov, Igor: 253, 257
Vinogradov, Iurii: 112n14, 117n28, 118n31, 119n34
Vinogradov, Pavel G.: 166
Vinogradskaia, Irina: 106n3, 111n10
Vititskii, Sergei: 289n1
Vitte, Sergei: 154n12, 170
Vlasenko, Aleksandr: 215n17
Vlasenko, Boris: 197–198
Vodovozov, Vasily I.: 166–167, 179
Vodovozova, Elizaveta N.: 179n67
Voice of the Past (journal), see: *Golos minuvshago*
Voinovich, Vladimir: 252
Volgin, Igor: 58, 60
Volkov, Sergei I.: 170n20
Voloshin, Maksimilian: 81n3, 260, 280
Voltaire: 92, 93, 98
Von Herzen, Michael: 7n15
Voronsky, Aleksandr: 212
Vylegzhanin, Rostislav: 346

Vysotsky, Vladimir: 343
Walicki, Andrzej: 127n13
Walker, Barbara: 14n44
Wallace, Martin: 247n7
Wallace-Murphy, Tim: 191n9
Warhol, Andy: 343
Warsaw: 178
Websites: 340
Wells, H.G.: 230, 235
Western Europe: 166, 191, 319; egotistic individualism: 124; ideals: 49; intellectual: xxix, 154n14; languages: x
Westernization: xi, xxv, 49, 52, 140, 192, 193
Westernizers: 59, 60
White Guard: 318
Whittaker, Cynthia: 5
Williams, Robert C.: 66n8
Wirtschafter, Elise, 4
Woehrlin, William: 142–143
Worrall, Nick: 112n12, 115, 118n33
Writers' Union (Union of Soviet Writers): 213, 214, 219–226, 230, 234–235, 241

Yasnaya Polyana: 44, 75, 180
Yatsenko, Aleksandr: 336
Yenukidze, Avel: 205
YouTube: xxiii, 277, 280, 338, 340, 341–342, 344, 345, 347
Yudin, Pavel: 251
Yurchak, Alexei: 292n8

Zabolotsky, Nikolai: 253
Zaichnevsky, Pyotr: 50
Zamyatin, Evgeny: 230; *We*: 231
Zanerv, Dmitry: 242, 243
Zaretsky, Robert: 18n52
Zavadskaya, Vera: 194, 196, 200, 201, 205
Zavadsky, Yuri (Georgy): 194, 200, 201, 204, 206
Zdravomyslova, Olga: 322, 327n63
Zemfira: xxii
Zhukovsky, Vasily: xi, xii, xiin6
Zlobin, Andrei: xxin30
Znamia, see: *Banner*
Zola, Émile: 92, 93, 97, 98, 99; "J'accuse!": 95, 96, 319
Zorin, Andrei: xxv
Zoshchenko, Mikhail: 217, 218, 225
Zubok, Vladislav: xxv, 269, 273, 289; *Zhivago's Children*: xivn12, 232n9, 239–240n29, 269, 289n3, 290, 291n7, 292
Zviagintsev, Andrei: xxi
Zygar, Mikhail: 342–343

www.ingramcontent.com/pod-product-compliance
Lightning Source LLC
Jackson TN
JSHW012336060225
78596JS00002B/3